BUSINESS IN ACTION

Courtland L. Bovée
Professor of Business Administration
C. Allen Paul Distinguished Chair
Grossmont College

John V. Thill
Chief Executive Officer
Communication Specialists of America

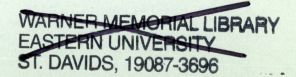

Prentice
Hall

Upper Saddle River, New Jersey 07458

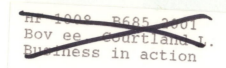
Library of Congress Cataloging-in-Publication Data
Bovée, Courtland L.
    Business in action / Courtland L. Bovée, John V. Thill.
        p. cm.
    Supplementary multi-media instructional materials are available. Book includes access
to interactive Internet-supported instructional resources.
    Includes bibliographical references and index.
    ISBN 0-13-017962-0 (pbk.)
    1. Business. 2. Commerce. 3. Industrial management. I. Thill, John V. II. Title.
HF1008.B685 2001
650—dc21   00-036759

Senior Editor: Linda Schreiber
Assistant Editor: Jennifer Surich
Media Project Manager: Michele Faranda
Senior Marketing Manager: Debbie Clare
Marketing Assistant: Jessica Pasquini
Managing Editor (Production): Judy Leale
Production Editor: Lynda P. Hansler
Production Assistant: Keri Jean
Manufacturing Manager: Arnold Vila
Associate Director, Manufacturing: Vincent Scelta
Senior Designer: Cheryl Asherman
Design Manager: Patricia Smythe
Interior Design: Donna Wickes
Photo Researcher: Melinda Alexander
Cover Design: Cheryl Asherman
Cover Photo: Ken Davies/Masterfile
Associate Director, Multimedia Production: Karen Goldsmith
Manager, Multimedia Production: Christina Mahon
Production Editor (Composition): Arik Ohnstad
Composition: Carlisle Communications, Ltd.

10 9 8 7 6 5 4 3 2 1
ISBN 0-13-017962-0

CONTENTS IN BRIEF

CONTENTS

PREFACE

Step into the world of opportunity in the 21st century. That's what students will experience as they turn the pages of *Business in Action* and learn about the dynamic world of business that awaits them. A world that will change more in the next ten years than it has in the last fifty. A world of velocity, complexity, mystery, success, failure, and never-ending opportunity.

Of course, we've been writing about the world of business for decades in *Business Today,* and this new textbook follows its respected tradition of excellence and currency. But it's different. In *Business in Action* we've simplified things a bit. And we've slimmed things down (including the price). Best of all, we've loaded the chapters with a wealth of innovative, real-world, skill-building, and highly involving activities so that beginning business students can learn the key business fundamentals in an intriguing and involving manner.

Students will appreciate the text's user-friendly magazine layout, manageable length, eye-catching graphics and exhibits, lively, conversational tone, entrepreneurial focus, and broad selection of featured companies—many of which are service-based and tie in with Business PlanPro software. Instructors will appreciate the students' stimulation, the lively classroom debates sparked by such features as "Business Mysteries," "Handling Difficult Situations on the Job," and "Building Your Team Skills," and the unsurpassed instructional resource and supplemental package that accompanies this text.

So step into the world of opportunity in the 21st century, and explore *Business in Action.* We think this is the text students have been looking for!

■ BUSINESS IN ACTION IS A PLUS!

Business in Action is a compelling model of today's most effective instructional techniques. This textbook is interactive + Internet-supported + integrated + innovative + intriguing, so that using this text adds up to a plus for both instructors and students.

Five i+ factors will make your classes livelier, more relevant, and more enjoyable—for you and your students.

- *interactive.* Prentice Hall's Learning on the Internet Partnership (PHLIP) Web site is the most advanced, text-specific site available on the Web!
- *Internet-supported.* "See It on the Web" and "Learn More Online" Internet exercises give students practice with the rich resources of the World Wide Web. *E-Business in Action,* the text's online supplement, extends chapter coverage of the all-important topic of electronic commerce.
- *integrated.* Integrated questions and exercises link chapter material with concepts covered previously in the text and require students to use critical-thinking skills to make important decisions.
- *intriguing.* A series of intriguing business mysteries at real companies promotes an exciting, active learning environment in the classroom.
- *innovative.* Only *Business in Action* has such a wide variety of innovative and involving real-world features and activities within a flexible and customizable framework.

■ REAL-WORLD FEATURES AND ACTIVITIES

Behind the Scenes

Facing Business Challenges Each chapter begins with a slice-of-life vignette that attracts student interest by vividly portraying the business challenges faced by a real businessperson. Each vignette ends with thought-provoking questions that draw students into the chapter. References to the company and businessperson throughout the chapter help students see the connection between the chapter content and the real world of business.

Meeting Business Challenges Each chapter ends with a case that expands on the chapter-opening vignette and describes a business problem. The case includes three critical-thinking questions that ask students to solve the problem by applying the concepts presented in the text. Plus, students can learn more about the company featured in the case by completing the "Learn More Online" exercises. Featured companies include AOL Time Warner, Whirlpool, Patagonia, Top of the Tree Baking Company, Virgin Group, Wainwright Industries, Kinko's, Starbucks, UPS, Harley-Davidson, Continental Airlines, Levi Strauss, Amazon. com, The Concrete Doctor, and E*Trade.

INTEGRATED APPROACH TO E-BUSINESS

Business in Action's six-way integrated approach to electronic business reinforces its importance to students:

1. *Chapter coverage.* Internet technology and its impact on the way companies do business are featured throughout the chapters and explored in detail in Component Chapter C.

2. *"Focus on E-Business" boxes.* Special feature boxes highlight the differences that exist between conducting business in the e-world versus conducting business in a traditional business environment.

3. *Featured e-businesses.* Chapter vignettes, case studies, boxes, business mysteries, and in-text and online examples feature popular e-businesses, such as AOL Time Warner, Cisco, Dell, E*Trade, eSchwab, Priceline, 1-800-Flowers, iPrint, eBay, Amazon, and more.

4. *Online supplement.* Written specifically to accompany this text, *E-Business in Action* focuses entirely on e-business hot topics and the latest trends in e-commerce.

5. *Video cases.* Professionally produced video cases give students a first-hand view of the challenges that BMC, a business animation company, faces as it transacts business electronically.

6. *Internet exercises.* Students become acquainted with the wealth of information on the Web by completing the text's "See It on the Web," "Learn More Online," and supplemental online Internet exercises.

BUSINESS MYSTERIES AND KEY PRINCIPLES

Students help two business detectives, Nick and Natasha, investigate and solve a series of intriguing business mysteries at the end of each text part. The goal is to find out why, when a company appears to be doing everything right, it surprisingly stumbles or falls, or suddenly changes its course of action. Featured companies include Intel, DaimlerChrysler, Boeing, PeopleSoft, Saturn, and Schwab.

To solve the company mysteries, students apply imaginative thinking to the evidence and use clues strategically placed in the margins throughout the textbook. These clues consist of key business principles that highlight the latest management thinking by today's most recognized and respected business leaders—Peter Drucker, Clayton Christensen, Gary Hamel, Bill Gates, Thomas Friedman, Arthur Levitt, Jr., Tom Peters, Al Ries, Jack Trout, and more.

The "Business Mystery" features continue with supplemental online exercises. Students are asked to solve the mysteries of e-business using the same chapter clues and featured companies.

SEE IT ON THE WEB FEATURES AND EXERCISES

Students become acquainted with the Web and its wealth of information that relates to the content of *Business in Action.* In each chapter, three "See It on the Web" features describe Web sites that reinforce and extend chapter material.

Three end-of-chapter exercises are directly tied to the showcased "See It on the Web" sites and give students experience with the rich resources of the Web. The exercises provide students with navigational directions, guidance, and hints. Students who complete these exercises will learn how to use the Internet proficiently and productively.

SPECIAL FEATURE BOXES

Special feature boxes make the world of business come alive with fresh, never-before-seen examples that are carefully placed in each chapter to further enhance student learning. Each box includes two critical-thinking questions that are ideal for developing individual or team problem-solving skills. Students will enjoy the variety of business topics, which include

Enterprise Rent-A-Car Tries Harder, and It Pays Off ■ How Cisco Bought Its Way to the Top ■ How Michael Dell Works His Magic ■ Office Ethics: Teams Make It Hard to Tattle ■ Mervyn's Calls SWAT Team to the Rescue ■ Chek Lap Kok's Turbulent Takeoff ■ Is Telecommuting Right for You? ■ Are Temp Workers Becoming a Full-Time Headache? ■ It's Okay to Fall Asleep on the Job ■ It's the Brand, Stupid ■ Auditors and Clients: Too Close for Comfort?

Special feature boxes titled "Focus on E-Business" highlight the many challenges companies are facing in the world of electronic commerce. Topics include

Here Comes the Electronic Highway ■ Roadblocks on the European Superhighway ■ Create a Winning Web Site ■ Is the End of the Beginning Near? ■ Seven Habits of Highly Effective E-Managers ■ This Cyberbazaar Is Strictly Business-to-Business ■ Living with the E-Cultures of Hype and Craft ■ Your Right to Privacy vs. the Marketing Databases ■ The Electronic Price Isn't Always Right ■ E-tailing: It Takes More Than a Web Site

SPOTLIGHT ON FIVE MAJOR BUSINESS CHALLENGES

Five business themes are woven into the chapter text. Real-world examples and discussion bring vivid insights into how businesspeople face these challenges on a daily basis. They are

- Keeping Pace with Technology and Electronic Commerce
- Supporting Quality Initiatives and Achieving Customer Satisfaction
- Starting and Managing a Small Business in Today's Competitive Environment
- Thinking Globally and Committing to a Culturally Diverse Work Force
- Behaving in an Ethically and Socially Responsible Manner

EXERCISES AND LEARNING TOOLS FOCUS ON REAL-WORLD COMPETENCIES AS RECOMMENDED BY SCANS

As described in the SCANS (Secretary's Commission on Achieving Necessary Skills) report from the Department of Labor, it is essential that students meet national standards of academic and occupational skill. Like no other introduction to business text, *Business in Action* empha-

sizes the skills and competencies necessary for students to make the transition from academia to the workplace.

To help accomplish the SCANS goal, this text offers extensive, specifically designed pedagogy that is grounded in real-world situations. This pedagogy includes features and exercises that stimulate critical thinking skills such as observation, interpretation, organization, decision making, analysis, and practical application of chapter concepts—at a level that students will understand and enjoy.

SKILL-BUILDING, PRACTICAL, REAL-WORLD EXERCISES

Business in Action includes an extraordinary number of pedagogical devices that simplify teaching, facilitate learning, stimulate critical thinking, maintain interest and enjoyment, and illustrate the practical application of chapter concepts. These include

- *Building Your Team Skills.* Chapter-related exercises teach students important team-building skills such as brainstorming, collaborative decision making, developing a consensus, debating, role-playing, and resolving conflict.
- *Handling Difficult Situations on the Job.* Short, experiential exercises expose students to real-world business situations in which they must use the knowledge they've gained from the text, along with their good judgment, to solve a challenging workplace situation. Taken from actual events, these exercises are designed to develop student problem-solving and critical-thinking skills.
- *Sharpening Your Communication Skills.* The ability to communicate well—whether listening, speaking, reading, or writing—is a skill students must possess to have a successful business career. These exercises call on students to practice a wide range of communication activities, including one-on-one and group discussions, personal interviews, panel sessions, oral and written papers, and letter-and memo-writing assignments.
- *Exploring Career Opportunities.* Students are given the opportunity to explore career resources on campus, observe businesspeople on their jobs, interview businesspeople, and perform self-evaluations to assess their own career skills and interests.
- *Developing Your Research Skills.* These exercises familiarize students with the wide variety of

business reference material available and give students practice in developing research skills.

LEARNING TOOLS THAT HELP DEVELOP SKILLS AND ENHANCE ■ COMPREHENSION

Business in Action uses a variety of helpful learning tools to reinforce and apply chapter material as well as stimulate higher-level thinking skills. These include

- *Learning Objectives.* Six chapter-opening learning objectives establish benchmarks for measuring success. Each numbered objective is clearly stated to signal important concepts students are expected to master. The numbered objectives reappear in the text margins close to the related material. The end-of-chapter "Summary of Learning Objectives" reinforces basic concepts by capsulizing chapter highlights for students.

- *Questions for Review.* Five end-of-chapter questions reinforce learning and help students review the chapter material.

- *Questions for Analysis.* Five end-of-chapter questions help students analyze chapter material. One of these questions is ethics-based and marked with a special icon.

- *Questions for Application.* Four end-of-chapter questions give students the opportunity to apply principles presented in the chapter material. Two of these questions are integrated and give students the opportunity to apply principles learned in earlier chapters. Marked with a special icon, these integrated questions encourage students to think about the "big picture."

- *Four-Way Approach to Vocabulary Development.* The text's four-way method of vocabulary reinforcement helps students learn basic business vocabulary with ease. First, each term is printed in boldface within the text. Second, a definition appears in the margin adjacent to the term. Third, an alphabetical list of key terms appears at the end of each chapter, with convenient cross-references to the pages where the terms are defined. Fourth, all marginal definitions are assembled in an alphabetical Glossary at the end of the book.

- *Team Building Exercises.* In addition to "Building Your Team Skills" exercises, many of the exercises included in *Business in Action* are designed to be worked on in teams. This is especially true for application and critical thinking questions, in addition to all cases, Web-based exercises, business mysteries, and research exercises.

- *Lively, Conversational Writing Style.* Read a few pages of this textbook and then read a few pages of another introduction to business textbook. We think you will immediately notice how the lucid writing style in *Business in Action* makes the material pleasing to read and easy to comprehend. We have carefully monitored the text's content and its reading level to make sure they are neither too simple nor too difficult.

- *Comprehensive Video Cases.* Brand new and professionally produced Video Cases feature BMC, a business animation company. Each video case includes questions and exercises that help students understand how business principles and chapter concepts apply to the workplace.

WHEN YOU ADOPT BUSINESS IN ACTION, YOU GET MUCH MORE ■ THAN A TEXTBOOK!

Welcome to the myPHLIP Companion Web site located at http://www.prenhall.com/bovee, your personal guide to the free online resources for your book.

Featuring one-click access to all of the new resources created by an award-winning team of educators, myPHLIP (Prentice Hall's Learning on the Internet Partnership) provides a personalized view of the great new resources available:

myPHLIP pages—Your personal access page unites all your myPHLIP texts.

Notes—Add personal notes to our resources for personal reminders and references.

Messages—Instructors can send messages to individual students, or all students linked to your course.

Student Resources—Add premium PHLIP resources for your students to view and download (such as our PowerPoints, videos, and spreadsheets).

Syllabus Tool—Improved online syllabus tools help you add your own personal syllabus to our site in minutes.

Business Headlines—Check out links to articles in today's business news.

Search—Search all PHLIP resources for relevant articles and exercises.

Instructor's Manual—myPHLIP Instructor's Manual provides tips and suggestions from our PHLIP faculty for integrating PHLIP resources into your course.

Online Resources You Have Trusted Throughout the Years

√ **In the News**—New current events articles are added throughout the year. Each article is summarized by our teams of expert professors and fully supported by exercises, activities, and instructor materials.

√ **Online Study Guide**—Results from the automatically graded questions for every chapter provide immediate feedback for students that can be e-mailed to the instructor.

√ **Research Area**—Your own personal resource library includes tutorials, descriptive links to virtual libraries, and a wealth of search engines and resources.

√ **Internet Resources**—Links connect you to discipline-specific sites, including preview information that allows you to review site information before viewing the site, ensuring that you visit the best available business resources found by our learning community.

For the Instructor

√ **Teaching Resources** include resources contributed by professors throughout the world, including teaching tips, techniques, academic papers, and sample syllabuses.

√ **Talk to the Team** is a moderated faculty chat room.

√ **Online faculty support** includes downloadable supplements, additional cases, articles, links, and suggested answers to Current Events Activities.

√ **What's New** gives you one-click access to all newly posted PHLIP resources.

For the Student

√ **Talk to the Tutor** has virtual office hours that allow students to post questions from any supported discipline and receive responses from the dedicated PHLIP/CW faculty team.

√ **Writing Resource Center** is an online writing center that provides links to online directories, thesauruses, writing tutors, style and grammar guides, and additional tools.

√ **Career Center** helps access career information, view sample résumés, even apply for jobs online.

√ **Study Tips** is an area for students to learn to develop better study skills.

E-Business Online Supplement— E-Business in Action

This outstanding, unique e-business online supplement was written specifically for *Business in Action*. Each electronic chapter is keyed to the seven text parts and includes learning objectives, real-world examples, discussion questions, a group activity, Internet exercises, and a mystery exercise. In-depth coverage of the latest trends and concepts in e-commerce include "Internet Privacy and Security," "Internet Davids vs. Goliaths," "Managing the Virtual Organization," "Virtual Training and Development," "Hot Online Pricing Strategies," "Internet IPOs," "Emerging Legal Issues In E-Commerce," and "Preparing for a Career in E-Commerce."

E-Biz: Prentice Hall Guide to E-Business and E-Commerce

Take your students behind the scenes to explore the dynamic world of e-business with this new multidisciplinary value-pack supplement. The supplement's printed component offers ten modules that examine the challenges and opportunities e-businesses face in such disciplines as strategy, marketing, management, finance, and more. Each module includes key-term definitions and one mini-case study. Special sections include career development on the Internet, distance learning on the Internet, and tips for successful online searches. The Web component to this supplement provides updated coverage of the latest trends, challenges, and hot concepts in e-commerce plus additional interactive exercises.

Business PlanPro Software and Exercises

Business PlanPro 4.0 (BPP) software provides students with a step-by-step approach to creating a comprehensive business plan. The software is designed to stimulate student thinking about the many tasks and decisions that go into planning and running a business. Preformatted report templates, charts, and tables do the mechanics so students can focus on the thinking. Business PlanPro software can be packaged with the textbook for a nominal fee of $10.

The end-of-part Business PlanPro exercises included in *Business in Action* focus on chapter-related material. Students will sharpen their business planning skills by reviewing six of the thirty sample plans featured in the software.

By working through the exercises, students will gain a practical business-planning skill as they begin to craft their own winning business plan.

Distance Learning Programs: WebCT, Blackboard, and E-College

Now you have the freedom to personalize your own online course materials as well as select the course management system that best meets your needs. Prentice Hall is proud to provide the content and support. Our content has been preloaded into the following course management systems: WebCT, Blackboard, and E-College. Contact your local representative for more information.

ADDITIONAL SUPPLEMENTS

Additional instructional materials include:

Study Guide

A *Study Guide for Business in Action* by Sarita Crawford, Colorado State University, is designed to increase your students' comprehension of the concepts presented in this text. The guide provides chapter-by-chapter explanations and exercises designed to reinforce comprehension of key terms and concepts, and to promote concept-application skills.

Threshold Competitor: A Management Simulation, Second Edition

This team-based introduction to business simulation gives students the opportunity to manage small manufacturing companies competing in the same marketplace. Each student team decides on company missions, goals, policies, and strategies in areas ranging from marketing to finance and manufacturing. Students practice skills in planning, organizing, directing, and controlling, and they get responses to both questions and decisions. Group performance is rated and ranked according to criteria determined by the instructor.

Beginning Your Career Search

This concise book by James S. O'Rourke IV offers some straightforward, practical advice on how to write a résumé, where and how to find company information, how to conduct oneself during an interview, and tips on the interview process. Included in the book are copies of sample introductory, cover, follow-up, and thank-you letters. This book is provided at no charge to students using *Business in Action.*

UNSURPASSED INSTRUCTIONAL RESOURCE PACKAGE

The instructional resource package accompanying this text is specially designed to simplify the task of teaching and learning.

Instructor's Resource Manual

This comprehensive manual by Anne Gogela, Colorado State University, with contributions by Marian Burk Wood, is a set of completely integrated support materials. It is designed to assist instructors in finding and assembling the resources available for each chapter of the text. Also available electronically from the book's Web site, the *Instructor's Resource Manual* for *Business in Action* includes

> ■ Summary of Learning Objectives ■ Course Planning Guide ■ Sample Syllabuses ■ Lecture Outlines and Teaching Suggestions ■ Answers to end-of-chapter questions, cases, exercises, and boxes ■ Answers to the Business Mystery ■ Answers to the Business PlanPro exercises ■ Instructor's Notes for the Video Cases ■ Instructor's Notes for the Study Guide.

Introduction to Business Insights Newsletter for Faculty

Delivered exclusively by e-mail every month, this newsletter provides interesting materials that can be used in class and offers a wealth of practical ideas about teaching methods. To receive a complimentary subscription, simply send an e-mail to join-ibi@mh.databack.com.

Authors' E-Mail Hotline for Faculty

Integrity, excellence, and responsiveness are our hallmarks. This means providing you with the textbooks that are academically sound, creative, timely, and sensitive to instructor and student needs. As an adopter of *Business in Action,* you are invited to use our E-Mail Hotline. We want you to be sure you're completely satisfied, so if you ever have a question or concern related to the text or its supplements, please e-mail us at bovee-thill@uia.net. We'll get back to you as quickly as possible.

Test Bank

A master test item file of approximately 1,500 quality questions is available for use with *Business in Action.* The test file consists of multiple-choice, true/false, and essay items. Each test question is ranked as easy, moderate, or difficult, to allow an instructor maximum flexibility in creating a test. The *Test Bank* was prepared by Bronwyn Becker of Colorado State University.

Prentice Hall Custom Test (Windows Version)

Based on a state-of-the-art test generation software program developed by Engineering Software Associates, *Prentice Hall Custom Test* is suitable for your course and can be customized to your class needs. This user-friendly software allows you to originate tests quickly, easily, and error-free. You can create an exam, administer it traditionally or online, and analyze the success of the examination—all with a simple click of the mouse.

Videos

The ability to drive home a point—to excite the human mind and to stimulate action—is what makes videos so incredibly powerful. Now this power can be yours when you experience the drama and immediacy of real-world business in your classroom with the *Business in Action* videos.

The seven high-quality videos available with this text feature BMC, a business animation company, and were produced especially for *Business in Action*. Most importantly, these videos challenge students with a unique set of instructive video case exercises located at the end of each text part. The videos are designed as in-class field trips to bring to life the concepts and issues covered in the textbook. The exercises are designed to help students understand how business principles and concepts are applied in the workplace.

Color Acetate Transparency Program

A set of approximately 300 color transparency acetates, available to instructors on request, highlights text concepts and supplies additional facts and information to help bring concepts alive in the classroom and enhance the classroom experience. All are keyed to the *Instructor's Resource Manual*.

PowerPoint Presentation Software

The overhead transparency program is also available on PowerPoint. The software is designed to allow you to present the overhead transparencies to your class electronically. PowerPoint slides can be downloaded from the text's Web site or are available on disk from your Prentice Hall representative.

■ ACKNOWLEDGMENTS

A special debt is owed to the following individuals who reviewed the manuscript for *Business in Action*:

> Donald L. Lester—Union University
> Linda Mitchell—Lyndon State College
> Edward J. McGee—Rochester Institute of Technology
> Judy Dietert—Southwest Texas State University
> Harry Alan Donicone—California Lutheran University

A very special acknowledgment goes to Barbara Schatzman for her truly remarkable talents, valuable contributions, and wise counsel.

Recognition and thanks to Marian Burk Wood for her inventive contributions; to Jackie Estrada for her excellent communication skills, and to Joe Glidden for his research efforts.

The supplements package for *Business in Action* also benefited from the able contributions of numerous individuals. We would like to express our thanks to them for creating the finest set of instructional supplements in the field.

We wish to extend a sincere appreciation to the devoted professionals at Prentice Hall. They include Sandra Steiner, President; James Boyd, Vice President/Editorial Director; Natalie Anderson, Editor-in-Chief; Linda Schreiber, Senior Editor; Debbie Clare, Senior Marketing Manager; Jenn Surich, Assistant Editor; all of the Prentice Hall Business Publishing Group; and the outstanding Prentice Hall sales representatives. Finally, we thank Judy Leale, Managing Editor, and Lynda Hansler, Production Editor, for their dedication; and we are grateful to Copyeditor Margo Quinto, Senior Designer Cheryl Asherman, Permissions Coordinator Suzanne Grappi, and Photo Researcher Melinda Alexander, for their superb work.

Courtland L. Bovee
John V. Thill

UNDERSTANDING THE FUNDAMENTALS OF BUSINESS AND ECONOMICS

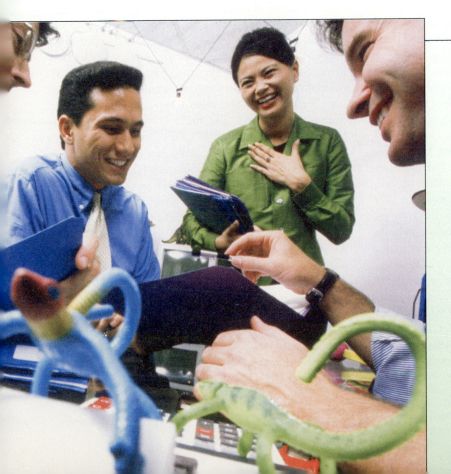

LEARNING OBJECTIVES

After studying this chapter, you will be able to

1 Identify four key social and economic roles that businesses serve

2 Differentiate between a free-market system and a planned economy

3 Explain how supply and demand interact to affect price

4 Name five strategies companies use to gain a competitive advantage

5 List the three major economic roles of the U.S. government

6 Identify five challenges that businesses are facing today

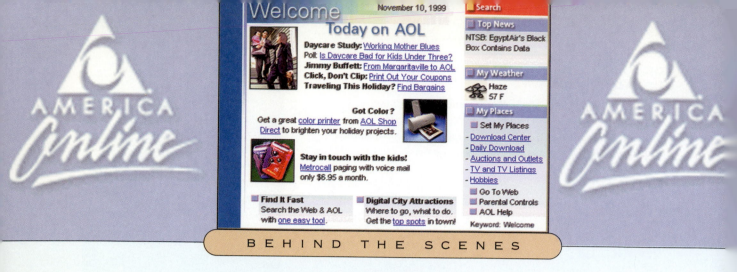

FACING BUSINESS CHALLENGES AT AMERICA ONLINE

Morphing America Online into a Media Mogul

Back in the days when modems creaked along at 300 bits per second and computers labored half an hour to download a small black-and-white photo, Steve Case imagined a service that would allow ordinary folk to find real utility in connected computers. In the early 1980s, this business concept seemed totally ridiculous to most people but not to Case, a lifelong entrepreneur. Growing up in Hawaii, he and his brother had operated a lemonade stand and then started a small business selling wristwatches and other products. Case got a taste of bigger business by working for Procter & Gamble and PepsiCo after college. But his imagination shifted into overdrive when he came home, turned on his computer, and began exploring the online world.

Intrigued by the world of bits and bytes, Case jumped at the chance to work at Control Video, a company that sent video games to computer users via telephone lines. The firm ran out of money two weeks later, but Case stayed on. He changed the firm's direction and began offering electronic bulletin board services for home computer users. Then in 1985, he pioneered the graphical interface for online communications—an innovation that allowed ordinary users to get what they wanted by pointing and clicking rather than typing lengthy, arcane codes.

Renaming the company America Online (AOL), Case set out to build his fledgling dial-up service. In 1992 he took the company public. Then he blanketed the country with millions of free AOL disks, introduced a flat monthly price for unlimited access to AOL's service, and signed up millions of customers. But the resulting surge in usage soon caused AOL's already strained communication network to back up like a kitchen sink. Angry customers complained and Case learned the hard way that online services required significant investments in phone lines, modems, computer servers, and software. To keep up with demand and regain consumer confidence, Case authorized heavy investments in technology and marketing. But these investments kept AOL profitless for years—even as the company steadily added customers and boosted revenues.

By 1995, AOL was in serious trouble. Bleeding cash, churning customers, and fierce competition from Microsoft, Netscape, and others kept Case awake at nights. Many of the high-tech elite had written off America Online. Nevertheless, from his unimpressive desk in an office park tucked behind a car dealership in suburban Northern Virginia, Case predicted to anyone who would listen that AOL would become one of the most powerful companies of the 21st century. "We could be bigger than AT&T," he said confidently to one reporter. "The future is online." If you were Steve Case, how would you morph AOL into the giant he envisioned? Would you limit your customer base to only U.S. customers, or would you reach out to customers around the globe? What new services would you offer to attract new customers? How would you make sure that AOL had the necessary resources to provide these new services?[1]

■ WHAT IS A BUSINESS?

Like Steve Case, many people start a new **business**—a profit-seeking activity that provides goods and services that satisfy consumers' needs. Businesses play a number of key roles in society and the economy: They provide society with necessities such as housing, clothing, food, transportation, communication, and health care; they provide people with jobs and a means to prosper; they pay taxes that are used to build highways, fund education, and provide grants for scientific research; and they reinvest their profits in the economy, thereby creating a higher standard of living and quality of life for society as a whole.

The driving force behind most businesses is the prospect of earning a **profit**—the difference between what it costs to produce and market something and what customers are willing to pay for it. However, some organizations exist to provide society with a social or educational service instead. Such **not-for-profit organizations** include museums, schools, public universities, symphonies, libraries, and government agencies. Even though these organizations do not have a profit motive, they must still run efficiently and effectively to achieve their goals. Thus, the business principles discussed throughout this textbook—competition, marketing, finance, management, quality, and so on—apply to both profit-seeking and not-for-profit organizations.

Most businesses can be classified into two broad categories (or industry sectors): service businesses and goods-producing businesses. **Service businesses** produce intangible products (ones that cannot be held in your hand) and include those whose principal product is finance, insurance, transportation, utilities, wholesale and retail trade, banking, entertainment, health care, repairs, and information. **Goods-producing businesses** produce tangible goods by engaging in activities such as manufacturing, construction, mining, and agriculture. Of course, many companies produce both services and goods. Consider IBM, for example. IBM manufactures computers and other business machines, but at least one-third of IBM's sales come from computer-related services such as systems design, consulting, and product support.[2] Similarly, a manufacturer of industrial and farm equipment such as Caterpillar must provide its customers with services such as product training and technical support. Even though it becomes more and more difficult to classify a company as either a goods-producing or a service business, such classification is useful for reporting and analysis purposes.

Whether you're running a service or a goods-producing business, keep in mind that many factors contribute to its success—management, research, innovation, timing, location, product appeal, pricing, and customer satisfaction, to name a few. Moreover, as Chapter 3 will show, world economic situations such as the turmoil in Asia's financial markets affect all businesses that compete in the global economy. Thus, running a successful business today requires a firm understanding of basic economic principles, of the different economic systems in the world, and of how businesses compete in the global economy.

■ WHAT IS AN ECONOMIC SYSTEM?

An **economic system** is the basic set of rules for allocating a society's resources to satisfy its citizens' needs. Economists call the resources that societies use to produce goods and services *factors of production*. To maximize a company's profit, businesses use five **factors of production** in the most efficient way possible:

- **Natural resources**—things that are useful in their natural state, such as land, forests, minerals, and water

---

business
Activity and enterprise that provides goods and services that a society needs

LEARNING OBJECTIVE 1
Identify four key social and economic roles that businesses serve

profit
Money left over after expenses and taxes have been deducted from revenue generated by selling goods and services

not-for-profit organizations
Firms whose primary objective is something other than returning a profit to their owners

service businesses
Businesses that provide intangible products or perform useful labor on behalf of another

goods-producing businesses
Businesses that produce tangible products

Sooner or later the battle in every industry revolves around a company's capacity to leverage limited resources.[3]

economic system
Means by which a society distributes its resources to satisfy its people's needs

factors of production
Basic inputs that a society uses to produce goods and services, including natural resources, labor, capital, and entrepreneurship

Manufacturers of resistance-training machines have characteristics of both goods-producing and service-producing businesses. In addition to producing high-quality equipment, they must provide product training, technical support, warranties, and on-site repair and maintenance.

The most valuable asset of a twenty-first century institution will be its knowledge workers and their productivity.[5]

natural resources
Land, forests, minerals, water, and other tangible assets usable in their natural state

human resources
All the people who work for an organization

capital
The physical, human-made elements used to produce goods and services, such as factories and computers; can also refer to the funds that finance the operations of a business

entrepreneurs
People who accept the risk of failure in the private enterprise system

- **Human resources**—anyone (from company presidents to grocery clerks) who works to produce goods and services
- **Capital**—resources (such as money, computers, machines, tools, and buildings) that a business needs to produce goods and services
- **Entrepreneurs**—people such as Steve Case who are innovative and willing to take risks to create and operate new businesses (see Exhibit 1.1)
- **Knowledge**—the collective intelligence of an organization

Some companies rely more heavily on one factor of production than another to operate. For instance, a **labor-intensive business** relies predominantly on human resources to prosper. A consulting firm is an example of a labor-intensive business because its existence is heavily dependent on the knowledge and skills of its consultants. Even though the firm requires money to operate, a group of consultants can go into business simply by purchasing some computers and some telephones. By contrast, a **capital-intensive business** requires large amounts of money or equipment to get started and to operate. Airlines, electric utilities, telecommunications companies, and automobile manufacturers are examples of capital-intensive businesses. Although each of these businesses requires a large pool of labor to operate, it would be difficult to start any of them without substantial initial investments in plants, machinery, and equipment.

Traditionally, a business was considered to have an advantage if it was located in a country with a plentiful supply of natural resources, human resources, capital, and entrepreneurs. But in a global economy, companies can obtain capital from one part of the world, purchase supplies from another, and locate production facilities in still another. Furthermore, companies can relocate their operations to wherever they find a steady supply of affordable workers. Thus, economists no longer point to the proximity of these four factors of production as a requirement for success. Instead, they consider knowledge to be the key economic resource.[4] Today, minds rather than mines are the source of economic prosperity.

How important is knowledge in the global economy? Consider this: Economists agree that the seven key industries of the next few decades will be microelectronics, biotechnology, composite materials, telecommunications, civilian aviation, robotics, and computers.[6] All of these are brainpower industries. Tomorrow's workers will be freelancers, contractors, and analysts-for-hire, and their work will be brain-intensive instead of labor-intensive. Thus, countries with the greatest supply of knowledge workers and ones with economic systems that give workers the freedom to pursue their own economic interests will have the greatest advantage in the global marketplace.

Types of Economic Systems

All societies must deal with the same basic questions: How should limited economic resources be used to satisfy society's needs? What goods and services should be produced? Who should produce them? How should these goods and services be divided among the population? In some countries these decisions are made by individuals (or households) when they decide how to spend or invest their income and by businesses when they decide what kinds of goods and services to produce; in other countries these decisions are made by governments.

EXHIBIT 1•1

THE COMPANY	ITS START
Clorox	In May 1913, five men pooled $100 each and started Clorox. The group had no experience in bleach-making chemistry but suspected that the brine found in salt ponds in San Francisco Bay could be converted into bleach.
The Limited	In 1963, 26-year-old Leslie Wexner left his family's retail store after having an argument with his father. He opened one small store in a strip mall in Columbus, Ohio. Today the company operates more than 5,000 stores in the United States.
Gateway 2000	Using $10,000 he borrowed from his grandmother, Ted Waitt started the company in his father's South Dakota barn in 1985. Because a typical computer-industry campaign would have been too costly, Waitt invented its now-famous faux-cowhide boxes. Today Gateway's revenues exceed $5 billion.
Coca-Cola	Pharmacist John Pemberton invented a soft drink in his backyard in 1886. Asa Chandler bought the company for $2,300 in 1891. Today it is worth over $170 billion.
E & J Gallo Winery	The brothers invested $6,000 but had no wine-making experience when they rented their first warehouse in California. They learned wine making by studying pamphlets at the local library.
Marriott	Willard Marriott and his fiancee-partner started a 9-seat A&W soda fountain with $3,000 in 1927. They demonstrated a knack for hospitality and clever marketing from the beginning.
Nike	In the early 1960s, Philip Knight and his college track coach sold imported Japanese sneakers from the trunk of a station wagon. Start-up costs totaled $1,000.
United Parcel Service	In 1907 two Seattle teenagers pooled their cash, came up with $100, and began a message and parcel delivery service for local merchants.
William Wrigley Jr.	In 1891 young Wrigley Jr. started selling baking soda in Chicago. To entice new customers, he threw in two packages of chewing gum with every sale. Guess what the customers were more excited about?

RAGS TO RICHES

Few start-up companies are resource rich. Often they become successful because ingenuity is substituted for capital.

The degree of individual freedom to make these decisions and the role that the government plays in allocating a society's resources depend on society's economic system. Two main economic systems exist in the world today: *free-market systems* and *planned economies*.

Free-Market System   In a **free-market system,** individuals are free to decide what products to produce, how to produce them, whom to sell them to, and at what price to sell them. Thus, they have the chance to succeed—or to fail—by their own efforts. **Capitalism** is the term most often used to describe the free-market system, which owes its philosophical origins to eighteenth-century philosophers such as Adam Smith. According to Smith, in the ideal capitalist economy (pure capitalism), the *market* (an arrangement between buyer and seller to trade goods and services) serves as a self-correcting mechanism—an "invisible hand" to ensure the production of the goods that society wants in the quantities that society wants, without regulation of any kind.[7]

Because the market is its own regulator, Smith was opposed to government intervention. He believed that if anyone's prices or wages strayed from acceptable levels that were set for everyone, the force of competition would drive them back. In modern practice, however,

knowledge
Expertise gained through experience or association

labor-intensive business
Businesses in which labor costs are more significant than capital costs

capital-intensive business
Businesses that require large investments in capital assets

free-market system
Economic system in which decisions about what to produce and in what quantities are decided by the market's buyers and sellers

capitalism
Economic system based on economic freedom and competition

the government sometimes intervenes in free-market systems to influence prices and wages or to change the way resources are allocated. This practice of limited intervention is called *mixed capitalism,* which is the economic system of the United States. Other countries with variations of this economic system include Canada, Germany, and Japan. Under mixed capitalism, the pursuit of private gain is regarded as a worthwhile goal that ultimately benefits society as a whole. This is not the case in a planned economy.

Planned Economy   In a **planned economy,** governments control all or part of the allocation of resources and limit the freedom of choice in order to accomplish government goals. Because social equality is a major goal of planned economies, private enterprise and the pursuit of private gain are generally regarded as wasteful and exploitative.

The planned system that allows individuals the least degree of economic freedom is **communism,** which still exists in such countries as North Korea and Cuba. (Keep in mind that even though communism and socialism are discussed here as economic systems, they can be political and social systems as well.) The degree to which communism is actually practiced varies. In its purest form, almost all resources are under government control. Private ownership is restricted largely to personal and household items. Resource allocation is handled through rigid centralized planning by a handful of government officials who decide what goods to produce, how to produce them, and to whom they should be distributed.[8] Although pure communism still has its supporters, the future of communism is dismal. As economists Lester Thurow and Robert Heilbroner put it, "It's a great deal easier to design and assemble the skeleton of a mighty economy than to run it."[9]

Look at Russia. After decades of economic failure and the associated public unrest, the republics that were formerly part of the Soviet Union began restructuring their communist economies. Overnight, the entire Soviet system—its ideology, institutions, and embracing party apparatus—was dismantled. Despite the fervent efforts of Westerners and Russian reformers to shift to a more market-driven system, internal financial and economic turmoil forced the country to throw on the brakes (as Chapter 3 will discuss in detail). As a result, Russia moved only partly down the path to a free-market economy. Now the country is operating on a system of barters and IOUs fueled by shortages of money and supplies—a system that some economists say grows stranger by the day.[10]

Socialism, by contrast, lies somewhere between capitalism and communism in the degree of economic freedom that it permits. Like communism, socialism involves a relatively high degree of government planning and some government ownership of land and capital resources (such as buildings and equipment). However, government involvement is limited to industries considered vital to the common welfare, such as transportation, utilities, medicine, steel, and communications. In these industries, the government owns or controls all the facilities and determines what will be produced and how the output will be distributed. Private ownership is permitted in industries that are not considered vital, and both businesses and individuals are allowed to benefit from their own efforts. However, taxes are high in socialist states because the government absorbs the costs of medical care, education, subsidized housing, and other social services.

LEARNING OBJECTIVE 2
Differentiate between a free-market system and a planned economy

planned economy
Economic system in which the government controls most of the factors of production and regulates their allocation

communism
Economic system in which all productive resources are owned and operated by the government, to the elimination of private property

Well over half of Russia's economy operates on a barter system. These shoppers at a Moscow market are trading goods for food.

socialism
Economic system characterized by public ownership and operation of key industries combined with private ownership and operation of less-vital industries

See It on the Web See It on the Web

FIND THE RIGHT STUFF

Getting information on a specific company can be a challenge, especially if you don't know where to begin. One of the best starting points is Hoover's Online. This Web site provides an incredible gateway to over 10,000 companies and the latest information on each (such as brief profiles, financial data, history, and current events). So log on and use the toolbox to browse company data. Type in the full name of a company and check it out. Be sure to explore the special Hoover Features. You might want to read about some of the emerging companies.
http://www.hoovers.com
Note: To reach the Web sites listed in this book, you don't have to type the URLs into your browser. Just go to the Web site for this book at http://www.prenhall.com/bovee. There, you'll find live links that take you straight to the site of your choice.

. . A tip for finding Web sites: If you get an error message when you try to get to a site, go to http://www.ixquick.com or http://www.brightgate.com. Insert the name of the site or the URL in the space provided, and press "search." If the site you're seeking is still operating, the results of this search will usually provide a hot link to it.

The Trend Toward Privatization

Although varying degrees of socialism and communism are practiced around the world today, several socialist and communist economies are moving toward free-market economic systems. Anxious to unload unprofitable businesses for badly needed cash and to experiment with free-market capitalism, countries such as Great Britain, Mexico, Argentina, Israel, France, Sweden, and China, are **privatizing** some of their government-owned enterprises by selling them to privately held firms. Great Britain, for example, has sold the national phone company, the national steel company, the national sugar company, Heathrow Airport, water suppliers, and the company that makes Rover automobiles. Hopes are high that converting certain industries to private ownership will enable them to compete more effectively in the global marketplace.[11]

privatizing
The conversion of public ownership to private ownership

Nevertheless, many planned economies are discovering that moving toward a free-market economic system and converting state-owned enterprises into world-class corporations is a formidable task without existing blueprints. Some countries are rushing forward without building effective banking or legal systems to protect their emerging private industries. Others, such as China, are being met with strong resistance from hard-line communists. Still, China's president plans to convert most of the country's 305,000 state-owned companies into shareholder-owned corporations while keeping key industries under state control. If successful in its privatization attempts, China will indeed serve as a role model.[12]

■ HOW DO FREE-MARKET ECONOMIES WORK?

Earlier in this chapter we noted that in a free-market economy the marketplace determines what goods and services get produced. In this section we will discuss the underlying elements or principles that must be present for the free market to work in an orderly fashion. These concepts include the theory of supply and demand, competition, and government intervention.

LEARNING OBJECTIVE 3
Explain how supply and demand interact to affect price

The Theory of Supply and Demand in Free-Market Economies

The theory of supply and demand is the immediate driving force of the free-market economy. It is the basic tool that economists use to describe how the market works in determining prices and the quantity of goods produced. **Demand** refers to the amount of a good or

demand
Buyers' willingness and ability to purchase products

EXHIBIT 1·2

EFFECT OF HIGHER AIR FARES ON DEMAND FOR BUSINESS TRAVEL

When airlines raise their ticket prices, demand for business travel softens as companies take these steps to reduce their travel costs.

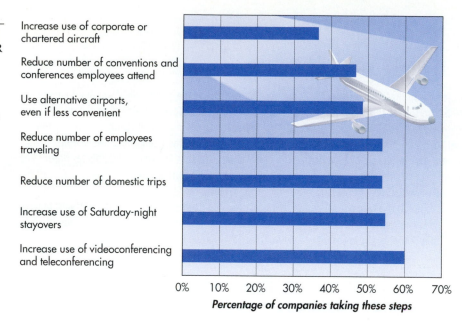

Increase use of corporate or chartered aircraft

Reduce number of conventions and conferences employees attend

Use alternative airports, even if less convenient

Reduce number of employees traveling

Reduce number of domestic trips

Increase use of Saturday-night stayovers

Increase use of videoconferencing and teleconferencing

0% 10% 20% 30% 40% 50% 60% 70%

Percentage of companies taking these steps

supply
Specific quantity of a product that the seller is able and willing to provide

service that consumers will buy at a given time at various prices. **Supply** refers to the quantities of a good or service that producers will provide on a particular date at various prices. Simply put, *demand* refers to the behavior of buyers, whereas *supply* refers to the behavior of sellers. Exhibit 1.2 shows how the two work together to impose a kind of order on the free-market system.

On the surface, the theory of supply and demand seems little more than common sense. Consumers would buy more when the price is low and buy less when the price is high. Producers would offer more when the price is high and offer less when the price is low. In other words, the quantity supplied and the quantity demanded would continuously interact, and the balance between them at any given moment would be reflected by the current price on the open market.

However, a quick look at any real-life market situation shows you that pricing isn't that simple. To a large degree, pricing depends on the type of product being sold. When the price of gasoline goes up, consumers may cut down a little, but most wouldn't stop driving, even if the price were to double. But a rise in housing prices could set off rumors that prices will rise even more. As a result consumers might rush to buy available homes, forcing the prices to rise higher still.

Nevertheless, in broad terms, the interaction of supply and demand regulates a free-market system by determining what is produced and in what amounts. For example, a movie studio might produce more comedies if ticket sales for similar films are brisk. On the other hand, it might decide to produce fewer comedies and more action adventure movies if attendance at comedies lags. The result of such decisions—in theory, at least—is that consumers will get what they want and producers will earn a profit by keeping up with public demand.

Buyer's Perspective   The forces of supply and demand determine the market price for products and services. Say that you're shopping for blue jeans, and the pair you want is priced at

EXHIBIT 1·3

THE RELATIONSHIP
BETWEEN SUPPLY AND
DEMAND

In a free-market economy,
prices aren't set by the
government; nor do
producers alone have the final
say. Instead, prices reflect the
interaction of supply (**S**) and
demand (**D**). The equilibrium
price (**E**) is established when
the amount of a product that
producers are willing to sell at
a given price equals the
amount that consumers are
willing to buy at that price.

$35. This is more than you can afford, so you don't make the purchase. When the store puts them on sale the following week for $18, however, you run right in and buy a pair.

But what if the store had to buy the jeans from the manufacturer for $20? It would have made a profit selling them to you for $35, but it would lose money selling them for $18. What if the store asks to buy more from the manufacturer at $10 or $15 but the manufacturer refuses? Is there a price that will make both the supplier and the customer happy? The answer is yes—the price at which the number of jeans demanded equals the number supplied.

This relationship is shown in Exhibit 1.3. A range of possible prices is listed vertically at the left of the graph, with the lowest at the bottom and the highest at the top. Quantity of blue jeans is represented along the horizontal axis. The points plotted on the curve labeled **D** indicate that on a given day the store would sell 10 pairs of jeans if they were priced at $35, 15 pairs if they were priced at $27, and so on. The curve that describes this relationship between price and quantity demanded is a **demand curve**. (Demand curves are not necessarily curved; they may be straight lines.)

Seller's Perspective   Now think about the situation from the seller's point of view. In general, the more profit the store can make on a particular item, the more of that item it will want to sell. This relationship can also be depicted graphically. Again, look at Exhibit 1.3. The line labeled **S** shows that the store would be willing to offer 30 pairs of jeans at $35, 25 pairs at $30, and so on. The store's willingness to carry the item increases as the price it can charge and its profit potential per item increase. In other words, as price goes up, quantity supplied goes up. The line tracing the relationship between price and quantity supplied is called a **supply curve.**

As much as the store would like to sell 30 pairs of jeans at $35, you and your fellow consumers are likely to want only 10 pairs at that price. If the store offered 30 pairs, therefore, it would probably be stuck with some that it would have to mark down. How does the store avoid this problem? It looks for the point at which the demand curve and the supply curve intersect, the point at which the intentions of buyers and sellers coincide. The point marked **E** in Exhibit 1.3 shows that when jeans are priced at $25, consumers are willing to buy 20 pairs of them and the store is willing to sell 20 pairs. In other words, at the price of $25, supply and demand are in balance. The price at this point is known as the **equilibrium price.**

demand curve
Graph of relationship between
various prices and the quantity
demanded at each price

supply curve
Graph of relationship between
various prices and the quantity
supplied at each price

equilibrium price
Point at which quantity supplied
equals quantity demanded

competition
Rivalry among businesses for the same customer

pure competition
Situation in which so many buyers and sellers exist that no single buyer or seller can individually influence market prices

barriers to entry
Factors that make it difficult to launch a business in a particular industry

monopoly
Market in which there are no direct competitors so that one company dominates

oligopoly
Market dominated by a few producers

monopolistic competition
Situation in which many sellers differentiate their products from those of competitors in at least some small way

competitive advantage
Ability to perform in one or more ways that competitors cannot match

LEARNING OBJECTIVE 4
Name five strategies companies use to gain a competitive advantage

It doesn't take long before innovative products like inline skates catch on. But just rolling a "me-too" product in today's competitive marketplace will not guarantee success. Today's products must be exciting and create perceived consumer value to catch the savvy buyer's eye.

Note that this intersection represents both a specific price—$25 in our example—and a specific quantity of goods—here, 20 pairs of jeans. It is also tied to a specific point in time. Note also that it is the mutual interaction between demand and supply that determines the equilibrium price.

Competition in Free-Market Economies

In a free-market economy, customers are free to buy whatever and wherever they please. Therefore, companies must compete with rivals for potential customers. **Competition** is the situation in which two or more suppliers of a product are rivals in the pursuit of the same customers.

In theory, the ideal type of competition is **pure competition,** which is characterized by marketplace conditions in which multiple buyers and sellers exist; a product or service with nearly identical features; and low **barriers to entry;** that is, firms can easily enter and exit the marketplace. Under these conditions no single firm or group of firms in an industry becomes large enough to influence prices and thereby distort the workings of the free-market system. By contrast, a **monopoly** is a scenario in which only a single seller controls the supply of the good and service and thus determines the price. A situation in which an industry (such as long-distance telephone services) is dominated by only a few providers is called an **oligopoly.**

Between pure competition and a monopoly lie a number of firms with varying degrees of competitive power. Most of the competition in advanced free-market economies is **monopolistic competition,** in which a large number of sellers (none of which dominates the market) offers products that can be distinguished from competing products in at least some small way. Toothpaste, cosmetics, soft drinks, and restaurants are examples of products with distinguishable features.

When markets become filled with competitors and products start to look alike, companies use price, speed, quality, service, or innovation to gain a **competitive advantage—** something that sets one company apart from its rivals and makes its products more appealing to customers. For example, fast-food restaurants such as McDonald's sell special meal deals at reduced prices, Coke sells 24-pak cans at $3.99, Ford offers rebates and discounts, AOL offers a 30-day free trial period, and American Airlines sends e-mail listing rock bottom fares for undersubscribed flights to more than a million Net SAAver subscribers.[13]

Competing on price may seem like an obvious and easy choice to make, but the consequences can be devastating to individual companies and to entire industries. During a three-year period in the early 1990s, price wars caused the U.S. airline industry to lose more money than it had made since the Wright brothers' first flight. Unfortunately, the harsh truth of many price wars is that, sooner or later, everybody sells at a loss. For this reason, companies try to find other ways to compete.

Jiffy Lube, for instance, competes on speed. Mechanics change a car's oil and filter in 15 minutes or less while customers wait. Starbucks competes on quality by delivering a premium product that has changed the definition of "a good cup of coffee." And Enterprise Rent-A-Car blows past its competitors by competing on service. The company establishes convenient rental offices just about everywhere. If your car needs repair service, Enterprise will provide you with a rental car right at the dealer's service center. And the company bets that you won't be in the mood to quibble about prices.[14]

ENTERPRISE RENT-A-CAR TRIES HARDER, AND IT PAYS OFF

How does a small, private company in a highly competitive industry enter the marketplace and blow past everybody in the industry? For Enterprise Rent-A-Car, the answer was "be different." Winner of the 1997 Ernst and Young Entrepreneur of the Year Award, and named one of the "100 Best Companies to Work For" by *Fortune* magazine, Enterprise now owns more cars (over 350,000) and operates in more locations than Hertz. Here's how Enterprise did it.

Enterprise is innovative. While Hertz, Avis, and lots of little companies were cutting one another's throats to win more business from corporate and vacation travelers at airports, Enterprise invaded the market with a completely different strategy and an astoundingly simple approach. Instead of massing 10,000 cars at a few dozen airports, Enterprise recognized that many people can't live a day without their car. So the company set out to deliver wheels to people whose family cars were being repaired or whose cars were too small or unreliable for special occasions.

Enterprise is convenient. The company sets up inexpensive rental offices just about everywhere. As soon as an Enterprise site grows to about 150 cars, another is opened a few miles away. Enterprise now claims to be within 15 minutes of 90 percent of the U.S. population. And at major accounts such as auto repair shops, the company sets up an office on the premises, staffs it during peak hours, and keeps a supply of cars parked outside so customers can fill out the paperwork and conveniently pick up and return rental cars.

Enterprise is aggressive. The company knows that when your car is being towed, you're in no mood to figure out which local rent-a-car company to use. Instead you'll probably rely on the recommendation of the garage service manager. So once Enterprise opens a new site, employees fan out to develop chummy relationships with the service managers of every good-sized auto dealership and body shop in the area—bringing them pizza and doughnuts on most Wednesdays.

Enterprise is affordable. It charges less than competitors but is able to generate high profits because it sets up operations away from expensive airport locations. And higher profits means that Enterprise won't be needing a jump start to keep its business running in the future.

QUESTIONS FOR CRITICAL THINKING

1. Use Enterprise as an example to explain why the free-market system works.
2. Which factors of production does Enterprise rely on to maximize its profit?

Product innovation is another way that companies compete in the free-market economy. Consider 3M. For nearly a century, 3M's management has fostered creativity and has given employees the freedom to take risks and try new ideas. Beginning with the invention of sandpaper in 1904, 3M has produced such staples as masking tape, cellophane tape, magnetic tape, and videotape—not to mention Scotchgard fabric and Post-it Notes. Sometimes product innovation can revolutionize an entire industry, just as Rollerblades, AbFlex, Atomic hour-glass skis, and Burton & Sims snowboards did by creating new market opportunities for the sporting goods industry.[15]

Government's Role in Free-Market Economies

Although the free-market system generally works well, it's far from perfect. If left unchecked, the economic forces that make capitalism succeed may also create severe problems for some groups or individuals. To correct these types of problems, the government intervenes in free-market economies by enforcing laws and regulations to protect consumers

LEARNING OBJECTIVE 5
List the three major economic roles of the U.S. government

and foster competition, by contributing to economic stability, and by spending for the public good.

Enforcing Laws and Regulations to Protect Consumers and Foster Competition

The U.S. federal government and state and local governments create thousands of new laws and regulations every year, many of which limit what businesses and consumers can and cannot do. These laws are intended to protect the consumer and foster competition (See Component Chapter A for a list of important consumer legislation).[16] As a consumer, for example, you can't buy some medications without a doctor's prescription; you can't buy alcoholic beverages without a certificate proving that you're old enough; and you can't buy certain products lacking safety features, such as cars without seatbelts and medication without childproof tops.

deregulation
Removal or relaxation of rules and restrictions affecting businesses

Just as governments can create laws, they can also remove or relax existing laws and regulations through a process known as **deregulation.** Industries such as airlines, banking, and telecommunications have been deregulated in order to promote industry competition in hopes of providing consumers with lower prices and improved products or services.

Because competition generally benefits the U.S. economy, the federal government tries to preserve competition and ensure that no single enterprise becomes too powerful. If a company has a monopoly, it can harm consumers by raising prices, cutting output, or stifling innovation. Furthermore, because monopolies have total control over certain products and prices and the total market share for those products, it's extremely difficult for competitors to enter markets where monopolies exist. For these reasons, true monopolies are prohibited by federal antitrust laws. (Some monopolies, such as utilities, are legal but closely regulated.)

The government's heavy hand with monopolies has been a subject of continuing concern since the turn of the century. One of the highest-profile antitrust cases of the 1990s involved the software giant Microsoft. Microsoft makes the operating-system software used by 90 percent of personal computers as well as a wide array of application software that runs on those operating systems. In the late 1990s, the U.S. Justice Department accused Microsoft of using its vast clout to give itself an unfair advantage in the application-software business by bundling its popular Internet Explorer Web browser with its Windows operating system. Competitors such as Netscape alleged that Microsoft was willing to use every tool at its disposal to damage competition by forcing or persuading companies to install its Internet Explorer as a condition of licensing the Windows operating system.

In 1998 the U.S. government and 19 states filed lawsuits claiming that Microsoft's practices were in violation of antitrust law. After a much-publicized two-year trial, Judge Thomas Jackson ruled that Microsoft was guilty of violating antitrust law by (1) maintaining its monopoly in PC operating systems through anticompetetive means, (2) attempting to monopolize the Web-browser market, and (3) tying its Internet Explorer Web browser to the company's Window's operating system to quash innovation. While Jackson's ruling lays the foundation for powerful remedies against Microsoft (including breaking up the company), any penalties remain uncertain while Microsoft appeals its case.[17] Experts believe that the final outcome of the Microsoft case will set the ground rules for competition in the digital age.

While monopolies are illegal, oligopolies are not. Still, the government has the power to prevent a combination of firms if it would reduce competition in the marketplace. In 1999, for example, bookstore chain Barnes & Noble scrapped its planned $600 million acquisition of Ingram Book Group, the largest book wholesaler in the United States, in the face of regulatory opposition. Critics alleged that the merger would stifle competition by giving Barnes & Noble an advantage over smaller booksellers.[18] Similarly, in 1997 the government opposed the $4 billion merger of Staples and Office Depot, asserting that the combination would substantially impair competition and force consumers to pay higher prices for office supplies.[19]

Contributing to Economic Stability   Another important role the government assumes in a free-market economy is to contribute to the economy's stability. An economy never stays exactly the same size. Instead, it grows and contracts in response to the combined effects of such factors as technological breakthroughs, changes in investment patterns, shifts in consumer attitudes, world events, and basic economic forces. These up-and-down swings are known as the **business cycle.** Although such swings are natural and to some degree predictable, they cause hardship. During periods of downward swing, or **recession,** consumers buy less and factories produce less, so companies must lay off workers, who in turn buy less—and so on.

In an attempt to avoid such problems and to foster economic stability, the government can levy new taxes or adjust the current tax rates, raise or lower interest rates, and regulate the total amount of money circulating in our economy. These government actions have two facets: fiscal policy and monetary policy. **Fiscal policy** involves changes in the government's revenues and expenditures to stimulate or dampen the economy. **Monetary policy** involves adjustments to the nation's money supply by increasing or decreasing interest rates to help control inflation. In the United States, monetary policy is controlled primarily by the Federal Reserve Board, a group of appointed government officials who oversee the country's central banking system. (Monetary policy is discussed more fully in Chapter 15.)

Spending for the Public Good   Although everybody hates to pay taxes, most of us are willing to admit they're a necessary evil. If the government didn't take your tax money and repair our nation's roads, would you be inclined to fix them yourself? Similarly, it might not be practical to rely on individual demand to provide police and fire protection or to launch satellites. Instead, the government steps in and collects a variety of taxes so it can supply such *public goods* (see Exhibit 1.4).

For many years the U.S. government spent more money than it took in, creating annual budget deficits on the order of several hundred billion dollars. The accumulated amount of annual budget deficits (the U.S. national debt) now amounts to almost $6 trillion.

business cycle
Fluctuations in the rate of growth that an economy experiences over a period of several years

recession
Period during which national income, employment, and production all fall

fiscal policy
Use of government revenue collection and spending to influence the business cycle

monetary policy
Government policy and actions taken by the Federal Reserve Board to regulate the nation's money supply

TYPE OF TAX	LEVIED ON
Income taxes	Income earned by individuals and businesses. Income taxes are the government's largest single source of revenue.
Real property taxes	Asessed value of the land and structures owned by businesses and individuals.
Sales taxes	Retail purchases made by customers. Sales taxes are collected by retail businesses at the time of the sale and then forwarded to the government.
Excise taxes	Selected items such as gasoline, tobacco, and liquor. Often referred to as "sin" taxes, excise taxes are implemented to help control potentially harmful practices.
Payroll taxes	Earnings of individuals to help fund Social Security, Medicare, and unemployment compensation. Corporations match employee contributions.

EXHIBIT 1·4

TYPES OF TAXES

From road repair to regulation, running a government is an expensive affair. To fund government operations and projects, national governments, states, counties, and cities levy and collect a variety of revenue-raising taxes.

See It on the Web See It on the Web

LEARN ABOUT YOUR BENEFITS

U.S. workers pay billions of dollars into the Social Security program each year. Do you know what that money is used for? Why not visit the Social Security Administration (SSA) Web site and satisfy your curiosity. Learn what FICA stands for. Find out the truth about this program. Begin your discovery now by clicking on the History of the SSA (from the SSA homepage). Be sure to play some Fun and Games before you leave.
http://www.ssa.gov

As a result, interest payments alone on the national debt cost U.S. taxpayers $340 billion a year—or $10,000 per second. In 1997 Congress approved a plan to pare down future deficits in order to balance the budget by 2002.[20] Strong economic growth accompanied by budget modifications, however, has put the United States ahead of schedule.

Although reducing government spending might seem like a practical step, keep in mind that such reduction can have rippling economic consequences. That's because government spending boosts the economy and has a *multiplier effect* as it makes its way through the economy. For example, if the government decides to fund new highway projects, thousands of construction workers will be gainfully employed and earn wages. If some of these workers decide to spend their extra income to buy new cars, car dealers will have more income. The car dealers, in turn, might spend their income on new clothes, and the salesclerks (who earn commissions) might buy compact disks, and so on. This *circular flow* of money through the economic system links all elements of the U.S. economy by exchanging goods and services for money, which is then used to buy more goods and services, and so on.

HOW DO ECONOMISTS KNOW IF THE SYSTEM IS WORKING?

Each day we are deluged with complex statistical data that depict the current status and past performance of the economy. Sorting, understanding, and interpreting these data are difficult tasks even for professional economists. **Economic indicators** are statistics such as interest rates and unemployment rates that are used to monitor and measure economic performance. Statistics that point to what may happen to the economy in the future are called *leading indicators;* statistics that signal a swing in the economy after the movement has begun are called *lagging indicators* (see Exhibit 1.5). Unemployment statistics, for example, are leading economic indicators because they are an early indicator of future changes in personal income. When unemployment rises, people have less income to spend, and the economy suffers. Two key indicators that economists closely monitor are a nation's output and price changes.

economic indicators
Statistics that measure variables in the economy

gross domestic product (GDP)
Dollar value of all the final goods and services produced by businesses located within a nation's borders; excludes receipts from overseas operations of domestic companies

Measuring a Nation's Output

The broadest measure of an economy's health is the **gross domestic product (GDP).** The GDP measures a country's output—its production, distribution, and use of goods and services—by computing the sum of all goods and services produced for final use in a market during a specified period (usually a year). The goods may be produced by either do-

EXHIBIT 1·5

MAJOR ECONOMIC INDICATORS

Businesses and government leaders rely on these major economic indicators to make decisions.

LEADING INDICATORS	LAGGING INDICATORS
Changes in the money supply in circulation	Changes in the prime rate
Number of building permits issued by private housing units	Number of commercial and industrial loans to be repaid
New orders for consumer goods	Change in the Consumer Price Index for services
Number of contracts and orders for equipment	Size of manufacturing and trade inventories
Weekly initial claims for unemployment insurance	Average length of unemployment
Average weekly hours for production workers in manufacturing	Labor cost per unit of output in manufacturing

mestic or foreign companies as long as these companies are located within a nation's boundaries. Sales from a Honda assembly plant in California, for instance, would be included in the GDP. A less popular measure of a country's output is the **gross national product (GNP).** This measure excludes the value of production from foreign-owned businesses within a nation's boundaries (such as Honda U.S.), but it includes receipts from the overseas operations of domestic companies—such as McDonald's in Switzerland. Put another way, GNP considers *who* is responsible for the production; GDP considers *where* the production occurs. Although far from perfect, the GDP enables a nation to evaluate its economic policies and to compare its current performance with prior periods or with the performance of other nations.[21]

gross national product (GNP)
Dollar value of all the final goods and services produced by domestic businesses, including receipts from overseas operations; excludes receipts from foreign-owned businesses within a nation's borders

Measuring Price Changes

Price changes, especially price increases, are another important economic indicator. In a period of rising prices, the purchasing power of a dollar erodes, which means that you can purchase fewer things with today's dollar than you could in a prior period. Over time, price increases tend to lead to wage increases, which in turn add pressures for higher prices, setting a vicious cycle in motion.

Inflation is a steady rise in the prices of goods and services throughout the economy. When the inflation rate begins to decline, economists use the term *disinflation*. **Deflation,** on the other hand, is the sustained fall in the general price level for goods and services. It is the opposite of inflation; that is, purchasing power increases because a dollar held today will buy more tomorrow. In a deflationary period, investors postpone major purchases in anticipation of lower prices in the future. Keep in mind that although prices in the overall economy tend to increase year after year, not all industries and product categories necessarily follow this trend. In the electronics industry, for instance, technological advances have the opposite effect; prices tend to drop as production increases.

inflation
Economic condition in which prices rise steadily throughout the economy

deflation
Economic condition in which prices fall steadily throughout the economy

The **consumer price index (CPI)** measures the rate of inflation by comparing the change in prices of a representative basket of goods and services such as clothing, food, housing, and utilities over time. A numerical weight is assigned to each item in the representative basket to adjust for each item's relative importance in the marketplace. As are most economic indicators, the CPI is far from perfect. For one thing, the representative basket of goods may not accurately represent the prices and consumption patterns of the area in which you live. For another, the mix in this basket may not include new innovations, which often play a major role in consumer spending patterns. Nonetheless, many businesses use the CPI to adjust rent increases and to keep employees' wages in line with the pace of inflation.

consumer price index (CPI)
Monthly statistic that measures changes in the prices of about 400 goods and services that consumers buy

See It on the Web See It on the Web

WHAT'S IN THE CPI?

The CPI is an important tool that allows analysts to track the change in prices over time. But the CPI doesn't always match a given individual's inflation experience. Find out why by visiting the official CPI Web site maintained by the U.S. Bureau of Labor Statistics. Be sure to check out how the CPI measures homeowners' costs, and don't leave without getting some data. Click on the Most Requested Series, find your region, and trace the CPI for your area by entering some information in the boxes.
http://stats.bls.gov/cpihome.htm

U.S. Economic Growth and the Challenges Ahead

By any objective measure, the U.S. economy is thriving today. GDP, jobs, trade, output productivity, and purchasing power all show the United States in the midst of a robust expansion. New technologies, the end of the Cold War, industry reinvention, and the information revolution have put the United States back into the driver's seat. However, a look into the history of the country's economic growth will show that getting there has been a long journey and a rough ride.

History of U.S. Economic Growth

The first economic base in the United States was the small family farm. People grew enough food for their families and used any surplus to trade for necessary goods provided by independent craftspeople and merchants. Business operated on a small scale, and much of the population was self-employed. With fertile, flat terrain and adequate rainfall, farmers soon prospered, and their prosperity spread to the townspeople who served them.

In the early nineteenth century, people began making greater use of rivers, harbors, and rich mineral deposits. Excellent natural resources helped businesspeople accumulate the capital they needed to increase production—fueling the transition of the United States from a farm-based economy to an industrial economy.

technology
Knowledge, tools, techniques, and activities used in the production of goods and services

economies of scale
Savings from manufacturing, marketing, or buying in large quantities

Age of Industrialization: 1900 to 1944   During the nineteenth century, new **technology** (the knowledge and processes used in the production of goods and services) gave birth to the factory and the industrial revolution. Millions of new workers came to the United States from abroad to work in factories where each person performed one simple task over and over. Separating the manufacturing process into distinct tasks and producing large quantities of similar products allowed businesses to achieve cost and operating efficiencies known as **economies of scale.**

As businesses increased in size, they also became more powerful. In the early 1920s more and more industrial assets were concentrated into fewer and fewer hands, putting smaller competitors, workers, and consumers at a disadvantage. By popular mandate, the government passed laws and regulations to prevent the abuse of power by big business. At the same time, workers began to organize into labor unions to balance the power of their employers. Meanwhile, U.S. businesses enjoyed such an enormously diverse market within the country's borders that they didn't need to trade overseas. But prosperity soon ended. In 1929 the U.S. stock market crashed, ushering in a period of economic collapse known as the Great Depression. Millions of people lost their jobs. By 1941, one in ten workers remained unemployed, the birthrate was stagnant, and the hand of the U.S. government strengthened as people lost confidence in the power of business to pull the country out of hard times.

World War II and the Postwar Golden Era: 1945 to 1979   World War II (which the United States entered in 1941) and the postwar reconstruction starting in 1945 revived the economy and renewed the trend toward large-scale enterprises. The G.I. Bill of Rights opened advanced education to the working classes. The middle class grew and prospered. By 1950 the birthrate had jumped, and the baby boom was on. Accustomed to playing a major role in the war effort, the government continued to exert a large measure of control over business and the economy. President Eisenhower's highway system fueled expansion and the growth of the suburbs. Sales of new homes and U.S.-manufactured automobiles skyrocketed.

Stimulated by a boom in world demand and an expansive political climate, the United States prospered throughout the 1960s. Expanding world trade provided limitless markets for U.S. goods. But once Europe and Japan had recovered from the war, they began challenging U.S. industries—Italy with shoes, Switzerland with watches, and Japan with cameras. By the end of the 1960s, Japanese transistor radios dominated the world market. Still, the more advanced technological industries and their products—televisions, copying machines, and aircraft—remained U.S. preserves.

In the early 1970s inflation depressed demand and U.S. economic growth began to slump. In 1973 the price of a barrel of oil skyrocketed from $3 to $11, forcing companies to invest in ways to save energy instead of investing in new manufacturing equipment. The U.S. economy had barely recovered from the 1973 oil shock when it got hit again in 1979 (oil jumped from $13 to $23 per barrel), resulting in galloping inflation and sky-high interest rates. Exports from Asia began to pour into the United States—some bearing U.S. labels—and the United States entered an era of diminishing growth.[22] Meanwhile, a takeover binge was changing the structure of corporate America. Giant organizations called *conglomerates* emerged as companies acquired strings of unrelated businesses to grow and diversify their enterprises.

Rise of Global Competition and Two Decades of Reinvention: 1980–1999   During the 1980s, global competition crept up slowly on the United States. Since the 1950s, Japanese firms had been refining their manufacturing processes to become more efficient, and by 1980 they had a 30-year head start on the United States. (Ironically, the United States had supplied its foreign competitors with the resources and know-how to stake a claim in the world marketplace.). Sony moved into the fast lane and introduced new product innovations such as the Walkman and the VCR, while pricing them affordably. By the mid-1980s, it became almost impossible to buy a consumer electronic device that was made in the United States.

To regain a competitive edge, many U.S. companies restructured their operations. Some corporations merged with others to produce economies of scale; others splintered into smaller fragments to focus on a single industry or a narrower customer base. Then, in the early 1990s, U.S. businesses got hit again. The U.S. economy went into full-blown recession, and many companies that had loaded up on debt in the 1980s to expand their operations or to acquire other companies went bankrupt. During this period of upheaval, unemployment soared as hundreds of thousands of jobs were eliminated. General Motors alone laid off 130,000 workers—enough to fill two football stadiums. Had the United States continued in the direction it was headed at the beginning of the 1990s, it might well have experienced the disaster that many economists feared. But it didn't.

 **Companies that adopt a "wait and see" attitude to introduce products with lower profit margins may wind up entering the market when it's too late.**[23]

Manufacturing improvements helped move the United States from a position of near-terminal decline to renewed world dominance.[24] Managers at IBM and AT&T breathed new life into these two U.S. manufacturing classics. Meanwhile, Motorola struck back with its pagers and cell phones, Hewlett-Packard took over the high-volume market in low-cost computer printers, and once-sleepy Kodak challenged the Japanese with digital and disposable cameras.[25] As more and more U.S. companies reengineered their operations to improve productivity and to focus on product quality, U.S. industries experienced remarkable turnarounds. But it was the growth of the U.S. service sector and the country's lead in the age of information that ultimately pushed the U.S. economy into a remarkable period of prosperity.

Growth of the Service Sector

Services have always played an important role in the U.S. economy. For more than 60 years, they accounted for half of all U.S. employment. In the mid-1980s services became the engine of growth for the U.S. economy (see Exhibit 1.6).[26] In fact, most of the increase in U.S. employment from 1985 to the present has been generated by the service sector. Today about half of the 1,000 largest U.S. companies are service-based.[27]

Economists project that the number of service-related jobs will continue to increase—from about 94 million (or 72 percent of the 130 million or so people at work today) to about 112 million by 2006. In contrast, employment growth in the goods-producing sector is projected to remain flat through 2006.[28] (See Appendix 2 for a discussion of the outlook for selected business careers in both the service and manufacturing sectors). The projected growth in the service sector is attributable to several factors:

- *More disposable income.* The 76 million baby boomers in the United States (people born between 1946 and 1964) are in their peak earning years. These consumers find themselves with more disposable income and look for services to help them invest, travel, relax, and stay fit.

- *Changing demographic patterns.* The United States has more elderly people, more single people living alone, more two-career households, and more single parents than ever before. These trends create opportunities for service companies that can help people with all the tasks they no longer have time for, including home maintenance, food service, and child care.[29]

EXHIBIT 1·6

SECTORS OF THE U.S. ECONOMY

The service sector accounts for 72 percent of U.S. economic output; the goods-producing sector accounts for the remaining 28 percent.

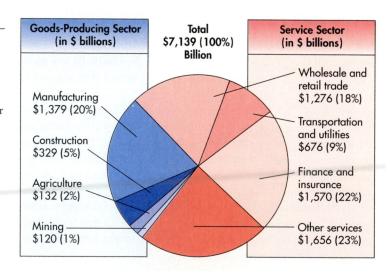

Goods-Producing Sector (in $ billions)	Total $7,139 (100%) Billion	Service Sector (in $ billions)

Manufacturing $1,379 (20%)
Construction $329 (5%)
Agriculture $132 (2%)
Mining $120 (1%)

Wholesale and retail trade $1,276 (18%)
Transportation and utilities $676 (9%)
Finance and insurance $1,570 (22%)
Other services $1,656 (23%)

- *Increasing number of complex goods.* Computers, home entertainment centers, recreational vehicles, security systems, and automated production equipment are examples of products that require specialized installation, repair, user training, or extensive support services. As new technology is incorporated into more and more products, companies will need to provide more of these types of product-support services to remain competitive.
- *Greater need for professional advice.* Many firms turn to consultants to find ways to cut costs, refine processes, and become more competitive. In addition, the continued growth of global marketing and manufacturing requires more international support services.[30]
- *Growing Internet opportunities.* Traditional service providers, such as retailers, brokers, lawyers, advertisers, and consultants, are building new businesses around the Internet technology. As one economist put it, "The Internet is the backbone of greater service trade."[31] (For a more in-depth look at the issues and challenges businesses are facing in the world of e-commerce, consult the E-Business in Action online supplement at http://www.prenhall.com/introductiontobusiness and your copy of *E-Biz: Prentice Hall Guide to E-Business and E-Commerce.*)

The Challenges Ahead

Even though the United States is beginning a new century in a position of great economic strength, doing business in the twenty-first century means working in a world of increasing uncertainty as the very nature of work, organizations, and economics is changing. Businesses today are facing a raft of new challenges. In the coming chapters we will explore each of these challenges in depth and will provide real-world examples of how companies are tackling and meeting these challenges in the global economy.

LEARNING OBJECTIVE 6
Identify five challenges that businesses are facing today

Keeping Pace with Technology and Electronic Commerce Everywhere we look, technology is reshaping the world. The Internet and innovations in computerization, miniaturization, telecommunication, and digitization (the process of turning sound, movies, pictures, documents, and other forms of data into computer bits to transfer them by phone lines, satellites, and cable around the world) have made it possible for people anywhere in the world to exchange information and goods. Such technologies are reshaping the global marketplace, collapsing boundaries, changing the way customers, suppliers, and companies interact, and revolutionizing all facets of business life.

Fledgling Internet companies are starting up businesses and becoming global competitors overnight. Furthermore, these Internet companies are forcing traditional enterprises to explore new ways of doing business—including launching products and services that compete with their existing ones.[33]

Electronic commerce (e-commerce), the buying and selling of goods and services over an electronic network, is a driving force behind U.S. economic growth. E-commerce, which is projected to contribute over six percent of the U.S. GDP by 2005, consists of two distinct facets.[34] *Business-to-business* e-commerce is the transaction of e-commerce between suppliers, distributors, manufacturers and stores, whereas *business-to-consumer* e-commerce (often referred to as e-tailing or online selling) involves interactions and transactions between a company and its consumers.

Some companies, such as Dell, Cisco, Amazon, and Ebay, are now taking e-commerce to the next level by becoming an **electronic business (e-business);** that is, they are reinventing their business practices, finding new ways to electronically market existing products, and developing new products and services to sell in the e-commerce marketplace.[35]

Traditional companies can master the Internet if they set up a completely independent organization and let that organization attack the parent.[32]

electronic commerce (e-commerce)
The general term for the buying and selling of goods and services on the Internet

electronic business (e-business)
A business that transforms its processes to take full advantage of Internet technology, generates a large share of its revenue from Internet sales, focuses on earning a profit, and is always open for business

Focus on E-Business

HERE COMES THE ELECTRONIC ECONOMY

Without a doubt, the Internet is ushering in an era of sweeping change. It is tearing down the walls of geography and allowing businesses to reach markets anywhere in the world. It's spawning new businesses, transforming existing ones, saving companies money, and creating enormous new wealth. It's changing the way people shop for books, cars, vacations, advice—just about everything. It's forcing companies of all sizes and types to face new competition, explore new business opportunities, and adopt new ways of conducting business. In the span of just a few years, the Internet has touched every business and industry. But that's not good news for everyone.

Operating at an accelerated pace dubbed Internet time, companies conducting e-commerce move quickly and aggressively to develop Internet products and services, find capital, and win Web customers. Those that take advantage of the Net to revamp their businesses or build brand new ones stand to reap the rewards; those that wait or ignore the Internet's force are being squeezed out. Travel agencies, stockbrokers, and physical retail stores are just a few of the casualties. After all, as human tasks such as selling airline tickets, stock, and all kinds of consumer goods are taken over by the dot-coms, there's not much additional work left for those businesses to do.

Even more frightful, or exciting (depending on which side of the casualty line you're on) is the fact that the e-commerce (the buying and selling of goods and services over a network) is only in its infancy and by all measures is expected to provide much of the fuel that will power the 21st century. Experts predict that revenues from e-commerce will exceed $1 trillion by 2005. That's a pretty impressive statistic considering the fact that only a handful of companies have figured out how to make money transacting business-to-consumer e-commerce, and nobody really knows its potential or its limits. Moreover, companies transacting e-commerce face many obstacles. For one thing, they must accept constant change as a reality. For another, they must redefine their relationships with suppliers, customers, and employees, and they must transform every aspect of their operations to become true e-businesses.

Fresh opportunities and big threats. That's the Web. In subsequent "Focus on E-Business" boxes, we'll take a closer look at how e-commerce is revolutionizing all facets of business life. You'll see that becoming an e-business in today's electronic economy takes much more than launching a Web site.

QUESTIONS FOR CRITICAL THINKING

1. Why must companies move at an accelerated pace in today's economy?
2. How is e-commerce facilitating the globalization of business?

Keep in mind that while many companies today transact e-commerce, few have become true e-businesses. Such transformation takes a lot of time and effort. (Consult Component Chapter C and Focus on E-Business feature boxes throughout this text for an in-depth discussion of the challenges businesses are facing as they position themselves to transact business in the electronic economy.)

Supporting Quality Initiatives and Achieving Customer Satisfaction   For many businesses, such as AOL, the challenge in the future will be to compete on the basis of *speed* (getting products to market sooner), *quality* (doing a better job of meeting customer expectations), and *customer satisfaction* (making sure buyers are happy with every aspect of the purchase, from the shopping experience until they're through using the product). In addition, as Steve Case discovered, one of the biggest challenges companies will face is to attract new customers by offering them innovative products before others do.

At times it's right *not* to listen to your customers and to invest in new products that your customers may not yet want or need.[36]

Starting and Managing a Small Business in Today's Competitive Environment   Starting a new business or successfully managing a small company in today's global economy will require creativity and a willingness to exploit new opportunities. Small companies often lack the resources to buffer themselves from competition. Furthermore, in the information age, once a new product or process is brought to the market, competitors need only a short time to be up and running with something similar. Thus, the biggest challenge for small businesses is to make a product or provide a service that is hard to imitate—or that competitors choose not to imitate. If something is easy for the large competitors to copy, they will.

Using technology to level the playing field, meeting an unsatisfied consumer need through better service or a higher-quality product, and thinking globally are some of the ways small businesses can compete successfully against big business.

Thinking Globally and Committing to a Culturally Diverse Work Force   Today, financial and product markets are far more interconnected than ever before. **Globalization**—the increasing tendency of the world to act as one market instead of a series of national ones—opens new markets for a company's goods and services while simultaneously producing tougher competition. Globalization also changes the composition of the work force into one that is more diverse in race, gender, age, physical and mental abilities, lifestyle, culture, education, ideas, and background. Thus, to be competitive in the global economy, companies must commit to a culturally diverse work force and adopt global standards of excellence.

globalization
Tendency of the world's economies to act as a single interdependent system

Behaving in an Ethically and Socially Responsible Manner   As businesses become more complex through global expansion and technological change, they face an increasing variety of ethical and social issues. These include the marketing of unhealthful products, the use of questionable accounting practices to compute financial results, and the pollution of the environment (as Chapter 2 will discuss). In the future, businesses can expect continued pressure from environmental groups, consumers, and government regulators to act ethically and responsibly.

Summary of Learning Objectives

1. **Identify four key social and economic roles that businesses serve.**
   Businesses provide society with necessities; they provide people with jobs and a means to prosper; they pay taxes that are used by the government to provide services for its citizens; and they reinvest their profits in the economy, thereby increasing a nation's wealth.

2. **Differentiate between a free-market system and a planned economy.**
   In a free-market system, individuals have a high degree of freedom to decide what is produced, by whom, and for whom. Furthermore, the pursuit of private gain is regarded as a worthwhile goal. In a planned economy, governments limit the individual's freedom of choice in order to accomplish government goals, control the allocation of resources, and restrict private ownership to personal and household

items. The pursuit of private gain is nonexistent under a planned system.

3. **Explain how supply and demand interact to affect price.**
   In the simplest sense, supply and demand affect price in the following manner: When price goes up, the quantity demanded goes down but the supplier's incentive to produce more goes up. When price goes down, the quantity demanded increases, whereas the quantity supplied may (or may not) decline. When the interests of buyers and sellers are in balance, an equilibrium price is established. However, pricing involves more than the simple notions of supply and demand, as the examples of gasoline and housing illustrate.

4. **Name five strategies companies use to gain a competitive advantage.**
   Companies compete on the basis of price, speed, quality, service, and innovation.

MEETING BUSINESS CHALLENGES AT AMERICA ONLINE

Steve Case was an entrepreneur with a vision of a high-tech service simple enough to be used by ordinary people. Well before *Internet* was a household word, Case wanted to help people get connected via computers quickly and easily. Following this vision, he reshaped a tiny Virginia company with the humdrum name of Control Video into an online giant with the catchier name of America Online (AOL).

To make AOL even more attractive to a wider audience, Case forged ahead with several acquisitions. First, he broadened the customer base by buying rival CompuServe. Next, he gained access to more business users with its $4.2 billion acquisition of Netscape Communications, maker of the popular Navigator Internet browser. Then Case followed up by acquiring Mirabilis, the Israel-based firm behind ICQ ("I seek you") instant messaging software, one of AOL's most popular communication features. Recognizing the global need for online access, Case began offering a version of AOL in Japan as early as 1985 and soon expanded into Canada, France, Germany, the United Kingdom, Austria, Switzerland, and Australia.

As the millennium closed, AOL was serving more than 22 million customers all over the world. Even though AOL was now profitable, the company faced a range of uncertainties: Upstarts were giving away Internet access—a service for which AOL charged customers $21.95 each month. Moreover, the company did not own the high-speed cable lines it needed to build the Web's next infrastructure. Rather than hashing out a series of joint ventures with other Internet and cable companies, Case made an audacious move: He orchestrated the largest merger in history by joining forces with Time Warner to form the world's first fully integrated media and communications company. Valued at $162 billion, the AOL Time Warner colossus would resolve both firms' strategic pickles. AOL could use Time Warner's high-capacity cable lines to zap services and content (including

Time Warner's world-class media) into homes at lightning speed. Meanwhile Time Warner, the world's biggest media company, could use AOL's infrastructure, e-commerce capabilities, and technological expertise to accelerate its digital metamorphosis. Together they would transform the media landscape of the new millennium and fundamentally change the way people get information, are entertained, communicate with others, and buy products.[37]

Critical Thinking Questions

1. How did AOL and Time Warner gain a competitive advantage by joining forces?
2. Explain how AOL, a service business, depends on other goods-producing businesses to deliver its service to customers.
3. Give examples of how AOL competes on price, speed, quality, service, and innovation.

■ LEARN MORE ONLINE

America Online remains a formidable competitor in the online industry. Launch your Internet browser and visit the corporate section of its Web site at http://www.aol.com/corp to find out more about the company's background, its merger with Time Warner, and its future plans. Click on the link to read the company profile and browse the most recent annual report. Then scan some of the latest press releases. What acquisitions has Steve Case made lately—and why? What are the trends in growth and profitability? How is new technology driving innovation at AOL?

5. **List the three major economic roles of the U.S. government.**
   The U.S. government enforces rules and regulations to foster competition, contributes to economic stability, and provides its citizens with public services.

6. **Identify five challenges that businesses are facing today.**
   The five challenges identified in the chapter are (1) the accelerating pace of technological change and the need to modify business practices to transact electronic commerce competitively; (2) the need to innovate and compete on the basis of speed, quality, and customer satisfaction; (3) the competition that small businesses face from industry giants and the global economy; (4) the increasingly global nature of the economy and the challenges of meeting the needs of a diverse work force; and (5) the continued public and government scrutiny of business's social, ethical, and environmental performance.

Key Terms

barriers to entry (10)

business (3)

business cycle (13)

capital (5)

capital-intensive business (6)

capitalism (6)

communism (6)

competition (10)

competitive advantage (10)

consumer price index (CPI) (15)

deflation (15)

demand (7)

demand curve (9)

deregulation (12)

economic indicators (14)

economic system (3)

economies of scale (16)

electronic business (e-business) (19)

electronic commerce (e-commerce) (19)

entrepreneurs (5)

equilibrium price (9)

factors of production (3)

fiscal policy (13)

free-market system (6)

globalization (21)

goods-producing businesses (3)

gross domestic product (GDP) (14)

gross national product (GNP) (15)

human resources (5)

inflation (15)

knowledge (5)

labor-intensive business (6)

monetary policy (13)

monopolistic competition (10)

monopoly (10)

natural resources (5)

not-for-profit organizations (3)

oligopoly (10)

planned economy (6)

privatizing (7)

profit (3)

pure competition (10)

recession (13)

service businesses (3)

socialism (6)

supply (8)

supply curve (9)

technology (16)

Test Your Knowledge

QUESTIONS FOR REVIEW

1. Why do businesspeople study economics?
2. Why will knowledge workers be the key economic resource in the future?
3. How is capitalism different from communism and socialism in the way it achieves key economic goals?
4. Define the demand curve, the supply curve, and the equilibrium price.
5. What role does competition play in the free-market economy?

QUESTIONS FOR ANALYSIS

6. Why is it often easier to start a service business than a goods-producing business?
7. Explain how a product like Rollerblades could revolutionize the sporting goods industry and how the economy as a whole benefits from new products like Rollerblades.
8. Why do governments intervene in a free-market economy?
9. How do economists know if the economic system is working?
10. A spokesperson for Ty, the maker of the Beanie Baby stuffed animal, admits that the company periodically "retires" Beanies to ensure scarcity and spike product demand.[38] Is this practice ethical? Please explain your answer.

QUESTIONS FOR APPLICATION

11. Company sales are skyrocketing, and projections show that your computer consulting business will outgrow its current location by next year. What factors should you consider when selecting a new site for your business?

12. How would a decrease in Social Security benefits to the elderly affect the economy?

13. Graph a supply and demand chart for America Online's monthly subscription pricing structure. Make up any data you need, but show the company's equilibrium price to be $23.95.

14. One of the five economic challenges in this century is "starting and managing a small business in today's global economy." Review "Enterprise Rent-A-Car Tries Harder, and It Pays Off" (see page 11) and explain how Enterprise Rent-A-Car is meeting this challenge.

Practice Your Knowledge

SHARPENING YOUR COMMUNICATION SKILLS

Select a local service business you are familiar with. How does that business try to gain a competitive advantage in the marketplace? Write a brief summary, as directed by your instructor, describing whether the company competes on speed, quality, price, innovation, service, or a combination of those attributes. Be prepared to present your analysis to your classmates.

HANDLING DIFFICULT SITUATIONS ON THE JOB: COPING WITH WAKEBOARD MANIA

Bill Porter, owner of the Performance Ski & Surf store, hasn't seen sporting equipment sell this rapidly in Orlando, Florida, since in-line skating became popular. But now his store, where you are the assistant manager, has been unable to keep wakeboards in stock. It doesn't seem to matter which brand—Wake Tech, Neptune, or Full Tilt—locals and tourists alike are snapping them up and heading out to the water. These boards are outselling traditional trick water skis by 20 to 1.

This unusually strong demand has been fueled, in part, by media coverage of professional wakeboarders such as Dean Lavelle, who recently exhibited his wakeboard skills at nearby Lake Butler. You and Porter saw a photo of Lavelle in action, holding the same kind of rope as any water skier—except he was 15 feet in the air. His short, stubby, fiberglass wakeboard (which was strapped to his feet) was higher than his head, and from the grimace on his face, it looked as if he was mid-flip.

Porter does not want to keep disappointing shoppers who come in asking for wakeboards, so he has asked you to order another 12 Wake Techs, 8 Neptunes, and 10 Full Tilts. "Don't worry about colors or models; we'll be lucky to get this order filled at all from what I hear," he says. With such strong demand, however, you wonder whether the store should adjust the price of these wakeboards to reflect the skimpy and uncertain supply.[39]

1. According to the theory of supply and demand, how do you think consumers would react if your store set higher prices on the new order of wakeboards? What are the advantages and disadvantages of increasing the price to customers? In the end, what would you advise Porter to do?

2. If you do mark a higher price on the next shipment of wakeboards, what will you tell shoppers who comment on the increase?

3. What would you do if a competitor started selling wakeboards over the Internet at a much lower price?

BUILDING YOUR TEAM SKILLS

Economic indicators help businesses and governments determine where the economy is headed. You may have noticed news headlines such as the following, each of which offers clues to the direction of the U.S. economy:

1. Housing Starts Lowest in Months
2. Fed Lowers Discount Rate and Interest Rates Tumble
3. Retail Sales Up 4 Percent Over Last Month
4. Business Debt Down from Last Year
5. Businesses Are Buying More Electronic Equipment
6. Industry Jobs Go Unfilled as Area Unemployment Rate Sinks to 3 Percent
7. Telephone Reports 30-Day Backlog in Installing Business Systems

Discuss each of those headlines with the other students on your team. Is each item good news or bad news for the economy? Why? What does each news item mean for large and small businesses? Report your team's findings to the class as a whole. Did all the teams come to the same conclusions about each headline? Why or why not? Back in your team, discuss how these different perspectives might influence the way you interpret economic news in the future.

Expand Your Knowledge

EXPLORING CAREER OPPORTUNITIES

The service sector is rapidly expanding, fueled by the high disposable income of baby boomers and their interest in services that help them relax, travel, feel safe, and stay healthy. This expansion means plenty of career opportunities for you to consider as you plan your future. Start by looking at *Occupational*

Outlook Handbook in your library or online at http://stats. bls.gov/ocohome.htm. This is an authoritative resource for information about all kinds of occupations.

1. What categories of service occupations are featured in this handbook? Read about two service occupations that interest you. What is the job outlook for each of these occupations? What training do you need to qualify for these jobs?
2. Select one of these service occupations, and list the education and skills this occupation requires. What can you do now to start preparing for this occupation?
3. What types of businesses, not-for-profit organizations, or government agencies typically hire employees in the service occupation you are exploring? How would you find out about job openings at these organizations?

DEVELOPING YOUR RESEARCH SKILLS

The gross domestic product (GDP) is a broad measure of the economy's health. How healthy has the U.S. economy been in recent years? To find out, use your research skills to identify the right questions and the right sources of information for investigating this topic.

1. Start by doing some background reading about the GDP to clarify the scope of your research and to narrow your focus. Scan printed sources such as the *Information Please Almanac* and the *Statistical Abstract of the United States,* looking up "GDP" and related keywords. What kind of information is available on GDP trends?
2. Select a specific period, such as the 1990s. What detailed information is available about year-by-year GDP figures during your chosen period? In addition to the printed sources noted in number 1, you can check online sources such as the U.S. Bureau of Economic Analysis Web site at http://www.bea.doc.gov/, which contains mountains of statistical data.
3. Look for patterns emerging from the data you have gathered from all these printed and online sources. On the basis of your research, do you think the U.S. economy has become healthier over the period you studied? Prepare a brief oral report, including a visual representation of your data, to share your conclusions and evidence with the entire class.

SEE IT ON THE WEB EXERCISES
Find the Right Stuff, page 7

Hoover's Online provides a wealth of company information. Browse Hoover's Online at http://www.hoovers.com to learn about the following companies: IBM, Wrigley, and Marriott International. (Be sure to enter the company name as shown under

the *power search.*) Use the information provided for these companies to answer the following.

1. Are these companies mainly service or goods-producing businesses? Find the names of the three main competitors for each company.
2. Review several press releases or news articles for these companies. Explore the other data given. How is Hoover's Online an effective tool for gathering information about companies?
3. Return to the Hoover's Online homepage (click Home) and, under Hoover Features, click on the List of Lists, click Select, and click on the Social Responsibility, Corporate Governance, and Workplace link. Click on America's 100 Most Admired Companies (Fortune), and click on any of the companies listed. On what categories are these companies judged? Which of those categories are discussed in this chapter?

Learn About Your Benefits, page 14

Social Security takes a big bite out of your paycheck. Find out what this government program is all about. Visit the Social Security Administration (SSA) Web site at http://www.ssa.gov, scroll down, and click on History of the SSA. Click on the FAQs (frequently asked questions) to answer the following questions.

1. Is there any significance to the numbers assigned in your Social Security number? Are Social Security numbers reused after a person dies?
2. Approximately how much has Social Security paid out in benefits since its inception?
3. Explore the Web site. Besides history, what types of helpful information does this site offer?

What's in the CPI?, page 16

Find out what's in the Consumer Price Index (CPI) and how it is calculated by visiting the CPI Web site at http://stats.bls.gov/ cpihome.htm. Click on the FAQs (frequently asked questions) to answer these questions (hint: sometimes you will need *more* information):

1. How is the CPI used?
2. What goods and services does the CPI cover, and how are they categorized?
3. Using the inflation calculator at http://www.westegg. com/inflation/, see the power of inflation by answering the following: If you had $100 in 1900, how much would it be worth today? (Use the latest year available.)

2

PRACTICING ETHICAL BEHAVIOR AND SOCIAL RESPONSIBILITY

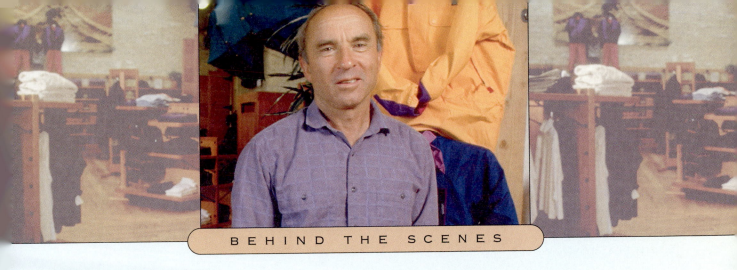

FACING BUSINESS CHALLENGES AT PATAGONIA

Can You Make a Profit and Protect the Environment Too?

Yvon Chouinard admits that he likes the rush of adrenaline that comes from scaling frozen waterfalls and steep mountains. Never one to refuse a challenge, the daredevil sportsman became an icon in the world of ice and rock climbing during the 1970s. But Chouinard faced another test of endurance in the 1990s when he encountered a business problem as challenging as the mountains he loved to climb.

As the founder and owner of Patagonia, a leading designer and distributor of outdoor gear, Chouinard worked hard to build a successful company that catered to extreme sports enthusiasts like himself. Along the way, he incorporated his personal passion for environmental protection into Patagonia's operating principles. As Chouinard explains, "We want it all. We want the best quality and the lowest environmental impact."

Under Chouinard's leadership, the company rigorously pursued its environmental values. In 1984 Patagonia created its own "earth tax" for donation to environmental causes, giving away the greater of either 1 percent of sales or 10 percent of pretax profits. As a result, the firm donated about $1 million each year to environmental groups—more money than the company allocated for advertising.

By the end of the 1980s, Patagonia had carved its own niche among sports enthusiasts by producing the best outdoor products in the marketplace at the lowest possible cost to the environment. Annual sales from Patagonia's quarterly catalog, retail centers, and international distributors topped $100 million. With an annual growth rate of 30 percent, the company expanded its offerings to 375 products, including a line of casual apparel that appealed to the masses. But adhering to rigid environmental standards in the production of its high-priced goods created enormous operating expenses. So when sales leveled off in the 1990s, Patagonia was forced to scale back its operations and lay off one-fifth of its work force.

Consultants advised Chouinard to sell the company and create a charitable foundation for environmental causes instead of donating a million or so from company profits each year. But Chouinard hadn't established Patagonia for the sole purpose of giving money away to environmental groups. He wanted to "use the company as a tool for social change," believing that Patagonia could lead the way in developing new, environmentally sensitive methods of producing high-quality goods.

Convinced that Patagonia could serve as an example for others to follow, Chouinard wanted to prove that a "green" company could help the environment. But no one would benefit from the environmental agenda of a business in bankruptcy, so Chouinard faced a challenging dilemma: How could Patagonia continue to grow, expand, and make a profit without compromising its commitment to the environment? If you were Yvon Chouinard, how would you balance Patagonia's economic needs with its environmental principles?[1]

◼ ETHICS IN THE WORKPLACE

Yvon Chouinard works hard to make sure that Patagonia does the right thing. But as Chouinard knows, a business can't take action or make decisions; only the individuals within a business can do that. From the CEO to the newest entry-level clerk, individuals make decisions every day that affect their company and its **stakeholders**—groups that are affected by (or that affect) a business's operations, including colleagues, employees, supervisors, investors, customers, suppliers, and society at large. These decisions ultimately shape the company's **ethics,** the rules or standards governing the conduct of a person or group.

What Is Ethical Behavior?

Ethical decisions can be divided into two general types. The first type is the **ethical dilemma,** in which one must choose between two conflicting but arguably valid sides. For example, Johnson & Johnson (J&J) faced an ethical dilemma when it had to decide how to keep its Tylenol customers well informed without scaring them away altogether. Tylenol is certainly safe enough for all the millions of people who take it each year without ill effects. However, more than 100 deaths a year are caused by acetaminophen, the active ingredient in Tylenol.[2]

Even though J&J strengthened label warnings about not giving Tylenol to children and not taking it in combination with alcohol, labels did not mention the possibility of death from liver failure when the recommended dose is exceeded. The company believed that such warnings would confuse people and that mentioning the risk of death would promote the use of Tylenol in suicides.[3] Should J&J include organ-specific warnings? Or is it enough to caution users about sticking to the proper dose? J&J decided to clarify the dangers by mentioning that mixing alcohol with painkillers can lead to liver damage and stomach bleeding.[4]

All ethical dilemmas have a common theme: the conflict between the rights of two or more important groups of people. Consumers have the right to be informed about any risks from using over-the-counter medications, and J&J has the right to profit by selling a beneficial medication that is used safely by millions.

The second type of decision is an **ethical lapse,** in which an individual makes a decision that is clearly wrong. Be careful not to confuse ethical dilemmas with ethical lapses. A company faces an ethical dilemma when it must decide whether to continue operating a production facility that is suspected, but not proven, to be unsafe. A company makes an ethical lapse when it continues to operate the facility even after the site has been proven unsafe. Other examples of ethical lapses would include inflating prices for certain customers or selling technological secrets to unfriendly foreign governments.

How Do Businesses Make Ethical Choices?

Determining what's right in any given situation can be difficult. One approach is to measure each act against certain absolute standards. In the United States, these standards are often grounded in religious teachings, such as "Do not lie" and "Do not steal." Another place to look for ethical guidance is the law. If saying, writing, or doing something is clearly illegal, you have no decision to make; you obey the law. However, even though legal considerations will resolve some ethical questions, you'll often have to rely on your own judgment and principles. When trying to decide the most ethical course of action, you might apply the Golden Rule: Do unto others as you would have them do unto you.

---

stakeholders
Individuals or groups to whom business has a responsibility

ethics
The rules or standards governing the conduct of a person or group

ethical dilemma
Situation in which both sides of an issue can be supported with valid arguments

LEARNING OBJECTIVE 1
Explain the difference between an ethical dilemma and an ethical lapse

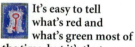 It's easy to tell what's red and what's green most of the time, but it's that yellow light that gives you some really tough decisions to make.[5]

ethical lapse
Situation in which an individual makes a decision that is morally wrong, illegal, or unethical

Or you might examine your motives: If your intent is honest, the decision is ethical, even though it may be factually or technically incorrect; however, if your intent is to mislead or manipulate, your decision is unethical, regardless of whether it is factually or technically correct.

You might also consider asking yourself a series of questions:

1. Is the decision legal? (Does it break any laws?)
2. Is it balanced? (Is it fair to all concerned?)
3. Can you live with it? (Does it make you feel good about yourself?)
4. Is it feasible? (Will it actually work in the real world?)

When you need to determine the ethics of any situation, these questions will get you started. You may also want to consider the needs of stakeholders, and you may want to investigate one or more philosophical approaches (see Exhibit 2.1).

These approaches are not mutually exclusive alternatives. On the contrary, most businesspeople combine them to reach decisions that will satisfy as many stakeholders as possible without violating anyone's rights or treating anyone unjustly. In any case, wanting to be an ethical corporate citizen isn't enough; people in business must actively practice ethical behavior.

LEARNING OBJECTIVE 2

List four questions you might ask yourself when trying to make an ethical decision

IS THE DECISION ETHICAL?	DOES IT RESPECT STAKEHOLDERS?	DOES IT FOLLOW A PHILOSOPHICAL APPROACH?
Is it legal?	Will outsiders approve?	Is it a utilitarian decision?
☑ Does it violate civil law?	☑ Does it benefit customers, suppliers, investors, public officials, media representatives, and community members?	☑ Does it produce the greatest good for the greatest number of people?
☑ Does it violate company policy?		Does it uphold individual, legal, and human rights?
Is it balanced?	Will supervisors approve?	☑ Does it protect people's own interests?
☑ Is it fair to all concerned, in both the short and the long term?	☑ Did you provide management with information that is honest and accurate?	☑ Does it respect the privacy of others and their right to express their opinion?
Can you live with it?	Will employees approve?	☑ Does it allow people to act in a way that conforms to their religious or moral beliefs?
☑ Does it make you feel good about yourself?	☑ Will it affect employees in a positive way?	
☑ Would you feel good reading about it in a newspaper?	☑ Does it handle personal information about employees discreetly?	Does it uphold the principles of justice?
Is it feasible?	☑ Did you give proper credit for work performed by others?	☑ Does it treat people fairly and impartially?
☑ Does it work in the real world?		☑ Does it apply rules consistently?
☑ Will it improve your competitive position?		☑ Does it ensure that people who harm others are held responsible and make restitution?
☑ Is it affordable?		
☑ Can it be accomplished in the time available?		

EXHIBIT 2·1

ITEMIZED LIST FOR MAKING ETHICAL DECISIONS

Companies with the most success in establishing an ethical structure are those that balance their approach to making decisions.

How Can Companies Become More Ethical?

Most companies are concerned about ethical issues, and many are trying to develop approaches for improving their ethics. More than 80 percent of large companies have adopted a written **code of ethics,** which defines the values and principles that should be used to guide decisions (see Exhibit 2.2). By itself, however, a code of ethics can't accomplish much. It must be supported by employee communications efforts, a formal training program, employee commitment to follow it, and a system through which employees can get help with ethically difficult situations.

In fact, Federal Sentencing Guidelines (1991) state that a company found to be violating federal law might not be prosecuted if it has the proper ethics policies and procedures in place. As Texas Instruments Ethics Officer Glenn Coleman explains, "If you have an active ethics program in place ahead of time, then bad things shouldn't happen; but if they do happen, it won't hurt you as badly."[6] Perhaps inspired by these guidelines, some companies have created an official position—the ethics officer—to guard morality. The ethics officer oversees corporate conduct, from pilfering company pens to endangering the environment to selling company secrets. Unfortunately, some ethics officers lack the power to truly make a difference.[7] Besides, encouraging ethical behavior means doing more than simply complying with laws. "Compliance is what you *have* to do; ethics is what you *should* do," says the former vice president in charge of ethics at Northrop (which has since merged with the Grumman Corporation).[8]

Keep in mind that ethical behavior starts at the top. The CEO and other senior managers must set the tone for people throughout the company. At Aveda, a cosmetics company, the cor-

code of ethics
Written statement setting forth the principles that guide an organization's decisions

LEARNING OBJECTIVE 3
Identify three steps that businesses are taking to encourage ethical behavior

EXHIBIT 2.2

IEEE CODE OF ETHICS

The Institute of Electrical and Electronics Engineers promotes the public policy interests of its U.S. members. The organization's code of ethics serves as a model for members to adopt.

THE INSTITUTE OF ELECTRICAL AND ELECTRONICS ENGINEERS, INC.

Code of Ethics

We, the members of the IEEE, in recognition of the importance of our technologies affecting the quality of life throughout the world, and in accepting a personal obligation to our profession, its members and the communities we serve, do hereby commit ourselves to the highest ethical and professional conduct and agree:

1. to accept responsibility in making engineering decisions consistent with the safety, health and welfare of the public, and to disclose promptly factors that might endanger the public or the environment;
2. to avoid real or perceived conflicts of interest whenever possible, and to disclose them to affected parties when they do exist;
3. to be honest and realistic in stating claims or estimates based on available data;
4. to reject bribery in all its forms;
5. to improve the understanding of technology, its appropriate application, and potential consequences;
6. to maintain and improve our technical competence and to undertake technological tasks for others only if qualified by training or experience, or after full disclosure of pertinent limitations;
7. to seek, accept, and offer honest criticism of technical work, to acknowledge and correct errors, and to credit properly the contributions of others;
8. to treat fairly all persons regardless of such factors as race, religion, gender, disability, age, or national origin;
9. to avoid injuring others, their property, reputation, or employment by false or malicious action;
10. to assist colleagues and co-workers in their professional development and to support them in following this code of ethics.

porate mission is to bring about positive effects through responsible business methods. "We do this, quite frankly, out of self-preservation," says founder and chairman Horst Rechebecher.[9]

Another way companies support ethical behavior is by establishing ethics hot lines that encourage *whistle-blowing*—an employee's disclosure of illegal, unethical, wasteful, or harmful practices by the company. Whistle-blowing can bring with it high costs: Public accusation of wrongdoing hurts the business's reputation, requires attention from managers, who must investigate, and damages employee morale. Moreover, whistle-blowers risk being fired or demoted, and they often suffer career setbacks, financial strain, and emotional stress. The fear of such negative repercussions allows many unethical or illegal practices to go unreported. However, "Any rational company that has something bad going on within it is going to want to know," says one expert on whistle-blowing.[10]

ACTIONS SPEAK LOUDER THAN CODES

Once you write a code of ethics and establish an ethics hot line, what more does your business need? A lot more, according to experts. When Walker Information surveyed 2,000 U.S. employees, it found that many people still didn't trust their employers' ethics. Nearly 30 percent of respondents said that employers sometimes ignored ethics and even deliberately broke the law. Fewer than half trusted employers: Only 46 percent believed leaders take responsibility for their actions; just 45 percent believed leaders act with fairness; and only 40 percent believed employers keep promises.

Some companies developed detailed codes of behavior and established ethics hot lines only to pay them lip service. Perhaps that's why 81 percent of top managers believe they use ethics in day-to-day decision making, whereas 43 percent of employees believe managers routinely overlook ethics. When leaders make decisions that clearly show profits winning out over ethics, employees become skeptical and mistrustful, attitudes that lead to unethical behavior.

To avoid the lip service trap, support your ethics programs with a dose of reality:

- *Inspire concretely.* Tell employees how they will personally benefit from participating in ethics initiatives. People respond better to personal benefits than to company benefits.
- *Acknowledge reality.* Admit errors. Discuss what went right and what went wrong. So-licit employee opinion: What do you think? What's your view? And act on those opinions.
- *Incorporate reality into your solutions.* Use practical strategies that can be accomplished in the time available. Obtain real feedback by asking employees to name three realities the company isn't facing, three reasons the company won't meet its goals, and three competitive weaknesses the company exhibits in the marketplace.
- *Be honest.* Tell employees what you know as well as what you don't know. Talk openly about real results, not about what you'd like them to be. Accept criticism—and listen to it.

Make personal benefits, company errors, and tactical solutions more concrete by being straightforward and specific. By acknowledging the realities in every situation, you turn your words into action and build trust with your employees.

QUESTIONS FOR CRITICAL THINKING

1. How does building trust encourage employees to be more ethical?
2. Some companies ask job candidates to take pre-employment tests such as drug tests or lie detector tests. Does such testing build trust with potential employees? Explain.

See It on the Web See It on the Web

■ SOCIAL RESPONSIBILITY IN BUSINESS

social responsibility
The idea that business has certain obligations to society beyond the pursuit of profits

In addition to practicing ethics in the workplace, companies such as Patagonia strive to create organizations that encourage social responsibility in their policies and among their employees. Of course, the ideal relationship between business and society is a matter of debate. Supporters of the concept of **social responsibility** argue that a company has an obligation to society beyond the pursuit of profits. Businesses such as Tom's of Maine (which produces natural personal-care products) and Working Assets (which provides long-distance telephone service) link the pursuit of socially responsible goals with their overall growth strategies.[11] Still, many other managers believe that their primary obligation is to the company's shareholders and that social responsibility is a secondary concern. Finding the right balance is challenging.

The Evolution of Social Responsibility

Social responsibility is a concept with decades-old roots. In the nineteenth and early twentieth centuries, the prevailing view among U.S. industrialists was that business had only one responsibility: to make a profit. "The public be damned," said railroad tycoon William Vanderbilt, "I'm working for the shareholders."[12] *Caveat emptor* was the rule of the day—"Let the buyer beware." If you bought a product, you paid the price and took the consequences. No consumer groups or government agencies would help you if the product was defective or caused harm.

By the early twentieth century, however, reformers were beginning to push politicians and government regulators to protect citizens from the abuses of big business. Their efforts paid off. Laws were passed to ensure the purity of food and drugs, limit the power of monopolies, and prevent unfair business practices, among other reforms. (See Component Chapter A for a list of early government regulations pertaining to business.)

During the Great Depression, which started in 1929, 25 percent of the work force was unemployed. Many people lost their faith in capitalism, and pressure mounted for government to fix the system. At the urging of President Franklin D. Roosevelt, Congress passed laws in the 1930s and 1940s that established the Social Security system, allowed employees to join unions and bargain collectively, set a minimum hourly wage, and limited the length of the workweek. New laws prevented unfair competition and false advertising and started the Securities and Exchange Commission (SEC) to protect investors.

Public confidence in U.S. business revived during World War II, and, throughout the 1950s, the relationship between business, government, and society was relatively tranquil. However, the climate shifted in the 1960s, as activism exploded on four fronts: environmental protection, national defense, consumerism, and civil rights. These movements have drastically altered the way business is conducted in the United States. Many of the changes have been made willingly by socially responsible companies such as Patagonia; others have been forced by government action; and still others have come about because of pressure from citizen groups.

Social Responsibility Versus Profits

A recent Business Week/Harris poll found that 95 percent of adults reject the notion that a corporation's only role is to make money. In fact, 76 percent of respondents said that if price and quality were equal, they would be likely to switch brands and retailers to support socially responsible companies.[13] Even so, combining business goals and social responsibility isn't easy, as Patagonia's Yvon Chouinard knows well. And yet, some businesses are finding that social responsibility doesn't have to cut into profits.

Consider Ben & Jerry's Homemade Ice Cream. Founders Ben Cohen and Jerry Greenfield were among the first CEOs to worry less about the bottom line and more about social causes. At Ben & Jerry's, shareholder profits melted in the heat of donating 7.5 percent of pretax profits to various causes (including saving the family farm, promoting world peace, saving the world's rain forests, and keeping French nuclear testing out of the South Pacific). Ben & Jerry's brand of social responsibility worked . . . for a while. Unfortunately, the company fell on hard times, nearly confirming the view that socially responsible companies would ultimately go out of business. But Perry D. Odak became CEO and proved the skeptics wrong.

When Odak took over, sales were down, and so was company morale. Employees didn't want to abandon Ben & Jerry's social mission in a search for profits. Many of them regretted the cancellation of efforts such as the Peace Pop program and its "One Percent for Peace." But as colorful as some of those programs were, they had also been inefficient. Take, for example, the company's arrangement to use nuts from a Brazilian cooperative in order to preserve the rain forest. The effort was publicized and highlighted on packages of Rainforest Crunch ice cream, but because of quality problems, the Brazilian cooperative ended up supplying only about 5 percent of the nuts used (a pretty small percentage to support the rain forest—as pointed out by an uncharitable media).

But things have changed under Odak, explains Elizabeth Bankowski, Ben & Jerry's social mission director. "We now meet and identify social mission objectives by function, and they're taken as seriously as every other business objective." By focusing on the balance sheet, CEO Odak has managed not only to tighten Ben & Jerry's business practices and improve its bottom line but also to enhance its ability to contribute to worthy causes.[14] When managed well, social responsibility can be achieved without hurting profits. In fact, it may even contribute to a company's bottom line.

With a 40 percent market share of top-tier ice cream brands, Ben and Jerry's has proven that companies with a social mission are very serious about their business. In fact, recent attempts to improve the company's bottom line have sent ice cream flavors such as Cool Britannia and products such as Peace Pops and Brownie Bars to the company's graveyard, a term the company uses for dropped products.

Efforts to Increase Social Responsibility

As the Ben & Jerry's example shows, today's businesses are about more than just making products or profits. Socially responsible businesses can indeed make a difference in the world. Moreover, those that give back to society are finding that their efforts can lead to a

LEARNING OBJECTIVE 4
Discuss three types of activity that socially responsible companies might engage in

social audit
Assessment of a company's performance in the area of social responsibility

philanthropic
Descriptive term for altruistic actions such as donating money, time, goods, or services to charitable, humanitarian, or educational institutions

more favorable public image and stronger employee morale. Thus, more and more organizations are attempting to be socially responsible citizens by conducting a *social audit*, by engaging in *cause-related marketing*, or by being *philanthropic*.

A **social audit** is a systematic evaluation and reporting of the company's social performance. The report typically includes objective information about how the company's activities affect its various stakeholders. For example, once a year Ben & Jerry's Homemade Ice Cream asks an outsider to conduct a social audit that assesses the impact of the company's operations on its employees, customers, communities, suppliers, and shareholders. The company announces the results of the audit in its annual report to shareholders.

Companies can also engage in *cause-related marketing*, in which a portion of product sales helps support worthy causes. For example, MCI offers businesses telephone service plans in which a percentage of the bill is donated to the Nature Conservancy or the Audubon Society. Similarly, Peaceworks encourages joint business ventures among people of different backgrounds who live in volatile regions of the world. One of the company's product lines is *spraté*, uniquely flavored spreads produced in Israel by a Jewish-owned company that buys all its ingredients from Israeli Arabs and Palestinians. When consumers buy a jar of spraté, they not only get a tasty spread, they also support the peace process in the Middle East.[15]

Some companies choose to be socially responsible corporate citizens by being **philanthropic;** that is, they donate money, time, goods, or services to charitable, humanitarian, or educational institutions. Corporations such as Microsoft, General Electric, Dell, and Wal-Mart donate billions of dollars in cash and products to charity each year. American Express employees in Phoenix, Arizona, donate time to repair the houses of elderly, disabled, and low-income residents.[16] And Wendy's founder, Dave Thomas, travels around the country, urging large companies to help employees with the costs associated with adopting children. "But writing a check is not enough," says Thomas. "You have to let people know that you are putting money where your heart is by giving your time, too."[17] Other businesses, such as Oxford Health Plans, support a spirit of giving not only by offering financial support to causes but also by motivating employees to decide whether, where, when, and how often to volunteer.

In short, businesspeople are doing whatever they can—donating computers, taking kids on field trips, supporting basketball teams, building houses for people, or helping people find jobs. "We try to function as though we live next door to everybody in our community," says the director of the Socially Responsible Banking Fund at Vermont National Bank.[18]

David Lubetzky, the founder of Peaceworks, is helping the Middle East peace process on two fronts: by encouraging cooperative business ventures between Jews and Arabs and by increasing awareness among American consumers.

BUSINESS'S RESPONSE TO THE NEEDS OF SOCIETY

Exactly how much can businesses contribute to social concerns? This is a difficult decision for most companies because they have limited resources. Thus, they must allocate their resources to a number of goals such as upgrading facilities and equipment, developing new products, marketing existing products, and rewarding employee efforts, in addition to contributing to social causes. This juggling act is a challenge that every business faces. For example, if a company consistently ignores its stakeholders, its business will suffer and eventually fold. If the company disregards society's needs (such as environmental concerns), voters will clamor for laws to limit the offensive business activities; consumers who feel their needs and values are being ignored will spend their money on a competitor's products; investors who are unhappy with the company's performance will invest elsewhere; and employees whose needs are not met will become unproductive or will quit and find other jobs.

As you can see, stakeholders' needs sometimes conflict. In such cases, which stakeholders should be served first—society, consumers, investors, or employees?

Responsibility Toward Society and the Environment

Environmental issues exemplify the difficulty that businesses encounter when they try to reconcile conflicting interests: Society needs as little pollution as possible from businesses that turn resources into products; however, consumers need quality products, and businesses cannot produce them without polluting to some degree. Workers need safe surroundings and fair wages to produce the goods and services that businesses sell; however, investors need lower costs and efficient production in order to realize higher profits. In addition, businesses must sometimes spend more in order to pollute less. Business executives such as Patagonia's Yvon Chouinard and Ben & Jerry's Perry Odak are trying to satisfy these diverse needs by making environmental management a formal part of their business strategy—along with quality, profits, safety, and other daily business operations. Even though many businesses are doing their utmost to preserve our environment by disclosing information on emissions releases, operational details, and environmental defects, overcoming the problem of pollution is not an easy task.[19]

The Pervasiveness of Pollution   Our air, water, and land can easily be tainted by **pollution** (the contamination of the natural environment by the discharge of harmful substances). Moreover, the pollution in any one element can easily taint the others. Environmental pollution pervades industrialized and developing nations alike. The emerging economies of Asia and Latin America have based much of their growth on loose environmental standards. However, Mexico, Malaysia, and other developing countries realize that their prosperity can be sustained only if their citizens can enjoy the quality of life that comes with a clean environment. At the same time, the countries of Eastern Europe are scrambling to reverse the decades of environmental neglect that occurred under communism.[20]

pollution
Damage to or destruction of the natural environment caused by the discharge of harmful substances

Air Pollution.   The most noticeable form of air pollution is smog, produced by the interaction of sunlight and hydrocarbons (gases released when fossil fuels are burned). Another kind of air pollution causes acid rain, created when emissions from coal-burning factories and electric utility plants react with air. Acid rain has been blamed for damaging lakes and forests in the northeastern United States and southeastern Canada.

Emissions from factories and cars also contribute to global warming. The greenhouse effect occurs when heated gases form a layer of unusually warm air around the earth, trapping the sun's heat and preventing the earth's surface from cooling. The United Nations' Intergovernmental Panel on Climate Change (IPCC), which includes over 900 scientists worldwide, recently reported that global warming will cause worldwide temperatures to rise by 1 to 3.5 degrees Celsius (about 34 to 38 degrees Fahrenheit) in the next century. This warming is expected to lead to increases in both droughts and floods in some regions and to raise the sea level about 50 centimeters (about 20 inches) by 2100. The report concludes that "the balance of evidence suggests a discernible human influence on global climate."[21] However, numerous other scientists refute the theory of global warming, claiming that no solid evidence yet exists to support a human influence on global climate change. The debate will continue.

ECO-INVASION: A GLOBAL THREAT TO THE ENVIRONMENT

As more people and goods travel between developed and developing nations, they are transporting small stowaways that can ultimately cause a great deal of environmental damage. The expansion of worldwide trade is erasing the mountains, deserts, and oceans as natural boundaries, so seeds, weeds, bugs, fish, birds, and animals are arriving from far-off shores by air, land, and sea. The spread of nonnative species is threatening ecosystems around the world, disrupting food and agriculture, destroying wetlands, interfering with shipping, and drastically altering natural habitats, not to mention its effect on human lives.

The United States loses more than $122 billion each year to invasive species such as noxious weeds, harmful insects, and organisms that cause human disease (such as AIDS and cholera). The invasion of nonnative species is already widespread, including beetles, pigeons, wild pigs, rats, and hundreds of plants—just to name a few. A truck carrying beehives brought red fire ants to California. World War II cargo ships brought the brown tree snake to Guam, where it eliminated 9 of the 11 native bird species, and now the same snake has been found in Hawaii (on or around planes from Guam). Killer bees have come to the United States from Latin America, and the Mediterranean fruit fly rides in on produce from Mexico. Brought back by the navy during World War II, Formosan termites have caused some $100 million in damage to New Orleans each year—more than hurricanes, tornadoes, or floods. And the Asian long-horned beetle emerged from cargo holds of ships in 1996 to decimate more than 2,000 trees in Brooklyn and begin a similar infestation in Chicago.

Unlike pollution, biological invaders multiply. Moreover, what was once a problem for neighboring ecosystems is now a global one. "Every ship, every plane, every truck is a potential carrier," warns a specialist with the America Lands Alliance. But so far, attempts to control eco-invasion are fragmented and ineffective. Getting government and public support is difficult.

However, the destruction from the zebra mussel is changing attitudes. This bean-sized mollusk from Eastern Europe arrived in 1986 in Lake St. Clair in a freighter's ballast water. Since then, it has effectively taken over the Great Lakes and is found in every river in the Mississippi watershed. It could eventually show up "in every lake, river, and stream all the way to the West Coast," says one expert. Power and water plants in the area are already spending some $3 billion a year to keep these mollusks from clogging up their pipes and equipment. Ecologists hope this wake-up call will inspire decisive action.

QUESTIONS FOR CRITICAL THINKING

1. To protect U.S. ecology, what can we do to detect hidden stowaways such as seeds and bugs?
2. How can the United States encourage other countries to inspect and regulate their exports?

Experts also worry about airborne toxins emitted during some manufacturing processes. Large and small companies together release millions of pounds of chemical wastes into the air each year. Although the effects of many of these substances are unknown, some are carcinogenic (cancer-causing). Of special concern are microscopic particulates in the air that may be responsible for more than 150,000 deaths each year.[22]

Water Pollution. Our air is not the only part of our environment to suffer. Water pollution has damaged many U.S. lakes, rivers, streams, harbors, and coastal waters. Contamination comes from a variety of sources: manufacturing facilities, mining and construction sites, farms, and city sewage systems. Although dramatic accidents are widely publicized (such as the Exxon *Valdez* oil spill in Alaskan waters), the main threat is the careless day-to-day disposal of wastes from thousands of individual sources.

Land Pollution.   Even if all wastewater were purified before being discharged, our groundwater would still be endangered by leakage from the millions of tons of hazardous substances that have been buried underground or dumped in improper storage sites. Much of this pollution was created years ago by companies that carelessly—but legally—disposed of substances now known to be unhealthy. Cleaning up these wastes is extremely difficult and expensive.

In addition, companies and individuals alike generate enormous amounts of solid waste—over 200 million tons in the United States each year. Much of this waste ends up in landfills. A large part of the landfill problem comes from consumer demands for convenience and fashion. These demands lead to creating disposable items, manufacturing products with excess packaging, and discarding useful items that are no longer the hot style or color. Fortunately, recent efforts to conserve and recycle resources are helping to combat the land pollution problem.[23]

The Government Effort to Reduce Pollution   Widespread concern for the environment has been growing since the 1960s, with the popularization of **ecology,** or the study of the balance of nature. In 1963 federal, state, and local governments began enacting laws and regulations to reduce pollution. In December 1970 the federal government established the Environmental Protection Agency (EPA) to regulate air and water pollution by manufacturers and utilities, supervise the control of automobile pollution, license pesticides, control toxic substances, and safeguard the purity of drinking water. Congress is currently attempting to reform the EPA, because critics contend that the agency's tough restrictions actually prohibit companies from finding the most cost-effective ways to reduce pollution.

Even the CIA is "turning green." The agency already has spy photos of the great forests of Alaska and Siberia, which are considered a laboratory for studying global warming. By tracking the advance of Arctic forests, scientists can track global warming (as it allows trees to grow farther and farther north). The CIA is also establishing an environmental center to look at international tensions. The agency already monitors compliance with international environmental treaties, and it hopes to warn of impending catastrophes (such as the disastrous smog that resulted when Indonesian farmers cleared land by burning). In addition, the agency hopes to foresee future environmental problems (such as potential water shortages in the Middle East).[24]

Individual states have passed their own tough clean air laws. For example, California requires that 10 percent of all new vehicles sold in the state be pollution-free by 2003. In response, both large and small car manufacturers are working to produce electric vehicles. General Motors and Honda have already begun selling their first models.[25]

Progress has also been made in reducing water pollution. Both government and private business have made major expenditures to treat and reuse wastewater, as well as to upgrade sewage systems. As a result, the percentage of U.S. rivers and lakes that have become fishable and swimmable has almost doubled since 1970, and several major waterways that were once sewers have been cleaned up, including the Cuyahoga and Potomac rivers, Delaware Bay, and Boston Harbor.[26]

Unfortunately, the war on toxic waste has not been quite as successful. For years, many industrial wastes were routinely dumped in landfills, where few (if any) protective barriers could be counted on to prevent dangerous chemicals from leaking into the soil and the water supply. Government attempts to force businesses to clean up these sites have yielded many lawsuits and much expense but disappointing results. At some sites, the groundwater may never be restored to drinking-water purity.

Although many companies do a good job of regulating themselves, it is often pressure from the public and the government that causes businesses to clean up their acts. Companies

ecology

Study of the relationships between living things in the water, air, and soil, their environments, and the nutrients that support them that pollute excessively not only risk being charged with violating federal laws but also risk being sued by private citizens. Of course, such after-the-fact costs are ultimately passed on to consumers. Clearly, society benefits most when companies take it upon themselves to find cost-effective ways of reducing pollution.

The Business Effort to Reduce Pollution   Today's managers are learning from the mistakes of their predecessors and are taking steps to reduce and prevent pollution. Some use high-temperature incineration to destroy hazardous wastes, some recycle wastes, some give their wastes to other companies that can use them, some neutralize wastes biologically, and some have redesigned their manufacturing processes so that they don't produce the wastes in the first place. In Kahlundborg, Denmark, some companies practice what they call *industrial symbiosis,* which means that they work together in a mutually advantageous relationship. Manufacturers as diverse as a pharmaceutical company, an oil refinery, a farm, a building materials company, and a power plant are linked via pipes and ground transportation systems so that each can use the waste products from the others as fuel and raw materials for themselves. The idea started among the managers of the companies as a way to lower costs and boost profits. But the reduction of waste and pollution has been so substantial that the EPA has taken notice. It is now supporting the development of similar eco-industrial parks in the United States.[27]

Another innovative approach to reducing pollution is based on free-market principles. In certain cities, companies can buy and sell pollution rights. Each company is given an allowable "pollution quota" based on such factors as its size and industry. If a company voluntarily reduces pollution below its limit, it can sell its "credits" to another company. This system provides an incentive for companies to find efficient ways of reducing pollution. Evidence so far suggests that the plan is effective in reducing overall levels of pollutants such as sulfur dioxide.[28]

Many companies are also reducing the amount of solid waste they send to landfills by implementing companywide recycling programs. The EPA reports that over 20 percent of the solid waste generated in the United States is now recycled.[29] In addition, hundreds of thousands of tons of waste have been eliminated through conservation and more efficient production.[30]

Many businesses like Patagonia are recognizing the link between environmental performance and financial well-being and are addressing environmental problems by:[31]

LEARNING OBJECTIVE 5
Identify five of the eight steps that some businesses are taking to address environmental problems

- Considering them a part of everyday business and operating decisions
- Accepting environmental staff members as full-fledged partners in improving the company's competitiveness
- Measuring environmental performance
- Tying compensation to environmental performance
- Determining the long-term environmental costs *before* such costs occur
- Considering environmental impact in the product-development process
- Challenging suppliers to improve environmental performance
- Conducting training and awareness programs

More and more companies are discovering that spending now to prevent pollution can end up saving more money down the road (by reducing cleanup costs, litigation expense, and production costs). From building eco-industrial parks to improving production efficiency, these activities are a part of the *green marketing* movement, in which companies distinguish themselves by using less packaging materials, recycling more waste, and developing new products that are easier on the environment.

See It on the Web See It on the Web

GO FOR THE GREEN

Maybe you want to lead more of a green lifestyle, but you're not sure where to begin. The Web site of the Sustainable Business Network (SBN) is a good starting point. This site has valuable information on environmental business issues ranging from recycling and renewable energy to organic products, social investing, and certified forestry. You can also access databases of information on environmentally conscious companies, locate green business opportunities, and find jobs that let you put your business skills to work to help the environment. Then follow the link to the EnviroLink Network to learn even more about the latest environmental issues.

http://sbn.envirolink.org

Responsibility Toward Consumers

The 1960s activism that awakened business to its environmental responsibilities also gave rise to **consumerism,** a movement that put pressure on businesses to consider consumer needs and interests. Consumerism prompted many businesses to create consumer-affairs departments to handle customer complaints. It also prompted state and local agencies to set up bureaus to offer consumer information and assistance. At the federal level, President John F. Kennedy announced a "bill of rights" for consumers, laying the foundation for a wave of consumer-oriented legislation (see Component Chapter A for a list of major federal consumer legislation). These rights include the right to safety, the right to be informed, the right to choose, and the right to be heard.

consumerism
Movement that pressures businesses to consider consumer needs and interests

LEARNING OBJECTIVE 6
List four rights of consumers

The Right to Safe Products   As recently as the 1970s, hand irons could overheat into a melted mess, mower blades could continue turning even after users let go of the machine, over-the-counter drugs didn't come in childproof containers, and cars had so many problems that consumers expected to have trouble with them. Of course, today's irons turn off automatically, mowers shut off when the operator lets go, childproof caps are commonplace, and car quality has risen sharply.[32]

The U.S. government imposes many safety standards that are enforced by the Consumer Product Safety Commission (CPSC), as well as by other federal and state agencies. Theoretically, companies that don't comply with these rules are forced to take corrective action. However, many consumer advocates complain that some unsafe products slip through the cracks because regulatory agencies lack the resources to do an effective job. But even without government action, the threat of product-liability suits and declining sales motivates many

Faulty electrical components and wiring forced Fisher-Price to pull 10 million battery-driven Power Wheels cars and trucks off the market in 1998. The U.S. Consumer Product Safety Commission received about 700 consumer complaints of electrical problems (150 involved fires such as the one that damaged the toy shown here) before Fisher-Price recalled the product.

companies to meet safety standards. After all, a poor safety record can damage a company's reputation.

Nevertheless, some unsafe products remain on the market, even after decades of pressure to eliminate them. Scientists determined long ago that the tar and nicotine in tobacco are both harmful and addictive. In 1965 the Federal Cigarette Labeling and Advertising Act was passed, requiring all cigarette packs to carry the now-famous Surgeon General's warnings. Over the years, tobacco companies have spent billions of dollars to defend themselves in lawsuits brought by smokers suffering from cancer and respiratory diseases. As recently as 1996, the Liggett Group (a major U.S. tobacco company) admitted publicly that cigarettes cause cancer, are addictive, and have been promoted to encourage smoking among minors. And in 1997 the tobacco industry agreed to pay $368.5 billion over 25 years and an additional $15 billion per year after that to settle lawsuits brought by smoking victims and 40 state governments. Even so, RJR Nabisco chairman Steve Goldstone reminds us that "behind all the allegations . . . is the simple truth that we sell a legal product."[33] Should the consumer's right to safety dictate a ban on tobacco products? Even when a product has been proven to be dangerous, does the fact that it is legal justify its sale? Should the government take measures to make the product illegal, or should consumers be allowed to decide for themselves what they buy?

The Right to Be Informed   Consumers have a right to know what is in a product and how to use it. They also have a right to know the costs of goods or services and the details of any purchase contracts. The Food and Drug Administration, the Federal Trade Commission, and the Agriculture Department are the federal agencies responsible for regulating product labels to make sure no false claims are made. These agencies are concerned not only with safety but also with accurate information. Research shows that nearly three-quarters of shoppers read labels when deciding whether to buy a food product the first time, so labels are an important element in informing consumers.[34]

If a product is sufficiently dangerous, a warning label is required by law, as in the case of cigarettes. However, warning labels can be a mixed blessing for consumers. To some extent, the presence of a warning protects the manufacturer from product-liability suits, but the label may not deter people from using the product or from using it incorrectly. The billions of dollars a year still spent on cigarettes in the United States illustrate this point. Moreover, as the world economy becomes more and more service-oriented, consumers are buying items that don't necessarily carry a label. Therefore, consumers must take it upon themselves to ensure that they are getting what they pay for.

Recent media blitzes by anti-smoking organizations are cropping up in magazines, on billboards, and in television commercials. The hope is that ads such as this one will elevate consumer awareness about the health problems cigarette smoking causes.

The Right to Choose Which Products to Buy   Especially in the United States, the number of products available to consumers is truly amazing. But how far should the right to choose extend? Are we entitled to choose products that are potentially harmful, such as cigarettes, liquor, or guns? To what extent are we entitled to learn about these products? Should beer and wine ads be elimi-

See It on the Web See It on the Web

SURF SAFELY

Although the majority of telemarketing and online businesses are legitimate, unethical businesses bilk consumers out of billions of dollars every year. Fortunately, the National Fraud Information Center (NFIC) can help consumers fight back. The center was established by the National Consumers League (NCL) to safeguard consumers against telemarketing and Internet fraud. Resources on the center's Web site include reports about current online and telephone scams, tips for online safety, advice on how to file a fraud report, statistics about telemarketing fraud, and special advice for seniors, who are targeted by con artists. Even if you consider yourself a savvy consumer, the site contains a lot of valuable information to help you avoid being ripped off. http://www.fraud.org

nated from television, just as ads for other types of alcoholic beverages have been? Should advertising aimed at children be banned altogether?

Consumer groups are concerned about these questions, but no clear answers have emerged. In general, however, business is sensitive to these issues. Recent public concern about drunk driving, for example, has led the liquor industry to encourage responsible drinking. For example, Coors runs advertisements designed to discourage underage drinking and drinking on the job.[35] Similarly, several major broadcast television networks have implemented a rating system to help the public gauge whether a show is appropriate for a young audience. Most U.S. businesspeople prefer to help consumers make informed choices—rather than be told what choices to offer.

The Right to Be Heard   Many companies have established toll-free numbers for consumer information and feedback, and these numbers are often printed on product packages. In addition, more and more companies are establishing Web sites that provide product information and access for customer feedback. Of course, businesses benefit from gathering as much information about their customers as possible. Customer information allows companies to make informed decisions about changing current products and offering new ones. It also allows companies to target narrower, more-focused groups of consumers. However, the pursuit of information has given rise to a new ethical concern—maintaining customer privacy.

Credit-card companies have a lot of information about how much money individual consumers spend and where they spend it. Similarly, insurance companies have personal information about their policyholders. But neither industry is restricted from revealing this information. Only recently has the federal government passed legislation to restrict phone companies from using customer information (such as billing records and calling patterns) for marketing purposes.[36] As Internet commerce increases, the issue of consumer privacy has become even more important. For example, after privacy advocates protested, America Online backed out of a plan to make its customers' home telephone numbers available to telemarketing companies.[37] (Consult Part I of the *E-Business in Action* online supplement at http://www.prenhall.com/ebusinessinaction for additional discussion of Internet Privacy and Security.)

The right to be heard also covers a broad range of complaints about discrimination against customers. More than 4,000 African American customers complained to the U.S.

Justice Department about racial discrimination by some Denny's restaurants. Among their complaints: They were asked to pay for meals in advance (although other customers weren't asked to do so), and they received slower service than other customers did. Flagstar, the chain's owner, responded by making a public apology and paying $46 million to settle the claims. In addition, the number of African American–owned Denny's franchises has risen from 1 to 27 in three years, and 12 percent of the company's supplies are now purchased from minority-owned vendors.[38]

Responsibility Toward Investors

In addition to their other responsibilities, businesses are responsible to those who have invested in the company. Historically, investors have been primarily interested in a company's financial performance. Of course, any action that cheats the investors out of their rightful profits is unethical.

Misrepresenting the Investment   Every year tens of thousands of people are the victims of investment scams. Lured by promises of high returns, people sink more than a billion dollars per year into nonexistent oil wells, goldmines, and other fraudulent operations touted by complete strangers over the telephone and the Internet. Shady companies use other types of scams to take people's money, too. For example, in this era of high-tech companies that seem to skyrocket overnight, con artists can dupe unwary investors by offering shares in start-up companies that don't exist. Investors should be especially careful of opportunities advertised over the Internet because it's so difficult for regulators to control online scams.[39] Other ways of misrepresenting the potential of an investment fall within the law. For example, with a little "creative accounting," a business that is in financial trouble can be made to look reasonably good to all but the most astute investors. Companies have some latitude in their reports to shareholders, and some firms are more conscientious than others in representing their financial performance.

Companies should think twice before playing accounting games.[40]

Diverting Earnings or Assets   Business executives may also take advantage of the investor by using the company's earnings or resources for personal gain. Managers have many opportunities to indirectly take money that rightfully belongs to the shareholders. Perhaps the most common approach is to cheat on expense accounts. Padding invoices and then splitting the overcharge with the supplier is another common ploy. Other tactics include selling company secrets to competitors or using confidential, nonpublic information gained from one's position in a company to benefit from the purchase and sale of stocks. Such **insider trading** is illegal and is closely watched by the Securities and Exchange Commission (SEC).

insider trading
The use of unpublicized information that an individual gains from the course of his or her job to benefit from fluctuations in the stock market

Overdoing the Quest for Profits   Even though few companies knowingly break laws in an attempt to gain a competitive advantage, companies have taken questionable steps in their zeal to maximize profits. In order to protect earnings, some companies have used questionable methods to get bankrupt customers to sign repayment agreements. And to get ahead of the competition, some companies have engaged in corporate spying. Although businesses need to gather as much strategic information as they can, ethical companies steer clear of stealing patents, searching rivals' trash bins for sensitive information, accessing telephone records, hiring employees from competitors to gain trade secrets, and electronically eavesdropping.

Clearly, a business can fail its investors by depriving them of their fair share of the profits. But a business can also fail its shareholders by being too concerned about profits. Today a growing number of investors are concerned about the ethics and social responsibility of the companies in which they invest. One study found that 26 percent of investors consider social responsibility to be extremely important.[41]

The job of looking out for a company's shareholders falls to its board of directors. Lately, more investors are turning up the heat on the individuals who sit on those boards. Concerned investors are targeting board members who fail to attend meetings, who sit on the boards of too many companies, who are underinvested (own very little stock in the companies they direct), and who sit on boards of companies with which their own firms do business. Looking out for investors is no easy task, but investors are finding that holding individual directors more accountable improves overall performance.[42]

Responsibility Toward Employees

Patagonia's Yvon Chouinard has always emphasized employee relationships that are ethical and supportive. For some companies, the past 30 years have brought dramatic changes in the attitudes and composition of the work force. These changes have forced businesses to modify their recruiting, training, and promotion practices, as well as their overall corporate values and behaviors. (Consult Chapter 9 for an in-depth discussion of the staffing and demographic challenges employers are facing in today's workplace.)

The Push for Equality in Employment   The United States has always stood for economic freedom and the individual's right to pursue opportunity. Unfortunately, until the past few decades many people were targets of economic **discrimination,** relegated to low-paying, menial jobs and prevented from taking advantage of many opportunities solely on the basis of their race, gender, disability, or religion.

> **discrimination**
> In a social and economic sense, denial of opportunities to individuals on the basis of some characteristic that has no bearing on their ability to perform in a job

The Civil Rights Act of 1964 established the Equal Employment Opportunity Commission (EEOC)—the regulatory agency that battles job discrimination. The EEOC is responsible for monitoring the hiring practices of companies and for investigating complaints of job-related discrimination. It has the power to file legal charges against companies that discriminate and to force them to compensate individuals or groups who have been victimized by unfair practices. The Civil Rights Act of 1991 extended the original act by allowing workers to sue companies for discrimination and by granting women powerful legal tools against job bias.

Affirmative Action.   In the 1960s, **affirmative action** programs were developed to encourage organizations to recruit and promote members of minority groups. Proponents of the programs believe that minorities deserve and require preferential treatment to boost opportunities and to make up for years of discrimination. Opponents of affirmative action believe that creating special opportunities for women and minorities creates a double standard that infringes on the rights of other workers and forces companies to hire, promote, and retain people who are not necessarily the best choice from a business standpoint. Regardless, any company that does business with the federal government must have an affirmative action program.

> **affirmative action**
> Activities undertaken by businesses to recruit and promote women and minorities, based on an analysis of the work force and the available labor pool

Still, studies show that affirmative action has not been entirely successful. For one thing, efforts to hire more minorities do not necessarily change negative attitudes about differences among individuals. To combat this problem, about 75 percent of U.S. companies have established **diversity initiatives.** These initiatives often involve increasing minority employment and promotion, contracting with more minority vendors, including more minorities on boards of directors, and targeting a more diverse customer base. In addition, diversity initiatives use diversity training to promote understanding of the unique cultures, customs, and talents of all employees.

> **diversity initiatives**
> Company policies designed to enhance opportunities for minorities and to promote understanding of diverse cultures, customs, and talents

People with Disabilities.   In 1990 people with a wide range of physical and mental difficulties got a boost from the passage of the federal Americans with Disabilities Act (ADA), which guarantees equal opportunities for an estimated 50 million to 75 million people who have or have had a condition that might handicap them. As defined by the 1990 law, *disability* is a broad term that protects not only those with obvious physical handicaps but also those with less-visible conditions, such as cancer, heart disease, diabetes, epilepsy, AIDS, drug addiction, alcoholism, and emotional illness. In most situations, employers cannot legally require job applicants to pass a physical examination as a condition of employment. The law also forbids firing people who have serious drinking or drug problems unless their chemical dependency prevents them from performing their essential job functions.

Businesses serving the public are required to make their services and facilities accessible to people with disabilities. This requirement means that restaurants, hotels, stores, airports, buses, taxis, banks, sports stadiums, and so forth must try to accommodate people who have disabilities. A hotel, for example, must equip 5 percent of its rooms with flashing lights or other "visual alarms" for people with hearing impairments.[43]

Occupational Safety and Health Each day 17 workers lose their lives on the job while another 24,000 are injured in the workplace (See Exhibit 2.3).[44] During the activist 1960s, mounting concern about workplace hazards resulted in passage of the Occupational Safety and Health Act of 1970, which set mandatory standards for safety and health and which established the Occupational Safety and Health Administration (OSHA) to enforce them.

New concerns for employee safety have been raised by the international expansion of businesses. Many U.S. companies subcontract production to companies in foreign coun-

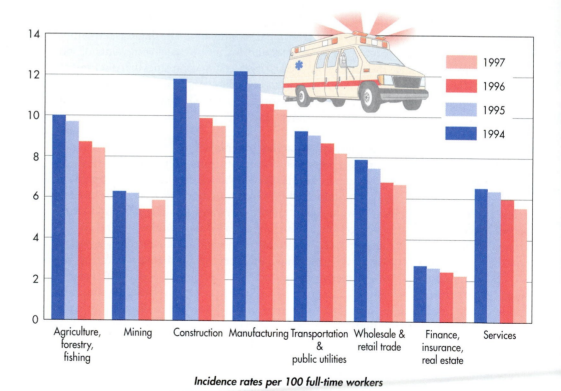

Incidence rates per 100 full-time workers

EXHIBIT 2·3

INJURIES ON THE JOB

The workplace injury and illness rate for 1997 was the lowest since the Bureau of Labor Statistics began reporting this information in the early 1970s. As the graph shows, manufacturing and construction jobs report the most incidents.

tries, making it more difficult to maintain proper standards of safety and compensation. For example, when a local labor advocacy group inspected a Nike factory in Vietnam, members discovered violations of minimum wage and overtime laws, as well as physical abuse of workers. Nike has been criticized in recent years for similar conditions in its other Southeast Asian and Chinese factories. Many other companies, including the Gap, Guess, and the Body Shop have come under similar criticism. In 1997 a presidential task force composed of apparel industry representatives, labor unions, and human rights groups drafted a code of conduct to uphold the rights of foreign workers of U.S. manufacturing companies. Among the provisions of the code are minimum wage requirements and limits on the number of hours employees work in a week.[45]

ETHICS AND SOCIAL RESPONSIBILITY AROUND THE WORLD

As complicated as ethics and social responsibility can be when talking about the United States, these issues grow even more complex when cultural influences are applied from country to country around the world. What does it mean for a business to do the right thing in Thailand? In Africa? In Norway? What may be considered unethical in the United States may be an accepted practice in another culture. Several areas of corruption are being addressed by international agreements: bribes, air pollution, and corporate behavior.

Consider bribes, for example. In the United States, bribing officials is illegal, but Kenyans consider paying such bribes a part of life. To get something done right, they pay *kitu kidogo* (or "something small"). In China businesses pay *huilu*. In Russia they pay *vzyatka;* in the Middle East it's *baksheesh;* and in Mexico it's *una mordida* ("a small bite").

The United States has lobbied other nations for 20 years to outlaw bribery, and at last the industrialized nations have signed a treaty that makes payoffs to foreign officials a criminal offense. The ban on bribes came after a string of high-level scandals around the world: Two South Korean presidents went to prison for accepting bribes. French cabinet ministers and mayors resigned during an investigation of kickbacks. The late dictator of Zaire (now Congo) actually merged his family's finances with those of the state. And corruption is such an obstacle in Ukraine and Russia that some U.S. companies quit trying to do business there. Of course, bribery won't end just because a treaty has been signed, but supporters are optimistic that countries will ratify the treaty, pass legislation, and enforce the new laws stringently.[46]

In a similar pact, 150 nations recently signed an agreement in Kyoto, Japan, to reduce worldwide emissions of carbon dioxide and other pollutants thought to be contributing to global warming. To comply with the agreement, countries around the world will be turning to energy from renewable sources, such as sun and wind—good news for companies like Houston-based Enron, which markets natural gas and oversees solar and wind projects.[47] The European Union (EU) had proposed a huge 15 percent cut in three of the best-known greenhouse gases by the year 2015, but the Kyoto compromise requires an 8 percent cut in six gases. Will Europe stand by its original offer? Europe would need to drop 800 million tons of carbon dioxide emissions at a cost of $15 billion to $21 billion. The region is looking to new Danish technology for installing windmills at sea, in waters up to 45 feet deep. Over the ocean, winds will be stronger and more reliable. Plus, the new windmills avoid the kind of "landscape pollution" found in California's controversial windmill forests at Palm Springs.[48]

Espionage is another issue on the U.S. agenda for global ethics. The American Society for Industrial Security surveyed U.S. companies, asking which foreign country poses the greatest economic-espionage threat. The 1,300 respondents ranked the five top countries as (1) China, (2) Japan, (3) France, (4) the United Kingdom, and (5) Canada. In 1998 FBI Director Louis

Freeh testified before Congress, saying that the companies or governments of 23 countries were currently involved in the illicit acquisition of U.S. trade secrets.[49]

The foreign piracy of intellectual property is also a huge problem for U.S. companies. When Disney released its animated film *Mulan* in Hong Kong, the city's shopping arcades had already been selling the illegal video compact disk (VCD) for a week—complete with Chinese subtitles. Asian pirates are active not only in Hollywood but also in Silicon Valley and in the music business. In the Philippines, according to the Software Publishers Association, 83 percent of business software is pirated; even government offices openly use illegally copied programs. In fact, Asian pirates sell far more illegal copies of Microsoft's popular programs than Microsoft itself. But even though laws against piracy exist, enforcing them is as difficult for Asian countries as it was for the United States to enforce Prohibition in the 1920s. As soon as one operation is shut down, another pops up in its place.[50]

Summary of Learning Objectives

1. **Explain the difference between an ethical dilemma and an ethical lapse.**
    An ethical dilemma is an issue with two conflicting but arguably valid sides. An ethical lapse occurs when an individual makes a decision that is illegal, immoral, or unethical.

2. **List four questions you might ask yourself when trying to make an ethical decision.**
    When making ethical decisions, ask yourself: (1) Is the decision legal? (Does it break any law?); (2) Is it balanced? (Is it fair to all concerned?); (3) Can you live with it? (Does it make you feel good about yourself?); (4) Is it feasible? (Will it work in the real world?)

3. **Identify three steps that businesses are taking to encourage ethical behavior.**
    Businesses are adopting codes of ethics, appointing ethics officers, and establishing ethics hot lines to encourage whistle-blowing.

4. **Discuss three types of activity that socially responsible companies might engage in.**
    Companies can conduct social audits to assess whether their performance is socially responsible, engage in cause-related marketing by using a portion of product sales to help support worthy causes, and engage in philanthropy by donating their money, time, goods, or services to charitable, humanitarian, or educational institutions.

5. **Identify five of the eight steps that some businesses are taking to address environmental problems.**
    All eight steps are: (1) making environmental problems part of everyday decisions, (2) making environmental staff members full-fledged partners in improving competitiveness, (3) measuring environmental performance, (4) tying compensation to environmental performance, (5) determining environmental costs *before* they occur, (6) considering the environmental impact of the product-development process, (7) helping suppliers improve their environmental performance, (8) conducting training and awareness programs.

6. **List four rights of consumers.**
    Consumers have the right to safety, the right to be informed, the right to choose, and the right to be heard.

Key Terms

affirmative action (43)	ecology (37)	philanthropic (34)
code of ethics (30)	ethical dilemma (28)	pollution (35)
consumerism (39)	ethical lapse (28)	social audit (34)
discrimination (43)	ethics (28)	social responsibility (32)
diversity initiatives (43)	insider trading (42)	stakeholders (28)

MEETING BUSINESS CHALLENGES AT PATAGONIA

A mountain of obstacles blocked Patagonia's path to success during the 1990s. Faced with sagging sales and a severe cash crunch, owner Yvon Chouinard was determined to put Patagonia back on solid ground without compromising environmental values. To solve immediate problems, Chouinard focused his attention on the company's founding philosophy: produce the best outdoor gear in the market at the lowest possible cost to the environment.

First he got the company "back to the basics" by eliminating one-third of its 375 products and by reducing the work force by 20 percent. Then Chouinard took his case to the public. He informed customers about plans to limit Patagonia's growth by designing and developing products that emphasized function rather than fashionable styles, and he educated consumers on environmental issues. Lengthy catalog essays by Chouinard explained the company's philosophies about saving the earth's resources and Patagonia's rationale for developing environmentally sensitive techniques in the production of merchandise. The ultimate aim behind the messages, of course, was to generate product demand as consumers recognized the added environmental value of Patagonia's merchandise.

To reinforce the sincerity of Patagonia's commitment to the environment, Chouinard established numerous internal procedures that validated its public image of a "green" business. For instance, the company built a new distribution center with recycled materials and equipped it with an energy-saving heating system. Furthermore, it established an internal assessment group that studied the environmental impact of everything from production methods to office procedures and then offered suggestions for improvement. And to ensure that suppliers and contractors shared Patagonia's environmental values, the company invited input from their outside sources on the development of smoother operating procedures.

At the same time, Patagonia managers monitored working conditions of outside contractors and helped them develop techniques for meeting the company's environmental standards. For example, the company worked with outside contractors to create a new fabric, Synchilla fleece, from recycled soda bottles. Patagonia not only incorporated the fabric into many of its own products but also shared the development with the clothing industry. Today 8 million plastic soda bottles are recycled each year in the production of Synchilla fleece.

Patagonia also introduced 100 percent organic cotton for clothing. To offset higher production costs for the cotton, the company split the increased costs with consumers, hoping that they would find value in an environmentally sensitive product. They did. Patagonia immediately sold out of the new line of all-organic cotton sweaters once the catalogs hit the streets.

Today, Patagonia is a proven leader and pioneer of "green" profits. With annual sales exceeding $170 million, Chouinard has succeeded in his attempt to prove that Patagonia could achieve success without compromising environmental values.[51]

Critical Thinking Questions

1. Which of the company's stakeholders are most affected by Patagonia's environmentalism?

2. How does Patagonia's environmentalism exemplify the consumer's right to safety?

3. The California electricity market recently opened its doors to competition, allowing businesses and consumers to choose their own energy providers. Patagonia now has the option to obtain electricity from "green" providers that use nonpolluting sources, such as wind, solar, or geothermal sources, to generate energy, but these are costly. With Patagonia's need to balance economics with environmental concerns, what course of action should the company take?

■ LEARN MORE ONLINE

Patagonia's environmentalism is communicated through the company's catalog, product labels, and Web site. Go to the company's main page http://www.patagonia.com and click on the Enviro Action and About Us links to read current and older reports on environmental issues. What types of environmental concerns are being addressed? How are proceeds from the Earth Tax being distributed? Do you agree with the causes Patagonia supports? Explain your answer.

Test Your Knowledge

QUESTIONS FOR REVIEW

1. Who shapes a company's ethics?

2. How do companies support ethical behavior?

3. How has business's sense of social responsibility evolved since the turn of the century?

4. How are businesses responding to the environmental issues facing society?

5. What can a company do to assure customers that its products are safe?

QUESTIONS FOR ANALYSIS

6. Why can't legal considerations resolve every ethical question?

7. How do individuals employ philosophical principles in making ethical business decisions?

8. Why does a company need more than a code of ethics to be ethical?

9. Explain how Ben & Jerry's managed to balance its social responsibility efforts with its need to make profits.

10. If you discovered that a company initiated ethics programs only to avoid prosecution under the Federal Sentencing Guidelines of 1991, would you conclude that its actions were unethical because its motives were self-serving? Would you consider the company's actions manipulative or misleading? Explain your answer.

QUESTIONS FOR APPLICATION

11. You sell musical gifts on the Web and in quarterly catalogs. Your two-person partnership has quickly grown into a 27-person company, and you spend all your time on quality matters. You're losing control of important environmental choices about materials suppliers, product packaging, and even the paper used in your catalogs. What steps can you take to be sure your employees continue making choices that protect the environment?

12. At quitting time, you see your new colleague filling her briefcase with expensive software programs that aren't supposed to leave the premises. What do you do? Explain your answer.

13. In Chapter 1 we identified knowledge workers as the key economic resource of the twenty-first century. If an employee leaves a company to work for a competitor, what types of knowledge would be ethical for the employee to share with the new employer and what types of knowledge would be unethical to share?

14. Is it ethical for state and city governments to entice businesses to relocate their operations to that state or city by offering them special tax breaks that are not extended to other businesses operating in that area?

Practice Your Knowledge

SHARPENING YOUR COMMUNICATION SKILLS

In one page or less, explain why you think each of the following is or is not ethical.

- Deemphasizing negative test results in a report on your product idea
- Taking a computer home to finish a work-related assignment
- Telling an associate and close friend that she'd better pay more attention to her work responsibilities or management will fire her
- Recommending the purchase of excess equipment to use up your allocated funds before the end of the year so that your budget won't be cut next year

HANDLING DIFFICULT SITUATIONS ON THE JOB: ETHICS, SOCIAL RESPONSIBILITY, AND KETCHUP

Peggy Charen, founder of Action for Children's Television, was upset when H.J. Heinz invited children to help design new labels for ketchup bottles. "I don't think children are the proper target for marketing efforts," she wrote Heinz. Working in Heinz's consumer relations department, you've heard some ripples of concern ever since the firm began sending art posters and label-design contest rules to classrooms and promoting the contest in magazine ads across the United States.

Heinz wanted the new ketchup labels to appeal to families—especially to children, who influence family buying decisions, according to experts. But the contest was designed to be educational, as well. A senior product manager told your department: "Heinz took great care to minimize the commerciality, so to speak, of this program. The materials sent to schools were packed with art facts and art history and art learning." Heinz also donated $450,000 to the National Endowment for the Arts for children's art programs. The entries were judged by a distinguished panel; the three winners each received $5,000 and the satisfaction of seeing their art on Heinz ketchup bottles.

Charen praised Heinz's NEA grant but remained worried. "I don't want my grandchildren thinking ketchup is an important part of their lives," she said. She wanted Heinz to stop using children's artwork in a commercial way. You have been assigned to respond.[52]

1. How will you respond to Charen's request?
2. Do you consider this situation an ethical dilemma or an ethical lapse? Why?
3. In writing a letter to Ms. Charen, what can you say about the benefits of the label-design contest and the way Heinz is seeking to balance social responsibility and profits?

BUILDING YOUR TEAM SKILLS

All organizations, not just corporations, can benefit from having a code of ethics to guide decision making. But who should a code of ethics protect, and what should it cover? In this exercise, you and your team are going to draft a code of ethics for your school.

Start by brainstorming about who will be protected by this code of ethics. What stakeholders should the school consider when making decisions? What negative effects might decisions have on these stakeholders?

Then think about the kinds of situations you want your school's code of ethics to cover. One example might be employment decisions; another might be disclosure of confidential student information.

Next, using Exhibit 2.2 as a model, draft your school's code of ethics. Write a general introduction explaining the purpose of the code and who is being protected. Next, write a positive statement to guide ethical decisions in each situation you identified earlier in this exercise. Your statement about promotion decisions, for example, might read: "School officials will encourage equal access to job promotions for all qualified candidates, with every applicant receiving fair consideration."

Compare your code of ethics with the codes drafted by other teams. Did all the teams' codes seek to protect the same stakeholders? What differences and similarities do you see in the statements guiding ethical decisions?

Expand Your Knowledge

EXPLORING CAREER OPPORTUNITIES

Businesses, government agencies, and not-for-profit organizations offer numerous career opportunities related to ethics and social responsibility. How can you learn more about these careers?

1. Search through Appendix 2 to identify jobs related to ethics and social responsibility. One example is Occupational Health and Safety Manager, a job concerned with a company's responsibility toward its employees. What are the duties and qualifications of the jobs you have identified? Are the salaries and future outlooks attractive for all of these jobs?
2. Select one job for further consideration. Following the suggestions in Appendix 1, what sources of employment information might provide more details about this job? Which of these sources are available in your school or public library? What additional sources can you consult for more information about the daily activities of this job and for ideas about locating potential employers?
3. What skills, educational background, and work experience do you think employers are seeking in applicants for the specific job you are researching? What key words do you think employers would search for when scanning electronic résumés submitted for this position?

DEVELOPING YOUR RESEARCH SKILLS

What environmental problems threaten your community, city, or state? Using library, government, or Internet sources, find out whether your area is dealing with pollution caused by fuel spills, toxic manufacturing emissions, leaking underground oil tanks, contaminated drinking water, acid rain, or similar sources. Keep track of your sources and your search methodology as you research these pollution problems.

1. What kind of environmental pollution problems did your research reveal? Who or what caused each pollution problem? How long has your area been grappling with these problems?
2. What dangers are associated with the local pollution problems? What is the estimated cost of cleaning up the damage? What is the estimated cost of preventing such problems in the future?
3. What local, state, and federal laws apply to your area's pollution problems? Do you think these laws are adequately addressing these environmental threats? Why or why not?

SEE IT ON THE WEB EXERCISES
Build a Better Business, page 32

The Better Business Bureau Web site has a lot of useful information for businesses and consumers alike. Go to the bureau's site at http://www.bbb.org and click on the links to answer the following questions.

1. Click on About the BBB. What are "BBB Reliability Reports"? What does it mean when the BBB does not have a report on a particular company? How are these reports related to the consumer's right to be informed?

2. From the homepage, follow the link to Programs and Services of the Better Business Bureau. What is BBB Auto Line? What kind of disputes are handled by the program? What right does a consumer forfeit when accepting the decision of an Auto Line arbitrator? As a consumer, what primary benefits would you expect from this program?

3. From the homepage, click on Advertising Review Programs and then on BBB Advertising Guidelines to access the Code of Advertising. According to the code, when is it acceptable for BBB members to use the word *sale* in advertising? How should BBB members handle "extra charges" in their advertising? Why is it in the best interest of advertisers to comply with the ethical principles of the BBB's guidelines, even if they are not BBB members?

Go for the Green, page 39

The Sustainable Business Network makes it easier for businesses and consumers to find the information that will enable them to make environmentally responsible choices. Visit the network's Web site at http://sbn.envirolink.org/ to answer the following questions.

1. Click on SBN Library, then scroll down to click on the link to Business for Social Responsibility (BSR). What is this organization's mission? What products and services does BSR provide its members? As a future businessperson, do you support the goals of BSR? Would you want to work for a company that supports those goals? Why or why not?

2. Return to the SBN Library and click on Green Seal. What is Green Seal, and how does it help protect the environment? Why would a business want to have the Green Seal label on its products? Why might a business not want to be associated with Green Seal?

3. From the SBN homepage, click on SBN Job Center and then search by level of job for internships. Browse through the list and look for any internships that interest you. What skills or experience would help you obtain these positions? What can you do to develop such skills while you are a student?

Surf Safely, page 41

Visit the Web site of the National Fraud Information Center (NFIC) at http://www.fraud.org to learn how to protect yourself from telephone and Internet scams. Answer the following questions by navigating the links on the site.

1. Click on Telemarketing Fraud. What percentage of U.S. adults have reported receiving fraudulent telephone offers? According to FBI estimates, how many illegal telephone sales companies are operating in the United States? Why should legitimate businesses be concerned about these high rates of telephone fraud?

2. Find Internet Tips under Internet Fraud Watch. After reading the Basic Internet Tips, what do you think are the three most important tips for staying safe in cyberspace? Given the increase in the number of Internet businesses, how easy or difficult is it for consumers to follow these guidelines?

3. Click on How to Report Fraud and Ask Questions at the bottom of the screen. What two ways can you report fraud to the NFIC? What information should you supply in your report? How does the government benefit from consumers' taking action against fraudulent businesses? How does this action indirectly affect all consumers?

3

COMPETING IN THE GLOBAL ECONOMY

LEARNING OBJECTIVES

After studying this chapter, you will be able to

1 Highlight the opportunities and challenges of conducting business in other countries

2 Identify five forms of international business activity

3 Explain the theory of comparative advantage

4 Highlight the arguments for and against protectionism

5 Discuss the function, advantages, and disadvantages of trading blocs

6 Explain why a country might devalue its currency

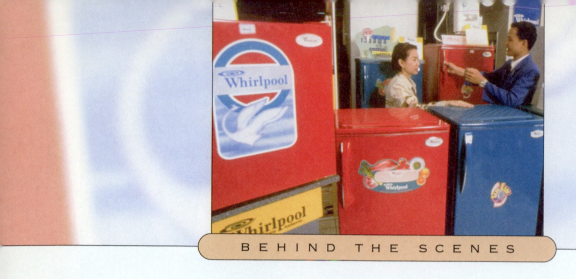

FACING BUSINESS CHALLENGES
AT WHIRLPOOL

Caught in the Wringer of Global Business?

Everybody is talking about going global these days, but most people don't understand what that really means. David Whitwam, chairman and CEO of Whirlpool, does. When he first began eyeing the global marketplace, this Michigan-based appliance maker was concentrating only on the U.S. market, producing and marketing washers, refrigerators, and other household appliances under the Whirlpool, KitchenAid, Roper, and Kenmore brand names.

Determined to convert Whirlpool from essentially a U.S. company to a major global player, Whitwam purchased N. V. Philips's floundering European appliance business in 1989. The CEO's first challenge was to integrate and coordinate the many European operations with the U.S. operation. Some companies accomplish this task by imposing the parent's systems on the acquired companies, but Whitwam started down a more ambitious path. He created cross-cultural teams with members from the European and North American operations, and together they designed a program to ensure quality and productivity throughout Whirlpool's worldwide operation. In the eyes of other corporate leaders, Whirlpool was doing everything right. The company was even featured in a 1994 *Harvard Business Review* article titled "The Right Way to Go Global."

Still, Whitwam soon discovered that developing global strategies was far easier than executing them.

Whirlpool had not counted on the difficulty in marketing appliances—a largely homogeneous process in the United States—to the fragmented cultures of Europe, Asia, and Latin America. For instance, clothes washers sold in northern European countries such as Denmark must spin-dry clothes much better than in southern Italy, where consumers often line-dry clothes in warmer weather. And consumers in India and southern China prefer small refrigerators because they must fit in tight kitchens. Meanwhile, Whitwam was also caught off guard by poor economic conditions in Europe, Asia, and Brazil. There, because of economic downturns, consumers were postponing appliance purchases or buying lower-priced models—and cutting deeply into Whirlpool's profits.

Despite these challenges, Whitwam was convinced that he could remake Whirlpool into a truly global company. Of course, to capitalize on the projected double-digit growth of developing countries, he knew that Whirlpool would have find a way to respond to national and regional product preferences. But how? If you were Whitwam, what would you do to help Whirlpool navigate the rough waters of the global marketplace? How would you learn more about consumer needs to develop suitable appliances for each market? What steps would you take to boost sales of the Whirlpool brand around the world?[1]

■ THE GLOBAL BUSINESS ENVIRONMENT

Like Whirlpool, more and more enterprises are experiencing the excitement of conducting business in the global marketplace. Although selling goods and services in foreign markets can generate increased sales, produce operational efficiencies, expose companies to new technologies, and provide greater consumer choices, venturing abroad also exposes companies to many new challenges, as David Whitwam discovered. For instance, each country has unique ways of doing business, which must be learned: Laws, customs, consumer preferences, ethical standards, labor skill, and political and economic stability vary from country to country, and all have the potential to affect a firm's international prospects. Furthermore, volatile currencies and international trade relationships can indeed make global expansion a risky proposition.

Still, in most cases the opportunities of the global marketplace greatly outweigh the risks. Consider UPS. When this company began its rapid global expansion program in the 1980s, it had to attain air rights into each country, unravel a patchwork of customs laws, learn how to deal with varying work ethics and employment policies, and so on. But the company's efforts paid off. Today UPS delivers over 3.14 billion packages and documents in more than 200 countries around the globe.[2]

Cultural Differences in the Global Business Environment

As David Whitwam learned, managing operations in more than one country can be tricky. For one thing, companies must recognize and respect the many cultural differences that distinguish people in one country from people in another. These include differences in social values, ideas of status, decision-making habits, attitudes toward time, use of space, body language, manners, and ethical standards. Such differences can lead to misunderstandings in international business relationships, particularly if language differences also exist. Furthermore, companies that sell their products overseas often must adapt the products to meet the unique needs of international customers, just as Whirlpool does.

The best way to prepare yourself to do business with people from another culture is to study that culture in advance. Learn everything you can about the culture's history, religion, politics, and customs—especially its business customs. Who makes decisions? How are negotiations usually conducted? Is gift giving expected? What is the proper attire for a business meeting? In addition to learning about the culture, seasoned international businesspeople suggest the following techniques for improving intercultural communication:

- *Deal with the individual.* Don't stereotype the other person or react with preconceived ideas. Regard the person as an individual first, not as a representative of another culture.

- *Be alert to the other person's customs.* Expect him or her to have values, beliefs, expectations, and mannerisms different from yours. For instance, don't be surprised when businesspeople in Pakistan excuse themselves in the middle of a meeting to conduct prayers. Moslems pray five times a day.

- *Be aware that gestures and expressions mean different things in different cultures.* The other person's body language may not mean what you think, and he or she may read unintentional meanings into your message. Clarify your true intent by repetition and examples. Ask questions and listen carefully. The Japanese are generally appreciative when foreigners ask what is proper behavior, because it shows respect for the Japanese way of doing things.[5]

- *Adapt your style to the other person's.* If the other person appears to be direct and straightforward, follow suit. If not, adjust your behavior to match. In many African

countries, for example, people are suspicious of others who seem to be in a hurry. Therefore, you should allow plenty of time to get to know the people you are dealing with.

- *Show respect.* Learn how respect is communicated in various cultures—through gestures, eye contact, and so on. For example, in Spain let a handshake last five to seven strokes; pulling away too soon may be interpreted as a rejection. In France, however, the preferred handshake is a single stroke.

Legal Differences in the Global Business Environment

All U.S. companies that conduct business in other countries must be familiar with U.S. law, international law, and the laws of the specific countries where they plan to trade or do business. For example, all companies doing international business must comply with the 1978 Foreign Corrupt Practices Act. This U.S. law outlaws actions such as bribing government officials in other nations to approve deals. It does, however, allow certain payments, including small payments to officials for expediting routine government actions.

Critics of this U.S. law complain that payoffs are a routine part of world trade, so forbidding U.S. companies to follow suit cripples their ability to compete. Others counter that U.S. exports haven't been affected by this law and that companies can conduct business abroad without violating antibribery rules. Regardless of whether they agree with the law, some companies have had to forgo opportunities as a result of it. For example, a U.S. power-generation company recently walked away from a $320 million contract in the Middle East because government officials demanded a $3 million bribe. The contract went to a Japanese company instead.[6]

Forms of International Business Activity

LEARNING OBJECTIVE 2
Identify five forms of international business activity

Once a company decides to operate in the global marketplace, it must decide on the level of involvement it is willing to undertake. Five common forms of international business activities are *importing and exporting, licensing, franchising, strategic alliances and joint ventures,* and *wholly owned facilities.* Each has a varying degree of ownership, financial commitment, and risk.

importing
Purchasing goods or services from another country and bringing them into one's own country

exporting
Selling and shipping goods or services to another country

Importing and Exporting   **Importing,** the buying of goods or services from another country, and **exporting,** the selling of products outside the country in which they are produced, have existed for centuries. In the last few decades, however, the increased level of these activities has caused the economies of the world to become tightly linked. Currently, the United States exports some $700 billion of merchandise each year.[7] Considering the fact that 95 percent of the world's consumers live outside the United States, and many consumers in these areas are just beginning to buy products from the United States, you can see why exporting is indeed an attractive growth option for U.S. businesses.[8]

Companies that choose to export their products may do so directly by calling on potential customers overseas, or they may rely on intermediaries at home or abroad. Such intermediaries include *export management companies,* domestic firms that specialize in performing international marketing services on a commission basis, and *export trading companies,* general trading firms that will buy your products for resale overseas as well as perform a variety of importing, exporting, and manufacturing functions. Still another alternative is to use foreign distributors.

Working through someone with connections in the target country is often helpful to both large and small companies because such intermediaries can provide you with the expertise and knowledge you will need to conduct business in a foreign market.[9] In addition, many countries now have foreign trade offices to help importers and exporters interested in doing business within their borders. Other helpful resources include professional agents, local businesspeople, and the International Trade Administration of the U.S. Department of Commerce. This trade organization offers a variety of services, including political and credit-risk analysis, advice on entering foreign markets, and financing tips.

Licensing Licensing is another popular approach to international business. License agreements entitle one company to produce or market another company's product or to utilize its technology in return for a royalty or fee. For example, a U.S. business might obtain the rights to manufacture and sell a Scandinavian skin lotion in the United States, using the Scandinavian formula and packaging design. The U.S. company would be responsible for promoting and distributing the product, and it would pay the Scandinavian company a percentage of its income from sales in exchange for the product rights.

China is becoming too big a PC market for anyone to ignore. Dell, which recently opened its fourth PC factory in the world on China's southeastern coast, can now deliver PCs to Chinese customers as fast as it does to North American ones.

Licensing deals can also work the other way, with the U.S. company acting as the licenser and the overseas company as the licensee. The U.S. firm would avoid the shipping costs, trade barriers, and uncertainties associated with trying to enter other markets, but it would still receive a portion of the revenue from overseas sales. Of course, licensing agreements are not restricted to international business. A company can also license its products or technology to other companies in its domestic market.

licensing
Agreement to produce and market another company's product in exchange for a royalty or fee

Franchising Some companies choose to expand into foreign markets by *franchising* their operation. Under this arrangement, a franchisor enters into an agreement whereby the franchisee obtains the rights to duplicate a specific product or service—perhaps a restaurant, photocopy shop, or a video rental store—and the franchisor obtains a royalty fee in exchange. Holiday Inn Worldwide has used this approach to reach customers in over

See It on the Web See It on the Web

GOING GLOBAL

Have you ever thought about getting into the world of exporting? Where would you go for information and help? Many small and large companies have gotten valuable export assistance from the U.S. government through the International Trade Administration (ITA). You can find a wealth of information about export procedures; foreign markets, industries, companies, and products; export financing; unfair trade practices; trade statistics; and more by visiting the ITA's Web page. The site is also a great starting point for links to many other trade-related sites. Select Regions and Countries to find out more about markets all over the world.
http://www.ita.doc.gov

65 countries. Smaller companies have also found that franchising is a good way for them to enter the global marketplace. For example, Ziebart Tidy-Car, which franchises car-improvement outlets from its headquarters in Michigan, has arranged to open more than 300 outlets in 40 countries.[10] By franchising its operations, a firm can minimize the costs and risks of global expansion and bypass certain trade restrictions. (The advantages and disadvantages of franchising will be discussed in detail in Chapter 4.)

Strategic Alliances and Joint Ventures   *Strategic alliances* and *joint ventures* offer another practical approach to international business. A **strategic alliance** is a long-term partnership between two or more companies aimed at helping each establish competitive advantages in the marketplace. To reach their individual but complementary goals, the companies may share ideas, resources, and technologies. Consider the strategic alliance between Northwest Airlines and Continental Airlines, for example. By merging passengers, routes, frequent flier programs, and marketing while keeping their employees and airplanes separate, the two companies will be in a better position to compete with such megacarriers as United Airlines and American Airlines.[11]

In contrast, a **joint venture** is a partnership in which one company cooperates with other companies or governments to jointly develop, produce, or sell products. Companies involved in a joint venture typically share the investment costs, risks, management, and profits of their business venture. In some countries, foreign companies are prohibited from owning facilities outright or from investing in local business. Thus, establishing a joint venture with a local partner may be the only way to do business in that country. In other cases, foreigners may be required to move some of their production facilities to the country to earn the right to sell their products there. For instance, the Chinese government would not allow Boeing to sell airplanes in China until the company agreed to move half of the tail-section production for its 737s to Xian.[12]

Wholly Owned Facilities   The most comprehensive form of international business is a wholly owned operation run in another country, without the financial participation of a local partner. Many U.S. firms conduct business this way, as do companies based in other countries. These operations vary in form, size, and purpose. Some are started from scratch; others are acquired from local owners. Some are small sales offices; others are full-scale manufacturing facilities. Some are set up to exploit the availability of raw materials; others take advantage of low wage rates; still others minimize transportation costs by choosing locations that give them direct access to markets in other countries. In almost all cases, at least part of the work force is drawn from the local population.

Companies with a physical presence in numerous countries are called **multinational corporations (MNCs)**. Because they operate on such a worldwide scale, at times it's difficult to determine exactly where home is (see Exhibit 3.1). Since 1969, the number of multinational corporations in the world's 14 richest countries has more than tripled, from 7,000 to 24,000.[13] Some multinational corporations increase their involvement in foreign countries by establishing **foreign direct investment (FDI)**. That is, they either establish production and marketing facilities in the countries where they operate or purchase existing foreign firms, as Wal-Mart did in the late 1990s, when it acquired large retail stores in Germany and Great Britain and later converted them into Wal-Mart supercenters. Such foreign direct investment constitutes the highest level of international involvement.[14]

The U.S. Commerce Department reports that foreign direct investment in the United States has been rising steadily over the past few years.[15] For example, Daimler-Benz's $40 billion acquisition of Chrysler and British Petroleum's $48 billion acquisition of Amoco

strategic alliance
Long-term relationship in which two or more companies share ideas, resources, and technologies in order to establish competitive advantages

joint venture
Cooperative partnership in which organizations share investment costs, risks, management, and profits in the development, production, or selling of products

multinational corporations (MNCs)
Companies with operations in more than one country

foreign direct investment (FDI)
Investment of money by foreign companies in domestic business enterprises

1998 RANK	COMPANY	FOREIGN REVENUE ($US IN MILLIONS)	TOTAL REVENUE ($US IN MILLIONS)	FOREIGN AS PERCENT OF TOTAL
1	Exxon	$ 80,705	$ 100,697	80
2	IBM	46,364	81,667	57
3	Ford Motor	43,819	144,416	30
4	General Motors	40,918	132,863	31
5	Texaco	31,313	39,497	79
6	General Electric	31,278	100,469	31
7	Mobil	28,009	47,678	59
8	Citigroup	26,276	76,431	34
9	Hewlett-Packard	25,531	47,061	54
10	Philip Morris Companies	19,814	57,813	34
11	Chevron	19,008	40,216	47
12	Procter & Gamble Company	17,928	37,154	48
13	American International Group	17,478	33,296	53
14	Compaq Computer	17,188	31,169	55
15	Intel	14,610	26,273	56

EXHIBIT 3·1

FIFTEEN LARGEST U.S. MULTINATIONALS

On average, the 15 largest U.S. multinational corporations earn about 46 percent of their revenue from foreign sales.

propelled Germany and the United Kingdom to the top two foreign countries investing in the United States.[16]

In addition to the United States, areas such as the Chinese Economic Area (China, Hong Kong, and Taiwan), South Korea, Singapore, Thailand, Malaysia, Indonesia, Vietnam, India, South Africa, Turkey, and Brazil are becoming attractive spots for foreign investment. Labeled *big emerging markets*, these countries make up 70 percent of the world's land, 85 percent of the world's population, and 99 percent of the anticipated growth in the world's labor force.[17] As such, they have been identified by the U.S. International Trade Administration as having the greatest potential for large increase in U.S. exports over the next two decades.

FUNDAMENTALS OF INTERNATIONAL TRADE

Once the target of a U.S. embargo, Vietnam is now an emerging economy with great potential for U.S. companies.

The success of U.S. businesses such as Whirlpool, Wal-Mart, UPS, and others that operate in the global marketplace depends, in part, on the international economic relationships the United States maintains with other countries. Basically, the objective of the United States is to devise policies that balance the interests of U.S. companies, U.S. workers, and U.S. consumers.

Other countries, of course, are trying to do the same thing. As you might expect, the many players in world trade sometimes have conflicting goals.

Why Nations Trade

LEARNING OBJECTIVE 3
Explain the theory of comparative advantage

No single country has the resources to produce everything its citizens want or need. Countries specialize in the production of certain goods and trade with other countries for those they do not produce. Most countries, however, try to remain reasonably self-sufficient in certain essential industries, such as agriculture and energy, so they can provide for the basic needs of their citizens in the event of an international conflict.

absolute advantage
A nation's ability to produce a particular product with fewer resources per unit of output than any other nation

Apart from supplying a country's basic needs, how does a country know what to produce and what to trade for? In some cases the answer is easy: a nation may have an **absolute advantage,** which means it can produce a particular item more efficiently than *all* other nations, or, it is virtually the only country producing that product. Saudi Arabia, for example, is seen as having an absolute advantage in crude oil production because of its huge, developed reserves. Similar in scope to a global monopoly, it makes sense for Saudi Arabia to specialize in providing the world with oil, and to trade for other items its country needs.

comparative advantage theory
Theory which states that a country should produce and sell to other countries those items it produces most efficiently

Nevertheless, absolute advantages are rare today. In most cases, a country can produce many of the same items that other countries can produce. The **comparative advantage theory** explains how a country chooses which items to produce and which items to trade for; the theory states that a country should produce and sell to other countries those items it produces more efficiently and trade for those items it can't produce efficiently. To see how the theory works, imagine two countries, East and West. Each can produce both bicycles and wheat, but East is more efficient at producing bicycles than wheat, while West is more efficient at producing wheat than bicycles. According to the comparative advantage theory, the two countries will be better off if each specializes in the industry where it is more efficient and if the two trade with each other—East sells bicycles to West and West sells wheat to East.[18]

The basic argument behind the comparative advantage theory is that such specialization and exchange will increase a country's total output and allow both trading partners to enjoy a higher standard of living. Still, the theory is only one explanation for why countries trade. International trade has many benefits: it increases a country's total output, offers lower prices and greater variety to consumers, subjects domestic oligopolies and monopolies to competition, and allows firms to attain economies of scale.[19]

How International Trade Is Measured

In Chapter 1 we discussed how economists monitor certain key economic indicators to evaluate how well their country's economic system is performing. One trend that economists watch carefully is the level of a nation's imports and exports. For instance, at any given time, a country may be importing more than it is exporting. As Exhibit 3.2 illustrates, the United States imports more consumer goods than it exports, but it exports more services than it imports. Two key measurements of a nation's level of international trade are the *balance of trade* and the *balance of payments*.

balance of trade
Total value of the products a nation exports minus the total value of the products it imports, over some period of time

The total value of a country's exports *minus* the total value of its imports, over some period of time, determines its **balance of trade.** In years when the United States exports more goods and services than it imports, its balance of trade is favorable, creating a **trade surplus:** People in other countries buy more goods and services from the United States than the United States buys from them. As a result, money flows into the U.S. economy, a situation that is good for U.S. businesses. Conversely, when the people of the United States buy more from foreign countries than the foreign countries buy from the United States, imports

trade surplus
Favorable trade balance created when a country exports more than it imports

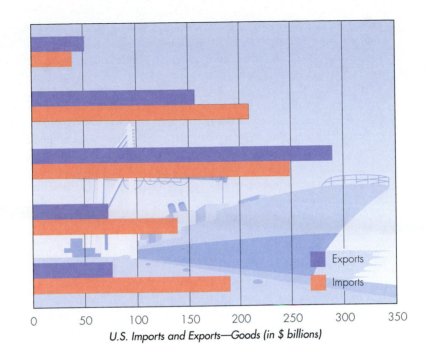

Foods, feeds, and beverages

Industrial supplies and materials

Machinery and transport equipment (except automotive)

Automotive vehicles, engines, and parts

Consumer goods (nonfood)

■ Exports
■ Imports

0   50   100   150   200   250   300   350

U.S. Imports and Exports—Goods (in $ billions)

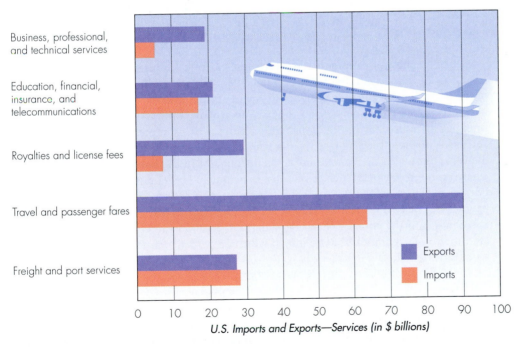

Business, professional, and technical services

Education, financial, insurance, and telecommunications

Royalties and license fees

Travel and passenger fares

Freight and port services

■ Exports
■ Imports

0   10   20   30   40   50   60   70   80   90   100

U.S. Imports and Exports—Services (in $ billions)

ExHIBIT 3·2

U.S. EXPORTS AND IMPORTS

The United States actively participates in global trade by exporting and importing goods and services.

trade deficit
Unfavorable trade balance created when a country imports more than it exports

exceed exports, money flows out of the U.S. economy, and its balance of trade is unfavorable, creating a **trade deficit.** In 1998 the U.S. trade deficit soared to a record $164 billion (produced by a $246 billion trade deficit in goods and an $82 billion trade surplus in services). Economists attribute this deficit to a falloff in U.S. exports rather than a surge in foreign imports.[20]

Bear in mind that the excess of imports over exports does not necessarily mean that U.S. companies are not competitive in the world market. The balance of trade is obscured by several factors. One such factor is the change in the value of the dollar compared with the value of other currencies. When the dollar is strong, products from other countries seem relatively inexpensive in the United States, and U.S. products seem relatively expensive overseas. As U.S. consumers buy more of the relatively inexpensive imported goods and consumers overseas buy less of the relatively expensive U.S. goods, the U.S. trade deficit grows. When the situation is reversed and U.S. consumers buy fewer imported goods while people in other countries buy more U.S. exports, the U.S. trade deficit narrows and may even turn into a trade surplus. (Currency valuations and their impact on global trade will be discussed later in this chapter.)

intrafirm trade
Trade between global units of a multinational corporation

Another reason that the balance of trade can be misleading is **intrafirm trade,** which is trade between the various units of a multinational corporation. In fact, intrafirm trade now accounts for one-third of all the goods traded around the world.[21] Multinational corporations such as Whirlpool, AT&T, Texas Instruments, and General Electric set up factories to make components in countries where wage rates are low, then ship the components back to the United States for assembly. These shipments to the United States are counted as imports even though they are used by the same company. By contrast, products produced by subsidiaries of foreign companies in the United States for the U.S. market are not considered imports. As you can see, by itself, the balance of trade does not paint a complete picture of a nation's global competitiveness.

balance of payments
Sum of all payments one nation receives from other nations minus the sum of all payments it makes to other nations, over some specified period of time

The **balance of payments** is the broadest indicator of international trade. It is the total flow of money into the country *minus* the total flow of money out of the country over some period of time. The balance of payments includes the balance of trade plus the net dollars received and spent on foreign investment, military expenditures, tourism, foreign aid, and other international transactions. For example, when a U.S. company such as Whirlpool buys all or part of a company based in another country, that investment is counted in the balance of payments but not in the balance of trade. Similarly, when a foreign company such as Daimler-Benz buys a U.S. company such as Chrysler or purchases U.S. stocks, bonds, or real estate, those transactions are part of the balance of payments. The goal is to have a favorable balance of payments. That means more money is coming into the country than is flowing out. In 1998 the U.S. balance of payments amounted to a deficit of $220 billion, of which 75 percent was attributable to the country's trade deficit.[22]

LEARNING OBJECTIVE 4
Highlight the arguments for and against protectionism

protectionism
Government policies aimed at shielding a country's industries from foreign competition

Protectionist Measures

Even though international trade has many economic advantages, sometimes countries practice **protectionism;** that is, they restrict international trade for one reason or another. Sometimes they restrict trade to shield their industries from foreign competition and the possible loss of jobs. Other times, they try to protect certain industries that are key to their national defense and the health and safety of their citizens. In the case of some emerging economies, such as China, protectionist measures may also be designed to give new or weak industries an opportunity to grow and strengthen so they can compete with bigger players.[24]

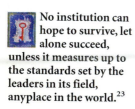 **No institution can hope to survive, let alone succeed, unless it measures up to the standards set by the leaders in its field, anyplace in the world.**[23]

EXHIBIT 3·3

PROTECTIONISM PROS
AND CONS

Although arguments can be
made both for and against
protectionism, most experts
agree that it is damaging to a
nation's economy in the long
run.

PROS	CONS
Boosts domestic economies by restricting foreign competition	Raises price of both foreign and domestic goods by removing competition
Protects local jobs because demand for domestically produced goods remains strong	Creates problems for U.S. companies that depend on imported parts
Helps new industries get started and weak industries get stronger	Stifles product innovation because companies have no incentive to improve quality or advance technologically
Keeps technology out of the hands of potential enemies	Prevents companies from developing production and distribution synergies and economies of scale

Is protectionism a good idea or a bad idea? Although proponents of both sides of the issue can make convincing arguments (see Exhibit 3.3), study after study has shown that in the long run, protectionism hurts everyone. In fact, many developing countries that once imposed trade barriers to shield their emerging industries are now opening up their markets because they found that trade restrictions were stifling their economies. The most commonly used forms of trade restrictions include:

- *Tariffs.* **Tariffs** are taxes, surcharges, or duties levied against imported goods. Sometimes tariffs are levied to generate revenue for the government, but more often they are levied to raise the price of imported goods, giving domestic producers a cost advantage. Unfortunately, it is usually the consumer who pays the price, because without foreign competition, producers can charge more for their goods.

- *Quotas.* **Quotas** limit the amount of a particular good that countries can import during a year. Limits may be set in quantities, such as bushels of wheat, or in values, such as total dollars' worth of peanuts.

- *Embargoes.* In its most extreme form, a quota becomes an **embargo,** a complete ban on the import or export of certain products. For example, Canada forbids the importation of oleomargarine in order to protect its dairy industry, and the U.S. bans the importation of toys with lead paint because of health concerns.

- *Sanctions.* Sanctions are politically motivated embargoes that revoke a country's normal trade relations status: They are often used as forceful alternatives short of war. Sanctions can include arms embargoes, foreign-assistance reductions and cutoffs, trade limitations, tariff increases, import-quota decreases, visa denials, air-link cancellations, and more. About two dozen countries are now subject to U.S. sanctions, including Iraq (for its invasion of Kuwait) and India (for conducting nuclear tests). Still, most governments today (including the United States) use sanctions sparingly, because studies show that sanctions are ineffective at getting countries to change. More often, they hurt the innocent instead of those responsible for the undesirable behavior. Furthermore, sanctions can permanently harm a country's export opportunities if countries against which they are imposed can obtain the sanctioned goods or services elsewhere.[25]

- *Restrictive import standards.* Another way countries give their domestic producers an edge is to establish restrictive import standards, such as requiring special licenses for doing certain kinds of business and then making it difficult for foreign

tariffs
Taxes levied on imports

quotas
Fixed limits on the quantity of imports a nation will allow for a specific product

embargo
Total ban on trade with a particular nation (a sanction) or of a particular product

companies to obtain such a license. For example, Saudi Arabia restricts import licenses for a variety of products, including chemicals, pasteurized milk, and information technology products.[26] Other countries restrict imports by requiring goods to pass special tests.

- *Subsidies.* Rather than restrict imports, some countries subsidize domestic producers so that their prices will be substantially lower than import prices. The goal is to help build up an industry until it is strong enough to compete on its own in both domestic and foreign markets. Airbus, for example, is a subsidized joint venture in aircraft manufacturing supported by Germany, France, England, and Spain. Although plans to privatize the company are already under way, support from these countries helps Airbus compete against Boeing, which holds a majority of the world's passenger airplane market.[27] Worldwide, agriculture receives the largest subsidies. However, in the United States new agricultural policies are gradually reducing price supports until the year 2002.[28]

Sometimes countries justify protectionism beyond the need for security and safety reasons because of anticompetitive behavior on the part of the foreign producer. Under Section 301 of the Trade Act of 1988, for example, the U.S. president is legally obligated to retaliate against foreign producers that use questionable tactics in approaching the U.S. market. These tactics can include international price discrimination and **dumping,** the practice of selling large quantities of a product at a price lower than the cost of production or below what the company would charge in its home market. Dumping is often used to quickly gain a larger share of the market or to reduce inventories. It puts pressure on competitors to cut their own prices in order to maintain sales. Even though reducing prices may benefit consumers, it can greatly damage a company's competitive position. At least 200 antidumping cases have been brought against China by the United States and the European Union in recent years. Among the products China is accused of dumping are shoes and bicycles.[29]

dumping
Charging less than the actual cost or less than the home-country price for goods sold in other countries

Agreements and Organizations Promoting International Trade

To prevent trade disputes from escalating into full-blown trade wars and to ensure that international business is conducted in a fair and orderly fashion, countries worldwide have created trade agreements and organizations. Philosophically, most of these agreements and organizations support the basic principles of **free trade;** that is, each nation will ultimately

free trade
International trade unencumbered by restrictive measures

See It on the Web See It on the Web

LEADING THE WAY TO FOREIGN TRADE

How do products from all over the world find their way into the hands of consumers? The process can take a long time, but it may begin with a *trade lead*—a sort of classified ad to buy or sell products internationally. World Trade Markets lists many current trade leads on its Web page. Here you will find product and contact information from companies and agents all over the world. You can view the leads by date, country, or product. Follow the links to products or areas of the world that interest you—who knows what opportunities you will find.
http://www.wtm.com

benefit by freely exchanging the goods and services it produces most efficiently for the goods and services it produces less efficiently. The major trade agreements and organizations include the GATT, the WTO, the APEC, the IMF, and the World Bank.

- *The General Agreement on Tariffs and Trade (GATT).* The GATT is a worldwide pact that was first established in the aftermath of World War II. The pact's guiding principle has been one of nondiscrimination: Any trade advantage a GATT member gives to one country must be given to all GATT members, and no GATT nation can be singled out for punishment. In 1995 GATT established the World Trade Organization (WTO), which has now replaced GATT as the world forum for trade negotiations.

- *The World Trade Organization (WTO).* The WTO is a permanent forum for negotiating, implementing, and monitoring international trade procedures and for mediating trade disputes among its 135 member countries. The organization's goals include facilitating free trade, lowering the costs of doing business, enhancing the international investment environment, simplifying customs, and promoting technical and economic cooperation. Experts believe that the WTO should ultimately prove to be more effective than the GATT because the WTO has a formal legal structure for settling disputes. Admission to the organization is by unanimous consent. For instance, even though a recent agreement between the United States and China cleared the way for China's entry into the WTO (after 13 years of on-and-off negotiations), China must still reach agreement with other member governments.[30]

- *The Asia Pacific Economic Cooperation Council (APEC).* The APEC is an organization of 18 countries that are making efforts to liberalize trade in the Pacific Rim (the land areas that surround the Pacific Ocean). Among the member nations are the United States, Japan, China, Mexico, Australia, South Korea, and Canada. In 1994 the members agreed to eliminate all tariffs and trade barriers among industrialized countries of the Pacific Rim by 2010 and among developing countries by 2020.[31]

- *The International Monetary Fund (IMF).* The IMF was founded in 1945 and is now affiliated with the United Nations. Its primary function is to provide short-term loans to countries that are unable to meet their budgetary expenses. As such, the IMF is often looked upon as a lender of last resort. For example, the IMF has provided well over a combined total of $150 billion in loans to South Korea, Indonesia, Brazil, Thailand, and other countries to help rescue them from a global financial crisis at the end of the twentieth century.[32]

- *The World Bank.* Officially known as the International Bank for Reconstruction and Development, the World Bank was founded to finance reconstruction after World War II. It now provides low-interest loans to developing nations for the improvement of transportation, telecommunications, health, and education. Currently the World Bank is focused on bringing the Internet to the less-developed regions of the world, such as Africa. World Bank officials and telecommunication executives hope that Internet connections will attract more companies to the region, and thus lead to more rapid economic development.[33]

Although both the IMF and the World Bank are affiliated with the United Nations, their membership is separate. They are funded by deposits from their 182 member nations. The bulk of the funds come from the United States, western Europe, and Japan.

Trading Blocs **Trading blocs** are another type of organization that promotes international trade. Generally comprising neighboring countries, trading blocs promote free trade among regional members. Although specific rules vary from group to group, their primary

LEARNING OBJECTIVE 5
Discuss the function, advantages, and disadvantages of trading blocs

trading blocs
Organizations of nations that remove barriers to trade among their members and that establish uniform barriers to trade with nonmember nations

objective is to ensure the economic growth and benefit of members. As such, trading blocs generally promote trade inside the region while creating uniform barriers against goods and services entering the region from nonmember countries. Trading blocs are becoming a significant force in the global marketplace.[34]

Trading blocs can be advantageous or disadvantageous in promoting world trade, depending on one's perspective. Some economists are apprehensive about the growing importance of regional trading blocs. They fear that the world is splitting into three camps, revolving around the Americas, Europe, and Asia. Any nation that does not fall into one of these economic regions could suffer, they say, because members of the trading blocs could place severe restrictions on trade with nonmember countries. The critics fear that overall world trade could decline as members become more protective of their own regions. As a result, consumers could find themselves with fewer choices, and many producers could lose sales in lucrative foreign markets.

Others claim, however, that trading blocs could improve world trade. For one thing, the growth of commerce and the availability of customers and suppliers within a trading bloc could be a boon to smaller or younger nations that are trying to build strong economies. For another, the lack of trade barriers within the bloc could help their industries compete with producers in more developed nations, and, in some cases, member countries could reach a wider market than before.[35] Furthermore, close ties to more stable economies could help shield emerging nations from fluctuations in the global economy and could promote a greater sharing of knowledge and technology; both outcomes could aid future economic development.

The four most powerful trading blocs today are the Association of Southeast Asian Nations (ASEAN), South America's Mercosur, the NAFTA (North American Free Trade Agreement) countries, and the European Union (EU), with the latter two being the largest and most powerful organizations (see Exhibit 3.4). Because many trading nations see Latin America as an area for large-scale economic growth in the future, they are eager to establish ties with Mercosur, even though its member countries currently contribute only 0.3 percent of world trade. Some U.S. officials hope that Mercosur will eventually join the North American Free Trade Agreement (NAFTA) to form a Free Trade Area of the Americas (FTAA).[36]

NAFTA   In 1994 the United States, Canada, and Mexico formed a powerful trading bloc, the North American Free Trade Agreement (NAFTA), which incorporates 400 million people and an economic output of about $8 trillion. As outlined in the agreement, the three countries have been phasing out all of the tariffs and quotas that formerly restricted trade within the bloc. This process paves the way for the freer flow of goods, services, and capital within the three-nation region. In addition, talks are currently under way to expand NAFTA to include Chile, whose streamlined economy has become the envy of Latin America. Ultimately, NAFTA's supporters would like to see the agreement expanded to include all of Central and South America by 2005.

NAFTA has always been controversial. Debate still continues about whether the agreement is helping or hurting the U.S. economy. One primary concern is NAFTA's effect on U.S. jobs. Critics contend that many jobs have been lost because U.S. manufacturers have moved production to Mexico and Canada. Supporters, on the other hand, say that U.S. jobs have multiplied as a result of increased exports. Which side is right? It's still too early to tell whether NAFTA's overall impact on the U.S. economy will be positive or negative.[37] Over the coming years, U.S. trade policy and NAFTA will certainly continue to be watched closely.

EUROPEAN UNION (EU)*	NORTH AMERICAN FREE TRADE AGREEMENT (NAFTA)	ASSOCIATION OF SOUTHEAST ASIAN NATIONS (ASEAN)	MERCOSUR
Austria	Canada	Brunei	Argentina
Belgium	Mexico	Indonesia	Brazil
Finland	United States	Malaysia	Paraguay
France		Philippines	Uruguay
Germany		Singapore	
Ireland		Thailand	
Italy			
Luxembourg			
Netherlands			
Portugal			
Spain			
Denmark			
Great Britain			
Greece			
Sweden			

EXHIBIT 3.4

MEMBERS OF MAJOR TRADE BLOCS

As the economies of the world become increasingly linked, many countries have formed powerful regional trade blocs that trade freely with one another and limit foreign competition.

*Shaded countries are members of the Economic and Monetary Union (EMU).

The European Union   One of the largest trading blocs is the European Union (EU), which combines 15 countries and over 370 million people. Talks are under way to admit more countries, including the Czech Republic, Estonia, Hungary, Slovenia, and Poland.[38] EU nations are working to eliminate hundreds of local regulations, variations in product standards, and protectionist measures that limit trade between member countries. Eliminating barriers enables the nations of the EU to function as a single market, with trade flowing between member countries as it does between states in the United States.

In 1999, 11 of the 15 countries formed the Economic and Monetary Union (EMU) and turned over control of their individual monetary policies to the newly created European Central Bank. With a combined population of about 300 million people, these 11 countries account for 19.4 percent of the world's GDP (gross domestic product), making them a commanding force in the world economy.[39] The four countries that did not join the EMU are Greece, which did not meet the strict qualification requirements, and Britain, Denmark, and Sweden, which chose not to participate initially. One of the driving forces behind the decision to join forces was the anticipated advantages these 11 countries would enjoy by creating of a unified currency called the **euro.**

Officially launched in 1999 (with notes and coins available in 2002), the euro is expected to transform Europe's financial scene. Experts predict that the euro will wipe out some $65 billion annually in currency exchange costs among participants and will cut the middleman out of trillions of dollars' worth of foreign exchange transactions. U.S. businesses and travelers alone could save as much as 50 percent of the costs they now pay to convert dollars into multiple European currencies. Furthermore, as prices in these 11 nations become visible in one currency, consumers will get the biggest break because

euro
A planned unified currency used by European nations that meet certain strict requirements

Focus on E-Business

ROADBLOCKS ON THE EUROPEAN SUPERHIGHWAY

Until recently, Europe trailed far behind the United States in its use and enthusiasm for the Web. But that may change if individual countries can focus more on the "U" in European Union. Cited as the next-largest e-commerce market after the United States, experts say that European e-commerce is expected to soar from $20 billion to $430 billion by 2006. Nevertheless, roadblocks on the European superhighway exist.

For one thing, cultural and legislative differences among the European countries are restraining e-commerce growth. For another, some governments see e-commerce as an economic opportunity to be developed while others see it as a legislative challenge to be brought under control. As a result, e-commerce development has varied from country to country across Europe. Scandinavians, for example, are early adopters, driven partly by manufacturers such as Ericsson of Sweden and Nokia of Finland. France, on the other hand, has been slow to take to the Web partly because of cultural resistance and partly because 70 percent of French households use the country's less-sophisticated Minitel information terminals, so they are reluctant to switch. Things are also slower in Germany, where heavy discounting is illegal (to protect neighborhood stores), and two-for-one offers and lifetime guarantees are banned.

To take full advantage of the potential of e-commerce, European governments must learn to embrace the American speed and open spirit of the Internet. But that's a big challenge for countries such as Switzerland and Germany, which have strict privacy laws. Moreover, under the European Convention on Human Rights, European employees are entitled to e-mail privacy while employers are regarded by law as the publishers of their employees' e-mails and can be held legally responsible for their content. Copyright, on the other hand, is automatic in some European countries while in others it is established only by registration.

To attempt to resolve some of these differences, the 15 E.U. nations drafted an e-commerce directive in 1998. Consumer groups welcomed the directive, which requires companies transacting e-commerce to comply with the consumer protection laws of each country they sell to. But mail-order businesses were outraged because they would now have to cope with 15 different sets of rules. Meanwhile, as governments debate, the e-commerce clock is ticking away. Soon Europe will have to decide whether to enter the Digital Age with conviction or suffer the consequences.

QUESTIONS FOR CRITICAL THINKING

1. How will the euro help facilitate European and global e-commerce?
2. How should global companies handle language differences on their e-commerce Web sites?

they will be able to compare prices on similar items whether they are sold in Lisbon or Vienna.[40]

Some observers think the euro may even have a chance to unseat the dollar as the international currency of trade and eventually become the dominant player. But given the euro's rocky launch, others aren't as confident. They claim that the dollar can hold its own because of the size of the U.S. economy and the safety and liquidity of the U.S. government-bond market. Still others predict that the two currencies will share the crown.[41]

INTERDEPENDENCE OF ECONOMIES IN THE ■ GLOBAL MARKETPLACE

As more and more companies such as Whirlpool and UPS seek international markets for their goods and services, or search for the most cost-effective locations to produce their goods or to transact business, they become even more tangled in the global marketplace. As mentioned earlier, the opportunities in the global marketplace are many, but these opportunities are not without risks. A worldwide economic crisis at the end of the twentieth century dramatically demonstrates just how risky the global marketplace can be. In this section, we'll show how one small country's decision to *float* its currency set a spark that ignited a regional economic crisis that sent shock waves throughout the world. But we must first explain some important concepts about foreign exchange rates and currency valuations so that you can understand how the change in value of one country's currency could cause such global economic turmoil.

Foreign Exchange Rates and Currency Valuations

When companies buy and sell goods and services in the global marketplace, they complete the transaction by exchanging currencies. For instance, if a Japanese company borrows money from a U.S. bank to build a manufacturing plant in Japan, it must repay the loan in U.S. dollars. Or if a South Korean car manufacturer imports engine parts from Japan, it must pay for them in yen (Japan's currency). To do so, companies exchange their currency at any international bank that handles **foreign exchange,** the conversion of one currency into an equivalent amount of another currency. The number of yen, francs, or pounds that must be exchanged for every dollar, mark, or won is known as the **exchange rate** between currencies.

Most international currencies operate under a **floating exchange rate system;** thus, a currency's value or price fluctuates in response to the forces of global supply and demand (as we discussed in Chapter 1). The supply and demand of a country's currency are determined in part by what is happening in the country's own economy. For example, if Mexico's economy is suffering from severe inflation and unemployment, foreign investment in Mexico will decrease, thereby lessening the demand for Mexican currency and causing its value to be lower than the value of currencies in countries not experiencing economic problems. Because supply and demand for a currency are always changing, the rate at which it is exchanged for other currencies may change a little each day. For example, Japanese currency might be trading at 137.6 yen to the dollar on one day and 136.8 on the next.

foreign exchange
Trading one currency for the equivalent value of another currency

exchange rate
Rate at which the money of one country is traded for the money of another

floating exchange rate system
World economic system in which the values of all currencies are determined by supply and demand

See It on the Web See It on the Web

GET THE FOREIGN EXCHANGE FACTS

When you need basic data about currencies and economic conditions in other countries, turn to The World Factbook, prepared by the Central Intelligence Agency. In addition to providing the name of each country's currency, historical data about the exchange rate over recent years, and listings of the largest trading partners for import and export, this jam-packed publication offers a wealth of facts about the nations of the world, from Afghanistan to Zimbabwe. To access this valuable resource, select the Publications link on the CIA's homepage and go to The World Factbook. http://www.odci.gov

LEARNING OBJECTIVE 6
Explain why a country might devalue its currency

Even though most governments let the value of their currency respond to the forces of supply and demand, sometimes a government will intervene and adjust the exchange rate of its country's currency. Why would a government do this? One reason is to keep the price of a nation's goods and services more affordable in the global marketplace and to protect the nation's economy against trade imbalances. Another is to boost or slow down the country's economy.

Devaluation, or the drop in the value of a nation's currency relative to the value of other currencies, can at times boost a country's economy because it makes the country's products and services more affordable in foreign markets while it increases the price of imports. Because fewer units of foreign currency are required to purchase the devalued currency, such situations tend to raise a country's exports and lower its imports. Conversely, a strong currency boosts imports and dampens exports.

Some countries fix, or peg, the value of their currencies to the value of more stable currencies, such as the dollar or the yen, instead of letting it float freely. Hong Kong, for example, pegs its currency to the U.S. dollar. If a currency is pegged, its value fluctuates proportionately with the value of the foreign currency to which it is linked. So if the U.S. dollar declines, so will the Japanese yen and other currencies that are pegged to it. Of course, this system works well as long as the proportionate relationship between the two currencies remains valid. But if one partner suffers economic hardship, demand for its currency will decline significantly and the exchange rate at which the two are pegged will become unrealistic. Such was the case with many of the Southeast Asian currencies in the late 1990s.

The Global Economic Crisis at the End of the Twentieth Century

In July 1997 Thailand unpegged its currency (the baht) from the U.S. dollar to allow the currency to float and gradually seek its true value. Thailand anticipated that its currency would drop somewhat in value but was caught off guard when the currency went into a free fall. At about the same time, Indonesia unpegged the rupiah from the U.S. dollar, and the currency fell from 2,500 to 7,900 to the dollar, a devaluation of 300 percent in about 6 months.[42] Subsequent currency devaluations by other countries that felt pressured to keep the price of their exports competitive soon ignited an economic crisis that spread and infected nations as far flung as Guyana, Lebanon, Zimbabwe, Brazil, and Russia. One by one the crisis struck economies that were already weak as a result of internal economic problems. Currencies plunged, commodity prices fell, stock markets crashed, and investors panicked and fled—taking with them the capital these emerging countries needed to fund their growth.[43] What caused the crisis, and why did the contagion spread? Economists now cite a combination of factors that contributed to the global economic turmoil.

The global economic crisis drove down prices on the foreign stock markets. Two traders at the Tokyo Stock Exchange react to the plunge of the benchmark Nikkei index.

What Caused the Global Economic Crisis? As the currencies plunged, foreign investors, which had poured over $100 billion a year into the world's emerging markets, panicked. Overnight, they pulled their money out of these countries, and economic growth hit the brakes. Without this growth, the supply of local currencies exceeded their demand, forcing these currencies to fall even lower.[44]

As currencies devalued, consumers in the Southeast Asian countries were hit hard. Many could not afford to pay back their loans. Others lost their businesses. Still others watched their investments shrink in value overnight. As a result, Southeast Asia's demand for commodities such as oil, copper, aluminum, and gold tailed off, depressing world commodity prices to ten-year lows. This plunge in commodity prices transferred the economic crisis to other emerging markets and to Russia, because a large share of their exports are commodity-based. Meanwhile, to bail these countries out, the IMF and the World Bank lent them large sums of money: $17.2 billion to Thailand, $42 billion to Indonesia, $58.4 billion to South Korea, and $41.5 billion to Brazil.[45]

Although these loans were intended to stabilize the failing economies, some experts contend that the IMF's actions in fact made matters worse. That's because in exchange for the money, the IMF imposed tight fiscal and monetary conditions on the recipients.[46] One such condition required recipients to slash budget deficits. To accomplish this goal, governments had to raise taxes and cut government spending; both actions hurt consumers even more. Another condition required recipients to privatize inefficient state-owned industries. This pressure resulted in massive worker layoffs and further depressed economies that were already plagued by internal problems:[47]

- *Excessive amounts of foreign-denominated debt.* Because most emerging nations could not finance their own growth, they had borrowed large sums of money from the United States and Japan to build new roads, dams, and industries. This practice seemed safe as long as the exchange rate for their local currencies remained stable. But once the value of these currencies plummeted, the borrowers could not afford to pay back their dollar- or yen-denominated debts. For example, a $1 million U.S. loan (equivalent to 26 million baht) doubled after the currency's free fall to 52 baht to the dollar. This meant that borrowers would have to exchange 52 million baht to pay back the $1 million loan to U.S. banks.

- *Bad loans.* Many Southeast Asian and Japanese banks worked on a buddy system (called croney capitalism) and made risky loans to friends who were poor credit risks and whose businesses were not financially sound. This practice kept profitless enterprises alive and led to the misallocation of resources. South Korean chaebol (giant family-controlled conglomerates) with the right connections, for example, were granted loans by local banks often in return for under-the-table payoffs.[48]

- *Plunging real estate prices.* Global economic turmoil hit while Japan was experiencing a severe real estate recession. At its peak, the land beneath the Imperial palace in downtown Tokyo was said to be worth as much as all of California, and a parking space in Hong Kong sold for $517,000. Many Japanese banks relied on the overvalued real estate as collateral for loans. When real estate prices plunged—some falling to 10 percent of their peak values—banks were reluctant to call their loans in hopes that real estate values would rebound. With few good lending opportunities at home, Japanese banks began lending elsewhere in Southeast Asia, adding to the banks' own troubles.[49]

Today, many Southeast Asian economies have made a significant recovery: Currencies have stabilized; interest rates (which were boosted to attract foreign investors) have declined, and stock markets have recovered to near precrisis levels. Some experts contend that if these countries continue to restructure their economic systems as a result of the crisis, they could emerge as much stronger nations.[50] Still, others fear swift recoveries and restored optimism could sideline many of the meaningful reforms that are getting under way and cause Asia to suffer a relapse.[51]

THE RISE AND FALL OF A MIGHTY EMPIRE—GUM DEPARTMENT STORE

In the Soviet days, GUM (pronounced *goom*) was the best department store in Russia. Each morning, lines of people would eagerly wait outside the Moscow store for it to open. But they were banned from the special area on the third floor that was set aside for only Communist party officials. Inside Section 100, officials could pick up fine clothing unavailable anywhere else in Russia. Then things changed.

One of the first Russian companies to be privatized after the fall of the Soviet Union, GUM soon transformed into an upscale shopping mall that would rival even the finest in the United States. Suddenly the mall was filled with "this-just-in from western Europe and Manhattan." With more than 40 international retailers paying rents higher than anywhere else in Europe, the names Christian Dior, Lafayette, Nike, Reebok, and Revlon popped up all along the walkway. Business was excellent. The Samsonite luggage store reported more sales per square foot than in any of its other outlets around the world. And GUM's sales soared to an average of $US925 per square foot—one of the highest in the world. (By contrast, Bloomingdale's New York store sales average $256 per square foot.) GUM became a symbol of Russia's free-market hope—and a very attractive investment.

Some attribute GUM's success to its chairman, Yuri Solomatin, who ran the most open, market-oriented Western-style company in all Russia. In fact, Solomatin sold more than half of GUM's stock to foreigners, mostly Americans and Europeans, an unheard-of feat in nationalistic Russia. But when the Russian devaluation and market meltdown came in August 1998, investors dumped the ruble, and suddenly GUM crumbled. Its stock fell from $5.40 a share to 25 cents a share—overnight.

Meanwhile, shop managers spent two hours a day revising the prices of the shops' merchandise. Most of GUM'S inventory was imported, so as the ruble declined to one-third its value, prices for the merchandise tripled. Customers soon began resenting stores full of high-priced imports they could no longer afford—despite signs boasting 70 percent off.

Gone were the customers. Many had lost their jobs. Instead of buying designer goods, they were busy exchanging their rubles for U.S. dollars. Those who waited got less and less for their rubles each day. Overnight, Russians became paupers, and GUM went bankrupt. Today GUM is a candidate for a takeover by a foreign company. But Solomatin is skeptical. "Investor fear is so great," notes Solomatin, "who would take us over?"

QUESTIONS FOR CRITICAL THINKING

1. Why did stores with imported merchandise have to raise their prices when Russia devalued the ruble?
2. Why were Russians lining up to buy dollars instead of stocking up on food, blankets, clothing, and other necessities?

Effect of the Crisis on the United States

Ironically, the world's troubles had little negative impact on the United States economy. Although some businesses such as Boeing faced a slew of canceled orders from Asian carriers, others prospered.[52] Why did many U.S. businesses thrive during a period of global economic malaise? For one thing, the U.S. government lowered interest rates on several occasions to boost the U.S. economy. (Lower interest rates make it more affordable for companies and consumers to borrow money and purchase more goods.) For another, plunging commodity prices kept U.S. inflation low and saved U.S. businesses billions of dollars, while the strong dollar made imports cheaper. Moreover, a windfall of foreign money seeking investments in U.S. businesses boosted the U.S. economy and helped push the U.S. stock markets to record highs.[53]

Still, some economists warn that the United States cannot expect to remain "an oasis of prosperity" if global economic turmoil were to reignite.[54] They point to a decline in U.S. exports, evidenced by stacks of empty containers at U.S. shipping ports, as a warning sign. The Asian crisis has turned the once-vigorous two-way trade between Asia and the U.S. into predominantly one-way trade. Some fear that the costs and inefficiencies of sending back empty shipping containers to Asia to get more goods could eventually force shippers to raise their prices, an event that could in turn cause a series of price increases and inflation.[55] Of course, raising shipping prices could ignite economic problems for other nations. As the Asian crisis demonstrates, in the global marketplace—where economies of the world are entangled—problems in one country can indeed send shock waves around the globe.

In the aftermath of the Asian financial crisis, a growing imbalance of trade with Asia is creating difficulties for the shipping industry, especially between the West Coast and eastern Asia, the world's heaviest trade corridor.

Summary of Learning Objectives

1. **Highlight the opportunities and challenges of conducting business in other countries.**
   Conducting business in other countries can provide opportunities such as increased sales, operational efficiencies, exposure to new technologies, and consumer choices. At the same time, it poses challenges such as the need to learn unique laws, customs, and ethical standards. Furthermore it exposes companies to the risks of political and economic instabilities.

2. **Identify five forms of international business activity.**
   Importing and exporting, licensing, franchising, strategic alliances and joint ventures, and wholly owned facilities are five of the most common forms of international business activity. Each entails different levels of risk and provides a company with varying degrees of control.

3. **Explain the theory of comparative advantage.**
   The theory of comparative advantage contends that a country should produce and sell those products it produces most efficiently and trade for those it cannot produce as efficiently.

4. **Highlight the arguments for and against protectionism.**
   People who support protectionism believe that building in a preference for a country's home industries can boost local economies and save local jobs. It can also shield domestic industries from head-to-head competition with overseas rivals and help new industries get started. Those who argue against protectionism say that it leads to higher consumer prices because of lack of competition, creates problems for U.S. companies that depend on imported parts, and stifles product innovation and efficiencies.

5. **Discuss the function, advantages, and disadvantages of trading blocs.**
   The primary function of trading blocs is to ensure the economic growth and benefit of their members by promoting trade inside the region. The advantages include improved world trade, protection for smaller or younger countries that might not be able to compete in world markets on their own, a greater sharing of knowledge and technology, and a way to shield emerging nations from global economic instability. The disadvantages include the potential for exclusion of nonmember countries from world markets, decline of world trade if regional protectionism is practiced, and fewer consumer choices if lucrative foreign markets are closed to others.

6. **Explain why a country might devalue its currency.**
   Devaluation makes a country's products more affordable in foreign markets while raising the price of foreign goods at home. Thus, it can increase a country's exports and reduce its imports; both outcomes in turn can boost the country's economy and correct trade imbalances.

MEETING BUSINESS CHALLENGES AT WHIRLPOOL

David Whitwam's timing couldn't have been worse. Just as the company was planting its feet in international markets, economic turmoil hit Asia and Europe. Wildly fluctuating foreign exchange rates wreaked havoc in Asia, where Whirlpool had participated in several joint ventures. Fortunately, less than 5 percent of Whirlpool's sales came from Asia, so the company was not seriously hurt. Still, ongoing global economic woes contributed to Whirlpool's multimillion dollar losses overseas.

As a result, Whitwam fine-tuned his expansion plans. Whirlpool dropped one joint venture in China (costing the company $350 million) and rearranged others as intense competition and weak economic conditions drove appliance prices down and sapped profits. In Brazil, where Whirlpool had long been profitable, a currency crisis coupled with inflation worries slowed appliance sales to a trickle. Still, Whitwam remained committed to the market. Anticipating future growth opportunities in this emerging market, Whirlpool invested hundreds of millions of dollars to modernize operations, cut costs, and solidify its position as the country's market leader in refrigerators, room air conditioners, and washers.

Meanwhile, Whitwam reorganized the company into four geographical regions: North America, Asia, Latin America, and Europe. He restructured operations so that the vast majority of products sold in each region were made in that region, even though senior management would continue to report to the company's headquarters in Michigan. Whitwam also began focusing less on manufacturing its own products overseas and more on developing licensing arrangements and strategic alliances as a vehicle for growth. For example, Whirlpool formed strategic alliances with Tupperware to work jointly on marketing, branding, and product development in Europe, Africa, and the Middle East.

To develop suitable appliances for each market, Whirlpool developed product technology centers to share technological advances and engineering expertise across borders. Feature-rich German appliances were combined with efficient, low-cost Italian technologies to produce a "world washer" that could be modified to fit the unique requirements of different markets.

David Whitwam's global strategy was not widely copied by rivals. As Whirlpool continued to invest heavily to expand in Europe, Latin America, and Asia, the company's major competitor, Maytag, was selling its European and Australian businesses to refocus on the lucrative North American market. Nevertheless, Whitwam was willing to ride out the storm, even as global economic troubles dragged on.

Today, Whirlpool's future as a global player is still uncertain. In less than a decade, Whitwam has transformed the company into a $10 billion global giant, marketing 11 major brands in 170 countries around the world. But losses mount. And the interdependence of economies around the world results in the added risk that market conditions can change at the drop of a baht, ruble, or dollar. Of course, only time will tell whether Whirlpool will succeed in its global efforts or get caught in the wringer of global business.[56]

Critical Thinking Questions

1. What did Whirlpool find to be the advantages and disadvantages of doing business around the world?

2. How did global expansion affect Whirlpool's products?

3. Should Whirlpool be concerned about a currency crisis in a country where it sells few appliances?

■ LEARN MORE ONLINE

To find out how Whirlpool is faring with its global strategy, check the company's Web site at http://www.whirlpoolcorp.com. Click on Important Company Stuff and follow the Whirlpool News link to see the latest news releases about financial performance, international operations, and plans for expansion. How are Whirlpool's sales doing outside the United States? Where is the company strongest? Where is it struggling? What changes, if any, is Whitwam making to Whirlpool's global strategy?

Key Terms

absolute advantage (58)

balance of payments (60)

balance of trade (58)

comparative advantage theory (58)

dumping (62)

embargo (61)

euro (65)

exchange rate (67)

exporting (54)

floating exchange rate system (67)

foreign direct investment (FDI) (56)

foreign exchange (67)

free trade (62)

importing (54)

intrafirm trade (60)

joint venture (56)

licensing (55)

multinational corporations (MNCs) (56)

protectionism (60)

quotas (61)

strategic alliance (56)

tariffs (61)

trade deficit (60)

trade surplus (58)

trading blocs (63)

Test Your Knowledge

QUESTIONS FOR REVIEW

1. How can a company use a licensing agreement to enter world markets?

2. What is the balance of trade, and how is it related to the balance of payments?

3. What is intrafirm trade?

4. What is dumping, and how does the United States respond to this practice?

5. What is a floating exchange rate?

QUESTIONS FOR ANALYSIS

6. Why would a company choose to work through intermediaries when selling products in a foreign country?

7. How do companies benefit from forming international joint ventures and strategic alliances?

8. What types of situations might cause the U.S. government to implement protectionist measures?

9. How do tariffs and quotas protect a country's own industries?

10. Should the U.S. government more closely regulate the practice of giving trips and other incentives to foreign managers to win their business? Is this bribery?

QUESTIONS FOR APPLICATION

11. Suppose you own a small company that manufactures baseball equipment. You are aware that Russia is a large market, and you are considering exporting your products there. What steps should you take? Who might be able to give you assistance?

12. Because your Brazilian restaurant caters to Western businesspeople and tourists, much of the food you buy is imported from the United States. Lately, the value of the real (Brazil's currency) has been falling relative to the dollar. This change makes your food imports much more costly, and it negatively affects your profitability. You have three options: Which one will you choose? (a) Raise menu prices across the board. (b) Accept only U.S. dollars from customers. (c) Try to purchase more of your food items locally. Please explain your selection.

13. Review the theory of supply and demand discussed in Chapter 1. Using this theory, explain how a country's currency is valued and why governments sometimes adjust the values of their currency.

14. You just received notice that a large shipment of manufacturing supplies you have been waiting for has been held up in customs for two weeks. A local business associate tells you that you are expected to give customs agents some "incentive money" to see that everything clears easily. How will you handle this situation? Evaluate the ethical merits of your decision by answering the questions outlined in Exhibit 2.1.

Practice Your Knowledge

SHARPENING YOUR COMMUNICATION SKILLS

Languages never translate on a word-for-word basis. When doing business in the global marketplace, choose words that convey only their most specific denotative meaning. Avoid using slang or idioms (words that can have meanings far different from their individual components when translated literally). For example, if a U.S. executive tells an Egyptian executive that a certain product "doesn't cut the mustard," chances are that communication will fail.

Team up with two other students and list ten examples of slang (in your own language) that would probably be misinterpreted or misunderstood during a business conversation with someone from another culture. Next to each example, suggest other words you might use to convey the same message. Make sure the alternatives mean *exactly* the same as the original slang or idiom. Compare your list with those of your classmates.

HANDLING DIFFICULT SITUATIONS ON THE JOB
Exporting Runs the Gamut from Ripe to Rotten

When President Carlos Menem of Argentina took office, he and his economy minister, Domingo Cavallo, decided that competition from foreign producers would stimulate Argentine businesses to provide better products at competitive prices. To the delight of Argentine shoppers, import tariffs were lowered and goods began pouring in from all over the world: calculators, bicycles, toothpicks—and peaches.

California peach growers responded eagerly to the opening of the Argentine market. Individual growers joined forces and formed the California Peach Growers Association to ship their fruit to Edcadassa, the Argentine firm that oversees all imported goods awaiting customs clearance at Ezeiza international airport. As president of the growers association, you were pleased that the initial shipments arrived in great shape. But then things soured. Angry Argentine retailers complained that instead of fresh, firm California peaches, fruit was arriving ready for the garbage bin. They refused to pay for rotten fruit, and your association lost $50,000.

Investigating, you discovered that Edcadassa was at fault. Overwhelmed by the high level of imported goods flowing into Argentina, Edcadassa lost your shipments in the confusion; by the time the fruit cleared customs, it was rotten. Now your organization wants Edcadassa to pay for the fruit.[57]

1. What might you want to know about Argentine culture and law before you approach Edcadassa?

2. Assuming your association wants to continue exporting to Argentina, should you insist that Edcadassa pay the entire cost of the spoiled fruit, or should you ask for partial payment? Why?

3. What recommendations can you make to Edcadassa and to your growers to help prevent similar problems in the future?

BUILDING YOUR TEAM SKILLS

In today's interdependent global economy, fluctuations in a country's currency can have a profound effect on the flow of products across borders. The U.S. steel industry, for example, has been feeling intense competition from an influx of Korean, Brazilian, and Russian steel imports. After the currencies of those countries plummeted in value, the price of steel products exported to the United States dropped as well, making U.S. steel much more expensive by comparison.

Fueled by low prices, steel flooded into the United States, hurting sales of U.S. steel. Over the course of several months, the volume of steel imports nearly doubled. Stung, U.S. steelmakers slashed production and laid off more than 10,000 U.S. workers. U.S. trade officials charge that the cheap imported steel is being dumped, and they are considering protectionist measures such as imposing quotas on steel imports.[58]

With your team, brainstorm a list of at least four additional ways the United States might handle this situation. Once you have your list, consider the probable effect of each option on these stakeholders:

- U.S. businesses that buy steel
- U.S. steel manufacturers
- U.S. businesses that export to Korea, Brazil, or Russia
- Employees of U.S. steel manufacturers

On the basis of your analysis and discussion, which option will your team recommend? Select a spokesperson to explain your selection and your team's reasoning to the other teams. Compare your recommendation with those of your classmates.

Expand Your Knowledge

EXPLORING CAREER OPPORTUNITIES

If global business interests you, consider working for a U.S. government agency that supports or regulates international trade. For example, here are the duties performed by an international

trade specialist at the International Trade Administration of the U.S. Department of Commerce: "The incumbent will assist senior specialists in coordination and support of government trade programs and events; perform research and analysis of trade data and information on specific topics or issues within a larger project or assignment; and disseminate trade information and materials on government products/services to U.S. businesses and associations. Incumbent will attend meetings and engage in other activities for developmental purposes. As a condition of employment, applicants must be available for reassignment and relocation within the United States."[59]

1. On the basis of this description, what education and skills (personal and professional) would you need to succeed as an international trade specialist? Why? How does this job description fit your qualifications and interests?

2. Given their duties, where would you expect international trade specialists to be situated or transferred? Would you be willing to move to another city or state for this type of position?

3. What sources would you contact to locate trade-related jobs with government agencies such as the International Trade Administration?

DEVELOPING YOUR RESEARCH SKILLS

Every business involved in international trade has to watch the foreign exchange situation. Use your research skills to locate and analyze information about the value of the Japanese yen relative to the U.S. dollar. As you complete this exercise, make a note of the sources and search strategies you used.

1. How many Japanese yen does one U.S. dollar buy right now? Find yesterday's foreign exchange rate for the yen in the *Wall Street Journal* or, if you are using Internet sources, on the Bloomberg site or another financial information site.

2. Investigate the foreign exchange rate for the yen against the dollar over the past month. Is the dollar growing stronger (buying more yen) or growing weaker (buying fewer yen)?

3. If you were a U.S. exporter selling to Japan, how would a stronger dollar be likely to affect demand for your products? How would a weaker dollar be likely to affect demand?

SEE IT ON THE WEB EXERCISES
Going Global, page 55

There are many factors to consider when you want to export a product, but the information at the International Trade Administration's Web page can help you make sense of it all. Explore the links to information about individual countries found on the Regions and Countries page at http://www.ita.doc.gov. Drawing on this information as well as on what you've learned in the text, answer the following questions about trading with emerging economies.

1. What are five of the leading U.S. industry sectors exporting to India? How can U.S. firms form joint ventures in India?

2. How is the political situation in Poland affecting privatization and international trade?

3. What are the current economic trends in Brazil? How do you think the economy is affecting imports from the United States?

Leading the Way to Foreign Trade, page 62

Trade leads are an excellent way for manufacturers and professional export agents to learn about international trade opportunities. Go to World Trade Markets at http://www.wtm.com, and follow either the date, country, or product link to trade leads. Select a particular lead that interests you and answer the following questions.

1. What is the company's name, and where is it located? What product does the company wish to import or export?

2. Could this particular request be handled by a small company, or does it require the experience and resources of a large firm? What types of business arrangements would be most applicable to handling this lead (i.e., direct importing or exporting, joint venture, licensing, franchising, or running a wholly owned facility), and why?

3. What contact information is given for the company? Does the contact person speak English? If you were a small importer or exporter, what kind of information would you want to know about this individual or company before you transact any business?

Get the Foreign Exchange Facts, page 67

The CIA's primary purpose is to gather information. Fortunately for businesspeople, the agency shares a lot of its information about foreign countries in publications available on its Web site at http://www.odci.gov. Select The World Factbook from the list of publications, then follow the country links to research economic information about foreign exchange and trade issues.

1. What is the five-year trend in foreign exchange between the Mexican peso and the U.S. dollar? How do you think this trend is affecting U.S. companies that import goods from Mexico?

2. Does Japan import more than it exports or export more than it imports?

3. What is Cuba's currency called? How does Cuba handle foreign exchange of this currency against the U.S. dollar? What are the implications for U.S.-based exporters?

P A R T   I   V I D E O   C A S E

Conducting Business in the Global Economy

Learning Objectives

1. Explore the key economic and competitive challenges and opportunities facing a small business in the global economy.
2. See how a small business handles its commitment to social responsibility.
3. Understand some of the constraints and considerations that can shape a small business's future.

Background Information

In today's boundaryless global marketplace, small businesses such as Blausen Medical Communications find themselves competing with companies across town, across the country, or even across the ocean. Growing demand for many goods and services in free-market economies has opened the way for new business opportunities—and fiercer competition. In response, more sellers are using the Internet and advanced technology to communicate more efficiently with buyers, locate suppliers, and create products geared to customers' needs.

The Video

Bruce Blausen founded Houston-based Blausen Medical Communications (BMC) in 1991. Trained in biology, art, and medical illustration, Blausen recognized a market need for three-dimensional medical and scientific graphics and animation. Now his company targets eight markets, from pharmaceuticals firms such as Abbott Laboratories to museums such as the Stockholm Museum of Natural Science. Because BMC fills orders from customers around the world, Blausen and his staff have to pay close attention to cultural differences. As a small business owner, Blausen is concerned about balancing the need

to reinvest in his business with the need to earn profits. He demonstrates his social responsibility by donating his firm's animations and graphics to the Houston Museum of Health and Medical Science.

Discussion Questions

1. What is BMC's competitive advantage?
2. What are some ways Blausen can reinvest in his business to boost future profitability?
3. How might Blausen use franchising to expand his business nationally and internationally?

Next Steps

Some industries have higher barriers to entry than other industries. Consider the medical animation industry in which BMC operates. Identify some of the barriers to entry facing companies that want to compete with BMC. Does this industry have high or low barriers to entry? What are the implications for companies seeking to enter the industry?

■ LEARN MORE ONLINE

Explore BMC's Web site and then visit the site of LifeHouse Productions, a company offering three-dimensional biomedical animation and computer graphics. What are the differences and similarities between the products and services offered by these companies? What is the competitive advantage of each firm?
http://www.imagesofhealth.com/start.htm (BMC site)
http://www.lifehouseproductions.com/
(LifeHouse Productions site)

Business in Action Story

Have Your Students Experience *Business in Action*—It's a Real Plus

From the global economy to the economics of a small business, *Business in Action* takes your students on an engaging exploration of the fundamental rules, strategies, and dynamics that make the business world work. Through motivating activities and timely examples, students experience firsthand the different functional areas of business and how they all work together.

This new paperback text, written by respected and experienced authors, Court Bovée and John Thill, is interactive + Internet-supported + integrated + innovative + intriguing and will be a real plus for professors and students!

 **nteractive**

The book's hands-on activities and Prentice Hall's Learning on the Internet Partnership (PHLIP) make learning a truly interactive experience.

 **nternet-supported**

Internet exercises give students practice with the rich resources of the World Wide Web.

 **ntegrated**

Review questions and exercises link chapter material with concepts covered previously in the text.

 **nnovative**

Only *Business in Action* has such a wide variety of innovative and involving features and activities within a highly flexible framework.

 **ntriguing**

Business Mysteries at real companies promote an exciting, active-learning environment in the classroom.

Nick: Hey Natasha, did you know there are over 7.5 million transistors in an Intel Pentium computer chip and that the company chairman, Andy Grove, expects to deliver chips packed with a cool one billion transistors by 2011?

Natasha: Sounds pretty fast to me. Wasn't Andy Grove the genius responsible for changing Intel's direction from making memory chips to producing microprocessors back in the 1980s?

Nick: Yes, and he was also part of the team responsible for slapping "Intel Inside" stickers on computers, a move that helped turn Intel into the eighth most profitable company in the world.

Natasha: So if he's got such foresight, why do you have that puzzled look, Nick?

Nick: Here's what I don't get. After a decade of selling high-priced fast, faster, and fastest microprocessor chips and watching the profits roll in, now Intel wants to be like everybody else. The company is heading downstream, slashing chip prices faster than day-old bakery goods.

Natasha: Sounds like the company is trying to play catch up. You know, I just bought a really swift computer last month for less than $1000—monitor, CD player, and the works. Now that I think about it, I'm pretty sure there wasn't an "Intel Inside." I wonder why.

Nick: Let's see if we can find the answers.

THE MYSTERY OF A SPEED DEMON CAUGHT FLAT FOOTED

For years, Intel had a business model that was its ticket to success. Every nine months or so the company would build a new $2 million state-of-the-art factory (or "fab") to manufacture the next generation of microprocessor chips. Of course, each new fab was a bet that consumers would want the fastest, most powerful computer chip to run newer, speedier computers jammed with all the latest features, including upgraded versions of popular software. And they did.

But owning the fast lane required Intel to build the fabs two years in advance of needing them—a risky venture, indeed. To fund the construction, the company sold new processors at sky-high prices. Customers didn't care, however. Those who wanted the fastest machines were willing to pay the premium. Others would wait a year or two until these machines were superseded by yet faster ones, and then they would purchase the older models at more affordable prices. And so the cycle continued: Build a fab, sell latest chips at a premium, discount yesterday's chip, plow profits into a new fab, start the cycle again. Competitors couldn't even come close to perfecting this model. As long as customers wanted chips with more functions and more speed to do some very cool things, it was almost impossible to make a dent in Intel's lock on the high-end market.

So competitors focused their resources in a different direction. Several lower-tier PC makers began to hawk personal computers priced below $1000. Intel wasn't concerned, however. Referring to them as "Segment Zero," or a dumping ground for inventory close-outs, the king of chips held to the high ground, pushing pricey chips at juicy profits. But when Compaq joined the sub-$1000 market with its highly touted Presario model, the market changed overnight.

Soon, lower-priced PCs captured 5 percent of unit sales in the United States. Intel was caught flat-footed. Because Intel's chips were far too expensive for the new sub-$1000 machines, PC manufacturers turned to competitors Advanced Micro Devices (AMD) and Cyrix for affordable chips. Reacting quickly, Intel developed Celeron. But this new chip got poor reviews, and Intel initially priced it too high. After all, cheap chips hadn't been figured into Intel's business model for success. But neither was walking away from a market whose size promised to be at least tens of millions of units a year. Eventually, though, Intel got it right. Aggressive marketing and steep price cuts in the Celeron chip delivered big market share gains to Intel and forced some rivals to withdraw from the market. Now Intel would have to count on higher sales volume to compensate for the thinner profit margins of low-priced chips. And that's a risky business—even for this speed demon.[60]

SOLVING THE MYSTERY OF A SPEED DEMON CAUGHT FLAT-FOOTED

1. Why did customers change their buying habits overnight? What did Intel fail to see that others saw clearly?
   CLUE: HOW WAS THE PRIMARY FUNCTION OF PCS CHANGING DURING THE 1990s?

2. Intel has invested more than $500 million in new companies that create the latest computer software or Internet-related products. Why wouldn't Intel use that money to build a new factory instead?
   CLUE: THINK ABOUT THE FORCES OF SUPPLY AND DEMAND.

3. Look back at the margin clues in Part I of this textbook. What business principles did Intel overlook?

4

STARTING, FINANCING, AND EXPANDING A SMALL BUSINESS

LEARNING OBJECTIVES

After studying this chapter, you will be able to

1 List four important functions of small businesses in the economy

2 Identify three factors contributing to the increase in the number of small businesses

3 Cite the key characteristics common to most entrepreneurs

4 Name 12 topics that should be covered in a formal business plan

5 List five things you should know before starting a business

6 List three ways of getting into business for yourself

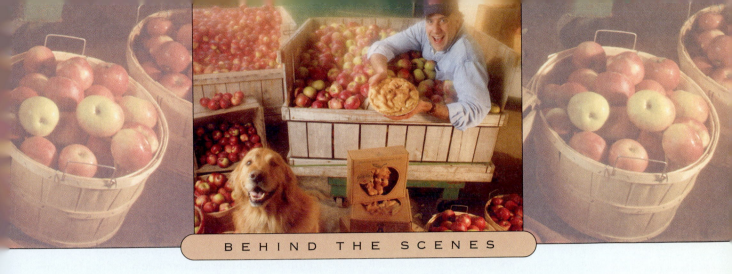

FACING BUSINESS CHALLENGES AT TOP OF THE TREE BAKING COMPANY

Baking Up Millions

Gordon Weinberger became an entrepreneur at an early age, running the proverbial lemonade stand, as well as a candy stand and a bicycle repair shop, while still in his teens. During college, he founded a window-washing company, and after college he co-founded a promotions agency. After a stint in nonprofit public relations, Weinberger joined a major Boston advertising agency. Then a pie recipe changed his life. Working from his great-grandmother's recipe, Weinberger baked apple pies that won blue ribbons in a New Hampshire contest two years in a row. These victories aroused his entrepreneurial instinct: Could an award-winning apple pie be his recipe for success?

Researching the pie industry, Weinberger identified a potential niche for fresh-tasting pies, a tiny slice of the market between the well-known brands sold in the freezer case and the store brands sold in the bakery department. Once Weinberger found his niche, he polished up his great-grandmother's recipe, drafted a detailed business plan, and talked with supermarket executives. But he needed money—$100,000 to be exact—to put his plan into action.

So Weinberger took to the phones, calling more than 70 friends, family members, and colleagues who might invest in his Top of the Tree Baking Company. Every night, he would set aside 6 P.M. to 11 P.M. for dialing potential investors and catching up with the latest family news before explaining his proposition. By the end of the night, his ear would be sore and his vocal cords scratchy. But it was worth the trouble. Over the course of several months, he convinced 11 people to invest about $10,000 each. The investors agreed they would have no direct control over or say in the affairs of the business, in exchange for Weinberger's promise to double their money in five years.

Although entrepreneurs are often strong on developing their ideas, many stumble when it comes to raising money. Not Weinberger. Even though he had little financial experience beyond negotiating a home mortgage, he was able to convince 11 investors to back his business. But to grow the operation, Weinberger would need more money. If you were Gordon Weinberger, how would you find additional investors? What would you include in your business plan to excite investors about your ideas? And how would you translate your plan into reality?[1]

UNDERSTANDING THE WORLD OF SMALL BUSINESS

Small businesses are the cornerstone of the U.S. economic system. The country was originally founded by people involved in small businesses—the family farmer, the shopkeeper, the craftsperson. Successive waves of immigrants carried on the tradition, launching restaurants and laundries, providing repair and delivery services, and opening newsstands and bakeries.

This trend continued for many years, until improvements in transportation and communication enabled large producers to manufacture goods at low costs and pass the savings on to consumers. As a result, many small, independent businesses could not compete. Scores of them closed their doors, and big business emerged as the primary economic force. The trend toward bigness continued for several decades; then it reversed.

The 1990s were a golden decade for entrepreneurship in the United States. Small companies have, in fact, turned the U.S. economy into the growth engine for the world. Today, being a small business is equated with being nimble and dynamic.[2] Even so, defining what constitutes a small business is surprisingly tricky, because *small* is a relative term. For example, a manufacturing firm with 500 employees might be considered small if it competes against much larger companies, but a retail establishment with 500 employees might be classified as big compared with its competitors.

small business
Company that is independently owned and operated, is not dominant in its field, and meets certain criteria for the number of employees and annual sales revenue

One reliable source of information for small businesses is the Small Business Administration (SBA). This government agency serves as a resource and advocate for small firms, providing them with financial assistance, training, and a variety of helpful programs. The SBA defines a **small business** as a firm that is (a) independently owned and operated, (b) not dominant in its field, (c) relatively small in terms of annual sales, and (d) with fewer than 500 employees. In fact, according to SBA figures, 80 percent of all U.S. companies have annual sales of less than $1 million.[3]

Economic Role of Small Businesses

Small businesses are of two distinct types: lifestyle businesses and high-growth ventures. Roughly 80 to 90 percent are modest operations with little growth potential (although some have attractive income potential for the solo businessperson). The self-employed consultant working part-time from a home office, the corner florist, and the neighborhood pizza parlor fall into the category of **lifestyle businesses**—firms built around the personal and financial needs of an individual or a family.[4] Lifestyle businesses aren't designed to grow into large enterprises.

lifestyle businesses
Small businesses intended to provide the owners with a comfortable livelihood

In contrast to lifestyle businesses, some firms are small simply because they are new. Many companies—such as FedEx, Microsoft, and E*Trade—start out as small entrepreneurial firms but quickly outgrow their small-business status. These **high-growth ventures** are usually run by a team rather than by one individual, and they expand rapidly by obtaining a sizable supply of investment capital and introducing new products or services to a large market.

high-growth ventures
Small businesses intended to achieve rapid growth and high profits on investment

Both lifestyle businesses and high-growth ventures play a number of important roles in the economy:

LEARNING OBJECTIVE 1

List four important functions of small businesses in the economy

- *They provide jobs.* Small businesses are a principal source of new jobs. Some 24 million small businesses employ almost half of the private U.S. work force and generate more than half of the U.S. gross domestic product. Furthermore, small businesses provide 67 percent of workers with their first jobs and initial on-the-job training in basic skills.[5]

- *They introduce new products.* The National Science Foundation estimates that 98 percent of the nation's "radical" new-product developments spring from small firms, a staggering percentage given the fact that small companies spend less than 5 percent of the nation's research-and-development money.[6]

- *They supply the needs of large corporations.* Many small businesses act as distributors, servicing agents, and suppliers to large corporations. Consider Parallax. This 160-employee firm inspects nuclear power plants, implements safety procedures, and cleans up hazardous and nuclear waste at power plants and weapons complexes across the nation. Seventy percent of Parallax's business comes from large corporations such as Westinghouse and Lockheed Martin. Not bad for a company launched out of the founder's home with $10,000 in personal savings.[7]

- *They provide specialized goods and services.* When Mike Woods tried to teach his son how to read he couldn't find any toys on the market that helped teach phonics. So he left his job as a partner in a big law firm and started LeapFrog. The company's initial product was the Phonics Disk, a $50 toy that teaches children shapes, sounds, and pronunciation of letters and words. Today LeapFrog, a division of Knowledge Universe, produces 17 toys geared toward teaching children to read and write.[8]

Innovation in Small Business

Ever wonder why so many innovations like LeapFrog toys come from small businesses, or why once-small companies such as Yahoo!, America Online, Dell, and Amazon.com have literally changed the way we do business? One reason is that the attitude in big companies is to say *no* more often than *yes,* whereas the attitude in smaller companies tends to be "Let's try it."[9] Another reason is that small businesses tend to innovate more easily than larger ones. Case studies show that (1) small businesses can make decisions faster; (2) the owners are more accessible; and (3) employees have a greater opportunity for individual expression.

An enterprise that does not innovate will not survive long. Even the most successful companies must constantly reinvent themselves.[10]

Moreover, in big companies, putting an idea into action often means filing formal proposals, preparing research reports, and attending lots of meetings. This process could kill an idea before it has a chance to take off. Consider Microsoft, for example. One manager recently quit out of frustration with the company's snail's pace for decision making. It took ten meetings and three months to act on his suggestion to add a feature to Hot Mail (the company's freebie Internet e-mail service) that would quickly take 40 million users to Microsoft's MSN Web site. In contrast, it took only 30 minutes to write the code for this feature.[11]

To stimulate innovation, many big companies are dividing their organizations into smaller work units. Xerox, AT&T, du Pont, Motorola, and Hewlett-Packard have launched their own small enterprises to keep new ideas from falling through the cracks. Run by *intrapreneurs*—people who create innovation of any kind *within* an organization (not to be confused with *entrepreneurs*—risk takers in the private enterprise system)—these ventures get funding and support from the parent organization. Nevertheless, some intrapreneurial ventures continue to face giant obstacles, because the parent corporation continues to burden them with strict reporting requirements and formal procedures.[12]

Factors Contributing to the Increase in the Number of Small Businesses

Three factors are contributing to the increase in the number of small businesses today. They are: technological advances, an increase in the number of women and minority business owners, and corporate downsizing and outsourcing.

LEARNING OBJECTIVE 2
Identify three factors contributing to the increase in the number of small businesses

In the global marketplace, new technology provides the means for the smallest players to benefit in ways never before possible.[14]

Technology and the Internet It is estimated that over 13 percent of small businesses have a Web site on the Internet, and this number is expected to increase to over 30 percent in the near future.[13] The Internet allows small companies to compete on a level playing field with larger companies by taking advantage of the collapse of time and distance. For instance, companies can communicate with customers and suppliers all over the world—any time of the day—and access the types of resources and information that were previously available only to larger firms.

Moreover, the advent of computer-aided manufacturing equipment and affordable data processing systems enables small companies to customize their products and deliver them as efficiently as their larger rivals. Look at Isis, a small pharmaceutical company. Being first to introduce a new drug in the market is critical in the pharmaceutical industry. But it takes years of research and data analysis to get the required agency approvals. In the past, small companies could not afford to spend millions of dollars on data-crunching systems to process the information efficiently. But today, less expensive versions of these sophisticated systems are available. As a result, a small firm like Isis can file its 40,000-page reports with the U.S. Food and Drug Administration in one-third the time by compressing the information onto one CD-ROM.[15]

Technology also makes it easier to work at home. With the Internet and online resources such as Lexis-Nexis, Dun & Bradstreet, Electric Library, and Commerce Clearing House's Business Owners' Toolkit, accountants, writers, lawyers, and consultants can set up shop at home, on the road, or just about anywhere. According to one recent study, about 24 million home-based businesses exist in the United States, and an additional 11 million people telecommute.[16] Some predict that by 2003 as much as half the work force may be involved in full- or part-time home-based businesses.[17]

Rise in Number of Women and Minority Small Business Owners Studies show that women now own roughly 40 percent of the 24 million businesses in the United States; these firms employ more than 18.5 million people and ring up more than $2.3 trillion in annual sales.[18] Similar advances are also showing up in minority segments of the population. Estimates from the National Foundation for Women Business Owners show that between 1987 and 1996, business start-ups with African American, Hispanic, or Asian women at the helm grew 153 percent—more than triple the 47 percent rate of U.S. businesses overall.[18]

Women are turning to small business for two main reasons: Some women choose to run their own companies so they can enjoy a more flexible work arrangement; others leave the corporate world because of advancement barriers—known as the glass ceiling. Take Josie Natori, for a perfect example. By her late twenties, Natori was earning six figures as the first female vice president of investment banking at Merrill Lynch. Where could she go from there? Today Natori is the owner of a $33 million fashion empire that sells elegant lingerie and evening wear.[19] Nevertheless, going solo does not guarantee success. Many women business owners still struggle to be taken seriously. In addition, the hours can be grueling, and failure rates are high.

Downsizing and Outsourcing Beginning in the late 1980s and continuing through the 1990s, many big corporations downsized, reducing their number of employees to improve their profits. Some, such as Procter & Gamble, were able to function with fewer people once they redesigned their businesses to operate more efficiently.[20] Other companies turned to **outsourcing,** or subcontracting special projects and secondary business functions to experts outside the organization, to make up for the layoffs of permanent staff. Still others used outsourcing on a permanent basis to eliminate entire departments.

Regardless of the reason, the increased use of outsourcing provides opportunities for smaller businesses to service the needs of larger enterprises. Many employees who leave the

outsourcing
Subcontracting work to outside companies

Focus on E-Business

CREATE A WINNING WEB SITE

These days anyone can learn to design and construct Web pages. All you need is the right Web-authoring software and a reasonably good PC to create pages with text, photos, and animated graphics. But if you want to create a winning Web site, here are a few tips to consider:

- *Present a professional corporate image.* Be sure to provide a corporate profile that tells people a little bit about your company. Include news releases or articles about your business so that customers can see how well known or dynamic you are in the industry. Make sure your material is accurate, interesting, and related to your products. Identify the key benefits of your product (include product details on a second page). Check out other Web sites for inspiration—especially your competitors' sites—and decide what you like or dislike about their appearance. Think of ways to distinguish your site.

- *Don't forget the basics.* Always give visitors a person to call and a place to send for information. Be sure to list your postal and e-mail addresses and phone and fax numbers. And remember, because the Internet is international, list the nation where your company or its dealers are located.

- *Make your Web site easy to use.* Web surfers have a short attention span, so keep large graphics (which take forever to load) to a minimum. If you must include any large, embedded graphics or photos, provide an option for users to select a text-only interface, or provide small images of photos (called thumbnails) for users to click on if they want to view larger, more detailed versions. Always provide hot links at the bottom of each page to allow users to move backward and forward through a multipage site.

- *Anticipate your customers' needs.* Plan ahead. By including answers to frequently asked questions, chances are you'll cover about 90 percent of your customers' concerns. Remember, users tend to provide both frank and useful input, but only if you ask them for it. So be sure to include an active customer feedback mechanism such as e-mail, open feedback forms, or structured survey forms. Don't require users to register before they can see your site. You may drive them away.

- *Promote your Web site.* Be sure to list with numerous search engines—giant indexes that allow Web users to find information by entering key words. Most of these listings are free. Maximize the number of times your site will be listed by jamming in as many words as you can that best describe your site. Take out an ad in the newspaper and list your company in the Internet yellow pages. Finally, don't just sit back and expect your Web site to perform magic. Use it to find out as much as possible about your customers. Ask yourself: How can I benefit from all this customer information?

QUESTIONS FOR CRITICAL THINKING

1. When designing your Web site, why might you want to minimize the number of hot links you include that take users to other Web sites?

2. List some of the ways companies can benefit from having a Web site on the Internet.

corporate world find it more fulfilling to work as independent contractors or to join smaller firms. Some, like Harold Jackson, are even wooing their former employers as customers. After working several years as Coca-Cola's manager of media relations in Atlanta, Jackson left to found JacksonHeath Public Relations International, taking Coke with him as his most valuable client.[21]

■ STARTING A SMALL BUSINESS

Not only are people in the United States starting new businesses at dizzying rates, but a study by the Entrepreneurial Research Consortium shows that more than 35 million U.S. households—roughly one in three—"have had an intimate involvement in a new or small business."[22] Could you or should you join the thousands of men and women like Gordon Weinberger and Harold Jackson who start new businesses every year? What qualities would you need?

Laid-off executives who are used to running multibillion-dollar enterprises sometimes have trouble adjusting to the unglamorous details of daily life in a small business. Many miss the support services and fringe benefits they enjoyed in large corporations.[23] Furthermore, because small companies generally have limited resources, many owners and employees must learn how to do more with less. Each must perform a variety of job functions in order to get the work done. And this jack-of-all-trades mentality is not for everyone (see Exhibit 4.1). Unfortunately, some people find that out the hard way. They discover that running a small business takes a lot of hard work and that being a successful corporate employee doesn't necessarily translate into being a successful small-business owner.

When Bob Hammer and Sue Crowe purchased Blue Jacket Ship Crafters, a mail-order model-ship-kit manufacturer, they quickly learned that running a small company was not like running Motorola, where the two had been senior managers for the better part of their careers. It took a lot more work and time than they had imagined. Even Crowe admits, "You will put in more money than you thought you would, you will take out a lot less, and you will work harder than you did when you were making a six-figure salary at your large corporation."[24] In fact, three out of four people who start their own company spend at least

EXHIBIT 4·1

HOW ENTREPRENEURS SPEND THEIR TIME

The men and women who start their own companies are jacks-of-all-trades, but they devote the lion's share of their time to selling and producing the product.

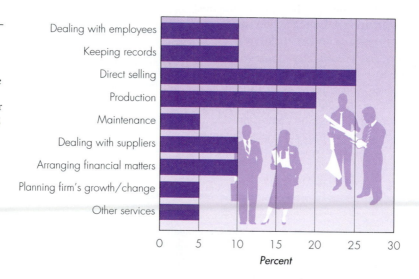

Dealing with employees
Keeping records
Direct selling
Production
Maintenance
Dealing with suppliers
Arranging financial matters
Planning firm's growth/change
Other services

0   5   10   15   20   25   30
Percent

50 hours a week on the job; a quarter of them put in 70 hours or more.[25] On the other hand, Carlos Montero knew exactly what he was getting into when he used $300,000 in savings to buy three Burger Kings several years ago. After attending rigorous training sessions to learn everything from cooking burgers to cleaning windows, Montero worked almost 21 hours a day for many, many weeks. Today he owns 22 restaurants with annual revenues approaching $18 million.[26]

Characteristics of Entrepreneurs

LEARNING OBJECTIVE 3
Cite the key characteristics common to most entrepreneurs

What drives people like Carlos Montero, Sue Crowe, Harold Jackson, Josie Natori, and others to take the entrepreneurial plunge in the first place? Contrary to what you might expect, most of these people are not glamorous adventurers; in fact, they are often ordinary people like Gordon Weinberger who have a good idea. While many are anxious to become their own boss, surprisingly they cite making money as the secondary reason for starting their own business.[27]

Still, studies show that it takes more than a good idea to launch a successful business. In fact, most entrepreneurs have these qualities in common: They prefer excitement, are highly disciplined, like to control their destiny, listen to their intuitive sense, relate well to others, are eager to learn whatever skills are necessary to reach their goal, learn from their mistakes, stay abreast of market changes, are willing to exploit new opportunities, seldom follow trends (rather, they spot and interpret trends), are driven by ambition, think positively, and prefer the excitement and potential rewards of risk taking over security.[28] Exhibit 4.2 lists some successful entrepreneurs and the key factor contributing to their success.

Recuperating from a broken ankle while vacationing in Lake Tahoe, Perry Klebahn decided to try out a pair of snowshoes he found in a friend's closet. Today his company, Atlas Snowshoe, sells high-end snowshoes in more than 1,000 stores across the United States, ringing in annual sales of about $12 million.

Many entrepreneurs start with relatively small sums of money and operate informally from their homes, at least for a while.[29] Most have diverse backgrounds in terms of education and business experience. Some come from companies unlike the ones they start; others use their prior knowledge and skills—such as editing, telemarketing, public relations, or selling—to start their own businesses. Still others have less experience but an innovative idea or a better way of doing something. Like Gordon Weinberger, they find an overlooked corner of the market, exploit a demographic trend unnoticed by others, or meet an unsatisfied consumer need through better service or a higher-quality product. Moreover, they often develop their product quickly, while the rest of the business world ponders whether a market for the product exists. Regardless, starting and managing a business today takes motivation, desire, and talent. It also takes lots of research and planning.

 To compete with small, fast-moving companies in the global economy, giant companies have got to behave like small companies.[30]

Importance of Preparing a Business Plan

Although many successful entrepreneurs claim to have done little formal planning, even the most intuitive of them have *some* idea of what they're trying to accomplish and how they hope to do it. No amount of hard work can turn a bad idea into a profitable one: The health-food store in a meat-and-potatoes neighborhood and the childcare center in a retirement

EXHIBIT 4·2

ENTREPRENEURIAL
SUCCESS

If you like a product, chances
are an entrepreneur is
behind it.

KEY SUCCESS FACTOR	COMPANY
Persistence	*Breed Technologies:* It took Allen Breed over ten years to convince carmakers that air bags could save several thousand lives a year. Today Breed Technologies is one of the most profitable suppliers in the automotive industry—his company makes the sensors that trigger the air-bag system. With more than 5,000 employees and branches in eight countries, this company's sales went from zero to nearly half a billion dollars in less than a decade.
Skill	*La Tempesta:* Using Aunt Isa's recipe for biscotti (twice-baked Italian cookies), Bonnie Tempesta baked them and sold them at a fancy San Francisco chocolate shop. While attending a fancy-foods trade show one day, she noticed that she was the only one there with biscotti. Today she sells over $9 million worth through 65 separate regional distributors to 5,000 stores, including Starbucks, Nordstrom, and Neiman Marcus.
Passion	*Transmissions by Lucille:* Lucille Treganowan didn't grow up yearning to repair cars. In fact, she didn't know a transmission from a turnip. So she began asking mechanics questions, reading, and working on cars. In 1973 she started her business. Today, transmissions are more than a business; they are a passion.
Hobby	*Rusty Cos:* Russell Preisendorfer is an avid surfer. To support his habit he began shaping surfboards. Last year his privately owned Rusty Cos grossed $57 million from sales of surfboards and royalties from a line of surfing apparel he helps design.
Common Sense	*Auntie Anne's:* To bring in some extra cash, Anne Beiler managed a food stand at a farmer's market in Maryland. She noticed that the fastest-selling items at the stand were hand-rolled pretzels that sold for 55 cents each. Not bad for 7 cents worth of ingredients. So Beiler decided to try the pretzel business herself. Today Beiler's mini-empire consists of over 300 franchised pretzel shops in about 35 states.
Talent	*Anthony Mark Hankins Ltd.:* When Anthony Hankins was only seven years old, he sat down at a sewing machine and made a suit for his mother to wear to a wedding. At 27, he was still making clothes for his mother—and millions of other women. After just one year in business, retail sales for his clothing collections had reached $40 million.

community are probably doomed from the beginning. Before you rush in to supply a product, you need to be sure that a market exists.

You must also try to foresee some of the problems that might arise and figure out how to cope with them. What will you do if one of your suppliers suddenly goes out of business? Can you locate another supplier quickly? What if the neighborhood starts to change—even for the better? An influx of wealthier neighbors may cause such a steep increase in rent that your business must move. Also, tough competition may move into the neighborhood along with the fatter pocketbooks. Do you have an alternative location staked out? What if fashions suddenly change? Can you switch quickly from, say, hand-painted T-shirts to some other kind of shirt?

One of the first steps you should take toward starting a new business is to develop a **business plan,** a written document that communicates a company's goals and how it intends to achieve those goals. Preparing a business plan will help you decide how to turn your idea into reality, and if you need outside financing, the plan will help you persuade lenders and investors to back your business. In fact, without a business plan, many investors won't even grant you an interview.

business plan
A written document that provides an orderly statement of a company's goals and how it intends to achieve those goals

See It on the Web See It on the Web

INCREASE YOUR CHANCES FOR SUCCESS

Starting a new business is not for everyone. Find out whether you have the "right stuff" to be a successful entrepreneur. Do you know how to network effectively? Explore the world of small business now by visiting the Small Business Advisor. While you're at it, check out Biz FAQs and find the answers to some of the most frequently asked questions about small business. Then select The Advisor and scroll down to click on Start-Up Topics and learn nine important ways to increase your chances for success.

http://www.isquare.com

If you are starting out on a small scale and using your own money, your business plan may be relatively informal. But at a minimum, you should describe the basic concept of the business and outline its specific goals, objectives, and resource requirements. Although the business plan has a simple, straightforward purpose, it still requires a great deal of thought. For example, before you even open your doors, you have to make important decisions about personnel, marketing, facilities, suppliers, and distribution. A written business plan forces you to think about those issues and develop programs that will help you succeed.

A formal plan, suitable for use with banks or investors, should cover these points (keep in mind that your audience wants short, concise information, not lengthy volumes):[31]

- *Summary.* In one or two pages, summarize your business concept. Describe your product or service and its market potential. Highlight some things about your company and its owners that will distinguish your firm from competition. Summarize your financial projections and the amount of money investors can expect to make on their investment. Be sure to indicate how much money you will need and for what purpose.

- *Company and industry.* Give full background information on the origins and structure of your venture and the characteristics of its industry.

- *Products or services.* Give a complete but concise description, focusing on the unique attributes of your products or services. Explain how customers will benefit from using your products or services instead of those of your competitors.

- *Market.* Provide data that will persuade the investor that you understand your market and can achieve your sales goals. Be sure to identify the strengths and weaknesses of your competition.

- *Management.* Summarize the background and qualifications of the principals, directors, and key management personnel in your company. Include résumés in the appendix.

- *Marketing strategy.* Provide projections of sales and market share, and outline a strategy for identifying and contacting customers, setting prices, providing customer services, advertising, and so forth. Whenever possible, include evidence of customer acceptance, such as advance product orders.

- *Design and development plans.* If your product requires design or development, describe the nature and extent of what needs to be done, including costs and possible problems.

LEARNING OBJECTIVE 4
Name 12 topics that should be covered in a formal business plan

- *Operations plan.* Provide information on the facilities, equipment, and labor needed.
- *Overall schedule.* Forecast development of the company in terms of completion dates for major aspects of the business plan.
- *Critical risks and problems.* Identify all negative factors and discuss them honestly.
- *Financial information.* Include a detailed budget of start-up and operating costs, as well as projections for income, expenses, and cash flow for the first three years of business.
- *Exit strategy.* Explain how investors will be able to cash out or sell their investment, such as through a public stock offering, sale of the company, or a buyback of the investors' interest.

What distinguishes a winning business plan from others? According to the MIT Enterprise Forum, a national clinic providing assistance to emerging growth companies, a winning plan must explain what the company expects to accomplish in three to seven years, show how the user will benefit from the company's products or services, present hard evidence of the demand for the company's products or services, portray the partners as a team of experienced managers with complementary business skills, and show how investors can earn (relatively quickly) a substantial profit. In addition, a winning business plan must present both the company's strengths and anticipated weaknesses. Finally, it must be realistic in its projections for growth.[32]

Why Businesses Fail

Even if you write a winning business plan, you have no guarantee for success. In fact, you may have heard some depressing statistics about the number of new businesses that fail. Some reports say your chances of succeeding are only one in three; others claim that the odds are even worse, stating that 85 percent of all new business ventures fail within ten years. Roughly 83,000 U.S. companies closed their doors in 1997. But the true failure rate is much lower if you remove those operations that Dun & Bradstreet (D&B) business analysts say aren't "genuine businesses." For instance, a freelancer who writes one article for a magazine and then stops writing would be counted as a failed business under the traditional measurement (which is based on tax returns).[33]

Despite these compelling statistics, most business owners refuse to contemplate the possibility of failure. W. David Waters, for instance, never expected his new business to fail. Instead, he expected his business, Honolulu-based Centaur Zone Café, to be the prototype for a chain of international coffeehouses. With a Georgetown University dual degree in management and finance and years of management experience under his belt, Waters set about researching the industry and preparing his business plan. A local banker was so impressed with Waters's plan that he decided to nominate him as SBA entrepreneur of the year. Once Waters opened the café's doors, however, patronage was much lower than anticipated. The café did become a hangout for college students, but when summer hit, students departed and business dragged. Furthermore, Hawaii's poor economy was taking its toll on coffeehouses as it was on other businesses. Unable to pay the rent, Waters closed up shop.

Some entrepreneurs, like Jeff Schwarz, make this common mistake: They fail to establish a time limit for a new business to generate a profit and then stick to it. When Schwarz's business failed, what bugged him the most was that he hadn't pulled the plug soon enough. Instead, he went three years without a salary and burned through $100,000 of his personal savings before calling it quits.[35]

Mistakes are a part of learning. They tell us that whatever we're doing is not working. Making mistakes is not a crime—not learning from them is.[34]

ARE YOU CRAZY?

If you've ever thought about quitting your job and starting a business, it's almost certain that someone—a spouse, a co-worker, a friend—uttered these three words: "Are you crazy?" The reason is that risk taking, an essential quality of entrepreneurship, scares most people. But you're different. You're forging ahead because you have a dream. And you're not afraid, because, after all, you're about to embark on the greatest voyage of your life—just as the following entrepreneurs did.

Edward DuCoin: $100 was more than enough for this entrepreneur when, at 18, he launched Impact Telemarketing. Inspired by his telemarketing job for a lawn-care company, DuCoin found a used desk, bought a really inexpensive, old answering machine, and set up shop in his bedroom. He began drumming up business by answering help-wanted ads for telephone salespeople in the local newspaper. He pointed out to companies that it would be more economical for them to use his services than to hire and train a new employee. Soon he had a team of telemarketers working for him out of their homes. With gross revenues near $12 million, in 1997 DuCoin merged his company with four other collection firms and mailing services and took the company public as Compass International.

Kelly Dunn: In 1996 this single mother and Pillsbury secretary scoured Minneapolis for a concierge who might relieve her of household chores. She couldn't find one. So after attending a one-day seminar on the concierge business, Dunn quit her job and started her own concierge company, Consider It Dunn. She knocked on doors for months at downtown offices, asking whether they needed a concierge. Nobody did. Meanwhile, she combed Minneapolis for topflight vendors—shoe repair shops, jewelers, and so on—comparing prices, quality, and speed. Her big break came when Pillsbury (her former employer) hired her as its first concierge. Today she employs ten workers and is projecting a gross profit of $80,000 on revenues of $237,000.

Kate Spade: When Spade quit her job as accessories editor for *Mademoiselle* and launched her own handbag company in 1991, even her mother said she had gotten cocky. Priced at $100 to $400, Spade's nylon bags weren't cheap, and she had a tough time getting them into trade shows because she didn't "do leather." But Spade's instincts were better than the stylemakers'. On an impulse the night before her first trade show, Spade ripped the labels "kate spade new york" from the inside of her bags and stitched them on the outside, sewing until her fingers got puffy. Good move. Barneys ordered 18 of her bags, and *Vogue* decided to feature them on the glossy's accessories page. It wasn't long before Julia Roberts and Gwyneth Paltrow (who saw the bags in fashion magazines) had them on their shoulders. Nevertheless, the company didn't become profitable until 1996, when Saks and Neiman Marcus each ordered 3,000 bags for all their stores. Today Kate Spade, Inc. has its own retail outlets with a new line of clothing. Sales are projected to top $30 million.

QUESTIONS FOR CRITICAL THINKING

1. What key entrepreneurial characteristics did each of these individuals exhibit?
2. Which of these businesses would be considered lifestyle businesses and which, if any, would be considered high-growth ventures? Why?

Keep in mind that failure can happen to anyone. It's what happens afterward that often matters the most. Many presidents of big, successful companies, including Fred Smith of FedEx, can spin long tales about how failure got them where they are today. In fact, failure is often part of the learning experience, as some experts advise. But while some entrepreneurs lick their wounds and find a new focus incredibly quickly, not everybody bounces back.[36]

According to small-business consultants, the top three small-business killers are inadequate financing, inability to find clients or customers, and lack of good management skills. Also high on the list are a lack of realism about one's own abilities and not having the right information to work with. Before embarking on your entrepreneurial journey, experts recommend that you think about these important points:[37]

- *Know yourself and what you want to accomplish.* Ask yourself whether you have what it takes to start and operate a business. Consider whether you like dealing with people, enjoy the intricacies of making or selling the product or service, and get satisfaction from meeting the needs of your customers. Find out whether you have the technical knowledge and business management skills to do a better job than your competitors.

- *Know how to find the money you need.* Financing is one of the biggest challenges small businesses face. Many banks shy away from lending money to new businesses because they consider new businesses risky investments. (Financing the enterprise will be discussed later in this chapter.)

- *Know how to register and insure your business.* Having all the proper registrations, certifications, licenses, and insurance protects you from violations that could eventually shut down your business. In Chapter 5 we will discuss the requirements for different forms of business ownership. Insurance and risk management are discussed in Component Chapter B.

- *Know who your customers are and how to reach them.* Most businesspeople make the mistake (as W. David Waters did) of assuming that all you need is a good idea and that as soon as you open your doors, customers will come rushing in. Resist the thought. One of the most important parts of preparing a business plan is to learn who your customers are and to develop strategies for reaching those customers.

- *Know where to go for help.* In the next section we will discuss a variety of business resources that can help you with your undertaking. Besides using these resources, you'll also need to pull together a team of professionals and consultants to whom you can turn for advice on a regular basis. These experts include a good lawyer, accountant, bookkeeper, banker, insurance agent, and marketing expert.

Sources of Small-Business Assistance

Experts advise that you always seek professional assistance before beginning your entrepreneurial journey. A number of small-business resources are available to help you evaluate your business idea, develop a business plan, locate start-up funding sources, and even teach you how to package your business image professionally. Many local business professionals are willing to serve as mentors and can help you avoid the pitfalls of business. These small-business resources include SCORE representatives, incubators, and the Internet.

After a friend referred John and Lynelle Lawrence to SCORE, counselor Joe Geller (right) helped the couple through each stage of preparation for their Mudhouse Café in Charlottesville, Virginia.

SCORE Some of the best advice available to small businesses costs little or nothing. It's delivered by volunteers with the Service Corps of Retired Executives (SCORE), a resource partner of the SBA. SCORE's 12,000 volunteers are working and retired executives and active small-business owners who offer advice and one-to-one counseling sessions on topics such as developing a business plan, securing financing, and managing business growth. To date, more than 3.5 million clients, such as New York Bagel, have been helped by SCORE counselors.[38]

Whether you use a SCORE counselor or find a private mentor, having someone to bounce your ideas off or help you create a five-year financial forecast can increase the chances of your business's surviving, as Lynelle and John Lawrence discovered. Owners of the Mudhouse Café in Charlottesville, Virginia, the Lawrences used a SCORE representative to help them prepare a detailed business plan and obtain financing. "There's no way we would be here without SCORE," confesses the couple.[39]

Incubators Incubators are centers that provide "newborn" businesses with low-cost offices and basic business services. Nearly 90 percent of incubators are started and operated by not-for-profit alliances, which usually include government agencies and universities. In a typical incubator, new companies can lease space at bargain rates and share secretaries, receptionists, telephone equipment, financial and accounting advice, marketing support, and credit-checking services. Because the goal is to convert "tenant" firms into "graduates," most incubators set limits—from 18 months to five years—on how long a company can stay in the nest.[40]

Several successful businesses have been hatched from incubators. Create-A-Saurus, producer of a line of playground equipment assembled from recycled and reconditioned tires, is one. The company got its start in the Oakland (California) Small Business Growth Center, one of the 800-plus business incubators in the United States and Canada. Similarly, a Milwaukee, Wisconsin, business incubator gave Yolanda Cross the chance to move her catering-related business from her home into a more professional setting, where it has flourished.[41]

Recent studies show that incubator companies are much more likely to grow into viable job-creating businesses than firms without such support. In fact, these studies show that eight out of ten businesses nurtured in incubators succeed. Some incubators are open to businesses of all types; others specialize. For example, the Spokane Business Incubation Center operates the Kitchen Center, where small food-processing companies can share a commercial kitchen.[42]

The Internet Sometimes the key to unlocking valuable advice, business leads, or other small-business assistance is right at your fingertips. Sonja Edmond, owner of Heavenly Bounty Giftbaskets, a hand-crafted gift-basket business, had to look no farther than her computer screen when she needed help. Although she enjoyed making gift baskets as a hobby, she wasn't sure whether a viable market existed to support a home-based business. So she posted a price-setting question on CompuServe's Working from Home and Handcrafts forum. Within 24 hours, her e-mail box was flooded with answers from forum members, who "convinced me I could do this," she says. Edmond struck a resource goldmine: Not only did she find the encouragement she needed to plunge into entrepreneurship; she also got valuable business leads and advice on licensing her product.[43]

Small-Business Ownership Options

If you decide to take the risk, you can get into business for yourself in three ways: Start from scratch, buy an existing operation, or obtain a franchise. Roughly two-thirds of business founders begin **start-up companies;** that is, they start from scratch rather than buying an existing operation or inheriting the family business. Although starting from scratch is the most common route, it's probably the most difficult as well. Exhibit 4.3 provides a checklist of some of the many tasks involved in starting a new business.

Another way to go into business for yourself is to buy an existing business. This approach tends to reduce the risks—provided, of course, that you check out the company carefully. When you buy a business, you instantly acquire a known product or service and a system for producing it. You don't have to go through the painful period of building a reputation, establishing a clientele, and hiring and training employees. In addition, financing an existing business is often much easier than funding a new one; lenders are reassured by the company's history and existing assets and customer base. With these major details already settled, you can concentrate on making improvements.

incubators
Facilities that house small businesses during their early growth phase

LEARNING OBJECTIVE 6
List three ways of getting into business for yourself

start-up companies
New ventures

EXHIBIT 4·3

BUSINESS START-UP CHECKLIST

You have many tasks to perform before you start your business. Here are just a few.

✓ Choose a business name, verify the right to use it, and register it.
✓ Reserve a corporate name if you will be incorporating.
✓ Register or reserve state or federal trademarks.
✓ Apply for a patent if you will be marketing an invention.
✓ Write a business plan.
✓ Choose a location for the business.
✓ File partnership or corporate papers.
✓ Get any required business licenses or permits.
✓ Have business phone lines installed.
✓ Check into business insurance needs.
✓ Apply for sales tax number.
✓ Apply for employee identification number if you will have employees.
✓ Open business bank account(s).
✓ Have business cards and stationery printed.
✓ Purchase equipment and supplies.
✓ Order inventory.
✓ Order signage.
✓ Order fixtures.
✓ Print brochures and other sales literature.
✓ Send out publicity releases.
✓ Call everyone you know and tell them you are in business.

Still, buying an existing business is not without disadvantages. For one thing, it can be more expensive to buy an existing business than to start one from scratch. Furthermore, inventories and equipment may be obsolete, your personality may clash with those of existing managers and employees, and outstanding bills owed by customers may be difficult to collect. Keep in mind that no matter how fast you learn and how much investigating you do, you're likely to find that the challenges of running an existing business are far greater than you anticipated.[44]

The Franchise Alternative

An alternative to buying an existing business is to buy a **franchise** in somebody else's business. This approach enables the buyer to use a larger company's trade name and sell its products or services in a specific territory. In exchange for this right, the **franchisee** (the small-business owner who contracts to sell the goods or services) pays the **franchisor** (the supplier) an initial fee (and often monthly royalties as well).

Franchises are a factor of rising importance in the U.S. economy. About every six minutes of every business day, a new franchise opens somewhere in the United States. Fran-

franchise
Business arrangement in which a small business obtains rights to sell the goods or services of the supplier (franchisor)

franchisee
Small-business owner who contracts for the right to sell goods or services of the supplier (franchisor) in exchange for some payment

franchisor
Supplier that grants a franchise to an individual or group (franchisee) in exchange for payments

chising now accounts for roughly $1 trillion, or about 50 percent of all U.S. retail sales.[45] Franchised businesses employ more than 8 million people; their suppliers employ another 2.4 million.[46]

Corporate downsizing and early retirement have yielded a rich crop of qualified franchisee prospects in recent years. Over 30 percent of all new franchisees are ex-employees of big companies, and many are equipped with MBAs. In addition, many immigrants, with their unmatched entrepreneurial spirit and their drive to succeed, turn to franchising as a way of starting their own business.[47] However, owning a franchise is no guarantee that your business will succeed. According to one study, your chances are no better with a franchise operation than with a start-up.[48]

Franchises are of three basic types. A *product franchise* gives you the right to sell trademarked goods, which are purchased from the franchisor and resold. Car dealers and gasoline stations fall into this category. A *manufacturing franchise,* such as a soft-drink bottling plant, gives you the right to produce and distribute the manufacturer's products, using supplies purchased from the franchisor. A *business-format franchise* gives you the right to open a business using a franchisor's name and format for doing business. Fast-food chains such as KFC, Taco Bell, and Pizza Hut typify this form of franchising. As you are well aware, franchises such as these are popping up all over the country—on military bases and college campuses and in supermarkets, hospitals, airports, zoos, sports arenas, theme parks, and shopping malls.

Advantages of Franchising   Why is franchising so popular? For one thing, when you invest in a franchise, you know you are getting a viable business, one that has "worked" many times before. If the franchise is well established, you get the added benefit of instant name recognition. Besides, when it comes to marketing and advertising—the things that most businesses don't have time for—the franchise company does that for you. An independent hamburger stand can't afford a national television advertising campaign, but McDonald's, Burger King, and Wendy's can.

In addition to giving you a proven formula, buying a franchise gives you instant access to a support network along with a ready-made blueprint for building a business. For an initial investment (from a few thousand dollars to upward of a million, depending on

See It on the Web See It on the Web

GET SMART

It seems as if one-stop shopping is the way to go these days—everything under one roof, or on one page if you're on the 'Net. Smartbiz puts the world of business resources at your fingertips with business articles, resources, hot tips, franchise information, home office ideas, Internet links, and more. Thinking about buying an existing franchise? Better check out the franchisor first. Perhaps starting a home business sounds more appealing. Where should you begin? What are some of the advantages or disadvantages? Be sure to Browse SBS for some answers. Do you have a Web site? It takes only five minutes to build one. Find out how by visiting Smartbiz, click Business on the Net, and scroll down to the hot link The Home Page Maker. Don't forget to e-mail us your URL.
http://www.smartbiz.com

the franchise), you get services such as site-location studies, market research, training, and technical assistance, as well as assistance with building or leasing your structure, decorating the building, purchasing supplies, and operating the business for 6 to 12 months. Few franchisees are able to write a check for the amount of the total investment. Most obtain a loan to cover at least part of the cost. In some cases, the lender is actually the franchisor.

Disadvantages of Franchising Although franchising offers many advantages, it is not the ideal vehicle for everyone. First of all, owning a franchise is no guarantee of wealth. Even though it may be a relatively easy way to get into business, it isn't necessarily the cheapest. According to some analysts, it costs 10 to 30 percent more to buy a franchise than to open a business independently.[49] In addition, not all franchises are hugely profitable. Some franchisees barely survive, in fact. One of the biggest disadvantages of franchising is the monthly payment, or royalty, that must be turned over to the franchisor. This fee varies from nothing at all to 20 percent of sales. High royalties are not necessarily bad as long as the franchisee gets ongoing assistance in return.

Another drawback of franchises is that many allow individual operators little independence. Franchisors can prescribe virtually every aspect of the business, down to the details of employee uniforms and the color of the walls. Furthermore, when a chain loses its cutting edge in the marketplace, being stuck with a franchise can be painful. By contrast, if independent retailers run into trouble with their product lines, they can change suppliers or perhaps switch rapidly to a whole new line of business. Franchisees can't. They're usually bound by contracts to sell only authorized goods, often supplied by the franchisor itself at whatever price the franchisor wants to charge.

Although franchisors can also make important decisions without consulting franchisees, the days of franchisors' exercising such control are ending. In many cases the relationship between franchisor and franchisee is becoming more of a joint venture. Some franchisors are rewriting contracts to become less dictatorial, says the CEO of U.S. Franchise Systems. Newer contracts offer stock options, automatic contract renewals, and empowerment through franchise advisory boards. Some are adding "give and take" clauses. Others are even giving franchisees more of a say in issues such as how territories are protected and how advertising funds are handled. Furthermore, legislative proposals are being considered that would require franchisors to meet certain criteria (something like an accreditation) before they can sell a franchise in the United States.[50]

How to Evaluate a Franchise How do you protect yourself from a poor franchise investment? The best way is to study the opportunity carefully before you commit. Since 1978 the Federal Trade Commission has required franchisors to disclose information about their operations to prospective franchisees. By studying this information, you can determine the financial condition of the franchisor and ascertain whether the company has been involved in lawsuits with franchisees. Before signing a franchise agreement, it's also wise to consult an attorney. Exhibit 4.4 suggests some points to consider as you study the package of information on the franchise.

Nevertheless, some people find out too late that franchising isn't the best choice for them. They make a mistake common among prospective franchisees—buying without really understanding the day-to-day business. Often, prospects simply don't get beyond the allure of the successful name or concept—or the mistaken notion that a franchise brings instant success. "People go into a sub shop at the noon hour and see the cash register opening and closing," says the president of Franchise Solutions. "What they don't see is having to

EXHIBIT 4·4

TEN QUESTIONS TO ASK BEFORE SIGNING A FRANCHISE AGREEMENT

1. What does the initial franchise fee cover? Does it include a starting inventory of supplies and products?
2. How are the periodic royalties calculated and when are they paid?
3. Are all trademarks and names legally protected?
4. Who provides and pays for advertising and promotional items?
5. Who selects the location of your business?
6. Are you assigned an exclusive territory?
7. If the territory is not exclusive, does the franchisee have the right of first refusal on additional franchises established in nearby locations?
8. Is the franchisee required to purchase equipment and supplies from the franchisor or other suppliers?
9. Under what conditions can the franchisor and/or the franchisee terminate the franchise agreement?
10. Can the franchise be assigned to heirs?

A franchise agreement is a legally binding contract that defines the relationship between the franchisee and the franchisor. Because the agreement is drawn up by the franchisor, the terms and conditions generally favor the franchisor. Before signing the franchise agreement, be sure to consult an attorney.

get there at 4 A.M. to bake the bread." Buying a franchise is much like buying any other business: It requires analyzing the market, finding capital, choosing a site, hiring employees, and buying equipment. The process also includes an element not found in other businesses—evaluating the franchisor.[51]

One of the best ways to evaluate a prospective franchisor is by talking to other franchisees. At a minimum, you should find out what other franchisees think of the opportunity. If they had it to do over again, would they still invest? You might even want to spend a few months working for someone who already owns a franchise you're interested in. Fabiola Garcia did. She worked at a 7-Eleven evenings and swing shifts, learning all aspects of the business as part of the screening and training process for prospective 7-Eleven franchise owners. This was in addition to a two-week special session at headquarters, where Garcia learned the franchisor's paperwork procedures.[52]

Nevertheless, as Jim and Laura White discovered, evaluating a franchise means more than assessing the current operation. What the market will be like tomorrow is just as important an issue to address. For example, when the Whites opened their Body Shop franchise in 1994, they expected to earn a comfortable living on their $300,000 investment. Instead, the outlet lost money every year. What they hadn't taken into account was that less than a year after the Whites' Body Shop opened, Bath & Body would come into the same mall. So did Crabtree & Evelyn, followed a year later by Garden Botanika (these chains sell products that compete directly with Body Shop's, and each of the stores was bigger than the Whites').[53]

For 23 years, the Body Shop, a high-quality skin and hair care product manufacturer and retailer with nearly $1 billion in sales and more than 1,700 outlets in 48 countries, has served consumers for whom natural, no-frills cosmetics products have been both beneficial and culturally relevant. But competition from savvy, better-looking, and in some cases, lower-priced competitors has seriously eroded the Body Shop's market share. To shake things up, the Body Shop has reduced the number of franchisees in favor of company-owned stores and has begun an extensive store renovation campaign.

■ FINANCING A NEW BUSINESS

Once you've decided whether you will build a business from scratch, buy an existing business, or invest in a franchise, you will probably need some money to get started. How much money will you need, and where should you turn first for capital? The answers depend on the size and type of business you want to launch. Retail and service businesses generally require less start-up cash than manufacturing companies or hi-tech research-and-development ventures.

Private Financing Assistance

Most firms initially choose to borrow money from private sources simply because they are not ready to sell their stock on the open market, or *go public*. In Chapter 5 we'll explain the process of selling stock to the public. In Component Chapter B, we'll discuss the advantages, the disadvantages, and the risk of financing with borrowed money (debt financing) versus financing by selling shares of stock in your firm to the public (equity financing).

Keep in mind that finding private financing sources is not an easy task. While bank loans and owner's equity are the principal sources of financing, many banks tend to shy away from lending money to new businesses. For one thing, banks consider a start-up very risky. For another, the risk inherent in some start-ups justifies higher interest rates than banks are allowed to charge by law. Thus, most banks will finance a start-up only if they can obtain payment guarantees from other financially sound parties or to the extent that the business has marketable collateral, such as buildings and equipment, to back the loan.[54] So what do you do if you can't obtain a bank loan and you can't call on friends and relatives as Gordon Weinberger did? Other alternatives for private financing assistance include venture capitalists, angel investors, credit cards, and the SBA.

venture capitalists
Investment specialists who provide money to finance new businesses or turnarounds in exchange for a portion of the ownership, with the objective of making a considerable profit on the investment; also called VCs

Venture Capitalists   **Venture capitalists** are investment specialists who raise pools of capital from large private and institutional sources (such as pension funds) to fund ventures that have a high, rapid growth potential and a need for large amounts of capital. Venture capitalists, or VCs as they're called in entrepreneurial circles, do not simply lend money to a small business as a bank would. Instead they provide money in return for a sizable ownership interest in the business, and some help run the business as well. Once the business becomes profitable, venture capitalists reap the reward by selling their interest to other long-term investors for a sizable profit.

The problems with venture capital are that it's extremely hard to find and the price of financing through a venture capital firm is high. To catch the eye of a typical venture capitalist, you need a business with pizzazz that has the potential to reach $50 million in sales within five years and provide an annualized rate of return of 20 to 40 percent over five to seven years.[55] If you're looking for only $1 or 2 million, you might want to find an angel instead. (Consult Part II of the *E-Business in Action* online supplement at http://www.prenhall. com/ebusinessinaction for additional discussion of venture funding for e-businesses.)

Angel Investors   Comfortable with risks that scare off many banks, *angel investors* put their own money into start-ups with the goal of eventually selling their interest for a large profit. These wealthy individuals are willing to loan smaller amounts of money than are VCs and to stay involved with the company for a longer period of time.

According to the SBA, 30,000 companies (needing between $250,000 and $5 million) are funded each year by angels. Start-ups that seek out angels typically have spent the $50,000–$100,000 raised from family and friends and are now looking for the next $250,000 to prove their concept.[56] In addition to providing financing, angels can be a great source of business expertise and credibility. For instance, Bill Gates (chairman of Microsoft) is an angel who has invested millions of dollars in biotech start-ups such as Darwin Molecular, which is trying to create artificial molecules that attack diseases.[57]

Credit Cards   More and more people are using credit cards to finance their small businesses. According to a recent study by Arthur Andersen Company, one-third of businesses with 19 or fewer employees use credit cards to fund their new business ventures.[58] Many people turn to credit cards because credit card companies don't care how borrowers spend the money just as long as they pay the bill. But with high interest rates, credit cards are a risky way to finance a business, as Jorge de la Riva discovered. He used personal credit cards to start up his industrial wholesale business—an experience he calls "playing with the tiger." As de la Riva put it, "You can make it work only if you have a definite plan to pay back the debt."[59] Unfortunately, many do not. (Credit cards are discussed in greater detail in Chapter 15.)

Small Business Administration Assistance

If your business doesn't fit the profile of high-powered venture-capital start-ups, or you can't find an angel, you might be able to qualify for a bank loan backed by the SBA. To get an SBA-backed loan, you apply to a regular bank, which actually provides the money; the SBA guarantees to repay 85 to 90 percent of the loan if you fail to do so. The average SBA-backed loan is about $100,000; the upper limit is $750,000. Guaranteed loans provided by the SBA launched FedEx, Intel, and Apple Computer. These three now pay more annual taxes to the federal government than the entire yearly cost of running the SBA.[60] In addition to operating its loan guarantee program, the SBA provides a limited number of direct loans to minorities, women, and veterans.[61]

From the businessperson's standpoint, SBA-backed loans are especially attractive because most have longer repayment terms than conventional bank loans—nine years as opposed to two or three. A longer repayment term translates into lower monthly payments. Unfortunately, demand for SBA loans vastly outstrips the agency's budget. Consequently, getting an SBA loan is difficult. In a typical year, only about 17,000 businesses are lucky enough to get one.[62]

Karla Brown is one of the lucky ones. With plenty of perseverance and a $19,000 microloan from the SBA, Brown was able to start her business, Ashmont Flowers Plus. The SBA microloan program began in 1992 to help people realize the American dream—to own a business and

Aspiring entrepreneurs like Karla Brown, who might not qualify for regular bank loans, can apply for SBA microloans to make their dreams come true.

be self-sufficient. Microloans range from $100 to $25,000, with the average loan of $10,000 paid back over four years.[63]

Another option for raising money is one of the investment firms created by the Small Business Administration. Small Business Investment Companies (SBICs) and Minority Enterprise Small Business Investment Companies (MESBICs), which finance minority-owned businesses, are similar in operation to venture-capital firms, but they tend to make smaller investments and are willing to consider businesses that VCs may not want to finance.[64]

See It on the Web See It on the Web

START A SMALL BUSINESS

Thinking about starting your own small business? The U.S. Small Business Administration (SBA) Web site puts you in touch with a wealth of resources to assist you in your start-up. Perhaps you would like some professional business counseling, financial assistance, or advice on developing a business plan. Starting a new business or buying an existing one can be an overwhelming process. But you can increase your chances for success by taking your first steps with the SBA's Startup Kit. So log on to find out if entrepreneurship is for you. Then do your research and discover some of the secrets to success.
http://www.sba.gov

■ MANAGING GROWTH SUCCESSFULLY

Growing from an entrepreneurial business into a professionally managed company creates another level of challenges for most small businesses. In a typical scenario, an entrepreneur has a good idea, turns it into a successful company, and expands it—perhaps by adding new products or new locations. While the upsides of growth are many—it creates jobs, provides a stimulating and exciting environment to work in, and offers a potential for new wealth—growth has its downsides too. When growth is too rapid, for instance, chaos can prevail. And nothing can kill a successful business faster than chaos.

Doug and Jill Smith learned this the hard way. With a 50 percent increase in sales—in one year alone—their company, Buckeye Beans & Herbs, was spinning out of control. They needed more people to take the orders, fill them, package the product, and so on. It took them a while to realize they weren't running a little mom-and-pop operation anymore. "We just couldn't do it all, and we didn't have the people in place yet," note the Smiths, who eventually got things back on the right track.[65]

Like the Smiths, many entrepreneurs find they know little about managing a larger company. "There are times I have moments of sheer panic," notes the president of Creedon Controls, an electrical contractor. "Where am I going to get the money? How am I going to cover the payroll? How am I going to get the job done?"[66] These are just a few of the challenges owners of a growing business must face. Bigger companies need new systems, processes, computers, employees, advisers, and often more sophisticated management. Owners have to staff positions that never existed and learn to delegate responsibilities and control. Sometimes they even lose what they like most about being small—the ability to work closely with employees in a hands-on environment.

Roger Miller, president of DependiCare, a supplier of medical equipment for home health care, found this out. When annual company revenues were $1.5 million, it was easy to take a hands-on approach and do without a lot of systems, processes, and procedures. But when DependiCare went from $6 million to $8 million and then to $12 million, things changed, and he had to give up some control.

As you move from one level to the next in a growing company, experts advise that you take these steps:[67]

- *Get help.* Although some entrepreneurs are good at launching companies, they sometimes lack the skills needed to manage companies over the long term. The person who excels during the start-up phase might know the industry and the product or service very well but may have problems figuring out how to run the expanded business. Therefore, as a company grows, you need to hire advisers with good business expertise.

- *Prepare to change your role.* As a company grows, the owner's role must change. The leader of a growing concern needs to become the strategic thinker and the planner— and must learn to delegate day-to-day responsibilities. The CEO needs to be in charge of tomorrow; he or she has to have other people who are in charge of today.

- *Modify the infrastructure.* A growing company usually needs new technology, more inventory, new product-ordering systems, and new communication systems. Growth means there will be many more vendors, more bills, and more checks to write. "If you double the size of the company, the number of bills you have to pay goes up by a factor of six," notes one entrepreneur.[68]

- *Stay focused.* One of the biggest mistakes entrepreneurs make is straying too far from the original product or market. Take Lifeline Systems, a provider of personal-response systems for the elderly. Fewer than ten years after it was founded, the company went public and was distributing its monitoring devices in more than 700 hospitals across the United States. Fearing that its focus was too small, the company diversified by introducing a new version of its monitoring device that could be used by children and college students in emergencies. It sold these devices to drug, electronics, and department stores at roughly half the price of the original model. But the mass market strategy found few buyers. Worse, it alienated the company's hospital customers, whose demand for the original product was already falling as a result of slashed hospital budgets. Lifeline began reporting losses. When a new CEO was hired to turn things around, one of the first things he did was undo the company's diversification efforts and restore the company's original focus.[69]

Of course, one of the biggest challenges you may face as the owner of a new business is handling success. Some companies are so successful in marketing their products or services that they are not able to keep up with customer demand. Look at Grandmother Calendar. When orders for elaborate cut-rate personalized calendars came in faster than the company could fill them, the company rushed production and quality suffered. Eventually the backlog overwhelmed them. The company had to notify customers that their orders would not be filled in time—and that was for Christmas presents. Angry customers canceled their orders and took their business elsewhere, forcing Grandmother Calendar to close up shop.[70]

Summary of Learning Objectives

1. **List four important functions of small businesses in the economy.**
   Small businesses provide jobs, introduce new goods and services, supply the needs of large corporations, and provide specialized goods and services.

2. **Identify three factors contributing to the increase in the number of small businesses.**
   The affordability and advancement of technology, an increase in the number of women and minority entrepreneurs entering the work force, and corporate downsizing and outsourcing are three factors contributing to the growth in the number of small businesses today.

3. **Cite the key characteristics common to most entrepreneurs.**

Entrepreneurs are highly disciplined, intuitive, innovative, ambitious individuals who are eager to learn, like to set trends, and prefer taking risks over having security.

4. **Name 12 topics that should be covered in a formal business plan.**
   In a formal business plan you should (1) summarize your business concept, (2) describe the company and its industry, (3) explain the product or service, (4) analyze the market, (5) summarize the background and qualifications of management, (6) describe your marketing strategy, (7) discuss design and development plans, (8) explain your operations plan, (9) provide an overall schedule, (10) identify risks and potential problems, (11) provide detailed financial information,

MEETING BUSINESS CHALLENGES AT TOP OF THE TREE BAKING COMPANY

Gordon Weinberger, founder of Top of the Tree Baking Company, knew he had his work cut out for him. After all, the pie industry was very competitive. But taking a cue from Ben & Jerry's Homemade ice cream, Weinberger believed people would be willing to pay slightly more for a fresh, tasty apple pie. Some people agreed—including Jerry Weissman, a businessman and friend of the family.

Weissman took Weinberger's business plan to a few friends, who were enthralled. The plan had short-term goals, long-term goals, and a ladder-type path to reach those goals. And Weissman liked something else, something far less tangible than Weinberger's well-thought-out plan. He sensed that Weinberger had the character and commitment to carry out the plan. And he was right.

To develop interest in his pies, Weinberger approached individual branches of New England supermarkets and conducted in-store tastings and pie-eating contests. For meetings with supermarket buyers, Weinberger spread checkered tablecloths on the executives' desks, played a tape-recorded jingle, and served up warm pie and cold milk. To attract the attention of pie lovers, Weinberger and company hitched an 11-foot-tall fiberglass apple to the back of their truck for a tour through five New England cities. At each stop, they handed out thousands of free pies and pints of frozen yogurt. This public relations coup earned Weinberger coverage on the evening news and in local newspapers.

By the end of the first year, Top of the Tree was churning out 6,000 pies a week and was racking up about $1 million in annual sales, almost exactly in line with the business plan projections. First-year sales got an expected boost from Weinberger's appearance on the QVC home shopping network, where he sold 2,700 pies in less than two minutes. The following year, Top of the Tree tripled its sales, in part because the founder continued making monthly appearances on QVC.

Weinberger used some unusual methods to market his pies and raise funds for expansion. For example, he and his staff toured the United States in a refurbished school bus, serving up apple pie to potential customers. Not only was it an effective marketing tool, but the bus became a mobile fund-raiser for more capital. This and other imaginative methods helped Weinberger raise $1 million in additional capital, and he plans to raise more—without giving up control of his company. Looking ahead, the entrepreneur is working on more dynamic strategies to achieve his goal of reaching $20 million in pie sales within the next few years.[71]

Critical Thinking Questions

1. Which entrepreneurial success factors seem to have contributed to Gordon Weinberger's achievement in founding and growing Top of the Tree into a thriving business?

2. Some business owners choose to expand by franchising. What issues should Weinberger consider before making a decision about franchising Top of the Tree?

3. As a potential investor, what questions would you ask Weinberger before deciding whether to invest in his company?

■ LEARN MORE ONLINE

Gordon Weinberger's Web site is an integral part of his plan to woo consumers and inform potential investors about the company. Point your browser to Top of the Tree's homepage http://www.gordonpies.com and click on the mission, the pie bus, and other features that describe the latest company doings. Why would Weinberger post his mission statement on this site? Why would Weinberger choose not to post sales and profit results on this site?

and (12) explain how investors will cash out on their investment.

5. **List five things you should know before starting a business.**

Before starting a business, know what you want to accomplish, how to find the money you need, how to

register and insure your business, where to go for help, and who your customers are and how to reach them.

6. **List three ways of getting into business for yourself.**

You can start a new company from scratch, you can buy a going concern, or you can invest in a franchise.

Key Terms

business plan (87)
franchise (92)
franchisee (92)
franchisor (92)

high-growth ventures (80)
incubators (91)
lifestyle businesses (80)
outsourcing (82)

small business (80)
start-up companies (91)
venture capitalists (96)

Test Your Knowledge

QUESTIONS FOR REVIEW

1. What is the difference between an intrapreneur and an entrepreneur?
2. What distinguishes a winning business plan from unsuccessful ones?
3. How do SCORE volunteers assist small businesses?
4. What is a business incubator?
5. What are the pros and cons of owning a franchise?

QUESTIONS FOR ANALYSIS

6. Why is writing a business plan an important step in starting a new business?
7. Why is it important to establish a time limit for a new business to generate a profit?
8. Why is it important to identify critical risks and problems in a business plan?
9. How is technology leveling the playing field between big and small companies?
10. You're thinking about starting your own hotdog and burger stand. You've got the perfect site in mind, and you've analyzed the industry and all the important statistics. It looks as if all systems are go. Uncle Pete is even going to back you on this one. You really understand the

fast-food market. In fact, you've become a regular at a competitor's operation (down the road) for over a month. The owner thinks you're his best customer. He even wants to name a sandwich creation after you. But you're not there because you love Frannie's fancy fries. No, you're actually spying. You're learning everything you can about the competition so you can outsmart them. Is this behavior ethical? Explain your answer.

QUESTIONS FOR APPLICATION

11. Briefly discuss an incident in your life when you learned from failure.
12. If you were starting a new business, how would you go about finding a mentor or an adviser?
13. Entrepreneurs are one of the five factors of production as discussed in Chapter 1. Review that material plus Exhibit 1.1 (Rags to Riches; see page 5), and explain why entrepreneurs are an important factor for economic success.
14. Pick a local small business or franchise that you visit frequently and discuss whether that business competes on price, speed, innovation, convenience, quality, or any combination of those factors. Be sure to provide some examples.

Practice Your Knowledge

SHARPENING YOUR COMMUNICATION SKILLS

One of the most important things in communicating effectively is to identify your primary audience and adapt your message to your audience's needs. This is true even for business plans. One of

the primary reasons for writing a business plan is to obtain financing. With that in mind, what do you think are the most important things the audience will want to know? How can you convince them that the information you are providing is accurate?

What should you assume the audience knows about your specific business or industry?

HANDLING DIFFICULT SITUATIONS ON THE JOB: DECIDING TO MOVE FROM A LARGE TO A SMALL BUSINESS

Your brother, Ruben N. Rodriguez Jr., started the family-owned Los Amigos Tortilla Manufacturing, Inc., in 1969 with only $12,000. While Los Amigos developed, you were able to help support the family with your income from your job at IBM. Today, the Atlanta-based tortilla business enjoys annual sales of about $4.5 million—and its prospects look bright.

Ruben has asked you to leave your position as head of marketing for IBM's Latin American Division to join the family business. Before answering, you conduct some research into the matter. You find that Hispanic-owned businesses have outstripped U.S. business growth in general. You know that many Hispanic corporate executives are leaving big companies and starting their own businesses. Now you're excited about becoming part of this amazing trend, not only because of the profit potential but also because you love your family and want to help your brother expand the company. Maybe someday your children will join the business as well.

Still, resigning from a key position at IBM is a major step. Are you ready to give up the responsibilities and respect that come with your corporate position? On the other hand, can you disappoint your brother and your entire family when they are asking for your help?[72]

1. What are some of the advantages you see in moving from IBM, a giant corporation, to Los Amigos Tortilla Manufacturing? What are some of the disadvantages?

2. How do you think your IBM experience might help you address the problems of managing small-business growth in the family business?

3. What kinds of questions should you ask your brother before making your final decision? What kinds of questions should you ask yourself?

BUILDING YOUR TEAM SKILLS

The ten questions shown in Exhibit 4.4 cover major legal issues you should explore before plunking down money for a franchise. In addition, however, there are many more questions you should ask in the process of deciding whether to buy a particular franchise.

With your team, think about how to investigate the possibility of buying a 7-Eleven convenience store franchise. Franchisees operate roughly 3,000 7-Eleven stores in the Midwest, in the Northeast, and on the West Coast. If you or your teammates have shopped in a 7-Eleven store or have seen 7-Eleven advertising, you may already know something about this company. Now is your chance to dig deeper and find out whether buying a 7-Eleven franchise might make sense for you.

First, brainstorm with your team to draw up a list of sources (such as printed sources, Internet sources, and any other suitable sources) where you can locate basic background information about the franchisor. Also list at least two sources you might consult for detailed information about buying and operating a 7-Eleven franchise. Next, generate a list of at least ten questions any interested buyer should ask about this potential business opportunity.

Choose a spokesperson to present your team's ideas to the class. After all the teams have reported, hold a class discussion to analyze the lists of questions generated by all the teams. Which questions were on most teams' lists? Why do you think those questions are so important? Can your class think of any additional questions that were not on any teams' lists but seem important?

Expand Your Knowledge

EXPLORING CAREER OPPORTUNITIES

Would you like to own and operate your own business? Whether you plan to start a new business from scratch or buy an existing business or a franchise, you will need certain characteristics to be successful. Start your journey into the personal side of entrepreneurship by rereading this chapter's section on characteristics of entrepreneurs and studying Exhibit 4.2. Now you are ready to delve deeper into the career opportunities of owning and running a small business.

1. Which of the entrepreneurial characteristics mentioned in the chapter and in Exhibit 4.2 describe you? Which of those characteristics can you develop more fully in advance of running your own business?

2. Using library sources, find a self-test on entrepreneurial qualities or use the entrepreneurial test at the Web site http://www.onlinewbc.org/docs/starting/test.html. Analyze the test's questions. Which of the characteristics discussed in this chapter are mentioned or suggested by the questions included in the test?

3. Answer all the questions in the self-test you have selected. Which questions seem the most critical for entrepreneurial success? How did you score on this self-test—and on the questions you think are most critical? Before you go into business for yourself, which characteristics will you need to work on?

DEVELOPING YOUR RESEARCH SKILLS

A good way to find out more about the personal and professional challenges of entrepreneurship is to talk with small-business owners. Make an appointment with a franchise owner or a small-business owner in your area to conduct a brief informational interview. In preparation for a brief report to the class, summarize the answers you received to each question and explain how this interview affected your view of entrepreneurship.

1. How and why did this small-business or franchise owner decide to become an entrepreneur? What did this person do before starting or buying a small business?

2. What does this entrepreneur think are the advantages and disadvantages of owning and running a small business?

3. What advice does this entrepreneur have for people who are considering whether to go into business for themselves?

SEE IT ON THE WEB EXERCISES
Increase Your Chances for Success, page 87

Many Web sites publish answers to their most frequently asked questions (FAQs). Check out the Biz FAQs under the Contents section of the Small Business Advisor at http://www.isquare.com to find the answers to these questions.

1. If you are a sole proprietor without employees, do you need to get a federal identification number from the IRS?

2. What is DBA?

3. Where can you find out the minimum hourly wage for your state? Why is this information important to small-business owners?

Get Smart, page 93

Buying a franchise is sometimes easier than starting from scratch—provided of course, that you understand what you're getting into. Use this Web site to help in your investigation. Go to Smartbiz http://www.smartbiz.com, click on the Browse SBS icon, highlight the category Franchising, and click Go To Selected Topic.

1. Find the Checklist for Evaluating Your Suitability as a Franchisee. Explain why the following items appear on this checklist: (a) Are you prepared to give up some independence of action in exchange for the advantages the franchise offers you? (b) Is it possible for either you or your spouse to become employed in the type of business you seek to buy before any purchase?

2. Find the Checklist of Information to Secure from a Franchisor. Why is it important to know whether you will have the right of first refusal to adjacent areas?

3. Visit a related Web site, Fran Info, by entering the following URL: http:\\www.franinfo.com. Take Self Test #1 to determine whether you are suited to become a franchise owner.

Start a Small Business, page 98

Starting a new business or buying an existing one can be an overwhelming process. But you can increase your chances for success if you do your research and plan ahead. Go to the SBA Web site at http://www.sba.gov. Click on Starting and explore the site's wealth of information for small business owners.

1. Click on Success Series and take the quiz for success. After you've worked through the entire quiz, go back and add up your points. Then compare your total with the Success Quotient table to see how you compare with some of California's most successful business people.

2. Go back to the SBA and click on the Startup Kit. Then click on Ask Yourself: Is Entrepreneurship for You? Answer the questions. Would you classify yourself as an entrepreneur? Why or why not?

3. Now click on Business Plans (left side of screen) and review the SBA Business Plan Outline. What information should you include in a business plan when describing your business or products? What information should you provide about your competitors? What questions should you answer about your management team?

5

SELECTING THE PROPER FORM OF BUSINESS OWNERSHIP AND EXPLORING MERGERS, CONSOLIDATIONS, AND ACQUISITIONS

LEARNING OBJECTIVES

After studying this chapter, you will be able to

1 Discuss the three basic forms of business ownership

2 List five advantages and four disadvantages of forming a sole proprietorship

3 Explain the differences between common and preferred stock from a shareholder's perspective

4 Delineate the three groups that govern a corporation and describe the role of each

5 Cite four advantages and three disadvantages of corporations

6 List six main synergies companies hope to achieve by combining their operations

FACING BUSINESS CHALLENGES AT KINKO'S

Restructuring the Partnerships to Duplicate Success

Paul Orfalea knew he would run a big company someday. He just never envisioned Kinko's as that dream. At 22, Orfalea borrowed enough money to open a copying service near the University of California, Santa Barbara. The store was so small that he had to wheel the single copier onto the sidewalk to make room for customers. Nevertheless, it serviced the needs of local college students.

By 1995 (some 25 years later), Kinko's—named after Orfalea's reddish, curly hair—had grown into a chain of 815 stores operating in five countries. But Kinko's wasn't managed as a single entity. Instead, the business consisted of 130 separate partnerships, each operating groups of stores. Even though Orfalea retained a majority interest in each partnership, the partners were free to operate their stores as they saw fit. As a result, not all Kinko's were the same. And that was a problem. Some reinvested their earnings in high-tech equipment; others cashed in their profits. This meant that traveling customers would find color copiers and high-speed Internet access at spruced-up outlets in one city and dilapidated storefronts with little more than black-and-white copy machines in another.

Kinko's ad hoc management structure was hobbling its growth. Orfalea knew that to succeed in a high-tech marketplace, all Kinko's stores would have to look alike and offer comparable services. Moreover, with more and more people working at home, in cars, in airports, or in other remote locations, the stores would have to invest in expensive equipment such as digital printers, high-speed copiers, fast Internet connections, and even video conferencing equipment to service the growing needs of these virtual workers. Such services, of course, would require lots of money and a shift in focus for many Kinko's partners.

Seeking financial acumen and managerial expertise, Orfalea selected private investors Clayton, Dublier & Rice (CD&R) in 1997 to help turn things around. Orfalea sold one-third of his partnership interests to the leveraged-buyout firm for $220 million. Meanwhile, CD&R organized a massive "roll-up" whereby individual partnerships swapped their interests for shares of stock in the new private Kinko's corporation. This structure allowed CD&R to centralize all management functions.

Now CD&R's challenge was to harness, not destroy, Kinko's entrepreneurial culture—the engine of its success. But how? What programs could management implement to keep the new private shareholders motivated? What new services could they offer to attract the growing customer base of business travelers and home-office workers? How could they convince Kinko's 23,000 co-workers at 900 branches worldwide that changing to a corporate structure would provide the operating efficiencies and funds the shops would need to survive and thrive?[1]

■ CHOOSING A FORM OF BUSINESS OWNERSHIP

As Paul Orfalea knows, one of the most fundamental decisions you must make when starting a business is selecting a form of business ownership. This decision can be complex and have far-reaching consequences for your business. Furthermore, as your business grows, chances are you may change the original form you selected, as Orfalea did.

The three most common forms of business ownership are sole proprietorship, partnership, and corporation. Each form has its own characteristic internal structure, legal status, size, and fields to which it is best suited. Each has key advantages and disadvantages for the owners, and each offers employees a distinctive working environment with its own risks and rewards. Exhibit 5.1 contrasts the characteristics of the three forms of business ownership.

Sole Proprietorships

A **sole proprietorship** is a business owned by one person (although it may have many employees), and it is the easiest and least expensive form of business to start. Many farms, retail establishments, and small service businesses are sole proprietorships, as are many home-based businesses (such as caterers, consultants, and computer programmers).

Advantages of Sole Proprietorships   A sole proprietorship has many advantages. One is ease of establishment. All you have to do to launch a sole proprietorship is to obtain necessary licenses, start a checking account for the business, and open your doors. Another advantage is the satisfaction of working for yourself. As a sole proprietor, you can make your own decisions, such as which hours to work, whom to hire, what prices to charge, whether to expand, and whether to shut down. Best of all, you can keep all the after-tax profits, and profits are taxed at individual income tax rates not at the higher corporate rates.

As a sole proprietor, you also have the advantage of privacy; you do not have to reveal your performance or plans to anyone. Although you may need to provide financial information to a banker if you need a loan, and you must provide certain financial information when you file tax returns, you do not have to prepare any reports for outsiders as you would if the company were a public corporation.

Disadvantages of Sole Proprietorships   One major drawback of a sole proprietorship is the proprietor's **unlimited liability.** From a legal standpoint, the owner and the business are one and the same. Any legal damages or debts incurred by the business are the owner's responsibility. As a sole proprietor, you might have to sell personal assets, such as your home, to satisfy a business debt. And if someone sues you over a business matter, you might lose everything you own if you do not have the proper types and amount of business insurance (see Component Chapter B).

In some cases, the sole proprietor's independence can also be a drawback because it means that the business depends on the talents and managerial skills of one person. If problems crop up, the sole proprietor may not recognize them or may be too proud to seek help, especially given the high cost of hiring experienced managers and professional consultants. Other disadvantages include the difficulty of a single-person operation to obtain large sums of capital and the limited life of a sole proprietorship. Although some sole proprietors pass their business on to their heirs as part of their estate, the owner's death may mean the demise of the business. And even if the business does transfer to an heir, the founder's unique skills may have been crucial to the successful operation of the business.

LEARNING OBJECTIVE 1
Discuss the three basic forms of business ownership

sole proprietorship
Business owned by a single individual

LEARNING OBJECTIVE 2
List five advantages and four disadvantages of forming a sole proprietorship

unlimited liability
Legal condition under which any damages or debts attributable to the business can also be attached to the owner because the two have no separate legal existence

CORPORATE STRUCTURE	OWNERSHIP RULES AND CONTROL	TAX TREATMENT	RISK OF LOSSES	EASE OF ESTABLISHMENT AND TERMINATION
Sole proprietorship	One owner has complete control.	Profits and losses flow directly to the owners and are taxed at individual rates.	Owner has unlimited personal liability for business debts.	Easy to set up but leaves owner's personal finances at risk. Owner must generally sell the business to get his or her investment out.
General partnership	Two or more owners; each partner is entitled to equal control unless agreement specifies otherwise.	Profits and losses flow directly to the partners and are taxed at individual rates. Partners share income and losses equally unless the partnership agreement specifies otherwise.	Personal assets of any operating partner are at risk from business creditors.	Easy to set up but requires written partnership agreement. Partners must generally sell their share in the business to recoup their investment.
Limited partnership	Two or more owners; the general partner controls the business; limited partners don't participate in the management.	Same as for general partnership.	Limited partners are liable only for the amount of their investment.	Same as for general partnership.
Corporation	Unlimited number of shareholders; no limits on stock classes or voting arrangements. Ownership and management of the business are separate. Shareholders in public corporations are not involved in daily management decisions; in private or closely held corporations, owners are more likely to participate in managing the business.	Profits and losses are taxed at corporate rates. Profits are taxed again at individual rates when they are distributed to the investors as dividends.	Investors' liability is limited to the amount of their investment.	Expense and complexity of incorporation vary from state to state; can be costly from a tax perspective. In a public corporation, shareholders may trade their shares on the open market; in a private corporation, shareholders must find a buyer for their shares to recoup their investment.

EXHIBIT 5•1

CHARACTERISTICS OF THE FORMS OF BUSINESS OWNERSHIP

The "best" form of ownership depends on the objectives of the people involved in the business.

Partnerships

If starting a business on your own seems a little intimidating, you might decide to share the risks and rewards of going into business with a partner. In that case, you would form a **partnership**—a legal association of two or more people as co-owners of a business for profit. You and your partners would share the profits and losses of the business and perhaps the management responsibilities. Your partnership might remain a small, two-person operation; it might have multiple partners as Kinko's did; or it might grow into an international

partnership
Unincorporated business owned and operated by two or more persons under a voluntary legal association

business with 1,000 partners, 50,000 employees, and operations on six continents like Andersen Consulting.[2]

Partnerships are of two basic types. In a **general partnership,** all partners are considered equal by law, and all are liable for the business's debts. In a **limited partnership,** one or more people act as general partners who run the business, while the remaining partners are passive investors (that is, they are not involved in managing the business). These partners are called limited partners because their liability (the amount of money they can lose) is limited to the amount of their capital contribution.

general partnership
Partnership in which all partners have the right to participate as co-owners and are individually liable for the business's debts

limited partnership
Partnership composed of one or more general partners and one or more partners whose liability is usually limited to the amount of their capital investment

Advantages of Partnerships   Proprietorships and partnerships have some of the same advantages. Like proprietorships, partnerships are easy to form, although it's always wise to get a lawyer's advice on the partnership agreement—the legal document that spells out the partners' rights and responsibilities. A key element of this document is the buy/sell agreement, which defines what will happen if one of the partners dies. Partnerships also provide the same tax advantages as proprietorships, because profits are taxed at individual income-tax rates rather than at corporate rates.

However, in a couple of respects, partnerships are superior to sole proprietorships, largely because there's strength in numbers. When you have several people putting up their money, you can start a more ambitious enterprise. In addition, the diversity of skills that good partners bring to an organization leads to innovation in products, services, and processes, which improves your chances of success.[3] As a partner, you may also have better luck than a sole proprietor in obtaining financing, because you and your partners are all legally responsible for paying off the debts of the group. Finally, by forming a partnership you increase the chances that the organization will endure, because new partners can be drawn into the business to replace those who die or retire. For example, even though the original partners of the accounting firm KPMG Peat Marwick (founded in 1897) died many years ago, the company continues. Provisions for handling the departure and addition of partners are usually covered in the partnership agreement.

Disadvantages of Partnerships   A fundamental drawback of a general partnership arrangement is the unlimited liability of the active partners. If one of your partners makes a serious business or professional mistake and is sued by a disgruntled client, you are financially accountable. At the same time, you are responsible for any debts incurred by the partnership. Even though malpractice insurance or business-risk insurance offers some financial protection, you pay a premium for your peace of mind.

Another disadvantage of partnerships is the potential for interpersonal problems. Difficulties often arise because each partner wants to be responsible for managing the organization. Electing a managing partner to lead the organization may diminish the conflicts, but disagreements are still likely to arise. Moreover, the partnership may have to face the question of what to do with unproductive partners. And if a partner wants to leave the firm, conflicts can arise over claims on the firm's profits and on capital the partner invested. If the partner goes to work for a competitor, the other partners will be concerned that she will take proprietary information with her. As a result, increasing numbers of partnerships are requiring their partners to sign covenants that make it difficult for them to join competitors.[4] Finally, in the ranks of the aspiring partners, competition is often fierce. The junior employees are vying for a limited number of partnership slots, and they view each other as rivals. This situation may lead to political maneuvering or may create a pressure-cooker environment in which everyone is working 80-hour weeks in hopes of looking good.

Tom and Kate Chappell are partners in their business, Tom's of Maine, a manufacturer of all-natural health and beauty products.

Corporations

A **corporation** is a legal entity with the power to own property and conduct business. Unlike the case with sole proprietorships and partnerships, a corporation's legal status and obligations exist independently of its owners. The modern corporation evolved in the nineteenth century when large sums of capital were needed to build railroads, coal mines, and steel mills. Such endeavors required so much money that no single individual or group of partners could hope to raise it all. The solution was to sell shares in the business to numerous investors, who would get a cut of the profits in exchange for their money. These investors got a chance to vote on certain issues that might affect the value of their investment, but they were not involved in managing day-to-day operations. The investors were protected from the risks associated with such large undertakings by having their liability limited to the amount of their investment.

It was a good solution, and the corporation quickly became a vital force in the nation's economy. As rules and regulations developed to define what corporations could and could not do, corporations acquired the legal attributes of people. Like you, a corporation can receive, own, and transfer property, make contracts, sue and be sued.

The relationship between a corporation and its **shareholders,** or owners, is a source of enormous strength. Because ownership and management are separate, the owners may get rid of the managers (in theory, at least) if the owners vote to do so. Conversely, because shares of the company, known as **stock** and evidenced by a **stock certificate,** may be bequeathed or sold to someone else, the company's ownership may change drastically over time while the company and its management remain intact (as long as the company is economically sound). The corporation's unlimited life span, combined with its ability to raise capital, gives it the potential for significant growth, which is often instrumental in achieving economies of scale.

Common versus Preferred Stock   Most stock issued by corporations is **common stock,** securities that represent an ownership interest in the corporation. Owners of common stock get to elect the company's board of directors in addition to voting on major policies that will affect ownership—such as mergers, acquisitions, and takeovers. Besides conferring voting privileges, common stock frequently pays **dividends,** payments to shareholders from the company's profits, and the market value of common stock rises and falls in value along with the success and failure of the company. So if shareholders sell their stock in good times for more than they paid for it, they stand to pocket a handsome gain.

In contrast, **preferred stock** does not usually carry voting rights. It does, however, give stockholders the right of first claim on the corporation's assets (in the form of dividends) after all the company's debts have been paid. This right is especially important if the company ever goes out of business. Furthermore, because preferred stockholders do not share directly in the success (or failure) of a business, dividends paid on this class of stock tend to be higher than those paid on common stock. In other words, preferred stock pays more dependable dividends than common stock, but common stock typically gives the shareholder a greater say in how the company is run and a better chance to profit from the company's success.

Dividends   After a company has paid all expenses and taxes out of revenues, its board of directors can pay a dividend. There is no law that requires them to do so, however. The decision is up to the board, who may decide—for good reasons—to omit the dividend or keep it to a minimum.

In the case of a small, young company, for instance, the best course is usually to put all the profits back into the business. This practice enables the company to grow without

corporation
Legally chartered enterprise having most of the legal rights of a person, including the right to conduct business, to own and sell property, to borrow money, and to sue or be sued; owners of the corporation enjoy limited liability

shareholders
Owners of a corporation

stock
Shares of ownership in a corporation

stock certificate
Document that proves stock ownership

common stock
Shares whose owners have voting rights and have the last claim on distributed profits and assets

dividends
Distributions of corporate assets to shareholders in the form of cash or other assets

preferred stock
Shares that give their owners first claim on a company's dividends and assets after all debts have been paid and whose owners do not have voting rights

LEARNING OBJECTIVE 3
Explain the differences between common and preferred stock from a shareholder's perspective

using expensive outside financing. In the long run, the shareholders stand to benefit more from the growth of the company and the resulting increase in the value of their stock than they do solely from the dividend.

Sometimes, large, well-established companies cut or omit dividends if profits decline. The company hangs on to its cash in order to cover operating expenses. Unfortunately, shareholders not only lose out on their dividends in such situations but frequently lose out on the value of the stock as well—because when a big company cuts its dividend, it sends a message to investors that there may be financial problems, which causes the stock price to fall, at least temporarily.

Dividends may be paid in cash, but rapidly growing companies often issue dividends in the form of additional company stock. By doing so, they conserve the firm's cash for capital investments, research and development, and similar types of expenditures. Another option for increasing shareholder value is to repurchase the outstanding common stock. This option reduces the amount of issued stock and increases the value of each share because fewer shares now have a piece of the same company value.

Public versus Private Corporations   Corporations have evolved into various types. The first variation is whether a company is public or private. The stock of a **public corporation** is held by and available for sale to the general public. Shares of Amazon.com, E*Trade, and Boeing, for example, are sold to anyone who is willing to pay the market price for them; they are said to be *publicly traded.* Whenever the stock of a closely held corporation is offered to the public for the first time, the company is said to be *going public,* and the initial shares sold are the company's *initial public offering,* or IPO. (Consult Part VI of the *E-Business in Action* online supplement at http://www.prenhall.com/ebusinessinaction for a detailed discussion of how e-businesses raise money and the IPO process.)

By contrast, the stock of a **private corporation** such as Kinko's is held by only a few individuals or companies and is *not publicly traded.* By withholding their stock from public sale, the owners retain complete control over their operations and protect their businesses from unwelcome takeover attempts. Such famous companies as Hallmark and Hyatt Hotels have opted to remain private corporations (also referred to as *closed corporations* or *closely held companies*). These companies finance their operating costs and growth from either company earnings or other sources, such as bank loans.

Advantages and Disadvantages of Going Public   Among the advantages of going public are increased liquidity (there is now a public market for your shares), voluntary dividend payments (unlike creditors, stockholders do not have to be repaid at a fixed rate or time), and enhanced visibility. In addition, it establishes an independent market value for the company. Moreover, having a publicly traded stock gives companies flexibility to use such stock to acquire other firms. This was one of the primary reasons UPS decided to sell 10 percent of its stock to the public in 1999, after nearly a century of remaining a privately held organization.[5]

Nevertheless, selling your stock to the public has distinct disadvantages: (1) the cost of going public is high (ranging from $50,000 to $500,000), and the filing requirements with the SEC (Securities and Exchange Commission) are burdensome; (2) public ownership does little good unless your business has sufficient investor awareness and appeal; (3) you lose ownership control; (4) management must be ready to handle the administrative and legal demands of widespread public ownership; and (5) nothing guarantees that the public will buy the shares at the initial offering price. Keep in mind that an IPO is one of the most difficult transactions that a business can undertake. Going public requires advance planning—sometimes as long as five years before the target date. Furthermore, IPO candidates

public corporation
Corporation that actively sells stock on the open market

private corporation
Company owned by private individuals or companies

Hyatt's owners, the Pritzker family, have opted to retain control of their enterprise because they appreciate the long-term value of doing so. That status also has a profound effect on the way Hyatt runs its 190 hotels and resorts worldwide. Public companies, which have an eye trained on the stock price, tend to overlook the long-term effects of decisions in favor of short-term gains. But Hyatt general managers have the freedom from concern about quarterly earning reports and stock prices. This gives them a certain entrepreneurial attitude that other hotel managers might not enjoy.

must have a history of solid and sustained growth, strong earning records, three to five years of audited financial reports, and solid management (including a strong board of directors).[6]

Direct Public Offerings   Because of the high costs and complexity of an IPO, when Spring Street Brewing decided to offer its stock to the public for the first time, the company did not use traditional investment bankers or venture capitalists to market its stock. Instead, the company sold its stock directly to the public—a practice known as a *direct public offering,* or DPO.[7] The number of DPOs is steadily growing, thanks to the Internet, and DPOs are expected to become an increasingly popular funding option. Still, reaching out directly to investors on the Internet will not be as easy for others as it was for Spring Street Brewing, as the company benefited from unusually high levels of publicity because it was the first Internet DPO.[8]

Although DPOs provide businesses with fresh capital for expansion at less than half the cost of an IPO, most companies still go the traditional IPO route. One reason is that DPO shares are not traded on public security exchanges, making it difficult for shareholders to find subsequent buyers for their shares. Another is that even if a company chooses to go the DPO route, it must still follow rules and regulations for selling securities privately. For example, Rule 504 of Regulation D of the Securities and Exchange Commission (also known as "504 offerings" or "Regulation D" offerings) allows companies to raise up to $1 million every 12 months by selling stock, provided they register the securities with the state. Regulation A extends the size of the offering to $5 million but requires a registration with the Small Business Office of the SEC.[9]

Special Types of Corporations   Certain types of corporations enjoy special privileges provided they adhere to strict guidelines and rules. One type of corporation, known as the **S corporation** (or subchapter S corporation), is a cross between a partnership and a corporation. S corporations can be attractive to business owners who plan to sell stock to no more than 75 investors; the owners receive the tax advantages of a partnership while they raise money through the sale of stock. In addition, income and tax deductions from the business flow directly to the owners, who are taxed at individual income-tax rates, just as they are in a partnership. Moreover, the shareholders in an S corporation, like the shareholders in a regular corporation, have limited liability.

Limited liability companies (LLCs) are another special type of corporation. These flexible business entities combine the tax advantages of a partnership with the personal liability protection of a corporation. Furthermore, LLCs are not restricted in the number of shareholders they can have, and members' participation in management is not restricted as it is in limited partnerships. Members of an LLC normally adopt an operating agreement (similar to a partnership agreement) to govern the entity's operation and management. These agreements generally are flexible and permit owners to structure the allocation of income and losses any way they desire, so long as certain tax rules are followed. In addition, the agreements can be designed to meet the special needs of owners, such as special voting rights, management controls, and buy-out options. The only limit to what can be done is the owners' imagination.[10]

Some corporations are not independent entities; that is, they are owned by a single entity. **Subsidiary corporations,** for instance, are partially or wholly owned by another corporation, known as a **parent company,** which supervises the operations of the subsidiary. A **holding company** is a special type of parent company that owns other companies for investment reasons and usually exercises little operating control over those subsidiaries.

Corporations can also be classified according to where they do business. An *alien corporation* operates in the United States but is incorporated in another country. A *foreign*

S corporation
Corporations with no more than 75 shareholders that may be taxed as a partnership; also known as a subchapter S corporation

limited liability companies (LLCs)
Organizations that combine the benefits of S corporations and limited partnerships without the drawbacks of either

subsidiary corporations
Corporations whose stock is owned entirely or almost entirely by another corporation

parent company
Company that owns most, or all, of another company's stock and that takes an active part in managing that other company

holding company
Company that owns most, or all, of another company's stock but that does not actively participate in the management of that other company

Focus on E-Business

IS THE END OF THE BEGINNING NEAR?

It's a brand new e-world. The Internet is creating a new generation of entrepreneurial firms that are using a window of opportunity to create value for customers and wealth for investors before the big, old, slow-moving companies get their acts together. New e-commerce companies are springing up like dandelions in the summer. We've never seen such an explosion of new companies before. But other generations have. And if history repeats itself, the Internet economy may soon change its course.

From 1884 to 1903, an estimated 20,000 telephone companies were started in the United States. Now we're down to a few big baby bells. Between 1855 and 1861, the number of telegraph companies in the United States shrank by 88 percent from 50 companies to 6. In less then four years, the number of large electrical companies dwindled by 87 percent—from 15 to 2. And only three of the thousands of automobile startups survived. So, if the Internet follows the same course as those technological breakthroughs did, then today's 400 or so *public* Internet companies could eventually be reduced to under 50.

We have nearly 10,000 Internet companies too many, says one Silicon Valley venture capitalist. We already have 400 auction sites, 1,500 e-commerce shoe sites, 50 major beauty sites, and thousands of mom-and-pop operations selling vitamins and drugs online. How many do we really need? An Armageddon is going to happen once all these e-companies spend their huge advertising budgets and still come out broke. The Internet will not escape a shakeout of its own. At some point, there will be many losers, but only a few winners.

Of course, that carnage day may still be far ahead. But when it does happen, using the history of the railroads as a guide, the big winners may not even be the originators of the ideas. The pieces could very well be picked up by the people who stood on the sidelines in the first place—you know, those big, old, stupid companies that couldn't get their acts together. After all, Commodore Vanderbilt never built a railroad in his life. Instead, he bought badly run ones, restructured them, merged them into efficient operations, and managed them superbly.

QUESTIONS FOR CRITICAL THINKING

1. What advantages do small entrepreneurial firms have over big firms in the new world of e-commerce?

2. Why are experts predicting an eventual Internet shakeout?

---

corporation, sometimes called an *out-of-state corporation,* is incorporated in one state (frequently the state of Delaware, where incorporation laws are lenient) but does business in several other states where it is registered. And a *domestic corporation* does business only in the state where it is chartered (incorporated).

LEARNING OBJECTIVE 4
Delineate the three groups that govern a corporation and describe the role of each

Corporate Structure and Governance   Although a corporation's shareholders own the business, they are rarely involved in managing it, particularly if the corporation is publicly traded. Instead, the shareholders elect a board of directors to represent them, and the directors, in turn, select the corporation's top officers, who actually run the company.

Shareholders   Shareholders can be individuals, other companies, not-for-profit organizations, pension funds, and mutual funds. All shareholders who own voting shares are invited to an annual meeting to choose directors, select an independent accountant to audit the company's financial statements, and attend to other business. Those who cannot attend the annual meeting in person vote by **proxy,** signing and returning a slip of paper that authorizes management to vote on their behalf. Because shareholders elect the directors, in theory they are the ultimate governing body of the corporation. In practice, however, most individual shareholders in large corporations—where the shareholders may number in the millions—accept the recommendations of management.

Typically, the more shareholders a company has, the less tangible the influence each shareholder has on the corporation. However, some shareholders have more influence than others. In recent years, *institutional investors,* such as pension funds, insurance companies, mutual funds, and college endowment funds, have accumulated an increasing number of shares of stock in U.S. corporations. As a result, these large institutional investors are playing a more powerful role in governing the corporations in which they own substantial shares, especially with regard to the election of a company's board of directors.[11] Furthermore, at companies such as Avis and United Airlines, employees are major shareholders and so have a significant voice in how the company is run. For example, when United Airlines employees did not endorse management's decision to promote company president John Edwardson to the CEO position, Edwardson resigned.[12]

Board of Directors   Representing the shareholders, the **board of directors** is responsible for guiding corporate affairs and selecting corporate officers. The board has the power to vote on major management decisions, such as building a new factory, hiring a new president, or buying a new subsidiary. Depending on the size of the company, the board might have anywhere from 3 to 35 directors, although 15 to 25 is the typical range. In some corporations, several of the directors may be inside directors, people who are also employees of the company. Outside directors are often large shareholders, and many serve on the boards of several companies.

The board's actual involvement in running a corporation varies from one company to another. Some boards are strong and independent and serve as a check on the company's management. Others act as a "rubber stamp," simply approving management's recommendations. Assertive boards are becoming far more common these days, mainly because of pressure from institutional investors who want the value of their stock to increase. Today's directors are expected to be involved in corporate strategy, management succession, evaluation of executive performance, and other issues that are crucial to the company's success. To accomplish such involvement, many companies are seeking more outside directors who own large shares in the company. In addition, more companies are compensating directors with company stock instead of salaries and pension plans. In this way, the directors' interests are aligned with the interests of other shareholders.

Companies today are also seeking directors experienced in corporate management, such as chief executives of other firms. Evidence shows that companies in which directors own large amounts of stock and take an active role in guiding the company usually outperform those with more passive boards consisting of company insiders. The value of Time Warner's stock increased immediately when it announced that its two new board nominees were the chief executives of Hilton Hotels and United Airlines.[13] Companies around the world are also looking for foreign directors to bring international perspectives into the boardroom. In fact, a recent study found that about 20 percent of U.S. firms now have at least one non-U.S. citizen on their board.[14]

Officers   The center of power in a corporation often lies with the **chief executive officer,** or **CEO.** Together with the chief financial officer (CFO) and the chief operating officer (COO),

proxy
Document authorizing another person to vote on behalf of a shareholder in a corporation

board of directors
Group of people, elected by the shareholders, who have the ultimate authority in guiding the affairs of a corporation

chief executive officer (CEO)
Person appointed by a corporation's board of directors to carry out the board's policies and supervise the activities of the corporation

See It on the Web See It on the Web

THE DECLARATION OF DIRECTOR INDEPENDENCE

When CalPERS talks, corporations listen. The California Public Employees' Retirement System, the largest U.S. public pension system, wields considerable power because, as an institutional investor, it holds large blocks of shares in numerous corporations. Always pushing for better corporate management, CalPERS has drafted model governance principles about the selection and responsibilities of directors for the boards of U.S. and international corporations. Take a peek at the role CalPERS thinks independent directors should play in supervising corporate management.
http://www.calpers-governance.org/principles/

the CEO is responsible for establishing company policies, managing corporate direction, and making the big decisions that will affect the company's growth and competitive position. In Chapter 6, we'll discuss in detail the functions and roles of management. Keep in mind that the chief executive officer may also be the chairman of the board, the president of the corporation, or both.

LEARNING OBJECTIVE 5

Cite four advantages and three disadvantages of corporations

Advantages of Corporations No other form of business ownership can match the success of the corporation in bringing together money, resources, and talent; in accumulating assets; and in creating wealth. As it grows, a corporation gains from a diverse labor pool, greater financing options, expanded research-and-development capabilities, and economies of scale. The corporation has certain inherent qualities that make it the best vehicle for reaching those objectives. One such quality is limited liability. Although a corporate entity can assume tremendous liabilities, it is the corporation that is liable and not the private shareholders. Take Johannes Schwartlander, who ran his San Francisco marble and granite business as a sole proprietorship for seven years. When the company began to grow, Schwartlander decided to incorporate to protect himself. "When we had so many employees and started installing marble panels ten stories up, I realized that if five years later something fell down, I would be responsible," he says.[15] Incorporation also protects him from personal liability should his business go bankrupt.

liquidity
The level of ease with which an asset can be converted to cash

In addition to limited liability, corporations that sell stock to the general public have the advantage of **liquidity,** which means that investors can easily convert their stock into cash by selling it on the open market. This option makes buying stock in a corporation attractive to many investors. In contrast, liquidating the assets of a sole proprietorship or a partnership can be difficult.

Corporations are also often in a better position than proprietorships and partnerships to make long-term plans as a result of their unlimited life span and the funding available through the sale of stock. As they grow, corporations can benefit from the diverse talents and experience of a large pool of employees and managers. Moreover, large corporations are often able to finance projects internally.

Keep in mind that a company need not be large to incorporate. Most corporations, like most businesses, are relatively small, and most small corporations are privately held, which means that the company's stock is not traded publicly. The big ones, however, are *really* big. The 500 largest corporations in the United States, as listed by *Fortune* magazine, have combined sales of over $5.7 trillion. Wal-Mart stores alone employ 910,000 people, which is greater than the population of San Jose, California.[16]

FOLLOWING THE FORTUNES OF THE FORTUNE 500

Quick! Name the largest corporation in the United States, as measured by annual revenues. Give up? Just check *Fortune* magazine's yearly ranking of the 500 largest U.S. companies. For years, General Motors has topped the list with its $160 billion-plus in annual revenues, but Ford, Wal-Mart, General Electric, and other giants have also been strong contenders in recent years. The Fortune 500 not only ranks corporations by size but also offers brief company descriptions along with industry statistics and additional measures of corporate performance. You can search the list by ranking, by industry, by company name, or by CEO. And to help you identify the largest international corporations, there's a special Global 500 list as well.

http://www.pathfinder.com/fortune/fortune500/500list.html

Disadvantages of Corporations   Corporations are not without some disadvantages. For one thing, publicly owned companies are required by the government to follow certain rules and to publish information about their finances and operations. These reporting requirements increase the pressure on corporate managers to achieve short-term growth and earnings targets in order to satisfy shareholders and to attract potential investors. In addition, having to disclose financial information increases the company's vulnerability to competitors and to those who might want to take over control of the company against the wishes of the existing management.

The paperwork and costs associated with incorporation can also be burdensome, particularly if you plan to sell stock. The complexity varies from state to state, but regardless of where you live, it is wise to consult an attorney and an accountant before incorporating. In addition, individual shareholders must pay income taxes on their share of the company's profits received as dividends. Because dividend payments are not a deductible expense for corporate income-tax purposes, essentially owners are taxed twice, once at the corporate level and again at the individual level. By contrast, profits in a sole proprietorship or partnership are taxed only once, at the individual level.

UNDERSTANDING MERGERS, CONSOLIDATIONS, AND ACQUISITIONS

Companies have been combining in various configurations since the early days of business. Nevertheless, joining two companies is a complex process because it involves every aspect of both companies. For instance, executives have to agree on how the combination will be financed and how the power will be transferred and shared. Marketing departments often need to figure out how to blend advertising campaigns and sales forces. Data processing and information systems, which seldom mesh, must be joined together seamlessly. And companies must deal with layoffs, transfers, and changes in job titles and work assignments.

Two of the most popular forms of business combinations are mergers and consolidations. The difference between a merger and a consolidation is fairly technical, having to do with how the financial and legal transaction is structured. Basically, in a **merger,** one company buys another company, or parts of another company, and emerges as the

merger
Combination of two companies in which one company purchases the other and assumes control of its property and liabilities

HOW CISCO BOUGHT ITS WAY TO THE TOP

In an industry where buying companies for their technology is routine, Cisco Systems has turned that strategy into a successful way of life. Armed with over $12 billion in annual revenue, this San Jose supplier of computer networking equipment for the Internet and corporations knows how to spot a good company when it sees one. In fact, its masterly buying methods have spurred the company's success.

In the past six years, Cisco has spent $18.8 billion on 42 acquisitions and plans to make 10-15 new acquisitions each year. Why? Cisco recognizes that it can't build everything it needs to grow, so it swallows innovative start-up firms to enhance its high-tech arsenal. In doing so, it also obtains some highly talented people. Still, few companies can integrate acquired firms into their existing operation as smoothly as Cisco does. What's the company's secret?

According to Mike Volpi, vice president of business development, Cisco looks for five things in an acquisition candidate: "We look at a company's vision; its short-term success with customers; its long-term strategy; the chemistry of the people with ours; and its geographic proximity." Then there's one final test: "We pick companies that are old enough to have finished and tested their product, yet young enough to be privately held and flexible in their ways."

Even though Cisco leaves much of the acquired firm's infrastructure in place, it makes sure the acquired employees know who their new employer is. "I don't believe a merger of equals works," notes CEO John Chambers. "In a merger you can't blend resources and cultures—only one can survive." Which is why Cisco prefers to focus on smaller, start-up firms. These companies are easier to integrate. "You know exactly what everybody does," says Volpi. Big firms can result in duplicate functions and culture clashes. "Acquire a business that's too mature, and risk soars," Volpi explains. Moreover, figuring out how to integrate a company with existing customers, product flaws, and entrenched systems could take nine months—and that's a lifetime in the high-tech industry. After all, as Volpi puts it: "When you adopt a very young child, they become your kid pretty quickly. But if you adopt a 16-year old who is set in their ways, it's pretty hard to get them to be your son or daughter."

QUESTIONS FOR CRITICAL THINKING

1. When Cisco absorbs a company, it usually makes a no-layoffs pledge. Why would the company promise to keep the acquired firm's employees?
2. Why does Cisco prefer to buy start-up companies?

---

consolidation
Combination of two or more companies in which the old companies cease to exist and a new enterprise is created

acquisition
Form of business combination in which one company buys another company's voting stock

controlling corporation. The acquiring company also assumes all the debts and contractual obligations of the company it acquires, and the acquired company ceases to exist. A **consolidation** is similar to a merger except that an entirely new firm is created by two or more companies who pool their interests. In a consolidation, both the acquiring firm and the acquired firm terminate their previous legal existence and become part of the new firm. Thus, the distinction between the acquiring and the acquired firm is not important.

A third way that a company may acquire another firm is by purchasing that firm's voting stock. This transaction is generally referred to as an **acquisition** and is completed when the shareholders of the acquired firm tender their stock for either cash or shares of stock in the acquiring company. Keep in mind that the purpose and outcome of these three business combinations are basically the same, which is why you will often hear these terms used interchangeably.

Advantages of Mergers, Consolidations, and Acquisitions

Business combinations provide several financial and operational advantages. Combined entities hope to eliminate expenditures for redundant resources; increase their buying power as a result of their larger size; increase revenue by cross-selling products to each other's customers; increase market share by combining product lines to provide more comprehensive offerings; eliminate manufacturing overcapacity; and gain access to new expertise, systems, and teams of employees who already know how to work together.

LEARNING OBJECTIVE 6
List six main synergies companies hope to achieve by combining their operations

Often these advantages are grouped under umbrella terms such as *economies of scale, efficiencies,* or *synergies,* which generally mean that the benefits of working together will be greater than if each company continued to operate independently. For instance, when WorldCom and MCI merged, they expected to gain competitive advantages that were not available to either before the merger. Now, MCI World Com, one of the largest providers of Internet services in the world and the second largest long-distance telephone company in the United States, hopes to achieve even more economies of scale when it completes its $129 billion acquisition of Sprint.[17] Similarly, the 1998 merger of the American Stock Exchange (Amex) with the Nasdaq stock exchange promised to combine the best features of each while producing substantial cost savings in addition to a number of advantages for customers. Amex, for example, expected to gain technological expertise and cost efficiencies, while Nasdaq hoped to build market share in the lucrative stock options market.[18]

Trading experts say Nasdaq may choose to close the Amex's stock-trading floor in lower Manhattan to produce operating economies of scale now that the two exchanges have merged.

Disadvantages of Mergers, Consolidations, and Acquisitions

Despite these many advantages, studies of merged companies show that 65 to 85 percent of these deals fail to actually achieve promised efficiencies.[19] One such study even found that the profitability of acquired companies on average declined.[20] Furthermore, while some analysts equate "bigger" with success, others disagree. They quickly point to companies such as Honda, which at only a fraction of GM's size has consistently outperformed GM for the past 20 years. In addition, a recent study by Andersen Consulting found that, since 1995, small banks have consistently operated more efficiently per customer than their much larger competitors.[21] As one expert put it, if you combine two lumbering companies, you get one that runs worse, not better.[22]

One of the biggest obstacles that companies face when combining forces is *culture clash.* In Chapter 6 we will discuss how a company's culture is the way people in the organization do things. Culture clash occurs when two joining companies have different beliefs about what is really important, how to make decisions, how to supervise people, how to communicate, and so on. Experts note that in too many deals the acquiring company imposes its values and management systems on the acquired company without any regard to what worked well there. When Quaker Oats acquired Snapple, for example, it immediately dismantled Snapple's distribution system, a key factor in Snapple's success. Ultimately, Quaker Oats paid the price by discovering that if you destroy another company's systems, you often end up buying nothing.[24]

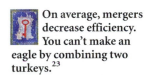

On average, mergers decrease efficiency. You can't make an eagle by combining two turkeys.[23]

People never fit together as easily as flowcharts.[25]

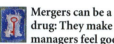
Under the best circumstances, power sharing is not a natural thing for corporate executives. Such arrangements have seldom worked in the past.[28]

Mergers can be a drug: They make managers feel good in the short term but ultimately sap the energy and creativity of the firm.[30]

trusts
Monopolistic arrangements established when one company buys a controlling share of the stock of competing companies in the same industry

horizontal mergers
Combinations of companies that are direct competitors in the same industry

vertical mergers
Combinations of companies that participate in different phases of the same industry (e.g., materials, production, distribution)

conglomerate mergers
Combinations of companies that are in unrelated businesses, designed to augment a company's growth and to diversify risk

Keep in mind that culture includes not only management style and practices but also the way people dress, how they communicate, or whether they punch a time clock. Recent studies have shown that underestimating the difficulties of merging two cultures was the major factor in failed mergers, and experts contend that the increasing number of worldwide mergers, consolidations, and acquisitions will make culture clash an even bigger challenge.[26] When Ford acquired Volvo, for example, Swedish car workers were nervous that they might lose their health club benefits and other perks that Swedish companies give to workers to compensate them for the high income taxes they pay the government.[27] Similarly, culture clash has been an issue at DaimlerChrysler. Since their 1998 merger, Chrysler's U.S. employees and Daimler-Benz's German employees have had to learn how to work together.

To minimize these obstacles, some merged entities such as Citigroup (formerly Citicorp and Travelers) and DaimlerChrysler are jointly running their operations by creating co-chairperson positions—giving equal power to the heads of both companies involved in the merger. Still, most experts note that even when top leaders agree to share power, the pact seldom lasts long.[29]

Besides cultural issues, critics argue that mergers create an immense burden of high-risk corporate debt and that they divert investment from productive assets. Furthermore, mergers tend to distract managers' attention from the company's day-to-day operations. Finally, even in friendly deals there are bound to be losers: executives whose careers come to a crashing halt, workers who are laid off through no fault of their own, communities that suddenly find themselves with empty factories because operations are consolidated elsewhere, and consumers who face higher prices when competition diminishes.

Types of Mergers

Mergers tend to happen in waves, in response to changes in the economy. One of the biggest waves of merger activity occurred between 1881 and 1911, when capitalists created giant monopolistic **trusts,** buying enough stock of competing companies in basic industries such as oil and steel to control the market. These trusts were **horizontal mergers,** or combinations of competing companies performing the same function. The purposes of a horizontal merger are to achieve the benefits of economies of scale and to fend off competition. The rise of a government antitrust movement and the dissolution of Standard Oil in 1911 marked the end of this wave.

A second great wave occurred in the boom decade of the 1920s. This era was marked by the emergence of **vertical mergers,** in which a company involved in one phase of an industry absorbs or joins a company involved in another phase of the same industry. The aim of a vertical merger is often to guarantee access to supplies or to markets. For example, until fairly recently, both Ford and General Motors owned the companies that supplied most of the parts for their cars.

A third wave of mergers occurred in the late 1960s and early 1970s, when corporations acquired strings of unrelated businesses, often in an attempt to moderate the risks of a volatile economy. These **conglomerate mergers** were designed to augment a company's growth and to diversify its risks. Theoretically, when one business was down, another would be up, thus creating a balanced performance picture for the company as a whole. At their peaks, some of these conglomerates had hundreds of companies. TLC Beatrice (formerly Beatrice Foods Company), for example, at one time owned companies as diverse as Tropicana (juice), Samsonite (luggage), Stiffle (lamps), and Eckrich (meats). Since the late 1960s, many of the superconglomerates have been dismantled or slimmed down to streamline operations, to build up capital for other endeavors, or to get rid of unprofitable subsidiaries.

In the 1980s, a wave of **leveraged buyouts (LBOs)** also occurred. In an LBO, one or more individuals purchase a company or a division of a company by using borrowed funds. The debt is expected to be repaid with funds generated by the company's operations and, often, by the sale of some of its assets. Unfortunately, in many cases, such as Denny's and Montgomery Ward, the enormous amount of debt sucked up cash that should have been used to run the company's operations, causing significant problems and, in cases such as Wards, bankruptcy.[31]

Also during the 1980s, some investors purchased large companies because they were actually worth more by the piece than by the whole. These purchasers, often referred to as "corporate raiders," would buy undervalued companies and quickly sell off divisions to realize a quick and handsome gain.[32] Consider Beatrice. In 1986 investors Kohlberg Kravis Roberts bought the giant conglomerate and shortly thereafter broke it into pieces by selling off the subsidiaries.[33]

Current Trends in Mergers, Consolidations, and Acquisitions

Beginning in the 1990s, a new wave of mergers, consolidations, and acquisitions began that were motivated by long-term strategies. Instead of using debt to take over and dismantle a company for a quick profit, corporate buyers used cash and stock to selectively acquire businesses to enhance their position in the marketplace.

This decade witnessed the return of horizontal mergers and consolidations in many industries among both large and small companies. More than 7,700 transactions with a combined value exceeding $1.8 trillion were announced in 1998. Nine of the top ten largest deals in history were also announced in 1998, and many observers expect this megamerger trend to continue.[34] Some even predict that mergers that looked like earthquakes in the past may look like mere tremors years from now.[35] Consider, for instance, the $160 billion merger of America Online (the world's biggest online company) and Time Warner (the world's biggest media company). This megadeal, announced only 10 days into the new millennium, will link AOL's twenty-some million subscribers and unmatched e-commerce capabilities with Time Warner's sprawling cache of world-class media, entertainment, news brands, and broadband delivery systems to produce the world's first fully-integrated media and communications company. Many industry analysts expect this deal to shock competitors into motion and fan an already heated merger mania.[36]

Part of the reason for this merger frenzy is the fierce global competition that has created an environment in which large domestic companies must vie with foreign competitors even in their home markets. Tough competitive conditions have also led the U.S. government to be more lenient about regulating the growth of companies. Rather than opposing any merger that might allow a company to develop a dominant position in the market, the Federal Trade Commission and the Anti-Trust Division of the Justice Department are seeking new ways to ensure that industries remain open to new competitors.

As Chapter 1 and Component Chapter A discuss, the relaxation of existing industry regulations is designed to make industries more competitive and to provide consumers with improved products and lower prices. But some think industry deregulation has backfired by spurring mass consolidation instead. Take the telecommunications industry, for example. Critics contend that the MCI WorldCom-Sprint merger is likely to transform the telecommunications infrastructure into a duopoly with WorldCom-Sprint and AT&T fighting a two-way battle.[37] Similarly, some see the 1999 consolidation of SBC and Ameritech as nothing more than a reassembly of the Ma Bell monopoly splintered by the Justice Department in 1984. As one naysayer put it: "First there were seven Baby Bells, then six, then five, and now four."[38] Moreover, Bell Atlantic's proposed merger with GTE, if approved, will reduce the number of Baby Bells to three, and they won't be babies.[39]

leveraged buyout (LBO)
Situation in which individuals or a group of investors purchase a company primarily with debt secured by the company's assets

See It on the Web See It on the Web

TRACKING THE URGE TO MERGE

New mergers, consolidations, and acquisitions are announced almost daily in the ever-changing world of business. To stay on top of the latest news about companies gobbling companies, check The Online Investor Web site. This site summarizes the major deals that have been announced in recent weeks, including the total value. When you want to dig even deeper, just click on the link to read the acquiring company's news release about the reasoning behind that deal. But remember that, as the site's disclaimer notes, not all business combinations go through. As is any engagement, the announcement is just the first formal step toward the altar—and anything can happen before companies say "I do."
http://www.investhelp.com/mergers.shtml

hostile takeover
Situation in which an outside party buys enough stock in a corporation to take control against the wishes of the board of directors and corporate officers

tender offer
Invitation made directly to shareholders by an outside party who wishes to buy a company's stock at a price above the current market price

The banking industry is also undergoing mass consolidation as a result of relaxed industry regulation. Since 1990 some 3,356 banks have been gobbled up by larger ones. Furthermore, the recent acquisition of Travelers by Citicorp (valued at $83 billion) spliced together a global bank, insurance company, brokerage firm, credit-card operation, and some 100 million customers in 100 countries.[40] As Chapter 15 will point out, the repeal of the Glass-Steagall Act paves the way for banking, securities, and insurance industries to expand into one another's businesses and sets the stage for another wave of consolidations.[41]

This megamerger trend is also occurring in the oil and automobile industries. The $81 billion marriage of Exxon and Mobil in 1999 created the world's largest oil company, whereas the $36 billion combination of Daimler-Benz and Chrysler in 1998 was the biggest acquisition of any U.S. company by a foreign buyer—and one that is destined to transform the way the auto industry operates worldwide. Some believe that by combining product and sales networks, DaimlerChrysler has set the pace for the global car wars to come. As one economist put it, "If you don't play the game as a global company, you're going to wind up a niche player."[42]

Merger, Consolidation, and Acquisition Defenses

About 95 percent of all business combinations are friendly deals, as opposed to **hostile takeovers,** where one party fights to gain control of a company against the wishes of the existing management.[43] Still, every corporation that sells stock to the general public is potentially vulnerable to takeover by any individual or company that buys enough shares to gain a controlling interest. Basically, a hostile takeover can be launched in one of two ways: by tender offer or by proxy fight.

In a **tender offer,** the raider offers to buy a certain number of shares of stock in the corporation at a specific price. The price offered is generally more than the current stock price so that shareholders are motivated to sell. The raider hopes to get enough shares to take control of the corporation and to replace the existing board of directors

Juergen Schrempp, left, and Robert Eaton show off official DaimlerChrysler NYSE stock certificates on the company's first day of business as a merged entity.

and management. In a **proxy fight,** the raider launches a public relations battle for shareholder votes, hoping to enlist enough votes to oust the board and management. Proxy fights sound easy enough, but they are tough to win. The insiders have certain advantages: They can get in touch with shareholders, and they can use money from the corporate treasury in their campaign.

proxy fight
Attempt to gain control of a takeover target by urging shareholders to vote for directors favored by the acquiring party

During the 1980s, when many takeovers were uninvited and even openly hostile, corporate boards and executives devised a number of schemes to defend themselves against unwanted takeovers:

- *The poison pill.* This plan, triggered by a takeover attempt, makes the company less valuable in some way to the potential raider; the idea is to discourage the takeover from actually happening. A good example is a special sale of newly issued stock to current stockholders at prices below the market value of the company's existing stock. Such action increases the number of shares the raider has to buy, making the takeover more expensive. Many shareholders believe that poison pills are bad for a company because they can entrench weak management and discourage takeover attempts that would improve company value.[44]

- *The golden parachute.* This method is designed to benefit a company's top executives by guaranteeing them generous compensation packages if they ever leave or are forced out after a takeover. These packages often total millions of dollars for each executive and therefore make the takeover much more expensive for the acquiring company. In this way, a golden parachute has an effect similar to that of a poison pill.

- *The shark repellent.* This tactic is more direct; it is simply a requirement that stockholders representing a large majority of shares approve of any takeover attempt. Of course, such a plan is viable only if the management team has the support of the majority of shareholders.

- *The white knight.* This tactic uses a friendly buyer to take over the company before a raider can. White knights usually agree to leave the current management team in place and to let the company continue to operate in an independent fashion. Starwood Lodging Trust, a large hotel investment firm, used this tactic to block the hostile takeover attempt of ITT by Hilton Hotels.[45]

Sometimes a group of investors is able to take a publicly traded company off the open market by purchasing all of the company's stock. This tactic is known as "taking the company private." Descendants of Levi Strauss, for example, borrowed $3 billion to buy back all the shares of Levi's stock so that the family could maintain control of the company.[46]

Companies sometimes go private to thwart unwanted takeovers. But this is a radical action. First of all, stockholders must be willing to sell, and second, buyers must have enough cash on hand to repurchase all the company's stock. Moreover, going private eliminates the firm's ability to raise future capital by selling authorized shares to the public; so it's not a move that many corporations make.

Summary of Learning Objectives

1. **Discuss the three basic forms of business ownership.**
   A sole proprietorship is a business owned by a single person. A partnership is an association of two or more people who share in the ownership of an enterprise. The dominant form of business is the corporation, a legally chartered entity having many of the same rights and duties as a person.

2. **List five advantages and four disadvantages of forming a sole proprietorship.**
   Sole proprietorships have five advantages: (1) They are easy to establish; (2) they provide the owner with control and independence; (3) the owner reaps all the profits; (4) income is taxed at individual rates; and (5) the company's plans and financial performance remain private. The four main disadvantages of a sole proprietorship are (1) the company's financial resources are usually limited; (2) management talent may be thin; (3) the owner is liable for the debts and damages incurred by the business; and (4) the business may cease when the owner dies.

3. **Explain the differences between common and preferred stock from a shareholder's perspective.**
   Common stockholders can vote and share in the company's profits (or losses) through dividends and adjustments in the market value of their stock. In contrast, preferred shareholders get a fixed return on their investment and a priority claim on assets after creditors, but they cannot vote.

4. **Delineate the three groups that govern a corporation and describe the role of each.**
   Shareholders are the basis of the corporate structure. They elect the board of directors, who in turn elect the officers of the corporation. The corporate officers carry out the policies and decisions of the board. In practice, the shareholders and board members have often followed the lead of the chief executive officer. However, board members are becoming increasingly active in corporate governance.

5. **Cite four advantages and three disadvantages of corporations.**
   Corporations have the power to raise large sums of capital; they offer the shareholders protection from liability; they provide liquidity for investors; and they have an unlimited life span. In exchange for these advantages, they pay large fees to incorporate; they pay higher taxes and are taxed on company profits distributed as dividends; and, if publicly owned, they must adhere to strict government reporting requirements.

6. **List six main synergies companies hope to achieve by combining their operations.**
   By combining their operations, companies hope to eliminate redundant costs, increase their buying power, increase their revenue, improve their market share, eliminate manufacturing overcapacity and gain access to new expertise and personnel.

Key Terms

acquisition (116)
board of directors (113)
chief executive officer (CEO) (113)
common stock (109)
conglomerate mergers (118)
consolidation (116)
corporation (109)
dividends (109)
general partnership (108)
holding company (111)
horizontal mergers (118)
hostile takeover (120)

leveraged buyout (LBO) (119)
limited liability companies (LLCs) (111)
limited partnership (108)
liquidity (114)
merger (115)
parent company (111)
partnership (107)
preferred stock (109)
private corporation (110)
proxy (113)
proxy fight (121)

public corporation (110)
S corporation (111)
shareholders (109)
sole proprietorship (106)
stock (109)
stock certificate (109)
subsidiary corporations (111)
tender offer (120)
trusts (118)
unlimited liability (106)
vertical mergers (118)

MEETING BUSINESS CHALLENGES AT KINKO'S

Plunking down $220 million in exchange for a 33 percent share of Kinko's, Clayton, Dublier & Rice rolled the 130 individual partnerships into a single privately held corporation and centralized all management functions. The firm replaced Kinko's founder and chief executive, Paul Orfalea, with Joseph Hardin Jr., the former CEO of Wal-Mart's Sam's Club discount supermarket chain. Orfalea moved into the position of chairman of the board, where he assumed the role of chief idea man. It took the original partners some time to adjust to the new corporate structure; after all, they were accustomed to being their own bosses. But eventually they came around. Besides, they realized that having a private equity stake in Kinko's could be worth a sizable fortune if the company went public some day.

To recruit and motivate managers to make the many changes that would help Kinko's grow, Hardin used an instrument called "phantom stock," which is essentially a bookkeeping device. Fictional shares are rewarded to those responsible for helping the company reach certain financial and market share benchmarks. Here's how it works: Once a year Kinko's uses outside consultants to determine what these phantom shares would sell for if they were publicly traded. For example, the first 120,000 shares of Kinko's phantom stock were rewarded to managers and higher-level employees for meeting company goals. The phantom shares were priced at $70 each; that is, if the company were to go public at $300 per share, managers could purchase an equivalent number of real company shares at $70 per share, sell them for $300 each, and make a tidy profit of $225 per share.

Now Hardin had everyone working in the same direction. The store managers lobbied aggressively for new equipment and expanded their services to include on-site computer rentals, document binding and finishing, custom printing, passport photos, mailing services (including overnight delivery drop-off), videoconference facilities, and more. In addition, the company launched KinkonetSM, a proprietary document distribution and print network that allows customers to transmit information from one Kinko's site to another. Now customers can pick up finished projects at any location, eliminating shipping costs or the inconvenience of lugging boxes on an airplane. Furthermore, they can go into any of the 1,000 Kinko's in such far-flung places as Australia, Japan, South Korea, or the United Kingdom and find the same equipment, supplies, and services, making it possible for small-business owners and travelers to rely on Kinko's as their office away from home.

With annual sales topping $1 billion, Kinko's is indeed the leader in the $7 billion copy-services market. Still, the company is always looking for new ways to expand its market. Actively seeking corporate clients who outsource their printing and opening mini Kinko's in airports and hotel lobbies are two promising growth vehicles. But both require large amounts of capital. Of course, one way to fund growth and expansion is by taking the company public. And that's something Kinko's intends to do—soon.[47]

Critical Thinking Questions

1. Why is it important for all Kinko's stores to have the same equipment and offer the same services?
2. Why did Kinko's change its structure from individual partnerships to a single corporate entity?
3. How does the issuance of phantom stock keep Kinko's entrepreneurial spirit alive?

■ LEARN MORE ONLINE

Log on to Kinko's Web site at http://www.kinkos.com/topframeset.html to learn about Kinko's many services. Why does Kinko's provide extensive information on how to prepare brochures, posters, presentations, and more? Click on the Online link to learn about online ordering. Also, enter your city and state to find the nearest Kinko's location. Why does Kinko's offer both online ordering information and a store locator?

Test Your Knowledge

QUESTIONS FOR REVIEW

1. What is a sole proprietorship? Why is it the most common type of business in the United States?
2. What is the difference between a general and a limited partnership?
3. What is a closely held corporation, and why do some companies choose this form of ownership?
4. What is the role of a company's board of directors? How is this role changing?
5. What is culture clash?

QUESTIONS FOR ANALYSIS

6. Why is it advisable for partners to enter into a formal partnership agreement?
7. To what extent do shareholders control the activities of a corporation?
8. How might a company benefit from having a diverse board of directors that includes representatives of several industries, countries, and cultures?
9. Why do so many mergers fail?
10. ▨ Your father sits on the board of directors of a large, well-admired, public company. Yesterday, while looking for an envelope in his home office, you stumbled on a confidential memorandum. Unable to resist the temptation to read the memo, you discovered that your father's company is talking with another publicly traded company about the possibility of a merger, with Dad's company being the survivor. Dollar signs flashed in your mind. Should the merger occur, the value of the other company's stock is likely to soar. You're tempted to log on to your E*Trade account in the morning and place an order for 1,000 shares of that company's stock. Better still, maybe you'll give a hot tip to your best friend in exchange for the four Dave Matthews Band tickets he's been flashing in your face all week. Would either of those actions be unethical? Explain your answer.

QUESTIONS FOR APPLICATION

11. Suppose you and some friends want to start a business to take tourists on wilderness backpacking expeditions. None of you has much extra money, so your plan is to start small. However, if you are successful, you would like to expand into other types of outdoor tours and perhaps even open up branches in other locations. What form of ownership should your new enterprise take, and why?
12. Carco, the leading automobile parts manufacturer, is considering acquiring Parts Plus, the nation's third largest automobile parts retailer. Both companies are financially solid, and both have dedicated employees, strong management, and good reputations in their industries. Carco expects to offer Parts Plus shareholders a 20 to 25 percent premium over the company's current stock price. What do you think the chances of success will be if the acquisition goes through? What issues might arise that could limit the transaction's success?
13. ▨ In Chapter 2 we discussed strategic alliances and joint ventures. Why might a company want to enter into those types of arrangements instead of merging?
14. ▨ Review the Chapter 3 discussion of "How International Trade is Measured." Briefly discuss how the DaimlerChrysler merger impacts the U.S. balance of trade and the U.S. balance of payments.

Practice Your Knowledge

SHARPENING YOUR COMMUNICATION SKILLS

Find a current news article discussing a merger, a consolidation, an acquisition, or a hostile takeover. In your own words, write a short summary explaining (1) what steps or events led to this development and (2) what results you expect this development to have on the company, consumers, and the industry in which the company operates.

HANDLING DIFFICULT SITUATIONS ON THE JOB: FINDING THE RIGHT BOARD OF DIRECTORS

Robert Hedin, the owner of Paradise Sportswear in Hawaii, has finally hit "pay dirt." His first business, silk-screening and airbrushing T-shirts, was all but destroyed in 1992 by Hurri-cane Iniki. When he set up the company again, Hawaii's red dirt started seeping into his warehouse and ruining his inventory. Finally, a friend suggested that Hedin stop fighting Mother Nature. So the entrepreneur mortgaged his condo and began producing Red Dirt Shirts with dye created from the troublesome local dirt. "You can make 500 shirts with a bucket of dirt," says Hedin.

All the Red Dirt Sportswear designs were quickly snapped up by locals and tourists in Hedin's eight Paradise Sportswear retail outlets. Soon the company was selling Red Dirt clothing in every Kmart in the Hawaiian islands, as well. Then Hedin added a new line of clothing he called Lava Blues because the colors come from local lava rock.

With the growing popularity of Red Dirt, Hedin had his hands full managing the entire operation and selling his apparel throughout the islands. Nevertheless, with local sales at over $2 million, the owner has decided to expand to the mainland.[48] As part of his expansion, Hedin is searching for four people to enlarge his board of directors from six to ten members. He has approached your recruiting firm to help identify suitable candidates. You don't know whether the entrepreneur really wants the guidance and challenge of a strong, independent board or whether he is putting together a rubber-stamp board that will simply approve his plans.

1. What are some of the decisions Hedin's board might have to make in the near future?

2. When Hedin asks for your professional advice, will you recommend all outsiders or a mix of employees and outsiders to fill the director positions? Why?

3. What kinds of expertise would you suggest Hedin seek in outside directors to make the board an even more valuable resource as Red Dirt expands? Why?

BUILDING YOUR TEAM SKILLS

Directors often have to ask tough questions and make difficult decisions, as you will see in this exercise. Imagine that the president of your college or university has just announced plans to retire. Your team, playing the role of the school's board of directors, must decide how to choose a new president to fill this vacancy next semester.

First, generate a list of the qualities and qualifications you think the school should seek in a new president. What background and experience would prepare someone for this key position? What personal characteristics should the new president have? What questions would you ask to find out how each candidate stacks up against the list of credentials you have prepared?

Now list all the stakeholders that you, as directors, must consider as you decide on a replacement for the retiring president. Of these stakeholders, whose opinions do you think are most important? Whose are least important? Who will be directly and indirectly affected by the choice of a new president? Of these stakeholders, which should be represented as participants in the decision-making process?

Select a spokesperson to deliver a brief presentation to the class summarizing your team's ideas and the reasoning behind your suggestions. After all the teams have completed their presentations, discuss the differences and similarities among credentials proposed by all the teams for evaluating candidates for the presidency. Then compare the teams' conclusions about stakeholders. Do all teams agree on the stakeholders who should participate in the decision-making process? Lead a classroom discussion on a board's responsibility to its stakeholders.

Expand Your Knowledge

EXPLORING CAREER OPPORTUNITIES

Are you best suited to working as a sole proprietor, as a partner in a business, or in a different role within a corporation? For this exercise, select three businesses with which you are familiar: one run by a single person, such as a dentist's practice or a local landscaping firm; one run by two or three partners, such as a small accounting firm; and one that operates as a corporation, such as a Toys "R" Us store.

1. Write down what you think you would like about being the sole proprietor, one of the partners, and the corporate manager or an employee in the businesses you have selected. For example, would you like having full responsibility for the sole proprietorship? Would you like being able to consult with other partners in the partnership before making decisions? Would you like having limited responsibility when you work for other people in the corporation?

2. Now write down what you might dislike about each form of business. For example, would you dislike the risk of bearing all legal responsibility in a sole proprietorship? Would you dislike having to talk with your partners before spending the partnership's money? Would you dislike having to write reports for top managers and shareholders of the corporation?

3. Weigh the pluses and minuses you have identified in this exercise. On balance, which form of business most appeals to you?

DEVELOPING YOUR RESEARCH SKILLS

Choosing the right location for your new business is just as important as choosing the right form of ownership. You'll want to select a location that will ensure a good volume of business. But you'll also want to be sure that your chosen location is properly zoned for what you want to do. Even when you've found the perfect spot, reading over your commercial lease may make you wish you had a law degree. So before you hire an attorney, familiarize yourself with some zoning and commercial lease basics. One good place to start your research is the Small Business Law Center at Nolo Press, http://www.nolo.com. Click on Choosing a Business Location to answer these questions.

1. What is zoning ordinance and how does it impact a firm's operation?

2. What are some key items typically addressed in a commercial lease?

3. When negotiating a commercial lease, what items might you want to pay particular attention to?

SEE IT ON THE WEB EXERCISES
The Declaration of Director Independence, page 114

When it comes to corporate boards, CalPERS strongly favors directors who are independent, not insiders who are beholden to management. Go to the CalPERS site http://www.calpers-governance.org/principles/ and read about the governance principles proposed for domestic and international corporations.

1. In Appendix B-1, what is the CalPERS definition of an independent director? In Appendix B-2, what is the definition of an independent director under the Internal Revenue Code?

2. Under International Corporate Governance, click Global Corporate Governance Principles and read about CalPERS's strategic objective. How does CalPERS define corporate governance?

3. Under Other Corporate Governance Principles, follow the link to Barriers to Good Corporate Governance under the U.S. heading. What are the three questions pointing to barriers to good corporate governance?

Following the Fortunes of the Fortune 500, page 115

Look at the online Fortune 500 list for this year at http://www.pathfinder.com/fortune/fortune500/500list.html for a snapshot of the titans of U.S. industry. Notice the kinds of corporations at the top and bottom of the list—and how much revenue is generated by the top five alone. Then explore some of the other links to find out more about the Fortune 500 list.

1. What corporation heads this year's list of the Fortune 500? What corporation is number 500 on the list?

2. Click on the Introduction link. What are some of the most significant changes in the most recent list compared with the previous year's list?

3. Click on the Top Performers link. What company had the biggest increase in revenues? What company had the highest profits?

Tracking the Urge to Merge, page 120

A new day, a new deal. Visit The Online Investor at http://www.investhelp.com/mergers.shtml to track the largest mergers and acquisitions announced today, yesterday, last week, and possibly the week before.

1. What acquisitions were announced today (or, if none were posted for today, yesterday)? What is the value of the largest acquisition? When is the expected completion date?

2. Click on the link to the acquiring corporation in the highest-value deal of today or yesterday and read the news release. What reason does this acquirer give for taking over the other company?

3. Get more news about this deal by searching for the acquirer's name on the Marketwatch site at http://www.marketwatch.com/. What additional details about the acquisition can you find at this site?

Starting a Small Business

Learning Objectives

1. Understand how a small business innovates, operates, and evolves.
2. Become familiar with the challenges of financing a small business.
3. Learn about an entrepreneur's decisions regarding forms of business ownership and mergers and acquisitions.

Background Information

Small businesses such as Blausen Medical Communications (BMC) have always played a vital role in the U.S. economy. In addition to creating new jobs and new—often specialized—products, they supply the needs of much larger businesses, the way BMC supplies medical animations and graphics to Pfizer and other corporate giants. Although entrepreneurs strike out on their own for a variety of reasons, launching a new business entails more than a good idea. Financing is a major consideration; even after a business is up and running, funding day-to-day operations can be a constant struggle. Money is also a key factor in decisions about the form of business ownership and possible mergers or acquisitions.

The Video

Bruce Blausen, BMC's founder, didn't start out to build a business. After graduate school, he worked in television production and in medical animation, gaining experience with sophisticated equipment and honing his technical skills. When one employer fired him and offered to hire him on a freelance basis for certain projects, Blausen turned entrepreneurial. In his view, entrepreneurs must be willing to take risks; they also need patience and discipline. Money is always a concern, as Blausen strives to meet his payroll, invest in new equipment, and grow his business. BMC is an S corporation, which limits the owner's liability while

allowing income from the business to be taxed at individual income-tax rates. And the company has such growth potential that Blausen is not yet ready to sell it, despite several tempting offers.

Discussion Questions

1. Was BMC started as a lifestyle business or a high-growth venture? How do you know?
2. What steps is Blausen taking to more effectively manage BMC's growth?
3. What was Blausen trying to achieve by repeatedly borrowing from banks and repaying these loans earlier than required?

Next Steps

Public corporations have a board of directors to represent the shareholders and assist management in running the company. Outside directors, in particular, can offer valuable insights and help guide a company. Although BMC is not a public corporation, how could it benefit from an unofficial board of directors? What kinds of outside directors might Blausen seek out as advisors on such a board? Would you suggest that Blausen include any international experts?

■ LEARN MORE ONLINE

On BMC's Web site, follow the Company link to the Personnel page to locate Bruce Blausen's biography. Based on this biography and the video, which of the key characteristics common to most entrepreneurs does Blausen appear to possess? Now follow the Clients link to see which companies have purchased BMC's goods and services. Why would a potential customer want to see this list? Why would a bank, an angel investor, or a venture capital firm want to see this list?

http://www.imagesofhealth.com/start.htm (BMC site)

Natasha: Nick, do you remember when Daimler-Benz and Chrysler announced their merger in 1998—wasn't it touted as a marriage of equals?

Nick: Something like that. To keep things equal both Daimler's chairman, Jürgen Schrempp, and Chrysler's chairman, Robert Eaton, agreed to share the power for three years—until Eaton retired.

Natasha: I heard it took Schrempp only 17 minutes to convince Eaton that merging to create a $140 billion global automotive colossus was a good idea. Sort of like love at first sight.

Nick: Actually, Natasha, I think they married for money. Industry experts calculated that by joining forces they could achieve economies of scale and save over $1.4 billion annually.

Natasha: Yes, but saving money was only part of the attraction. The companies were a perfect fit—one was strong where the other was weak. Daimler's engineering was legendary, and it was strong in technology. Chrysler excelled at new-product design and development. Complementary products and geographical mix would allow them to challenge rivals around the world.

Nick: So with all this talk about synergies, why did it take so long for the two entities to combine their operations?

Natasha: Perhaps we can find the answers.

THE MYSTERY OF THE $140 BILLION GLOBAL FENDER BENDER

The champagne was on ice at the Dorchester Hotel in London when the boards of Chrysler and Daimler-Benz agreed to the merger. Headquartered in Germany, DaimlerChrysler would be the world's third-largest automaker. Schrempp and Eaton would co-manage the 440,000-employee colossus. In the first few weeks, executives on both sides enjoyed the honeymoon. Stoked with excitement and curious about each other's cars and culture, the two companies held marathon meetings in Switzerland to discuss how to integrate their operations. But the morning after came soon—once the novelty of the merger wore off.

Being six time zones apart complicated the postmarriage adjustment period, of course. So did the fundamental differences in Daimler's and Chrysler's management, operational, and decision-making styles. The Germans wanted to expedite the integration. They wanted to put the unpopular issues on the table right from the start. After all, Schrempp believed it was "much better to move fast, and make mistakes occasionally, than to move too slowly." But the Americans preferred to edge into changes. Chrysler's managers valued consensus building and shared decision making, and like the Germans, they were used to having their own way.

As the teams from both sides began the nitty-gritty of melding the two companies, the infighting began. Instead of jointly creating new ways of doing things, managers from both sides would compare existing practices and pick the one they thought worked best. Turf battles bogged down the combination process. Issues that should have been resolved by managers were bumped up to the company's board of directors. The travel policy alone took six months to settle. Daimler-Benz employees were accustomed to flying first class to preserve the company's image—a perk reserved for only top officers at Chrysler. Similar frictions led to the departure of talented Chrysler midlevel managers, engineers, and several top Chrysler executives—including Chrysler's president, Thomas Stallkamp, who had played an instrumental role in orchestrating the merger.

As Chrysler's leverage was whittled away, the power gravitated more toward the Germans. Soon the reality became clear. DaimlerChrysler wasn't a merger of equals. Instead, Daimler-Benz had bought Chrysler. Not only was DaimlerChrysler 58 percent owned by former Daimler shareholders but former Daimler executives were indeed running the show. The transition wasn't going as smoothly as the two had planned. So Schrempp and Eaton slammed on the breaks and ran operations separately for a while.[49]

SOLVING THE MYSTERY OF THE $140 BILLION GLOBAL FENDER BENDER

1. With billions of dollars at stake, why did Schrempp and Eaton decide to temporarily halt the transition and operate Chrysler and Daimler-Benz separately? What was preventing the company from achieving the promised synergies?

   CLUE: WHAT IS ONE OF THE BIGGEST OBSTACLES COMPANIES FACE WHEN THEY COMBINE FORCES?

2. Why did Eaton and Schrempp agree to share the top position of the new entity?

   CLUE: WHAT MESSAGE DID JOINT LEADERSHIP SEND TO THE STAKEHOLDERS?

3. Look back at the margin clues in Parts I and II. What business principles did DaimlerChrysler overlook?

UNDERSTANDING THE FUNCTIONS AND ROLES OF MANAGEMENT

LEARNING OBJECTIVES

After studying this chapter, you will be able to

1 Explain the purpose of a mission statement
2 Identify and explain the three types of managerial skills
3 Define the four basic management functions
4 Explain the role that goals and objectives play in management
5 Cite three leadership styles and explain why no one style is best
6 Clarify how total quality management (TQM) is changing the way organizations are managed

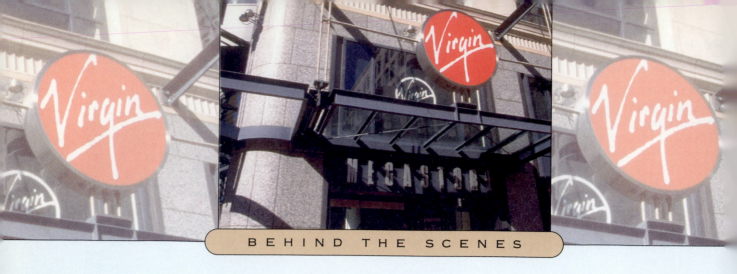

FACING BUSINESS CHALLENGES
AT VIRGIN GROUP

Richard Branson Plays David to Business Goliaths

What do businesses specializing in air travel, beverages, financial services, books, entertainment, and hotels have in common? Perhaps not much. But Richard Branson, founder and head of London-based Virgin Group, doesn't see it that way. Branson's credo is if you know one business you know any business. And he loves nothing more than a daunting challenge.

Branson, who heads nearly 200 diverse companies with operations in 24 countries and revenues estimated at $4 billion, views the impossible as just another business opportunity. He specializes in playing David to the Goliaths of the business world, starting companies to attack well-established competitors. For example, Virgin Atlantic Airways, the most successful of Branson's enterprises, is a high-quality, low-fare trans-Atlantic carrier competing against British Airways and other deep-pocketed giants. The Virgin Megastore chain, another cash cow, goes up against HMV, Tower, and other music superstores.

Not all the Branson businesses are doing as well, however. Virgin Cola has made little headway against the global dominance of Coca-Cola and Pepsi, and service headaches plague Virgin Rail, the public train system Branson bought from Great Britain during the government's drive toward privatization. Nevertheless, Branson is not afraid to take risks or to fail, for that matter. Twice named Britain's best business leader by KPMG Management Consultants, Branson is anything but a typical buttoned-down corporate executive. He is convinced that his unconventional management approach is the most effective for his growing organization.

In fact, rarely a week goes by without Branson's staging an outlandish publicity stunt to promote the Virgin brand. On one occasion, he rolled through New York City in a tank to herald Virgin Cola's initial marketing attack against U.S. colas; more than once, he tried (unsuccessfully) to be the first to fly around the world in a hot-air balloon. Time and again, Branson's brash ambitions and flamboyant style have put him at odds with the business establishment. Still, even he acknowledges that putting so much emphasis on public relations may not be to the corporation's long-term benefit. "My weaknesses really go back to the fact that I have spread myself too thin," he told the press. "In a purely business sense, I suspect that if I just wanted to maximize profits, I should have stayed more focused on one area. That's the conventional way, and I'm sure that's what most business schools teach. Perhaps it's right. But it wouldn't have been half as much fun."

As a manager—sometimes an absentee manager—what should Branson do to ensure the ongoing survival and performance of the companies within his Virgin Group? How can he reach out to his 20,000 employees and spread his vision? How can he apply his unique management style to the demands of running a highly diverse, geographically dispersed organization?[1]

■ THE SCOPE OF MANAGEMENT

Much of Richard Branson's success centers on his ability to find the best people to run his diverse empire. "If you can find people who are good at motivating others and getting the best out of people, they are the ones you want," he says. Still, Branson knows that **management** is a complex, challenging activity. It entails four basic functions: planning, organizing, leading, and controlling resources (land, labor, capital, and information) to efficiently reach a company's goals.[2] To perform these four basic functions and a number of other duties, managers must possess strong interpersonal, technical, and conceptual skills. Furthermore, they must maintain a high level of **quality**—a measure of how closely goods or services conform to predetermined standards and customer expectations.

Some companies adopt a **total quality management (TQM)** approach, which means they focus on delivering the optimum level of quality to customers by building quality into every organizational activity. TQM (which will be discussed later in this chapter) is both a strategic management process and a management philosophy—one that companies communicate through their mission statement.

The Importance of Communicating a Vision and a Mission

Why do organizations such as Virgin Group, Microsoft, and the United Way exist? Like most organizations they were formed in order to realize a **vision,** a realistic, credible, and attainable view of the future that grows out of and improves on the present.[3] Henry Ford envisioned making affordable transportation available to every person. Steve Case (founder of America Online) envisioned a world where everyone was connected by computers. Fred Smith (founder of FedEx) envisioned making FedEx an information company (besides being a transportation company), and now Bill Gates (chairman of Microsoft) envisions empowering people through great software, anytime, anyplace, and on any device.[4] Without such visionaries, who knows how the world would be different. In fact, companies that strive to envision and define the future often have an advantage over those that simply react to the present.

Nevertheless, having a vision is no guarantee of success. To transform vision into reality, managers must define specific organizational goals, objectives, and philosophies. A starting point is to write a company **mission statement,** a brief document that defines why the organization exists, what it seeks to accomplish, and the principles that the company will adhere to as it tries to reach its goals (see Exhibit 6.1). Typical components of a mission statement include the company's product or service; primary market; fundamental concern for survival, growth, and profitability; managerial philosophy; and commitment to quality and social responsibility.

Another important function of a mission statement is to bring clarity of focus to members of the organization. A mission statement helps employees understand how their role is tied to the organization's greater purpose. Thus, it should inspire and guide employees and managers in a way that they can understand the firm's vision and identify with it. Furthermore, the statement must be congruent with the organization's core values. Managers should refer to it to assess whether new project proposals are within the scope of the company's mission.[6]

Consider Edge Learning Institute, an employee-training firm based in Tempe, Arizona. Edge executives were considering mass-marketing their training videos through television "infomercials." However, they realized that this was contrary to the company's mission of using "the human touch when providing individuals and organizations with information." So they decided instead to expand Edge's reach by developing a network of franchises that follow the company's training methods.[7]

---

management
Process of coordinating resources to meet organizational goals

quality
A measure of how closely a product conforms to predetermined standards and customer expectations

total quality management (TQM)
Comprehensive, strategic management approach that builds quality into every organizational process as a way of improving customer satisfaction

vision
A viable view of the future that is rooted in but improves on the present

LEARNING OBJECTIVE 1
Explain the purpose of a mission statement

mission statement
A statement of the organization's purpose, basic goals, and philosophies

 Companies that learn to cannibalize themselves today will rule tomorrow's business jungle; those that don't will find themselves in someone else's pot.[5]

EXHIBIT 6•1

MISSION STATEMENT

The mission statement for Dell Computer embodies the firm's high standards for quality and customer service.

Dell's mission is to be the most successful computer company in the world at delivering the best customer experience in the market we serve. Dell will meet customer expectations of:

- **Highest quality**
- **Leading technology**
- **Competitive pricing**
- **Individual and company accountability**
- **Best in-class service and support**
- **Flexible customization capability**
- **Superior corporate citizenship**
- **Financial stability**

management pyramid
Organizational structure comprising top, middle, and lower management

top managers
Those at the highest level of the organization's management hierarchy; they are responsible for setting strategic goals, and they have the most power and responsibility in the organization

middle managers
Those in the middle of the management hierarchy; they develop plans to implement the goals of top managers and coordinate the work of first-line managers

Managerial Structure

In all but the smallest organizations, more than one manager is necessary to guide the organization's activities. That's why many companies form a **management pyramid** with top, middle, and bottom management levels. Even though more managers are at the bottom level than at the top, as illustrated in Exhibit 6.2, today's leaner companies tend to have fewer levels, flattening the organizational structure, as Chapter 7 will point out.

In general, **top managers** are the upper-level managers who have the most power and who take overall responsibility for the organization. An example is the chief executive officer (CEO). Top managers establish the structure for the organization as a whole, and they select the people who fill the upper-level positions. Top managers also make long-range plans, establish major policies, and represent the company to the outside world at official functions and fund-raisers.

Middle managers have similar responsibilities, but usually for just one division or unit. They develop plans for implementing the broad goals set by top managers, and they coordi-

See It on the Web See It on the Web

CATCH THE BUZZ!

Buzzwords. You may hear them often in your business classes, but they will come at you from all sides when you enter the business world. How can you stay on top of all of these management terms? You can look them up in the Management and Technology Dictionary. This online dictionary of management terms includes definitions of both established terms and trendy buzzwords. The site classifies each word as either a management term or a technology term, and it includes descriptions of leading-edge companies as well. In addition, unlike a standard dictionary, this online dictionary invites you to interact with the authors by sending your comments on a particular definition or on the site in general.
http://www.euro.net/innovation/Management_Base/Mantec.Dictionary.html

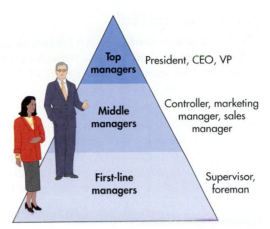

EXHIBIT 6·2

THE MANAGEMENT PYRAMID

Separate job titles are used to designate the three basic levels in the management pyramid.

nate the work of first-line managers. In traditional organizations, managers at the middle level are plant managers, division managers, branch managers, and other similar positions—reporting to top-level managers. But in more innovative management structures, middle managers often function as team leaders who are expected to supervise and lead small groups of employees in a variety of job functions. Similar to consultants, they must understand every department's function, not just their own area of expertise. Furthermore, they are granted decision-making authority previously reserved for only high-ranking executives.[8]

At the bottom of the management pyramid are **first-line managers** (or *supervisory managers*). They oversee the work of operating employees, and they put into action the plans developed at higher levels. Positions at this level include supervisor, department head, and office manager.[9]

Managerial Roles

In addition to performing the four basic managerial functions and developing and communicating a company's vision, managers perform a number of duties to coordinate the organization's work. These duties, or **roles,** fall into three main categories:

- *Interpersonal roles.* Managers perform ceremonial obligations; provide leadership to employees; build a network of relationships with bosses, peers, and employees; and act as liaison to groups and individuals both inside and outside the company (such as suppliers, competitors, government agencies, consumers, special-interest groups, and interrelated work groups).

- *Informational roles.* Managers spend a fair amount of time gathering information by questioning people both inside and outside the organization. They also distribute information to employees, other managers, and outsiders.

- *Decisional roles.* Managers use the information they gather to encourage innovation, to resolve unexpected problems that threaten organizational goals (such as reacting to an economic crisis), and to decide how organizational resources will be used to meet planned objectives. They also negotiate with many individuals and groups, including suppliers, employees, and unions.[10]

Although certain managerial roles may be emphasized more than others, depending on a manager's organizational level, being able to move among these roles is a skill that serves managers well throughout their career.

first-line managers
Those at the lowest level of the management hierarchy; they supervise the operating employees and implement the plans set at the higher management levels; also called supervisory managers

roles
Behavioral patterns associated with or expected of certain positions

Key Managerial Skills

Effective managers need skills that fall into three basic categories: *interpersonal, technical,* and *conceptual.* As managers rise through the organization's hierarchy, they may need to strengthen their abilities in one or more of these skills; fortunately, managerial skills can usually be learned.[11]

LEARNING OBJECTIVE 2
Identify and explain the three types of managerial skills

interpersonal skills
Skills required to understand other people and to interact effectively with them

Interpersonal Skills   The various skills required to communicate with other people, work effectively with them, motivate them, and lead them are **interpersonal skills.** Because they mainly get things done through people, managers at all levels of the organization use interpersonal skills in countless situations. Encouraging employees to work together toward common goals, interacting with employees and other managers, negotiating with partners and suppliers, developing employee trust and loyalty, and fostering innovation—all these activities require interpersonal skills.

Communication, or exchanging information, is the most important and pervasive interpersonal skill that managers use. Employees at Virgin Group, for example, do not hesitate to air grievances directly to Branson because he has proved with his actions that he listens and responds.[12] Branson knows that the ability to communicate increases the manager's own productivity as well as the organization's. It also shapes the impressions made on colleagues, employees, supervisors, investors, and customers. Communication allows you to perceive the needs of these stakeholders (your first step toward satisfying them), and it helps you respond to those needs.[13]

technical skills
Ability and knowledge to perform the mechanics of a particular job

administrative skills
Technical skills in information gathering, data analysis, planning, organizing, and other aspects of managerial work

Technical Skills   A person who knows how to operate a machine, prepare a financial statement, program a computer, or pass a football has **technical skills;** that is, he or she has the knowledge and ability to perform the mechanics of a particular job. Technical skills are most important at lower organizational levels because managers at these levels work directly with employees who are using the tools and techniques of a particular specialty, such as automotive assembly or computer programming. In addition, managers at all levels use **administrative skills,** which are the technical skills necessary to manage an organization. Administrative skills include the abilities to make schedules, gather information, analyze data, plan, and organize. Managers often develop such skills through education and then improve them by working in one or more functional areas of an organization, such as accounting or marketing.[14]

conceptual skills
Ability to understand the relationship of parts to the whole

decision making
Process of identifying a decision situation, analyzing the problem, weighing the alternatives, choosing an alternative and implementing it, and evaluating the results

Conceptual Skills   Managers need **conceptual skills** to see the organization as a whole, in the context of its environment, and to understand how the various parts interrelate. Conceptual skills are especially important to top managers. These managers are the strategists who develop the plans that guide the organization toward its goals. Entrepreneurs such as Richard Branson use their conceptual skills to acquire and analyze information, identify both problems and opportunities, understand the competitive environment in which their companies operate, develop strategies, and make decisions.

A key managerial activity requiring conceptual skills is **decision making,** a process that has five distinct steps: (1) recognizing the need for a decision, (2) analyzing and defining the problem or opportunity, (3) developing alternatives, (4) selecting an alternative and implementing it, and (5) evaluating the results. Managers monitor the results of decisions over time to see whether the chosen alternative works, whether any new problem or opportunity arises because of the decision, and whether a new decision must be made (see Exhibit 6.3).[15]

EXHIBIT 6·3

GREATEST MANAGEMENT DECISIONS EVER MADE

Great decisions change things. Here are some of the greatest management decisions made in the twentieth century.

During WWII, Robert Woodruff, president of Coca-Cola, committed to selling bottles of Coke to members of the armed services for a nickel a bottle. Customer loyalty never came cheaper.

In 1950 when Frank McNamara found himself in a restaurant with no money, he came up with the idea of the Diners Club Card. The first credit card changed the nature of buying and selling throughout the world.

When the Wilson family of Memphis went on a motoring vacation, they discovered it was not much fun staying in motels that were either too expensive or too slovenly. So Kemmons Wilson built his own. The first Holiday Inn opened in Memphis in 1952.

When Honda arrived in America in 1959 to launch its big motor bikes, customers weren't keen on their problematic performance. However, they did admire the little Supercub bikes Honda's managers used. So Honda bravely changed direction and transformed the motorbike business overnight.

When Jean Nidetch was put on a diet by the Obesity Clinic at New York Department of Health, she invited six dieting friends to meet in her apartment every week. In 1961 she created Weight Watchers and launched the slimming industry.

Ignoring market research, Ted Turner launched the Cable News Network in 1980. No one thought a 24-hour news network would work.

Sony chief Akito Morita noticed that young people liked listening to music wherever they went. So in 1980 he and the company developed what became the Walkman. There was no need for market research, because according to Morita, "The public does not know what is possible. We do."

When Johnson & Johnson pulled Tylenol from store shelves in 1982 after capsules were found to be poisoned, the company put customer safety before corporate profit. And it provided a lesson in media openness.

In 1984 Michael Dell decided to sell PCs direct and built to order. Now everybody in the industry is trying to imitate Dell Computer's strategy.

Keep in mind that a company's managerial structure defines the way decisions are made. Today's flatter organizations, for example, allow information to flow more freely between all levels of the organization, and they push decision making down to lower organizational levels. As Chapter 7 will discuss in detail, more and more organizations are empowering their employees and teams by giving them increasing discretion over work-related issues.[16] This is especially true for e-businesses whose organizational and management structures must facilitate independent decision-making flexibility, risk taking, and open communication.

THE FOUR BASIC FUNCTIONS OF MANAGEMENT

Richard Branson demonstrates that when managers possess the right combination of vision, skill, experience, and determination, they can lead an organization to success. To do this, however, they must perform the four basic functions of management: (1) planning, (2) organizing, (3) leading, and (4) controlling (see Exhibit 6.4). These functions are not discrete; they overlap and influence one another.

LEARNING OBJECTIVE 3
Define the four basic management functions

The Planning Function

Planning is the primary management function, the one on which all others depend. Managers engaged in **planning** establish goals and objectives for the organization and determine the best ways to achieve them. To establish effective goals, managers consider budgets, schedules, data about the industry and the economy, the company's existing resources, and

planning
Establishing objectives and goals for an organization and determining the best ways to accomplish them

Focus on E-Business

SEVEN HABITS OF HIGHLY EFFECTIVE E-MANAGERS

Think fast. The pace of the Web is breathless. It's built for speed. Deals happen, competitors spring up, and consumers provide feedback, all in the course of a typical afternoon. To an Internet company, a week is equivalent to a quarter in the traditional business world, which is why managers of e-businesses can't relax for even a minute. They must be willing to make decisions with far less data and analysis than they had in the traditional business world. They must rely on their instincts and process information quickly. There simply isn't time for day-to-day decisions to go up and down the hierarchy.

Moreover, because the pace is so hectic, everyone must be a leader in an e-business and each leader must help create other leaders within the organization. This model of cascading leadership is not a luxury; it's the only way an e-business can survive. Of course, e-leaders must possess the same key managerial skills characteristic of effective traditional managers. But in addition to these skills, they must practice these habits to survive in the e-environment:

- **Make customer obsession a top priority.** In traditional businesses, conducting customer surveys and performing other forms of marketing research could take three to six months. In e-businesses, this process must accelerate because customers change their minds with a click of the mouse. Companies must quickly learn what their customers want so they can make their Web sites more productive and engaging to the people who use them day after day.
- **Build a flat, cross-functional organization.** The command-and-control style of traditional management structures does not work in e-businesses. These organizations need cross-functional collaboration so all employees have the information they need to make fast decisions.
- **Plan often.** In traditional businesses, strategic planning is an annual event. In e-businesses, strategic planning must be an ongoing event. That's because Web sites are linked and companies are integrated. One change can set off a rippling effect throughout the entire chain.
- **Communicate the vision.** All effective leaders have a vision. In e-businesses this vision must be communicated throughout the entire organization to keep all parts of the e-organization in alignment.
- **Be willing to take risks.** In the e-world, barriers to entry are low, but rewards for success are huge. E-managers must be willing to take risks and invent new approaches to continuously stay ahead.
- **Work hard.** Every manager must work hard these days, regardless of the type of organization. But e-managers typically tally 80 to 100 hours each week, and they must learn how to do more with less.
- **Commit.** Many e-business "failures" are a result of leaders who only pay lip service to Internet initiatives. To be a successful e-leader, you must commit 100 percent to the Web effort.

QUESTIONS FOR CRITICAL THINKING

1. Why must e-businesses have a flat, cross-functional organization structure?
2. Why must leaders of e-businesses obsess about the customer?

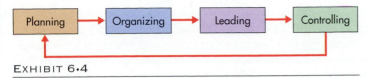

EXHIBIT 6·4

THE FOUR BASIC FUNCTIONS OF MANAGEMENT
Some managers, especially those in smaller organizations, perform all four managerial functions. Although these functions tend to occur in a somewhat progressive order, sometimes they occur simultaneously, and often the process is ongoing.

resources that may realistically be obtained. They also carefully evaluate basic assumptions: Just because a business has developed along certain lines in response to previous conditions doesn't mean that another way might not be appropriate given today's conditions. The planning process encompasses many tasks, which include establishing organizational goals and objectives, forecasting and preparing for the future, and planning for a crisis.

Establishing Organizational Goals and Objectives   Establishing goals and objectives is a key task in the planning process. Although these terms are often used interchangeably, a **goal** is a broad, long-range accomplishment that the organization wishes to attain in typically five or more years, whereas an **objective** is a specific, short-range target designed to help reach that goal. For Virgin Atlantic, a goal might be to surpass British Airways in the number of daily trans-Atlantic flights, and an objective might be to add three new trans-Atlantic routes by year-end.

To be effective, organizational goals and objectives should be specific, measurable, relevant, challenging, attainable, and time-limited. For example it is better to state "increase our customer base by 10 percent over the next three years" than "substantially increase our customer base." Setting appropriate goals increases employee motivation, establishes standards for measuring individual and group performance, guides employee activity, and clarifies management's expectations. By establishing organizational goals, managers set the stage for the actions needed to achieve those goals. If actions aren't planned, the chances of reaching company goals are slim.

Organizations establish three levels of goals or objectives to help fulfill their mission:

- **Strategic goals** focus on broad issues, apply to the company as a whole, and aim to enhance the company's performance. These long-term goals encompass eight major areas of concern: market standing, innovation, human resources, financial resources, physical resources, productivity, social responsibility, and financial performance.[17]
- **Tactical objectives** focus on departmental issues and define the short-term results necessary to achieve the organization's strategic goals.
- **Operational objectives** focus on short-term issues and define the results necessary to achieve both the tactical objectives and the strategic goals.

Strategic, Tactical, and Operational Plans   Each level of goals or objectives has a corresponding plan that defines how the goals or objectives will be achieved.[18] **Strategic plans** define the actions and the allocation of resources necessary to achieve strategic goals over a period of two to five years. Strategic plans are typically established by a company's board of directors and key managers who consult with board members and middle managers. A good strategic plan answers: Where are we going? What is the environment? How do we get there?

LEARNING OBJECTIVE 4
Explain the role that goals and objectives play in management

goal
Broad, long-range target or aim

objective
Specific, short-range target or aim

strategic goals
Goals that focus on broad organizational issues and aim to improve performance

tactical objectives
Objectives that focus on departmental issues and describe the results necessary to achieve the organization's strategic goals

operational objectives
Objectives that focus on short-term issues and describe the results needed to achieve tactical objectives and strategic goals

strategic plans
Plans that establish the actions and the resource allocation required to accomplish strategic goals; usually defined for periods of two to five years and developed by top managers

tactical plans
Plans that define the actions and the resource allocation necessary to achieve tactical objectives and to support strategic plans; usually defined for a period of one to three years and developed by middle managers

operational plans
Plans that lay out the actions and the resource allocation needed to achieve operational objectives and to support tactical plans; usually defined for less than one year and developed by first-line managers

management by objectives (MBO)
A motivational tool whereby managers and employees work together to structure goals and objectives for every individual, department, and project to mesh with the organization's goals

Tactical plans lay out the actions and the allocation of resources necessary to achieve short-term tactical objectives that support the company's strategic plan. Usually developed by middle managers (who consult with first-line managers before committing to top management), tactical plans typically cover a period of one to three years. **Operational plans** designate the actions and resources required to achieve operational objectives and to support tactical plans. Operational plans usually define actions for less than one year. They are developed by first-line managers, who consult with middle managers.

Management by Objectives   Management by objectives (MBO) is a companywide process that emphasizes the results of managerial actions rather than the activities themselves. Management by objectives shifts management's focus to goals and to the purpose of the activity by asking, "What is the objective toward which I am working?" instead of "What am I supposed to do?"[19]

One key feature of MBO is that managers and employees have control over the goals that are set and how they are achieved. Together they define the goals, the responsibility for achieving those goals, and the means of evaluating individual and group performance so that all employees' activities are directly linked to achieving organizational goals. The MBO process consists of four steps: setting goals, planning action, implementing plans, and reviewing performance.[20] Because employees at all levels are involved in these four steps, they learn more about company objectives and feel that they are an important part of the companywide team. Furthermore, they understand how even their small job function contributes to the organization's success.

Many organizations, including Xerox, Intel, and duPont, use MBO to improve performance at all company levels. Because this process ties the goals of each manager to those of managers at levels above and below, MBO acts as a coordinating system that facilitates teamwork throughout the organization, improves communication, encourages participation, and motivates employees through a sense of shared responsibility. However, MBO must have the involvement and commitment of top management to succeed. In addition, problems can result if employees or managers focus too narrowly on their own operational objectives at the expense of the company's strategic goals or the objectives of other departments. Also, if too much paperwork is required for goal setting, performance standards, and reviews, employees may lose their enthusiasm for meeting their objectives. Finally, if the MBO process is administered too rigidly, managers may lose the flexibility to respond to change effectively.[21]

Industry foresight allows a company to control its own destiny.[22]

forecasting
Making educated assumptions about future trends and events that will have an impact on the organization

Forecasting and Preparing for the Future   Technology, culture, product development, service offerings, competition, government priorities, social values, laws, the environment, and the economy are constantly changing. Because any one of these external factors can affect a company's success, managers must continually analyze these factors and interpret their potential impact on an organization's goals and objectives. Such analysis is especially important when planning for the future, or **forecasting**, because it helps managers make wise use of a company's limited resources. Forecasting is, of course, not an exact science. Managers must make a number of educated assumptions about future trends and events and modify those assumptions once new information becomes available.

Managers can use any number of published forecasting tools available to them, such as *Industry Week*'s "Trends and Forecasts," *Business Week*'s "Survey of Corporate Performance," and Standard & Poor's *Earnings Forecast.* These publications depend on accurate forecasts for their continued success, so they usually offer some of the best projections available. However, published forecasts may not always include certain key variables specific to an individual company or industry. Moreover, because these forecasts are public docu-

See It on the Web See It on the Web

SEE THE FUTURE

Managers sometimes wish they had a crystal ball that would allow them to see the future of the business environment. Of course, no such tool exists, but Dun & Bradstreet online might just be the next best thing. On the Dun & Bradstreet Web site, the Economic Analyses & Trends link under News & Events contains many helpful forecasts and charts, including reports about consumer spending, manufacturing production, economic growth, global economic developments, and employment. The future looks much less cloudy when managers have access to these kinds of thoughtful analyses.

http://www.dnb.com

ments, competitors have access to them as well. Therefore, managers must also develop their own forecasts.

Managerial forecasts fall under two broad categories: *quantitative forecasts,* which are typically based on historical data or tests and which involve complex statistical computations; and *qualitative forecasts,* which are based on intuitive judgments or consumer research. Statistically analyzing the cycles of economic growth and recession over several decades to predict when the economy will take a downward turn is an example of quantitative forecasting. Making predictions about sales of a new product on the basis of experience and consumer responses to a survey is an example of qualitative forecasting. Neither method is foolproof, but both are valuable tools, enabling managers to fill in the unknown variables that inevitably crop up in the planning process.

Planning for a Crisis No matter how well a company is managed on a daily basis, any number of problems can arise to threaten its existence. An ugly fight for control of a company, a product failure, a breakdown in routine operations (as a result of fire, for example), or an environmental accident could develop into a serious and crippling crisis. Managers can help a company survive these setbacks through **crisis management,** a plan for handling such unusual and serious problems.

The goal of crisis management is to keep the company functioning smoothly both during and after a crisis. Successful crisis management requires comprehensive contingency plans in addition to speedy, open communication with all who are affected by the crisis. TWA was criticized for not promptly sharing information with the public when Flight 800 crashed off the coast of Long Island in July 1996, killing 230 people. Critics accused TWA of taking too long to release the names of people onboard the airplane and being unresponsive to the media. The company suffered a huge public relations blow.[23]

Crisis planning is not only for large corporations, as Rocket USA will attest. Ready for take-off in 1997, this five-person manufacturer of collectible windup toys had planned for everything—except a UPS strike. The company found itself with orders streaming in and inventory stacked high in the warehouse, yet no way to fill orders. "We were totally in the dark about how we were going to ship," confesses the company president. The company had no backup plan.[24]

Responding to a crisis is much easier when management has prepared for problems by actively looking for signs of a disaster in the making. When Belgian and French consumers became ill after drinking cans of Coke produced with substandard carbon dioxide,

crisis management
System for minimizing the harm that might result from some unusually threatening situations

Cans of banned Coke were dumped at the Coca-Cola depot in Evere, Belgium, as part of the largest recall in the company's history.

organizing
Process of arranging resources to carry out the organization's plans

leading
Process of guiding and motivating people to work toward organizational goals

Coca-Cola officials were caught off guard. "No one would have thought that this would happen to Coke. But they should have planned for it," notes one beverage industry expert. Consumers, who were dissatisfied with late apologetic statements by Coca-Cola's CEO Douglas Ivester, felt management should have done more to calm people's fears and to restore the product's image.[25]

The Organizing Function

Organizing, the process of arranging resources to carry out the organization's plans, is the second major function of managers. During the organizing stage, managers think through all the activities that employees carry out (from programming the organization's computers to mailing its letters), as well as all the facilities and equipment employees need in order to complete those activities. They also give people the ability to work toward organizational goals by determining who will have the authority to make decisions, to perform or supervise activities, and to distribute resources. As does the planning function, the organizing function requires a manager to have strong conceptual skills. The organizing function will be discussed in detail in Chapter 7.

The organizing function is particularly challenging because most organizations undergo constant change. Long-time employees leave, and new employees arrive. Equipment breaks down or becomes obsolete, and replacements are needed. The public's tastes and interests change, and the organization has to reevaluate its plans and activities. Shifting political and economic trends can lead to employee cutbacks—or perhaps expansion. Long-time competitors take unexpected actions, and new competitors enter the market. Every week the organization faces new situations, so management's organizing tasks are never finished. Consider Microsoft. The company continually challenges itself by asking: "Are we making what customers want and working on products and technologies they'll want in the future? Are we staying ahead of all our competitors? What don't our customers like about what we do, and what are we doing about it? Are we organized most effectively to achieve our goals?"[26]

The Leading Function

Leading—the process of influencing and motivating people to work effectively and willingly toward company goals—is the third basic function of management. Leading becomes even more challenging in today's business environment, where individuals who have different backgrounds and unique interests, ambitions, and personal goals are melded into a productive work team. Managers with good leadership skills have greater success in influencing the attitudes and actions of others, both through the demonstration of specific tasks and through the manager's own behavior and spirit. Furthermore, effective leaders are good at *motivating,* or giving employees a reason to do the job and to put forth their best performance (see Chapter 9).

What makes a good leader? When early researchers studied leadership, they looked for specific characteristics, or *traits,* common to all good leaders. At the time, they were unable to prove any link between particular traits and leadership ability. However, researchers found that leaders who have specific traits, such as decisiveness and self-confidence, are likely to be more effective.[27] Additional studies have shown that managers with strong interpersonal skills and high emotional quotients (EQs) tend to be more effective leaders. The characteristics of a high EQ include:[28]

- *Self-awareness.* Self-aware managers have the ability to recognize their own feelings and how they, their job performance, and other people are affected by them. Moreover, someone who is highly self-aware knows where he or she is headed and why.

- *Self-regulation.* Self-regulated managers have the ability to control or reduce disruptive impulses and moods. They can suspend judgment and think before acting.
- *Motivation.* Motivated managers are driven to achieve beyond expectations—their own and everyone else's.
- *Empathy.* Empathetic managers thoughtfully consider employees' feelings, along with other factors, in the process of making intelligent decisions.
- *Social skill.* Socially skilled managers tend to have a wide circle of acquaintances, and they have a knack for finding common ground with people of all kinds. They assume that nothing important gets done by one person alone and have a network in place when the time for actions comes.

Keep in mind that these traits alone do not define a leader. Different leadership traits are appropriate under different leadership situations.[29] Many highly admired CEOs have stumbled, not because they didn't have effective leadership skills or strategies for success, but because they couldn't execute their strategies or deliver on their commitments. Furthermore, effective leaders refrain from launching a new initiative until current ones are embedded in the company's DNA. Take GE's Jack Welch, for example. He has introduced just five major initiatives in his 18 years as CEO.[30] That's because developing a strategy or vision is less than half the battle. It's executing it that counts. In today's information age, strategies quickly become public property. Everyone knows Dell's direct business model, for example, yet few companies, if any, have successfully copied its execution.

Adopting an Effective Leadership Style   *Leadership style* is the way a manager uses authority to lead others. Every manager, from the baseball coach to the university chancellor, has a definite style. The three broad categories of leadership style are *autocratic, democratic,* and *laissez-faire.*

Autocratic leaders make decisions without consulting others. "My way or the highway" summarizes this style, which tends to go with traditional, hierarchical organizational structures. Although autocratic leadership can be highly effective when quick decisions are necessary, it does little to empower employees or encourage innovation.

In contrast, **democratic leaders** delegate authority and involve employees in decision making. Even though their approach can lead to slower decisions, soliciting input from people familiar with particular situations or issues may result in better decisions. As more companies adopt the principles of teamwork, democratic leadership continues to gain in popularity. For example, managers at Rhone-Poulenc, the U.S. subsidiary of France's leading chemical and pharmaceutical manufacturer, gradually made the transition from autocratic to democratic leadership as the organization moved from a hierarchical structure to a team-based environment. CEO Peter Neff says, "I don't look over people's shoulders anymore. . . . My role now is to enable people to do the best they know how to do." For Neff, this means acting as an opportunity seeker, coach, facilitator, motivator, and mentor rather than as a controller or problem solver.[31]

The third leadership style, laissez-faire, is sometimes referred to as free-rein leadership. The French term *laissez faire* can be translated as "leave it alone," or more roughly as "hands off." **Laissez-faire leaders** take the role of consultant, encouraging employees' ideas and offering insights or opinions when asked. The laissez-faire style may fail if workers pursue goals that do not match the organization's. However, the style has proven effective in some situations. Managers at Hewlett-Packard's

LEARNING OBJECTIVE 5
Cite three leadership styles and explain why no one style is best

autocratic leaders
Leaders who do not involve others in decision making

democratic leaders
Leaders who delegate authority and involve employees in decision making

laissez-faire leaders
Leaders who leave the actual decision making up to employees

Lou Gerstner's transformational leadership has changed IBM from a slow-moving "dinosaur" to a cutting-edge company once again. This employee's casual dress looks nothing like the IBM of a decade ago, and neither does the product he is working on.

North American distribution organization adopted a laissez-faire style when they were given nine months to reorganize their order-fulfillment process. The managers eliminated all titles, supervision, job descriptions, and plans, and they made employees entirely responsible for the project. At first there was chaos. However, employees soon began to try new things, make mistakes, and learn as they went. In the end, the team finished the reorganization ahead of schedule, reduced product delivery times from 26 days to 8 days, and cut inventory by 20 percent. Moreover, the employees experienced a renewed sense of challenge, commitment, and enjoyment in their work.[32]

More and more businesses are adopting democratic and laissez-faire leadership as they reduce management layers and increase teamwork. However, experienced managers know that no one leadership style works every time. In fact, a recent study found that in the most successful companies, the CEO adapts his or her leadership approach to match the requirements of the particular situation.[33] The best approach depends on the leader's personality, the employees' skills and backgrounds, and the situations the company is facing. Adapting leadership style to current business circumstances is called **contingency leadership.** You can think of leadership styles as existing along a continuum of possible leadership behaviors, as suggested by Exhibit 6.5.

contingency leadership
Adapting the leadership style to what is most appropriate, given current business conditions

Coaching and Mentoring   Managers can provide effective leadership by coaching and mentoring their employees. On a winning sports team, the coach focuses on helping all team members perform at their highest potential. In a similar way, *coaching* managers strive to bring out the best in their employees. **Coaching** involves taking the time to meet with employees, discussing any problems that may hinder their ability to work effectively, and offering suggestions and encouragement to help them work through these difficulties. This process requires keen powers of observation, sensible judgment, and both a willingness and an ability to take appropriate action. However, just as a sports coach cannot play the game for team members, a coaching manager must step back and let employees perform when it's "game time." Coaching managers develop a solid game plan and empower their team to

coaching
Helping employees reach their highest potential by meeting with them, discussing problems that hinder their ability to work effectively, and offering suggestions and encouragement to overcome these problems

Boss-centered leadership						Employee-centered leadership
Use of authority by the manager						**Area of freedom for workers**
Manager makes decision, announces it.	Manager "sells" decision.	Manager presents ideas, invites questions.	Manager presents tentative decision subject to change.	Manager presents problems, gets suggestions, makes decisions.	Manager defines limits, asks group to make decision.	Manager permits workers to function within defined limits.

EXHIBIT 6.5

CONTINUUM OF LEADERSHIP BEHAVIOR

Leadership style occurs along a continuum, ranging from boss-centered to employee-centered. Situations that require managers to exercise greater authority fall toward the boss-centered end of the continuum. Other situations call for a manager to give workers leeway to function more independently.

carry it out. If the team gets behind, the manager offers encouragement to boost morale. And when team members are victorious, the manager recognizes and praises their outstanding achievement.[34]

Acting as a mentor is similar to coaching, but mentoring also emphasizes helping employees understand how the organization works. A **mentor** is usually an experienced manager or employee who can help guide other employees through the corporate maze. Mentors have a deep knowledge of the business and a useful network of industry colleagues. In addition, they can explain office politics, serve as a role model for appropriate business behavior, and provide valuable advice about how to succeed within the organization.

Your mentor won't necessarily be your boss. Relationships with mentors often develop informally between the individuals involved. However, some companies have established formal mentoring programs. In the program at Xerox, women employees can spend a few hours every month discussing work or career issues with any of the participating women executives.[35] Mentoring offers benefits for both parties: The less experienced employee gains from the mentor's advice and ideas; the mentor gains new contacts for his or her networks, in addition to personal satisfaction.

Managing Change   Another important function of leaders is to manage the process of change. As competitive pressures get worse, the pace of change accelerates while companies search for even higher levels of quality, service, and overall speed. Sometimes managers initiate change; other times change imposes itself from outside the company. No matter what propels company evolution, effective leaders provide a powerful vision to pull people in a desired direction. They often begin by envisioning where they want the company to go; then they look backward from the future and ask, "What will it take to create that future?"[37] They also work effectively with employees to ensure that the change process goes smoothly.

Resistance to change often arises because people don't understand how it will affect them. Mention change and most people automatically feel victimized. Some worry that they may have to master new skills—ones that might be difficult. Others fear that their jobs will be in jeopardy. Experts advise that if managers want less resistance to change, they should build trust with employees long before the change arrives and, when it does, explain to them how it will affect their jobs. Moreover, cultivating constant change on a small scale can prepare employees for even larger changes; it's the difference between asking someone to run a race who has never even practiced before versus asking someone to run a race who jogs every day.[38]

Building a Strong Organizational Culture   Strong leadership is a key element in establishing a productive **organizational culture**—the set of underlying values, norms, and practices shared by members of an organization. When you visit an organization, observe how the employees work, dress, communicate, address each other, and conduct business. Each organization has a special way of doing things. In corporations, this force is often referred to as *corporate culture.*

A company's culture influences the way people treat and react to each other. It shapes the way employees feel about the company and the work they do; the way they interpret and perceive the actions taken by others; the expectations they have regarding changes in their work or in the business; and how they view those changes.[39] Look at Southwest Airlines. As one manager puts it, "Our whole culture drives everything. So many companies, while they don't put it in writing, create a culture that says, 'Leave your personality at home; all we want you to do is work.' At Southwest, we say, 'Bring your personality and your sense of humor to work.' Our ads, our recruitment techniques, and our interview process—all of it attracts a certain type of individual who values hard work, family, and, yes, fun."[40]

mentor
Experienced manager or employee with a wide network of industry colleagues who can explain office politics, serve as a role model for appropriate business behavior, and help other employees negotiate the corporate structure

 An effective change leader puts every product, every service, every customer on trial for its life and regularly asks, "If we did not do this already, should we do it now?"[36]

organizational culture
A set of shared values and norms that support the management system and that guide management and employee behavior

How Michael Dell Works His Magic

Michael Dell wasn't *Industry Week*'s CEO of the Year just because of Dell Computer's resounding financial success or because of his contributions to the community where he and his family live. He was chosen because of the way he keeps Dell Computer one step ahead of its competitors by constantly pushing the envelope of change. Dell has the ability to visualize and then capitalize on changes in the business world before they occur. As a result, he has propelled Dell Computer to the top with an unconventional business model for selling and manufacturing, which his competitors are now scrambling to copy.

"You have to be self-critical to succeed," says Dell. "If you sat in on our management meetings, you would find that we are a remarkably self-critical bunch with a disdain for complacency that motivates us. We are always looking to do things more efficiently. We are 99 percent focused on what is going to happen and what could change the business in the future. We ask ourselves, what are the risks to the business, what could go wrong."

From day one, the company's mission has been the same: Build better computers and sell them at lower prices. And it is this simple mission that has kept the company's management focused on doing what it does best. Furthermore, it drives management to continually ask, "What is the most efficient way to do things?" Pretty basic stuff for an $18 billion global corporation. Nevertheless it keeps Dell Computer on track. When the company has deviated from the direct-sales model in the past, business has suffered. So if you ask Michael Dell whether the company would consider taking some of his billions and branching out beyond the computer business today, he'll flat out tell you no. "You have to be careful about expanding into new businesses, because if you get into too many too quickly, you won't have the experience or the infrastructure to succeed," he explains.

So what drives the fourth-richest person in the country, whose company stock has increased 29,600 percent in one decade, to go to work each day? "Not money," says Dell. "Do you have any idea how much fun it is to run a billion-dollar company?" In fact, walk into his executive suite and chances are you'll see a man standing behind a podium desk, both absorbed in and invigorated by his work. Michael Dell's office has chairs, of course, but they are only for visitors. Dell works standing up.

QUESTIONS FOR CRITICAL THINKING

1. What leadership style do you think Michael Dell practices, and why?
2. How does Michael Dell successfully manage change?

The Controlling Function

controlling
Process of measuring progress against goals and objectives and correcting deviations if results are not as expected

Controlling is the fourth basic managerial function. In management, **controlling** means monitoring a firm's progress toward meeting its organizational goals and objectives, resetting the course if goals or objectives change in response to shifting conditions, and correcting deviations if goals or objectives are not being attained. Managers use their technical skills for the controlling function, comparing where they are with where they should be.

The controlling function is an important part of total quality management, which is sometimes referred to as *total quality control*. In the past, *control* often meant those little sticky tags attached to new items that say, "inspected by #47." Companies would inspect finished products and rework or discard items that didn't meet quality standards. Today, this inspection step is only one small part of the total control process. Control methods are examined in greater detail in Chapter 8. The remainder of this section will focus on the relationship between management and the controlling function.

See It on the Web See It on the Web

LINKING TO ORGANIZATIONAL CHANGE

Looking for more information on every aspect of organizational change management? You'll find a comprehensive collection of links on the Web site of the Management Assistance Program for Nonprofits. This is the place to access articles, discussion groups, and other resources related to organizational change in businesses and in nonprofit organizations. Start with the overview, which sets the stage for browsing the many links devoted to exploring management and employee perspectives on the challenges and goals of managing change.

http://www.mapnp.org/library/mgmnt/orgchnge.htm

Many firms control for quality through a four-step cycle that involves all levels of management and all employees (see Exhibit 6.6). In the first step, top managers set **standards,** or criteria for measuring the performance of the organization as a whole. At the same time, middle and first-line managers set departmental quality standards so they can meet or exceed company standards. Establishing control standards is closely tied to the planning function and depends on information supplied by employees, customers, and other external sources. Examples of specific standards might be "Produce 1,500 circuit boards monthly with less than 1 percent failures." "Open three new trans-Atlantic routes by year-end that experience a combined passenger load factor of 60 percent or higher."

In the second step of the control cycle, managers assess performance, using both quantitative (specific, numerical) and qualitative (subjective) performance measures. In the third step, managers compare performance with the established standards and search for the cause of any discrepancies. If the performance falls short of standards, the fourth step is to take corrective action, which may be done by either adjusting performance or reevaluating the standards. If performance meets or exceeds standards, no corrective action is taken. As

standards
Criteria against which performance is measured

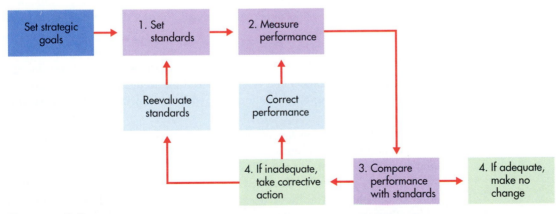

EXHIBIT 6.6

THE CONTROL CYCLE

The control cycle has four basic steps: (1) On the basis of strategic goals, top managers set the standards by which the organization's overall performance will be measured. (2) Managers at all levels measure performance. (3) Actual performance is compared with the standards. (4) Appropriate corrective action is taken (if performance meets standards, nothing other than encouragement is needed; if performance falls below standards, corrective action may include improving performance, establishing new standards, changing plans, reorganizing, or redirecting efforts).

Exhibit 6.6 shows, if everything is operating smoothly, controls permit managers to repeat acceptable performance. If results are below expectations, controls help managers take any necessary action.

Take Virgin Airways. Suppose the company does not reach its objectives of adding three new profitable trans-Atlantic routes by year-end. With proper control systems in place, managers will evaluate why these objectives were not reached. Perhaps they will find that a shortage of airplanes, landing slots, or pilots prevented expansion. Or perhaps the market where expansion was targeted became saturated with carriers. Regardless, management will search for the cause of the discrepancies before deciding whether to modify the company's objectives or try a different approach in order to achieve the company's long-term goal of becoming the number one trans-Atlantic carrier.

■ TOTAL QUALITY MANAGEMENT

LEARNING OBJECTIVE 6
Clarify how total quality management (TQM) is changing the way organizations are managed

Earlier in this chapter we defined total quality management (TQM) as a strategic management process and philosophy that focuses on delivering the optimum level of quality to customers. Total quality management draws its ideas, principles, and tools from psychology, sociology, statistics, management, and marketing. The goal of TQM is to create an environment that encourages people to grow as individuals and to learn to bring about continuous and breakthrough improvements. Companies that adopt TQM create a value for all stakeholders—customers, employees, owners, suppliers, and the community.[41] The four key elements of TQM are employee involvement, customer focus, benchmarking, and continuous improvement.

participative management
Sharing information with employees and involving them in decision making

- *Employee involvement.* Total quality management involves every employee in quality assurance. Workers are trained in quality methods and are empowered to stop a work process if they feel that products or services are not meeting quality standards. Managers also encourage employees to speak up when they think of better ways of doing things. This approach exemplifies a **participative management** style, the sharing of information at all levels of the organization (also known as *open-book management*). By directly involving employees in decision making, companies increase employees' power in an organization and improve the flow of information between employees and managers.

- *Customer focus.* Focusing on the customer simply means finding out what customers really want and then providing it. This approach requires casting aside assumptions about customers and relying instead on accurate research. It also requires developing long-term relationships with customers, as Chapter 11 will discuss in detail.

- *Benchmarking.* This element of TQM involves comparing your company's processes and products against the standards of the world's best companies and then working to match or exceed those standards. This process entails rating the manufacturing process, product development, distribution, and other key functions against those of acknowledged leaders; analyzing how those role models achieve their outstanding results; and then applying that knowledge to make quality improvements. Among the world-class organizations frequently cited as benchmarks for production are Toyota, IBM, and Hewlett-Packard; for distribution, L. L. Bean and FedEx; and for customer service, American Express and Nordstrom.[42]

- *Continuous improvement.* This key feature of TQM requires an ongoing effort to reduce defects, cut costs, slash production and delivery times, and offer customers innovative products. Improvements are often small, incremental changes that add up to greater competitiveness over the long run. Because responsibility for such improvement often falls on employees, it becomes management's job to provide employee incentives that will motivate them to want to improve.

Although many U.S. companies are enjoying greater success as a result of total quality initiatives, a recent study of Fortune 500 companies indicates that such initiatives have fallen short of expectations in a large number of companies. However, the fact that total quality principles played a significant role in propelling Japanese businesses from postwar ruins to pillars of innovation and productivity suggests that much can be gained from the process. What may be lacking in the United States is a firm commitment to TQM. Many companies have jumped on the TQM bandwagon hoping for a quick boost in performance without really thinking about how to make total quality a part of their long-term strategy. Such companies often fail to provide the necessary managerial and financial support for the programs. In about half of the firms studied, less than 40 percent of workers and less than 80 percent of management teams were sufficiently knowledgeable about TQM philosophy, concepts, and tools.[43] Experts agree that the entire organization—from the bottom all the way up to the CEO—must be actively and visibly involved for TQM to work. Companies that make a halfhearted commitment should not expect dramatic improvements.[44]

At the same time, pursuing TQM is not necessarily a prerequisite for success. Many successful companies do not have TQM programs.[45] However, no business that operates in a competitive environment can expect long-term success unless managers strive to meet customers' needs, improve processes, lower costs, and empower employees in one way or another. Managers should keep this in mind while they pursue the four functions of management.

L. L. Bean's distribution employees, like the one pictured here, recently traded jobs with stockers in retail stores to learn how to serve each other better.

Summary of Learning Objectives

1. **Explain the purpose of a mission statement.**
   A mission statement defines why the organization exists, what it does, what it hopes to achieve, and the principles it will abide by to meet its goals. It is used to bring clarity of focus to members of the organization and to provide guidelines for the adoption of future projects.

2. **Identify and explain the three types of managerial skills.**
   Managers use (1) interpersonal skills to communicate with other people, work effectively with them, and lead them; (2) technical skills to perform the mechanics of a particular job; and (3) conceptual skills (including decision making) to see the organization as a whole, to see it in the context of its environment, and to understand how the various parts interrelate.

3. **Define the four basic management functions.**
   The four management functions are (1) planning—establishing objectives and goals for the organization and determining the best ways to achieve them; (2) organizing—arranging resources to carry out the organization's plans; (3) leading—influencing and motivating people to work effectively and willingly toward company goals; and (4) controlling—monitoring progress

toward organizational goals, resetting the course if goals or objectives change in response to shifting conditions, and correcting deviations if goals or objectives are not being attained.

4. **Explain the role that goals and objectives play in management.**
   Goals and objectives establish long- and short-range targets that help managers fulfill the company's mission. Setting appropriate goals increases employee motivation, establishes standards by which individual and group performance can be measured, guides employee activity, and clarifies management's expectations.

5. **Cite three leadership styles and explain why no one style is best.**
   Three leadership styles are autocratic, democratic, and laissez-faire (also called free-rein). Each may work best in a different situation: autocratic when quick decisions are needed, democratic when employee participation in decision making is desirable, and laissez-faire when fostering creativity is a priority. Good leaders are flexible enough to respond with the best approach for the situation.

MEETING BUSINESS CHALLENGES AT VIRGIN GROUP

Richard Branson's passion is starting businesses that directly challenge established competitors, no matter what the odds against success. "I really do believe that fighting competition is exciting—and it's good for business," he said in a recent interview. "There's no point in going into a business unless you can shake up the whole industry. Then you are not just making a difference for yourself. You find the whole industry has to react to your being there and change the way it does business." This is the vision behind Branson's Virgin Atlantic Airways, and it has also pervaded every other Virgin enterprise, motivating employees to work harder to topple complacent industry leaders.

Branson's leadership is an effective engine for launching new businesses that are then turned over to a hand-picked group of leaders who manage actual day-to-day operations. (The exception is Virgin Atlantic, one of his favorites and the beneficiary of many of his high-profile publicity stunts.) In selecting managers, Branson puts more emphasis on interpersonal skills than on technical skills. "What makes somebody good is how good they are at dealing with people," he explains. "There are plenty of so-called experts, but not as many great motivators of people."

This emphasis on people is reflected in Virgin's corporate culture, where employees—not customers or shareholders—always come first. "If your employees are happy and smiling and doing their work, they will perform well," notes Branson. "Consequently, the customers will enjoy their experience with your company. If your employees are sad and miserable and not having a good time, the customers will be equally miserable."

Branson goes to great lengths to stay in touch with his employees and motivate them toward higher performance. He encourages employees to contact him with gripes or ideas; he not only responds, he makes a point of taking action. He gives employees big discounts at all Virgin businesses, and he hosts an annual summer party at his home for the entire staff. Top-performing Virgin employees, from switchboard operators to pilots, receive invitations to vacation with Branson at his private Caribbean island. "The idea is to have fun, but by talking to employees, you learn a lot, as well," he notes.

Attending new-employee orientation sessions allows Branson to spread his vision and initiate employees into Virgin's work-hard, play-hard culture. In general, when communicating with employees, he prefers to encourage performance by offering praise rather than criticism. "I will praise, praise, praise, and only criticize if they are going to kill themselves crossing the road," he says. "People know when they've done things wrong; they don't need to be told. When I write my letters to employees, you'll never see a line of criticism."

Critical Thinking Questions

1. Which managerial roles are exemplified by Richard Branson's hosting an annual summer party at his private island for all company employees? Explain your answer.

2. When Branson plans the launch of a new business to challenge established companies in an industry, which category of managerial skills is he applying?

3. What mission statement would you suggest to express the purpose of Branson's Virgin Group?

■ LEARN MORE ONLINE

Visit the company's Web page at http://www.virgin.com/about/richards_diary/index.html and look at "Richard's Diary," which covers a number of Branson's internal and external activities on behalf of Virgin. Also browse the site to find news about the company's latest business ventures and charitable works. How does this site convey the founder's vision? How does it reflect his emphasis on people?[46]

6. **Clarify how total quality management (TQM) is changing the way organizations are managed.**
Total quality management is both a management philosophy and a management process that focuses on delivering quality to customers. TQM redirects management to focus on four key elements: (1) Employee involvement includes team building and soliciting employee input on decisions. (2) Customer focus involves gathering customer feedback and then acting on that feedback to better serve customers. (3) Benchmarking involves measuring the company's standards against the standards of industry leaders. (4) Continuous improvement requires an ongoing commitment to reducing defects, cutting costs, slashing production and delivery times, and offering customers innovative products.

Key Terms

administrative skills (134)

autocratic leaders (141)

coaching (142)

conceptual skills (134)

contingency leadership (142)

controlling (145)

crisis management (139)

decision making (134)

democratic leaders (141)

first-line managers (133)

forecasting (138)

goal (137)

interpersonal skills (134)

laissez-faire leaders (141)

leading (140)

management (131)

management by objectives (MBO) (138)

management pyramid (132)

mentor (143)

middle managers (132)

mission statement (131)

objective (137)

operational objectives (137)

operational plans (138)

organizational culture (143)

organizing (140)

participative management (146)

planning (135)

quality (131)

roles (133)

standards (145)

strategic goals (137)

strategic plans (137)

tactical objectives (137)

tactical plans (138)

technical skills (134)

top managers (132)

total quality management (TQM) (131)

vision (131)

Test Your Knowledge

QUESTIONS FOR REVIEW

1. What is management? Why is it so important?

2. Why are interpersonal skills important to managers at all levels?

3. What is forecasting, and how is it related to the planning function?

4. What is the goal of crisis management?

5. What are some common characteristics of effective leaders?

QUESTIONS FOR ANALYSIS

6. How do the three levels of management differ?

7. Explain whether the following statement is an example of a strategic goal, a tactical objective, or an operational objective: "To become the number one retailer of computers and computer accessories in terms of revenue, growth, and customer satisfaction."

8. Why are coaching and mentoring effective leadership techniques?

9. How are the four main elements of total quality management related to the goal of delivering quality to customers?

10. When an organization learns about a threat that could place the safety of its workers and its customers at risk, is management obligated to immediately inform these parties of the threat? Explain your answer.

QUESTIONS FOR APPLICATION

11. Develop a set of long-term career goals for yourself and several short-term objectives that will help you reach those goals. Make sure your goals are specific, measurable, and time-limited.

12. Suppose you are a middle manager of a chair-manufacturing company. Top management has asked you to organize a team to redesign the process of getting finished chairs from the warehouse to the customer. Your objectives are to reduce delivery times and inventory levels, and you have only three months to complete the task.

What leadership style do you think would work best to motivate your team and meet the stated objectives?

13. [■] Using Dell Computer's mission statement in Exhibit 6.1 as a model and the material you learned in Chapter 3, develop a mission statement for a socially responsible company such as Patagonia or Ben & Jerry's.

14. [■] What is the principal difference between a business plan (as discussed in Chapter 4) and a strategic plan?

Practice Your Knowledge

SHARPENING YOUR COMMUNICATION SKILLS

Interview the owner or manager of a local business to learn about the organization's culture, and summarize your findings in a brief memo to your instructor. Some of the questions you might want to ask include:

- How does the company define success?
- How is the company organized, and how do people report to each other?
- How are decisions made? Is the emphasis on individual or group responsibility?
- How do people dress and address each other?
- How are goals and objectives established?
- How are employee learning and innovation encouraged?

HANDLING DIFFICULT SITUATIONS ON THE JOB: COOKING UP PLANS FOR THE UNEXPECTED

A few months ago you landed the most exciting job you could imagine, as a production assistant for Meg McComb, one of the best-known movie food stylists in Hollywood. But some days it's just a little too exciting. Like today. McComb has just been hired to concoct a twelfth-century feast for a period costume drama directed by Kenneth Branagh. That means food for 150 actors that must look authentic and be on the movie set by 1 P.M. tomorrow. McComb is a pro, and you have full confidence in her as she races around the office handing out assignments. You've seen her juggle all kinds of unforeseen problems, such as what to do with a banquet for 150 when shooting is canceled at the last minute (feed it to friends).[47]

Now McComb tosses you a catalog of food suppliers and shouts "asparagus" as she zips on to the next food item in the feast. You know she means asparagus for 150. Luckily, most produce suppliers are here in California, so you are pretty sure you can get fresh, jumbo spears overnight. Aside from worrying about the cost, which you'll just have to pass on to Branagh, you are nervous about what the asparagus will look like and whether it will arrive on time. Failure is definitely not an option. You know that Branagh is depending on your company—and may very well hire another firm for his next movie if things don't work out. All this pressure starts you thinking: Is there a better way the company can prepare for the unexpected?

1. What can you say to convince McComb that the company needs to do a better job of planning? Do you think organizing, leading, and controlling should be taken into consideration as part of this planning process? Why?

2. Do you consider rush projects (like this last-minute order) a crisis? Is crisis management appropriate for such situations? Explain your answers.

3. Knowing that directors are likely to want anything at a moment's notice, what can you, in your role as McComb's assistant, do to better prepare the company for the unexpected?

BUILDING YOUR TEAM SKILLS

A good mission statement should define the organization's purpose and ultimate goals and outline the principles that are to guide managers and employees in working toward those goals. Using library sources such as annual reports or Internet sources such as organizational Web sites, locate mission statements from one not-for-profit organization, such as a school or a charity, and one company with which you are familiar.

Bring these statements to class and, with your team, select four mission statements to evaluate. How many of the mission statements contain all five of the typical components (product or service; primary market; concern for survival, growth, and profitability; managerial philosophy; commitment to quality and social responsibility)? Which components are most often absent from the mission statements you are evaluating? Which components are most often included? Of the mission statements your team is analyzing, which is the most inspiring? Why?

Now assume that you and your teammates are the top management team at each organization or company. How would you improve these mission statements? Rewrite the four mission statements so that they cover the five typical components, show all organization members how their roles are related to the vision, and inspire commitment among employees and managers.

Summarize your team's work in a written or oral report to the class. Compare the mission statement that your team found the most inspiring with the statements that other teams found the most inspiring. What do these mission statements have in common? How do they differ? Of all the inspiring mission statements reported to the class, which do you think is the best? Why? Does this mission statement inspire you to consider working for or doing business with this organization?

Expand Your Knowledge

EXPLORING CAREER OPPORTUNITIES

If you become a manager, how much of your day will be spent performing each of the four basic functions of management? This is your opportunity to find out. Arrange to shadow a manager (such as a department head, a store manager, or a shift supervisor) for a few hours. As you observe, categorize the manager's activities in terms of the four management functions and note how much time each activity takes. If observation is not possible, interview a manager in order to complete this exercise.

1. How much of the manager's time is spent on each of the four management functions? Is this the allocation you expected?

2. Ask whether this is a typical work day for this manager. If it isn't, what does the manager usually do differently? Does this manager tend to spend most of her or his time on one particular function during a typical day?

3. Of the four management functions, which does the manager believe is most important for good organizational performance? Do you agree?

DEVELOPING YOUR RESEARCH SKILLS

Managers know that a productive organizational culture can help a company succeed. On the other hand, a strong culture can also cause problems, such as slowing a company down when changes are needed or causing conflict when two companies merge. Use your research skills to find one article or example about how corporate culture helped a company succeed and another about how corporate culture caused problems for a company. You may want to check library sources such as the *Reader's Guide to Periodical Literature* or search Web sites such as *American City Business Journal*'s http://www.amcity.com. Other good sources include back issues of popular business magazines such as *Business Week, Fortune,* and *Forbes*. Note what sources and search strategies you use.

1. In the successful example, what was the role of culture? What characteristics of this company's culture contributed to its success?

2. In the other example, what characteristics of this company's culture contributed to the problem?

3. What do you think top management could have done about the culture that contributed to the company's problem?

SEE IT ON THE WEB EXERCISES
Catch the Buzz! page 132

The online Management and Technology Dictionary can help you identify business terms that are unfamiliar to you and can keep you current on management buzzwords. Explore the dictionary at http://www.euro.net/innovation/Management_Base/Mantec.Dictionary.html to answer the following questions.

1. What is the definition of *dependent demand?* Give an example.

2. What are *knowledge workers,* and what challenges do they present to managers?

3. Explain what a *learning organization* is and how it is related to the concept of total quality management.

See the Future, page 139

Managers rely on solid information to help them forecast future trends as part of the planning function. Dun & Bradstreet online is one of many useful Web sites that offer information to help managers forecast and prepare for the future. From Dun & Bradstreet's main Web page http://www.dnb.com, select News & Events and then choose the Economic Analyses & Trends link to answer these questions.

1. Examine the information comparing weekly business starts this year with weekly business starts last year. Were there more starts in week 4 this year than last year? Does the report indicate more or fewer year-to-date business starts this year compared with the same point last year? What conclusions might managers draw from such data?

2. Scroll down to the section on International Business Expectations and browse the most recent quarterly report. What regions or countries are expected to experience higher growth in the near future?

3. Browse the most recent quarterly report on the U.S. Business Expectations section. Are U.S. executives optimistic or pessimistic about the outlook for sales, profits, and employment? Why would managers find this information valuable?

Linking to Organizational Change, page 145

Leaders in all kinds of organizations must be able to effectively handle change management. Luckily, help is available at the Web site of the Management Assistance Program for Nonprofits http://www.mapnp.org/library/mgmnt/orgchnge.htm. Read "Basic Context for Organizational Change" and then explore some of the links before answering these questions.

1. What is the distinction between organizational change and smaller-scale change in an organization? What are some examples of organization-wide change?

2. Why do employees and managers often resist change? What can top management do to address such resistance to organizational change?

3. Scroll down to "Related Library Links," click on the "Change Management" link, and read about "selling" change. Based on this material, what mistakes do managers frequently make in their attempts to sell managing change? What three positive steps can management take to facilitate change?

7

ORGANIZING TO FACILITATE TEAMWORK AND COMMUNICATION

After studying this chapter, you will be able to

1 Discuss the function of a company's organization structure

2 Explain the concepts of accountability, authority, and delegation

3 Define four types of departmentalization

4 Highlight the advantages and disadvantages of working in teams

5 Describe the five primary formats of cross-functional teams

6 Review the five stages of team development

FACING BUSINESS CHALLENGES AT WAINWRIGHT INDUSTRIES

Open Communication Plus Teamwork Equals Award-Winning Quality

Did the owners and managers of Wainwright Industries, a family-run manufacturer of components for automotive and aerospace companies, sincerely trust and believe in their employees? CEO Arthur D. Wainwright first faced the question of trust in the early 1990s. He and several other managers were listening to a presentation by a winner of the Malcolm Baldrige National Quality Award. When the speaker mentioned "trust and belief," a Wainwright plant manager became intrigued. He wrote the phrase down and passed it to the other managers with the notation, "What is that?" Another manager scribbled, "I don't know. Do we have it at Wainwright?" The plant manager wrote back, "If we don't know what it is, we probably don't have it."

That exchange, captured on a napkin, changed Wainwright Industries forever. "We had a lot of discussions after that day," the CEO said later, "and we realized that no matter what we said about our commitment to involve employees, managers were still running the show." Indeed, prior to that day, CEO Wainwright had taken some basic steps to improve participation, communication, and teamwork. Managers were trained in world-class operations; everyone, from assembly workers to senior managers, wore uniforms with "Team Wainwright" embroidered above the pocket; and employees had been renamed "associates" as part of a companywide team-building effort. Still, something wasn't right. Even though the business was growing, profits weren't keeping pace. Furthermore, frustration was building up and down the hierarchy because, despite Wainwright's efforts, decision-making power was still firmly concentrated at the very top.

So Wainwright decided to make a daring, public break from the past. He and the other owners began with a confession: "We stood up in front of all the associates and told them we knew they were committed to us but that we were still trying to make decisions for them." From now on, he told them, the company would have "sincere trust and belief" in its employees, treating them like "responsible, adult human beings" who, with proper training, could do an even better job of applying their talents and energies.

With promises such as these, Wainwright certainly had his work cut out for him. What could he do to foster more effective teamwork and employee participation in the company's decisions, plans, and operations? How could he show employees that the company genuinely valued their ideas and involvement? How could he encourage more open communication within the organization?[1]

DESIGNING AN EFFECTIVE ORGANIZATION STRUCTURE

LEARNING OBJECTIVE 1
Discuss the function of a company's organization structure

organization structure
Framework enabling managers to divide responsibilities, ensure employee accountability, and distribute decision-making authority

organization chart
Diagram showing how employees and tasks are grouped and where the lines of communication and authority flow

informal organization
Network of informal employee interactions that are not defined by the formal structure

As Arthur Wainwright can tell you, the decision-making authority of employees and managers is supported by the company's **organization structure.** This structure helps the company achieve its goals by providing a framework for managers to divide responsibilities, hold employees accountable for their work, and effectively distribute the authority to make decisions. Managers rely on a formal organization structure to coordinate and control the organization's work. In some organizations, this structure is a relatively rigid, vertical hierarchy like the management pyramid described in Chapter 6. In other organizations, teams of employees and managers from across levels and functions work together to make decisions and achieve the organization's goals.[2]

When managers design the organization's structure, they use an **organization chart** to provide a visual representation of how employees and tasks are grouped and how the lines of communication and authority flow. Exhibit 7.1 shows the organization chart for a grocery store chain. An organization chart depicts the official design for accomplishing tasks that lead to achieving the organization's goals, a framework known as the *formal organization.* Every company also has an **informal organization**—the network of interactions that develop on a personal level among workers. Sometimes the interactions among people in the informal organization parallel their relationships in the formal organization, but often interactions transcend formal boundaries. Crossing formal boundaries can help establish a

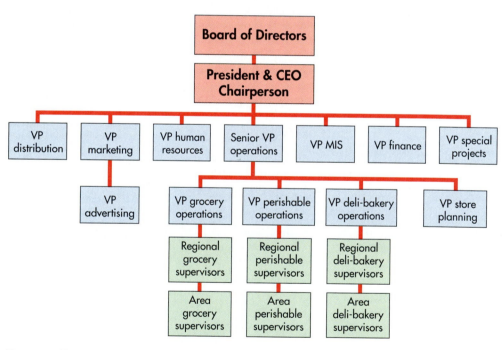

EXHIBIT 7•1

ORGANIZATION CHART FOR FOOD LION GROCERY STORE CHAIN

At first look, organization charts may appear very similar. In fact, the traditional model of an organization is a pyramid in which numerous boxes form the base and lead up to fewer and fewer boxes on higher levels, ultimately arriving at one box at the top. A glance at Food Lion's organization chart reveals who has authority over whom, who is responsible for whose work, and who is accountable to whom.

more pleasant work environment, but it can also undermine formal work processes and hinder a company's ability to get things done.[3]

How do companies design an organization structure, and which organization structure is the most effective? As management guru Peter Drucker sees it, "There is no such thing as one right organization. Each has distinct strengths, distinct limitations, and specific applications." Drucker further notes that managers of the future will require a toolbox full of organization structures and will have to select the right tool for each specific task: on some tasks employees will be working in teams; on others, under a traditional command-and-control hierarchy.[4] Nevertheless, four factors must be taken into consideration when designing an effective organization structure: work specialization, chain of command, vertical organization, and horizontal organization and coordination.

Work Specialization

Work specialization, also referred to as *division of labor,* is the degree to which organizational tasks are broken down into separate jobs.[6] Few employees have the skills to perform every task a company needs. Therefore, work specialization can improve organizational efficiency by enabling each worker to perform tasks that are well defined and that require specific skills. For example, in 1776 Scottish economist Adam Smith found that if each of ten workers went through every step needed to make a pin, the entire group could make 200 pins a day. However, if each worker performed only a few steps and no one made a pin from start to finish, the same ten workers could make 48,000 pins a day. When employees concentrate on the same specialized tasks, they can perfect their skills and perform their tasks more quickly. A classic example of work specialization is the automobile assembly line.

However, organizations can overdo specialization. If a task is defined too narrowly, employees may become bored with performing the same tiny, repetitive job over and over. They may also feel unchallenged and alienated. Managers must think carefully about how specialized or how broad each task should be. In fact, a growing number of companies are balancing specialization and employee motivation through teamwork. This approach enables group members to decide how to break down a complex task, and it allows employees to rotate among the jobs that the team is collectively responsible for. The team then shares credit for the results, and workers feel that they have created something of value. The team approach to organization is discussed in more depth later in this chapter.

Chain of Command

Besides incorporating work specialization into an organizational structure, companies must also establish a **chain of command,** the unbroken line of authority that connects each level of management with the next level. The chain of command helps organizations function smoothly by making two things clear: who is responsible for each task, and who has the authority to make official decisions.

All employees have a certain amount of **responsibility**—the obligation to perform the duties and achieve the goals and objectives associated with their jobs. As they work toward the organization's goals, employees must also maintain their **accountability,** their obligation to report the results of their work to supervisors or team members and to justify any outcomes that fall below expectations. Managers ensure that tasks are accomplished by exercising **authority,** the power to make decisions, issue orders, carry out actions, and allocate resources to achieve the organization's goals. Authority is vested in the positions that managers hold, and it flows down through the management pyramid. **Delegation** is the assignment of work and the transfer of authority and responsibility to complete that work.[7]

 To be effective, an organizational structure must be transparent.[5]

work specialization
Specialization in or responsibility for some portion of an organization's overall work tasks; also called division of labor

chain of command
Pathway for the flow of authority from one management level to the next

responsibility
Obligation to perform the duties and achieve the goals and objectives associated with a particular position

LEARNING OBJECTIVE 2
Explain the concepts of accountability, authority, and delegation

accountability
Obligation to report results to supervisors or team members and to justify outcomes that fall below expectations

authority
Power granted by the organization to make decisions, take actions, and allocate resources to accomplish goals

delegation
Assignment of work and the authority and responsibility required to complete it

EXHIBIT 7·2

SIMPLIFIED LINE-AND-STAFF STRUCTURE

A line-and-staff organization divides employees into those who are in the direct line of command (from the top level of the hierarchy to the bottom) and those who provide staff (or support) services to line managers at various levels. Staff reports directly to top management.

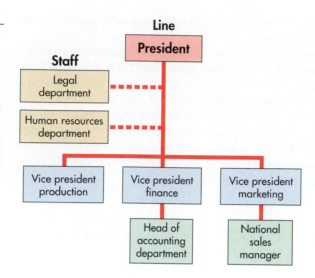

Look again at Exhibit 7.1. The senior vice president of operations delegates responsibilities to the vice presidents of grocery operations, perishable operations, deli-bakery operations, and store planning. These department heads have the authority to make certain decisions necessary to fulfill their roles, and they are accountable to the senior VP for the performance of their respective divisions. In turn, the senior VP is accountable to the company CEO.

The simplest and most common chain-of-command system is known as **line organization** because it establishes a clear line of authority flowing from the top down, as Exhibit 7.1 depicts. Everyone knows who is accountable to whom, as well as which tasks and decisions each is responsible for. However, line organization sometimes falls short because the technical complexity of a firm's activities may require specialized knowledge that individual managers don't have and can't easily acquire. A more elaborate system called **line-and-staff organization** was developed out of the need to combine specialization with management control. In such an organization, managers in the chain of command are supplemented by functional groupings of people known as *staff,* who provide advice and specialized services but who are not in the line organization's chain of command (see Exhibit 7.2).

Span of Management   The number of people a manager directly supervises is called the **span of management** or *span of control.* When a large number of people report directly to one person, that person has a wide span of management. This situation is common in **flat organizations** with relatively few levels in the management hierarchy. Sun Microsystems, Visa, and Oticon (a hearing-aid manufacturer in Denmark) are all companies that have flat organizations. In contrast, **tall organizations** have many hierarchical levels, usually with only a few people reporting to each manager. In such cases, the span of management is narrow (see Exhibit 7.3). General Motors has traditionally had a tall organization structure with as many as 22 layers of management. However, as are many companies, GM is flattening its organization structure by delegating some middle management responsibilities to work teams.[8]

No formula exists for determining the ideal span of management. How well people work together is more important than the number of people reporting to one person. Still, several factors affect the number of people a manager can effectively supervise, including the manager's personal skill and leadership ability, the skill of the workers, the motivation

line organization
Chain-of-command system that establishes a clear line of authority flowing from the top down

line-and-staff organization
Organization system that has a clear chain of command but that also includes functional groups of people who provide advice and specialized services

span of management
Number of people under one manager's control; also known as span of control

flat organizations
Organizations with a wide span of management and few hierarchical levels

tall organizations
Organizations with a narrow span of management and many hierarchical levels

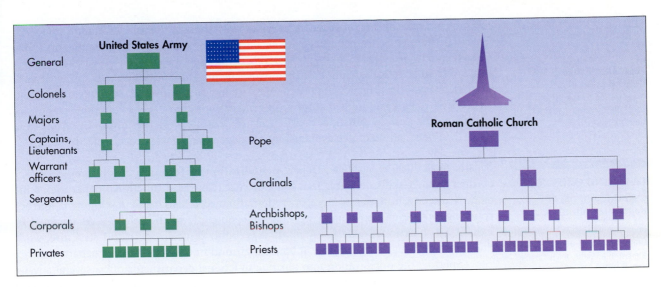

EXHIBIT 7·3

TALL VERSUS FLAT ORGANIZATIONS

A tall organization has many levels with a narrow span of management at each level so that relatively few people report to each manager on the level above them. In contrast, a flat organization has relatively few levels with a wide span of management so that more people report to each manager.

of the workers, and the nature of the job. In general, employees who are highly skilled or who are trained in many work tasks don't require as much supervision as employees who are less skilled.

Centralization Versus Decentralization   Organizations that focus decision-making authority near the top of the chain of command are said to be centralized. **Centralization** benefits a company by utilizing top management's rich experience and broad view of organizational goals. Both line organizations and line-and-staff organizations tend to be rather centralized.

However, the trend in business today is to decentralize. As Arthur Wainwright discovered, **decentralization** pushes decision-making authority down to lower organizational levels, thereby easing the burden on top executives and offering lower-level employees a greater challenge. Also, because decisions don't have to be referred up the hierarchy, decision making in a decentralized organization tends to be faster.[9] Consider General Electric. Managers at each of GE's 13 independent businesses have $25 million they can spend as they see fit without having to get the approval of the board of directors or the CEO. Giving each core business more decision-making authority has helped GE achieve tremendous growth in sales and profits.[10]

Keep in mind that decentralization does not work in every situation or in every company. At times, strong authority from the top of the chain of command may be needed to keep the organization focused on immediate goals. Managers should select the level of decision making that will most effectively serve the organization's needs given the individual circumstances.[11]

Vertical Organization

Choosing between a vertical and a horizontal model is one of the most critical decisions a company can make. Many organizations use a traditional vertical structure to define formal relationships and the division of tasks among employees and managers. **Vertical organization**

centralization
Concentration of decision-making authority at the top of the organization

decentralization
Delegation of decision-making authority to employees in lower-level positions

vertical organization
Structure linking activities at the top of the organization with those at the middle and lower levels

links the activities at the top of the organization with those at the middle and lower levels.[12] This structure also helps managers delegate authority to positions throughout the organization's hierarchy. Besides authority, the structure defines specific jobs and activities across vertical levels. In a vertical organization, companies define jobs and activities by using **departmentalization**—the arrangement of activities into logical groups that are then clustered into larger departments and units that form the total organization.[13] Four common ways of departmentalizing are by function, division, matrix, and network. An organization may use more than one method of departmentalization, depending on its particular needs.

departmentalization
Grouping people within an organization according to function, division, matrix, or network

Departmentalization by Function   **Departmentalization by function** groups employees according to their skills, resource use, and expertise. Common functional departments include marketing, human resources, operations, finance, research and development, and accounting, with each department working independently of the others.[14] As depicted in Exhibit 7.1, functional departmentalization is highly centralized. In this structure, work doesn't flow through the company, it bounces around from department to department.

Splitting the organization into separate functional departments offers several advantages: (1) Grouping employees by specialization allows for the efficient use of resources and encourages the development of in-depth skills; (2) centralized decision making enables unified direction by top management; and (3) centralized operations enhance communication and the coordination of activities within departments. Despite these advantages, functional departmentalization can create communication barriers between departments, thereby slowing response to environmental change, hindering effective planning for products and markets, and overemphasizing work specialization (which alienates employees).[15] For these reasons, most large companies have abandoned the functional structure in the past decade or so.

LEARNING OBJECTIVE 3
Define four types of departmentalization

departmentalization by function
Grouping workers according to their similar skills, resource use, and expertise

Departmentalization by Division   **Departmentalization by division** establishes self-contained departments that encompass all the major functional resources required to achieve their goals—such as research and design, manufacturing, finance, and marketing. These departments are typically formed according to similarities in product, process, customer, or geography.

departmentalization by division
Grouping departments according to similarities in product, process, customer, or geography

- *Product divisions.* Time Warner uses a structure based on **product divisions**—grouping companies that make similar products into appropriate divisions such as Cable Networks, Publishing, Entertainment, and Cable Systems (see Exhibit 7.4). Other companies that use product divisions include General Motors, duPont, and Procter & Gamble.[16]

product divisions
Divisional structure based on products

- *Process divisions.* **Process divisions,** also called *process-complete* departments, are based on the major steps of a production process. For example, a table-manufacturing company might have three divisions, one for each phase of manufacturing a table. Astra/Merck, a company that markets anti-ulcer and anti-hypertension drugs, is organized around six process divisions, including drug development and distribution.[17]

process divisions
Divisional structure based on the major steps of a production process

EXHIBIT 7·4

PRODUCT DIVISIONS

Time Warner employees are grouped according to what they produce, a grouping that brings together people of diverse skills.

- *Customer divisions.* The third approach, **customer divisions,** concentrates activities on satisfying specific groups of customers. For example, Johnson & Johnson devotes a separate division to each of its three main types of customers for health-care products: (1) consumer, (2) professional, and (3) pharmaceutical markets.
- *Geographic divisions.* **Geographic divisions** enable companies spread over a national or an international area to respond more easily to local customs, styles, and product preferences. For example, Quaker Oats has two main geographic divisions: (1) U.S. and Canadian Grocery Products and (2) International Grocery Products. Each division is further subdivided to allow the company to focus on the needs of customers in specific region.

customer divisions
Divisional structure that focuses on customers or clients

geographic divisions
Divisional structure based on location of operations

Divisional departmentalization offers both advantages and disadvantages. First, because divisions are self-contained, they can react quickly to change, thus making the organization more flexible. In addition, because each division focuses on a limited number of products, processes, customers, or locations, divisions can offer better service to customers. Moreover, top managers can focus on problem areas more easily, and managers can gain valuable experience by dealing with the various functions in their divisions. However, divisional departmentalization can also increase costs by duplicating the use of resources such as facilities and personnel. Furthermore, poor coordination between divisions may cause them to focus too narrowly on divisional goals and neglect the organization's overall goals. Finally, divisions may compete with one another for employees, money, and other resources, causing rivalries that hurt the organization as a whole.[18]

Departmentalization by Matrix **Departmentalization by matrix** is a structural design in which employees from functional departments form teams to combine their specialized skills. This structure allows the company to pool and share resources across divisions and functional groups. The matrix may be a permanent feature of the organization's design, or it may be established to complete a specific project. Consider Black & Decker, which formed a matrix organization in the early 1990s. Departments such as mechanical design, electrical engineering, and model shop assigned employees with specific technical skills to work on product-development projects in such categories as saws, cordless appliances, and woodworking.[19]

The major drawback of a matrix structure is that team members usually continue to report to their functional department heads as well as to a project team leader (see Exhibit 7.5). Black & Decker realized this soon after it implemented the matrix organization.

departmentalization by matrix
Assigning employees to both a functional group and a project team (thus using functional and divisional patterns simultaneously)

See It on the Web See It on the Web

HOW ORGANIZATIONS GET ORGANIZED

Want an inside peek at how real organizations are structured? A growing number of government agencies and companies are posting their organization charts on the Web for the world to see. Some show no names, just listing job titles in the individual boxes. Others, including the City of Sacramento, name names as well as positions. Looking at Sacramento's organization chart will show you the chain of command, the span of management, and the departmentalization method. And clicking on any name will lead you to detailed contact information for that part of the organization. In short, this chart's a virtual who's who for Sacramento government.
http://www.sacto.org/cityorg.htm

EXHIBIT 7·5

DEPARTMENTALIZATION BY MATRIX

In a matrix structure, each employee is assigned to both a functional group (with a defined set of basic functions, such as production manager) and a project team (which consists of members of various functional groups working together on a project, such as bringing out a new consumer product).

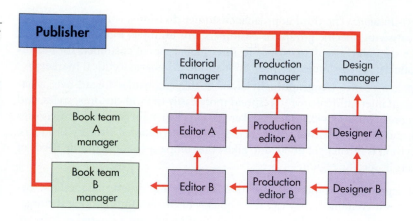

The manager with the most authority was always the functional department head, and the project team did not really hold any control. The company has since redesigned its organization structure, which is now based on product divisions that employ teams of people from many functional areas.[20]

In a matrix organization, excellent communication and coordination are necessary to avoid conflicts. In addition, companies may find it difficult to coordinate the tasks of diverse functional specialists so that projects are completed efficiently.[21] However, because it facilitates the pooling of resources across departments, a matrix organization can also enable a company to respond better to changes in the business environment.

departmentalization by network
Electronically connecting separate companies that perform selected tasks for a small headquarters organization

Departmentalization by Network   **Departmentalization by network** is a method of electronically connecting separate companies that perform selected tasks for a headquarters organization. Also called a *virtual organization,* the network organization *outsources* engineering, marketing, research, accounting, production, distribution, or other functions. This means that the organization hires other organizations under contracts to handle one or more of those functions. In fact, companies such as Nike, Liz Claiborne, and Dell Computer sell hundreds of millions of dollars' worth of products even though they don't own manufacturing facilities—they all outsource manufacturing. As these companies have learned, the network approach is especially appropriate for international operations, allowing every part of the business to draw on resources no matter where in the world they may be.[22]

A network structure can also enable small companies to compete on a large scale. For example, Barbara Schrager operates Attainment Marketing Partners with only one employee. By using a virtual staff of designers and copywriters who work under contract on specific projects, she is able to create marketing, advertising, and public relations campaigns for major clients in New York.[23]

As Barbara Schrager knows, a network structure is extremely flexible because it gives companies the ability to hire whatever services are needed and then change them after a short time. The limited hierarchy required to manage a network organization also permits the company to make decisions and react to change quickly. Additional advantages are that the organization can continually redefine itself, and a lean structure usually means employees have greater job variety and satisfaction. However, the network approach lacks hands-on control, because the functions are not in one location or company. Also, if one company in the network fails to deliver, the headquarters organization could suffer or even go out of business. Finally, strong employee loyalty and team spirit are less likely to develop, because the emotional connection between the employee and the organization is weak.[24]

Horizontal Organization

More and more businesses are transforming their traditional bureaucratic and hierarchical vertical structure into a horizontal organization.[25] The horizontal organization rejects the separation of people and work into functional departments by using the team concept to flatten hierarchies and integrate the many tasks of a business into a few smooth-flowing operations. British Petroleum (BP), for example, is amazingly flat and lean for an organization with $70 billion in revenues, 53,000 employees, and 90 business units that span the globe. At BP there is no level between the general managers of the business units and the group of nine operating executives who oversee the businesses.[26]

In a horizontal organization employees from various departments or functions are grouped around a few organizationwide, cross-functional core processes, and they are responsible for an entire core process from beginning to end. A typical core process group might include staff from finance, research and development, manufacturing, and customer service. All core processes lead to one objective: creating and delivering something of value to the cus-

tomer. For example, the Occupational Safety and Health Administration (OSHA), the U.S. agency charged with protecting the safety of workers, organized its 1,400 field employees around two basic core processes: (1) preventing workplace accidents and (2) responding to accidents and complaints.[27]

The biggest benefit of horizontal organization is that everyone works together. No longer can employees be concerned only with creating new product designs, for example, and letting others worry about whether those designs can be manufactured or marketed. Some companies are finding that a hybrid organization combining vertical and horizontal functions works best. In these firms, core processes are supported by organizationwide functional departments such as human resources and finance. The Xerox corporation, for example, organized its business operations around five core processes based on five types of products. The core processes are supported by two companywide vertical operations: technology management and customer service. This way researchers are not constrained by specific markets, and customers face only one customer service representative even if they buy different product types.[28]

A modular office layout such as this one at Continental Packaging Products encourages an open communication climate and the sharing of information among employees.

By now you can see that whether it uses a traditional vertical or an innovative horizontal organization structure, every organization must coordinate activities and communication among its employees. **Horizontal coordination** facilitates communication across departments without the need to go up and down the vertical chain of command. Horizontal coordination also gives employees the opportunity to share their views, which strengthens their willingness to understand, support, and implement innovative ideas. Without horizontal coordination, functional departments would be isolated from one another, and they would be unable to align their objectives.[29] Of course, one way to inject horizontal coordination into a vertical structure is by working in teams.

horizontal coordination
Coordinating communication and activities across departments

◼ WORKING IN TEAMS

Even though the vertical chain of command is a tried-and-true method of organizing for business, it is limited by the fact that decision-making authority is often located high up the management hierarchy. As a result, companies may become slow to react to change, and high-level managers may overlook many great ideas for improvement that originate in the lower levels of the organization. Many studies of individual industries show that companies using teamwork to organize, plan, and control activities enjoy greater productivity, increased profits, fewer defects, lower employee turnover, less waste, and even increased market value.[30]

team
A unit of two or more people who share a mission and collective responsibility as they work together to achieve a goal

A **team** is a unit of two or more people who work together to achieve a goal. Teams differ from other groups in that team members have a shared mission and are collectively responsible for their work. By coordinating their efforts, team members achieve performance levels that exceed what would have been accomplished if they had worked individually.[31] Teamwork also enables managers to delegate more authority and responsibility to lower-level employees, which inspires greater commitment and innovation in workers.

 The management pyramid can only be destroyed if managers are willing to share authority, responsibility, and power with employees.[32]

At Microsoft, almost all work is completed in teams. Two factors that have made Microsoft teams so successful are clear goals and strong leadership.[33] Although the team's goals may be set either by the team or by upper management, it is the job of the team leader to make sure the team stays on track to achieve those goals. Team leaders are often appointed by senior managers, but sometimes they emerge naturally as the team develops. Westinghouse Hanford, an electric power company, also uses teams. As one employee notes that, by using teams, "we come up with better ideas, work more cohesively and find better ways to solve problems." All of these factors help companies become more flexible and respond more quickly to the challenges of the competitive global environment.[34]

Similarly, at SEI Investments, administrator for $121 billion in investor assets, the defining unit of operation is the team. Finding itself indistinguishable from other competitors, SEI took a wrecking ball to the traditional corporate pyramid and formed 140 self-managed teams to speed up reaction time, innovate more quickly, and get closer to the customer. Some SEI teams are permanent, designed to serve big customers or important markets; others are temporary—they come together to solve a problem and disband when their work is done. This flexible team structure is supported by having all office furniture on wheels so that employees can create their own work areas to accommodate many different teams. In fact, employees move their desks so often that SEI has created software to map every employee's location.[35]

Earth and Environmental Services in San Francisco encourages its employees to work collaboratively so they can benefit from the knowledge of other team members.

According to a recent survey of Fortune 1000 executives, 83 percent said their firms are working in teams or moving in that direction.[36] Even though this approach sounds promising, shifting to a team structure often requires a fundamental shift in the organization's culture. As Wainwright Industries learned, management must show strong support for team concepts by empowering teams to make important decisions about the work they do. Teams must also have clear goals that are tied to the company's strategic goals, and their outcomes need to be measured and compared with benchmarks. In addition, employees must be motivated to work together in teams. Motivating employees often involves extensive training and a compensation system that is based, at least in part, on team performance. This last objective is sometimes accomplished through the use of stock options, profit sharing, and performance bonuses. At Wainwright, for instance, 25 percent of company profits are set aside and split equally. This means the chairman, plant manager, punch-press operator, janitor, and everyone else in the organization gets the same amount.[37]

LEARNING OBJECTIVE 4
Highlight the advantages and disadvantages of working in teams

Advantages and Disadvantages of Working in Teams

Even though teams can play a vital role in helping an organization reach its goals, they are not appropriate for every situation. Managers must weigh both the advantages and the disadvantages of teams when deciding whether to use them.[38]

Teams have the potential to unleash vast amounts of creativity and energy in workers. Motivation and performance are often increased as workers share a sense of purpose and mutual accountability. Teams can also fill the individual worker's need to belong to a group. Furthermore, they can reduce boredom, increase feelings of dignity and self-worth, and reduce stress and tension between workers. Finally, teams empower employees to bring more knowledge and skill to the tasks they perform and thereby often lead to greater efficiency and cost reduction. And, when employees work together in teams and are able to exchange jobs, the organization becomes more flexible. Workers can be reallocated as needed, and the company can meet changing customer needs more effectively.

All of this can add up to more satisfied employees performing higher-quality work that helps the organization achieve its goals. Consider Kodak. Using teams has allowed it to cut in half the amount of time it takes to move a new product from the drawing board to store shelves. Tennessee Eastman, a division of Eastman Chemical, increased labor productivity by 70 percent; Texas Instruments increased revenues per employee by over 50 percent; and Ritz-Carlton Hotels jumped to the top of the J. D. Power and Associates consumer survey of luxury hotels—all as a result of teamwork.[39]

Although teamwork has many advantages, it also has a number of potential disadvantages. For one thing, power within the organization sometimes becomes realigned with teams. Successful teams mean that fewer supervisors are needed, and usually fewer middle and front-line managers. Adjusting to their changing job roles, or even to the loss of their jobs, is understandably difficult for many people. Another potential disadvantage is **free riders**—team members who don't contribute their fair share to the group's activities because they aren't being held individually accountable for their work. The free-ride attitude can lead to certain tasks' going unfulfilled. Still another drawback to teamwork is the high cost of coordinating group activities. Aligning schedules, arranging meetings, and coordinating individual parts of a project can eat up a lot of time and money. Moreover, a team may develop *groupthink,* a situation in which pressures to conform to the norms of the group cause members to withhold contrary or unpopular opinions. Groupthink can hinder effective decision making because some possibilities will be overlooked.[40] Finally, teams aren't effective for all situations. As management guru Peter Drucker puts it, "When the ship goes down, you don't call a meeting. The captain gives an order or everybody drowns. One of the most important things for executives to learn is when to be in command and when to be a colleague."[41]

free riders
Team members who do not contribute sufficiently to the group's activities because members are not being held individually accountable for their work

Types of Teams

The type, structure, and composition of individual teams within an organization all depend on the organization's strategic goals. Companies may establish *informal teams* that are designed to encourage employee participation but that aren't part of the formal organization, or they can create *formal teams* that become part of the organization's structure.

Informal Teams   The most common type of informal team is the **problem-solving team.** This type of team usually consists of 5 to 12 employees from the same department who meet voluntarily to find ways of improving quality, efficiency, and the work environment. Any recommendations they come up with are then submitted to management for approval.[42] Such teams are sometimes referred to as *quality circles.* Land Rover, a manufacturer of luxury sport-utility vehicles, was able to save millions of dollars, improve productivity, and sell more vehicles by using this type of team.[43] If the problem-solving teams are able to successfully contribute to the organization, as Land Rover's were, they may evolve into formal teams, a change that represents a fundamental shift in the way the organization is structured.

problem-solving team
Informal team of 5 to 12 employees from the same department who meet voluntarily to find ways of improving quality, efficiency, and the work environment

OFFICE ETHICS: TEAMS MAKE IT HARD TO TATTLE

A co-worker fakes a document, steals from petty cash, or sneaks trade secrets to the competition. Do you tell the boss? That may depend on whether you work alone or on a team.

The rise in the use of employee teams has some experts worried that unethical behavior is going unreported. Members of a team often forge close ties. "You know them, and you're more dependent on one another," says the executive director of the Ethics Officer Association. Experts say that reluctance to blow the whistle on co-workers makes sense. It's truth versus loyalty. Is it right to tell the truth and risk losing friendships? Apparently not. At least that's what the statistics show.

A recent study found that 21 percent of workers did not report misconduct by a colleague. Furthermore, 96 percent of those who failed to turn in a co-worker for unethical behavior did so because they feared they would be accused of "not being a team player." Even people who want to do the right thing worry that turning in a team member reflects badly on the whole group.

So what's a manager to do? Experts suggest managers begin by fostering an open environment where workers feel safe voicing concerns. Managers should also (1) draft ethics policies and share them with all employees; (2) give team members a way to provide confidential information without fear of retribution; (3) encourage workers to tell if something is amiss by assuring confidentiality; and (4) follow up with employees who do report unethical behavior so they will know their input was taken seriously. Finally, managers should keep their eyes and ears open. A recent study found that 48 percent of employees admitted to illegal or unethical actions in one year.

QUESTIONS FOR CRITICAL THINKING

1. One of your teammates just informed you that she has accepted a new job with the company's key competitor. The project you're both working on is confidential, and you're concerned that if she stays on the team, she'll learn some trade secrets to take to her new employer. What should you do?

2. Last month you reported to the human resources department that two of your teammates called in sick when they were really on vacation. Now all of your teammates are giving you the cold shoulder. How should you handle this situation?

---

functional teams
Teams whose members come from a single functional department and that are based on the organization's vertical structure

Formal Teams   Formal teams typically fall into two categories: functional and cross-functional teams. **Functional teams,** or *command teams,* are organized along the lines of the organization's vertical structure and thus may be referred to as vertical teams. They are composed of managers and employees within a single functional department. For example, look again at Exhibit 7.1. Functional teams could be formed in Food Lion's marketing, human resources, and finance departments. The structure of a vertical team typically follows the formal chain of command. In some cases, the team may include several levels of the organizational hierarchy within the same functional department.[44]

cross-functional teams
Teams that draw together employees from different functional areas

In contrast to functional teams, **cross-functional teams,** or horizontal teams, draw together employees from various functional areas and expertise. Boeing, for example, used hundreds of "design-build" teams that integrated design engineers and production workers to develop its new 777 airplane. In the past, the two groups worked independently, and engineers often came up with designs that production workers thought were either too costly or unbuildable. But now, Boeing is trying to destroy all the old functional hierarchies.[45]

Cross-functional teams have also become a way of life at Chrysler (now Daimler-Chrysler). Under the old setup, the company relied on functional departmentalization in

See It on the Web See It on the Web

BUILDING TEAMS IN THE CYBER AGE

If you want to learn more about building effective teams, you can read many excellent books on the subject. But you might be surprised by just how much information on team building you can find on the Internet. One good starting point is the Self Directed Work Teams page. This site's designers are passionate about teamwork, and they want to make it easier for people to work effectively in teams. Read the Frequently Asked Questions (FAQs) to better understand the site's purpose. Then explore some of the links to discover more about teams and teamwork.
http://users.ids.net/~brim/sdwth.html

which each function (such as design, engineering, manufacturing, and so on) handed the results of its work to the next function in essentially a sequential process that was time-consuming, costly, and prone to errors. Now team members from various functions work simultaneously and communicate frequently to ensure, for instance, that the shape of a particular body part will accommodate adjacent components. As a result, the company has reduced the time it takes to bring a new vehicle to market from five years to less than three years.[46]

Cross-functional teams are a good way to inject horizontal coordination into a typical vertical organization structure: (1) They facilitate the exchange of information between employees; (2) they generate ideas for how to best coordinate the organizational units that are represented; (3) they encourage new solutions for organizational problems; and (4) they aid the development of new organizational policies and procedures.[47] In many cross-functional teams, employees are cross-trained to perform a variety of tasks. At Pillsbury, for instance, the most experienced workers can handle 23 different jobs.[48] Keep in mind that cross-functional teams such as ones used at DaimlerChrysler and Pillsbury can take on a number of formats:

- *Self-directed teams.* In addition to cross-training all team members, a **self-directed team** must obtain all the information, equipment, and supplies necessary to perform its assigned tasks. As the name implies, self-directed teams manage their own activities and require minimum supervision. For instance, the team has the authority to make decisions such as how to spend money, whom to hire, and what plans to make for the future. As you might imagine, many managers are reluctant to embrace this approach because it means they must give up much of the control they have grown accustomed to.

- *Task forces.* A **task force** is a type of cross-functional team formed to work on a specific activity with a completion point. Several departments are usually involved so that all parties who have a stake in the outcome of the task are able to provide input. However, once the goal has been accomplished, the task force is disbanded.[49] Saint Francis Hospital in Tulsa, Oklahoma, established a task force to find ways to reduce the cost of supplies. The team members came from many departments, including surgery, laboratory, nursing, financial planning, administration, and food service. The team not only helped the hospital save money by curbing supply waste but also generated excitement among hospital employees about working together for common goals.[50]

LEARNING OBJECTIVE 5
Describe the five primary formats of cross-functional teams

self-directed team
Teams in which members are responsible for an entire process or operation

task force
Team of people from several departments who are temporarily brought together to address a specific issue

committee
Team that may become a permanent part of the organization and is designed to deal with regularly recurring tasks

special-purpose teams
Temporary teams that exist outside the formal organization hierarchy and are created to achieve a specific goal

virtual team
Team that uses communication technology to bring geographically distant employees together to achieve goals

- *Committees.* In contrast to a task force, a **committee** usually has a long life span and may become a permanent part of the organization structure. Committees typically deal with regularly recurring tasks. For example, a grievance committee may be formed as a permanent resource for handling employee complaints and concerns. Because committees often require official representation in order to achieve their goals, committee members are usually selected on the basis of their titles or positions rather than their personal expertise.

- *Special-purpose teams.* Like task forces, **special-purpose teams** are created as temporary entities to achieve specific goals. However, special-purpose teams are different because they exist outside the formal organization hierarchy. Such teams remain a part of the organization but they have their own reporting structures, and members view themselves as separate from the normal functions of the organization. A special-purpose team might be used to develop a new product when complete creative freedom is needed. By operating outside the formal organization, the team would be able to test new ideas and new ways of accomplishing tasks.[51]

- *Virtual teams.* As a result of both globalization and advances in technology, another type of cross-functional team, the **virtual team,** has emerged as a way of bringing together geographically distant employees to accomplish goals. A company may have plants and offices around the world, but it can use computer networks, teleconferencing, e-mail, and global transportation to build teams that are as effective as those in organizations functioning under a single roof. At British Petroleum, for example, virtual teams link workers in the Gulf of Mexico with teams working in the eastern Atlantic and around the globe. By using a virtual team network, the company has decreased the number of helicopter trips to offshore oil platforms, has avoided refinery shutdowns because technical experts at other locations were able to handle problems remotely, and has experienced a significant reduction in construction rework, among other benefits.[52] (Consult Part III of the *E-business in Action* online supplement at http://www.prenhall.com/ebusinessinaction for additional discussion of virtual collaboration, teams, and management of the virtual organization.)

Team Characteristics

When developing teams of any type, managers must consider certain team characteristics, such as size and member roles. The optimal size for teams is generally thought to be between 5 and 12 members. Teams smaller than 5 may be lacking in skill diversity and may therefore be less effective at solving problems. Teams of more than 12 may be too large for group members to bond properly and may discourage some members from sharing their ideas. Larger groups are also prone to disagreements and factionalism because so many opinions must be considered, so the team leader's job is more difficult. Moreover, studies have shown that turnover and absenteeism are higher in larger teams because members tend to feel that their presence makes less of a difference.

For a team to be successful over time, it must be structured to accomplish its task and to satisfy its members' needs for social well-being. Effective teams usually fulfill both requirements with a combination of members who assume one of four roles: task specialist, socioemotional role, dual role, or nonparticipator. People who assume the *task-specialist* role focus on helping the team reach its goals. In contrast, members who take on the *socio-emotional role* focus on supporting the team's emotional needs and strengthening the team's social unity. Some team members are able to assume *dual roles,* contributing to the task and still meeting members' emotional needs. These members often make effective team leaders.

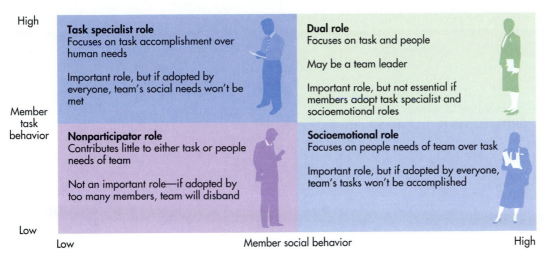

High

Task specialist role
Focuses on task accomplishment over human needs

Important role, but if adopted by everyone, team's social needs won't be met

Dual role
Focuses on task and people

May be a team leader

Important role, but not essential if members adopt task specialist and socioemotional roles

Member task behavior

Nonparticipator role
Contributes little to either task or people needs of team

Not an important role—if adopted by too many members, team will disband

Socioemotional role
Focuses on people needs of team over task

Important role, but if adopted by everyone, team's tasks won't be accomplished

Low

Low   Member social behavior   High

EXHIBIT 7·6

TEAM MEMBER ROLES
Team members assume one of these four roles. Members who assume a dual role often make effective team leaders.

At the other end of the spectrum are members who are *nonparticipators,* contributing little either to reaching the team's goals or to meeting members' emotional needs. Exhibit 7.6 outlines the behavior patterns associated with each of these roles.

Team Development

Like the members who form them, teams grow and change as time goes by. You may think that each team evolves in its own way. However, research shows that teams typically go through five definitive stages of development: forming, storming, norming, performing, and adjourning.[53] The *forming stage* is a period of orientation and breaking the ice. Members get to know each other, determine what types of behaviors are appropriate within the group, identify what is expected of them, and become acquainted with each other's task orientation. In the *storming stage,* members show more of their personalities and become more assertive in establishing their roles. Conflict and disagreement often arise during the storming stage as members jockey for position or form coalitions to promote their own perceptions of the group's mission. During the *norming stage,* these conflicts are resolved, and team harmony develops. Members come to understand and accept one another, reach a consensus on who the leader is, and reach agreement on what each member's roles are. In the *performing stage,* members are really committed to the team's goals. Problems are solved, and disagreements are handled with maturity in the interest of task accomplishment. Finally, if the team has a limited task to perform, it goes through the *adjourning stage* after the task has been completed. In this stage, issues are wrapped up and the team is dissolved.

As the team moves through the various stages of development, two things happen. First, the team develops a certain level of **cohesiveness,** a measure of how committed the members are to the team's goals. The team's cohesiveness is reflected in meeting attendance, team interaction, work quality, and goal achievement. Cohesiveness is influenced by many factors. Two primary factors are competition and evaluation. If a team is in competition with other teams, cohesiveness increases as the team strives to win. In addition, if a team's efforts and accomplishments are recognized by the organization, members tend to be more

LEARNING OBJECTIVE 6
Review the five stages of team development

cohesiveness
A measure of how committed the team members are to their team's goals

MERVYN'S CALLS SWAT TEAM TO THE RESCUE

The situation is tense. The stakes are high. Time is short. So who do you call for help if you're an executive at Mervyn's California facing the Christmas rush or the loss of a key manager? You call the company's SWAT team, of course.

Mervyn's is a department store chain with 32,000 employees and 270 locations in 14 states. Its SWAT team consists of 19 managers who race from division to division, usually at a moment's notice, to help with the kinds of crises that inevitably erupt in a high-pressure retail environment. SWAT team members must have experience in at least one specific discipline: buying, merchandising, or advertising. Assignments are as short as a week or as long as six months. Even though SWAT team members don't travel around in armored vehicles, life on the team can be pretty hectic.

This group of highly trained people can be deployed anywhere in the company's buying divisions, at any time, wherever they are needed. They can perform jobs quickly and efficiently, without a long learning curve. They help the company manage its unpredictable staffing needs, meet the requirements of its erratic markets, and seize unanticipated opportunities.

Originally created as an experiment to fill in for vacancies created by managers working flextime or on family leave, Mervyn's SWAT team has become something bigger. It has become an effective vehicle for moving talent around the company. SWAT team members aren't just good at learning fast; they're good at sharing what they've learned in other departments. And because team members have had a lot of exposure to various areas in the company, they're the most valued and highly sought after employees in the organization.

It's no surprise that the team's biggest problem is turnover: Members are frequently hired away for full-time positions by managers whom they've impressed. In fact, joining the SWAT team has become a high-priority career tactic for young people who want to move up or for veterans who want a change of pace.

QUESTIONS FOR CRITICAL THINKING

1. How could Mervyn's parent company, Dayton Hudson, use the SWAT team concept to benefit all its stores—Target, Dayton's, Hudson's, and Marshall Fields? (Hint: Think about the benefits of cross-functional teams.)

2. How does Mervyn's benefit from using the SWAT team concept on both a short-term and a long-term basis?

---

committed to the team's goals. Strong team cohesiveness generally results in high morale. Moreover, when cohesiveness is coupled with strong management support for team objectives, teams tend to be more productive.

norms
Informal standards of conduct that guide team behavior

The second thing that happens as teams develop is the emergence of **norms**—informal standards of conduct that members share and that guide their behavior. Norms define what is acceptable behavior. They also set limits, identify values, clarify what is expected of members, and facilitate team survival. Norms can be established in various ways: from early behaviors that set precedents for future actions, from significant events in the team's history, from behaviors that come to the team through outside influences, and from a leader's or member's explicit statements that have an impact on other members.[54]

Team Conflict

Managing a team requires many skills. However, none is more important than the ability to handle *conflict*—the antagonistic interactions resulting from differences in ideas, opinions, goals, or ways of doing things. Conflict can arise between team members or between different teams. Conflict interferes with the productive exchange of information and can destroy a team's cohesiveness.

Causes of Team Conflict   Team conflicts can arise for a number of reasons. First, teams and individuals may feel they are in competition for scarce or declining resources, such as money, information, and supplies. Second, team members may disagree about who is responsible for a specific task; this type of disagreement is usually the result of poorly defined responsibilities and job boundaries. Third, poor communication can lead to misunderstandings and misperceptions about other team members or other teams. In addition, intentionally withholding information can undermine trust among members. Fourth, basic differences in values, attitudes, and personalities may lead to clashes. Fifth, power struggles may result when one party questions the authority of another or when people or teams with limited authority attempt to increase their power or exert more influence. Sixth, conflicts can arise because individuals or teams are pursuing different goals.[55] For example, a British cardboard-manufacturing company switched from a hierarchical, functionally oriented organization to a team-based structure with the hope of empowering employees and reducing scrap. However, once they got started, the teams realized that the company had many problems to solve. Conflicts resulted when team members couldn't agree on which problems to tackle first.[56]

How to Resolve Team Conflict   Each team member has a unique style of dealing with conflict, but the members' styles are primarily based on how competitive or cooperative team members are when a conflict arises. Depending on the particular situation, the same individual may use one of several styles, which include avoidance, defusion, and confrontation.[57] *Avoidance* may involve ignoring the conflict in the hope that it will subside on its own, or it may even involve physically separating the conflicting parties. *Defusion* may involve several actions, including downplaying differences and focusing on similarities between team members or teams, compromising on the disputed issue, taking a vote, appealing to a neutral party or higher authority, or redesigning the team. *Confrontation* is an attempt to work through the conflict by getting it out in the open, which may be accomplished by organizing a meeting between the conflicting parties.

These three styles of conflict resolution come into play after a conflict has developed, but teams and team leaders can take several steps to prevent conflicts. First, by establishing clear goals that require the efforts of every member, the team reduces the chance that members will battle over their objectives or roles. Second, by developing well-defined tasks for each member, the team leader ensures that all parties are aware of their responsibilities and the limits of their authority. And finally, by facilitating open communication, the team leader can ensure that all members understand their own tasks and objectives as well as those of their teammates. Keep in mind that communication builds respect and tolerance, and it provides a forum for bringing misunderstandings into the open before they turn into full-blown conflicts.

The important thing to remember about resolving conflict is that people can usually get what they want if they are willing to work together. In many cases, the resolution process is an exchange of opinions and information that gradually leads to a mutually acceptable solution.

MANAGING THE FLOW OF INFORMATION ◼ IN THE ORGANIZATION

Whether an organization has a tall, vertical structure or is made up of cross-functional teams, communication provides the crucial link between individuals, teams, departments, and divisions. The sharing of information among the parts of an organization, as well as between the organization and the outside world, is the glue that binds the organization together. In a large organization, transmitting the right information to the right people at the right time is a real challenge. To meet this challenge, organizations depend on both formal and informal communication channels.

Formal and Informal Communication Channels

formal communication network
Communication network that follows the official structure of the organization

The **formal communication network** is aligned with the official structure of the organization. As we have seen, this structure is illustrated by an organization chart such as the one in Exhibit 7.1. Each box in the chart represents a link in the chain of command, and each line represents a formal channel for the transmission of official messages. Information may travel down, up, and across channels in the organization's formal hierarchy.

distortion
Misunderstanding that results when a message passes through too many links in the organization

When managers depend too heavily on formal channels for communicating, they risk encountering **distortion,** or misunderstanding. Every link in the communication chain opens up a chance for error. So by the time a message makes its way all the way up or down the chain, it may bear little resemblance to the original idea. As a consequence, people at lower levels may have only a vague idea of what top management expects of them, and executives may get an imperfect picture of what's happening lower down the chain. This is less of a problem in flat organizations than it is in tall organizations, as fewer levels means fewer links in the communication chain.

informal communication network
Communication network that follows the organization's unofficial lines of activity and power

Formal organization charts illustrate how information is supposed to flow; in actual practice lines and boxes on a piece of paper cannot prevent people from developing other communication channels. The **informal communication network** is the invisible side of the organization: It consists of who talks to whom, who listens to whom, and who is really making the decisions and moving the work forward. This informal network isn't reflected in the formal chart. The formal and informal organizations coexist in the same space and time, but they are often independent entities, operating sometimes in concert and sometimes at cross-purposes.[58]

See It on the Web See It on the Web

COMMUNICATIONS MASTER CLASS ONLINE

With a click of your mouse, you can delve deeper into the topic of organizational communication. Spotlight Communications, a U.K. firm, offers an online Communications Master Class with many valuable tips about becoming a good communicator. From planning to audience analysis to effective listening, this cyberclass covers all the basics. So click your way to better communication by browsing the lessons at this informative site.
http://www.spotlightcommunications.co.uk/frameset.htm

Barriers to Communication

Executives say that 14 percent of each 40-hour workweek is wasted because of poor communication between staff and management. Part of the problem stems from today's time crunch. Often, ideas are shared over the telephone lines instead of over lunch. Dashed-off e-mail has replaced thoughtful letters.[59] Nevertheless, in most cases the biggest barrier to communication is simply a lack of attention on the receiver's part. We all let our minds wander now and then, regardless of how hard we try to concentrate, especially if we are tired or if we feel that the information is too difficult or is unimportant. Communication can also break down if either the sender or the receiver has strong emotions about a subject.

Additional communication barriers include:

Learning as much as possible about another culture will enhance your ability to communicate with its members.

- *Perceptual differences.* How people perceive meanings of words, gestures, tone of voice, and other symbols is affected by their background, including age, culture, education, gender, economic position, religion, or political views.

- *Incorrect filtering.* People often screen out or abbreviate information before passing a message on to someone else. In business, secretaries, assistants, associates, and voice mail are just a few of the filters that exist between you and your receiver.

- *Language.* Even among people of the same culture, language can become a barrier to communication. If you have ever tried to read a legal contract, you know the problem. Lawyers, doctors, accountants, and computer programmers all use specialized vocabularies that affect their ability to communicate ideas.

Of course, many other factors can distort both the messages you send and those you receive in an organization. However, through a conscious commitment to quality communication, almost any barrier can be overcome. Moreover, as Arthur Wainwright discovered, designing an organization structure that facilitates teamwork and communication is an important first step.

Summary of Learning Objectives

1. **Discuss the function of a company's organization structure.**
   An organization structure provides a framework through which a company can coordinate and control the work, divide responsibilities, distribute authority, and hold employees accountable.

2. **Explain the concepts of accountability, authority, and delegation.**
   Accountability is the obligation to report work results to supervisors or team members and to justify any outcomes that fall below expectations. Authority is the power to make decisions, issue orders, carry out actions, and allocate

resources to achieve the organization's goals. Delegation is the assignment of work and the transfer of authority and responsibility to complete that work.

3. **Define four types of departmentalization.**
   Companies may departmentalize in any combination of four ways: (1) by function, which groups employees according to their skills, resource use, and expertise; (2) by division, which establishes self-contained departments formed according to similarities in product, process, customer, or geography; (3) by matrix, which assigns employees from functional departments to interdisciplinary project teams and requires them to report to both a

BEHIND THE SCENES

MEETING BUSINESS CHALLENGES AT WAINWRIGHT INDUSTRIES

In the early 1990s, Wainwright Industries was growing, but its employees and middle managers were frustrated because top managers controlled all the decisions. After hearing a Baldrige Award winner talk about trust and belief in employees, Wainwright's owners and senior managers realized that they were not acting as if they trusted and believed in their own work force. CEO Arthur Wainwright announced that the company was going to change. Now he had to follow through.

First, he designated worker safety and skills as a top priority. This was a tangible way for the company to demonstrate its commitment to its employees. Wainwright set aside 6 to 7 percent of the yearly payroll budget for training on safety, interpersonal skills, math, reading, and writing. New employees received a day-long orientation on the company and its safety procedures, followed by two weeks of on-the-job training with a trainer and one or more experienced employees.

Next, with training in place and ongoing management reinforcement, the company was able to implement a more effective team structure. Instead of following managers' orders, employees would participate in making and implementing decisions through a new team structure, with leaders serving as trainers and coaches to six members. This shift was initially unsettling to both managers and employees, but employees soon developed confidence in their abilities. "I can't imagine going back to the old way of doing things now," commented one employee. "If I say something isn't safe, nobody second-guesses me or tells me to go back to work."

Wainwright also implemented a new communication philosophy, which he summed up in two words: no secrets. "If you try to hide vital information," said the CEO, "you're wasting your money on training, because people can't make sound decisions. Furthermore, they won't trust that you are committed to equipping them with what they need to do a good job." The company jump-started the formal communication process by asking employees what was important to their per-

formance. In addition, the CEO met with each new employee to explain company priorities and discuss any concerns. The result: Safety, involvement, customer satisfaction, quality, and financial performance were incorporated into Wainwright's goals and plans, and these new policies reduced the number of accidents, the amount of lost time, and the amount spent on workers' compensation.

Once all these changes were in place, the company went through the arduous process of applying for a Baldrige Award. Winning that award put Wainwright in the major leagues, alongside such award-winning giants as IBM. It also showed that trust, open communication, and participative teamwork can really make a difference.[60]

Critical Thinking Questions

1. What effect do you think the "no secrets" policy had on internal communication at Wainwright?

2. How was the company's new team structure likely to affect accountability and authority?

3. Is Wainwright's drive for more employee involvement in decision making an example of centralization or decentralization?

■ LEARN MORE ONLINE

Effective teamwork and communication have helped Wainwright and many other companies win the prestigious Baldrige Award. Visit the "winner's showcase" page of the Baldrige Award Web site at http://www.baldrige.org/show.htm and read through the profiles of recent winners. How have the winners improved quality through better teamwork? How have they boosted quality by paying closer attention to internal and external communication?

E-Business Integration

Business in Action's six-way integrated approach to electronic business reinforces its importance to students:

✓ E-Business Special Feature Boxes

Special "Focus On E-Business" boxes show students the many challenges successful e-companies must address to gain a competitive advantage in the world of electronic commerce. Students will discover that becoming an e-business takes much more than launching a Web site; it requires new skills, innovative thinking, new rules, speed, and flexibility. Each box contains two critical thinking questions, which guide students to think about the differences that exist between doing business in the e-world versus the traditional business environment.

Focus on e-business

HERE COMES THE ELECTRONIC ECONOMY

Without a doubt, the Internet is ushering in an era of sweeping change. It is tearing down the walls of geography and allowing businesses to reach markets anywhere in the world. It's spawning new businesses, transforming existing ones, saving companies money, and creating enormous new wealth. It's changing the way people shop for books, cars, vacations, advice—just about everything. It's forcing companies of all sizes and types to face new competition, explore new business opportunities, and adopt new ways of conducting business. In the span of just a few years, the Internet has touched every business and industry. But that's not good news for everyone.

Operating at an accelerated pace dubbed Internet time, companies conducting e-commerce move quickly and aggressively to develop Internet products and services, find capital, and win Web customers. Those that take advantage of the Net to revamp their businesses or build brand new ones stand to reap the rewards; those that wait or ignore the Internet's force are being squeezed out. Travel agencies, stockbrokers, and physical retail stores are just a few of the casualties. After all, as human tasks such as selling airline tickets, stock, and all kinds of consumer goods are taken over by the dot-coms, there's not much additional work left for those businesses to do.

Even more frightful, or exciting (depending on which side of the casualty line you're on) is the fact that the e-commerce (the buying and selling of goods and services over a network) is only in its infancy, and by all measures is expected to provide much of the fuel that will power the 21st century. Experts predict that revenues from e-commerce will exceed $1 trillion by 2005. That's a pretty impressive statistic considering the fact that only a handful of companies have figured out how to make money transacting business-to-consumer e-commerce, and nobody really knows its potential or its limits. Moreover, companies transacting e-commerce face many obstacles. For one thing, they must accept constant change as a reality. For another, they must redefine their relationships with suppliers, customers, and employees, and they must transform every aspect of their operations to become true e-businesses.

Fresh opportunities and big threats. That's the Web. In subsequent "Focus on E-Business" boxes, we'll take a closer look at how e-commerce is revolutionizing all facets of business life. You'll see that becoming an e-business in today's electronic economy takes much more than launching a Web site.

QUESTIONS FOR CRITICAL THINKING

1. Why must companies move at an accelerated pace in today's economy?
2. How is e-commerce facilitating the globalization of business?

For more examples see pages 20, 66, 83, 112, 136, 190, 210, etc...

✓ E-Business Chapter (Information Management, the Internet, and E-Business)

The Internet has forever changed the way companies transact business with each other and with customers. Component Chapter C discusses these changes in detail; it focuses on current trends and hot topics in e-commerce such as pricing, security, logistics, channel conflict, and legal issues; and explores the benefits and challenges e-businesses experience in the fast-paced e-world.

more ➔

✓ Outstanding & Unique Online Supplement called E-Business in Action

This outstanding, e-commerce online supplement was written specifically for *Business in Action*. Each electronic chapter is keyed to the seven text parts and includes learning objectives, real-world examples, discussion questions, a group activity, Internet exercises, and a mystery exercise. In-depth coverage of the latest trends and concepts in e-commerce include "Internet Privacy and Safety," "Virtual Training and Development," "Hot Online Pricing Strategies," "Internet IPOs," "Emerging Legal Issues in E-Commerce," and "Preparing for a Career in E-Commerce."

✓ Featured E-Businesses

Chapter vignettes, case studies, boxes, business mysteries, and in-text and online examples feature popular e-businesses such as AOL Time Warner, Cisco, Dell, E*Trade, eSchwab, Priceline, 1-800 Flowers, iPrint, eBay, Amazon, and more.

✓ Video Cases

Professionally produced video cases give students a first-hand view of the challenges that BMC, a business animation company, faces as it transacts business electronically.
For some examples see pages 77, 128, 203, 251, etc…

✓ Internet Exercises

Students become acquainted with the wealth of information on the Web by completing the text's "See it on the Web," "Learn More Online," and supplemental online Internet exercises.
For some examples see pages 4, 14, 16, 25, 32, 39, 41, 49, 55, 62, 67, 75, 87, 93, 98, 103, etc…

ADDED BONUS—E-BIZ: PRENTICE HALL GUIDE TO E-BUSINESS AND E-COMMERCE SUPPLEMENT

Take your students behind the scenes to explore the dynamic world of e-business with this new multidisciplinary supplement. The supplement's printed component offers ten modules that examine the challenges and opportunities e-businesses face in such disciplines as strategy, marketing, management, finance, and more. Each module includes key-term definitions and one mini-case study. Special sections include: career development on the Internet, distance learning on the Internet, and tips for successful online searches.

department head and a team leader; and (4) by network, which connects separate companies that perform selected tasks for a headquarters organization.

4. **Highlight the advantages and disadvantages of working in teams.**
   Teamwork has the potential to increase creativity, motivation, performance, and satisfaction of workers and thereby can lead to greater company efficiency, flexibility, and cost savings. The potential disadvantages of working in teams include the difficulties of managing employees' changing roles, the possibilities of free riders and groupthink, and the costs and time needed to coordinate member's schedules and project parts.

5. **Describe the five primary formats of cross-functional teams.**
   The five primary formats of cross-functional teams are (1) self-directed teams, which manage their own activities and seldom require supervision; (2) task forces, which work

on a specific activity and disband once the work has been completed; (3) committees, which typically deal with recurring tasks and have a long life span; (4) special-purpose teams, which are temporary entities created to achieve a specific goal and which exist outside the formal hierarchy and the normal functions of the organization; and (5) virtual teams, which bring together employees from distant locations.

6. **Review the five stages of team development.**
   Teams typically go through five stages of development. In the forming stage, team members become acquainted with each other and with the group's purpose. In the storming stage, conflict often arises as coalitions and power struggles develop. In the norming stage, conflicts are resolved and harmony develops. In the performing stage, members focus on achieving the team's goals. In the adjourning stage, the team dissolves upon completion of its task.

Key Terms

accountability (155)	departmentalization by network (160)	organization structure (154)
authority (155)	distortion (170)	problem-solving team (163)
centralization (157)	flat organizations (156)	process divisions (158)
chain of command (155)	formal communication network (170)	product divisions (158)
cohesiveness (168)	free riders (163)	responsibility (155)
committee (166)	functional teams (164)	self-directed team (165)
cross-functional teams (164)	geographic divisions (159)	span of management (156)
customer divisions (159)	horizontal coordination (161)	special-purpose teams (166)
decentralization (157)	informal communication network (170)	tall organizations (156)
delegation (155)	informal organization (154)	task force (165)
departmentalization (158)	line organization (156)	team (162)
departmentalization by division (158)	line-and-staff organization (156)	vertical organization (157)
departmentalization by function (158)	norms (168)	virtual team (166)
departmentalization by matrix (159)	organization chart (154)	work specialization (155)

Test Your Knowledge

QUESTIONS FOR REVIEW

1. Why is organization structure important?
2. What are the characteristics of tall organizations and flat organizations?
3. What are the advantages and disadvantages of work specialization?
4. What are the advantages and disadvantages of functional departmentalization?

5. How can using the informal communication network help a manager be more effective?

QUESTIONS FOR ANALYSIS

6. Why would you expect a manager of a group of nuclear physicists to have a wide span of management?
7. How does horizontal organization promote innovation?
8. What can managers do to help teams work more effectively?

9. How can companies benefit from using virtual teams?

10. You were honored that they selected you to serve on the Y2K problem-solving team. As a member of that team, you reviewed pages upon pages of computer code in addition to all sorts of confidential company documents. One document included the salaries of all department managers. You discovered that managers at your level are earning $5,000 more than you, even though you've been at the company the same amount of time. You feel that a raise is justified on the basis of this information. How will you handle this situation?

QUESTIONS FOR APPLICATION

11. You are the leader of a cross-functional work team whose goal is to find ways of lowering production costs. Your team of eight employees has become mired in the storming stage. They disagree on how to approach the task, and they are starting to splinter into factions. What can you do to help the team move forward?

12. Your warehouse operation is currently functioning at capacity. To accommodate anticipated new business, your company must either build a major addition to your current warehouse operation or build a new warehouse that would be located at a distant site. As director of warehouse operations, you would like several people to participate in this decision. Should you form a task force, committee, or a special-purpose team? Explain your choice.

13. One of your competitors has approached you with an intriguing proposition. The company would like to merge with your company. The economies of scale are terrific. So are the growth possibilities. There's just one issue to be resolved. Your competitor is organized under a horizontal structure and uses lots of cross-functional teams. Your company is organized under a traditional vertical structure that is departmentalized by function. Using your knowledge about culture clash, explain the likely issues you will encounter if these two organizations are merged.

14. In Chapter 6 we discussed three styles of leadership: autocratic, democratic, and laissez-faire. Using your knowledge about the differences in these leadership styles, indicate which style you would expect to find under the following organization structures: (a) vertical organization—departmentalization by function; (b) vertical organization—departmentalization by matrix; (c) horizontal organization; (d) self-directed teams.

Practice Your Knowledge

SHARPENING YOUR COMMUNICATION SKILLS

Write a brief memo to your instructor describing a recent conflict you had with a peer at work or at school. Be sure to highlight the cause of the conflict and steps you took to resolve it. Which of the three conflict resolution styles discussed in this chapter did you use? Did you find a solution that both of you could accept?

HANDLING DIFFICULT SITUATIONS ON THE JOB: GOING THE DISTANCE WITH TEAMWORK

Dettmers Industries was cruising at an altitude of $3 million in annual sales when co-founder Michael Dettmers introduced self-directed teams. Employees at the Florida-based firm, which makes furnishings for private planes, were initially skeptical. So Dettmers started small, setting up one experimental self-directed team with the authority to hire new members, schedule work, handle customer service, supervise quality, and manage cash flow. As an incentive, Dettmers promised to pay members 25 percent of the revenues from sales of products made by the team—and guaranteed that members' incomes wouldn't be less than the previous year's earnings.

Dettmers required team members to attend 13 hours of quarterly training in teamwork, communication, and business skills. And to help teams get up to speed, Dettmers walked the shop floor for hours, coaching team leaders, facilitating meetings, and resolving conflicts.

By the end of the first year, members' earnings were averaging $45,000, compared with $32,000 the year before. Skepticism gave way to enthusiasm, once people could see that by working together effectively as a team they would make more money.

Even though teamwork is now a way of life, disputes still pop up. The members of your team are grumbling about one member who has become a free rider. She's no longer keeping up with her share of the production output. As team leader, you want to quickly resolve this conflict, before it threatens cohesiveness. But how?[61]

1. To defuse the conflict, should you suggest first asking other teams about their experience with free riders, or should you immediately call a team meeting to confront the free rider?

2. As a last resort, should you ask Dettmers how to handle the free-rider conflict? Why or why not?

3. To avoid this kind of conflict in the future, should you work as a team to draft rules for publicly reporting each member's output every week, or should you suggest delegating the process of tracking weekly member output to a few team members?

BUILDING YOUR TEAM SKILLS

What's the most effective organization structure for your college or university? With your team, obtain a copy of your school's organization chart. If this chart is not readily available, gather information by talking with people in administration, and then draw your own chart of the organization structure.

Analyze the chart in terms of span of management. Is your school a flat or a tall organization? Is this organization structure appropriate for your school? Does decision making tend to be centralized or decentralized in your school? Do you agree with this approach to decision making?

Finally, investigate the use of formal and informal teams in your school. Are there any problem-solving teams, task forces, or committees at work in your school? Are any teams self-directed or virtual? How much authority do these teams have to make decisions? What is the purpose of teamwork in your school—what kinds of goals do these teams have?

Share your team's findings during a brief classroom presentation, and then compare the findings of all teams. Is there agreement on the appropriate organization structure for your school?

Expand Your Knowledge

EXPLORING CAREER OPPORTUNITIES

Because every employee is a vital link in the organization's information chain, good communication skills are essential to your career—especially when you choose a career path in business communications. What do professional communicators do for their organizations? This is your opportunity to find out.

1. Visit your school's career center or use printed or online sources to research a list of at least three organizational jobs directly related to communications, such as webmaster and media relations specialist. Do these positions deal with internal or external communications?

2. Locate someone in your area who holds one of the jobs you have researched, and arrange a brief telephone interview. What are the duties and goals of this position? What training, education, and skills are needed for this job?

3. What about this job interests you? What else would you need to do or learn to be qualified for this kind of position?

DEVELOPING YOUR RESEARCH SKILLS

Although teamwork can benefit many organizations, introducing and managing team structures can be a real challenge. Using business publications in print or online, locate articles about how an organization has overcome problems with teams. For example, *Fast Company* often covers teamwork in its print and online editions; "Four Rules for Fast Teams," appeared in the August 1996 issue and is available on the Web at http://www.fastcompany.com/online/04/speed3.html. As you do this research, list the sources and the search strategy you are following:

1. Why did the organization originally introduce teams? What types of teams are being used?

2. What problems did the organization encounter in trying to implement teams? How did the organization deal with these problems?

SEE IT ON THE WEB EXERCISES
How Organizations Get Organized, page 159

The organization chart is your road map to who does what in any organization. A good case in point is the organization chart of the City of Sacramento, which you can access at http://www.sacto.org/cityorg.htm to answer the following questions.

1. Who is the city manager of Sacramento, and what is this person's span of management? Why do you think there are so many deputy city managers? What is the span of management for the deputy city manager in charge of neighborhoods, planning, and development services?

2. What departmentalization method does Sacramento seem to be using for positions that report to the city manager? Why is this departmentalization method appropriate?

3. What is the chain of command connecting the fire chief with the mayor and city council? How many levels in the hierarchy separate the fire chief and the mayor? Do you consider this a flat or a tall organization? Why?

Building Teams in the Cyber Age, page 165

The wealth of information on the Internet makes it convenient to learn more about almost any topic, and teamwork is no exception. Visit the Self Directed Work Teams page at http://users.ids.net/~brim/sdwth.html and click through the links to get a feel for the many resources available. Then answer the following questions.

1. From the main page, click on Sites on Team Basics and then on Core Competencies of Team. Do high-performing teams prefer dialogue or debate? What two types of balance do these teams maintain?

2. From the Sites on Team Basics page, click on Essential Questions—Poynter. Read through this list of the major issues facing teams. How might each issue's importance vary among different types of teams? Which three issues are most important to the assigned in-class teams in which you've participated? Which three do you think are

most important to a team of production workers looking for ways to cut costs and production time?

3. From the main page, click on Sites on Skills/Steps and then on Assess Your Team. What aspects of teamwork are these questions measuring? Take this test (using your experience on a school or work team) and submit your answers. What response do you get? Which areas do you think are most important for your team to focus on?

Communications Master Class Online, page 170

Sharing information through communication is the glue that binds together all the employees of an organization. An easy way to learn more about good communication is to take Spotlight Communications' Communications Master Class at http://www.spotlightcommunications.co.uk/frameset.htm and answer these questions.

1. Click on The Communications Plan to read about planning. What are the three questions of stages one and two? What activities make up stage three? Why is this last stage important? Should you follow this planning process in all communications situations?

2. Go back to the main page and click on Understanding Your Audience. What may differ from group to group? In the example in which the restaurant owner communicates about longer hours, what three audiences are identified? How does the message differ for each audience?

3. Return to the main page and click on Don't Talk—Listen. What are the four stages of effective listening? What can you do to set the scene for effective listening? Why should you ask questions?

8

PRODUCING QUALITY GOODS AND SERVICES

FACING BUSINESS CHALLENGES
AT HARLEY-DAVIDSON

Racing Toward Higher Output, Productivity, and Global Sales

Based in Milwaukee, Wisconsin, Harley-Davidson had long enjoyed an unprecedented level of customer loyalty. Its reputation as the outstanding maker of heavyweight motorcycles was legendary—until it hit a deep pothole in the 1970s. Cutting costs to battle stiff competition from imports, the company let production quality slip. Unwilling to tolerate constant oil leaks and frequent breakdowns, motorcycle buyers reluctantly turned to the smooth-riding imports. The company's market share tumbled.

Over the next two decades, Harley rebuilt its production processes from the ground up, putting more emphasis on quality than on quantity. By the early 1990s, the company had quality firmly under control. With its reputation mended, demand rebounded so strongly that dealers reported long waiting lists of riders eager to climb back on a Harley. Management responded to the surge of orders by carefully ratcheting up annual motorcycle production while maintaining quality. But products were snapped up as quickly as they could be cranked out.

By 1995, annual production had reached the milestone 100,000 mark, and the company's stock price was setting new highs. Some fiercely loyal customers even tattooed the company's logo on their chests. Moreover, projections indicated a strong increase in demand for the coming years. So with every reason to celebrate, why were Harley-Davidson's top managers planning a major retooling of the motorcycle manufacturing production processes?

Harley's managers wanted to rev up output and expand sales in Europe, Scandinavia, Australia, Japan, and other global markets without cutting back on domestic distribution. They set an ambitious companywide goal: to be able to produce 200,000 motorcycles annually by the time the company marked its centennial in 2003. But meeting this goal would require a top-to-bottom revamping of the entire production process, from supplies to purchasing to inventory and beyond. Consider warehousing and order fulfillment, for instance. Harley's 84-year-old distribution warehouse was cramped and outdated; its equipment, decades old. The warehouse was still operating on an antiquated paper-based system that hampered productivity and led to countless errors. Worse, when a dealer ordered a part, it sometimes took as long as 12 days for the part to be delivered from the warehouse—while competitors were delivering in three days or less.

Facing a 2003 deadline for boosting production output, what could CEO Jeff Bleustein and his top managers do to wring much more efficiency out of the production process without sacrificing quality? How could they apply technology to improve the company's production process? How could the company work hand in hand with its suppliers to meet Harley's centennial goal?[1]

■ UNDERSTANDING THE PRODUCTION PROCESS

The managers at Harley-Davidson faced the same situation that managers around the world are facing today: The extremely competitive nature of the global business environment requires companies to produce high-quality goods in the most efficient way possible or else be shredded by the competition. In almost every industry you can name, this global challenge has caused companies to reexamine their definition of quality and reengineer their production processes. High efficiency, few defects, fast production, low costs, excellent customer service, broad market reach, innovative products and processes, low waste, and high flexibility are just some of the objectives companies are building into their processes to improve quality, add value to the good or service being produced, and maintain a competitive advantage. After all, as Harley-Davidson's managers learned, the level of quality that a company aspires to is a strategic decision that affects the production process.[2]

What exactly is the *production process,* and what does it involve? To begin with, **production** is the transformation of resources into goods or services that people need or want. It involves all the processes and activities that make sure both goods and services are produced according to specifications, in the amounts and by the schedule required, and at a minimum cost. For example, think about all the organized processes and activities involved in completing a banking transaction, delivering a package, making a movie, providing medical care, or manufacturing a computer or an automobile. Producing those services or goods requires a series of coordinated steps that can include nonmanufacturing or manufacturing activities.

At the core of production is the *conversion process,* the sequence of events that convert resources into products or services. The conversion process can be diagrammed simply as:

Input		Transformation		Output
• Materials	⟶	• Mechanical	⟶	• Products
• Parts		• Assembly		• Services
• Customers		• Inspection		
		• Personal contact		
		• Shipping		

This formula applies to both intangible services and tangible goods (see Exhibit 8.1). For an airline to serve its customers, for example, it must transform tangible and intangible resources—the plane, the pilot's skill, the fuel, and a passenger—into the intangible service of transporting the customer to the final destination. For a clothing manufacturer to produce a shirt, the resources that are converted—cloth, thread, and buttons—are tangible, and so is the output—the shirt.

Although many individuals are involved in managing the production process, *operations managers* are directly responsible for designing, improving, managing, and controlling the production process. Moreover, if new products are developed or if existing products or production equipment become obsolete, operations managers must redesign systems to keep production running smoothly and efficiently. **Production efficiency**—lowering costs by optimizing output from each resource used in the production process—is one of the principal goals of **operations management,** which encompasses managing all the activities involved in producing goods and services.

One way organizations can achieve production efficiency is through **mass production**—manufacturing goods in great quantities. Mass production reduces production costs per unit and makes products available to more people. Some service companies also use

production
Transformation of resources into goods or services that people need or want

LEARNING OBJECTIVE 1
Explain what operations managers do

production efficiency
Minimizing cost by maximizing the level of output from each resource

operations management
Management of the conversion process that transforms inputs into outputs in the form of finished goods and services

mass production
Manufacture of uniform products in great quantities

SYSTEM	INPUTS	TRANSFORMATION COMPONENTS	TRANSFORMATION FUNCTION	TYPICAL DESIRED OUTPUT
Hospital	Patients, medical supplies	Physicians, nurses, equipment	Health care	Healthy individuals
Restaurant	Hungry customers, food	Chef, waitress, environment	Well-prepared and well-served food	Satisfied customers
Automobile factory	Sheet steel, engine parts	Tools, equipment, workers	Fabrication and assembly of cars	High-quality cars
College or university	High school graduates, books	Teachers, classrooms	Impart knowledge and skills	Educated individuals
Department store	Shoppers, stock of goods	Displays, salesclerks	Attract shoppers, promote products, fill orders	Sales to satisfied customers

EXHIBIT 8·1

INPUT-TRANSFORMATION-OUTPUT RELATIONSHIPS FOR TYPICAL SYSTEMS
The transformation of inputs into some desired output is called the conversion process.

mass production techniques. For example, fast-food chains, hotels, accounting firms, car-rental agencies, and some real estate firms mass produce their services through standardized and automated procedures.

Even though mass production has several advantages, the competitive pressures of the global economy often require production techniques that are flexible, customer-focused, and quality-oriented. Sometimes these techniques replace traditional mass production, and sometimes they simply improve on it. Consider Andersen Windows. Throughout most of its long history, Andersen made a range of standard windows in large batches. However, in the early 1990s customer demands and an increasing error rate caused Andersen to rethink the way it built windows. To better meet customer needs, the company developed an interactive computer catalog that allows customers to add, change, and remove features of Andersen's standard windows until they've designed the exact windows they want. Once the customers select their design, the computer automatically generates a price quote and sends the order to the factory, where standardized parts are tailored to customer specifications. The company now offers close to 200,000 different products that are virtually error-free. Andersen's new production system is known as **mass customization**—using mass production techniques to produce customized goods. The company's next goal is to use *batch-of-one manufacturing*, in which every product is made to order from scratch and virtually no standard inventory is kept on hand. Andersen is already achieving this goal in one factory that makes customized replacement windows.[3]

mass customization
Producing customized goods and services through mass production techniques

■ DESIGNING THE PRODUCTION PROCESS

When Jeff Bleustein and his management team at Harley-Davidson set out to return Harley to a competitive position, they learned that the way an organization designs its operations can dramatically affect a company's ability to deliver quality products. Designing an effective production process involves five important tasks: forecasting demand, planning for capacity, choosing a facility location, designing a facility layout, and scheduling work.

LEARNING OBJECTIVE 2
Identify key tasks involved in designing a production process

Forecasting Demand

Forecasting demand, the first step in designing an effective production process, involves determining how much product the company will need to produce in a certain time span. Using customer feedback, market research, past sales figures, industry analyses, and educated guesses about the future behavior of the economy and competitors, operations managers prepare **production forecasts,** or estimates of future demand for the company's products. These estimates are then used to plan, budget, and schedule the use of resources. Of course, many factors in the business environment cannot be predicted or controlled with certainty. For this reason, managers must regularly review and adjust their forecasts to account for these uncertainties.

Service companies must also forecast demand. For example, a dentist must be able to project approximately how many patients she will treat in a given time period to make sure that she staffs her office properly and has enough dental supplies on hand. Without such forecasts, she will not be able to run her production process (treating patients) efficiently. Similarly, cruise ship operators must forecast exactly how much food and supplies to stock for one week's journey, because once the ship sets sail, there are no last-minute deliveries. On the basis of years of experience, operation managers for Carnival's Elation Cruise Line can now forecast that a one-week Caribbean cruise will require some 10,000 pounds of meat, 10,080 bananas, and 41,600 eggs.[4]

Planning for Capacity

Once product demand has been estimated, management must determine the company's capacity to produce the goods or services. The term *capacity* refers to the volume of manufacturing or service capability that an organization can handle. For example, a doctor's office with only one examining room limits the number of patients the doctor can see each day. And a cruise ship with 750 staterooms limits the number of passengers that the ship can accommodate in any given week. Similarly, a beverage bottling plant with only one conveyor belt and one local warehouse limits the company's ability to manufacture beverage products.

Capacity planning is a long-term strategic decision that establishes the overall level of resources needed to meet customer demand.[5] The neighborhood convenience store needs to consider traffic volume throughout the day and night in order to plan staffing levels appropriately. At the other extreme of complexity, when managers at Boeing plan for the production of an airliner, they have to consider not only the staffing of thousands of people but also factory floor space, material flows from hundreds of suppliers, internal deliveries, cash flow, tools and equipment, and dozens of other factors. Because of the potential impact on finances, customers, and employees, capacity planning involves some of the most difficult decisions that managers have to make.

Top management uses long-term capacity planning to make significant decisions about an organization's ability to produce goods and services, such as expanding existing facilities, constructing new facilities, or phasing out unneeded ones. Such decisions entail a great deal of risk, for two reasons: (1) Large shifts in demand are difficult to predict accurately, and (2) long-term capacity decisions can be difficult to undo. For example, if a new facility is built to produce a new product that then fails, or if demand for a popular product suddenly declines, the company will find itself with expensive excess capacity. Managers must decide what they should do with this excess capacity. If they keep it, they might try to find an alternate use for this space. If they eliminate it and demand picks up again, the company will have to forego profits because it is unable to meet customer demand.[6]

Many of the newer, larger cruise ships have elegant restaurants, boutiques, luxury spas, high-tech fitness rooms, conference and meeting rooms, theaters, playrooms, ice-skating rinks, and even rock-climbing walls. With passenger counts of 2,600 and upward, managing an operation this large is like running a small village and every component in it.

production forecasts
Estimates of how much of a company's goods and services must be produced in order to meet future demand

capacity planning
A long-term strategic decision that determines the level of resources available to an organization to meet customer demand

See It on the Web See It on the Web

MAKE GLOVES, NOT WAR

The problem of excess manufacturing capacity is probably most apparent in the defense industries. When the nation is at war, factories may have to run at full speed, 24 hours a day just to keep up with the demand for weapons and ammunition. However, soon after the war ends, factories sit idle because there is no longer a need for producing in such quantities. Now the U.S. Army has found a way to get those facilities moving again. The Armament Retooling Manufacturing Support (ARMS) program encourages businesses to move in and use idle military facilities to manufacture peace-time products. To encourage participation, the U.S. government offers assistance with marketing, obtaining state and federal permits, guaranteeing loans, and planning grants. For a company looking to expand capacity, this could be just the ticket.

http://www.openterprise.com

Choosing a Facility Location

One long-term issue that management must resolve early when designing the production process is the location of production facilities. The goal is to choose a location that minimizes costs while increasing operational efficiencies and product quality. To accomplish this goal, management must consider such regional costs as land, construction, labor, local taxes, energy, and local living standards. In addition, management must consider whether the local labor pool has the skills that the firm needs. For example, firms that need highly trained accountants, engineers, or computer scientists often locate in areas near university communities, such as Boston. On the other hand, if most of the jobs can be filled by unskilled or semiskilled employees, firms can choose locations where such labor is available at a relatively low cost. The search for low-cost labor has led many U.S. companies to locate their manufacturing operations in countries such as Mexico, Taiwan, and Indonesia, where wages are much lower. However, companies that fail to compensate foreign workers fairly are risking strong consumer backlash in the United States.

Also affecting location decisions are transportation costs, which cover the shipping of supplies and finished goods. Almost every company needs easy, low-cost access to ground transportation such as highways and rail lines. Moreover, companies that sell a lot of products overseas must be able to arrange for efficient air or water transportation.

Finally, companies must consider raw materials costs. For example, the location of a coal-based power plant must be chosen to minimize the cost of distributing electrical power to customers and to minimize the cost and *lead time* of shipping coal to the plant.

Location considerations may be different for some service organizations. Although they may also take regional costs into consideration, the main objective for many service firms is to locate where profit potential is greatest. Unlike manufacturing operations, in which low production costs are an important consideration, services tend to focus on more customer-driven factors.[7] Because they often require one-on-one contact with customers, service organizations such as gas stations, restaurants, department stores, and charities must locate where their target market is large and sustainable. Therefore, market research often plays a central role in site selection. However, for service companies that reach customers primarily by telephone, mail, or the Internet, proximity to customers is less of a consideration.

Designing a Facility Layout

Once a site has been selected, managers must turn their attention to *facility layout,* the arrangement of production work centers and other elements (such as materials, equipment, and support departments) needed to process goods and services. Layout includes the efforts involved in selecting specific locations for each department, process, machine, support function, and other activity required for the operation or service. The need for a new layout design can occur for a number of reasons besides new construction; for instance, a new process or method might become available, the volume of business might change, a new product or service may be offered, an outdated facility may be remodeled, the mix of goods or services offered may change, or an existing product or service may be redesigned.[8]

Facility layout affects the amount of on-hand inventory, the efficiency of materials handling, the utilization of equipment, and the productivity and morale of employees. In goods manufacturing, the primary concern is the efficient movement of resources and inventory. In the production of services, facility layout controls the flow of customers through the system and influences the customer's satisfaction with the service.[9] In both services and goods operations, the major goals of a good layout design are to minimize materials-handling costs, reduce bottlenecks in moving material or people, provide flexibility, provide ease of supervision, use available space effectively and efficiently, reduce hazards, and facilitate ergonomics, coordination, and communications wherever appropriate.[10] Four typical facility layouts are the *process layout, product layout, cellular layout,* and *fixed-position layout* (see Exhibit 8.2).[11]

A **process layout** is also called a *functional layout* because it concentrates everything needed to complete one phase of the production process in one place. Specific functions, such as drilling or welding, are performed in one location for different products or customers (see Exhibit 8.2A). The process layout is often used in machine shops as well as in service industries. For example, a medical clinic might dedicate one room to X rays, another room to routine examinations, and still another to outpatient surgery.

An alternative to the process layout is the **product layout,** also called the assembly-line layout, in which the main production process occurs along a line, and products in progress move from one workstation to the next. Materials and subassemblies of component parts may feed into the main line at several points, but the flow of production is continuous. Electronics and personal-computer manufacturers are just two of many industries that typically use this layout (see Exhibit 8.2B).

Some production of services is also organized by product. For example, when you go to your local department of motor vehicles to get a driver's license, you usually go through a series of steps administered by several different people: registering, taking a written or computerized test, having an eye exam, paying a cashier, and getting your picture taken. You emerge from this system a licensed driver (unless, of course, you fail one of the tests).

A **cellular layout** groups dissimilar machines into work centers (or cells) to process parts that have similar shapes and processing requirements (see Exhibit 8.2C). Arranging work flow by cells can improve the efficiency of a process layout while maintaining its flexibility. At the same time, grouping smaller numbers of workers in cells facilitates teamwork and joint problem solving. Employees are also able to work on a product from start to finish, and they can move between machines within their cells, thus increasing the flexibility of the team. Cellular layouts are commonly used in computer chip manufacture and metal fabricating.[12]

Finally, the **fixed-position layout** is a facility layout in which labor, materials, and equipment are brought to the location where the good is being produced or the customer is being served. Buildings, roads, bridges, airplanes, and ships are examples of the types of

process layout
Method of arranging a facility so that production tasks are carried out in separate departments containing specialized equipment and personnel

product layout
Method of arranging a facility so that production proceeds along a line of workstations

cellular layout
Method of arranging a facility so that parts with similar shapes or processing requirements are processed together in work centers

fixed-position layout
Method of arranging a facility so that the product is stationary and equipment and personnel come to it

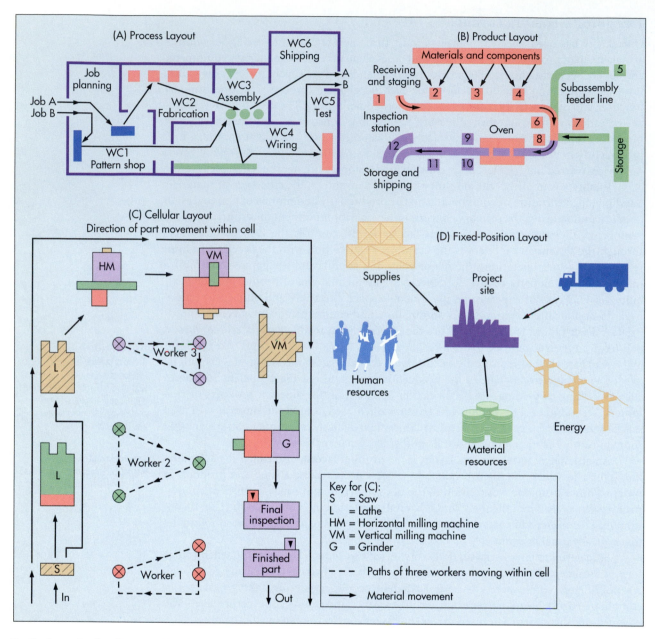

Facility layout is often determined by the type of product an organization is producing. Typically, a process layout is used for an organization producing made-to-order products. A product layout is used when an organization is producing large quantities of just a few products. A cellular layout works well in organizations that practice mass customization. And a fixed-position layout is used when the product is too large to move.

(A) A process layout is arranged according to the specialized employees and materials involved in various phases of the production process.

(B) In a product or assembly-line layout, the developing product moves in a continuous sequence from one workstation to the next.

(C) In a cellular layout, parts with similar shapes or processing requirements are processed together in work centers, an arrangement that facilitates teamwork and flexibility.

(D) A fixed-position layout requires employees and materials to be brought to the product.

EXHIBIT 8.2

TYPES OF FACILITY LAYOUTS

large products that are typically constructed using a fixed-position layout (see Exhibit 8.2D). Service companies also use fixed-position layouts: A plumber, for example, goes to a job site bringing the tools, material, and expertise needed to repair a broken pipe.

Routing is the task of specifying the sequence of operations and the path through the facility that the work will take. The way production is routed depends on the type of product and the layout of the plant. A table-manufacturing company, for instance, uses a process layout because it has three departments, each handling a different phase of the table's manufacture and each equipped with specialized tools, machines, and employees. Department 1 cuts wood into tabletops and legs. These pieces are then sent to department 2, where holes are drilled and rough finishing is done. Finally, the individual pieces are routed to department 3, where the tables are assembled and painted.

routing
Specifying the sequence of operations and the path the work will take through the production facility

Scheduling Work

In any production process, managers must use **scheduling**—determining how long each operation takes and setting a starting and ending time for each. A master schedule, often called a *master production schedule (MPS),* is a schedule of planned completion of items. In services such as a doctor's office, the appointment book serves as the master schedule.

When a job has relatively few activities and relationships, many production managers keep the process on schedule with a **Gantt chart.** Developed by Henry L. Gantt in the early 1900s, the Gantt chart is a bar chart showing the amount of time required to accomplish each part of a process. It allows managers to see at a glance whether the process is in line with the schedule they had planned (see Exhibit 8.3).

For more complex jobs, the **program evaluation and review technique (PERT)** is helpful. It is a planning tool that helps managers identify the optimal sequencing of activities, the expected time for project completion, and the best use of resources within a complex project. To use PERT, the manager must (1) identify the activities to be performed, (2) determine the sequence of activities, (3) establish the time needed to complete each activity, (4) diagram the network of activities, (5) calculate the longest path through the network that leads to project completion, and (6) refine the network's timing or use of resources as activities are completed. The longest path through the network is known as the **critical path** because it represents the minimum amount of time needed to complete the project.

scheduling
Process of determining how long each production operation takes and then setting a starting and ending time for each

Gantt chart
Bar chart used to control schedules by showing how long each part of a production process should take and when it should take place

program evaluation and review technique (PERT)
A planning tool that managers of complex projects use to determine the optimal order of activities, the expected time for project completion, and the best use of resources

critical path
In a PERT network diagram, the sequence of operations that requires the longest time to complete

ID	Task Name	Start Date	End Date	Duration	2000
1	Make legs	8/1/00	8/28/00	20d	
2	Cut tops	8/22/00	8/28/00	5d	
3	Drill	8/29/00	9/4/00	5d	
4	Sand	9/5/00	9/11/00	5d	
5	Assemble	9/12/00	9/25/00	10d	
6	Paint	9/19/00	9/25/00	5d	

EXHIBIT 8.3

A GANTT CHART

A chart like this one enables a production manager to see immediately the dates on which production steps must be started and completed if goods are to be delivered on schedule. Some steps may overlap to save time. For instance, after three weeks of cutting table legs, cutting tabletops begins. This overlap ensures that the necessary legs and tops are completed at the same time and can move on together to the next stage in the manufacturing process.

In place of a single time projection for each task, PERT uses four figures: an *optimistic* estimate (if things go well), a *pessimistic* estimate (if they don't go well), a *most likely* estimate (how long the task usually takes), and an *expected* time estimate, an average of the other three estimates.[13] The expected time is used to diagram the network of activities and determine the length of the critical path.

Consider the manufacture of shoes in Exhibit 8.4. At the beginning of the process, three paths deal with heels, soles, and tops. All three processes must be finished before the next phase (sewing tops to soles and heels) can be started. However, one of the three paths—the tops—takes 33 days, whereas the other two take only 18 and 12 days. The shoe tops, then, are on the critical path because they will delay the entire operation if they fall behind schedule. In contrast, soles can be started up to 21 days after starting the tops without slowing down production. This free time in the soles schedule is called *slack time* because managers can choose to produce the soles anytime during the 33-day period required by the tops.

dispatching
Issuing work orders and schedules to department heads and supervisors

Included in the scheduling process is the **dispatching** function, or the issuing of work orders to department supervisors. These orders specify the work to be done and the schedule for its completion. Work orders also inform department supervisors of their operational priorities and the schedule they must maintain.

Of course, once the schedule has been set and the orders dispatched, a production manager cannot just sit back and assume that the work will get done correctly and on time. Even the best scheduler may misjudge the time needed to complete an operation, and production may be delayed by accidents, mechanical breakdowns, or supplier problems. Therefore, the production manager needs a system for handling delays and preventing a minor disruption from growing into chaos. A successful system is based on good communication between the employees and the production manager.

Suppose a machine breakdown causes department 2 of a manufacturing company to lose half a day of drilling time. If the schedule is not altered to direct other work to department 3 (the next department), the employees and equipment in department 3 will sit idle

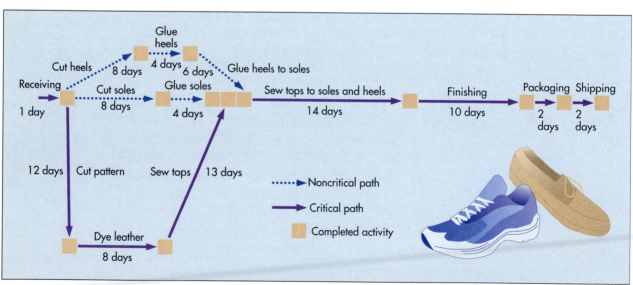

EXHIBIT 8·4

PERT DIAGRAM FOR MANUFACTURING SHOES

In the manufacture of shoes, the critical path involves receiving, cutting the pattern, dyeing the leather, sewing the tops, sewing the tops to soles and heels, finishing, packaging, and shipping—a total of 61 days.

for some time. However, if department 2 informs the production manager of its machine problem right away, the production manager can immediately reschedule some fill-in work for department 3.

■ IMPROVING PRODUCTION THROUGH TECHNOLOGY

Today more and more companies are taking advantage of new production technologies to improve their efficiency and productivity. Two of the most visible advances in production technology are computers and **robots**—programmable machines that work with tools and materials to perform various tasks. Although industrial robots may seem exotic, like some science fiction creation, they are quite common and are really nothing more than smart tools. Industrial robots can easily perform precision functions as well as repetitive, strenuous, or hazardous tasks.[14] When equipped with machine vision, or electronic eyes, robots can place doors on cars in precise locations, cull blemished vegetables from frozen-food processing lines, check the wings of aircraft for dangerous ice buildup, make sure that drug capsules of the right color go into the correct packages before they are shipped to pharmacies, and even assist with surgery.[15]

LEARNING OBJECTIVE 3
Discuss the role of computers and automation technology in production

Robots don't do everything these days. At this Chrysler plant in Detroit, polishing limited-edition Viper GTS-R is still done by human hands.

In addition to robots, other major developments in manufacturing automation include computer-aided design and engineering, computer-aided manufacturing, computer-integrated manufacturing, flexible manufacturing systems, and electronic information systems. Let's look a little closer at each of these.

Computer-Aided Design and Computer-Aided Engineering

Widely used today is **computer-aided design (CAD),** the application of computer graphics and mathematical modeling to the design of products. A related process is **computer-aided engineering (CAE),** in which engineers use computer-generated three-dimensional images and computerized calculations to test products. With CAE, engineers can subject proposed products to changing temperatures, various stresses, and even simulated accidents without ever building preliminary models. Moreover, the *virtual reality* capability of today's computers allows designers to see how finished products will look and operate before physical prototypes are built.

Using computers to aid design and engineering saves time and money because revising computer designs is much faster than revising hand-drafted designs and building physical models. In fact, computer technology allows companies to perfect a product or abandon a bad idea before production even begins. The result is better overall product quality. For example, when Boeing engineers designed the 777 airplane, they corrected problems and tried out new ideas entirely on their computer screens. Digitally preassembling the 3 million parts of the 777 allowed Boeing to exceed its goals for reducing errors, changes, and rework.[16]

Computer-Aided Manufacturing and Computer-Integrated Manufacturing

The use of computers to control production equipment is called **computer-aided manufacturing (CAM).** In a CAD/CAM system, computer-aided design data are converted automatically

robots
Programmable machines that can complete a variety of tasks by working with tools and materials

computer-aided design (CAD)
Use of computer graphics and mathematical modeling in the development of products

computer-aided engineering (CAE)
Use of computers to test products without building an actual model

computer-aided manufacturing (CAM)
Use of computers to control production equipment

into processing instructions for production equipment to manufacture the part or product. This integration of design and production can increase the output, speed, and precision of assembly lines, as well as make customized production much easier.[17] In addition, the latest CAD/CAM software allows company departments to share designs and data over intranets and the Internet, enabling geographically dispersed departments to work together on complex projects.[18] For example, Ford uses a CAD/CAM/CAE system it calls C3P to develop new vehicle prototypes. Whereas it once took two to three months to build, assemble, and test a car chassis prototype, with C3P the entire process can now be completed in less than two weeks. Although the program is still quite new, Ford expects it to improve engineering efficiency by 35 percent and reduce prototype costs by up to 40 percent.[19]

computer-integrated manufacturing (CIM)
Computer-based systems, including CAD and CAM, that coordinate and control all the elements of design and production

The highest level of computerization in operations management is **computer-integrated manufacturing (CIM),** in which all the elements of production—design, engineering, testing, production, inspection, and materials handling—are integrated into one automated system. Computer-integrated manufacturing is not a specific technology but rather a strategy that uses technology for organizing and controlling a factory. Its role is to link the people, machines, databases, and decisions involved in each step of producing a good.[20]

Flexible Manufacturing Systems

Advances in design technology have been accompanied by changes in the way the production process is organized. Traditional automated manufacturing equipment is *fixed* or *hard-wired*, meaning it is capable of handling only one specific task. Although fixed automation is efficient when one type or model of good is mass produced, a change in product design requires extensive equipment changes. Such adjustments may involve high **setup costs,** the expenses incurred each time a manufacturer begins a production run of a different type of item. In addition, the initial investment for fixed automation equipment is high because specialized equipment is required for each of the operations involved in making a single item. Only after much production on a massive scale can a company recoup the cost of that specialized equipment. For example, Harley-Davidson invested $4.8 million in fixed manufacturing to make a particular motorcycle—only to dismantle the operation when demand for that product faded.[21]

setup costs
Expenses incurred each time a producer organizes resources to begin producing goods or services

flexible manufacturing system (FMS)
Production system using computer-controlled machines that can adapt to various versions of the same operation

An alternative to a fixed manufacturing system is a **flexible manufacturing system (FMS).** Such systems link numerous programmable machine tools by an automated materials-handling system of conveyors or AGVs (driverless computer-controlled vehicles that move materials from any location on the factory floor to any other location). Changing from one product design to another requires only a few signals from a central computer. Each machine changes tools automatically, making appropriate selections from built-in storage carousels that can hold more than 100 tools. In addition, the sequence of events involved in building an item can be completely rearranged.[22] This flexibility saves both time and setup costs. Moreover, producers can outmaneuver less agile competitors by moving swiftly into profitable new fields. Flexible manufacturing also allows producers to adapt their products quickly to changing customer needs.[23] Such systems are particularly suited for *job shops*, such as small machine shops, which make dissimilar items or produce at so irregular a rate that repetitive operations won't help.

As a $10 million manufacturer of precision metal parts, Cook Specialty is one small company able to compete with larger manufacturers through flexible manufacturing. Cook used to make only certain products, such as basketball hoops and display racks. However, the company has transformed its production facilities so that it is now capable of manufacturing custom-engineered medical instruments and precision parts for high-tech equipment. Technical innovations for these devices advance rapidly, but Cook is able to adapt its production facilities to keep up with the changes. In fact, almost one-third of the products Cook manufactures each year are new.[24]

See It on the Web See It on the Web

SETTING STANDARDS

The National Institute of Standards and Technology (NIST) is a U.S. government agency that works "to assist industry in the development of technology . . . needed to improve product quality, to modernize manufacturing processes, to ensure product reliability . . . and to facilitate rapid commercialization . . . of products based on new scientific discoveries." The institute accomplishes its ambitious charter by partnering with business to conduct research, develop technology standards, provide technical assistance, share costs, and reward success. Visit the NIST Web site to learn more about how this public-private partnership is supporting technological improvements for production. http://www.nist.gov/

Electronic Information Systems

Of course, none of the production technologies mentioned so far will increase profits unless the company designs products to fit customer needs. Today, many companies recognized for their quality link themselves with their customers through information systems. These systems enable companies to respond immediately to customer issues, support rapid changes in customer needs, and offer "made-to-order" products. Moreover, information technology allows customers to track their products and obtain status reports throughout the production cycle. It can also promote better communication within the company, thereby increasing the efficiency of employees and machines alike. In fact, many companies now rely on information systems to help establish a competitive advantage. For example, Siemens, a global producer of goods and services in industries ranging from communications to health care, cites its use of information technology as the key to its rapid growth in productivity.[25]

One important type of information technology is **electronic data interchange (EDI).** Electronic data interchange systems transmit specially formatted documents (such as invoices and purchase orders) from one company's computers to another's. This process can greatly reduce the time, paperwork, and cost associated with placing and processing orders, thereby making it easier and more profitable for a customer to do business with the company.

electronic data interchange (EDI)
Information systems that transmit documents such as invoices and purchase orders between computers, thereby lowering ordering costs and paperwork

Wise Use of Technology

Even though robots, automation, and information systems can greatly improve the way a company designs, manufactures, and delivers goods, one of the worst mistakes a company can make is to automate a series of tasks without first examining the underlying process. If the basic process creates the wrong products or involves needless steps, nothing is gained by automating it without first cleaning it up. Otherwise a business runs the risk of simply doing the wrong things faster. Problems can also result from installing production technology without properly preparing the work force to implement and use the technology.

TRW is a global manufacturing and service company that targets the automotive, space, and defense industries. TRW regularly and carefully checks its automated production systems to make sure it is improving the production process without wasting capital. One employee focuses full-time on auditing machines for output mistakes, developing strategies for error reduction, and training other employees. Rather than automating for speed, the company focuses its efforts on designing "mistake-proofing" technology into its equipment, ensuring that it uses technology to work smarter as well as faster.[26]

Focus on E-Business

THIS CYBERBAZAAR IS STRICTLY BUSINESS-TO-BUSINESS

Why are General Motors, Ford, and DaimlerChrysler, the three biggest competitors in the automobile manufacturing industry, joining forces? They're building the world's largest e-company—a giant online marketplace where the three automakers can purchase raw materials, some $250 billion worth of parts, office supplies, and other goods they need each year.

The venture underscores just how powerful the promise of the Internet has become to traditional businesses. If successful, it could radically change the way cars are built and distributed. It could even fundamentally alter the way all organizations in all industries conduct business with each other in the future.

Automakers will use the new e-company to drive inefficiencies out of their systems. By converting the hurricane of blueprints, bids for some 10,000 parts that go into each car or truck, phone calls, endless meetings, and conferences into an online operation, manufacturers will slash billions of dollars of costs, save enormous amounts of time, and make operations more efficient for themselves and their suppliers.

Consumers stand to benefit, too. Traditionally, an auto plant cranks at full capacity building a predetermined mix of cars. Manufacturers assemble and paint most cars based on guesses of what combinations of options and colors customers will want. Then they ship the cars to dealers, who keep huge, expensive inventories. Few cars are "equipped to order" because custom cars take an additional two months to deliver, a lag that discourages most buyers. This is due to the logistical difficulties involved in ordering the correct combinations of parts from thousands of suppliers. But the new online marketplace will allow manufacturers to ship models with customer-specific options within 10 to 20 days, free a good chunk of the $60 billion now tied up in dealer inventories, and eliminate the fat rebates dealers must use to sell cars customers don't want.

Of course, reinventing automobile manufacturing while juggling high-tech alliances is a Herculean task for any industry—especially one more than a century old. To make the e-commerce venture work, a lot has to go on under the hood. Software and databases need to swap information and conduct transactions seamlessly, for one thing. But Ford CEO Jacques Nasser is ready for the challenge. "We're going to turn the old ways on their ears," he says. "It might not happen right away, but change is inevitable."

QUESTIONS FOR CRITICAL THINKING

1. What do automobile companies, suppliers, dealers, and customers stand to gain by this new e-business?
2. Why are the three companies joining forces instead of establishing their own independent online operations?

MANAGING AND CONTROLLING THE PRODUCTION PROCESS

During the production design phase, operations managers forecast demand, plan for capacity, choose facility locations, design facility layouts and configurations, and develop production schedules and sequences. Once the design of the production process has been completed, operations managers are responsible for managing and controlling these processes and systems. In this section, we will discuss three important management and control concepts: supply-chain management, inventory management, and quality assurance.

Supply-Chain Management

A company's ability to deliver products and services is often tied to the dynamics of its suppliers. One faulty part, one late shipment, can send rippling effects through the production system and can even bring operations to a grinding halt. When a surge of orders for new Boeing 747's stepped up demand for parts, for instance, Boeing's suppliers were caught flatfooted. "We had $25,000 engine mounts that couldn't be finished because we were waiting for $40 nuts and bolts," noted one Boeing supplier. As a result, promised aircraft delivery dates were delayed and Boeing suffered huge losses. To avoid such problems in the future, Boeing now works hand in hand with its suppliers to refine products and delivery schedules.[27]

 To build more flexible and efficient supply chains, manufacturers need to forge close, long-term ties with their suppliers.[28]

The group of firms that provide all the various processes required to make a finished product is called the *supply chain.* The chain begins with the provider of raw materials and ends with the company that produces the finished product that is delivered to the final customer. For example, if the finished product is a wood table, the supply chain going backward would include the retail store where it was sold, the shipping company that delivered it to the retail store, the furniture manufacturer, the hardware manufacturer, and the lumber company that acquired the wood from the forest.[29]

Through a process known as **supply-chain management,** many companies now integrate all of the facilities, functions, and activities involved in the production of goods and services going from suppliers to customers.[30] The process is based on the belief that because one company's output is another company's (or consumer's) input, all companies involved will benefit from working together more closely.[31] Building high-trust relationships was once thought possible only with internal suppliers. But today more and more companies are reducing the number of outside suppliers they use, working collaboratively with them, and even involving suppliers in the design process.

supply-chain management
Integrating all of the facilities, functions, and processes associated with the production of goods and services, from suppliers to customers

Honda, for example, has developed a process called Design In, which focuses directly on early supplier involvement. Honda will invite suppliers to work side by side with Honda's engineers, designers, and technologists in the very early stages of a new project. In addition, Honda believes in maintaining a frank, open, and collaborative relationship with its suppliers and even extends this philosophy to sharing cost data. "We show our suppliers our logic in coming up with the cost, and they show us theirs," notes Honda's senior purchasing manager.[32]

Some companies are taking things one step further and actually involving suppliers in the manufacturing of their product. For example, at Volkswagen's factory in Resende, Brazil, seven main suppliers build components and assemble them onto vehicles inside the Volkswagen factory, using the suppliers' own equipment and workers. Volkswagen figures that integrating the suppliers so deeply into the production process is a strong incentive for the suppliers to deliver high-quality components in unprecedented time.[33]

Inventory Management

Forward-thinking companies have realized that maintaining a competitive advantage requires continuously seeking ways to reduce costs, increase manufacturing efficiency, and improve customer value. They know how wasteful it is to tie up large sums of money in **inventory**—the goods and materials kept in stock for production or sale. On the other hand, not having an adequate supply of inventory can delay production and result in unhappy customers. That's why more and more companies are changing the way they purchase and handle the materials they use to produce goods and services.

LEARNING OBJECTIVE 4
Explain the strategic importance of managing inventory

 Think of inventory as dollar bills on your shelves.[34]

inventory
Goods kept in stock for the production process or for sales to final customers

Purchasing is the acquisition of the raw materials, parts, components, supplies, and finished products required to produce goods and services. The goal of purchasing is to make sure that the company has all of the materials it needs, when it needs them, at the lowest possible cost. To accomplish this goal, a company must always have enough supplies on hand

purchasing
Acquiring the raw materials, parts, components, supplies, and finished products needed to produce goods and services

lead time
Period that elapses between the ordering of materials and their arrival from the supplier

to cover a product's **lead time**—the period that elapses between placing the supply order and receiving materials.

In the past, companies would buy large enough supply inventories to make sure they would not run out of parts during peak production times. As soon as inventory levels dropped to a predetermined level, the purchasing department would order new parts. Many companies continue to operate this way, which does offer certain benefits. For example, companies typically get a better price when they buy inventory in bulk, and having a large supply on hand enables them to meet customer demand quickly. Unfortunately, carrying a large inventory also ties up the company's money and increases the risk that products will become obsolete.

inventory control
System for determining the right quantity of various items to have on hand and keeping track of their location, use, and condition

To minimize this risk and cost, and to increase manufacturing efficiency, many companies establish a system of **inventory control**—some way of (1) determining the right quantities of supplies and products to have on hand and (2) tracking where those items are. Two methods that companies use to control inventory and manage the production process are *material requirements planning* and *manufacturing resource planning.*

LEARNING OBJECTIVE 5
Distinguish among MRP, MRP II, and JIT systems

material requirements planning (MRP)
Method of getting the correct materials where they are needed, on time, and without carrying unnecessary inventory

Material Requirements Planning (MRP)   **Material requirements planning** (MRP) is an inventory-control technique that helps a manufacturer get the correct materials where they are needed, when they are needed, and without unnecessary stockpiling. Managers use computer programs to calculate when certain materials will be required, when they should be ordered, and when they should be delivered so that storage costs will be minimal. These systems are so effective at reducing inventory levels that they are used almost universally in both large and small manufacturing firms.

perpetual inventory
System that uses computers to monitor inventory levels and automatically generate purchase orders when supplies are needed

A more automated form of material requirements planning is the **perpetual inventory** system, in which computers monitor inventory levels and automatically generate purchase orders when supplies fall below a certain level. The price scanners found at the checkout counters of many stores are part of perpetual inventory systems. Every time a product is purchased, the scanner deletes that particular item from the computer system's inventory data. When inventory of the product reaches a predetermined level, the system generates an order for more. Often the store's system is linked to the supplier's own computer system, which enables the order to be placed with virtually no human involvement.

manufacturing resource planning (MRP II)
Computer-based system that integrates data from all departments to manage inventory and production planning and control

Manufacturing Resource Planning (MRP II)   The MRP systems on the market today are made up of various modules, including inventory control, purchasing, customer order entry, production planning, shop-floor control, and accounting. With the addition of more and more modules that focus on capacity planning, marketing, and finance, an MRP system evolves into a **manufacturing resource planning** (MRP II) system.

Because it draws together all departments, an MRP II system produces a company-wide game plan that allows everyone to work with the same numbers (see Exhibit 8.5). Employees can now draw on data, such as inventory levels, back orders, and unpaid bills, once reserved for only top executives. Moreover, the system can track each step of production, allowing managers throughout the company to consult other managers' inventories, schedules, and plans. In addition, MRP II systems are capable of running simulations (models of possible operations systems) that enable managers to plan and test alternative strategies.[35] And thanks to the Internet and some highly complex software, even geographically distant facilities can now be integrated into the planning system as though they were all under one roof.[36]

just-in-time (JIT) system
Continuous system that pulls materials through the production process, making sure that all materials arrive just when they are needed with minimal inventory and waste

Just-in-Time Systems   An increasingly popular method of managing operations, including inventory control and production planning, is the **just-in-time (JIT) system.** As with MRP,

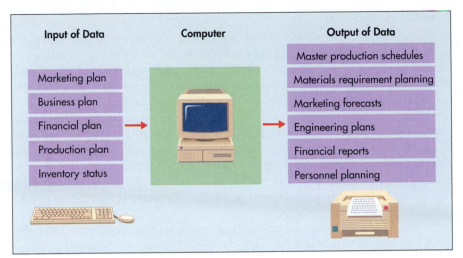

EXHIBIT 8·5

MRP II

An MRP II computer system gives managers and workers in every department easy access to data from all other departments, which in turn makes it easier to generate— and adhere to—the organization's overall plans, forecasts, and schedules.

the goal of just-in-time systems is to have only the right amounts of materials arrive at precisely the times they are needed. Because supplies arrive just as they are needed, and no sooner, inventories are eliminated and waste is reduced.

The maintenance of a "zero inventory" under JIT does have some indirect benefits. For instance, reducing stocks of parts to practically nothing encourages factories to keep production flowing smoothly, from beginning to end, without any holdups. And a constant production flow requires good teamwork. On the other hand, JIT exposes a company to greater risks, as a disruption in the flow of raw materials from suppliers can slow or stop the production process. A JIT system also places a heavy burden on suppliers because they must be able to meet the production schedules of their customers.

Thus, to be effective, JIT systems must be designed to include multifunctional teamwork, flexible manufacturing, small-batch production, strict production control, quick setups, consistent production levels, preventive maintenance, and reliable supplier networks. Furthermore, poor quality simply cannot be tolerated in a stockless manufacturing environment because one defective part can bring production to a grinding halt. In other words, JIT cannot be implemented without a commitment to total quality control.[37] When all of these factors work together in sync, the manufacturer achieves *lean production;* that is, it can do more with less.[38]

In those cases where it is difficult for manufacturers and suppliers to coordinate their schedules, JIT may not work. For example, shoemaker Allen-Edmonds cannot get its principal raw material whenever it wants because calfskin hides come on the market only at certain times each year.[39] Additional factors can also affect JIT: whether a product is seasonal or promotional or perishable; whether it has unusual handling characteristics; its size; its weight; and the volatility of the sales cycle.[40]

Keep in mind that JIT concepts can also be used to reduce inventory and cycle time for service organizations. Consider Koley's Medical Supply, which manages inventory for hospitals using what it calls "stockless distribution." Rather than making large, general deliveries to the stockroom, the company delivers specific items in just the right quantities to the various floors and rooms in the hospital. Doing so isn't always easy: At one hospital, Koley's has to make deliveries to 168 individual receiving points. But the system creates value for Koley's customers. For example, in Omaha, Nebraska, Bishop Clarkson Memorial Hospital reduced its annual inventory costs from $500,000 to just $7,000.

Quality Assurance

Companies today are more focused on quality than ever before. As was Harley-Davidson, many U.S. companies have been forced to examine the quality of their goods, services, and processes largely as a result of tough foreign competition. And just as Harley-Davidson was able to reestablish itself as the worldwide quality leader, many other U.S. companies are following in Harley's footsteps by setting new standards for quality.

Still, adopting high quality standards is not an easy task, because the manufacture of complex goods is not simply a matter of adding part A to part B to part C and so forth until a product emerges ready to ship. For example, the Mercedes M-Class sport-utility vehicle is assembled from subunits built by 65 major suppliers and many other smaller ones.[42] Making sure that all the pieces are put together in the proper sequence and at the proper time requires large-scale planning and scheduling. The same is true for the production of complex services.

The traditional means of maintaining quality is called **quality control**—measuring quality against established standards after the good or service has been produced and weeding out any defects. A more comprehensive approach is **quality assurance,** a system of companywide policies, practices, and procedures to ensure that every product meets preset quality standards. Quality assurance includes quality control as well as doing the job right the first time by designing tools and machinery properly, demanding quality parts from suppliers, encouraging customer feedback, training employees, empowering them, and encouraging them to take pride in their work. As discussed in Chapter 6, total quality management takes things to even a higher level by building quality into every activity within an organization.

Companies approach quality assurance in various ways. As a builder of sheet-metal components and electromechanical assemblies, Trident Precision Manufacturing empowers workers to make decisions on the shop floor, and it spends 4.7 percent of payroll on employee training.[43] High-end computer maker Sequent Computer Systems has a "customer process engineering manager" whose primary responsibility is to continually communicate with customers and identify any recurring problems. These companies know that eliminating only one inefficiency, such as a defect or an excessively complex process, can reduce total product costs because less money is spent on inspection, complaints, and product service.[44]

Statistical Quality Control and Continuous Improvement   Quality assurance also includes the now widely used concept of **statistical quality control (SQC),** in which all aspects of the

---

LEARNING OBJECTIVE 6

Highlight the differences between quality control and quality assurance

quality control
Routine checking and testing of a finished product for quality against an established standard

quality assurance
System of policies, practices, and procedures implemented throughout the company to create and produce quality goods and services

statistical quality control (SQC)
Monitoring all aspects of the production process to see whether the process is operating as it should

---

See It on the Web See It on the Web

MAKING QUALITY COUNT

In today's competitive business environment, companies have to be concerned about the quality of their goods and services. For information and advice, many turn to the American Society for Quality (ASQ), which maintains a Web site covering all things quality. You can find out about ISO 9000 and other quality standards, search an online glossary of quality-related terms, find out who won the latest Malcolm Baldrige awards, and follow links to numerous quality Web sites. At the ASQ, quality is only a click away.
http://www.asqc.org

production process are monitored so that managers can see whether the process is operating as it should. The primary tool of SQC is called **statistical process control (SPC),** taking samples from the process periodically and plotting observations of the samples on a *control chart.* A large enough sample provides a reasonable estimate of the entire process. By observing the random fluctuations graphed on the chart, managers and workers can identify whether such changes are normal or whether they indicate that some corrective action is required in the process. In this way SPC can prevent poor quality.[45]

Statistical quality control is not limited to goods-producing industries. For example, financial services provider GE Capital uses statistical control methods to make sure the bills it sends to customers are correct. The company's use of SQC lowers the cost of making adjustments while improving customer satisfaction.[46]

In addition to using SQC, companies can empower each employee to continuously improve the quality of goods production or service delivery. The Japanese word for continuous

statistical process control (SPC)
Use of random sampling and control charts to monitor the production process

CHEK LAP KOK'S TURBULENT TAKEOFF

Opening day at Chek Lap Kok, Hong Kong's new airport, was a monumental disaster. The state-of-the art facility, designed to handle 80 million passengers annually, was promoted as a symbol of Swiss-watch efficiency. But on the airport's first day of operations, every single thing broke down—or so it seemed (see photo, p. 196).

The airport lurched from crisis to crisis. Planes were stranded on the tarmac with no directions to parking gates. Passengers missed flights because of malfunctions in the Flight Information Display system. Some planes left without food for their passengers; others went without passengers altogether. Arriving passengers were imprisoned in the aircraft while mechanics repaired broken jetway doors. And baggage systems (designed to handle 13,700 pieces of luggage an hour) crashed, leaving passengers without luggage and loading luggage on planes without passengers—a serious security breach.

Then, just as the chaos in the passenger terminal seemed under control, computer glitches all but paralyzed air-cargo operations. A software bug disabled the computer system running the new $1.2 billion on-site automated cargo handling facilities—one of the largest in the world. Thousands of air freight containers were strewn across the tarmac. And perishable goods rotted in state-of-the art warehouses while new shipments were rerouted.

Poor communications, overconfidence, and lack of system testing and contingency planning—even incompetence—are just a few of the reasons why the July 6, 1998, debut of Hong Kong's new international airport at Chek Lap Kok turned into a nightmare. For example, communications systems and software on which the modern airport depended had not been thoroughly tested. Sample tests of 10,000 transactions had produced some minor problems, but when 70,000 actual transactions hit the systems on opening day, the systems were pushed to the breaking point. For another, political pressure forced officials to open the airport months before it should have been.

Chek Lap Kok is a good example of what can happen without sufficient quality control. Besides inflicting serious damage on Hong Kong's image, the airport's poor opening cost all parties involved over $5 billion—one-fifth the airport's $25 billion construction cost. The government wanted Chek Lap Kok to be world famous, and it was—but for all the wrong reasons.

QUESTIONS FOR CRITICAL THINKING

1. What steps might airport managers have taken to prevent Chek Lap Kok's disastrous opening?
2. Why did statistical quality control tests fail to produce the serious problems that occurred on opening day?

Numerous failures at Hong Kong's huge new airport, Chek Lap Kok, left cargo, including perishables, sitting on the tarmac for days.

ISO 9000
Global standards set by the International Organization for Standardization establishing a minimum level of acceptable quality

improvement is *kaizen.* Japanese manufacturers learned long before many U.S. manufacturers that continuous improvement is not something that can be delegated to one or a few people. Instead it requires the full participation of every employee. This means encouraging all workers to spot quality problems, halt production when necessary, generate ideas for improvement, and adjust work routines as needed.[47]

Global Quality Standards   Companies that do business in Europe have to leap an extra quality hurdle. Many manufacturers and service providers in Europe require that suppliers comply with **ISO 9000,** a set of international quality standards that establishes a minimum level of acceptable quality. Set by the International Organization for Standardization, a nongovernment entity based in Geneva, Switzerland, ISO 9000 focuses on internal production and process issues that affect quality, but it doesn't measure quality in terms of customer satisfaction or business results. Usually the standards are applied to products that have health- and safety-related features. However, even companies that manufacture products not covered by ISO 9000 standards are being forced to gain accreditation by customers seeking quality assurance. The standards are now recognized in over 100 countries, and one-fourth of all of the world's corporations insist that all their suppliers be ISO 9000 certified. Even the U.S. Navy requires its suppliers to meet ISO 9000 standards.[48]

ISO 9000 helps companies develop *world-class manufacturing,* a term used to describe the level of quality and operational effectiveness that puts a company among the top performers in the world. Companies seeking world-class quality can use as benchmarks those companies that are globally recognized quality leaders. They can also follow the guidelines of various national quality awards. In Japan, the Deming Prize is a highly regarded industrial quality award, and in the United States, the Malcolm Baldrige National Quality Award honors the quality achievements of U.S. companies. Of course, even if an organization doesn't want to actually apply for an award, it can improve quality by measuring its performance against the award's standards and working to overcome any problems uncovered by this process.

■ OUTSOURCING THE MANUFACTURING FUNCTION

As companies strive to find better ways to produce goods, some are learning that outsourcing the manufacturing function can provide tremendous cost efficiencies. For one thing, outsourcing allows companies to redirect the capital and resources spent on manufacturing to new product research, marketing, and customer service. As a result, some manufacturers today don't really "manufacture" products at all. Instead, they design them, market them, and support them. This is especially true with high-tech products.[49]

At Solectron, a California contract manufacturer, for example, 24 production lines simultaneously assemble everything from pagers to printers to television decoding boxes for some of the biggest brand names in electronics. Similarly, Ingram Micro, the world's largest wholesale distributor of computers, does assembly work for archrivals that together control more than one-third of the U.S. computer market. In some cases these supercontractors even manage their customers' entire product lines by offering an array of services from design to inventory management and by providing delivery and after-sales service.[50]

Companies that outsource their manufacturing operations, of course, claim that their products are differentiated from those of their competitors (even if they are all assembled by the same contractor) because unique features and levels of quality are designed into a company's products. As one Hewlett-Packard vice president commented, "We own all the intellectual property; we farm out the direct labor; we don't need to screw the motherboard into the metal box and attach the ribbon cable." Still, others fear that outsourcing the manufacturing function could jeopardize a company's control over the product's intellectual property or quality. Intel, National Semiconductor, and Merck are among the corporate giants that have chosen to keep manufacturing in-house to protect their competitive edge.[51]

Solectron is a part of a new breed of U.S. supercontractors that make dozens of brand-name electronics at the same factory.

Besides outsourcing, another trend sweeping manufacturing organizations is relegating more work to suppliers. In some companies, in-house manufacturing operations consist of nothing more than bolting together fabricated chunks that have been manufactured by suppliers. Consider Airbus's jetliner factory in Toulouse, France, for example. Large sections of Airbus jets manufactured at factories throughout Europe are flown to Toulouse in giant modified cargo jets called Belugas. There, small teams "snap together" the largely complete components, attach the landing gear, and drill holes to fasten wings to fuselages. The result is a much more modern and efficient production system than the one used by the industry leader, Boeing. In fact, Airbus now produces more revenue per employee than Boeing's commercial airplane division and is narrowing the gap between the number one and two spots of this industry duopoly. As competition heats up, Airbus recognizes that the company's competitor is not the Boeing of today, rather "the Boeing that will be."[52]

Summary of Learning Objectives

1. **Explain what operations managers do.**
   Operations managers design, improve, manage, and control the production process of both goods and services.

2. **Identify key tasks involved in designing a production process.**
   Managers must first prepare production forecasts, or estimates of future demand for the company's products. Next they must consider capacity, which is a business's volume of manufacturing or service delivery. The next step is to find a facility location that minimizes regional costs (land, construction, labor, local taxes, leasing, energy), transportation costs, and raw materials costs. Once a location has been selected, managers need to consider facility layout—the arrangement of production work centers and other facilities (such as material, equipment, and support departments) needed for the processing of goods and services. Finally, managers must develop a master production schedule.

3. **Discuss the role of computers and automation technology in production.**
   Computers and automation technology improve the production process in several ways: (1) Robots perform repetitive or mundane tasks quickly and with great precision; (2) CAD and CAE systems allow engineers to design and test virtual models of products; (3) CAM systems easily translate CAD data into production instructions; (4) CIM systems link the people, machines, databases, and decisions involved in each step of producing a good; (5) flexible manufacturing systems (FMSs) reduce setup costs and time by linking programmable, multifunctional machine tools through a computer network and an automated materials-handling system; and (6) EDI systems make ordering supplies faster and easier.

4. **Explain the strategic importance of managing inventory.**
   The goods and materials kept in stock for production or sale make up inventory, which must be managed to minimize costs and ensure that the right supplies are in the right place at the right time.

5. **Distinguish among MRP, MRP II, and JIT systems.**
   Material requirements planning (MRP) and perpetual inventory systems are used to determine when materials are needed, when they should be ordered, and when they should be delivered. A more advanced system is

MEETING BUSINESS CHALLENGES AT HARLEY-DAVIDSON

During the 1970s, when attractive new imports were roaring into the U.S. motorcycle market, Harley-Davidson suffered a serious quality crisis. It took the company almost two decades to figure out how to maintain high quality standards while boosting output. But incorporating continuous improvement methods into the company's manufacturing processes eventually paid off. By the mid-1990s, Harley had won back market share and was selling $2 billion in motorcycles, parts, and accessories to loyal fans all over the world. Still, CEO Jeff Bleustein was anything but complacent. Eyeing the projected increase in domestic demand and the huge sales potential of markets outside North America, he was determined to overhaul the production process for higher output and productivity.

One key target was the company's inefficient supply chain. Nearly 1,000 suppliers provided Harley with raw materials, parts, and components. The head of purchasing soon narrowed the supplier list to just 425 and streamlined purchasing through a Web-based supply system. These steps strengthened supplier commitment and helped purchasing get more mileage out of the company's $1 billion yearly supply budget. The company also centralized purchasing and inventory into a single supply management department and in doing so improved Harley's buying power. Next, all purchasing agents were required to complete a structured materials planning and buying training course, capped by testing and formal certification.

The distribution warehouse was another key target. Crowded, old, and inefficient, the warehouse was simply inadequate. After some analysis, the company decided to build a gigantic new distribution center in a Milwaukee suburb with state-of-the-art technology to track and control the inbound and outbound movement of items. This new distribution center doubled productivity and sliced fulfillment time for orders from twelve days to two.

In the race to boost output and productivity, Harley invested $650 million in new production facilities and manufacturing equipment. One new plant, equipped with a sophisticated materials management system, could produce motorcycles 30 percent more efficiently than the older plant. Advanced technology was integrated throughout the production process, including a computer-aided design (CAD) system accessible to employees in many departments. Harley also allowed selected suppliers to access the CAD system so they could collaborate on product development.

Although Bleustein was investing heavily to expand capacity and update facilities and systems, the improvements were expected to shave $40 million from overall production and inventory costs. Output and productivity soared, as did sales around the world. By the turn of the century, Harley was exceeding its yearly output targets and quickly closing in on its goal of producing 200,000 motorcycles in 2003.[53]

Critical Thinking Questions

1. Why would Harley want to allow employees in the purchasing department as well as selected suppliers to access information in the CAD system used for new product design and development?

2. How do you think reducing the time needed to fulfill parts orders would affect Harley's inventory costs?

3. How might Bleustein's goal of producing 200,000 motorcycles by 2003 affect Harley's suppliers?

■ LEARN MORE ONLINE

To monitor Harley-Davidson's progress toward its output target, visit the company's Web site at http://www.harley-davidson.com and locate the section with company and investor information. Read the latest annual report. Then look at the current and historical production and sales statistics posted on the site. How many motorcycles did Harley produce in the most recent quarter? In the most recent year? What is the output trend? What is the trend in Harley's worldwide sales?

manufacturing resource planning (MRP II), which brings together data from all parts of a company (including financial, design, and engineering departments) to better manage inventory and production planning and control. Just-in-time (JIT) systems reduce waste and improve quality by producing only enough to fill orders when they are due, thus eliminating finished-goods inventory. Furthermore, under the JIT system, parts or materials are ordered only when they are needed, thus eliminating supplies inventories.

6. **Highlight the differences between quality control and quality assurance.**

Quality control focuses on measuring finished products against a preset standard and weeding out any defects. On the other hand, quality assurance is a system of companywide policies, practices, and procedures that build quality into a product and ensure that each product meets quality standards.

Key Terms

capacity planning (181)

cellular layout (183)

computer-aided design (CAD) (187)

computer-aided engineering (CAE) (187)

computer-aided manufacturing (CAM) (187)

computer-integrated manufacturing (CIM) (188)

critical path (185)

dispatching (186)

electronic data interchange (EDI) (189)

fixed-position layout (183)

flexible manufacturing system (FMS) (188)

Gantt chart (185)

inventory (191)

inventory control (192)

ISO 9000 (196)

just-in-time (JIT) system (192)

lead time (192)

manufacturing resource planning (MRP II) (192)

mass customization (180)

mass production (179)

material requirements planning (MRP) (192)

operations management (179)

perpetual inventory (192)

process layout (183)

product layout (183)

production (179)

production efficiency (179)

production forecasts (181)

program evaluation and review technique (PERT) (185)

purchasing (191)

quality assurance (194)

quality control (194)

robots (187)

routing (185)

scheduling (185)

setup costs (188)

statistical process control (SPC) (195)

statistical quality control (SQC) (194)

supply-chain management (191)

Test Your Knowledge

QUESTIONS FOR REVIEW

1. Explain the conversion process.
2. What is mass customization?
3. What factors need to be considered when selecting a site for a production facility?
4. Why is an effective system of inventory control important to every manufacturer?
5. Why might a company want to outsource its manufacturing function?

QUESTIONS FOR ANALYSIS

6. Why is capacity planning an important part of designing operations?
7. Explain how JIT systems go beyond simply controlling inventory.
8. Why have companies moved beyond quality control to quality assurance?

9. How can supply-chain management help a company establish a competitive advantage?
10. How does society's concern for the environment affect a company's facility-location and layout decisions?

QUESTIONS FOR APPLICATION

11. Assume you are the production manager for a small machine shop that manufactures precision parts for industrial equipment. How can you use CAD, CAE, CAM, CIM, FMS, and EDI to manufacture better parts more easily?
12. If your final product requires several unique subunits that are all produced with different machinery and in differing lengths of time, what facility layout will you choose and why?
13. From an operational perspective, why is purchasing a franchise such as Wendy's or Jiffy Lube an attractive alternative for starting a business?
14. What things could you learn about a company's culture by observing the layout and design of its production facility? Discuss both goods and services operations.

Practice Your Knowledge

SHARPENING YOUR COMMUNICATION SKILLS

As the newly hired manager of Campus Athletics—a shop featuring athletic wear bearing logos of colleges and universities—you are responsible for selecting the store's suppliers. Merchandise with team logos and brands can be very trendy. When a college team is hot, you've got to have merchandise. You know that selecting the right supplier is a task that requires careful consideration, so you have decided to host a series of selection interviews. Think about all the qualities you would want in a supplier, and develop a list of interview questions that will help you assess whether that supplier possesses those qualities.

HANDLING DIFFICULT SITUATIONS ON THE JOB: GIVING SUPPLIERS A REPORT CARD

Just when you thought there was nothing left to measure and evaluate, your boss at Microsoft, Roxanna Frost, suggested something new. Frost, who is the program manager for Microsoft's Executive Management and Development Group, recently led a discussion emphasizing the importance of employee performance reviews. "It's all about improving clarity in terms of goals and expectations," noted one manager. Frost agreed: "Right—so everyone can talk about accomplishments and improvements." Then Frost suggested that the same should go for suppliers. "There's a gap between what we want our suppliers to do and the feedback they're getting."

　　Thinking about this observation, you realize that 60 percent of the employee services your group monitors (travel assistance, retirement plans, the library at Microsoft's Redmond, Washington, campus) are outsourced to independent suppliers. This is nothing unusual at Microsoft, where many departments outsource both goods and services. What is new is Frost's idea of providing suppliers with feedback about their performance.

　　As the discussion continues, Frost points out that it would be a good idea to periodically evaluate *all* the outside suppliers that serve the company. When she asks for a volunteer to coordinate this new project, you raise your hand. This is just the kind of challenge you relish. Now, how will you get the project under way?[54]

1. You know that on-time delivery is important; what additional criteria should Microsoft departments use for supplier evaluation? Identify at least four but no more than six criteria.
2. Frost wants Microsoft to evaluate its suppliers more than once. How often would you recommend gathering feedback to send to suppliers? Why?
3. When Microsoft provides feedback, how might suppliers be expected to respond?

BUILDING YOUR TEAM SKILLS

Facility layout is one of the most critical decisions production managers must make. In this exercise, you and your team are playing the role of production managers for the following companies, some producing a specific good and some producing a specific service:

- Mountain Dew—soft drinks
- H & R Block—tax consultation
- Bob Mackie—custom-made clothing
- Burger King—fast food
- Boeing—commercial jets
- Massachusetts General Hospital—medical services
- Hewlett-Packard—fax machines
- Toyota—sport-utility vehicles

For each company on the list, discuss and recommend a specific facility layout, referring to Exhibit 8.2 for an overview of the four layouts. Why does your team believe the recommended layout is best suited to the product or service each company produces? How would the recommended layouts affect the movement of resources and inventory for the manufacturers on the list? How would the layouts affect customer interaction for the service providers on the list?

Expand Your Knowledge

EXPLORING CAREER OPPORTUNITIES

Whether you prefer to work with products or services, many possible careers await you in production and operations. From input to transformation to output, companies are looking for resourceful, results-oriented employees able to meet the demands of ever-changing schedules and specifications. Start your research by scanning the help-wanted classified and display ads in your local newspaper and in the *Wall Street Journal;* also check help-wanted ads in business magazines such as *Industry Week.* If you have Internet access, search the production and manufacturing jobs listed on America's Job Bank (http://www.ajb.dni.us).

1. As you read through these want ads, note all the production-related job titles you find. How many of these jobs include quality or technology (or both) among the duties and responsibilities?

2. Select two job openings that interest you. Reread the ads for those jobs to find out what kind of work experience and educational background are required. What further preparation will you need to qualify for these jobs?

3. Assume you have the qualifications for the two jobs you have selected. What key words should you include on your electronic résumé to show the employers that you are a good job candidate?

DEVELOPING YOUR RESEARCH SKILLS

Seeking increased efficiency and productivity, a growing number of producers of goods and services are applying technology to improve the production process. Use library or online sources to find an article about how one company used CAD, CAE, robots, electronic information systems, or other technological innovations to refit or reorganize its production operations. As you complete this research, jot down the sources and search methodology you use.

1. What problems led the company to rethink its production process? What kind of technology did it choose to address these problems? What goals did the company set for applying technology in this way?

2. Before adding the new technology, what did the company do to analyze its existing production process? What changes, if any, were made as a result of this analysis?

3. How did technology-enhanced production help the company achieve its goals for financial performance? For customer service? For growth or expansion?

SEE IT ON THE WEB EXERCISES
Make Gloves, Not War, page 182

The Armament Retooling Manufacturing Support (ARMS) program helps manufacturers solve their capacity problems by using idle ammunition factories. Visit the Operation Enterprise Web site at http://www.openterprise.com/ and read more about this innovative public-private partnership. Then answer the following questions.

1. Follow the link to The ARMS Program: An Overview to learn more about this program. Who owns the facilities operated under ARMS? What kinds of businesses or industries do you think would be particularly attracted to this program?

2. Click on the link to The ARMS Program: Success Stories and read one of the success stories. What goods or services are being produced at the ARMS site you read about? Why did the business choose this facility? Why is this situation considered a success for both the business and the government?

3. Follow the link to Facility Amenities and read about what each ARMS site has to offer. Why would businesses need

to know these details at the outset? On the basis of these amenities, which sites would seem best suited to companies planning for international sales? Why?

Setting Standards, page 189

The National Institute of Standards and Technology (NIST) works with private industry to develop standards for emerging industries and to improve U.S. competitiveness in mature industries. Explore the NIST Web site at http://nist.gov/ so you can answer these questions:

1. From the main page, click on Advanced Technology Program. What is the goal of this program? Why does the federal government have an interest in promoting the development of advanced technologies?

2. Click on the ATP Focused Programs to learn about some of the advanced technology projects that NIST sponsors. As you can see, developing these technologies is a long and costly process. Why might private investors be reluctant to fund the development of such technologies? On the other hand, why might investors want to have a stake in developing them?

3. From the main page, click on the link to Measurement and Standards Laboratories. What benefits do NIST's Measurement and Standards Laboratories provide to businesses, industries, and the scientific community? Why is it important for all users of a particular technology to use a common language and standards?

Making Quality Count, page 194

Businesses can learn more about improving the quality of their goods and services by accessing the many resources on the American Society for Quality (ASQ) Web site at http://www.asqc.org. Point your browser to the ASQ site and respond to the following questions.

1. Click on the link to About ASQ and then on Ethics to read the society's code of ethics. How do you think an individual employee's attitude toward ethics can affect the overall level of quality in an organization? How are the society's ethical principles related to the principles of effective teamwork?

2. From the main page, follow the links in the About Quality to reach the Glossary. Search for a specific quality term such as "JIT." What definition does the glossary provide? How does the ASQ's definition compare with the definition in this text?

3. Go back to the main page and follow the link to ISO 14000. What is ISO 14000? What are its anticipated benefits? Can a company be considered a quality producer it if has a reputation for producing excellent goods or services but also has a spotty environmental record? Why or why not?

Managing a Business

Learning Objectives

1. See how an entrepreneur applies the four basic functions of management to a small business.
2. Follow the evolution of a fast-growing company's organizational structure.
3. Understand how a small business uses continuous improvement for competitive advantage.

Background Information

Like their counterparts in giant corporations, managers in small businesses such as Blausen Medical Communications (BMC) reach their organizations' goals through the four management functions of planning, organizing, leading, and controlling. Initially, a start-up may have fewer levels of management, and employees pitch in to handle a number of work tasks. As the business grows, however, it hires more employees and divides the workload into specialized tasks assigned to qualified employees. Eventually, the organization develops a hierarchy of first-line, middle, and top managers to supervise its larger staff and coordinate the increasingly specialized work activities. Regardless of size, no business can survive in today's highly competitive, global marketplace unless it can efficiently produce high-quality goods and services that meet customers' needs, such as the detailed medical animations and illustrations produced by BMC.

The Video

BMC is a young, growing company with a small group of upper-level managers at the top of its management pyramid. Because the company is small, employees pitch in when needed to work on all kinds of projects. BMC's founder, Bruce Blausen, gives his employees a great deal of responsibility and holds them accountable for completing projects on time and within budget. In the open environment of BMC's Houston headquarters, employees can easily see and comment on the work their colleagues are doing, which makes for closer collaboration. BMC ensures quality through its strong customer focus and emphasis on con-tinuous improvement. As its employees work on a project, they listen carefully to customers' ideas and make any needed revisions, without charge, until customers are satisfied. Over the years, BMC has created a huge library of medical animations that Blausen plans to tap for an ongoing succession of new and improved products and services.

Discussion Questions

1. Is BMC a flat organization or a tall organization? Does Blausen think this will change in the future—and why?
2. How is BMC's open environment likely to affect internal communication?
3. What elements form the input, the transformation, and the output in BMC's conversion process?

Next Steps

A mission statement helps the company define why it exists, what it seeks to accomplish, and the principles it will follow as it strives to achieve its goals. Draft a mission statement for BMC, covering the company's main products and services; its primary markets; its approach to survival, growth, and profitability; its managerial philosophy; and its commitment to quality and social responsibility. How can Blausen use this mission statement to make his organization more effective?

■ LEARN MORE ONLINE

Using a search site such as Google or Excite, use the key terms *medical animation* and *scientific animation* to locate the Web sites of at least three BMC competitors. Based on what you see on these sites, how large do these competitors seem to be? Do any of these competitors post mission statements on their sites? How do these competitors say they are using technology to produce quality products? What quality assurance techniques do they mention?

http://www.google.com (Google search site)

http://www.excite.com (Excite search site)

Nick: Say, Natasha, did you ever wonder how challenging it must be to manufacture a widebody jet? Next time I'm in Everett, Washington, I'm going to tour the Boeing 747 plant. I bet it's a real high-tech operation.

Natasha: Perhaps it is now, but it wasn't always that way. In the late 1990s many of the company's production techniques were still arcane. Every design alteration involved hundreds of pages of detailed drawings and cost hundreds of thousands of dollars to execute.

Nick: And Boeing's customers would pay for this?

Natasha: They did. That is, until competition between Boeing and its sole competitor, Europe's Airbus Industrie consortium, got savage. One day Airbus got smart, and the next it locked up 52 percent of all new aircraft orders.

Nick: Ouch! I bet that cut into Boeing's 60 percent market share and jolted it into making a change or two.

Natasha: Yes, but not before management made some pretty bad decisions—such as accepting more customer orders than Boeing could deliver on time.

Nick: Why would a company do that?

Natasha: Let's see if we can find the answers.

THE MYSTERY OF PILOT ERROR AND A SUDDEN DROP IN ALTITUDE

Boeing's engines were in full throttle when demand for new aircraft took off in the late 1990s. It was the industry's largest comeback in 50 years. And it should have been glorious times for Boeing, the world's biggest jetmaker, had it not been for management's overambition and miscalculations.

It all began when Airbus won 52 percent of new aircraft orders. Boeing feared that Airbus was closing in on its long-standing industry lead, so it adopted a close-as-many-deals-as-possible mentality. Banking on its ability to overhaul operations, cut production costs by 25 percent, and double production of its profitable 747 line, Boeing offered customers deep discounts on smaller planes to win their multiaircraft orders. The plan worked. A record number of new orders—712 to be exact—poured in, many of which were for 747s.

To meet its ambitious delivery schedule, Boeing cranked up production of its 747 line from two planes a month to three and a half and then to four. That's when the trouble began. Even though management shifted several hundred workers from its 767 line to help build the 747s, having workers was not enough. Boeing's systems were woefully inefficient—something Boeing's management had known for decades and was in the process of correcting. Moreover, management failed to communicate the surge of new orders to Boeing's suppliers, and a shortage of critical parts created bottlenecks just about everywhere. By September 1997, the 747 line was running more than 14,000 jobs behind schedule.

To get the 747 line back on schedule, management called a time-out. Boeing halted production of the 747 line for one month but still promised customers timely delivery of their new planes. Meanwhile, troubles mounted and Boeing failed to meet its ambitious delivery schedules. Late deliveries and cost overruns ultimately forced the Seattle giant to take a $178 million loss in 1997, its first red ink in 50 years. Investors were stunned.

While Boeing struggled to recover from its production woes, the Asian economic crisis dealt the company another blow. Unable to pay for their aircraft, many Asian airlines canceled or deferred their orders. As much as 30 percent of Boeing's 747 backlog had been earmarked for Asian customers. Now Boeing had to park 34 finished aircraft in the Arizona desert and wait for the economy to recover. The trouble was that management had counted on the cash from sales of 747s to compensate for the deep discounts it offered customers on Boeing's smaller models.[55]

SOLVING THE MYSTERY OF PILOT ERROR AND A SUDDEN DROP IN ALTITUDE

1. Why did Boeing's management accept more orders than it could deliver on time?
   HINT: AIRPLANES HAVE A 20-YEAR USEFUL LIFE.
2. What valuable lessons do you think Boeing's management learned from this incident?
   HINT: A CHAIN IS AS STRONG AS ITS WEAKEST LINK.
3. Look back at the margin clues in Parts I through III. What business principles did Boeing overlook?

MOTIVATING TODAY'S WORK FORCE AND HANDLING EMPLOYEE-MANAGEMENT RELATIONS

LEARNING OBJECTIVES

After studying this chapter, you will be able to

1 Identify and explain three important theories of employee motivation

2 List four staffing challenges employers are facing in today's workplace

3 List three demographic challenges employers are facing in today's workplace

4 Highlight three popular alternative work arrangements companies are offering their employees

5 Cite three options that unions have when negotiations with management break down

6 Cite three options management can exercise when negotiations with the union break down

FACING BUSINESS CHALLENGES AT UNITED PARCEL SERVICE

Delivering Better Employee-Management Relations

In the 80-plus years since United Parcel Service (UPS) founder Jim Casey had declared, "You can be a good Teamster and a good UPSer," the company had enjoyed generally good relations with the International Brotherhood of Teamsters. Despite economic ups and downs and competitive pressures, employees, managers, and union officials had usually worked collaboratively to keep the Atlanta-based company running smoothly and profitably. UPS—the world's largest package delivery service, handling over 12 million parcels every day—was known for offering good pay. Its employees rarely left; in fact, turnover was less than half the industry average.

Still, in the mid-1990s Teamsters officials had become increasingly concerned about the company's growing reliance on part-time employees. More than half of the jobs at UPS were part-time, paying half the hourly rate of full-time positions. So the union geared up to fight for better pay for part-timers, more full-time jobs, and better pension benefits. But when these issues boiled over in August 1997, the union called a national strike against UPS.

CEO Jim Kelly and his top managers—including many ex-Teamsters who had risen through the ranks—thought the strike would be short-lived because most employees would cross the picket lines. They were wrong. The vast majority of UPS employees joined the strike. And for the first time in 20 years, a nationwide poll found that the U.S. public overwhelmingly supported the strike, even though it caused major inconveniences for millions of people. As the days passed and customers took their business elsewhere, UPS laid off drivers to help offset the losses. Finally forced back to the negotiating table, management settled the strike by agreeing to nearly every union demand, including the creation of 2,000 full-time positions annually for the duration of the five-year contract.

The Teamsters union was widely viewed as the winner in this 15-day labor dispute, which cost UPS up to $1 billion in lost revenues. Within a year, however, it became clear that the union had failed to achieve its objective of creating more full-time jobs. Because sales volume remained below prestrike levels, management was not contractually obligated to create more full-time jobs. Instead, management reduced the number of full-time positions by roughly 6 percent, and union officials fumed. They accused management of trying to wiggle out of their promise on a contractual technicality.

Even though the strike was over, things remained tense. What could Jim Kelly and his managers do to renew the spirit of cooperation between employees, management, and union officials? How could management monitor its employees' attitudes toward the company and keep them motivated? What could they learn from the strike that could help them prevent a second labor dispute, this one with their pilots' union?[1]

205

■ MOTIVATING EMPLOYEES

When it comes to attracting and keeping talented people, CEO Jim Kelly knows that money alone won't do it. Although compensation and employee benefits are indeed important, employees, regardless of their status, want and expect their employers to treat them fairly. Furthermore, they want to be part of something they can believe in, something that confers meaning on their work and on their lives. They want to be motivated.[2]

What Is Motivation?

motivation
Force that moves someone to take action

Motivation is the force that moves individuals to take action. In some cases, fear of management or of losing a job may move an employee to take action, but such negative motivation is much less effective than encouraging an individual's own sense of direction, creativity, and pride in doing a good job. Positive motivators, such as setting clear and challenging—but achievable—goals, can encourage employees to reach higher levels of performance. At Aptar Group, a manufacturer of aerosol valves, finger pumps, and other caps for bottles, employee work teams set their own goals and report on their progress to senior management. Rob Revak, director of human resources at one of Aptar's divisions, finds that employees who set their own goals strive hard to reach them.[3] Empowering employees and involving them in goal setting and decision making is the essence of management by objectives, discussed in Chapter 6.

 If you want to spark innovation, rethink how you motivate, reward, and assign work to people.[4]

behavior modification
Systematic use of rewards and punishments to change human behavior

Some companies try to control or change employee actions by using **behavior modification.** They systematically encourage those actions that are desirable and discourage those that are not. Others rely on various kinds of rewards to motivate and reinforce the behavior of hardworking employees. These rewards include gifts, certificates, medals, dinners, trips, and so forth. Still others motivate their employees by providing a culture that makes it enjoyable to come to work. Research shows that employees who maintain a high **morale** or a positive attitude toward both their job and organization perform better.[5]

morale
Attitude an individual has toward his or her job and employer

As you can see, humans are motivated by many factors. Thus, the challenge for managers is to select motivators that will inspire employees to achieve organizational goals. But which ones are the most effective? Several theories of motivation have attempted to answer that question.

Theories of Motivation

Motivation has been a topic of interest to managers for more than a hundred years. Frederick W. Taylor was a machinist and engineer from Philadelphia who became interested in employee efficiency and motivation late in the nineteenth century. Taylor developed **scientific management,** an approach that seeks to improve employee efficiency through the scientific study of work. In Taylor's view, people were motivated almost exclusively by money, so he set up pay systems that rewarded employees when they were productive.

scientific management
Management approach designed to improve employees' efficiency by scientifically studying their work

Although money has always been a powerful motivator, scientific management fails to take into account other motivational elements, such as opportunities for personal satisfaction or individual initiative. Thus, scientific management can't explain why a person still wants to work even though his or her spouse already makes a good living or why a Wall Street lawyer will take a hefty pay cut to serve in government. Therefore, other researchers have looked beyond money to discover what else motivates people.

LEARNING OBJECTIVE 1
Identify and explain three important theories of employee motivation

Maslow's Hierarchy of Needs   In 1943 psychologist Abraham Maslow proposed the theory that behavior is determined by a variety of needs. He organized these needs into five categories and then arranged the categories in a hierarchy. As Exhibit 9.1 shows, the most basic

EXHIBIT 9•1

MASLOW'S HIERARCHY OF NEEDS

According to Maslow, needs on the lower levels of the hierarchy must be satisfied before higher-level needs can be addressed.

needs are at the bottom of this hierarchy, and the more advanced needs are toward the top. In Maslow's hierarchy, all of the requirements for basic survival—food, clothing, shelter, and so on—fall into the category of *physiological needs*. These basic needs must be satisfied before the person can consider higher-level needs such as *safety needs, social needs* (the need to give and receive love and to feel a sense of belonging), and *esteem needs* (the need for a sense of self-worth and integrity).

At the top of Maslow's hierarchy is *self-actualization*—the need to become everything one is capable of. This need is also the most difficult to fulfill. Employees who reach this point work not only to make money or to impress others but also because they feel their work is worthwhile and satisfying in itself. Self-actualization needs partially explain why some people make radical career changes or strike out on their own as entrepreneurs.

Although Maslow's hierarchy is a convenient way to classify human needs, it would be a mistake to view it as a rigid sequence. A person need not completely satisfy each level of needs before being motivated by a higher need. Indeed, at any one time, most people are motivated by a combination of needs.

Two-Factor Theory   In the 1960s, Frederick Herzberg and his associates undertook their own study of human needs. They asked accountants and engineers to describe specific aspects of their jobs that made them feel satisfied or dissatisfied. Upon analyzing the results, they found that two entirely different sets of factors were associated with satisfying and dissatisfying work experiences: *hygiene factors* and *motivators* (see Exhibit 9.2).

What Herzberg called **hygiene factors** are associated with dissatisfying experiences. The potential sources of dissatisfaction include working conditions, company policies, and job security. Management can lessen worker dissatisfaction by improving hygiene factors that concern employees, but such improvements won't influence satisfaction. On the other hand, managers can help employees feel more motivated and, ultimately, more satisfied, by paying attention to **motivators** such as achievement, recognition, responsibility, and other personally rewarding factors. Herzberg's theory is related to Maslow's hierarchy of needs: The motivators closely resemble the higher-level needs, and the hygiene factors resemble the lower-level needs.

Should managers concentrate on motivators or on hygiene factors? It depends. A skilled, well-paid, middle-class, middle-aged employee may be motivated to perform better if motivators are supplied. However, a young, unskilled worker who earns low wages, or an

hygiene factors
Aspects of the work environment that are associated with dissatisfaction

motivators
Factors of human relations in business that may increase motivation

EXHIBIT 9·2

TWO-FACTOR THEORY

Hygiene factors such as working conditions and company policies can influence employee dissatisfaction. On the other hand, motivators such as opportunities for achievement and recognition can influence employee satisfaction.

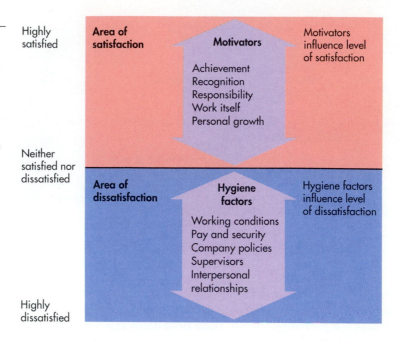

employee who is insecure, will probably still need the support of strong hygiene factors to reduce dissatisfaction before the motivators can be effective.[6]

Theory X
Managerial assumption that employees are irresponsible, unambitious, and distasteful of work and that managers must use force, control, or threats to motivate them

Theory Y
Managerial assumption that employees like work, are naturally committed to certain goals, are capable of creativity, and seek out responsibility under the right conditions

Theory X and Theory Y In the 1960s, psychologist Douglas McGregor identified two radically different sets of assumptions that underlie most management thinking. He classified these sets of assumptions into two categories: *Theory X* and *Theory Y* (see Exhibit 9.3).

According to McGregor, **Theory X**–oriented managers believe that employees dislike work and can be motivated only by the fear of losing their jobs or by *extrinsic rewards* such as money, promotions, and tenure. This management style emphasizes physiological and safety needs and tends to ignore the higher-level needs in Maslow's hierarchy. In contrast, **Theory Y**–oriented managers believe that employees like work and can be motivated by working for goals that promote creativity or for causes they believe in. Thus, Theory Y–oriented managers seek to motivate employees through *intrinsic rewards*.

The assumptions behind Theory X emphasize authority; the assumptions behind Theory Y emphasize growth and self-direction. It was McGregor's belief that, although

EXHIBIT 9·3

THEORY X AND THEORY Y

McGregor proposed two distinct views of human beings: The assumptions of Theory X are basically negative, whereas those of Theory Y are basically positive.

THEORY X	THEORY Y
1. Employees inherently dislike work and will avoid it whenever possible.	1. Employees like work and consider it as natural as play and rest.
2. Because employees dislike work, they must be threatened with punishment to achieve goals.	2. People naturally work toward goals they are committed to.
3. Employees will avoid responsibilities whenever possible.	3. The average person can learn to accept and even seek responsibility.
4. Employees value security above all other job factors.	4. The average person's intellectual potential is only partially realized.

some employees need the strong direction demanded by Theory X, those who are ready to realize their social, esteem, and self-actualization needs will not work well under Theory X assumptions.[7]

■ KEEPING PACE WITH THE CHANGING WORK FORCE

Although these theories shed some light on what managers can do to motivate employees to work efficiently and effectively toward achieving the organization's goals, managers must also recognize that employees have interests and obligations outside of work, such as family, volunteer activities, and hobbies. Furthermore, every employee, by human nature, needs to feel valued, challenged, and respected. In organizations, the goal of **human relations**—interactions among people within the organization—is to balance these diverse needs. Achieving this balance becomes increasingly difficult when taking into account the many staffing and demographic challenges faced by employers today.

Staffing Challenges

More than 4.6 million job cuts were announced in the 1990s. Factors contributing to *downsizing* decisions included company reorganizations, business downturns, elimination of unprofitable product lines, outsourcing, mergers and acquisitions, and a general mismatch between employee job skills and job demands. Even though corporate downsizing continues today, what is puzzling is a concurrent trend toward "upsizing," or massive hiring—and often within the same firm.[8]

This phenomenon can best be explained by the needs of companies to *rightsize,* or realign their work forces into business growth areas. For example, employees from Department A are let go while new hires are sought to keep up with the growth demands of Department B. Look at defense electronics giant Raytheon. Even though this company slashed 8,700 defense jobs, or 10 percent of its work force, it planned to redeploy 5,000 engineers to its booming commercial units.[9] The increasing demand for educated workers and the continuing conversion from a manufacturing-based economy to a service-based economy (as discussed in Chapter 1) are also forcing companies to pull apart their work force and then piece it back together differently. Complicating this scenario are four staffing challenges: a shortage of

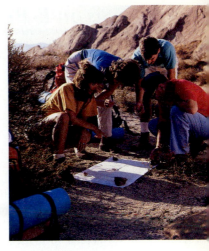

General Electric applies Theory Y in global operations. Here, GE managers in an Outward Bound workshop practice team-building skills to achieve a common goal.

human relations
Interaction among people within an organization for the purpose of achieving organizational and personal goals

See It on the Web See It on the Web

MEASURING EMPLOYEE SATISFACTION

Motivating employees to perform at their highest potential is one of the many daily challenges all managers face. However, it is often difficult to judge just how satisfied and motivated employees are, especially when a manager must oversee a large number of workers. Therefore, many managers ask about their employees' true feelings through anonymous surveys. Employees answer questions about their duties, work objectives, management support, relations with co-workers, and other pertinent issues. The responses give managers insights into the satisfaction levels of their employees. You can view a brief employee satisfaction survey at the *Inc.* magazine Web site and even answer the questions yourself to better understand what factors can affect employee morale.
http://www.inc.com/interactive/vc/01039825.html

Focus on E-Business

LIVING WITH THE E-CULTURES OF HYPE AND CRAFT

Anyone who has tried to create a corporate culture knows that it can't be done on Internet time. Cultures aren't designed. They simmer, they fester, and they brew continually while people learn what kind of behavior works or doesn't work in the company. The core problem faced by most e-businesses is not that they lack a culture; it's that they already have two—one of hype and one of craft.

The culture of hype is representative of the 20-something-year-old CEO wannabes pitching their business plans, living out of their cars, unable to pay their cellular phone bills one week, and guaranteed millions in stock options the next. These people are propelled at Internet speed to expand their concept, dominate the market, fend off voracious competitors, and pay for the immense start-up costs of their enterprise.

Meanwhile, the work has to be done by someone. Thus, enter the second culture, the culture of craft. These are the Web programmers, designers, and technology gurus that put together a Web site in a way that no one else can and develop the guts of the e-business. Craft people are not necessarily motivated by money in the same way that hype people are. Craft people are delighted by the idea of stock options, but most of all they want the chance to see their work evolve; they want praise and recognition for their accomplishments, and a chance to feel proud of their work. Thus, they are motivated to build something elegant, and can't be overly concerned about meeting a deadline if it requires them to compromise their work.

Now the conflict. While hype people agree with "elegance" in principal, they have much more to worry about. They must take on new business, raise more cash, and yes, pay their bills. To motivate the craft people and keep talented workers on board, they pay them higher salaries and give them more stock options (even if this is not what they really want). But such perks are costly, which in turn adds to the urgency to generate more cash. So hype people put more pressure on the craft people, and the pattern continues until the e-business culture spins into a frantic whirl of misunderstanding.

How can e-businesses avoid this culture clash? One way is to cultivate a team culture. By keeping craft teams together through various projects and even various corporate parents, they learn to work through these awkward phases, they begin to build their collective capabilities, they learn how to think together, and their energy curve increases substantially. Bottom line: the craft people produce faster and the hype people can slow down—a bit.

QUESTIONS FOR CRITICAL THINKING

1. Where on Maslow's hierarchy of needs would you place craft people?
2. In general, would you classify hype people as Theory X or Theory Y managers? Why?

---

skilled labor, a decrease in job security and employee loyalty, heightened job stress, and employees' attempts to balance their work life with their family life and outside interests.

LEARNING OBJECTIVE 2

List four staffing challenges employers are facing in today's workplace

Shortage of Skilled Labor   While some companies are cutting employees, others can't seem to find enough. In fact, if you ask business leaders what their biggest challenge is today, you will most likely get the same answer: finding, attracting, and keeping talented people.[10]

By one estimate there are already 190,000 unfilled high-tech jobs, and the demand for people with engineering, computer, and other technical skills is mushrooming. An additional 1 million such jobs are expected to be created in this decade, with virtually no increase in supply.[11] Furthermore, the gap is widening between what employers will require of new employees in the years ahead and the actual skills of these employees. A close look at Appendix 2 confirms that many of the growing occupations require specialized skills or training, whereas the shrinking occupations involve activities that require fewer skills or ones that are increasingly being automated. In fact, nearly all jobs today require computer literacy. Machinists, for example, need computer skills to operate chip-controlled equipment. Telemarketers must know how to keyboard. Even package delivery involves data entry.

Part of the skilled labor-shortage problem has resulted from the robust U.S. economy. An increasing demand for U.S. goods and services has put pressure on U.S. companies to operate at breakneck speeds. But with unemployment hovering at around 5 percent, the economy is considered to be at full employment.[12] This leaves employers in a quandary. Take Boeing, for example. To meet enormous demand for new airplanes, the company hired 150–200 employees each week during 1998 and had to turn to its prime suppliers as one source for qualified candidates.[13]

UPS faced a similar labor shortage but managed to solve its problem creatively. The city of Louisville could not supply the 6,000 additional employees the company needed to staff its growing $6 billion air-freight business. Rather than moving its main U.S. air hub from Louisville to another location, the company partnered with the city of Louisville to build its own "UPS University." To attract new employees to the area, the partners built special dormitories so student-workers could sleep during the day, attend classes taught by professors from the University of Louisville at night, and then work the UPS graveyard shift (from 11:30 P.M. to 3:30 A.M.) and still have time to study.[14]

Other businesses are also instituting educational programs to attract and keep skilled employees. Cisco Systems, a manufacturer of computer network routers, runs its own Networking Academy. This in-house vocational program teaches students how to build and manage the computer-server networks the company sells. Cisco hopes that eventually the students will return to the company for permanent jobs.[15]

Finding and keeping good workers has become especially hard for small-company owners, who often trail bigger companies in salary, benefits, job security, and other criteria that lead workers to choose one company over another. Larger companies can woo top job applicants with hiring bonuses, flexible work schedules, job training, and other incentives. But because such enticements are costly, they are not feasible for smaller concerns.

Declining Job Security and Employee Loyalty   The U.S. work force has been through nearly a decade of corporate downsizing, restructuring, and reengineering. Devastated by the lack of job security, as Exhibit 9.4 shows, employees quickly learned to "do what's best for me." But after several years of a tight labor market and employee turnover rates at a 10-year high, some employers are now going to great lengths to persuade employees that they want them to stay for years. Without promising lifelong employment, they're revamping rigid

> Employees need continuity. They do not function well if the environment is not predictable, not understandable, not known.[16]

EXHIBIT 9·4

THE COMMITTED EMPLOYEE—THEN AND NOW

Employee loyalty isn't what it used to be. A 1998 survey confirms that even today's most valuable committed workers often put career development and life and family issues ahead of company goals.

CHARACTERISTIC	THEN	NOW
Attachment to employer	Long-term	Near-term
Readiness to change jobs	Not interested	Not looking (but will listen)
Priorities on the job	The firm and its goals	Personal life and career
Devotion to employer goals	Follows orders	Buys in (usually)
Effort on the job	100 percent	110 percent
Motto	Always faithful	Seize the day

pay systems to make it easier for employees to move laterally and enhance their skills. And they're installing new career-development programs to help employees plan their career moves. Managers at International Paper, for example, sit down with every employee once a year to discuss their career desires, separate from their annual performance reviews.[17]

Despite such good intentions, today's employees are cautious. They recognize that the old idea of a paternal company taking care of employees has, for the most part, died. Employee expectations are now more realistic. Hardworking, loyal employees no longer expect to move up the organizational hierarchy. They realize that companies are going to do whatever they have to do to succeed and to survive. And this may mean manufacturing in South America, eliminating three layers of management, or closing down plants.[18] Even the Japanese tradition of lifetime employment is under attack. After years of severe economic recession and intense global competition, the Japanese are realizing that unconditional loyalty is becoming too expensive to justify. To remain competitive, Japanese companies are chipping away at their seniority-based management system and are forcing executives to perform or go—bringing Japan a little closer to the U.S. model.[19]

Increasing Job Stress and Desire for Work-Life Balance Today's employees want more than a good paycheck and satisfying work. They want to balance their careers and their family lives. "This is the most difficult generation ever to manage," says Marilyn Moats Kennedy, a career consultant. "The traditional appeals—money, prestige—have no appeal. People want to do their job, get home, and have a life."[20]

Achieving a work-life balance is especially difficult when both parents work or in situations where downsizing and restructuring have left remaining employees with heavier workloads than in the past. When 3M spun off its data-storage and medical-imaging divisions, for example, some employees began putting in 80 hour weeks. One 3M customer service consultant summed up the feelings of many employees when he said, "I always perceived work to be a means to an end, but not *the* end."[21] Others are working longer hours just to keep up. "It seems like you work, work, work," says one Michigan chemist.[22]

The Bureau of Labor Statistics says the proportion of professionals and managers working extremely long hours—49 or more a week—has risen by as much as 37 percent since 1985.[23] Such long hours can lead to employee *burnout,* which is characterized by emotional exhaustion, depersonalization, and lower levels of achievement. Severe burnout may even lead to clinical depression.[24] Other causes of employee burnout are job insecurity, technological advancements, and information overload:

- *Job insecurity.* Workers anxious about job security feel they have to give 150 percent (or more) or risk being seen as expendable. What once were considered crises-mode workloads have now become business as usual. These extra hours, which don't always bring extra pay, can leave employees feeling burned out and resentful.[25]

- *Technological advancements.* New technology allows employees to work from home, but being wired to the office 24 hours a day can add extra pressure. Employees feel compelled to answer that voice mail or e-mail whatever the hour. "We have all these great tools to save our time," notes one career expert. "Instead, it just extends our week. We're never out of touch anymore."[26]

- *Information overload.* Managers claim they're unable to handle the vast amounts of information they now receive. In fact, more information has been produced in the last 30 years than the previous 5,000, and the total quantity of printed material is doubling every five years, and accelerating.[27]

Employees aren't the only ones suffering. Employee turnover, unscheduled absenteeism, and waning morale cost companies an estimated $200 billion or more annually, says one report.[28]

See It on the Web See It on the Web

WORKING HARD ON THE WEB

Frustrated workers and managers now have a place to go to voice their opinions, commiserate with others, and get advice on how to motivate employees. The place is Hard@Work, a Web site created "to reduce the oversupply of fear and alienation in the workplace by meeting the pent-up demand for constructive communication about what's happening on the job." Visitors can hang around the "Water Cooler" to chat with others about work issues; play "Stump the Mentor," which offers suggestions for handling sticky work situations; or dig into the "Rock Pile," which features realistic case studies. Hard@Work offers something for workers and job seekers alike.
http://www.hardatwork.com

To help employees balance the demands of work and family, businesses are offering childcare assistance, family leave, flexible work schedules, telecommuting, and other solutions that are explored later in this chapter. Many are also focusing on improving the **quality of work life (QWL),** the environment created by work and job conditions.[29] An improved QWL benefits both the individual and the organization. Employees gain the chance to use their specialized abilities, improve their skills, and balance their lives. The organization gains a more motivated and loyal employee.

Two common ways of improving QWL are through **job enrichment,** which reduces specialization and makes work more meaningful by expanding each job's responsibilities, and through **job redesign,** which restructures work to provide a better fit between employees' skills and their jobs. Quality of work life can be improved in other ways, too. Andersen Consulting, for instance, will send someone to pick up an employee's car from the repair shop; Pepsi has an on-site dry cleaning drop-off at its New York headquarters; and American Banker's Insurance Group and Hewlett-Packard have sponsored schools at company sites that allow employees to visit their children during lunchtime and after school. All of these measures can improve employees' lives by freeing up their time and by making work a more enjoyable place to be.[30]

quality of work life (QWL)
Overall environment that results from job and work conditions

job enrichment
Reducing work specialization and making work more meaningful by adding to the responsibilities of each job

job redesign
Designing a better fit between employees' skills and their work to increase job satisfaction

Demographic Challenges

The U.S. work force is also undergoing significant demographic changes. Three of the most significant trends affecting human resource departments are increasing work-force diversity, an aging population, and increasing attention to gender-related issues.

LEARNING OBJECTIVE 3
List three demographic challenges employers are facing in today's workplace

Work-Force Diversity A growing percentage of the U.S. work force is made up of people with diverse cultural and ethnic backgrounds, a trend that will continue in the years ahead. These employees bring with them a wide range of skills, traditions, and attitudes toward work that can affect their behavior on the job. The challenge for managers is to communicate with and motivate this diverse work force while fostering cooperation and harmony among employees.

Many companies are recognizing the importance of diversity awareness and promotion by instituting diversity-training programs. At Allstate Insurance, for example, all nonagent employees with service of more than one year are expected to complete diversity training—a company investment in excess of 540,000 hours of classroom time.[31] And at the Marriott Marquis Hotel in New York, mandatory diversity-training classes teach managers how to avoid defining problems in terms of gender, culture, or race. These classes also help managers become more sensitive to the behavior and communication patterns of employees with diverse backgrounds.

Putting more people of color on the floor—and in executive positions—is a no-brainer for Wal-Mart, which was recently ranked by *Fortune* magazine as one of American's 50 best companies for Asian, black, and Hispanic Americans. This group, for instance, includes two senior vice presidents, four vice presidents, and two corporate counsels.

Although encouraging sensitivity to employee differences is important, a company stands to benefit most when it incorporates its employees' diverse perspectives into the organization's work. This assimilation enables the company to uncover new opportunities by rethinking primary tasks and redefining markets, products, strategies, missions, business practices, and even cultures. Consider the small public-interest law firm of Dewey & Levin. In the mid-1980s the firm had an all-white legal staff. Concerned about its ability to serve ethnically diverse populations, the firm hired a Hispanic female attorney. She introduced Dewey & Levin to new ideas about what kinds of cases to take on, and many of her ideas were pursued with great success. Hiring more women of color brought even more fresh perspectives. The firm now pursues cases that the original staff members would never have considered because they would not have understood the link between the issues involved in the cases and the firm's mission.[32] In short, diversity is an asset, and one of the challenges of corporate human relations is to make the most of this asset.

Aging Population   The population in the United States is aging. This situation creates new challenges and concerns for employers and employees alike. When the 76 million baby boomers—people born between 1946 and 1964—began entering the work force, the average age of U.S. employees fell. Now that they are approaching mid-career, the average age is again rising. The general aging of the population and the declining number of young people entering the work force is largely due to baby boomers' decisions to marry later, to postpone or forgo starting a family, and to have fewer children.

Experts predict that because of inadequate pensions, high medical costs, and a general desire to stay active, baby boomers will put off retirement until they are in their seventies. But widespread delayed retirement will present challenges for all parties involved. For one thing, companies today have less and less tolerance for people they believe are earning more than their output warrants. "For my salary, the company could hire two twenty-somethings," says a 41-year-old. "I'm good at what I do. But am I better than two people? Even I know that's not true." Older employees cost companies more money in other ways, too. Not only do they earn more, but benefits such as medical, insurance, and pension rise as well.[33] Besides, as the lives of products get shorter and the speed of change gets faster, it can be difficult for older employees to keep up unless they have the stamina of a 25-year-old.

Age has its advantages of course. According to a recent study, older employees have more experience, better judgment, and a greater commitment to quality. They are also more likely to show up on time and are less likely to quit. But these traits pale by comparison with the highly desired traits characteristic of younger workers who appear more flexible, more adaptable, more accepting of new technology, and better at learning new skills. Studies also show that the difference in job performance between someone with 20 years' experience and someone with just 5 years are often negligible.[34]

Even though the 1967 Age Discrimination in Employment Act (ADEA) makes workers over 40 a protected class, many suspect that age discrimination is widespread. For one thing, it's difficult to prove. In 1997 the Equal Employment Opportunity Commission (EEOC) handled over 18,000 complaints filed under the ADEA. Of those, 61 percent were found to have "no reasonable cause." Of course, these statistics can be misleading, because an estimated 90 percent of all age-discrimination charges are settled long before complaints are filed with the EEOC.[35]

sexism
Discrimination on the basis of gender

Gender-Related Issues   Although men do face some sexual discrimination in the workplace, women are more likely than men to feel the effects of **sexism,** discrimination on the basis of gender. In recent years, women have made significant strides toward overcoming sexism on the job, thanks to a combination of changing societal attitudes and company commitments to workplace diversity. Still, a disturbing gender gap in compensation persists, with women earning about 76 percent of men's median pay.[36] Moreover, even though women now hold 46 percent of executive, administrative, and managerial positions (up from 34 percent in 1983), only 10 percent of the top managerial positions at the nation's 500 largest companies are held by women. At levels of vice president or higher, the figure is only 2.4 percent. Some attribute this inequality to the *glass ceiling.*

The Glass Ceiling The **glass ceiling** is an invisible barrier that keeps women and minorities from reaching the highest-level positions. One theory about the glass ceiling suggests that top management has long been dominated by white males who tend to hire and promote employees who look, act, and think as they do. Another theory states that stereotyping by male middle managers leads them to believe that family life will interfere with a woman's work. As a result, women are relegated to less visible assignments in the company, so their work goes unnoticed by top executives and their careers stagnate.[37]

glass ceiling
Invisible barrier attributable to subtle discrimination that keeps women out of the top positions in business

Nevertheless, diversity initiatives are helping shatter the glass ceiling. Such initiatives include long-term commitments to hiring more women, company-sponsored networking and career planning for women, diversity training and workshops, and mentoring programs designed to help female employees move more quickly through the ranks. Pitney Bowes's long-term commitment to diversity has resulted in women holding 5 of the top 11 jobs at the company. Patagonia boasts that women now hold more than half of the company's top-paying jobs and almost 60 percent of managerial jobs. And the recent appointment of Carly Fiorina to CEO of Hewlett-Packard (HP) was hailed by many as a milestone for women. With more than a quarter of HP's managers being women, it seems that the glass ceiling at this company has been shattered.[38]

Sexual Harassment Another sensitive issue that women often face in the workplace is sexual harassment. As defined by the EEOC, **sexual harassment** takes two forms: the obvious request for sexual favors with an implicit reward or punishment related to work and the more subtle creation of a sexist environment in which employees are made to feel uncomfortable by off-color jokes, lewd remarks, and posturing.

sexual harassment
Unwelcome sexual advance, request for sexual favors, or other verbal or physical conduct of a sexual nature within the workplace

Research shows that 50 to 85 percent of all working women experience some sexual harassment during their careers, and 90 percent of the top 500 U.S. firms have received complaints of sexual harassment. Moreover, 5 out of 10 men say they've done or said something at work that could be considered sexual harassment by a female colleague.[39] Male employees may also be targets of sexual harassment, and both male and female employees may experience same-sex harassment. However, sexual harassment of female employees by male colleagues continues to make up the majority of reported cases.

Recent Supreme Court rulings explain (for the first time) how all employers—both large and small—can insulate themselves from potential sexual harassment lawsuits. In short, a company can defend itself successfully if it can prove that it had an effective policy against sexual harassment in place and that the employee alleging harassment failed to take advantage of this policy. To be effective, the policy must be in writing, communicated to all employees, and enforced.[40] This means that the company must train all employees on the policy, and the company must have clear procedures for reporting such behavior—including allowing employees access to management other than their supervisors. Without such policies, companies can be held indirectly responsible for a harasser's actions even when top managers had no idea that such practices were going on.[41]

Alternative Work Arrangements

flextime
Scheduling system in which employees are allowed certain options regarding time of arrival and departure

To meet today's staffing and demographic challenges, many companies are adopting alternative work arrangements. Three of the most popular arrangements are flextime, telecommuting, and job sharing. Many organizations find that a mix of these arrangements and other employee benefits work better than a one-size-fits-all approach (see Exhibit 9.5).[42]

Flextime   **Flextime** is a scheduling system that allows employees to choose their own hours within certain limits. For instance, a company may require everyone to be at work between 10:00 A.M. and 2:00 P.M., but employees may arrive or depart whenever they want as long as they work a total of 8 hours every day. Another popular schedule is to work four 10-hour days each week. The sense of control employees get from arranging their own work schedules is motivating for many.

Approximately 66 percent of all companies now offer some form of flextime.[43] Among the companies nationally recognized for having superior flextime policies are Pillsbury, Deloitte & Touche, and Aetna Life & Casualty.[44] Of course, flextime is more feasible in white-collar businesses that do not have to maintain standard customer-service hours. For this reason, it is not usually an option for employees on production teams, in retail stores, or in many offices where employees have to be on hand to wait on customers or answer calls.

Many companies have found that flextime reduces turnover, enables the company to adapt to business cycles, allows operation of a round-the-clock business, and helps maintain morale and performance after reengineering or downsizing. However, flextime is not without drawbacks. They include supervisors who feel uncomfortable and less in control when employees are coming and going, and co-workers who resent flextimers because they assume that people who work flexible hours don't take their jobs seriously enough.[45]

telecommuting
Working from home and communicating with the company's main office via computer and communication devices

Telecommuting   Related to flexible schedules is **telecommuting**—working from home or another location using computers and telecommunications equipment to stay in touch with the employer's offices. Depending on which study you read, between 20 and 58 percent of employers now offer telecommuting arrangements for their employees. In fact, current estimates now put the number of U.S. telecommuters at about 16 million.[46]

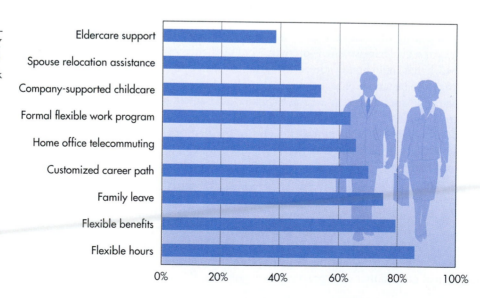

Of course, some company operations clearly are not designed for telecommuting. For example, a printer who runs giant color presses can't run the presses from home. But for the kinds of jobs that can be performed from remote sites, telecommuting helps meet employees' needs for flexibility while boosting their productivity as much as 20 percent. Half of AT&T's 50,000 managers worldwide now telecommute.[47] Companies such as AT&T, IBM, and Lucent Technologies provide employees with laptops, dedicated phone lines, software support, fax-printer units, help lines, and full technical backup at the nearest corporate facility. Some even provide employees who work at home with a generous allowance for furnishings and equipment to be used at their discretion.[48]

Telecommuting offers many advantages. For one thing, it can save the company money in equipment and space costs. Since 1991, AT&T has freed up some $550 million by eliminating offices people don't need, consolidating others, and reducing related overhead costs.[49] Telecommuting also enables a company to hire talented people in distant areas without requiring them to relocate. This option expands the company's pool of potential job candidates while benefiting employees who have an employed spouse, children in school, or elderly parents to care for.[50] Employees also like telecommuting because they can set their own hours, reduce job-related expenses such as commuting costs, and spend more time with their families.

Telecommuting does have its limitations. The challenges of managing the cultural changes required by telecommuting are substantial. In telecommuting situations, mid-level managers relinquish direct, visual employee supervision. Some find it scary to be in the position of managing people they can't see. Others are concerned that people working at home will slack off. Regardless, companies are learning that you can't just give people computers, send them home, and call them telecommuters. You have to teach an employee how to think like a telecommuter.

Merrill Lynch recognizes this fact. Prospective telecommuters at Merrill Lynch must submit a detailed proposal that covers when and how they're going to work at home, and even what their home office will look like. Next they participate in a series of meetings. Finally, they spend two weeks in a simulation lab that lets employees and their managers experience the change. Once at home, telecommuters are required to document their at-home working hours and submit weekly progress reports.[51] But even for those companies that provide support, some telecommuters are finding that this "ideal set-up" is not for everyone.

Job Sharing **Job sharing,** which lets two employees share a single full-time job and split the salary and benefits, has been slowly gaining acceptance as a way to work part-time in a full-time position. According to a recent survey by Hewitt Associates (a firm specializing in employee benefits), 37 percent of employers offer job-sharing arrangements to their employees.[52] But such arrangements are usually offered to people who already work for the company and who need to cut back their hours. Rather than lose a good employee or have to find and train someone new, the company finds a way to split responsibilities.

Consider UNUM Life insurance. When two of its employees approached the company about sharing a job, the company decided to let them do it. Now one employee works all day Monday and Tuesday, the other works all day Thursday and Friday, and the two overlap on Wednesday. The personal benefits are exactly what the employees hoped for—more time at home. The added benefit is that there's always someone available who understands the work. The company benefits because the position is rarely left uncovered because of vacation or illness and because two people, instead of just one person, bring their ideas and creativity to the job.[53]

job sharing
Splitting a single full-time job between two employees for their convenience

IS TELECOMMUTING RIGHT FOR YOU?

Telecommuting sounds like the perfect life. No commute. No morning rush to get ready for. No expensive wardrobe. No day care for kids. But for many people, telecommuting also means no social life.

Many home-based workers soon find that they miss interacting with colleagues. Some worry that if they're not in the office—if they're not seen—they'll be forgotten. Others find that they actually put in longer hours or they encounter too many distractions, such as young children requiring attention. Still others discover that it takes a lot of willpower and self-discipline to be productive when the refrigerator and a nice warm bed are just a few feet away.

Is telecommuting right for you? Here's a checklist to help you determine whether you'd be a good candidate. If you answer yes to all the questions, go for it. But if you answer no to any of them, you need to think the issue through carefully before taking the leap.

Have you worked at your company long enough to thoroughly understand its culture and expectations?

Can others perform their jobs without your being physically available?

Are you content to work in isolation?

Can you perform your job, complete projects, and meet your deadlines without supervision?

Can you physically take your work home with you in a briefcase?

Can you communicate everything you need for your daily workload via phone or e-mail?

Does your home have a separate room in which to work, with a door that shuts?

Does your home work space have a separate phone line for a fax/modem, computer, and other equipment?

If you have a child, will you have day care available while you work?

If you live with someone else who works at home, will this situation pose any problems?

Are you disciplined enough to stop working at the end of the day?

If you were your boss, would you let you telecommute?

QUESTIONS FOR CRITICAL THINKING

1. What can companies do to prepare employees for the challenges of telecommuting?
2. Why is it important to understand a company's culture before you begin telecommuting?

■ WORKING WITH LABOR UNIONS

labor unions
Organizations of employees formed to protect and advance their members' interests

Many companies take great pains to provide employees with safe and comfortable working conditions, pay that rewards their contributions to the organization, and alternative work arrangements. Nevertheless, owners and managers of businesses must also balance the use of their resources to increase productivity and profits. In the best of times and in the most enlightened companies, these two sets of needs can often be met simultaneously. However, when the economy slows down and competition speeds up, the needs of employees and management can differ. Because of this potential for conflict, many employees join **labor unions,** organizations that seek to protect employee interests by negotiating with employers for better wages and benefits, improved working conditions, and increased job security. (See Exhibit 9.6 for a summary of the most significant laws relating to labor unions).

By using their combined bargaining strength, as the UPS strike shows, union employees can put more pressure on management than they could as individuals. Keep in mind that employees are most likely to turn to unions if they are deeply dissatisfied with their cur-

LEGISLATION	PROVISION
Norris–La Guardia Act of 1932	Limits companies' ability to obtain injunctions against union strikes, picketing, membership drives, and other activities.
National Labor Relations Act of 1935 (Wagner Act)	Gives employees the right to form, join, or assist labor organizations; the right to bargain collectively with employers through elected union representatives; and the right to engage in strikes, pickets, and boycotts. Prohibits certain unfair labor practices by the employer and union. Establishes the National Labor Relations Board to supervise union elections and to investigate charges of unfair labor practices by management.
Labor-Management Relations Act of 1947 (Taft-Hartley Act)	Amends Wagner Act to reaffirm employees' rights to organize and bargain collectively over working conditions. Establishes specific unfair labor practices both for management and for unions, and prohibits strikes in the public sector.
Landrum-Griffin Act of 1959	Amends Taft-Hartley Act and Wagner Act to control union corruption and to add the secondary boycott as an unfair labor practice. A secondary boycott occurs when a union appeals to firms or other unions to stop doing business with an employer who sells or handles goods of a company whose employees are on strike. The act requires all unions to file annual financial reports with the U.S. Department of Labor, making union officials more personally responsible for the union's financial affairs. The act guarantees individual member rights such as the right to vote in union elections, the right to sue unions, and the right to attend and participate in union meetings.
Plant-Closing Notification Act of 1988	Requires employers to give employees and local elected officials 60 days advance notice of plant shutdowns or massive layoffs.

EXHIBIT 9·6

KEY LEGISLATION RELATING TO UNIONS

Most major labor legislation was enacted in the 1930s and 1940s. However, some more recent legislation has also been passed to protect organized labor.

rent job and employment conditions, if they believe that unionization can be helpful in improving those job conditions, and if they are willing to overlook negative stereotypes that have surrounded unions in recent years.[54]

On the other hand, companies that have most successfully resisted unionization seem to have adopted participative management styles and an enhanced sense of responsibility toward employees. Still, even the best working conditions are no guarantee that employees won't seek union representation. For instance, although Starbuck's is renowned for its generous employee benefit programs and supportive work environment, employees of stores in Vancouver, British Columbia, recently organized and successfully bargained for higher wages.[55] Not all employees support labor unions, however. Many believe that unions stifle individual initiative and are not necessary to ensure fair treatment from employers. Nevertheless, unions remain a significant force in employee-management relations in the United States.

The Labor Movement Today

Unions now represent only 14 percent (16.3 million) of workers in the United States (down from 20 percent in 1983). The decline in union power has also been felt in many other countries.[56] One key reason for the decrease in union membership is the shift from a manufacturing-based economy to one dominated by service industries, which tend to appeal less to unions. Another factor contributing to the decline in union power is the changing nature of the labor force. Women, young workers, and highly skilled workers have been harder to organize with traditional methods, as have workers in less hierarchical organizations.[57]

Does this mean that unions are dying out? The answer is no. Today's unions fight for many of the same goals unions have always sought: good wages, safe conditions, and benefits. But, as the UPS strike shows, a rapidly changing workplace raises many new issues, such as job security, increasing health-care costs, dual pay scales, labor involvement in decisions, and more job training. Many of these issues now serve as the unions' rallying cry. In addition, because of their efforts to sign up more women and minorities, unions have begun to focus on issues such as child care, affirmative action, and sexual harassment.[58] Moreover, dynamic labor leaders have recognized that their own inertia is partly to blame for the unions' decline, and they are taking corrective measures. In the United States, AFL-CIO president John Sweeney has beefed up recruiting efforts, especially among low-wage service workers, minorities, and women. In addition, new industries are being targeted, including high technology and health care. Sweeney has also launched a highly visible public relations campaign and has begun to target people in smaller businesses and self-employed workers to bring them into the union fold. Some unions have already begun to show increases in membership as a result.[59]

What does the future hold for employee-management relations? It is difficult to make predictions. Although John Sweeney's leadership is boosting enthusiasm and political action among union members, as well as generating a new wave of recruiting and organizing, many experts agree that today's global economic conditions severely limit the ability of unions to regain the strength they once had. This is the case both in the United States and in other countries. Nevertheless, the union promise of better pay, benefits, and working conditions, as well as more equitable treatment by management, has a strong appeal for many downsized workers. And even though unions are sticking to their traditional causes, progressive labor leaders are pursuing new workplace issues and targeting different employees, and they are doing so in unique ways.

The Collective-Bargaining Process

collective bargaining
Process used by unions and management to negotiate work contracts

As long as a union has been recognized as the exclusive bargaining agent for a group of employees, its main job is to negotiate employment contracts with management. In a process known as **collective bargaining,** union and management negotiators work together to forge the human resources policies that will apply to the unionized employees—and other employees covered by the contract—for a certain period, usually three years.

See It on the Web See It on the Web

SPREADING THE UNION MESSAGE

Of all the Web sites devoted to union causes, the AFL-CIO's site offers perhaps the most extensive collection of statistics, information, and commentaries on union issues and programs. The site is designed to educate members and prospective members about union activities and campaigns. Topics include union membership campaigns, safety and family issues, and much more. The AFL-CIO also maintains online directories with the e-mail addresses of members of Congress plus sample letters to encourage communication with legislators. Browse this site to get the latest on union initiatives as well as information about trends in the labor movement today.
http://www.aflcio.org

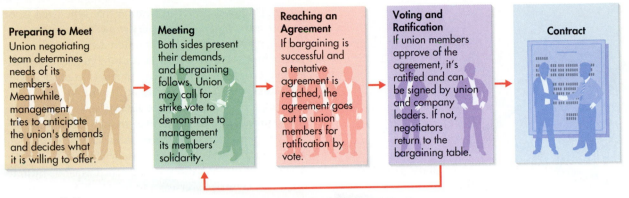

Preparing to Meet
Union negotiating team determines needs of its members. Meanwhile, management tries to anticipate the union's demands and decides what it is willing to offer.

Meeting
Both sides present their demands, and bargaining follows. Union may call for strike vote to demonstrate to management its members' solidarity.

Reaching an Agreement
If bargaining is successful and a tentative agreement is reached, the agreement goes out to union members for ratification by vote.

Voting and Ratification
If union members approve of the agreement, it's ratified and can be signed by union and company leaders. If not, negotiators return to the bargaining table.

Contract

EXHIBIT 9·7

THE COLLECTIVE-BARGAINING PROCESS

Contract negotiations go through the four basic steps shown here.

Most labor contracts are a compromise between the desires of union members and those of management. The union pushes for the best possible deal for its members, and management tries to negotiate agreements that are best for the company (and the shareholders, if a corporation is publicly held). Exhibit 9.7 illustrates the collective-bargaining process.

Meeting and Reaching an Agreement   When the negotiating teams made up of representatives of the union and management actually sit down together, they state their opening positions and each side discusses its position point by point. Labor usually wants additions to the current contract. In a cooperative atmosphere, the real issues behind the demands gradually come to light. For example, management may begin by demanding the right to determine the sizes of work crews when all it really wants is smaller crews; the union, however, wants to protect the jobs of its members and keep crew sizes as large as possible but may agree to certain reductions in exchange for, say, higher pay. After many stages of bargaining, each party presents its package of terms, and any gaps between labor and management demands are then dealt with.

If negotiations reach an impasse, outside help may be needed. The most common alternative is **mediation**—bringing in an impartial third party to study the situation and make recommendations for resolution of the differences. Mediators are generally well-respected community leaders whom both sides will listen to. However, the mediator can only offer suggestions, and his or her solutions are not binding. When a legally binding settlement is needed, the negotiators may submit to **arbitration**—a process in which an impartial referee listens to both sides and then makes a judgment by accepting one side's view. In *compulsory arbitration*, the parties are required by a government agency to submit to arbitration; in *voluntary arbitration*, the parties agree on their own to use arbitration to settle their differences.

Exercising Options When Negotiations Break Down   The vast majority of management-union negotiations are settled quickly, easily, and in a businesslike manner. Nevertheless, sometimes negotiations reach an impasse, and neither side is willing to compromise. Both labor and management are able to draw on many powerful options when negotiations or mediation procedures break down.

Labor's Options   Strikes and picket lines are perhaps labor's best-known tactics, but other options are also used.

mediation
Process for resolving a labor-contract dispute in which a neutral third party meets with both sides and attempts to steer them toward a solution

arbitration
Process for resolving a labor-contract dispute in which an impartial third party studies the issues and makes a binding decision

LEARNING OBJECTIVE 5
Cite three options that unions have when negotiations with management break down

Picketers outside GM's plant believe that jobs for U.S. autoworkers are on the line as the company increasingly shifts production to foreign factories.

strike
Temporary work stoppage by employees who want management to accept their union's demands

picketing
Strike activity in which union members march before company entrances to persuade nonstriking employees to walk off the job and to persuade customers and others to cease doing business with the company

boycott
Union activity in which members and sympathizers refuse to buy or handle the product of a target company

LEARNING OBJECTIVE 6
Cite three options management can exercise when negotiations with the union break down

strikebreakers
Nonunion workers hired to replace striking workers

- *Strike.* The most powerful weapon that organized labor can use is the **strike,** a temporary work stoppage aimed at forcing management to accept union demands. The basic idea behind the strike is that, in the long run, it costs management more in lost earnings to resist union demands than to give in. A 54-day strike at General Motors (GM) in 1998, for instance, cost the automaker over $2 billion in lost production revenues. Even though the union eventually won temporary reprieves on the closing of unprofitable plants, the settlement agreement failed to directly address important national issues, such as GM's push to open new factories overseas and trim its U.S. work force. As a result, some observers pegged this costliest strike in decades as a lose-lose situation for both the company and the union.[60] An essential part of any strike is **picketing,** in which union members positioned at entrances to company premises march back and forth with signs and leaflets, trying to persuade nonstriking employees to join them and to persuade customers and others to stop doing business with the company.

- *Boycott.* A less direct union weapon is the **boycott,** in which union members and sympathizers refuse to buy or handle the product of a target company. Millions of union members form an enormous bloc of purchasing power, which may be able to pressure management into making concessions. One of the best-known boycotts was the grape boycott organized by Cesar Chavez in the early 1970s. To pressure California growers into accepting the United Farm Workers (UFW) as the bargaining agent for previously unorganized farm laborers, he and his colleagues persuaded an estimated 17 million people in the United States to stop buying grapes. Eventually, the California legislature passed the country's first law guaranteeing farmworkers the right to hold union elections.[61]

- *Publicity.* Increasingly, labor is pressing its case by launching publicity campaigns, often called *corporate campaigns,* against the target company and companies affiliated with it. These campaigns might include sending to investors alerts that question the firm's solvency, staging rallies during peak business hours, sending letters to charitable groups questioning executives' motives, handing out to customers leaflets that allege safety and health-code violations, and stimulating negative stories in the press.

Labor's other options include *slowdowns,* in which employers continue to do their jobs but at a snail's pace, and *sickouts,* in which employees feign illness and stay home. Both can cripple a company. American Airlines was forced to cancel more than 6,600 flights when its pilots staged a sickout in 1999 to protest a lower wage scale for pilots of newly acquired Reno Air. A federal judge later ordered the pilots' union at American Airlines to pay the carrier more than $45 million to compensate the company for the lost business.[62]

Management's Options As powerful as the union's tactics are, companies are not helpless when it comes to fighting back. Management can use a number of legal methods to pressure unions when negotiations stall:

- *Strikebreakers.* When union members walk off their jobs, management can legally replace them with **strikebreakers,** nonunion workers hired to do the jobs of striking workers. (Union members brand them as "scabs.") For example, when over

2,000 union workers struck at the *Detroit News* and *Detroit Free Press* newspapers, management kept the presses rolling by hiring 1,400 replacement workers. Although the strike caused both papers to lose customers, advertisers, and profits, the papers persevered for 19 months until the union gave in. By that time, many temporary replacements had been hired permanently, an action that management is legally permitted to take if it's necessary to keep a business going.[63]

- *Lockouts.* The U.S. Supreme Court has upheld the use of **lockouts,** in which management prevents union employees from entering the workplace in order to pressure the union to accept a contract proposal. But lockouts are legal only if the union and management have come to an impasse in negotiations and the employer is defending a legitimate bargaining position. During a lockout, the company may hire temporary replacements as long as it has no antiunion motivation and negotiations have been amicable.[64]

- *Injunctions.* An **injunction** is a court order prohibiting union workers from taking certain actions. Management used this weapon without restriction in the early days of unionism, when companies typically sought injunctions to order striking employees back to work on the grounds that the strikers were interfering with business. Today injunctions are legal only in certain cases. For example, the president of the United States has the right, under the Taft-Hartley Act, to obtain a temporary injunction to halt a strike deemed harmful to the national interest. In 1997 Bill Clinton used that power to intervene in an American Airlines labor dispute with its pilots' union. The president designated a 60-day period during which a specially appointed arbitration panel was to help the two sides reach an agreement. Although the workers were free to strike after 60 days, an agreement was reached and the strike was avoided.[65]

lockout
Management tactic in which union members are prevented from entering a business during a strike in order to force union acceptance of management's last contract proposal

injunction
Court order prohibiting certain actions by striking workers

Summary of Learning Objectives

1. **Identify and explain three important theories of employee motivation.**
Malsow's hierarchy organizes individual needs into five categories and proposes that the individual must satisfy the most basic needs before being able to address higher-level needs. Herzberg's two-factor theory suggests that hygiene factors—such as working conditions, company policies, and job security—can influence employee dissatisfaction, but an improvement in these factors will not motivate employees. Only motivational factors such as recognition and responsibility can improve employee performance. McGregor's theory proposes two distinct views of individuals: Theory X–oriented managers believe that people dislike work and can be motivated only by fear, whereas Theory Y–oriented managers believe that people like work and are motivated by exposure to opportunities and challenges.

2. **List four staffing challenges employers are facing in today's workplace.**
A shortage of skilled labor, a decrease in job security and employee loyalty, an increase in employee job stress, and

employees' desire to balance work and life responsibilities are making it difficult for employers to find and keep talented people.

3. **List three demographic challenges employers are facing in today's workplace.**
An increase in work-force diversity, an aging population, and a number of gender-related issues such as sexism, the glass ceiling, and sexual harassment are causing employers to develop diversity- and sensitivity-training programs, provide opportunities and benefits for older employees, and implement policies to curb discrimination and sexual harassment.

4. **Highlight three popular alternative work arrangements companies are offering their employees.**
To meet today's staffing and demographic challenges, companies are offering their employees flextime (the ability to vary their work hours), telecommuting (the ability to work from home or another location), and job sharing (the ability to share a single full-time job with a co-worker).

MEETING BUSINESS CHALLENGES AT UNITED PARCEL SERVICE

CEO Jim Kelly and his management team were on the hot seat during the Teamsters strike in August 1997. They had not expected the strike to last, nor had they expected the public to side with the union. UPS finally ended the strike by agreeing to most of the union's demands. Even as UPS employees went back to work, managers faced the challenge of patching up strained relations and getting everyone back on track toward the company's goals. They were also concerned about winning back customers who had defected to other carriers during the strike.

"At issue was do we continue to talk about the fact that we had this disagreement, or do we move forward," said Lea Soupata, senior vice president for human resources at UPS. "All of us on the management team communicated that we were going to look forward, that we don't look back, and that what we should be focusing on is not this aberration, but what the future can hold for us working together."

Eager to repair working relationships, CEO Kelly videotaped a speech urging all 330,000 employees to get back to business as usual. Then other top managers fanned out to meet with employees and supervisors in the 60 UPS regional districts, answering questions and soliciting comments. They also unveiled a new program designed to reward drivers and supervisors for wooing customers back to UPS.

Although the meetings helped to generate goodwill, some employees and union personnel felt that UPS supervisors remained hostile and bitter about the strike. They accused supervisors of "riding the drivers constantly" to get even for the walkout. Nevertheless, UPS's Soupata insisted that such claims were unfounded, noting that the number of complaint calls logged in by employees over a special toll-free hot line (which allows employees to anonymously report such problems), had not increased significantly. Furthermore, union officials were heartened by Soupata's statement that top management would

straighten out any manager who continued to hold a grudge. And a companywide survey of employee attitudes, conducted two months after the strike, indicated that, although morale had gone down, employees were still committed to UPS.

While the fires smoldered, UPS managers found themselves defusing another tense labor situation. Its pilots, members of the Independent Pilots Association, had wrangled with UPS for nearly two years over pay, hours, and conditions. They wanted an agreement similar to the contract that FedEx had with its pilots' union. This time UPS and the union quickly settled the dispute by entering into 30 hours of nonstop talks under the supervision of the National Mediation Board. They agreed on terms that were comparable to the FedEx pilots' contract and kept UPS flying high without interruption.[66]

Critical Thinking Questions

1. How did the UPS strike affect employee morale?
2. Apart from calling another strike, how might the Teamsters put pressure on UPS to create the 2,000 full-time jobs that are in dispute?
3. Why was it important for UPS to reach a quick settlement with its pilots' union?

■ LEARN MORE ONLINE

Visit the Teamsters Web site at http://www.teamster.org/ and search sections of the Teamster News pages for updates on relations with UPS. Also look at one or two news articles about the union's initiatives in other industries. What kinds of issues are the Teamsters fighting for? How are UPS and other companies responding to the Teamsters?

5. **Cite three options that unions have when negotiations with management break down.**
   Unions can conduct strikes, organize boycotts, and use publicity to pressure management into complying with union proposals.

6. **Cite three options management can exercise when negotiations with the union break down.**
   To pressure a union into accepting its proposals, management may continue running the business with strikebreakers, institute a lockout of union members, or seek an injunction against a strike or other union activity.

Key Terms

arbitration (221)

behavior modification (206)

boycott (222)

collective bargaining (220)

flextime (216)

glass ceiling (215)

human relations (210)

hygiene factors (207)

injunction (223)

job enrichment (213)

job redesign (213)

job sharing (217)

labor unions (218)

lockouts (223)

mediation (221)

morale (206)

motivation (206)

motivators (207)

picketing (222)

quality of work life (QWL) (212)

scientific management (206)

sexism (214)

sexual harassment (215)

strike (222)

strikebreakers (222)

telecommuting (216)

Theory X (208)

Theory Y (208)

Test Your Knowledge

QUESTIONS FOR REVIEW

1. What is the goal of human relations?

2. What is rightsizing?

3. What is quality of work life, and how does it influence employee motivation?

4. What are the principal causes of employee burnout?

5. Why do employees choose to join labor unions? Why do they not join labor unions?

QUESTIONS FOR ANALYSIS

6. Why do managers often find it difficult to motivate employees who remain after downsizing?

7. How can diversity initiatives benefit a company?

8. What are some of the advantages and disadvantages of alternative work arrangements?

9. How are labor leaders trying to promote union membership?

10. You've got a golf game scheduled for Sunday afternoon, and you've worked all weekend to write a proposal to be presented Monday morning. The proposal is more or less finished, but a few more hours of work would make it polished and persuasive. Do you cancel the game?[67]

QUESTIONS FOR APPLICATION

11. One of your talented and hardworking employees comes to you one day and says she does not feel challenged. When she took the job a year ago, she expected to be able to diversify her skills more and take on greater responsibility than she now has. How do you respond?

12. Assume you are the plant manager for a company that manufactures tires for cars and light trucks. To compete more economically in the global market, the company is seriously considering closing the plant within the next year and moving manufacturing operations to Southeast Asia. Upon hearing about the possible plant closing, the union votes to launch a strike in one week if its demands for job security aren't met. Because of a recent surge in orders, the company is not in a position to close the plant yet. What are your options as you continue to negotiate with union representatives? Which option would you choose and why?

13. ■ How do economic concepts such as profit motive and competitive advantage (see Chapter 1) affect today's work force?

14. ■ Why are companies that practice management by objectives (see Chapter 6) more likely to have a motivated work force than companies that use more traditional approaches? Be sure to discuss MBO in the context of Maslow's, Herzberg's, and McGregor's motivational theories.

Practice Your Knowledge

SHARPENING YOUR COMMUNICATION SKILLS

As the director of public relations for a major airline your job is to prepare news releases should the pilots decide to strike. This is a challenging task because many people will be affected by the strike. Being a good communicator, you know that one of the first things you must do before preparing a message is to analyze the audience. Think about an airline strike and answer these questions briefly to practice this important communication technique:

1. What groups of people do you think would be interested in the information about the airline strike?

2. What do you think each of these groups would want to know about most?

3. How might they react to the information you will provide?

Summarize your answers to these three questions in a short memo to your instructor.

HANDLING DIFFICULT SITUATIONS ON THE JOB: SERVING UP STAFF SATISFACTION

This is the second summer you've worked as a food server at Ed's, a health-conscious eatery on Old Highway 101 in Cardiff, California. Normally, beach crowds cross the highway in the late afternoons for Ed's $4 smoothies and gourmet organic dinners. But with beach erosion, there haven't been as many sunbathers this year. Still, as far as you can tell, people are lining up in healthy numbers to order the sunset dinner specials and watch the dolphins play in the surf.

To save on overhead, Ed has cut back on the number of servers and kitchen staff. This means that during busy periods, customers wait longer for their food and for their tables (or leave in anger), while orders back up in the kitchen. You're working twice as hard and making fewer tips, since your customers now have to wait up to half an hour for their dinners. You've even lost some regulars you remember from last year, people who brought in all their out-of-town guests and left you hefty tips.

Clearly, being short-staffed is as bad for the long-term health of the business as it is for the satisfaction and motivation of the servers—including yourself. Rumors are flying that a new restaurant is going to open down the street, so you may yet be able to salvage some tips for the season. As the restaurant empties out, the manager heads your way. This is your chance to speak up.[68]

1. Should you tell your manager what angry customers have said or mention how many customers have left without ordering? If you decide to tell the manager, what should you say—and how?

2. Think about the hygiene factors and motivators that influence your job as a server. How are these affecting your motivation and your satisfaction with the policies at Ed's?

3. Assuming that Ed's wants Theory Y employees, can you offer a suggestion for keeping costs down while improving the motivation of the servers and kitchen staff?

BUILDING YOUR TEAM SKILLS

Debate the pros and cons of union membership within a group of four students (two students take the pro side, and the other two take the con side). As you prepare for this debate, consider the relevance of unions at a time when legislation is becoming more protective of employees' rights and companies are staying lean to compete more effectively. Are unions necessary now that participatory management and employee involvement in organizational decision making are more commonplace? What about the role of unions in professions such as medicine? Are unions more relevant in some industries or businesses than in others?

During your team's debate, let one side present its arguments while the other side takes notes on the major points. After both sides have completed their presentations, discuss all the supporting points and come to an agreement about the relevance of unions. Draft a one-page statement outlining your team's conclusion and reasoning, and share it during a class discussion.

Compare your team's conclusion and reasoning with those of other teams. Do most teams believe that unions are relevant or not? What issues do most teams agree on? What issues do they disagree on?

Expand Your Knowledge

EXPLORING CAREER OPPORTUNITIES

Is an alternative work arrangement such as telecommuting or flextime in your career future? This exercise will help you think about whether these work arrangements fit into your career plans.

1. Look at the list of possible business careers in Appendix 2. Of the careers that interest you, which seem best suited to telecommuting? To flextime?

2. Select one of the careers that seems suited to telecommuting. With this career in mind, answer the questions in this chapter's box "Is Telecommuting Right for You?" Did you answer no to any questions? Is there any way to turn that no into a yes?

3. Thinking about the same career, do you think it would be possible to split the job's responsibilities with a co-worker

under a job-sharing arrangement? What issues, if any, might you need to resolve first?

DEVELOPING YOUR RESEARCH SKILLS

With more people from diverse backgrounds and cultures—and an aging population—the U.S. work force continues to change. Use your research skills to take a closer look at the demographic challenges affecting the work force available to U.S. employers. As you complete this assignment, track the information sources and search tactics you use.

1. Using library or online sources such as the *Statistical Abstract of the United States* (http://www.census.gov/statab/www/), locate recent and historical data about the country's age distribution. What age categories have increased in size over the past five years? What age categories have decreased in size?

2. Look at population projections for the coming decade. Which age group will be the largest in ten years? Which will be the smallest? How do these projections compare with the historical data you just analyzed?

3. Now research immigration trends to find out where newcomers to the United States tend to come from. How many foreign-born people came to the United States in the most recent year for which statistics are available? What are the top three countries of origin? In addition to possible language barriers, what kinds of issues do you think employers would face in hiring these recent immigrants?

SEE IT ON THE WEB EXERCISES
Measuring Employee Satisfaction, page 209

Managers use surveys to gain a better understanding of how satisfied and motivated employees are at work. Look at the survey that was conducted by *Inc.* magazine and Gallup on *Inc.*'s Web site, at http://www.inc.com/interactive/vc/01039825.html.

1. Complete the 16 questions in the survey on the basis of your current or most recent work experience. Did all the survey questions make sense in the context of your work situation? How did you answer the question about your overall satisfaction with your place of employment?

2. Click "Continue" to compare your answers with those of other visitors who have taken the survey and with the answers of those who responded to the Gallup poll. How similar were your answers? How can you account for these similarities or differences?

3. Which of the motivation theories is reflected in Question 3, which asks about your supervisor's attitude toward you

as a person? Which of the needs in Maslow's hierarchy is reflected in Question 7, which asks about your personal development? Which of Herzberg's factors is reflected in Question 9, which asks about the materials and equipment needed to do your job?

Working Hard on the Web, page 213

Visitors to the Hard@Work Web site, at http://www.hardatwork.com, can get help with difficult work situations and chat with others about work and careers. Browse the site and then answer the questions below.

1. Follow the link at the bottom of the page to the Rock Pile, and select a case to review. Draft a paragraph in response to your selected case. Then compare your response with those suggested by other students who selected the same case. How do your responses differ? What does this difference say about the challenges of managing and motivating different employees?

2. Follow the link to Stump the Mentor. Look at the issues posted in this section. Have you or any of your classmates faced these types of situations at work? Select one case and read through the mentor's comments. Do you agree with the mentor? Why or why not?

3. After exploring the Water Cooler and other links on the site, write a paragraph or two evaluating the content and presentation. Would managers, employees, or job seekers most benefit from visiting this site? Do you find the information on this site valuable? Why?

Spreading the Union Message, page 220

The AFL-CIO maintains one of the most comprehensive Web sites dedicated to union activities and issues. Explore the site at http://www.aflcio.org and then respond to these questions.

1. Follow the link to How and Why People Join Unions. Read The Union Difference and the Work in Progress weekly e-letter. What worker issues and advantages of union membership are being highlighted?

2. Follow the link to Safety and Health on the Job. Are any new legislative initiatives being tracked? If so, what issues are these bills addressing? What is the AFL-CIO's position on these bills? Do you agree with its position?

3. Under the Executive PayWatch link, read about AFL-CIO's comments on executive compensation. What actions does the union suggest to limit executive pay? As a business student, what is your reaction to the union's stand? What are some of the positive and negative effects that might result from union activities on this issue?

10

MANAGING HUMAN RESOURCES

FACING BUSINESS CHALLENGES
AT STARBUCKS

Brewing Up People Policies for Chainwide Success

Hiring, training, and compensating a diverse work force of 27,000 employees worldwide would be a difficult task for any company. But it was an especially daunting challenge in an industry whose annual employee turnover rate approached 300 percent. It was even more of a challenge for a company that was striving to open a new store every day, despite a tight labor market, an uncertain global economy, and increasingly intense competition.

This was the high-pressure situation facing Starbucks Coffee Company in the 1990s, when CEO Howard Schultz set a torrid pace for global expansion. Starbucks wanted to perk past $1 billion in yearly sales and spread its gourmet coffee cult across more continents. Already, the rich aroma of fresh-brewed espresso was wafting through neighborhoods all over North America, with new stores planned for the United Kingdom, Japan, even China. To keep up with this ambitious schedule of new store openings, Starbucks had to find, recruit, and train 500 new employees every month, no easy feat "when there is a shortage of labor and few people want to work behind a retail counter," as Schultz noted.

But good locations and top-quality coffee were just part of the company's formula for success. Schultz and his management team knew that Starbucks' employees also had to deliver consistently superior customer service in every store and every market. "It's ironic that retailers and restaurants live or die on customer service," the CEO said, "yet their employees have some of the lowest pay in any industry. That's one reason so many retail experiences are mediocre for the public." And Starbucks wanted its employees (known internally as *partners*) to do more than simply pour coffee; it wanted them to believe passionately in the product and pay attention to all the details that can make or break the retail experience for the chain's 5 million weekly customers.

Schultz knew that it would take more than good pay and company declarations to "provide a great work environment and treat each other with respect and dignity," to motivate and inspire employees. But what other human resources policies and practices could Starbucks implement to achieve this goal? How could the company's managers train and motivate employees to give topnotch service? To reduce personal stress and minimize turnover, what could Starbucks do to help its employees juggle the conflicting demands of work and family?[1]

UNDERSTANDING WHAT HUMAN RESOURCES MANAGERS DO

human resources management (HRM)
Specialized function of planning how to obtain employees, oversee their training, evaluate them, and compensate them

As Starbucks' Schultz knows, employees are an important component of every business. In fact, most successful companies recognize that employees are indeed their most valuable asset. Such attitudes have fueled the rising emphasis on hiring the right people to help a company reach its goals and then overseeing their training and development, motivation, evaluation, and compensation. This specialized function, formerly referred to as *personnel management,* is now termed **human resources management (HRM)** to reflect the importance of a well-chosen and well-managed work force in achieving company goals. Because of the accelerating rate at which today's work force, economy, and corporate cultures are being transformed, the role of HRM is increasingly viewed as a strategic one.

Human resources (HR) managers must figure out how to attract qualified employees from a shrinking pool of entry-level candidates; how to train less educated, poorly skilled employees; how to keep experienced employees when they have few opportunities for advancement; and how to lay off employees equitably when downsizing is necessary. They must also retrain employees to enable them to cope with increasing automation and computerization, manage increasingly complex (and expensive) employee benefits programs, shape workplace policies to address changing work-force demographics and employee needs (as discussed in Chapter 9), and cope with the challenge of meeting government regulations in hiring practices and equal opportunity employment.

LEARNING OBJECTIVE 1

List six main functions of human resources departments

In short, human resources managers and staff members keep the organization running smoothly at every level by planning for a company's staffing needs, recruiting and hiring employees, training and developing employees and managers, and appraising employee performance. The HR staff also administers compensation and employee benefits and oversees changes in employment status (promotion, reassignment, termination or resignation, and retirement). This chapter explores each of these human resources responsibilities, beginning with planning (see Exhibit 10.1).

EXHIBIT 10·1

THE FUNCTIONS OF THE HUMAN RESOURCES DEPARTMENT

Human resources departments are responsible for these six important functions.

1. Planning for staffing needs
2. Recruiting and hiring
3. Training and development
4. Appraising performance
5. Administering compensation and benefits
6. Overseeing changes in employment status

■ PLANNING FOR A COMPANY'S STAFFING NEEDS

One of the six functions of the human resources staff members is to plan for a company's staffing needs. Proper planning is critical because a miscalculation could leave a company without enough employees to keep up with demand, resulting in customer dissatisfaction and lost business. Yet if a company expands its staff too rapidly, profits may be eaten up by payroll, or the firm may have to lay off people who were just recruited and trained at considerable expense. The planning function consists of two steps: forecasting supply and demand and evaluating job requirements (see Exhibit 10.2).

Forecasting Supply and Demand

Planning begins with forecasting *demand,* the numbers and kinds of employees that will be needed at various times. For example, suppose Starbucks is planning to open another store in San Diego within six months. The HR department would forecast that the store will need a store manager and an assistant manager as well as part-time salespeople. Although Starbucks might start looking immediately for someone as highly placed as the manager, hiring salespeople might be postponed until just before the store opens.

The next task is to estimate the *supply* of available employees. In many cases, that supply is within the company already—perhaps just needing training to fill future requirements. Starbucks may well find that the assistant manager at an existing store can be promoted to manage the new store, and one of the current salespeople can be named assistant manager. If existing employees cannot be tapped for new positions, the human resources manager must determine how to find people outside the company who have the necessary skills. In some cases, managers will want to consider strategic staffing alternatives such as hiring part-time and temporary employees or outsourcing the work to avoid drastic overstaffing or understaffing.

Part-Time and Temporary Employees   More and more businesses try to save money and increase flexibility by building their work forces around part-time employees, whose schedules can be rearranged to suit the company's needs. As a result, the part-time labor force has increased by leaps and bounds in recent years.

In addition to using part-time workers, some 85 percent of U.S. firms use temporary employees, or "temps," to handle a variety of jobs at all levels of the organization. Moreover, two-thirds of executives surveyed expect their use of temps to increase. The temporary ranks include computer systems analysts, human resources directors, accountants, doctors, and even CEOs. In fact, the Labor Department says that the professional

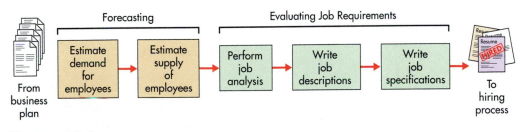

EXHIBIT 10·2

STEPS IN HUMAN RESOURCES PLANNING

Careful attention to each phase of this sequence helps ensure that a company will have the right human resources when it needs them.

and technical fields are the fastest-growing areas of temporary employment.[2] The use of temps has also become a recruiting technique because it allows companies to try out employees before hiring them permanently. Thus, what often begins as a temp assignment can turn into multiyear employment.

Some 29 percent of workers employed by temp agencies remain on the job assignment for one year or more, says the Bureau of Labor Statistics. Many of these "permatemps" hold high-prestige, high-skilled technology jobs at firms such as Microsoft. If fact, they often do the same work as the company's permanent employees, but because they are temps, they do not qualify for the benefits enjoyed by regular workers. Of course, for many, using permatemps is a win-win situation. Companies get a steady, knowledgeable labor supply, and workers have the flexibility to work for six months and then take some time off. But a recent

ARE TEMP WORKERS BECOMING A FULL-TIME HEADACHE?

They get no sick days or personal days. They don't get paid for holidays such as the day after Thanksgiving or Christmas. And the company on their paycheck doesn't read Microsoft or IBM but the name of the employment agency that places them. Still, many temporary workers are content with this arrangement—in the beginning, anyway.

Some see temporary work as a win-win situation for both the worker and the company. Temp workers (also known as noncore staff, the flexible work force, contingent employees, and permatemps) can get challenging work at leading companies, earn top hourly rates, and job-hop at will, learning new skills at each stop. Companies can staff their work force strategically, secure hard-to-find talent, move them from project to project, and save big dollars by not paying temporary workers employee benefits.

But with short-term projects turning into years of service, some temporary workers are rebelling. They want the same benefits as their full-time counterparts. And a recent ruling by the U.S. Court of Appeals for the Ninth Circuit concurs. The court ruling concluded that some Microsoft temporary workers were entitled to benefits that included company stock options, of course. Moreover, the ruling makes workers who are on a company's payroll for more than a few months "common-law employees" (even if they're signed up with a temp agency). This classification entitles them to the same benefits permanent staffers get.

Although some permatemps are excited about the recent court decision (which Microsoft intends to appeal), others are concerned. They fear that the ruling could backfire and create fewer opportunities for workers who want to take time off or move freely from job to job. Some experts predict that the ruling could cause a major shakeout in the temporary services business and get rid of permatemps permanently.

In the meantime, resourceful companies are finding ways to keep things legal. Microsoft, for example, requires part-time workers who complete an assignment of one year or longer to leave the company for 31 days. Others are putting pressure on employment agencies they contract with to offer benefits to their contingent work force and are even refusing to do business with any agency that doesn't comply. However, exactly how those benefits are implemented is left to the agencies. And they seldom match the lucrative benefits full-time employees receive—especially at companies like Microsoft, which claims to offer "more perks than Seattle has coffeehouses."

QUESTIONS FOR CRITICAL THINKING

1. How might a decline in the use of temporary workers affect company staffing?
2. Besides employee benefits, what other human resources challenges might the use of permatemps create?

spate of lawsuits could undo this mutually beneficial work arrangement. Some permatemps are suing companies, saying that they are, in fact, full-time employees and as such deserve employee benefits.[3]

Outsourcing Outsourcing is another way that companies fulfill their human resources needs without hiring permanent employees. A recent poll of 26 major companies including duPont, Exxon, and Honda found that 86 percent outsource some portion of their work. Outsourcing has many advantages: It gives companies access to new resources and world-class capabilities; it shares the risk of getting the work done; and it frees company resources for other purposes. Still, because companies that outsource their work give up direct control over the employees doing that work, problems do occur. Some companies have experienced work delays, loss of quality, unhappy customers, and labor union battles as a result of outsourcing.[4]

Evaluating Job Requirements

The second step of the planning function is to evaluate job requirements. If you were the owner of a small business, you might have a good grasp of the requirements of all the jobs in your company. However, in large organizations where hundreds or thousands of employees are performing a wide variety of jobs, management needs a more formal and objective method of evaluating job requirements. That method is called **job analysis.**

To obtain the information needed for a job analysis, the human resources staff asks employees or supervisors several questions: What is the purpose of the job? What tasks are involved in the job? What qualifications and skills are needed to do it effectively? In what kind of setting does the job take place? Is there much public contact involved? Does the job entail much time pressure? Sometimes they obtain job information by observing employees directly. Other times they ask employees to keep daily diaries describing exactly what they do during the workday.

Once job analysis has been completed, the human resources staff develops a **job description,** a formal statement summarizing the tasks involved in the job and the conditions under which the employee will work. In most cases, the staff will also develop a **job specification,** a statement describing the skills, education, and previous experience that the job requires.

■ RECRUITING, HIRING, AND TRAINING NEW EMPLOYEES

Having forecasted a company's supply and demand for employees and evaluated job requirements, the next step is to match the job specification with an actual person or selection of people. This task is accomplished through **recruiting,** the process of attracting suitable candidates for an organization's jobs. Recruiters are specialists on the human resources staff who are responsible for locating job candidates. They use a variety of methods and resources, including internal searches, newspaper and Internet advertising, public and private employment agencies, union hiring halls, college campuses and career offices, trade shows, corporate "headhunters" (people who try to attract people at other companies), and referrals from employees or colleagues in the industry (see Exhibit 10.3).

One of the fastest-growing recruitment resources for both large and small businesses is the Internet. Today many companies recruit online through their Web sites in addition to using popular online recruiting services such as Career Mosaic, Monster Board, and Career Path (as discussed in Appendix 1). In comparison with the other recruiting methods, online

job analysis
Process by which jobs are studied to determine the tasks and dynamics involved in performing them

job description
Statement of the tasks involved in a given job and the conditions under which the holder of the job will work

job specification
Statement describing the kind of person who would be best for a given job—including the skills, education, and previous experience that the job requires

recruiting
Process of attracting appropriate applicants for an organization's jobs

LEARNING OBJECTIVE 2
Cite eight methods recruiters use to find job candidates

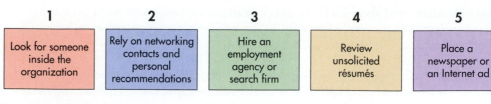

EXHIBIT 10·3

HOW EMPLOYERS APPROACH THE RECRUITING PROCESS

Studies show that employers prefer to fill job openings with people from within their organization or from an employee's recommendation. Placing want ads is often viewed as a last resort. In contrast, typical job hunters begin their job-search process from the opposite direction (starting with want ads).

recruiting allows companies to access a broader selection of applicants, target specific types of applicants more easily, reach highly skilled applicants more efficiently, and give applicants quicker responses to their queries. However, there are drawbacks. The biggest complaint is that companies must process more applications than ever before. Another is that not everyone has Internet access, making it especially difficult to reach nontechnical people.[5]

The Hiring Process

After exploring at least one—but usually more—of the available recruitment channels to assemble a pool of applicants, the human resources department may spend weeks and sometimes months on the hiring process. Most companies go through the same basic stages in the hiring process as they sift through applications to come up with the person (or persons) they want.

The first stage is to select a small number of qualified candidates from all of the applications received. Finalists may be chosen on the basis of a standard application form that all candidates fill out or on the basis of a *résumé*—a summary of education, experience, and personal data compiled by each applicant (see "Preparing Your Résumé" in Appendix 1 for further details). Sometimes both sources of information are used. Many organizations now use computer scanners to help them quickly sort through résumés and weed out those that don't match the requirements of the job.

The second stage in the hiring process is to interview each candidate to clarify qualifications and to fill in any missing information (see "Interviewing with Potential Employers" in Appendix 1 for further detail). Another goal of the interview is to get an idea of the applicant's personality and ability to work well with others. Depending on the type of job at stake, candidates may also be asked to take a test or a series of tests.

After the initial interviews comes the third stage, when the best candidates may be asked to meet with someone in the human resources department who will conduct a more probing interview. For higher-level positions, candidates may go through a series of interviews with managers, potential co-workers, and the employees who will make up the successful candidate's staff. In the fourth step, the position's supervisor evaluates the candidates, sometimes in consultation with a higher-level manager, the human resources department, and staff. During the fifth stage, the employer checks the references of the top few candidates. The employer may also research the candidates' education, previous employment, and motor vehicle records. A growing number of employers are also checking candidates' credit histories, a practice that is drawing criticism as a violation of privacy.[6] In the sixth stage, the supervisor selects the most suitable person for the job. Now the search is over—provided the candidate accepts the offer.

LEARNING OBJECTIVE 3
Identify the six stages in the hiring process

The way to handle an interview depends on what stage of the interview process you are in. For instance, in the screening stage, your main objective is to differentiate yourself from the other candidates. In later stages, your objective is to highlight your strengths and explain three or four of your best qualifications in depth.

Hiring and the Law Federal and state laws and regulations govern many aspects of the hiring process. In particular, employers must be careful to avoid discrimination in the wording of their application forms, in interviewing, and in testing. They must also obtain sufficient information about employees to avoid becoming the target of a negligent-hiring lawsuit. For example, a trucking company must check applicants' driving records to avoid hiring a new trucker with poor driving skills. As we will see, striking the right balance can be quite a challenge.

> You can encourage innovation by hiring, working with, and promoting people who think differently from you.[7]

Asking questions about unrelated factors such as marital status, age, and religion violate the Equal Employment Opportunity Commission's regulations because they may lead to discrimination. In addition, questions about whether the person is married or has children, whether he or she owns or rents a home, what caused a physical disability, whether the person belongs to a union, whether he or she has ever been arrested, and when the person attended school are not allowed. The exception is when such information is related to a bona fide occupational qualification for the specific job.

Since the Immigration Reform and Control Act was passed in 1986, employers must also be wary of asking too few questions. Almost all U.S. companies are forbidden to hire illegal aliens and must verify that the newly hired are legally eligible to work. However, the act also prohibits discrimination in hiring on the basis of national origin or citizenship status, resulting in a sticky situation for many employers trying to determine their applicants' citizenship.

Negligent Hiring Violence in the workplace is an increasing threat that can harm employees and customers, hurt productivity, and lead to expensive lawsuits and higher health-care costs. More than 1 million physical assaults and thousands of homicides occur at work each year. If an employer fails to prevent "preventable violences," that employer will likely be found liable. This means that companies need to be especially careful about negligent hiring.[8] In one case, Saks Fifth Avenue hired an undercover security officer at its flagship store in New York without adequately checking his background. After he raped a young woman executive twice in her office, it was discovered that the security officer had been convicted of sexually abusing an 11-year-old girl in Kentucky.[9]

This and similar cases emphasize the need for employers to conduct thorough background checks on job applicants, including verifying all educational credentials and previous jobs, accounting for any large time gaps between jobs, and checking references. Background checks are particularly important for jobs in which employees are in a position to possibly harm others. In these situations, the human resources department has to weigh the need for uncovering information against a respect for the privacy of applicants.

Testing One much-debated aspect of the hiring process is testing—using not only the tests that prospective employers give job applicants but any devices that can evaluate employees when making job decisions. Tests are used to gauge abilities, intelligence, interests, and sometimes even physical condition and personality.

Many companies rely on preemployment testing to determine whether applicants are suited to the job and whether they'll be worth the expense of hiring and training. Companies use three main procedures: job-skills testing, psychological testing, and drug testing. Job-skills tests are the most common type, designed to assess competency or specific abilities needed to perform a job. Psychological tests usually take the form of questionnaires. These tests can be used to assess overall intellectual ability, attitudes toward work, interests, managerial potential, or personality characteristics—including dependability, commitment, and motivation. People who favor psychological testing say that it can predict how well employees will actually perform on the job. However, critics say that such tests are ineffective and potentially discriminatory.

To avoid the increased costs and reduced productivity associated with drug abuse in the workplace (estimated to cost industry some $100 billion a year), many employers require applicants to be tested for drug use. Studies show that substance abusers have two to four times as many workplace accidents as do people who do not use drugs. Moreover, drug use can be linked to over 40 percent of industry fatalities. Nevertheless, some employers prefer not to incur the extra expense to administer drug tests; others consider such tests an invasion of privacy.[10]

Training and Development

orientation
Session or procedure for acclimating a new employee to the organization

To make sure that all new employees understand the company's goals, policies, and procedures, most large organizations and many small ones have well-defined **orientation** programs. Although they vary, such programs usually include information about company background and structure, equal opportunity practices, safety regulations, standards of employee conduct, company culture, employee compensation and benefit plans, work times, and other topics that newly hired employees might have questions about.[11] Orientation programs help new employees understand their role in the organization and feel more comfortable.

At Intel, all new hires participate in a six-month "integration" curriculum. Day One begins when new hires receive a packet at their home. The packet contains material about the company's culture and values, along with some forms to fill out. During the first month, all new hires attend a class called "Working at Intel," a formal eight-hour introduction to the company's corporate culture. At the end of the six-month period, each new hire participates in a two-hour structured question-and-answer session, in which an executive reviews the employee's transition into Intel and then asks a final long-term question: "What do you think it will take to succeed at Intel?"[12]

In addition to orientation programs, most companies offer training (and retraining), because employee competence has a direct effect on productivity and profits. At Wal-Mart, senior vice president of human resources Coleman Peterson believes that training is the most important part of human resources management. "Wal-Mart is in the business of keeping and growing talent," he says.[13] Although some employers worry that employees who develop new or improved skills might leave them for higher-paying jobs, studies show that the contrary is true. The more training given to employees, the more likely they will want to stay, because training gives them a sense that they are going somewhere in their careers, even if they're not getting a promotion.[14]

At this employee orientation session, new employees review the company's mission statement, policies, procedures, benefits, and safety regulations before they meet with their department managers.

In most companies, training takes place at the work site, where an experienced employee oversees the trainee's on-the-job efforts, or in a classroom, where an expert lectures groups of employees. Northeast Tool & Manufacturing is one of a growing number of companies that invests heavily in employee training to become more competitive. Some of its employees are sent to a community college; others take remote courses via computers; and still others attend classes by instructors brought into the plant.[15]

Employee training may also involve a self-study component using training manuals, computers, and tests. For example, employees at Fred Meyer discount stores use Computer Based Learning (CBL), a CD-ROM or Internet-based tool whereby employees indepen-

See It on the Web See It on the Web

STAYING ON TOP OF THE HR WORLD

Like all areas of business, the world of human resources changes quickly. To stay informed about trends in recruiting, compensation, benefits, and employee satisfaction, turn to HR Live. This comprehensive online resource provides HR professionals with information about layoffs, employment markets and trends, labor statistics, recruiting methods, and much more. The site also offers convenient links to job fairs and conventions in a variety of industries so recruiters (and job seekers) can plan ahead.

http://www.hrlive.com

dently access a series of multimedia training modules via computer terminals.[16] Other companies such as SGI distribute training and orientation materials via their intranets.[17] Southwest Airlines offers continuing training through its "University for People," where employees can choose courses that will help them to do their jobs more effectively and be more flexible in the tasks they can perform.[18] (Consult Part IV of the *E-Business in Action* supplement at http:www.prenhall.com/ebusinessinaction for a detailed discussion of virtual training and employee development.

■ APPRAISING EMPLOYEE PERFORMANCE

How do employees know whether they are doing a good job? How can they improve their performance? What new skills should they learn? Most human resources managers attempt to answer these questions by developing **performance appraisal** systems to objectively evaluate employees according to set criteria. Such systems promote fairness because their standards are usually job-related.

performance appraisal
Evaluation of an employee's work according to specific criteria

The ultimate goal of performance appraisals is not to judge employees but rather to improve their performance. Thus, experts recommend that performance reviews be an ongoing discipline—not just a once-a-year event linked to employee raises. Periodic performance evaluations are especially important in today's project-driven, results-oriented workplace. Employees need fast feedback so they can correct their deficiencies in a timely manner.[19]

Most companies also require regular, written evaluations of each employee's work. To ensure objectivity and consistency, firms generally use a standard company performance appraisal form to evaluate employees. The evaluation criteria are in writing so that both employee and supervisor understand what is expected and are therefore able to determine whether the work is being done adequately. Written evaluations provide a record of the employee's performance, which may protect the company in cases of disputed terminations. Finally, many performance appraisal systems require the employee to be rated by several people (including more than one supervisor and perhaps several co-workers). This practice further promotes fairness by correcting for the possible bias that might influence one person's appraisal.

One of the biggest problems with appraisal systems is finding a way to measure productivity. In a production job, the person who types the most pages of acceptable copy or who assembles the most defect-free microprocessors in a given amount of time is clearly the most productive. However, how does an employer evaluate the productivity of the registration clerk at a hotel or the middle manager at a large television station? Although the organization's overall productivity can be measured (number of rooms booked per night, number of viewers per hour), often the employer can't directly relate the results to any one employee's efforts.

Evaluating productivity becomes an even greater challenge in organizations where employees work in teams. Some companies, such as Con-Way Transportation Services, meet this challenge by having teams evaluate themselves. About every three months a neutral facilitator leads a discussion in which team members rate team performance on a 1–5 scale for 31 criteria, which can include customer satisfaction, the ability to meet goals, employee behavior toward co-workers and customers, job knowledge, motivation, and skills. During the meetings, members discuss the team's performance. Individual performance is also discussed but only in the context of the team. Each person creates two columns on a sheet of paper, one labeled "strengths" and the other, "something to work on." Team members self-assess and then pass the list around the room so other team members can add their comments.[20]

ADMINISTERING COMPENSATION AND EMPLOYEE BENEFITS

On what basis should employees be paid? How much should they be paid? When should they be paid? What benefits should they receive? Every day, company leaders confront these types of decisions. Administering **compensation,** a combination of payments in the form of wages or salaries, incentive payments, employee benefits, and employer services, is another major responsibility of a company's human resources department.

compensation
Money, benefits, and services paid to employees for their work

Wages and Salaries

Many blue-collar (production) and some white-collar (management and clerical) employees receive compensation in the form of **wages,** which are based on calculating the number of hours worked, the number of units produced, or a combination of both time and productivity. Wages provide a direct incentive to an employee: The more hours worked or the more pieces completed, the higher the employee's paycheck. Moreover, employers in the United States must comply with the Fair Labor Standards Act of 1938, which sets a minimum hourly wage for most employees and mandates overtime pay for employees who work

wages
Cash payment based on the number of hours the employee has worked or the number of units the employee has produced

See It on the Web See It on the Web

DIGGING DEEPER AT THE BUREAU OF LABOR STATISTICS

By now you're probably aware that the U.S. government has an agency for almost every purpose. Many of these agencies gather facts and statistics on trends in the United States, and the Bureau of Labor Statistics is no exception. When you need to research detailed information about national or regional employment conditions—such as wages, unemployment, productivity, and benefits—point your Web browser to this site.
http://www.bls.gov

longer than 40 hours a week. Most states also have minimum wage laws intended to protect employees not covered by federal laws or to set higher wage floors.[21]

Employees whose output is not always directly related to the number of hours worked or the number of pieces produced are paid **salaries.** As with wages, salaries base compensation on time, but the unit of time is a week, two weeks, a month, or a year. Salaried employees such as managers normally receive no pay for the extra hours they sometimes put in; overtime is simply part of their obligation. However, they do get a certain amount of leeway in their schedules.

Both wages and salaries are, in principle, based on the contribution of a particular job to the company. Thus, a sales manager, who is responsible for bringing in sales revenue, is paid more than a secretary, who handles administrative tasks but doesn't sell or supervise. However, as the tables in Appendix 2 show, pay varies widely by position, industry, and location. Among the best-paid employees in the world are chief executive officers of large U.S. corporations.

salaries
Fixed weekly, monthly, or yearly cash compensation for work

LEARNING OBJECTIVE 4
List seven popular types of employee incentive programs

Incentive Programs

To encourage employees to be more productive, innovative, and committed to their work, companies often provide managers and employees with **incentives,** cash payments that are linked to specific individual, group, and companywide goals; overall productivity; and company success. In other words, achievements, not just activities, are made the basis for payment. The success of these programs often depends on how closely incentives are linked to actions within the employee's control:

- *Bonuses.* For both salaried and wage-earning employees, one type of incentive compensation is the **bonus,** a payment in addition to the regular wage or salary. As an incentive to reduce turnover during the year, some firms pay an annual year-end bonus, amounting to a certain percentage of each employee's wages. Other cash bonuses are tied to company performance.

- *Commissions.* In contrast to bonuses, **commissions** are a form of compensation that pays employees a percentage of sales made. Used mainly for sales staff, they may be either the sole compensation or an incentive payment in addition to a regular salary.

- *Profit sharing.* Employees may be rewarded for staying with a company and encouraged to work harder through **profit sharing,** a system in which employees receive a portion of the company's profits. Depending on the company, profits may be distributed quarterly, semiannually, or annually.

- *Gain sharing.* Similar to profit sharing, **gain sharing** ties rewards to profits (or cost savings) achieved by meeting specific goals such as quality and productivity improvement. The financial incentive encourages employees to find better ways of doing their jobs and to improve their own skills, outcomes that also make the company more competitive.[23]

- *Pay for performance.* A variation of gain sharing, **pay for performance,** requires employees to accept a lower base pay but rewards them if they reach production targets or other goals. Experts estimate that 30 percent of U.S. companies have already adopted at least some pay-for-performance measures. Many have realized productivity gains as well as greater flexibility in keeping employees during hard times.[24] However, some critics point out that such incentives can actually lead to lower quality because employees become focused on working fast rather than working well.

incentives
Cash payments to employees who produce at a desired level or whose unit (often the company as a whole) produces at a desired level

bonus
Cash payment, in addition to the regular wage or salary, that serves as a reward for achievement

commissions
Payments to employees equal to a certain percentage of sales made

 Money, alone, doesn't make employees passionate about their jobs. A cash reward can't magically prompt people to find their work interesting if in their hearts they feel it is dull.[22]

profit sharing
System for distributing a portion of the company's profits to employees

gain sharing
Plan for rewarding employees not on the basis of overall profits but in relation to achievement of goals such as cost savings from higher productivity

pay for performance
Accepting a lower base pay in exchange for bonuses based on meeting production or other goals

knowledge-based pay
Pay tied to an employee's acquisition of skills; also called skill-based pay

broadbanding
Payment system that uses wide pay grades, enabling the company to give pay raises without promotions

- *Knowledge-based pay.* Another approach to compensation being explored by companies is **knowledge-based pay,** or skill-based pay, which is tied to employees' knowledge and abilities rather than to their job per se. Typically, the pay level at which a person is hired is pegged to his or her current level of skills; as the employee acquires new skills, the pay level goes up. Because employees do not compete with each other to increase their pay through promotions, knowledge-based pay enhances teamwork, flexibility, and motivation.[25]

- *Broadbanding.* Like knowledge-based pay, **broadbanding** gives pay raises without promoting employees. Instead of having many narrow pay grades, the company has fewer, broader pay grades. For example, instead of a range of $30,000 to $40,000 for a particular job, a broadband range may be $20,000 to $50,000. This approach allows today's flatter organizations to reward employees without having to move them up a hierarchy. It also allows companies to move employees to different positions without being restricted by the pay grades normally associated with specific jobs.

Employee Benefits and Services

employee benefits
Compensation other than wages, salaries, and incentive programs

Companies also regularly provide **employee benefits**—financial benefits other than wages, salaries, and incentives. For example, Starbucks offers medical and dental insurance, vacation and holiday pay, stock options, discounts on Starbucks products, and a free pound of coffee every week. The benefits package is available to part-time as well as full-time employees, so Starbucks attracts and retains good people at every level.[26]

Until recently, employee benefits came as a preset package in most companies. Once hired, the employee got whatever insurance, paid holidays, pension plan, and other benefits the company had set up. However, a newer flexible benefit approach allows employees to pick their benefits—up to a certain dollar amount—to meet their particular needs. An employee with a young family might want extra life or health insurance, for example, and might feel no need for a pension plan. A single employee might choose to "buy" an extra week or two of vacation time by giving up some other benefit. Such flexible plans help smooth out imbalances in benefits received by single employees and workers with families.[27]

Some of the benefits most commonly provided by employers are insurance, retirement benefits, employee stock-ownership plans, stock options, and family benefits. These benefits and services are undergoing considerable change to meet the shifting needs of today's work force.

LEARNING OBJECTIVE 5
Highlight five popular employee benefits

Insurance   Although it is entirely optional, insurance is the most popular employee benefit. Many businesses offer substantial compensation in the form of life and health insurance, but dental plans, disability insurance, and long-term-care insurance are also gaining in popularity (see Component Chapter B for a discussion of types of employee insurance coverage.) Today only about 61 percent of employees are covered by a company health plan. The number is expected to dip even further as costs rise.[28]

Often a company will negotiate a group insurance plan for employees and pay most of the premium costs. However, faced with exploding health costs, many companies now require employees to pay part of their insurance premiums or more of the actual doctor bills. In addition, more companies are hiring part-time and temporary workers, who typically receive very few company benefits. Nonetheless, some companies, such as Starbucks, provide benefits because doing so discourages employee turnover. Starbucks' CEO Howard Schultz figures that recruiting, interviewing, and training a new employee costs more than two years of medical coverage for an employee who stays with the company.[29]

Retirement Benefits   In the past, few people were able to save enough money in the course of their working years for their retirement. The main purpose of the Social Security Act was to provide basic support to those who could not accumulate the retirement money they would need later in life. Today, nearly everyone who works regularly has become eligible for Social Security payments during retirement. This income is paid for by the Social Security tax, part of which is withheld by the employer from employees' wages and part of which is paid by the employer.

A variety of company-sponsored **pension plans** have been developed as a way of providing additional retirement security. Most pension plans are funded by companies who set aside enough money on a regular basis to cover future retirement benefits. However, the cost and complexity of such plans have increased so dramatically during the past two decades that some employers have cancelled them or have modified them significantly. As a result, fewer companies offer pension plans today than in the past.[30]

Studies show that workers who exercise have fewer sick days and job-related injuries. As a result, more companies are offering fitness programs, including health club memberships. Drivers at Waste Management, for example, do morning exercises before climbing into their trucks. Injury incidents at this company have dropped 15 percent since the program started in 1997.

Employee Stock-Ownership Plans and Stock Options   Another employee benefit being offered by a number of companies is the **employee stock-ownership plan (ESOP),** under which a company places a certain amount of its stock in trust for some or all of its employees, with each employee entitled to a certain share. These plans allow employees to later purchase the shares at a fixed price. If the company does well, the ESOP may be a substantial employee benefit.

A related method for tying employee compensation to company performance is the **stock option plan.** Stock options grant employees the right to purchase a certain amount of stock at a fixed price based on the trading price at the time the option is granted. Options typically "vest" over five years, at a rate of 20 percent annually. This means that at the end of one year you can purchase up to 20 percent of the shares in the original grant, at the end of two years 40 percent, and so on.

Stock options can be a win-win situation for employers and employees. From the employer's perspective, stock options cost very little and they provide long-term incentives for good people to stay with the company. From the employee's perspective, stock options can generate a handsome profit if the stock's market price exceeds the grant price. When Cisco's stock started taking off in 1998, for example, employees of this producer of Internet switches and routers were high-fiving one another in the halls. In one month alone, many at Cisco saw the value of their company stock options increase by tens of thousands of dollars.[31]

pension plans
Company-sponsored programs for providing retirees with income

employee stock-ownership plan (ESOP)
Program enabling employees to become partial owners of a company

stock option plan
Program enabling employees to purchase a certain amount of stock at a discount after they have worked for the company a specified length of time or after the company's stock reaches a specific market price

See It on the Web See It on the Web

UNDERSTANDING EMPLOYEE OWNERSHIP

In recent years, employee ownership through ESOPs and stock options has become a popular way for companies to reward and motivate employees. The National Center for Employee Ownership (NCEO) is a not-for-profit organization dedicated to improving awareness of and participation in employee ownership programs. The NCEO Web site contains free interactive educational activities and reports plus fee-based publications and services. Explore the site to learn more about the ownership programs covered in this chapter.
http://www.nceo.org

Keep in mind, however, that stock options lose their appeal when the stock does not perform as expected. Employees could lose considerable profits if the stock's price falls below the option grant price.[32]

Family Benefits   The Family Medical and Leave Act (FMLA), signed into law in 1993, requires employers with 50 or more workers to provide them with up to 12 weeks of unpaid leave per year for childbirth, adoption, or the care of oneself, a child, a spouse, or a parent with serious illness.[33] Although the intent of the law is noble, the fact is that the average person can't afford to take extended periods of time off without pay.

Day care is another important family benefit, especially for two-career couples. Although only 10 percent of companies provide day-care facilities on the premises, 86 percent of companies surveyed by Hewitt & Associates offer child-care assistance. Types of assistance include dependent-care spending accounts and resource and referral (R&R) services, which help em-

IT'S OKAY TO FALL ASLEEP ON THE JOB

Nodding off at work? You're not alone. It is estimated that 70 to 80 million people in the United States are sleep-deprived—which means they just don't get enough of the stuff. But take heart. While afternoon siestas have long been the norm in many foreign countries, the nap is now slowly inching its way into the U.S. corporate culture. Skip the coffee or coke break, advise experts, and instead put your head down for 15 to 20 minutes.

Being sleepy impairs judgment and slows down reaction time. In fact, work-force fatigue is one of the key causes behind costly accidents, productivity lapses, and poor decision making. But a 20-minute snooze can earn you three to four hours more of peak alertness. Power napping, or napping for a short period of time, can help you quickly regain creativity and problem-solving skills "without the crash you suffer once the caffeine buzz wears off," says sleep expert Dr. Martin Moore-Ede. Furthermore, napping allows you to cope with a longer work day, and it increases productivity. Which is why experts are now advising companies to provide the ultimate employee benefit—the nap room.

Corporate nap rooms are popping up in the strangest places—and so are nappers. Take Russ Klettke, for example. Before he owned his own public relations firm, he used to try to hide his nap habit by sneaking siestas in his office cubicle. Now Klettke stretches out at least once a day in the company's storage closet, which doubles as a napping nook. And he's not the only one. While getting some fax paper, he once stepped on a slumbering co-worker.

Some companies are even going all out in designing their sleep space. Gould Evens Goodman Associates, a Kansas City architectural firm, uses "spent tents" instead of a traditional nap room—which reminded company executives of a nurse's station. These one-person tents are equipped with blankets and alarm clocks. "It's like a little village," notes one employee. Others are building nap rooms outfitted with recliners, couches, cots, earplugs, relaxing music, alarm clocks, and phones—just in case you have to take a call.

So next time you find yourself dropping your eyelids for a couple of ZZZZZs, rather than crawl under your desk or hide in a bathroom stall, tell your boss about the hottest employee benefit—nap rooms. After all, sleeping on the job can indeed be a good thing.

QUESTIONS FOR CRITICAL THINKING

1. Should employees be paid for the time they spend napping in a company nap room? Why or why not?
2. How can companies minimize employee abuse of benefits such as nap rooms?

ployees find suitable child care. Firms estimate that they save anywhere from $2.00 to $6.75 in lost productivity and employee absenteeism for every $1.00 they spend on R&R programs.[34]

A related family issue is care for aging parents. An estimated 77 percent of large corporations offer some form of elder-care assistance, ranging from referral services that help find care providers to dependent-care allowances. Some companies will even agree to move elderly relatives when they transfer an employee to another location.

Other Employee Benefits   Although sometimes overlooked, paid holidays, sick pay, premium pay for working overtime or unusual hours, and paid vacations are important benefits.[35] Companies handle holiday pay in various ways. To provide incentives for employee loyalty, most companies grant employees longer paid vacations after they've been with the organization for a prescribed number of years. Some companies let employees buy additional vacation time or sell unused days back to the employer. Sick-day allowances also vary from company to company and from industry to industry. Some U.S. companies, including Texas Instruments, have begun offering paid-time-off banks that combine vacation, personal use, and sick days into one package. Employees can then take a certain number of days off each year for whatever reason necessary, with no questions asked.[36]

■ OVERSEEING CHANGES IN EMPLOYMENT STATUS

Of course, providing competitive compensation and good employee benefits is no guarantee that employees will stay with the company. A recent survey shows that, all things being equal, 25 percent would leave their current jobs for a pay increase of 10 percent or less, and more than 55 percent would leave for an increase of at least 20 percent.[37] Employees may also leave for reasons other than compensation. Some may decide to retire or may resign voluntarily to pursue a better opportunity. On the other hand, the company may take the initiative in making the change—by promoting, reassigning, or terminating employees. Whatever the reason, losing an employee usually means going to the trouble and expense of finding a replacement, whether from inside or outside the company. Overseeing changes in the employment status is another responsibility of the human resources department.

LEARNING OBJECTIVE 6
Describe five ways an employee's status may change

Promoting and Reassigning Employees

When a person leaves or is promoted to a position of more responsibility, the company has to find someone else for the open job. Many companies prefer to look within the organization for such candidates. In part, this "promote from within" policy allows a company to benefit from the training and experience of its own work force. This policy also rewards employees who have worked hard and demonstrated the ability to handle more challenging tasks. In addition, morale is usually better when a company promotes from within because employees see that they can advance.

However, a potential pitfall of internal promotion is that a person may be given a job beyond his or her competence. A common practice is for someone who is good at one kind of job to be made a manager. Yet managing often requires a completely different set of skills. Someone who consistently racks up the best sales in the company, for example, is not necessarily a good candidate for sales manager. If the promotion is a mistake, the company not only loses its sales leader but also risks losing the employee altogether. People who can't perform well in a new job generally become demoralized and lose confidence in the abilities they do have. At the very least, support and training are needed to help promoted employees perform well.

One big issue these days is *relocation* of promoted and reassigned employees. In the past, companies transferred some employees fairly often, especially those being groomed for higher management positions. Now, however, fewer and fewer employees are willing to accept transfers. The reasons are many: disruption of a spouse's career; strong ties to family, friends, and community; the expense of relocating (buying and selling homes, planning around the reduction of a spouse's income, facing a higher cost of living in the new location); availability of good schools and child care; and the possibility that relocating won't be good for the employee's career. A recent survey of relocated employees found that 83 percent felt the move benefited the company, but only 53 percent felt that it personally benefited them.[38]

To encourage employee relocation, many employers today are covering the costs of house-hunting trips, moving, storage, transportation, and temporary living expenses. In addition, many employers are now helping spouses find good jobs in new locations, assisting transferees with home sales, providing school and day-care referral services, and sometimes reimbursing employees for spouses' lost wages or for financial losses resulting from selling and buying houses. Many companies are also reconsidering their transfer policies and asking employees to transfer only when it is absolutely necessary.

Terminating Employees

termination
Act of getting rid of an employee through layoffs or firing

A company invests time, effort, and money in each new employee it recruits and trains. This investment is lost when an employee is removed by **termination**—permanently laying the employee off because of cutbacks or firing the employee for poor performance. Many companies facing a downturn in business have avoided large-scale layoffs by cutting administrative costs (curtailing travel, seminars, and so on), freezing wages, postponing new hiring, implementing job-sharing programs, or encouraging early retirement. However, sometimes a company has no alternative but to reduce the size of its work force, leaving the human resources department to handle layoffs and their resulting effects on both the terminated and the remaining employees.

layoffs
Termination of employees for economic or business reasons

Layoffs   **Layoffs** are the termination of employees for economic or business reasons unrelated to employee performance. To help ease the pain of layoffs, many companies are now providing laid-off employees with job-hunting assistance. *Outplacement* aids such as résumé-writing courses, career counseling, office space, and secretarial help are offered to laid-off executives and blue-collar employees alike. For example, AT&T has seven career resource centers that help laid-off workers match their qualifications with more than 100,000 job leads from other companies. The centers offer courses and tests to help employees decide what types of jobs are best for them. AT&T also recently offered 4,000 laid-off managers $10,000 each to be used for retraining, relocation, or financing a small business.[39]

Some companies have adopted no-layoff, or guaranteed-employment, policies. In an economic downturn, employees may be shifted to other types of jobs, perhaps at reduced pay, or given the chance to participate in work-sharing programs. Such no-layoff policies help promote employee loyalty and motivation, which benefit the company over the long run. Rhino Foods realized the benefit of this policy when the company hit a downturn in the mid-1990s. Employees voluntarily took temporary jobs with other companies, which Rhino helped them find. If the new companies paid lower wages than the employees normally received, Rhino made up the difference. Employees also kept their Rhino seniority, benefits, and accrued vacation time. When business picked up again, the employees returned. As a result of the exchange program, Rhino enjoys much higher employee morale, loyalty, and trust than it would had it laid off workers.[40]

Firings and Employment at Will   It has long been illegal for any U.S. company to fire employees because they are would-be union organizers, have filed a job-safety complaint, or are of a particular race, religion, gender, or age. Beyond those restrictions, the courts have traditionally held that any employee not covered by a contract may be fired "at will." **Employment at will** is the right of the employer to keep or terminate employees as it sees fit. Recently, however, a number of legal decisions have begun to alter this doctrine. The most far-reaching decisions have held that there may be an implied contract between employer and employee requiring that any firing be done "fairly." **Wrongful discharge** suits—lawsuits that contend the employee was fired without adequate advance notice or explanation—have been plentiful in light of the massive layoffs in recent years. Some fired employees have even argued that their being called "permanent" employees by the company should protect them from firing—or at least from unfair firing. To combat this problem, many companies require employees to sign an "employment at will" statement acknowledging that they may be fired at any time at the company's discretion.

Retiring Employees

The U.S. population is aging rapidly. For the business community, an aging population presents two challenges. The first is to give job opportunities to people who are willing and able to work but who happen to be past the traditional retirement age. Many older citizens are concerned about their ability to live comfortably on fixed retirement incomes. Others simply prefer to work. For several decades, many companies and industries had **mandatory retirement** policies that made it necessary for people to quit working as soon as they turned a certain age. Then in 1967 the federal Age Discrimination in Employment Act outlawed discrimination against anyone between the ages of 40 and 65. In 1986 Congress amended the act to prohibit mandatory retirement for most employees. As a corollary, employers are also forbidden to stop benefit contributions or accruals because of age.

The second challenge posed by an aging work force is to find ways to encourage older employees to retire early. One method a company may use is to offer older employees financial incentives to resign, such as enhanced retirement benefits or one-time cash payments. Inducing employees to depart by offering them financial incentives is known as a **worker buyout.** This method can be a lot more expensive than firing or laying off employees. For example, the $10,000 incentive included in the buyout packages offered to the 4,000 AT&T managers would cost the company $40 million if they all accepted it. However, the method also has several advantages: The morale of the remaining employees is preserved because they feel less threatened about their own security, younger employees see a rise in their chances for promotion, and the risk of age-discrimination lawsuits is minimized.

employment at will
Employer's right to keep or terminate employees as it wishes

wrongful discharge
Firing an employee with inadequate advance notice or explanation

The number of U.S. workers over 65 has edged up during the past decade from 3 million to 3.8 million and is expected to rise to 4.3 million by 2005. In the meantime, the number of workers aged 25–44 is falling.

mandatory retirement
Required dismissal of an employee who reaches a certain age

worker buyout
Distribution of financial incentives to employees who voluntarily depart, usually undertaken in order to reduce the payroll

Summary of Learning Objectives

1. **List six main functions of human resources departments.**
Human resources departments plan for a company's staffing needs, recruit and hire new employees, train and develop employees, appraise employee performance, administer compensation and employee benefits, and oversee changes in employment status.

2. **Cite eight methods recruiters use to find job candidates.**
Recruiters find job candidates by (1) promoting internal candidates, (2) advertising in newspapers and on the Internet, (3) using public and private employment agencies, (4) contacting union hiring halls, (5) recruiting at college campuses and career placement offices, (6) attending trade shows, (7) hiring corporate

"headhunters," and (8) soliciting referrals from employees or colleagues in the industry.

3. **Identify the six stages in the hiring process.**
The stages in the hiring process are (1) narrowing down the number of qualified candidates, (2) performing initial screening interviews, (3) administering a series of follow-up interviews, (4) evaluating candidates, (5) conducting reference checks, and (6) selecting the right candidate.

4. **List seven popular types of employee incentive programs.**
The most popular employee incentive programs are bonuses, commissions, profit sharing, gain sharing, pay for performance, knowledge-based pay, and broadbanding.

MEETING BUSINESS CHALLENGES AT STARBUCKS

On the fast track toward global growth, the Starbucks chain transformed the ordinary cup of coffee into a wide variety of taste choices for millions of coffee lovers. Along the way, the company's astonishing success encouraged competitors to join the fray. Now expansion-minded companies like The Second Cup, Seattle's Best Coffee, and Barnie's were turning up the heat in the upscale coffee category. To stay on top, Starbucks managers had to ensure that their stores provided the best service along with the best coffee—which meant attracting, training, and compensating a diverse and dedicated work force.

Guided by the company mission statement, CEO Howard Schultz and his managers designed a variety of human resources programs especially for Starbucks partners (employees). In addition to offering good base pay, management bucked the trend in the industry by offering full medical, dental, life insurance, and disability insurance benefits to every partner who worked at least 20 hours per week. These partners were also eligible for paid vacation days and retirement savings plans, benefits not commonly available to part-time restaurant workers.

Another Starbucks innovation was Bean Stock, a program offering stock options not just to upper-echelon managers but to all partners who worked 20 or more hours per week. "We established Bean Stock in 1991 as a way of investing in our partners and creating ownership across the company," explained Bradley Honeycutt, vice president of human resource services. "It's been a key to retaining good people and building loyalty." For those who wanted to enlarge their financial stake in Starbucks, management devised a program that permitted partners to buy company stock at a discount. Owning a piece of the company motivated employees to take customer service to an even higher level of excellence.

Starbucks invested in its work force by providing new hires with 24 hours of training about the finer points of coffee brewing as well as the company's culture and values. To encourage more and better feedback and communication, management began holding a series of open forums in which company performance, results, and plans were openly discussed. They also instituted a program to honor employees whose achievements exemplified the company's values.

Helping partners better balance their work and family obligations was another priority for Starbucks. To accomplish this goal, the human resources department designed a comprehensive work-life program featuring flexible work schedules, access to employee assistance specialists, and referrals for child-care and elder-care support. In all, putting the focus on partners has helped Starbucks expand by attracting an energetic, committed work force and keeping turnover to a minimal 60 percent, much lower than the industry average.[41]

Critical Thinking Questions

1. Why do Starbucks' human resources managers need to be kept informed about any changes in the number and timing of new store openings planned for the coming year?

2. How does Starbucks benefit from using a part-time labor force?

3. How does Starbucks' liberal employee-benefits program help its employees balance their work and family obligations?

■ LEARN MORE ONLINE

Visit the job section of the company's Web site at http://www.starbucks.com/company/jobs/ to see how Starbucks presents its HR policies to potential employees. Browse the pages that discuss working at Starbucks. Read about company culture, diversity, benefits, and learning and career development. Why would Starbucks post information about company culture in this section of the Web site? Why would job candidates be interested in learning about the culture as well as the employee benefits and training at Starbucks?

5. **Highlight five popular employee benefits.**
The two most popular employee benefits are insurance (health, life, disability, and long-term care) and retirement benefits, such as pension plans that help employees save for later years. Employee stock-ownership plans and stock options, two additional benefits, allow employees to receive or purchase shares of the company's stock, and thus obtain a stake in the company. Family benefits programs, also popular, include maternity and paternity leave, child-care assistance, and elder-care assistance.

6. **Describe five ways an employee's status may change.**
An employee's status may change through promotion to a higher-level position, through reassignment to a similar or lower-level position, through termination (removal from the company's payroll), through voluntary resignation, or through retirement.

Key Terms

bonus (239)

broadbanding (240)

commissions (239)

compensation (238)

employee benefits (240)

employee stock-ownership plan (ESOP) (241)

employment at will (245)

gain sharing (239)

human resources management (HRM) (230)

incentives (239)

job analysis (233)

job description (233)

job specification (233)

knowledge-based pay (240)

layoffs (244)

mandatory retirement (245)

orientation (236)

pay for performance (239)

pension plans (241)

performance appraisal (237)

profit sharing (239)

recruiting (233)

salaries (238)

stock option plan (241)

termination (244)

wages (238)

worker buyout (245)

wrongful discharge (245)

Test Your Knowledge

QUESTIONS FOR REVIEW

1. What are some strategic staffing alternatives that organizations use to avoid overstaffing and understaffing?

2. What is the purpose of conducting a job analysis? What are some of the techniques used for gathering information?

3. What are some of the benefits and drawbacks to Internet recruiting?

4. What are the three types of preemployment tests administered by companies, and how is each of these tests used to assist with the hiring decision?

5. What functions do orientation programs serve?

QUESTIONS FOR ANALYSIS

6. How do incentive programs encourage employees to be more productive, innovative, and committed to their work?

7. Why do some employers offer comprehensive benefits even though the costs of doing so have risen significantly in recent years?

8. Several smaller companies outsource their human resources functions to professional HR management companies. What are some of the advantages and disadvantages of doing so?

9. The 1986 Immigration Reform and Control Act forbids companies to hire illegal aliens but at the same time prohibits discrimination in hiring on the basis of national origin or citizenship status. How can companies satisfy both requirements of this law?

10. Corporate headhunters have been known to raid other companies of their top talent to fill vacant or new positions for their clients. Is it ethical to contact the CEO of one company and lure him or her to join the management team of another company?

QUESTIONS FOR APPLICATION

11. If you were on the human resources staff at a large health-care organization that was looking for a new manager of information systems, what recruiting method(s) would you use and why?

12. Assume you are the manager of human resources at a manufacturing company that employs about 500 people. A recent cyclical downturn in your industry has led to financial losses, and top management is talking about

laying off workers. Several supervisors have come to you with creative ways of keeping employees on the payroll, such as exchanging workers with other local companies. Why might you want to consider this option?

13. ▮ Of the five levels in Maslow's hierarchy of needs, which is satisfied by offering salary? By offering health-care benefits? By offering training opportunities? By developing flexible job descriptions?

14. ▮ What are some of the human resources issues managers are likely to encounter when two companies (in the same industry) merge?

Practice Your Knowledge

SHARPENING YOUR COMMUNICATION SKILLS

Team up with a classmate to practice your responses to interview questions. Use the list of common interview questions provided in Exhibit A1.4 (see page 445) and take turns posing and responding to those questions. Which questions did you find most difficult to answer? What insights did you gain about your strengths and weaknesses by answering those questions? Why is it a good idea to rehearse your answers before going on an interview?

HANDLING DIFFICULT SITUATIONS ON THE JOB: BURGER MAKERS LEARN WHILE THEY EARN

Herb Schervish, owner of a Burger King in downtown Detroit, is worried about employee turnover. He needs to keep 50 people on his payroll to operate the outlet, but recruiting and retaining those people is tough. The average employee leaves after about seven months, which means that Schervish has to hire and train 90 people a year just to maintain a 50-person crew. At a cost of $1,500 per hire, the annual price tag for all that turnover is about $62,000.

Schervish knows that many employees quit because they think that flipping burgers is a dead-end job. But what if he offers to pay his employees' way through college if they remain with the store? Would that keep them behind the counter longer?

He's decided to give educational incentives a try. Employees who participate will earn their usual salary, but they will also get free books and college tuition, keyed to the number of hours they work each week. Those who work from 10 to 15 hours a week can take one free course at a nearby community college; those who work 16 to 25 hours can take two courses, and those who work 26 to 40 hours can take three courses. Schervish wants your advice about how to implement this voluntary program.[42]

1. Should Schervish pay only for employees who have worked at Burger King for six months or more to take courses? Why or why not?

2. Should Schervish publicize his educational program when recruiting? What effect do you think this program would have on his recruiting efforts?

3. How should Schervish handle payment for employees' tuition? If you recommend that he prepay for courses at the start of each semester, what should he do about employees who leave Burger King before the end of a course?

BUILDING YOUR TEAM SKILLS

How should the performance of a college or university instructor be evaluated? You and your team are going to design a performance appraisal form for this purpose. Working individually, generate a list of up to ten areas of performance that you would apply to this job, such as "knowledge of course material" and "communication skills." Compare your list with those of your teammates; discuss each item until your team has narrowed the focus to six basic criteria.

Now determine the rating system and period you will use. What would constitute an outstanding or unsatisfactory performance on the criteria you have set? How often do you think the performance of instructors should be evaluated?

In a presentation to the class, explain your team's ideas about areas of performance to be evaluated, performance ratings, and appraisal timing. What areas of performance were identified by other teams? Do you think all these areas are appropriate? Do you agree with the ratings and timing suggested by other teams? Why?

Expand Your Knowledge

EXPLORING CAREER OPPORTUNITIES

If you pursue a career in human resources, you'll be deeply involved in helping organizations find, select, train, evaluate, and retain employees. You have to like people and be a good communicator to succeed in HR. Is this field for you?

1. Using your local Sunday newspaper, the *Wall Street Journal,* or online sources such as Monster Board (http://www.monster.com), find ads seeking applicants for two or three of the HR jobs shown in Exhibit A2.5 (see page 452). What educational qualifications, technical knowl-

edge, or specialized skills are applicants for these jobs expected to have? How do these requirements fit with your background and educational plans?

2. Next, look at the duties mentioned in the ad for each job. What do you think you would be doing on an average day in these jobs? Does the work in each job sound interesting and challenging?

3. Now think about how you might fit into one of these positions. Do you prefer to work alone, or do you enjoy teamwork? How much paperwork are you willing to do? Do you communicate better in person, on paper, or by phone? Considering your answers to these questions, which of the HR jobs seems to be the closest match for your personal style?

DEVELOPING YOUR RESEARCH SKILLS

As you saw in Chapter 9, the work force is constantly changing. How are companies using human resources management to adapt to these changes? In the library or online, search through business magazines or HR publications to find an article about how a company changed its recruiting, selection, training, or compensation practices in response to work-force changes or employee needs. As you search, carefully note the sources and strategies you use.

1. What changes in the work force or employee needs caused the company to adapt? What did the company do to respond to these changes? Was the company's response voluntary or legally mandated?

2. Is the company alone in facing these changes, or is the entire industry trying to adapt? What are other companies in the industry doing to adapt to the changes?

3. What other changes in the work force or in employee needs do you think this company is likely to face in the next few years? Why?

SEE IT ON THE WEB EXERCISES
Staying on Top of the HR World, page 237

HR Live offers free online information about current human resources topics useful to more than just HR professionals. Visit the site at http://www.hrlive.com, take a look around, and respond to the following questions.

1. Click on the link to Markets and browse through some of the top recruiting markets for occupations that interest you. How might an HR manager with a growing company use this information to plan for recruiting new employees in the future? How might this information figure in senior management's decision about where to locate new facilities?

2. Click on Layoffs, and read one of the recent reports about a company that laid off employees. Why did the company lay off workers? How many were laid off, and over what time period?

3. Click on Reports and then on 'NetWorking to learn more about a survey on the use of the Internet in filling jobs. Read the executive summary for HR professionals. Are more HR professionals using the Internet to recruit this year than last year? What advantages and disadvantages are listed for this recruitment method?

Digging Deeper at the Bureau of Labor Statistics, page 238

The Bureau of Labor Statistics compiles data on workers, wages, employment, prices, and the economy in general. Explore the site at http://www.bls.gov to answer the following questions.

1. Click on Economy at a Glance. Look at the unemployment rate, average hourly earnings, and productivity for the past several months. What do these numbers say about the health of the economy?

2. From the main page, click on Surveys and Programs, then look for the link to Compensation and Working Conditions. Click to read one of the recent employee benefits surveys. How might this report be of use to HR professionals?

3. From the main page, click on Keyword Search of BLS Web Pages. Enter a search for "foreign labor statistics." When the results appear, scroll to the link to Foreign Labor Statistics Home Page. What kind of reports are available? How could HR managers use these reports?

Understanding Employee Ownership, page 241

The National Center for Employee Ownership (NCEO) provides valuable information about employee ownership programs. Find out more about this growing trend by visiting the NCEO's Web site at http://www.nceo.org, checking out some of the links, and answering these questions.

1. Read the brief introduction on the homepage, then click on the Interactive link to access the Interactive Introduction to ESOPs. What are the two types of ESOPs? How do they differ?

2. Still in the Interactive link, go to ESOP Nuts and Bolts to test your knowledge. Click on the topic link to see information if you're unsure of an answer. Are ESOPs usually accomplished through employee purchases or employer contributions?

3. Click on the Library link at the top, then scroll down to How ESOPs Work. Who is eligible to participate? How does vesting work?

Managing Human Resources and Labor Relations

Learning Objectives

1. See how a small company can effectively motivate its employees.
2. Understand the recruiting, hiring, and training challenges faced by a young business in a rapidly changing, high-tech industry.
3. Observe how a small business handles compensation and changes in employment status.

Background Information

Unless the business is a sole proprietorship, every company faces the twin tasks of motivating and managing employees. Employees are motivated by many factors, which means managers like Bruce Blausen of Blausen Medical Communications (BMC) need to consider ways of motivating different employees. Blausen, like other entrepreneurs, must also deal with a skilled-labor shortage, high stress on the job, and the drive for balance between work and family obligations. Careful recruiting, hiring, and training new employees allow companies to fill new positions during expansion and replace workers who leave. Once employees are on the job, their managers use periodic performance appraisals to objectively evaluate their performance. Appraisals help the company and the employee agree on areas for further development; in BMC, as in many other firms, managers also take appraisals into account when planning employee raises.

The Video

Managing and motivating employees is one of Bruce Blausen's main concerns. He rewards good work but is careful not to criticize or punish poor work, which might demoralize employees and prevent them from doing their best throughout a lengthy project. He also encourages employees to develop their skills by working on other types of projects, trying out new equipment, and staying abreast of new techniques in medical illustration and animation. As the founder, Blausen sometimes worked 100-hour weeks when he first started the business; now he spends the money to hire another employee instead of asking his staff to work more than 40 hours a week. In the course of recruiting and hiring new employees, Blausen sorts through a pile of résumés and holds a number of interviews to identify candidates who are qualified and genuinely interested in medical illustration. BMC is currently too small to have a vice president of human resources on staff, although Blausen plans to move someone into this position as the company grows.

Discussion Questions

1. What does Bruce Blausen do to improve the quality of work life for his employees?
2. Does Blausen appear to believe in Theory X or Theory Y? How do you know?
3. How has Blausen changed BMC's compensation and benefits over time? Why does he keep improving the compensation package?

Next Steps

Many companies are adopting alternative work arrangements to meet today's difficult staffing and demographic challenges. What are the advantages and disadvantages of offering flextime at BMC? What benefits would the company gain from allowing employees to telecommute? What problems might arise as a result of telecommuting at BMC? Under what circumstances might BMC agree to job sharing? What limitations might the firm place on the types of positions eligible for job-sharing arrangements—and why?

■ LEARN MORE ONLINE

Visit the BMC Web site and the sites of two competing firms you have identified. Browse several of the job openings posted on these sites looking for a listing that includes a job description or a job specification. How might a potential applicant use these statements when deciding whether to apply for a particular position? How can the companies use these statements when evaluating candidates for a particular position?

http://www.imagesofhealth.com/start.htm (BMC site)

Business Mystery

Natasha: Check out this Dave Duffield character. Did you know his employees were so enthralled with the business culture he established at PeopleSoft that they attached the company name to just about everything? Newborns were called "PeopleBabies," employees feasted on company-funded "PeopleSnacks," and they shopped at the company's "PeopleStore," which sold a variety of knickknacks with the PeopleSoft logo.

Nick: Sounds like overkill—especially the part about the company band, "The Raving Daves," named after CEO Duffield himself. Was this guy for real?

Natasha: Apparently so. His vision and leadership helped the company crank out record earnings one year after another. In fact, he made PeopleSoft one of the best places to work—until 1999, that is.

Nick: Yes, I remember that. The company posted another great year of sales in 1998 and then in early 1999 fired 6 percent of its workforce—430 employees were sent packing. What do you think happened, Natasha?

Natasha: Beats me. Look, here's a copy of the internal memo Duffield sent to employees announcing that he was searching for a new president to lead the company. Perhaps there are more clues in this file.

Nick: This looks like an interesting case to solve.

THE MYSTERY OF A COMPANY'S SALES GONE "SOFT"

David Duffield, a former IBM sales executive, sensed the coming boom in information-related software products—even before the Internet took off. To tap into the vast opportunity, Duffield founded PeopleSoft in 1987, launching one of the greatest success stories of the 1990s. One of the company's key products, enterprise resource planning (ERP) software, automates everything from manufacturing to human resources to payroll. Non-Internet based, it allows employees to share information by linking personal computers via a companywide internal computer network.

Duffield's hunch proved correct. Even at the lofty price of $1 million for the custom software, PeopleSoft could not keep up with customer demand. Going public in 1992 at an adjusted stock price of $1.81, the stock rose 32-fold over a six-year period. By 1998, revenue hit $1.3 billion, up 12-fold since 1994. Furthermore, at $54 a share, the company's stock had minted many stock-option millionaires.

From a managerial perspective, Duffield, an entrepreneur at heart, could do no wrong. He worked hard at developing an informal and sensitive corporate culture—one that emphasized caring and giving. "My focus has always been on innovation, making sure our customers are happy, and maintaining PeopleSoft's culture, which I view as a strategic asset," Duffield told the press. As a result, PeopleSoft's employees, which had grown from 914 in 1994 to over 7,000 in 1998, loved coming to work. Many worked 14 hours a day because this is what they wanted to do. Working at PeopleSoft was as good as it got.

Then in late 1998 the bottom fell out. In spite of Duffield's magic touch, sales of the company's software products came to a screeching halt, leaving the employees in "PeopleShock." Annual sales growth fell from 80 percent to zero. PeopleSoft's competitors' suffered, too. In fact, the entire ERP software industry was caught off guard.

Hoping to turn things around, Duffield stepped down as company president and hired Craig Conway in September 1999 to run the show. Then PeopleSoft acquired Vantive. But this high-flying maker of customer-relationship software suffered from its own internal difficulties: loss of market share, dismal earnings, and high personnel turnover, to name a few. Industry analysts and investors knew that two turkeys didn't make an eagle. But they were puzzled because the demand for software that facilitated the sharing of companywide information was indeed hot. So why had PeopleSoft's sales plummented?[43]

SOLVING THE MYSTERY OF A COMPANY'S SALES GONE "SOFT"

1. What did Duffield and others fail to see at the turn of the century that abruptly stopped PeopleSoft in its tracks?
   CLUE: WHAT TWO THINGS WERE COMPANIES FOCUSING ON AT THE TURN OF THE CENTURY THAT CONSUMED COMPANY RESOURCES?
2. Given Duffield's strong focus on maintaining an informal and sensitive corporate culture, which of the three leadership styles discussed in Chapter 6 do you think would best describe Duffield's actions? Support your answer.
3. Review the margin clues in Parts I through IV. What business principles did Duffield overlook?

11

MEETING CUSTOMERS' NEEDS IN THE CHANGING MARKETPLACE

LEARNING OBJECTIVES

After studying this chapter, you will be able to

1 Explain what marketing is

2 Highlight the benefits of learning about your customers

3 List five factors that influence the buyer's purchase decision

4 Outline the three steps in the strategic marketing planning process

5 Define market segmentation and review five factors used to identify segments

6 Identify the four basic components of the marketing mix

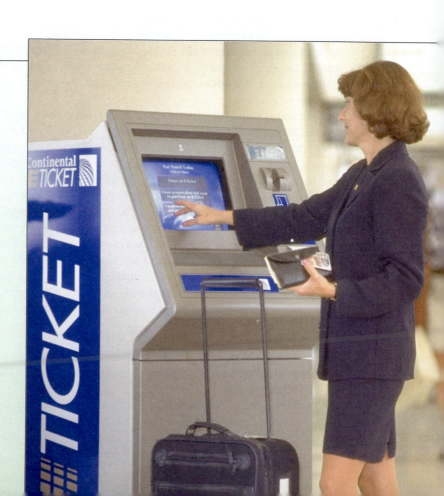

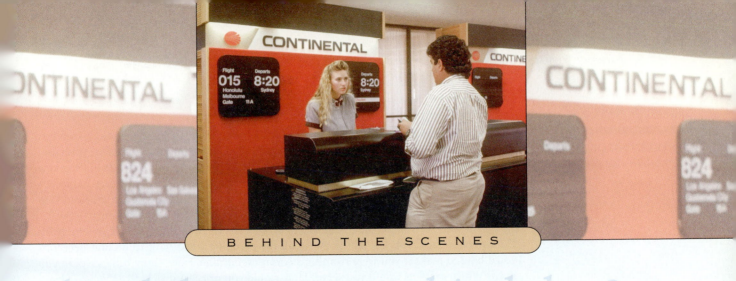

FACING BUSINESS CHALLENGES AT CONTINENTAL AIRLINES

Focus on Customer Guides Continental's Flight Plan for Success

When Gordon Bethune took the helm at Continental Airlines in 1994, the company ranked last on every measure of quality that mattered to customers—on-time performance, baggage handling, and customer service. In the previous decade, the company had burned through ten presidents and filed for bankruptcy twice. This prolonged turbulence was due, in part, to the airline's aggressive cost-cutting strategy, which eliminated the things customers cared about the most.

For example, the company pruned its frequent-flyer program because it cost too much. It discontinued first-class service on one-third of its U.S. flights and switched those planes to a new low-cost, low-fare subsidiary in an ill-fated attempt to compete with newer discount carriers. It cleaned all planes in 20 minutes, regardless of the appearance of the cabin. It eliminated food service on all flights under 2.5 hours to save $30 million per year. It even rewarded its pilots for fuel-saving measures such as cruising at economy speed. This practice caused many Continental flights to arrive late and ultimately cost the company an additional $6 million per month to accommodate passengers who missed their connections.

Angered by all these changes, 20 percent of the airline's regular customers fled to other carriers. Unfortunately, this valuable group accounted for 40 percent of Continental's revenue. Continental was in a steep tailspin—flying on autopilot—by the time Gordon Bethune became CEO. And employee morale was so low that maintenance workers ripped their company patches off their uniforms, ashamed to be identified with the carrier.

To address Continental's woes, Bethune devised a comprehensive, customer-focused "Go Forward Plan." His initial goal was on-time performance. "We figured that the most important thing to passengers was getting them where they were supposed to go on time," stated the CEO. To garner internal support for his plan, he promised employees a bonus for each month the airline was included among the top five carriers with the best on-time performance (according to the U.S. Department of Transportation). Within one month after the bonus was announced, Continental raised its performance ranking from seventh to fourth and was on a course toward becoming number one.

Next Bethune went after customer loyalty. He restored first-class service, upgraded meals, adjusted fares to be more affordable, and brought back the frequent-flyer program, with more relaxed rules. Even though Bethune's turnaround program had a smooth takeoff, he recognized that his work was not over. Rebuilding relationships with customers and reaching out to new ones was an ongoing challenge. To meet this challenge, Bethune would have to make more changes. But what? What else could he do to satisfy customers' changing needs? What customer groups should he target? What new marketing strategies should Continental adopt to keep the company flying high?[1]

253

◼ WHAT IS MARKETING?

LEARNING OBJECTIVE 1
Explain what marketing is

You probably already know quite a bit about marketing. People have been trying to sell you things for years, and you've learned something about their techniques—contests, advertisements, tantalizing displays of merchandise, price markdowns, and product giveaways, to name but a few. However, marketing involves much more than a fancy display of merchandise, a clever commercial, or a special contest. In fact, a lot of planning and execution are needed to develop a new product, set its price, get it into stores, and convince people to buy it.

The same is true for the marketing of services, as Gordon Bethune's experience with Continental Airlines shows. Think about all the planning you'd have to do and decisions you'd have to make if you were running a commuter airline. How many routes would you need? Which markets would you serve? How would you price your tickets? How would you get customers? What would you do if another commuter airline entered your market with substantially lower air fares? These are just a few of the many marketing decisions that companies must make in order to be successful. In fact, marketing is really an orderly and insightful process of thinking and planning. It involves understanding customers and their buying behaviors, analyzing the external forces that affect businesses, developing the best products, finding the most effective way to sell those products, creating consumer awareness, and outsmarting competitors.

marketing
Process of planning and executing the conception, pricing, promotion, and distribution of ideas, goods, and services to create and maintain relationships that satisfy individual and organizational objectives

The American Marketing Association (AMA) defines **marketing** as planning and executing the conception, pricing, promotion, and distribution of ideas, goods, and services to create exchanges that satisfy individual and organizational objectives.[2] Marketing involves all decisions related to determining a product's characteristics, price, production specifications, distribution, market-entry date, sales, and customer service. In fact, if you set out to personally handle all of a firm's marketing functions, you would be very busy indeed. In small companies, it's quite common for only one or two people to be responsible for all the marketing decisions. In larger organizations, however, the trend today is to involve cross-departmental teams of specialists from research to production to advertising—and even include the customers—in strategic marketing planning. As David Packard of Hewlett-Packard put it: "Marketing is too important to be left to the marketing department."[3]

Most people think of marketing in connection with selling tangible goods for a profit (the term *product* refers to any "bundle of value" that can be exchanged in a marketing transaction). But marketing applies to services, ideas, and causes as well. Continental Airlines has to market its flights. Politicians always market themselves. So do places like Paris or Portland, which want to attract residents, tourists, and business investment. **Place marketing** describes efforts to market geographical areas ranging from neighborhoods to entire countries. **Cause-related marketing** promotes a cause or a social issue—such as physical fitness, recycling, or highway safety.

place marketing
Marketing efforts to attract people and organizations to a particular geographical area

cause-related marketing
Identification and marketing of a social issue, cause, or idea to selected target markets

The Role of Marketing in Society

Take another look at the AMA definition of marketing. Notice that marketing involves an exchange between two parties—the buyer and the selling organization—both of whom must obtain satisfaction from the transaction. This definition suggests that marketing plays an important role in society by helping people satisfy their needs and wants and by helping organizations determine what to produce.

need
Difference between a person's actual state and his or her ideal state; provides the basic motivation to make a purchase

Needs and Wants   To survive, people need food, water, air, shelter, and clothing. A **need** represents a difference between your actual state and your ideal state. You're hungry and you don't want to be hungry; you need to eat. Needs create the motivation to buy products and are therefore at the core of any discussion of marketing.

Your **wants** are based on your needs but are more specific. Producers do not create needs, but they do shape your wants by exposing you to alternatives. For instance, when you need some food, you may want a Snickers bar or an orange. A fundamental goal of marketing is to direct the customer's basic need for various products into the desire to purchase specific brands. According to Al Ries and Jack Trout, co-authors of *The 22 Immutable Laws of Marketing,* customers' wants are directed by changing people's perception of products.[4] After all, what's the real difference between Viva and Bounty paper towels? Is one actually more absorbent than the other, or do you only perceive it that way?

Exchanges and Transactions   When you participate in the **exchange process,** you trade something of value (usually money) for something else of value, whether you're buying an airline ticket, a car, or a college education. When you make a purchase, you cast your vote for that item and encourage the producer of that item to make more of it. In this way, supply and demand are balanced, and society obtains the goods and services that are most satisfying.

When the exchange actually occurs, it takes the form of a **transaction.** Party A gives Party B $1.29 and gets a medium Coke in return. A trade of values takes place. Most transactions in today's society involve money, but money is not necessarily required. For example, when you were a child, you may have traded your peanut butter sandwich for a friend's bologna and cheese in a barter transaction that involved no money.

The Four Utilities   To encourage the exchange process, marketers enhance the appeal of their products and services by adding **utility,** something of value to customers (see Exhibit 11.1). When organizations change raw materials into finished goods, they are creating **form utility** desired by consumers. For example, when Nokia combines plastic, computer chips, and other materials to make digital phones, the company is providing form utility. In other cases, marketers try to make their products available when and where customers want to buy them, creating **time utility** and **place utility.** Overnight couriers such as Airborne Express create time utility, whereas coffee carts in offices and ATM machines in shopping malls create place utility. The final form of utility is **possession utility**—the satisfaction that buyers get when they actually possess a product, both legally and physically. First Union Mortgage, for example, creates possession utility by offering loans that allow people to buy homes they could otherwise not afford.

The Evolution of Marketing

The marketing function has changed significantly over the years. During the *production era* (which lasted until the 1930s), manufacturers were generally able to sell all that they produced. They relied on a good, solid product to sell itself, and they comfortably limited their

---

wants
Things that are desirable in light of a person's experiences, culture, and personality

exchange process
Act of obtaining a desired object from another party by offering something of value in return

transaction
Exchange between parties

utility
Power of a good or service to satisfy a human need

form utility
Consumer value created by converting raw materials and other inputs into finished goods and services

time utility
Consumer value added by making a product available at a convenient time

place utility
Consumer value added by making a product available in a convenient location

possession utility
Consumer value created when someone takes ownership of a product

---

UTILITY	EXAMPLE
Form utility	Sunkist Fun Fruits are nutritious, bite-sized snacks that appeal to youngsters because of their shapes—numbers, letters, dinosaurs, spooks, animals.
Time utility	LensCrafters has captured a big chunk of the market for eyeglasses by providing on-the-spot, one-hour service.
Place utility	By offering convenient home delivery of the latest fashion apparel and accessories, the Delia*s catalog and Web site have become favorites of teenaged girls.
Possession utility	RealNetworks, producer of software for listening to music from the Internet, allows customers to download and install its programs directly from the company's Web site.

EXHIBIT 11·1

EXAMPLES OF THE FOUR UTILITIES

The utility of a good or service has four aspects, each of which enhances the product's value to the consumer.

sellers' market
Marketplace characterized by a shortage of products

buyers' market
Marketplace characterized by an abundance of products

marketing concept
Approach to business management that stresses customer needs and wants, seeks long-term profitability, and integrates marketing with other functional units within the organization

marketing efforts to taking orders and shipping goods. In the production era, a **sellers' market** existed in many industries, meaning that demand for products exceeded supply.

Once technological advancements increased production capacity, however, the market for manufactured goods became more competitive. To stimulate demand for their products, firms spent more on advertising, but they still focused on selling whatever the company produced. Consequently, this period (1930s to 1950s) was labeled the *sales era*. It lasted until companies began facing a new challenge: an overabundance of products, or a **buyers' market**—that is, supply exceeded demand.

Faced with excess product, companies shifted from pushing whatever they produced on all consumers to finding out what buyers wanted and then filling that specific need. They became more customer-centered. This shift in focus began the *marketing era* that continues to develop and expand today.

Although some companies still operate with sales- or production-era values, most have adopted the **marketing concept.** They stress customer needs and wants; they concentrate on specific target markets; they seek long-term profitability; and they integrate the marketing function—that is, they hand marketing decisions over to cross-functional teams drawn from sales, advertising, product management, and other departments (see Chapter 12).[5] Companies that practice *permission marketing* take the marketing concept a step further by asking customers for permission before sending marketing messages. Continental Airlines, for example, invites travelers to sign up on its Web site for e-mailed air fare specials. Customers who give companies permission to send them e-mail announcements get more and better information about goods and services they really care about—and they tend to become loyal customers.[6]

How Technology Is Changing the Marketing Function

E-mail and Web sites are just two technological advances shaping marketing today. Just as mail-order catalogs changed the way companies sold products 100 years ago, Internet technology is opening a vast new channel for distributing tangible goods and intangible services worldwide. It's changing everything—the way we buy, sell, advertise, communicate with customers, and price products.

Other technologies are also changing the marketing function. Consider interactive *kiosks*. These small, free-standing electronic structures not only vend products and services but also provide marketers with the opportunity to find out more about customers' lifestyles, product preferences, and buying habits while introducing new products in dynamic ways.[7] Technology also means speedier, more convenient transactions. The Mobil

See It on the Web See It on the Web

FASTEN YOUR SEATBELT

Technology such as the Internet is changing the way consumers research and make purchases. Buying a car used to be a consumer headache, but going car shopping on the Internet is a breeze. Fasten your seatbelt and log on to CarSmart to get smart about car purchases. Imagine what you'll do with all this information when you enter the dealer's showroom. Will the salespeople be ready for you?
http://www.carsmart.com/autoadvr.htm

Speedpass, for example, is a tiny radio transmitter that attaches to a car window or a key chain and sends the user's credit card number to the gas station's computerized pump during a fuel stop.[8]

Technological advances also allow companies to give customers exactly what they want, when, where, and how they want it (as Component Chapter C discusses in detail). Companies can adapt their order entry, product design, production scheduling, manufacturing, inventory management, and product delivery to customize goods or services for individual customers at relatively low costs. For instance, Levi Strauss mass-customizes jeans by using an automated system to custom-cut the perfect fit once individual measurements and style preferences have been entered into the computer. In all, Levi's offers some 750 choices for customizing jeans—at a price slightly higher than that of ready-made jeans.[9]

Technology is also equalizing the marketplace. Small companies are using the Internet to reach potential customers all over the globe, and they are establishing databases to remember customers' favorite foods, authors, and clothing designers. Look at MiAmore Pizza and Pasta. This savvy, small company uses marketing databases to track customer purchases. If the regulars haven't stopped by in 60 days, this company's PC-based system generates a postcard to lure them back with a discount.[10]

THE IMPORTANCE OF UNDERSTANDING CUSTOMERS

LEARNING OBJECTIVE 2
Highlight the benefits of learning about your customers

According to management consultant Peter Drucker, "The aim of marketing is to know and to understand the customer so well that the product or service fits him and sells itself."[11] This is a challenge because customers today are sophisticated, demanding, quality-driven, and often difficult to understand. SkyMall, which sells gifts and other items through in-flight catalogs and the Web, got into trouble because it didn't really understand its customers. CEO Robert Worsley wanted to please customers by hand-delivering their in-flight purchases as soon as the airplane landed. This was a costly service, requiring large warehouses filled with inventory. As it turned out, however, customers, already burdened with luggage, were not eager to carry more packages. They enjoyed ordering from SkyMall while in the air, but they didn't want to pick up any packages on the ground.[13] Worsley's mistake was to offer costly extra services his customers didn't want.

 Even if you have your finger on your customers' pulse, if you don't make decisions quickly enough, you can be wiped out.[12]

SkyMall's experience shows that understanding customers is an important part of delivering quality and customer service. Whereas quality is the degree to which a product meets customer expectations and specifications, customer service encompasses everything a company does to satisfy its customers.[14] Consider how Virgin Atlantic treats people who fly first class from London to New York. These passengers have free car service at both ends of their trip; they can relax in the Virgin Clubhouse before boarding; and they can enjoy a massage while in the air.[15] Even though such perks may cost more, the payoff can be quite handsome. Satisfied customers are the best advertisement for a product. In addition, firms perceived to offer superior customer service find that they can charge as much as 10 percent more than their competitors.[16]

How do you balance giving customers what they want with keeping costs and operations under control? For many companies, including Continental Airlines, finding the right balance is a process of trial and error. Look at the $436 billion grocery industry, in which supermarkets were traditionally slow to respond to changing customer lifestyles. Threatened by new retail competitors and online grocery stores, supermarkets finally stepped up to the challenge. Many now offer freshly baked goods, takeout meals, eat-in restaurants, chef demonstrations, on-site banking, and home delivery. Still, as more customers try Streamline

Streamline field representatives like Dave Anderson do more than just deliver customers' groceries. This online grocery store (operating in Boston) picks up videos and dry cleaning, sells stamps, handles UPS shipments, and even collects returnable bottles and clothing donations for the homeless. "We're a one-stop solution for two-earner households," notes Timothy DeMello, founder and CEO.

and other Internet-based grocery stores, supermarkets will have to make further adjustments. Online shoppers want convenience; they are not being tempted by samples or displays, and they do not care whether their purchases come from a warehouse or a fancy store. In short, changes in consumer purchasing habits and lifestyles make it even more important for suppliers and retailers to understand their customers so they can satisfy them and keep them loyal.[17]

Satisfying Customers and Keeping Them Loyal

How do you know whether your customers are satisfied? One of the best ways to measure customer satisfaction is to analyze your customer base. Are you getting new customers? Are good ones leaving? What is your customer retention rate? In other words, are your customers loyal?

Many companies use customer satisfaction surveys to learn how happy their customers are with their products. However, if not carefully worded and administered, surveys can be misleading, as well as poor predictors of future buying behavior. For example, more than 90 percent of car buyers are either "satisfied" or "very satisfied" when they drive away from the dealer's showroom, but less than half wind up buying the same car the next time around.[18] In general, customer repurchase rates remain mired in the 30 to 40 percent range, and companies are finding that many satisfied customers don't come back. Plus, research shows that dissatisfied customers may tell as many as 20 other people about their bad experiences.[19]

No wonder so many companies put such a high priority on customer satisfaction. The software maker Intuit, for example, is so focused on customer satisfaction that every employee—including the president—spends a few hours each month working the customer-service phone lines. This intense focus helps Intuit make its Quicken program so user-friendly that customers are fiercely loyal. As one marketing consultant put it: "People would rather change their bank than switch from Quicken."[20]

Such customer loyalty is the exception, not the norm. On average, U.S. companies lose half their customers every five years. Why are customers less loyal today? First, they have more choices; more styles, options, services, and products are available than ever before. Second, customers have more information, from brochures, consumer publications, the Internet, and more, which empowers buyers and raises expectations. Third, when more and more products start to look the same, nothing stands out for customers to be loyal to. And fourth, time is scarce. If it's easier to buy gas at a different service station each week, customers will.[21] Furthermore, customer loyalty must be earned every day, because customer needs and buying habits change constantly (see Exhibit 11.2).

Despite these challenges, companies strive to keep their customers because acquiring a new customer can cost up to five times as much as keeping an existing one. Long-term customers buy more, take less of a company's time, bring in new customers, and are less price-sensitive.[22] That's why Hewlett-Packard, for example, guarantees 99.999 percent product reliability and availability. As a result, the company's customers are loyal and are willing to buying additional goods and services.[23] Companies such as A.T. Cross and Le Creuset satisfy customers and promote loyalty by offering extra-long product guarantees: Cross pens carry a lifetime guarantee, and Le Creuset cookware is guaranteed for 101 years.[24]

Nevertheless, not every customer is worth keeping. Some customers cost a great deal to service; others spend little but demand a lot. "We've gotten a lot smarter about separating the customers we do want from the customers we don't want," says C. Michael Armstrong, CEO of AT&T. Facing $500 million in yearly losses on the millions of customers who make few long-distance calls, AT&T routes customer service calls from low spenders to au-

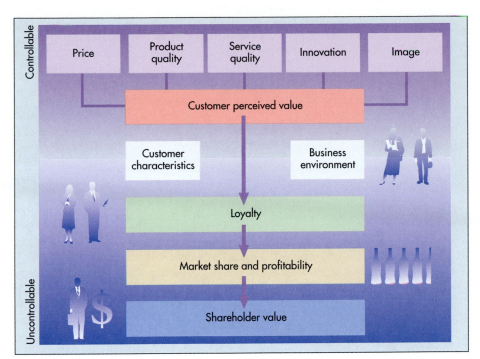

EXHIBIT 11·2

BEYOND CUSTOMER SATISFACTION

Satisfying the customer is no longer the ultimate business virtue. Companies today are looking for more and better ways of cementing customer loyalty to boost market share, profitability, and shareholder value.

tomated systems and lavishes human attention on higher-spending customers. The company also charges a minimum monthly fee, which customers must pay even when they make no long-distance calls in a given month.[25]

Building Relationships with Customers

One way companies keep customers coming back is by developing and maintaining close relationships with them. In the past, the relationship between customer and company often ended with the sales transaction. These days, however, it's more important to view the relationship as an ongoing process, not just a single transaction.[26] **Relationship marketing** is the process of building long-term satisfying relationships with key parties—customers, suppliers, distributors—in order to retain their long-term business.

Management expert Peter Drucker stresses that the most important sources of information for strategic decision making come from customers.[27] To tap into this valuable source of information, many companies today are using technology to engage in two-way, ongoing dialogues with customers through e-mail, Web pages, fax machines, and toll-free telephone numbers. Some are even involving their customers in the design and development of new products. For instance, Intuit's "follow-me-home" program sends company representatives home with Quicken buyers to observe them using the software for the first time. The representatives take notes and incorporate users' ideas in future software releases, making things easier for the next generation of first-time users.[28]

The Internet, of course, is a terrific vehicle for building relationships with customers. It brings the outside world closer and allows businesses to reach out and establish relationships with customers beyond their borders, find new suppliers, and market to the world. In addition, many companies are using the Internet to obtain support from vendors, collaborate on projects, answer customers' questions, test reaction to new products, sell products, and obtain customer feedback.

relationship marketing
A focus on developing and maintaining long-term relationships with customers, suppliers, and distributors for mutual benefit

For consumers, the Internet is a great way to find product information, check prices, and place orders—without going to a store. But as Component Chapter C points out, providing customers with these types of options shifts marketing control from sellers to buyers. As a result, attracting Web surfers and enticing them to stay and then buy is one of the biggest challenges online businesses now face. Many companies are meeting this challenge by using databases to gather as much information as possible about their customers' needs, preferences, and buying habits.

Using Databases to Learn About Customers

database marketing
Process of building, maintaining, and using customer databases for the purpose of contacting customers and transacting business

Database marketing is the actual recording and analysis of customer interactions, preferences, and buying behavior. Even though all customers share some common needs and characteristics, companies recognize that each customer has his or her own twist. By analyzing data collected on each customer's key attributes, companies can determine which customers to target, which to avoid, and how to customize marketing offers for the best response (see Exhibit 11.3).[29]

Allstate, for example, uses database marketing to amass huge amounts of data about applicants (credit reports, driving records, claims histories) in order to swiftly price a customer's insurance policy. Ritz Carlton records all customer requests, comments, and complaints in a worldwide database that now contains individual profiles of more than 500,000 guests. By accessing these profiles, employees at any Ritz Carlton hotel can accommodate the individual tastes of its customers from anywhere in the world.[30] Keep in mind that although database and relationship marketing are related, they are not the same. Database marketing is the act of gathering and analyzing customer information, whereas relationship marketing is the process of encouraging two-way communication between the company and the customer in order to build long-term relationships.

Some companies take database marketing a step further by gathering details about customer transactions, requests, and preferences from every department, adding external data such as market descriptions, and storing everything in computerized *data warehouses.* Through *data mining,* these companies analyze the data electronically and find meaningful patterns that lead the way to more effective, more targeted marketing. Wal-Mart's data warehouse, for example, contains five years of sales history plus data about weather patterns, local events, and other store-by-store information. The chain uses data mining to spot trends

EXHIBIT 11·3

TYPICAL DATABASE FOR CUSTOMERS' ORDERS

Designing a user-friendly database to record customer information is the key to building an effective database marketing program. The information from this simple order-entry screen will eventually be transferred to a customer history file so that the company can rank its customers by total dollars spent and other criteria.

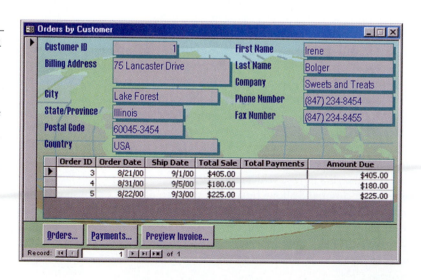

Customer ID	1	First Name	Irene
Billing Address	75 Lancaster Drive	Last Name	Bolger
		Company	Sweets and Treats
City	Lake Forest	Phone Number	(847) 234-8454
State/Province	Illinois	Fax Number	(847) 234-8455
Postal Code	60045-3454		
Country	USA		

Order ID	Order Date	Ship Date	Total Sale	Total Payments	Amount Due
3	8/21/00	9/1/00	$405.00		$405.00
4	8/31/00	9/5/00	$180.00		$180.00
5	8/22/00	9/3/00	$225.00		$225.00

Orders...   Payments...   Preview Invoice...

Record: |◄| ◄ | 1 | ► |►I|►*| of 1

Focus on E-Business

YOUR RIGHT TO PRIVACY VERSUS THE MARKETING DATABASES

Are all the details of your personal life really private? Consider this: Your bank knows your account balance, your credit history, and your mother's maiden name. Government agencies know how much money you made last year, the kind of car you own, and how many parking tickets you've gotten. Credit agencies know whom you owe money to, and how much. This list goes on and on, from video stores to insurance companies. Plus every time you enter your name in a registration field on the Web, or even click on a Web site, all sorts of data are being collected about you. By depositing "cookies" on your hard drive, Web marketers can follow your path and track the sites you visit. Right now, you are profiled in at least 25, and perhaps as many as 100, marketing databases.

Of course, there's nothing unethical about collecting data or maintaining a database. The ethical problems arise when marketers buy, borrow, rent, or exchange information, usually without your knowledge or permission. Who should have the right to see your records? The answer depends on where you live. In Europe, strict privacy regulations prevent companies from using data about individuals without asking permission and explaining how the data will be used. But in the United States and most other countries, marketers can easily buy information about who you are, where you live, how much you earn, and what you buy—for as little as a nickel. More Web marketers are posting privacy policies showing how they use personal data, but privacy advocates remain concerned, especially when sites collect information from children.

The consumer's right to privacy is an ongoing debate. Privacy advocates argue that people should have the right to be left alone, whereas marketers argue that they should have the right to freedom of speech—the right to inform customers about their offers. Thus, the ultimate dilemma: Do a marketer's needs and freedom of speech outweigh the consumer's right to privacy? What's your opinion?

QUESTIONS FOR CRITICAL THINKING

1. Should a marketer selling long-distance telephone service be allowed to see your telephone records without your knowledge or permission?
2. Should Web marketers be required to conspicuously post their privacy policies and ask consent before collecting and using visitors' personal data?

---

suggesting which products will sell in which stores, how much to stock, when to order or reorder, and even where to display merchandise. This is how Wal-Mart knows that Frito-Lay snacks sell well when set up next to a table of Star Wars and Teletubbies toys.[31] Data mining also helps companies understand consumer buying behavior. (Data warehousing and data mining are discussed further in Component Chapter C. Consult Part I of the E-Business in Action online supplement at http://www.prenhall.com/ebusinessinaction for additional discussion of Internet Privacy and Security.)

Analyzing Consumer Buying Behavior

Companies study **consumer buying behavior** to understand what induces individuals to buy. **Marketing research**—the process of gathering and analyzing information about customers, markets, and related marketing issues—is one tool companies use to analyze

consumer buying behavior
Behavior exhibited by consumers as they consider and purchase various products

marketing research
The collection and analysis of information for making marketing decisions

Marketing surveys are a common way of gathering data directly from consumers.

cognitive dissonance
Anxiety following a purchase that prompts buyers to seek reassurance about the purchase; commonly known as *buyer's remorse*

LEARNING OBJECTIVE 3
List five factors that influence the buyer's purchase decision

consumer buying behavior. For instance, when Israeli-based Sky Is the Ltd. needed to know where and how U.S. consumers buy crackers, its executives researched the behavior of U.S. shoppers. After conducting marketing research studies, they found that the firm's little-known brand would get lost among the sea of crackers on supermarket shelves but could attract some attention in gourmet food stores.[32] Similarly, Nabisco, Nintendo, the Gap, Ford, and other businesses use marketing research to better understand the buyer's decision process and factors that influence buying behavior.

The Buyer's Decision Process Suppose you want to buy a car. Do you rush to the dealer, plunk down money, and buy the first car you see? Of course not. Like most buyers, you go through a decision process, outlined in Exhibit 11.4, that begins with identifying a problem, which in this case is the need for a car. Your next step is to look for a solution to your problem. Possibilities occur to you on the basis of your experience (perhaps you recently drove a certain car) and on your exposure to marketing messages. If none of the obvious solutions seems satisfying, you gather additional information. The more complex the problem, the more information you are likely to seek from friends or relatives, magazines, salespeople, store displays, and sales literature.

Once you have all the information in hand, you are ready to make a choice. You may select one of the alternatives, such as a new Chevy Blazer or a used Ford Explorer. You might even postpone the decision or decide against making any purchase at all, depending on the magnitude of your desire, the outside pressure to buy, and your financial resources. If you decide to buy, you will evaluate the wisdom of your choice. If the item you bought is satisfying, you might buy the same product again under similar circumstances, thus developing a loyalty to the brand. If it is not satisfying, you will probably not repeat the purchase.

If the purchase was a major one, you will sometimes suffer from **cognitive dissonance,** commonly known as buyer's remorse. You will think about all the alternatives you rejected and wonder whether one of them might have been a better choice. At this stage, you're likely to seek reassurance that you have done the right thing. Realizing this tendency, many marketers try to reinforce their sales with guarantees, phone calls to check on the customer's satisfaction, user hot lines, follow-up letters, and so on. Such efforts help pave the way for repeat business.

Factors That Influence the Buyer's Decision Process Throughout the buying process, various factors may influence a buyer's purchase decision. An awareness of the following factors and consumer preferences enables companies to appeal to the group most likely to respond to its products and services:

- *Culture.* The cultures and subcultures people belong to shape their values, attitudes, and beliefs and influence the way people respond to the world around them.

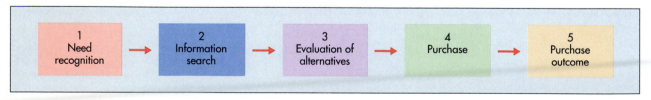

EXHIBIT 11·4

THE CONSUMER DECISION PROCESS
Consumers go through a decision-making process that can include up to five steps.

Understanding culture is therefore an increasingly important step in international business and in marketing to diverse populations within a country such as the United States.

- *Social class.* In addition to being members of a particular culture, people also belong to a certain social class—be it upper, middle, lower, or somewhere in between. In general, members of various classes pursue different activities, buy different goods, shop in different places, and react to different media.

- *Reference groups.* A reference group consists of people who have a good deal in common: family members, friends, co-workers, sports enthusiasts, music lovers, computer buffs. Individuals are members of many such reference groups, and they use the opinions of the appropriate group as a benchmark when they buy certain types of goods or services. For example, shopping malls are starting to lose what has long been their most faithful audience—teens. That's because many of today's teenagers think that malls are for parents and that malls have too many rules. So some retailers, including Urban Outfitters and Tower Records, refuse to open stores in most malls.[33]

- *Self-image.* The tendency to believe that "you are what you buy" is especially prevalent among young people. Marketers capitalize on people's need to express their identity through their purchases by emphasizing the image value of goods and services. That's why professional athletes and musicians frequently appear as product endorsers—so that consumers will incorporate part of these celebrities' public image into their own self-image.

- *Situational factors.* These factors include events or circumstances in people's lives that are more circumstantial but that can influence buying patterns. Such factors might include having a coupon, being in a hurry, celebrating a holiday, being in a bad mood, and so on.

Keep in mind that the buying behaviors of *organizational* and *consumer markets* differ considerably. The **organizational market** is made up of three main subgroups: the industrial/commercial market (companies that buy goods and services to produce their own goods and services, such as Toyota), the reseller market (wholesalers such as Ingram Micro, which wholesales computers, and retailers such as Fashion Bug, which sells women's clothing), and the government market (federal, state, and local agencies such as the state of Texas and the city of Dallas).[34]

organizational market
Customers who buy goods or services for resale or for use in conducting their own operations

Organizations buy raw materials (grain, steel, fabric) and highly technical and complex products (printing presses, management consultation, buildings). They also buy many of the same products that consumers do— such as food, paper products, cleaning supplies, and landscaping services—but they generally purchase larger quantities and use a more complex buying process. By contrast, the **consumer market** consists of individuals or households that purchase goods and services for personal use. In most cases, consumers purchase smaller quantities of items and use a process similar to the one outlined in Exhibit 11.3.

consumer market
Individuals or households that buy goods or services for personal use

■ HOW TO PLAN YOUR MARKETING STRATEGIES

By now you can see why successful marketing rarely happens without carefully analyzing your customers. Once you have learned about your customers, you're ready to begin planning your marketing strategies. *Strategic marketing planning* is a process that involves three steps: (1) examining your current marketing situation, (2) assessing your opportunities and setting your objectives, and (3) developing a marketing strategy to reach those objectives (see Exhibit 11.5).

LEARNING OBJECTIVE 4
Outline the three steps in the strategic marketing planning process

EXHIBIT 11·5

THE STRATEGIC
MARKETING PLANNING
PROCESS

Strategic marketing planning
covers three steps:
(1) examining your current
marketing situation,
(2) assessing your
opportunities and setting
objectives, and
(3) developing your
marketing strategy.

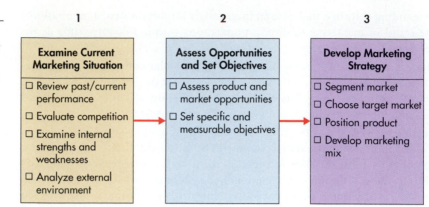

1

**Examine Current
Marketing Situation**

☐ Review past/current
performance

☐ Evaluate competition

☐ Examine internal
strengths and
weaknesses

☐ Analyze external
environment

2

**Assess Opportunities
and Set Objectives**

☐ Assess product and
market opportunities

☐ Set specific and
measurable objectives

3

**Develop Marketing
Strategy**

☐ Segment market

☐ Choose target market

☐ Position product

☐ Develop marketing
mix

The purpose of strategic marketing planning is to help you identify and create a competitive advantage, something that sets you apart from your rivals and makes your product more appealing to customers.[35] Most companies record the results of their planning efforts in a document called the *marketing plan*. Here's a closer look at the three steps in the process.

Step 1: Examining Your Current Marketing Situation

Examining your current marketing situation is the first step in the strategic marketing planning process; it includes reviewing your past performance (how well each product is doing in each market where you sell it), evaluating your competition, examining your internal strengths and weaknesses, and analyzing the external environment. The complexity of this step depends on the complexity of your business. Whereas giant multinational firms such as Xerox and Nestlé have to examine the current marketing situation for dozens of product lines and geographical divisions, smaller firms, such as individual Jiffy-Lube franchises, have far fewer products to think about.

Reviewing Performance   Unless you're starting a new business, your company has a history of marketing performance. Maybe sales have slowed in the past year; maybe you've had to cut prices so much that you're barely earning a profit; or maybe sales are going quite well and you have money to invest in new marketing activities. Reviewing where you are and how you got there is critical, because you will want to repeat your successes and learn from your past mistakes.

 Failure to forecast competitive reaction is a major cause of marketing failures.[36]

Evaluating Competition   In addition to reviewing past performance, you must also evaluate your competition. If you own a Burger King franchise, for example, you need to watch what McDonald's and Wendy's are doing. You also have to keep an eye on Taco Bell, KFC, Pizza Hut, and other restaurants in addition to paying attention to any number of ways your customers might satisfy their hunger—including fixing a sandwich at home. Furthermore, you need to watch the horizon for competitors that do not yet exist, such as the next big food craze.

Examining Internal Strengths and Weaknesses   Besides reviewing past performance and evaluating competition, successful marketers identify and examine their internal strengths and weaknesses. In other words they look at such things as management, financial resources, production capabilities, distribution networks, managerial expertise, and promotional capabilities. Next, they try to identify sources of competitive advantage or areas that need improvement. This step is important because you can't develop a successful marketing strategy if you don't know your strengths as well as your limitations. On the basis of your internal analysis, you will be able to decide whether your business should (1) limit itself to those opportunities for which it possesses the required strengths or (2) challenge itself to reach higher goals by acquiring and developing new strengths.

Understanding your strengths and weaknesses is especially important when evaluating the merits of global expansion. Selling products overseas requires not only managerial expertise and financial resources but also the ability to adjust your operation to different cultures, customs, legal requirements, and product specifications. Even selling on the Internet requires technological expertise and commitment as well as a thorough understanding of customer buying behavior.

Analyzing the External Environment   Marketers must also analyze a number of external environment factors when planning their marketing strategies. These factors include:

- *Economic conditions.* Marketers are greatly affected by trends in interest rates, inflation, unemployment, personal income, and savings rates. In tough times, consumers put off buying expensive items such as major appliances, cars, and homes. They cut back on travel, entertainment, and luxury goods. When the economy is good, consumers open their wallets and satisfy their pent-up demand for higher-priced goods and services.

- *Natural environment.* Changes in the natural environment can affect marketers, both positively and negatively. Interruptions in the supply of raw materials can upset even the most carefully conceived marketing plans. Floods, droughts, and cold weather can affect the price and availability of many products as well as the behavior of target customers.

- *Social and cultural trends.* Planners also study the social and cultural environment to determine shifts in consumer values. If social trends are running against a product, the producer might need more advertising to educate consumers about the product's benefits. After Campbell Soup saw its sales of condensed soups slump, it began running commercials and posting Web pages about the benefits of soup as a cooking ingredient.[37] Alternatively, businesses may have to modify their products to respond to changing tastes. Shiseido, for example, changed its nail polish line after studying what Japanese teens were using.[38]

- *Laws and regulations.* As is every other function in business today, marketing is controlled by laws at the local, state, national, and international levels. From product design to pricing to advertising, virtually every task you'll encounter in marketing is affected in some way by laws and regulations. For example, the Nutritional Education and Labeling Act of 1990 forced marketers to put standardized nutritional labels on food products. Although this regulation cost manufacturers millions of dollars, it was a bonanza for food-testing laboratories.

- *Technology.* When technology changes, so must your marketing. Look at Toys 'R' Us, which was slow to respond when eToys set up shop on the Internet. By the time Toys 'R' Us opened its own Web site, it was way behind eToys: during one recent December, eToys drew three times more Web visitors than Toys 'R' Us. "Being a land-based brand is becoming a handicap" in the world of online marketing, says the CEO of eToys.[39]

Keep in mind, however, that marketers must not only keep on top of today's external environment but must also think about tomorrow's changes. Coke is an example of a company that is staying ahead of the curve with technology. Each of its 800,000 vending

Successful companies **recognize that the marketing environment is constantly spinning new opportunities and threats; they understand the importance of continuously monitoring and adapting to the changing environment.**[40]

See It on the Web See It on the Web

FETCH IT!

Thinking about starting a new business? You'll need to do a lot of research to plan your marketing strategies. One of the quickest ways to search the Internet for information is by querying a metasearch engine such as *Dogpile.* Metasearch engines search several popular search engines with one click. Simply enter your search phrase or key terms and then click "fetch" to send this hound hunting.

http://www.dogpile.com

machines in Japan has an embedded computer chip. This chip can be used to record the number of cans left, the number of times a button was pressed for an item out of stock, and the time of day when purchases are highest. Looking ahead, Coke may use this chip to calculate the optimal product mix for each machine.[41]

Step 2: Assessing Your Opportunities and Setting Your Objectives

Once you've examined your current marketing situation, you're ready to assess your marketing opportunities and set your objectives. Successful companies are always on the lookout for new marketing opportunities, which can be divided into four groups: (1) selling more of your existing products in current markets, (2) creating new products for your current markets, (3) selling your existing products in new markets, and (4) creating new products for new markets.[42] These four groups are listed in order of increasing risk; trying new products in unfamiliar markets is usually the riskiest choice of all.

With opportunities in mind, you are ready to set your marketing objectives. A common marketing objective is to achieve a certain level of **market share,** which is a firm's portion of the total sales within a market. Objectives must be specific and measurable. Establishing a goal to "increase sales in the future" is not a good objective; it doesn't say by how much or by what date. On the other hand, a goal to "increase sales 25 percent by the end of next year" provides a clear target and a reference against which progress can be measured. Objectives should also be challenging enough to be motivating. As CEO Mitchell Leibovitz of the Pep Boys auto parts chain says: "If you want to have ho-hum performance, have ho-hum goals."[43] Whatever objectives you set, be sure all employees know and understand what the organization wants to accomplish. Every Ritz Carlton employee, for example, attends a daily 15-minute meeting in which managers reiterate the hotel chain's business goals and commitment to customer service.[44]

Step 3: Developing Your Marketing Strategy

Using your current marketing situation and your objectives as your guide, you're ready to move to the third step. This is where you develop your **marketing strategy,** which consists of dividing your market into *segments* and *niches,* choosing your *target markets* and the *position* you'd like to establish in those markets, and then developing a *marketing mix* to help you get there.

Dividing Markets into Segments and Niches A **market** contains all the customers or businesses who might be interested in a product and can pay for it. Most companies subdivide the mar-

market share
A firm's portion of the total sales in a market

marketing strategy
Overall plan for marketing a product

market
People or businesses who need or want a product and have the money to buy it

ket in an economical and feasible manner by identifying *market segments,* homogeneous groups of customers within a market that are significantly different from each other. This process is called **market segmentation;** its objective is to group customers with similar characteristics, behavior, and needs. Each of these market segments can then be targeted by offering products that are priced, distributed, and promoted differently for each segment—a practice known as *differentiated marketing.* By contrast, some companies practice *undifferentiated marketing.* That is, they ignore differences among buyers and offer only one product or product line to satisfy the entire market.

Here are five factors marketers frequently use to identify market segments:

- *Demographics.* When you segment a market using **demographics,** the statistical analysis of population, you subdivide your customers according to characteristics such as age, gender, income, race, occupation, and ethnic group. *People en Español,* for example, is targeted to the Hispanic-American segment.[45] Be aware, however, that according to recent studies, demographic variables are poor predictors of behavior.[46]

- *Geographics.* When differences in buying behavior are influenced by where people live, it makes sense to use **geographic segmentation.** Segmenting by geography can help companies decide where to sell products. For instance, Campbell Soup makes two types of nacho cheese sauce: spicy for customers in the Southwest and West and mild for everyone else.[47]

- *Psychographics.* Whereas demographic segmentation is the study of people from the outside, **psychographics** is the analysis of people from the inside, focusing on their psychological makeup, including activities, attitudes, interests, opinions, and lifestyle. Psychographic analysis focuses on why people behave the way they do by examining such issues as brand preferences, media preferences, reading habits, values, and self-concept.

- *Geodemographics.* Dividing markets into distinct neighborhoods by combining geographical and demographic data is the goal of **geodemographics.** The geodemographic system developed by Claritas Corporation divides the United States into 40 neighborhood types, with labels such as "Blue Blood Estates" and "Old Yankee Rows." This system, known as PRIZM, uses postal ZIP codes for the geographic segmentation part, making it easy to use specialized marketing programs to reach people in targeted neighborhoods.[48]

- *Behavior.* Markets can also be segmented according to customers' knowledge of, attitude toward, use of, or response to products or product characteristics. This

market segmentation
Division of total market into smaller, relatively homogeneous groups

LEARNING OBJECTIVE 5
Define market segmentation and review five factors used to identify segments

demographics
Study of statistical characteristics of a population

geographic segmentation
Categorization of customers according to their geographical location

psychographics
Classification of customers on the basis of their psychological makeup

geodemographics
Method of combining geographical data with demographic data to develop profiles of neighborhood segments

See It on the Web See It on the Web

DEMOGRAPHICS FOR YOUR MARKETING TOOLBOX

How much does the typical family spend on food away from home? On entertainment? Are these consumer expenditures increasing each year? Find out by visiting the American Demographics Marketing Tools Web site and explore its toolbox of useful information. Read some of the current marketing articles. Follow the link to the Bureau of Labor Statistics (BLS) Web site. With all these sources, no wonder marketers today have more and better data about their customers.
http://www.marketingtools.com

behavioral segmentation
Categorization of customers according to their relationship with products or response to product characteristics

approach is known as **behavioral segmentation.** Web-based BizTravel knows that business travelers have definite preferences and attitudes toward airlines, hotels, pricing, and schedules. So when a customer logs on to plan a trip, BizTravel's automated system is set up to recommend a customized itinerary based on that customer's previous choices and purchases.[49]

When you segment your market, you end up with several customer groups, each representing a potentially productive focal point for marketing efforts. However, keep in mind that a single segment includes customers with a variety of needs. For example, people from the same neighborhood may purchase Colgate toothpaste, but some will buy it for its flavor, others because it prevents decay, and others because it has whiteners. One way to recognize such differing needs is to segment your market into *niches.*[50]

Niche marketing takes segmentation one step further by dividing a market segment into microsegments. For example, offering an all-purpose athletic shoe is an example of servicing a market segment, whereas producing different kinds of athletic shoes—running,

MOVE OVER, BOOMERS AND GEN XERS: HERE COMES GENERATION Y

Coca-Cola is out, Mountain Dew is in; Estee Lauder is out, Hard Candy is in; Levi Strauss is out, Tommy Hilfiger is in. That's the brand assessment of Generation Y, the 60 million people in the United States born between 1979 and 1994. Generation Y is a smaller segment than the 72 million baby boomers (their grandparents' generation) but triple the size of Generation X. And this gigantic market segment has enormous buying power: They spend a whopping $150 billion annually on their own and influence household spending by another $500 billion. Given such attractive demographics, it's not surprising that marketers are racing to identify opportunities for hooking these younger consumers while they are still making up their minds about brands.

But reaching these consumers can be a daunting challenge. Studies show that traditional marketing tactics that clicked with baby boomers and Generation Xers are not the way to reach Generation Y. This techno-savvy segment, also known as the Net Generation, relies on the Internet to keep up with the latest styles and fads and to find out about goods and services. "If a company can't communicate via e-mail, the attitude is, 'What's wrong with you?'" observes John R. Samuel, director of interactive marketing at American Airlines. Reaching out to the college market, American has begun a special e-mail-only program to communicate information about discounted airfares to students who register for the service.

Like American, more and more businesses are using updated marketing tactics that mesh much better with Generation Y attitudes and lifestyles. "As a brand, you need to go where they are, not just pick a fashion statement, put it on TV, and wait for them to come to you," says the president of the Lee Apparel brand. But because the buying behavior of this market segment changes at the blink of a cursor, Lee and other marketers keep a close watch on trends that signal new opportunities for reaching Generation Y consumers.

QUESTIONS FOR CRITICAL THINKING

1. The Generation Y marketing segment can be identified by using which of the five popular marketing segmentation factors?

2. How are social and cultural trends in the external environment likely to influence marketing plans that target Generation Y?

Nick & Natasha Business Mysteries

Meet Nick and Natasha, two business detectives, who are trying to solve a series of business mysteries. They want to know why, when some companies appear to be doing everything right, they surprisingly stumble or fall. After several months of investigation, the detectives are beginning to notice a pattern. It appears that in each of the case files they have reviewed to date, the company they are investigating has violated at least one fundamental principle of business. One tiny slip up, one bad move, is all it took— at least that's what the evidence is showing.

Now Nick and Natasha need your students' help. Your students will review their case files—seven companies in total—and help them identify the fundamental principle(s) of business that each of these companies has violated. To assist students in solving these mysteries, the authors have left some clues. Students will have to put all the clues together to solve each mystery.

Fore more examples please see pages 77, 128, 203, 251, etc……

Business Mystery

Nick: Hey Natasha, did you know there are over 7.5 million transistors in an Intel Pentium computer chip and that the company chairman, Andy Grove, expects to deliver chips packed with a cool one billion transistors by 2011?

Natasha: Sounds pretty fast to me. Wasn't Andy Grove the genius responsible for changing Intel's direction from making memory chips to producing microprocessors back in the 1980s?

Nick: Yes, and he was also part of the team responsible for slapping "Intel Inside" stickers on computers, a move that helped turn Intel into the eighth most profitable company in the world.

Natasha: So if he's got such foresight, why do you have that puzzled look, Nick?

Nick: Here's what I don't get. After a decade of selling high-priced fast, faster, and fastest microprocessor chips and watching the profits roll in, now Intel wants to be like everybody else. The company is heading downstream, slashing chip prices faster than day-old bakery goods.

Natasha: Sounds like the company is trying to play catch up. You know, I just bought a really swift computer last month for less than $1000—monitor, CD player, and the works. Now that I think about it, I'm pretty sure there wasn't an "Intel Inside." I wonder why.

Nick: Let's see if we can find the answers.

THE MYSTERY OF A SPEED DEMON CAUGHT FLAT FOOTED

For years, Intel had a business model that was its ticket to success. Every nine months or so the company would build a new $2 million state-of-the-art factory (or "fab") to manufacture the next generation of microprocessor chips. Of course, each new fab was a bet that consumers would want the fastest, most powerful computer chip to run newer, speedier computers jammed with all the latest features, including upgraded versions of popular software. And they did.

But owning the fast lane required Intel to build the fabs two years in advance of needing them—a risky venture, indeed. To fund the construction, the company sold new processors at sky-high prices. Customers didn't care, however. Those who wanted the fastest machines were willing to pay the premium. Others would wait a year or two until these machines were superseded by yet faster ones, and then they would purchase the older models at more affordable prices. And so the cycle continued: Build a fab, sell latest chips at a premium, discount yesterday's chip, plow profits into a new fab, start the cycle again. Competitors couldn't even come close to perfecting this model. As long as customers wanted chips with more functions and more speed to do some very cool things, it was almost impossible to make a dent in Intel's lock on the high-end market.

So competitors focused their resources in a different direction. Several lower-tier PC makers began to hawk personal computers priced below $1000. Intel wasn't concerned, however. Referring to them as "Segment Zero," or a dumping ground for inventory close-outs, the king of chips held to the high ground, pushing pricey chips at juicy profits. But when Compaq joined the sub-$1000 market with its highly touted Presario model, the market changed overnight.

Soon, lower-priced PCs captured 5 percent of unit sales in the United States. Intel was caught flat-footed. Because Intel's chips were far too expensive for the new sub-$1000 machines, PC manufacturers turned to competitors Advanced Micro Devices (AMD) and Cyrix for affordable chips. Reacting quickly, Intel developed Celeron. But this new chip got poor reviews, and Intel initially priced it too high. After all, cheap chips hadn't been figured into Intel's business model for success. But neither was it walking away from a market whose size promised to be at least tens of millions of units a year. Eventually, though, Intel got it right. Aggressive marketing and steep price cuts in the Celeron chip delivered big market share gains to Intel and forced some rivals to withdraw from the market. Now Intel would have to count on higher sales volume to compensate for the thinner profit margins of low-priced chips. And that's a risky business—even for this speed demon.[60]

SOLVING THE MYSTERY OF A SPEED DEMON CAUGHT FLAT-FOOTED

1. Why did customers change their buying habits overnight? What did Intel fail to see that others saw clearly?
   CLUE: HOW WAS THE PRIMARY FUNCTION OF PCS CHANGING DURING THE 1990s?

2. Intel has invested more than $500 million in new companies that create the latest computer software or Internet-related products. Why wouldn't Intel use that money to build a new factory instead?
   CLUE: THINK ABOUT THE FORCES OF SUPPLY AND DEMAND.

3. Look back at the margin clues in Part 1 of this textbook. What business principles did Intel overlook?

tennis, aerobics, and so on—is an example of niche marketing. Of course, some companies, such as General Motors, aim their marketing efforts at multiple segments by manufacturing a variety of products that appeal to different customer types; others, such as Logitech, focus on a single segment—a practice known as *concentrated marketing*. Logitech has built a $450 million global business focusing only on specialized devices such as mice and keyboards for computer users.[51]

One-to-one marketing reduces market segmentation and niches to the tiniest segment—the individual. Because one-to-one marketing requires a thorough understanding of each customer's preferences and a detailed history of each customer's interactions with the company, the payoff is often increased customer loyalty: The more time and energy a customer spends in teaching a firm about his or her own tastes, the more trouble it will be for the customer to obtain the same level of customized service from a competitor.[52]

Technology, of course, is a critical component of one-to-one marketing. It allows businesses of all sizes to individualize their marketing efforts. One good example is the Custom Foot store in Connecticut, which invites customers to select a shoe style, pick a color, and have their feet measured with a computerized scanner. This information is then entered into a computer and used to make custom shoes that fit the individual perfectly—even if one foot is larger than the other.[53] Another example is CDuctive, an Internet music retailer that allows customers to browse categories of dance-club tunes, listen to samples, and order CDs customized with their choice of songs. This completely automated yet personalized approach helps CDuctive compete with online rivals such as CDnow and Tower.[54]

Choosing Your Target Markets   Once you have segmented your market, the next step is to find appropriate *target segments* or **target markets** to focus your efforts on. Deciding exactly which segment to target—and when—is not an easy task. Sometimes the answer will be obvious, such as when you lack the necessary technological skills or financial power to enter a particular market segment. At other times, you'll have the resources to compete in several segments but not enough resources to compete in all of them. In general, marketers use a variety of criteria to narrow their focus to a few suitable market segments. These criteria can include size of segment, competition in the segment, sales and profit potential, compatibility with company resources and strengths, costs, growth potential, and risks.[55]

Targeting is such a critical part of strategic marketing that missteps can be costly, as Motorola found out. The company stayed focused on the traditional cell phone market segment long after rivals Nokia and Ericsson had expanded into the digital phone segment. Furthermore, Motorola didn't respond when it was asked to develop digital phones for AT&T's digital network. By the time Motorola began to work on digital phones, its competitors had grabbed market share and brand loyalty in that fast-growing segment.[56]

Positioning Your Product   Regardless of the segmentation and targeting selections you make, your next step will be to stake out the position you'd like to occupy in the mind of buyers and potential buyers. **Positioning** your product is the act of designing your company's offering and image so that it occupies a meaningful and distinct competitive position in your target customers' minds.

Most companies position their products by choosing among several differentiating product factors, including features, performance, quality, durability, reliability, style, design, and customer service such as ordering ease, delivery and installation methods, and

target markets
Specific customer groups or segments to whom a company wants to sell a particular product

positioning
Using promotion, product, distribution, and price to differentiate a good or service from those of competitors in the mind of the prospective buyer

EXHIBIT 11•6

POSITIONING AND THE MARKETING ENVIRONMENT

When positioning products for target markets, you need to consider the four marketing mix elements plus the external environment.

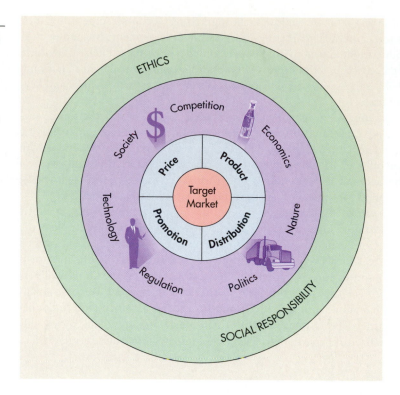

customer support. For example, Colgate Total is positioned as a toothpaste to prevent gum disease, cavities, and plaque, whereas Rembrandt's Dazzling White is positioned as a toothpaste to whiten teeth. By contrast, Aquafresh Whitening is positioned as a toothpaste that whitens, fights cavities, and tastes good.[57] Besides product factors, companies also differentiate their products on the basis of price, distribution, and promotion—the other elements in the firm's *marketing mix* (see Exhibit 11.6).[58]

marketing mix
The four key elements of marketing strategy: product, price, distribution (place), and promotion

Developing the Marketing Mix A firm's **marketing mix** (often called the *four Ps*) consists of product, price, place (or distribution), and promotion. The most basic marketing-mix element is *product,* which covers the product itself plus brand name, design, packaging, services, quality, and warranty. *Price,* the amount of money customers pay for the product (including any discounts) is the second marketing-mix element. *Place* (which is commonly referred to as *distribution*) is the third marketing-mix element. It covers the organized network of firms that move goods and services from the producer to the consumer. *Promotion,* the fourth marketing-mix element, includes all the activities the firm undertakes to communicate and promote its products to the target market. Among these activities are advertising, personal selling, public relations, and sales promotion.

LEARNING OBJECTIVE 6
Identify the four basic components of the marketing mix

We will take a closer look at each of these four marketing-mix elements in the remaining chapters of this text part. In Chapter 12 we will discuss product, price, and promotional strategies. Then in Chapter 13 we will focus on distribution strategies.

Summary of Learning Objectives

1. **Explain what marketing is.**
   Marketing is the process of planning and executing the conception, pricing, promotion, and distribution of ideas, goods, and services to create exchanges that satisfy individual and organizational objectives.

2. **Highlight the benefits of learning about your customers.**
   Companies learn about their customers so they can deliver quality products and provide good customer service in order to keep customers satisfied and retain their long-term loyalty.

3. **List five factors that influence the buyer's purchase decision.**
   The purchase decision is influenced by the buyer's culture, social class, reference groups, self-image, and situational factors.

4. **Outline the three steps in the strategic marketing planning process.**
   The three steps in the strategic marketing planning process are (1) examining your current marketing situation, which includes reviewing your past performance, evaluating your competition, examining your internal strengths and weaknesses, and analyzing the external environment; (2) assessing your opportunities and setting your objectives; and (3) developing your marketing strategy, which covers segmenting your market, choosing your target markets, positioning your product, and creating a marketing mix to satisfy the target market.

5. **Define market segmentation and review five factors used to identify segments.**
   Market segmentation is the process of subdividing a market into homogeneous groups in order to identify potential customers and to devise marketing approaches geared to their needs and interests. The five most common factors used to identify segments are demographics, geographics, psychographics, geodemographics, and behavior.

6. **Identify the four basic components of the marketing mix.**
   The marketing mix consists of the four Ps: product, price, place (distribution), and promotion.

Key Terms

behavioral segmentation (268)

buyers' market (256)

cause-related marketing (254)

cognitive dissonance (262)

consumer buying behavior (261)

consumer market (263)

database marketing (260)

demographics (267)

exchange process (255)

form utility (255)

geodemographics (267)

geographic segmentation (267)

market (266)

market segmentation (267)

market share (266)

marketing (254)

marketing concept (256)

marketing mix (270)

marketing research (261)

marketing strategy (266)

need (254)

organizational market (263)

place marketing (254)

place utility (255)

positioning (269)

possession utility (255)

psychographics (267)

relationship marketing (259)

sellers' market (256)

target markets (269)

time utility (255)

transaction (255)

utility (255)

wants (255)

Test Your Knowledge

QUESTIONS FOR REVIEW

1. How has marketing evolved over time?

2. How do market niches differ from market segments?

3. What external environmental factors affect strategic marketing decisions?

4. How does the organizational market differ from the consumer market?

5. What is strategic marketing planning, and what is its purpose?

QUESTIONS FOR ANALYSIS

6. Why do companies segment markets?

7. Why is it important for marketers to build relationships with customers?

MEETING BUSINESS CHALLENGES AT CONTINENTAL AIRLINES

CEO Gordon Bethune's "Go Forward Plan" was a customer-focused blueprint for bringing Continental Airlines out of a nosedive caused by excessive cost cutting. "We had cut costs so much that we simply had nothing to offer any more," Bethune observed. "Our service was lousy, and nobody knew when a plane might land. We were unpredictable and unreliable, and when you're an airline, where does that leave you? It leaves you with a lot of empty planes." The excessive cost cutting of the previous decade had alienated customers and employees alike. By listening to customers, the CEO engineered a stunning turnaround for an airline that had tottered on the financial brink for too long.

Bethune's top priority was restoring customer confidence. He knew that getting travelers to their destination on time was the single most important factor in satisfying these customers, and it was especially critical for the highly lucrative business traveler market segment. By initiating employee incentive bonuses for improved on-time performance rankings, Bethune and employees pushed Continental to the number-one slot (according to the Department of Transportation's ranking) within two months. Next, Bethune turned his attention to other criteria by which customers judge airline service quality, such as proper baggage handling and improved service for business travelers. He launched BusinessFirst amenities, which included roomier seating in a special cabin, better meals, and top-quality service.

Once rankings went up, customers came back, signaling that the turnaround was well under way. Still, Bethune had to keep the momentum going. But finding ways to grow revenue in a mature, highly competitive industry was a real challenge—one that Bethune knew he could meet by listening to what customers had to say. For instance, he learned that travelers wanted more options for travel to more destinations, so he forged a strategic global alliance with Northwest Airlines. The two carriers agreed to share route networks and frequent-flyer programs but to maintain their distinctive corporate identities and management operations. As a result, Continental's passengers were able to travel to more locations without switching airlines. At the same time, Continental was better positioned to compete with giants such as American Airlines and United, which already had global partnerships in place.

By the end of the 1990s, Continental was routinely achieving high ratings in service quality rankings. The airline was financially sound, and its employees had earned more than $270 million in profit-sharing bonuses. Moreover, its 2,200 daily flights were taking off to over 200 worldwide destinations with most of their seats filled, which meant that Continental was enjoying the highest load factor in its history. Gordon Bethune's customer-focused turnaround was a success.[59]

Critical Thinking Questions

1. Which of the four utilities did Bethune's turnaround plan emphasize? Explain your answer.

2. How did Continental Airlines segment its market for airline travel?

3. How did Bethune change Continental Airlines' marketing mix?

■ LEARN MORE ONLINE

To see how Continental Airlines is doing, visit its Web site at http://www.continental.com/corporate/ and click on the "About Continental" link to find the "Message from Gordon." Also follow the Investor Relations link to see the latest annual report and read about the global alliance. What is the CEO stressing? How has the global alliance been expanded?

8. How can data mining help companies better understand consumer buying behavior and improve their marketing efforts?

9. Why does a marketer need to consider its current marketing situation, including competitive trends, when setting objectives for market share?

10. ▨ When marketing researchers ask survey respondents to answer questions about family, friends, or neighbors, are they invading the respondents' privacy? Please explain.

QUESTIONS FOR APPLICATION

11. ▨ How might an airline use relationship and database marketing to improve customer loyalty?

12. ▨ Which of the five segmentation factors could PepsiCo use to segment the market for Doritos tortilla chips?

13. Review the discussion of leadership styles in Chapter 6 (see pages 141–143). Which style did Gordon Bethune use to turn Continental Airlines around? Why was this style effective?

14. Why is it important to analyze a firm's marketing plan before designing the production process for a service or a good? What kinds of information are generally included in a marketing plan that might affect the design of the production process as discussed in Chapter 8?

Practice Your Knowledge

SHARPENING YOUR COMMUNICATION SKILLS

Collect some examples of mail communications you have received from companies who are trying to sell you something. How do these communications try to get your attention? Highlight all the instances in which these communications use the word *you* or even your personal name. How is using the word *you* an effective way to communicate with customers? Does the communication appeal to your emotion or to your logic? How does the company highlight the benefits of its product or services? How does the company talk about price? Finally, how does the company motivate you to act? Bring your samples to class and be prepared to present your analysis of these factors to your classmates.

HANDLING DIFFICULT SITUATIONS ON THE JOB: TURNAROUND AT TRAVELFEST

As a travel agent with Travelfest Inc., in Austin, Texas, you have been both amazed and troubled by recent changes in the travel industry. The upset started when airlines stopped paying a 10 percent commission on airline tickets and set a new limit of a flat $25 commission on one-way domestic flights and $50 on round-trip domestic flights. Your boss, Gary Hoover, has been working night and day to make up for declining revenues caused by the loss of airline commissions. He has tried everything, from direct-mail campaigns to discount coupons to drawings for cruises and weekend getaways. Still, revenues remain flat, and no solution is in sight.

After researching your target markets and your customers' buying behavior, you noticed that about 70 percent of Travelfest's revenues comes from corporate and business travel, and 30 percent comes from leisure travel—mainly trips taken by your corporate customers. Many of your customers are middle- to high-income sophisticated travelers who, according to your sales records, are doing more traveling overseas. This research sparked some ideas about how Travelfest can increase revenue from existing customers.

Given the growth in foreign travel, you'd like to sell videos and audiotape courses in Spanish and other languages. You'd like to offer a complete line of travel products, including luggage, maps, and travel guides, in addition to offering travel seminars led by experienced travelers. These new products might not generate much direct profit, but you believe they will effectively position Travelfest as a full-service agency and will attract customers interested in leisure travel to foreign destinations.[60]

1. What questions do you think your boss might have about your ideas for selling travel-related products?

2. How do your ideas build on Travelfest's internal strengths?

3. How will these new products help you establish better relationships with your customers?

BUILDING YOUR TEAM SKILLS

In the course of planning a marketing strategy, marketers need to analyze the external environment to consider how forces outside the firm may create new opportunities and challenges. One important environmental factor for buyers at Kmart, for example, is weather conditions. When Dennis Charles, head of Kmart's $1.3 billion lawn and garden division, thinks about the assortment and number of products he needs for the chain's stores, he doesn't place any orders without poring over long-range weather forecasts for each market.

In particular, temperature and precipitation predictions for the coming 12 months are critical to Charles's marketing plans, because they offer clues to consumer demand for barbecues, lawn furniture, gardening tools, and other merchandise. By keying product orders and offers to weather patterns, Charles was able to boost profit margins for Kmart's lawn and garden division for five consecutive years.[61]

What other products would benefit from examining weather forecasts? With your team, brainstorm to identify at least three types of products (in addition to lawn and garden items) for which Kmart should examine the weather as part of their analysis of the external environment. Then select one product from your list and come up with five or more questions the buyer at Kmart would be better equipped to answer after studying weather forecasts. Indicate which of the four marketing-mix

elements each question is related to and how Kmart might use the answers to develop a more effective marketing plan.

Share your team's list and questions with the entire class. How many teams identified the same products your team did? What questions did the other teams suggest? What other marketing-mix variables were covered in the questions suggested by the rest of the teams?

Expand Your Knowledge

EXPLORING CAREER OPPORTUNITIES

Jobs in the four Ps of marketing cover a wide range of activities, including a variety of jobs such as personal selling, advertising, marketing research, product management, and public relations. You can get more information about various marketing positions by consulting the *Career Information Center* guide to jobs and careers, the U.S. Employment Service's *Dictionary of Occupational Titles,* and online job-search Web sites such as Career Mosaic http://www.careermosaic.com.

1. Select a specific marketing job that interests you. Using one or more of the above resources, find out more about this chosen job. What specific duties and responsibilities do people in this position typically handle?

2. Search through help-wanted ads in newspapers, specialized magazines, or Web sites to find two openings in the field you are researching. What educational background and work experience are employers seeking in candidates for this position? What kind of work assignments are mentioned in these ads?

3. Now think about your talents, interests, and goals. How do your strengths fit with the requirements, duties, and responsibilities of this job? Do you think you would find this field enjoyable and rewarding? Why?

DEVELOPING YOUR RESEARCH SKILLS

The strategic marketing planning process for any business involves a great deal of research. Consider the grocery industry. During the first stage in the process, a major supermarket chain such as Kroger must carefully examine its past performance, research its competitive situation, and analyze its internal strengths and weaknesses. All this research helps the chain make the most of its competitive advantages and plan better marketing strategies for serving attractive customer segments.

1. Find out about Kroger's performance and internal capabilities by examining sources such as the company's annual report and *Hoover's Handbook of American Business* (or Hoovers Online at http://www.hoovers.com). Are the company's sales and profits going up or down?

What are some of its strengths? What are some of its weaknesses?

2. Search through *Corporate and Industry Research Reports* and *Hoover's Handbook* or other sources to learn more about the grocery industry. Have industry sales and profits increased or decreased over the past five years? What are the projections for the near future?

3. Using the above sources, find out more about competition in the industry. Who are Kroger's main competitors? What new competitors are emerging? How is the Internet affecting the grocery industry?

SEE IT ON THE WEB
Fasten Your Seatbelt, page 256

Today's consumers can use technology such as the Internet to locate a wealth of information about both goods and services. Take, for example, the process of shopping for a car or truck. Go to CarSmart http://www.carsmart.com/autoadvr.htm to answer these questions.

1. Check out the Auto Buying Tips. Scroll down to the bottom of the page, click on Invoice Pricing Reports, and then click on View the Sample Report. How is this information useful to consumers?

2. Click to read How to Resolve a Dealer Service Complaint. Under what circumstances would consumers need this information? What part of the buying process does this section address?

3. Do you think car manufacturers and dealers like consumers' being armed with a great deal of information? Why or why not?

Fetch It!, page 266

Say you're thinking about opening a bicycle shop. You'll need to perform some industry, market, and product research. Dogpile, a metasearch engine at http://www.dogpile.com, can maximize your Internet search by searching several popular search engines with your key terms and phrases with one click. Log on to the Web site, enter *bicycle* and click on *fetch!* Be sure to review some of the links provided and check out listings from *all* the search engines Dogpile supports.

1. Which search engine(s) link(s) you to the most industry-related information?
2. Which search engine(s) link(s) you to the homepages of bicycle retailers and suppliers?
3. Which search engine(s) link(s) you to primarily local news, clubs, and non-industry-related sites?

Demographics for Your Marketing Toolbox, page 267

Learning about consumer demographics is one of the first steps in developing an effective marketing plan. To answer these questions, go to the American Demographics Marketing Tools Web site at http://www.marketingtools.com.

1. Review the publications *American Demographics* and *Marketing Tools*. Read some of the articles. How might these publications be helpful to marketers? Which has the most useful information? Why?
2. Scroll down to the Sources Page featuring Hot Links to Useful Government and Commercial Sites. Jump directly to the Bureau of Labor Statistics (BLS) Consumer Expenditure data. Click on the FAQs. What is the Consumer Expenditure Survey, and how is it used?
3. Go back to the Consumer Expenditure homepage, and click on the Standard Bulletin. Using the latest year of information, click on Composition of Consumer Unit. Review the table. How much did the "husband and wife only" spend on food away from home? How much did they spend on entertainment? Go back and review some of the other tables. How do data like these help marketers?

12

DEVELOPING PRODUCT, PRICING, AND PROMOTIONAL STRATEGIES

LEARNING OBJECTIVES

After studying this chapter, you will be able to

1 Describe the four stages in the life cycle of a product

2 Cite three levels of brand loyalty

3 List seven factors that influence pricing decisions

4 Identify the five basic categories of promotion

5. Explain the use of integrated marketing communications

6 Distinguish between push and pull strategies of promotion

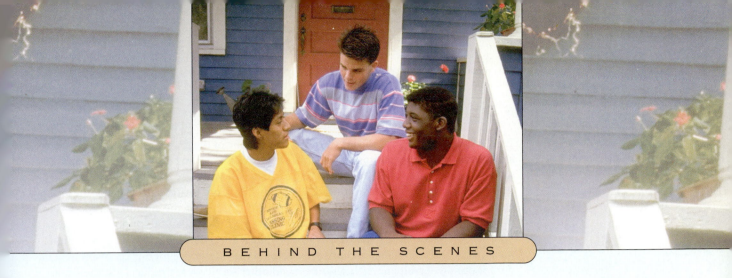

FACING BUSINESS CHALLENGES AT LEVI STRAUSS

Making a Once-Hot Brand Cool Again

One of the world's best-known companies was facing an unprecedented crisis. Levi Strauss, the darling of the denim set, had enjoyed more than a decade of skyrocketing sales growth. Its traditional jeans lines were selling well, and its Dockers apparel line, geared toward baby boomers who were growing out of their jeans, was a solid hit. Then, in the early 1990s, the external environment began showing signs of change. But Levi's marketers were not paying close attention to cultural trends, competitive threats, and shifts in their target markets; instead, they were continuing the same tried-and-true bluejeans marketing strategies that had built their business. The result was a sales disaster: Levi's share of the denim jeans market plummeted from a healthy 31 percent to just 17 percent in the course of eight years, dragging annual revenues from a height of nearly $7 billion to below the $6 billion mark.

To stop the downward slide in financial performance, Levi's top management closed more than two dozen factories, laid off thousands of employees worldwide, and put the brakes on an ambitious reengineering project that had soaked up much money and attention. At the same time, Levi's marketers conducted a study to determine what had gone wrong with their marketing strategy.

The marketing study found that Levi Strauss's products no longer appealed to the teen and 20-something consumer segments. These groups were growing in numbers and buying power, yet they were hardly fans of Levi's, which they saw as an unhip brand worn by their parents. So, while Levi Strauss was losing market share among consumers aged 14 to 19, other giant competitors such as the Gap, Lee, and Wrangler and up-and-comers such as Faded Glory were luring teens with newer styles. Jeans retailers also joined the competitive fray, creating private-brand products with more youthful fashion appeal.

Levi's longstanding policy of ignoring fashion trends had caused it to miss the sales potential of developments such as the movement toward baggier jeans. Maybe boomers wanted to wear the same jeans year in and year out, but younger consumers followed fashion by buying the very latest styles. As Levi ignored the call for wider pant legs and other styling updates, competitors of all sizes stepped into the void with a parade of new apparel products.

Now Levi Strauss had to develop a marketing plan for revitalizing sales and luring back customers. How could the company reach out to younger consumers? What product strategies could it use to address the diverse needs of various market segments? How could Levi make its brands more attractive to the segments it was targeting? How could the company use the Internet in these efforts?[1]

■ DEVELOPING PRODUCT STRATEGIES

product
Good or service used as the basis
of commerce

Products such as the jeans made by Levi Strauss are one of the four elements in a firm's marketing mix. From a marketing standpoint, a **product** is anything offered for the purpose of satisfying a want or a need in a marketing exchange. If you were asked to name three popular products off the top of your head, you might think of Doritos tortilla chips, the Volkswagen Beetle, and Gatorade drinks. You might not think of the Boston Celtics, Disney World, and the television show *60 Minutes*. That's because we tend to think of products as *tangible* objects, or things that we can actually touch and possess. Basketball teams, amusement parks, and television programs provide an *intangible* service for our use or enjoyment, not for our ownership; nevertheless, these and other services are products just the same.

Types of Products

Think again about Doritos tortilla chips and Disney World. You wouldn't market these two products in the same way, because buyer behavior, product characteristics, market expectations, competition, and other elements of the equation are entirely different. Acknowledging these differences, marketers most commonly categorize products on the basis of tangibility and use.

Tangible and Intangible Products   Although some products are predominantly tangible and others are mostly intangible, most products fall somewhere between those two extremes. When you buy software such as Norton Anti-Virus, for example, you get service features along with the product—such as virus updates, customer assistance, and so on. The *product continuum* indicates the relative amounts of tangible and intangible components in a product (see Exhibit 12.1). Political ideas are products at the intangible extreme, whereas salt and shoes are at the tangible extreme. TGI Friday's restaurants fall in the middle because they involve both tangible (food) and intangible (service) components.

Service products have some special characteristics that affect the way they are marketed. As we have seen, *intangibility* is one fundamental characteristic. You can't usually show a service in an ad, demonstrate it before customers buy, or give customers anything tangible to show for their purchase. Services marketers often compensate for intangibility

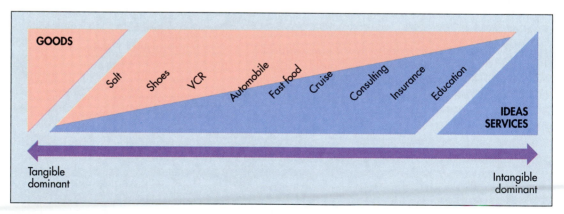

EXHIBIT 12·1

THE PRODUCT CONTINUUM

Products contain both tangible and intangible components; predominantly tangible products are categorized as goods, whereas predominantly intangible products are categorized as services.

by using tangible symbols or by adding tangible components to their products. Prudential Insurance, for example, uses the Rock of Gibraltar as a symbol of stability, and its ads invite you to get "your piece of the rock."

Another unique aspect of service products is *perishability.* Because services cannot usually be created in advance or held in storage until people are ready to buy, services present big challenges in terms of staffing and pricing. Look at movie theaters, for example. Once a scheduled feature has begun, the theater seldom fills the empty seats. For this reason, many movie theaters try to shift some customer demand from busy evenings and weekends by offering discounted tickets during the day and during the workweek.

Consumer Products Versus Organizational Products As you saw in Chapter 11, organizational and consumer markets use many of the same products for different reasons and in different ways. *Organizational products,* or products sold to firms, are generally purchased in large quantities and are not for personal use. Two categories of organizational products are expense items and capital items. *Expense items* are relatively inexpensive goods and services that organizations generally use within a year of purchase. These include supplies such as pencils and printer cartridges. *Capital items,* by contrast, are more expensive organizational products and have a longer useful life. Examples include desks, photocopiers, and bookshelves.

Even though many of these products are sold to both consumer and organizational markets, companies develop different marketing strategies to appeal to the unique buying behaviors and needs of these two groups. Nevertheless, some products—known as *consumer products*—are sold exclusively to consumers. Consumer products can be classified into four subgroups, depending on how people shop for them:

- *Convenience products* are the goods and services that people buy frequently, without much conscious thought, such as toothpaste, dry cleaning, film developing, and photocopying.
- *Shopping products* are fairly important goods and services that people buy less frequently: a stereo, a computer, or a college education. Such purchases require more thought and comparison shopping to check on price, features, quality, and reputation.
- *Specialty products* include CK perfume, Armani suits, and Suzuki violin lessons—particular brands that the buyer especially wants and will seek out, regardless of location or price. Specialty products are not necessarily expensive, but they are products that customers go out of their way to buy and rarely accept substitutes for.
- *Unsought goods* are products that people do not normally think of buying, such as life insurance, cemetery plots, and new products they must be made aware of through promotion.[2]

The Product Life Cycle

Whether you're buying Levi's jeans, Gatorade, an Armani suit, or a Dell computer, today's hot item may be yesterday's news in a couple of years or so—as Levi Strauss discovered. Most products go through a **product life cycle,** passing through four distinct stages in sales and profits: introduction, growth, maturity, and decline (see Exhibit 12.2). As the product passes from stage to stage, various marketing approaches become appropriate.

The amount of time that a product remains in any one stage depends on customer needs and preferences, economic conditions, the nature of the product, and the marketer's strategy. Still, the proliferation of new products, changing technology, globalization, and the ability to quickly imitate competitors is hurtling products through their life cycles much faster today. The pace is so frenetic that, in the words of GTE's president Kent Foster, "Companies are marketing products that are still evolving, delivered to a market that is

product life cycle
Four basic stages through which a product progresses: introduction, growth, maturity, and decline

LEARNING OBJECTIVE 1
Describe the four stages in the life cycle of a product

EXHIBIT 12·2

THE PRODUCT LIFE CYCLE

Most products and product categories move through a life cycle similar to the one represented by the curve in this diagram. However, the duration of each stage varies widely from product to product.

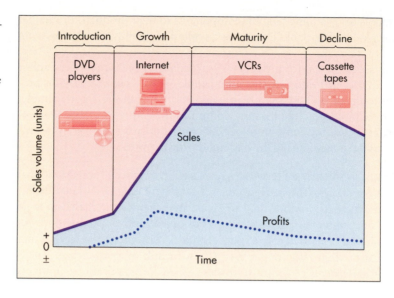

The product life cycle is shrinking for every business, whether it sells physical or information products.[3]

still emerging, via technology that is changing on a daily basis."[4] Consider electronics, where product life is now a matter of months; Panasonic replaces its consumer electronic products with new models every 90 days.[5] Why? Smart companies know that if they don't keep innovating, competitors who do will capture the business.

Introduction   The first stage in the product life cycle is the *introductory stage,* during which producers launch a new product and stimulate demand. In this stage, companies typically spend heavily on conducting research-and-development efforts to create the new product, on developing promotions to build awareness of the product, and on establishing the distribution system to get the product into the marketplace. Every product—from Hasbro's Pokemon cards to Gillette's Mach3 razors—gets its start in this stage. The producer makes little profit during the introduction; however, these start-up costs are a necessary investment if the new product is to succeed.

For example, Gillette spent $300 million to promote the launch of the Mach3 razor during its first year—on top of $750 million-plus in development costs. In expectation of rapid worldwide sales growth, the company also expanded its blade production facilities with multi-million-dollar machinery that can turn out 600 cartridges per minute. This aggressive strategy is designed to accelerate the Mach3's transition from the costly introduction stage to the profitable growth stage faster than any previous Gillette razors. So far this strategy has paid off. In just 18 months after the Mach3 was launched, sales for the product hit $1 billion, making it the company's most successful new product ever.[6]

In three months, many of the cameras and TVs displayed at this consumer electronics store will be replaced with newer models, each with state-of-the art features, making older products less desirable or, in some cases, obsolete.

Growth   After the introductory stage comes the *growth stage,* marked by a rapid jump in sales and, usually, an increase in the number of competitors. As competition increases, so does the struggle for market share. This situation creates pressure to maintain large promotional budgets and competitive prices. In fact, marketing in this stage is so expensive that it can drive out smaller, weaker firms. With enough growth, however, a firm can often produce and deliver its products more economically than in the introduction phase. Thus, the growth stage can reap handsome profits for those who survive.

Consider Apple Computer's colorful iMac personal computers. By the time this popular product line had reached the growth stage in its second year of sales, it had helped Apple grab badly needed market share from competitors. Just as important, the iMac line was giving Apple a healthy dose of higher revenues and profits. Looking ahead, the company plans to maintain sales momentum through ongoing upgrades, such as adding faster chips without increasing the price of future iMac computers.[7]

Maturity During the *maturity stage,* the longest in the product life cycle, sales begin to level off or show a slight decline. Competition increases and market share is maximized—making further expansion difficult. Because the costs of introduction and growth have diminished in this stage, most companies try to keep mature products alive so they can use the resulting profits to fund development of new products. Some companies even extend the life of a mature product by broadening its appeal or making minor improvements.

For example, Nike's mature athletic shoe line is facing steeper competition from other manufacturers as well as from fashion changes that have hurt sales. Now Nike, far and away the market leader, wants to renew interest in its athletic shoes. To do this, the company is making such improvements as boosting cushioning in the midsole, reducing shoe weight, and improving the heel.[8]

Decline Although maturity can be extended for many years, most products eventually enter the *decline stage,* when sales and profits slip and then fade away. Declines occur for several reasons: changing demographics, shifts in popular taste, product competition, and advances in technology. When a product reaches this point in the life cycle, the company must decide whether to keep it or discontinue it and focus on developing newer products. For instance, as digital photography moves ahead, some predict that the film business will dwindle into a small niche market. The challenge for Kodak will be to replace lost film sales with sales of newer products.[10]

> Dying products, services, or processes demand the greatest care and efforts. Most companies overestimate how much "life" still exists in an old product. Usually it is not dying; it's dead.[9]

Sometimes all a declining product needs is some innovation. The Dean Food Company, for example, decided to keep its chocolate-milk product despite a long-term decline in milk consumption. By introducing new single-serving plastic bottles called Chugs, the company increased sales for the product and brought new life to the entire chocolate milk category.[11] Mattel faced a similar decision about declining Barbie sales not long ago. For years, the company had been able to bring Barbie products back from periodic sales dips by introducing innovations such as limited-edition collectible Barbie dolls, customizable Barbie dolls, and even Barbie software. One of Mattel's biggest hits of the 1990s was Holiday Barbie, a limited-edition line of dolls that generated more than $100 million in sales during its peak year. After nearly a decade, however, Holiday Barbie sales began to decline. Long after the holidays were over, some retailers resorted to deep discounts to move any leftover dolls. Finally, Mattel decided to discontinue the line—but not the technique. Limited-edition dolls such as Millennium Barbie remain a major marketing tool for Mattel.[12]

Product-Mix and Product-Line Decisions

Anticipating the impact of product life cycles, most companies continually add and drop products to ensure that declining items will be replaced by growth products. In this way, they develop a **product mix,** a collection of goods or services offered for sale. Of course, the

product mix
Complete list of all products that a company offers for sale

READY-TO-EAT CEREALS	SNACK FOODS AND BEVERAGES	BAKING PRODUCTS AND DESSERTS	MAIN MEALS AND SIDE DISHES	DAIRY PRODUCTS
Cheerios	Bugles Corn Snacks	Betty Crocker Cake Mixes	Bac*Os	Colombo Yogurt
Cinnamon Toast Crunch	Chex Snack Mix	Bisquick	Chicken Helper	Yoplait Yogurt
Cocoa Puffs	Fruit by the Foot	Creamy Deluxe Frosting	Hamburger Helper	
Kix	Fruit Roll-Ups	Gold Medal Flour	Potato Buds	
Nature Valley Granola	Nature Valley Granola Bars	Softasilk Cake Flour	Suddenly Salad	
Oatmeal Crisp	Pop Secret Popcorn		Tuna Helper	
Raisin Nut Bran	Sweet Rewards Snack Bars			
Total				
Wheaties				

EXHIBIT 12·3

THE PRODUCT MIX AT GENERAL MILLS

Selected products from General Mills show a product mix that is fairly wide but that varies in depth within each product line.

product line
A series of related products offered by a firm

Could Dryel be the next big hit? Procter & Gamble thinks so. The company expects Dryel's sales to reach $500 million, making it as big as Downy or Bounce. But in order to sell a new kind of home dry-cleaning product, P & G must first convince consumers that they need a product they've never heard of.

simplest product mix is not really a mix at all, but rather a single product. However, most companies find that they need more than one product to sustain their sales growth, so they vary the width and depth of their product mix. For example, the General Mills product mix consists of cereals, baking products, desserts, snack foods, and so on (see Exhibit 12.3). When deciding on the width of its product mix, a company weighs the risks and rewards associated with various approaches. Some companies limit the number of product offerings to be economical: Doing so keeps the production costs per unit down and limits selling expenses to a single sales force. Other companies see a broader product mix as protection against shifts in technology, taste, and economic conditions.

Each component of a product mix is a **product line,** a group of products that are similar in terms of use or characteristics. The General Mills snack-food product line, for example, includes Bugles, Fruit Roll-Ups, Sweet Rewards Snack Bars, and Pop Secret Popcorn. Within each product line, a company confronts decisions about the number of goods and services to offer. Levi Strauss, for instance, must decide how many types of jeans it should produce, or Home Depot must decide how many types of garden hoses it should sell. A full-line strategy involves selling a wide number and variety of products, whereas a limited-line strategy focuses on selling a few selected items. In general, product lines tend to grow over time as companies look for new ways to boost sales. Look at Procter & Gamble. This company is spending millions to develop entirely new products such as Dryel, a home dry-cleaning product.[13] As Exhibit 12.4 shows, you can expand your product line in a number of ways.

Product Strategies for International Markets

In the course of developing strategies for marketing products internationally, companies must consider a variety of important factors, including unstable governments, market entry requirements, tariffs and other trade barriers, technology pirating, cultural and language differences, consumer preferences, foreign-exchange rates, and differing business customs. Because of these factors, launching a product in other countries requires careful thought and planning.

METHOD OF EXPANSION	HOW IT WORKS	EXAMPLE
Line filling	Developing items to fill gaps in the market that have been overlooked by competitors or have emerged as consumers' tastes and needs shift	Alka-Seltzer Plus cold medicine
Line extension	Creating a new variation of a basic product	Tartar Control Crest toothpaste
Brand extension	Putting the brand for an existing product category into a new category	Virgin Cola
Line stretching	Adding higher- or lower-priced items at either end of the product line to extend its appeal to new economic groups	Marriott Marquis hotel

EXHIBIT 12•4

EXPANDING THE PRODUCT LINE

Knowing that no product or category has an unlimited life cycle, companies use one or more of these methods to keep sales strong by expanding their product lines.

After the strategic marketing planning process, your first step in international marketing is to carefully examine your current marketing situation and assess opportunities to market your good or service in other countries. As you develop your marketing strategy, you must decide whether to *standardize* your product, selling the same product everywhere, or to *customize* your product to accommodate the lifestyles and habits of local target markets. Keep in mind that the degree of customization can vary. At times, you may change only your product's name or packaging; if you decide to customize, however, you will be offering a completely different product in different markets.

Many U.S. manufacturers have customized their products after learning that international customers are not all alike. For instance, Heinz now varies its ketchup recipe in different countries—after having discovered that consumers in Belgium and Holland use ketchup as a pasta sauce. In China, Cheetos are cheeseless because the Chinese people don't really like cheese.[14] On the other hand, Kellogg sells the same Corn Flakes in Europe that it sells in the United States. Only recently, however, has Kellogg made significant inroads in European markets, thanks to television advertising and lifestyle changes that favor bigger breakfasts.[15] The latest twist is for companies to adapt non-U.S. products for U.S. markets. For example, Haagen-Dazs has successfully introduced a caramel ice cream from Argentina into U.S. markets.[16]

When Heinz designs and promotes products such as mayonnaise for the Russian market, it needs to take cultural context into account.

▪ DEVELOPING BRAND AND PACKAGING STRATEGIES

Regardless of what type of product a company sells, it usually wants to create a **brand** identity by using a unique name or design that sets the product apart from those offered by competitors. Jeep, Levi's 501, and Apple are **brand names,** the portion of a brand that can be spoken, including letters, words, or numbers. McDonald's golden arches symbol is an

brand
A name, term, sign, symbol, design, or combination of those used to identify the products of a firm and to differentiate them from competing products

brand name
Portion of a brand that can be expressed orally, including letters, words, or numbers

See It on the Web See It on the Web

PROTECT YOUR TRADEMARK

Got a winning idea for a new product? Don't forget to protect your trademark by registering it with the U.S. Patent and Trademark Office. Visit this government agency's Web site and learn the basic facts about registering a trademark. Find out how the process works and how much it costs. In fact, why not search its database now to see whether anyone has already registered your trademark? http://www.uspto.gov/

brand mark
Portion of a brand that cannot be expressed verbally

trademark
Brand that has been given legal protection so that its owner has exclusive rights to its use

---

LEARNING OBJECTIVE 2
Cite three levels of brand loyalty

brand loyalty
Commitment to a particular brand

brand awareness
Level of brand loyalty at which people are familiar with a product; they recognize it

brand preference
Level of brand loyalty at which people habitually buy a product if it is available

brand insistence
Level of brand loyalty at which people will accept no substitute for a particular product

national brands
Brands owned by the manufacturers and distributed nationally

private brands
Brands that carry the label of a retailer or a wholesaler rather than a manufacturer

generic products
Products characterized by a plain label, with no advertising and no brand name

example of a **brand mark,** the portion of a brand that cannot be expressed verbally. The choice of a brand name and any associated brand marks can be a success factor. Brand names and brand symbols may be registered with the Patent and Trademark Office as trademarks. As Component Chapter A explains, a **trademark** is a brand that has been given legal protection so that its owner has exclusive rights to its use.

A brand name is often an organization's most valuable asset because it provides customers with a way of recognizing and specifying a particular product so that they can choose it again or recommend it to others. This notion of the value of a brand is also called *brand equity.* Strong brands often command a premium price in the marketplace, as Nike shoes, the North Face ski wear, Bobbie Brown cosmetics, and Evian water do. Sometimes companies, such as Warner Brothers, *license* or sell the rights to specific well-known names and symbols—such as Looney Tunes cartoon characters—and then manufacturers use these licensed labels to help sell products. In the United States and Canada alone, retail sales from licensing rights top $73 billion annually.[17]

Customers who buy the same brand again and again are evidence of the strength of **brand loyalty,** or commitment to a particular brand. Brand loyalty can be measured in degrees. The first level is **brand awareness,** which means that people are likely to buy a product because they are familiar with it. The next level is **brand preference,** which means people will purchase the product if it is available, although they may still be willing to experiment with alternatives if they cannot find the preferred brand. The third and ultimate level of brand loyalty is **brand insistence,** the stage at which buyers will accept no substitute.

Building Brands

Brands offered and promoted by a manufacturer, such as Procter & Gamble's Tide detergent and Pampers disposable diapers, are called **national brands. Private brands** are not linked to a manufacturer but instead carry a wholesaler's or a retailer's brand. DieHard batteries and Kenmore appliances are private brands sold by Sears. As an alternative to branded products, some retailers also offer **generic products,** which are packaged in plain containers that bear only the name of the product. Generic products can cost up to 40 percent less than brand-name products because of uneven quality, plain packaging, and lack of promotion. Yet generic goods have found a definite market niche, as a look at your local supermarket shelves will confirm.

Companies can take various approaches to building brands. One approach is to create separate brands for products targeted to different customer segments. For example, Second Cup Limited, a Canadian company, uses three distinct coffeehouse brands—Coffee Plantation, Gloria Jean's, and Coffee People—to target three geographical segments. The opposite approach is illustrated by Starbucks, which operates under one brand everywhere in the world.[18] Yet another approach is illustrated by the Gap. The $8 billion company has put its main brand on BabyGap and GapBody stores as well as its GapScents fragrances. Yet it has maintained separate brand identities for Banana Republic and Old Navy, two chains aimed at distinctly different customer segments.[19]

An increasing number of companies have been using **family branding** (using one brand on a variety of related products) to add to their product lines. Kraft, for example, has extended its Jell-O product line to include gelatin in a cup, pudding in a cup, and cheese-cake snacks in a cup. These products build on the convenience-with-quality image of the Jell-O family brand.[20]

family branding
Using a brand name on a variety of related products

IT'S THE BRAND, STUPID

Who's a dummy? Although few people would want to be called dummies, John Kilcullen's customers actually pay for the privilege. As CEO of IDG Books Worldwide, Kilcullen dreamed up the idea of a line of books for people who know nothing about computers. He recognized that many people needed basic information about computers and software, presented in a practical, no-nonsense way. His books, sporting titles such as *Windows for Dummies* and *Internet for Dummies,* became runaway hits, ringing up more than $80 million in annual sales.

Kilcullen didn't stop after launching his computer books. Viewing "Dummies" as more than a computer-book brand, he expanded the product line to cover more and more categories. Now know-nothings can prep themselves with hundreds of books under the Dummies brand, covering topics as diverse as alternative medicine, antiquing, baseball, chess, gardening, golf, home improvement, and even math. One of the biggest hits in the line is *Personal Finance for Dummies.* This lighthearted how-to book has gone through two editions, has sold more than 800,000 copies, and has been named as one of the top 15 best-selling business books by *Business Week.*

Looking ahead, Kilcullen sees the Dummies brand as a powerful, flexible umbrella capable of sheltering a wider range of products. "We don't look at the world as a book company," he explains. "We look at the world as a knowledge company." However, sales of Dummies books have slowed in recent years. Computer titles still account for nearly three-quarters of the company's sales, while the noncomputer titles are experiencing mixed results. Kilcullen is working to boost sales by investing more heavily in promotion and by signing more expensive deals with celebrity authors, even though these moves are cutting into profit margins. He also wants to cash in on the brand equity of Dummies through licensing agreements with toy companies and record labels. So far, licensing results have been fairly modest, adding up to only 3 percent of IDG Books' overall revenues.

Industry insiders worry that the brand has been stretched to the limit with so many extensions; some also say that customers may cheerfully admit ignorance of computers but not of other topics. Asked about the strength of the Dummies family brand, Kilcullen responds, "The brand is so entrenched it can be anywhere, just like Nike is in golf, skiing, and all types of shoes." In fact, the CEO has started to explore the idea of television programming based on the brand. Will people buy more Dummies books and watch Dummies shows? Stay tuned.

QUESTIONS FOR CRITICAL THINKING

1. How is Kilcullen using a brand name to create an identity for his books?
2. How far do you think Dummies can go with family branding? What products would not be suitable for this brand?

A lot of companies become too fuzzy, too diversified, too confused. Companies have to stand for something.[21]

co-branding
Partnership between two or more companies to closely link their brand names together for a single product

Building on the name recognition of an existing brand cuts the costs and risks of introducing new products. However, there are limits to how far a brand name can be stretched to accommodate new products. Snickers ice cream bars and Dr. Scholl's socks and shoes worked as brand extensions, but Bic perfume and Rubbermaid computer accessories did not. The secret is to extend with products that fit the buyer's perception of what the brand stands for.[22]

In addition, you can strengthen your brands and products by combining forces with another company. **Co-branding** occurs when two or more companies team up to closely link their names in a single product. Two examples of successful co-branding include Kellogg's Pop Tarts made with Smucker's jam and Nabisco Cranberry Newtons filled with Ocean Spray cranberries. Co-branding can help companies reach new audiences and tap the equity of particularly strong brands.[23]

Packaging and Labeling Your Products

Most products need some form of packaging to protect the product from damage or tampering and to make it convenient for customers to purchase. Packaging also makes products easier to display and facilitates the sale of smaller products. In addition, packaging can provide convenience, as with food products that are ready to eat right out of the wrapper. Quaker Oats, for example, has gained considerable market share by switching from bulky boxes to easy-open, lower-priced bags for its cereal products.[24] In some cases, packaging is an essential part of the product itself, such as microwave popcorn or toothpaste in pump dispensers.

Besides function, however, packaging plays an important role in a product's marketing strategy because most consumer buying decisions are made in the store. As a result, companies spend big bucks on packaging to attract consumer attention and to promote a product's benefits through the package's shape, composition, and design. Innovative packaging—such as Mentadent toothpaste's two-chamber package with pump—can give your product a powerful marketing boost, whereas a poorly designed package may drive consumers away.

Labeling is an integral part of packaging. Whether the label is a separate element attached to the package or a printed part of the container, it serves to identify a brand. Sometimes the label also gives grading information about the product or information about ingredients, operating procedures, shelf life, or risks. The labeling of foods, drugs, cosmetics, and many health products is regulated under various federal laws, which often require disclosures about potential dangers, benefits, and other issues consumers need to consider when making a buying decision.

Universal Product Codes (UPCs)
A bar code on a product's package that provides information read by optical scanners

Labels do more than communicate with consumers. They are also used by manufacturers and retailers as a tool for monitoring product performance and inventory. **Universal Product Codes (UPCs),** those black stripes on packages, give companies a cost-effective method of tracking the movement of goods. Store checkout scanners read UPC codes and relay the identity, sales, and prices of all products to the retailer's computer system. Such data can help retailers and manufacturers measure the effectiveness of promotions such as coupons and in-store displays.

▪ DEVELOPING PRICING STRATEGIES

Pricing, the second major component of a firm's marketing mix, is often one of the most critical decisions a company must make, because it's the one variable that actually generates income. In fact, pricing is sometimes the only element that differentiates your product from your competitor's. And nothing affects sales more quickly than a change in price. But determining the right price is not an easy task. If a company charges too much, it will make fewer sales; if it charges too little, it will sacrifice potential profits. The right price depends on many variables.

Factors Affecting Pricing Decisions

A company's pricing decisions are determined by manufacturing and selling costs, competition, consumer demand, and the needs of wholesalers and retailers who distribute the product to the final customer. In addition, pricing is influenced by a firm's marketing objectives, government regulations, and consumers' perceptions.

LEARNING OBJECTIVE 3
List seven factors that influence pricing decisions

- *Marketing objectives.* The first step in setting a price is to match it to the objectives you set in your strategic marketing plan. Is your goal to increase market share, increase sales, improve profits, project a particular image, or combat competition? Consider Intel. This Silicon Valley chipmaker slashed prices on its Pentium brand microprocessors to boost sales and fend off lower-priced rival brands.[25] Rolex takes a different approach, using premium pricing along with other marketing-mix elements to give its watches a luxury position.

- *Government regulations.* Government plays a big role in pricing in many countries. To protect consumers and encourage fair competition, the U.S. government has enacted various price-related laws over the years. Three important classes of pricing are regulated: (1) *price fixing*—an agreement among two or more companies supplying the same type of products as to the prices they will charge, (2) *price discrimination*—the practice of unfairly offering attractive discounts to some customers but not to others, and (3) *deceptive pricing*—pricing schemes that are considered misleading.

- *Consumer perceptions.* Another consideration is the perception of quality that your price will elicit from your customers. When people shop, they usually have a rough price range in mind. An unexpectedly low price triggers fear that the item is of low quality. South Korean car maker Hyundai, for example, decided not to cut prices when the dollar gained strength against the Korean won, because the company did not want to reinforce an image of shoddy goods.[26] On the other hand, an unexpectedly high price makes buyers question whether the product is worth the money.

Pricing Strategies

Developing an effective price for your product is like a game of chess: Those who make their moves one at a time—seeking to minimize immediate losses or to exploit immediate opportunities—will be beaten by those who plan a few moves ahead. In other words, every element in the marketing mix must be carefully coordinated to support an overall marketing strategy. Here are a few strategies that marketers use when setting their prices.

Cost-Based and Priced-Based Pricing   Many companies simplify the pricing task by using *cost-based pricing* (also known as cost plus pricing). They price by starting with the cost of producing a good or a service and then add a markup to provide a profit. Meanwhile, they watch competitors' prices to avoid exceeding them. Although cost-based pricing may ensure a certain profit, companies using this strategy tend to sacrifice profit opportunity.

Recent thinking holds that cost should be the last item analyzed in the pricing formula, not the first. Companies that use *priced-based pricing* can maximize their profit by first establishing an optimal price for a product or service. The product's price is based on an analysis of a product's competitive advantages, the users' perception of the item, and the market being targeted. Once the desired price has been established, the firm focuses its energies on keeping costs at a level that will allow a healthy profit. Keep in mind that few businesses fail from overpricing their products; many more fail from underpricing them.[27]

break-even analysis
Method of calculating the minimum volume of sales needed at a given price to cover all costs

variable costs
Business costs that increase with the number of units produced

fixed costs
Business costs that remain constant regardless of the number of units produced

break-even point
Sales volume at a given price that will cover all of a company's costs

Break-Even Analysis   How does a company determine the amount of profit it will earn by selling a certain product? **Break-even analysis** is a tool companies use to determine the number of units of a product they must sell at a given price to cover all manufacturing and selling costs, or to break even. In break-even analysis, you consider two types of costs. **Variable costs** change with the level of production. These include raw materials, shipping costs, and supplies consumed during production. **Fixed costs,** by contrast, remain stable regardless of the number of products produced. These costs include rent payments, insurance premiums, and real estate taxes. The total cost of operating the business is the sum of a firm's variable and fixed costs.

The **break-even point** is the minimum sales volume the company must achieve to avoid losing money. Sales volume beyond the break-even point will generate profits; sales volume below the break-even amount will result in losses. You can determine the break-even point in number of units with this simple calculation:

$$Break\text{-}even\ point = \frac{Fixed\ costs}{Selling\ price\ per\ unit - Variable\ costs\ per\ unit}$$

For example, if you wanted to price haircuts at $20 and you had fixed costs of $60,000 and variable costs per haircut of $5, you would need to sell 4,000 haircuts to break even:

$$Breaking\text{-}even\ point\ (in\ units) = \frac{\$60,000}{\$20 - \$5} = 4,000\ units$$

Of course, $20 isn't your only pricing option. Why not charge $30 instead? When you charge the higher price, you need to give only 2,400 haircuts to break even (see Exhibit 12.5). However, before you raise your haircut prices to $30, bear in mind that a lower price may attract more customers and enable you to make more money in the long run.

Break-even analysis doesn't dictate what price you should charge; rather, it provides some insight into the number of units you have to sell at a given price to make a profit. This analysis is especially useful when you are trying to calculate the effect of running a

EXHIBIT 12.5

BREAK-EVEN ANALYSIS

The break-even point is the point at which revenues just cover costs. After fixed costs and variable costs have been met, any additional income represents profit. The graph shows that at $20 per haircut, the break-even point is 4,000 haircuts; charging $30 yields a break-even point at only 2,400 haircuts.

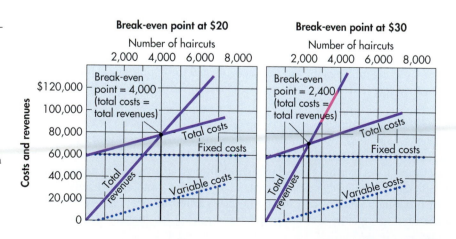

special pricing promotion; using spreadsheet software allows you to try different prices and see the results.

Skimming and Penetration   A product's price seldom remains constant and will vary depending on the product's stage in its life cycle. During the introductory phase, for example, the objective might be to recover product development costs as quickly as possible. To achieve this goal, the manufacturer might charge a high initial price—a practice known as **skimming**—and then drop the price later, when the product is no longer a novelty and competition heats up. Products such as HDTV and flat-screen monitors are perfect examples of this practice.

> **skimming**
> Charging a high price for a new product during the introductory stage and lowering the price later

Alternatively, a company might try to build sales volume by charging a low initial price, a practice known as **penetration pricing.** This approach has the added advantage of discouraging competition, because the low price (which competitors would be pressured to match) limits the profit potential for everyone. Penetration pricing can also help you expand the entire product category by attracting customers who wouldn't have purchased at higher, skim-pricing levels. Furthermore, if your company is new to a category pioneered by another company, this strategy can help you take customers away from the pioneer.[28]

> **penetration pricing**
> Introducing a new product at a low price in hopes of building sales volume quickly

Discounting and Value Pricing   When you use **discount pricing,** you offer various types of temporary price reductions, depending on the type of customer being targeted and the type of item being offered. You may decide to offer a trade discount to wholesalers or retailers as a way of encouraging orders, or you may offer cash discounts to reward customers who pay cash or pay promptly.

> **discount pricing**
> Offering a reduction in price

Sometimes discounts touch off price wars between competitors. Because price wars encourage customers to focus only on a product's pricing, and not on its value or benefits, they can hurt a business—even an entire industry—for years. Consider the price war that Web-based Amazon.com started when it began selling *New York Times* best-selling books at a 50 percent discount in an effort to bring more customers to its site. Online rivals Barnes andnoble.com and Borders.com quickly matched Amazon.com's prices, and smaller bookstores were forced to lower their prices on best-sellers. To offset the loss of revenue, some small bookstores stocked their shelves with more profitable book categories, such as specialty books. Others could not compete and eventually closed up shop.[29]

Another way to discount products is by *value pricing* them, charging a fairly affordable price for a high-quality offering. Many restaurants, including Friendly's, offer value menus for certain times of the day or certain customer segments, such as seniors. This strategy builds loyalty among price-conscious customers without damaging a product's quality image.

Dynamic Pricing   *Dynamic pricing* is the opposite of fixed pricing. Using Internet technology, companies continually reprice their products and services to meet supply and demand. Dynamic pricing not only enables companies to move slow selling merchandise instantly, but it also allows companies to experiment with different pricing levels. Because price changes are immediately posted to electronic catalogs or Web sites, customers always have the most current price information. Airlines are notorious for this type of continually-adjusted pricing. In addition to posting current fares on their home pages and many travel Web sites, many major airlines send customers weekly e-mail notifications listing special discount fares.[30]

Three popular dynamic pricing strategies are:

- *auction pricing,* where buyers bid against each other and the highest bid buys the product;

Focus on E-Business

THE ELECTRONIC PRICE ISN'T ALWAYS RIGHT

Among the Internet's many wonders is the speed in which it has overturned long-held assumptions about business. Take pricing, for example. It used to be that a seller would advertise a product in the marketplace at a specified price, and the buyer would take it or leave it. Not any more.

Today's customers are naming their price, and it's shaking up the way companies do business. Since Priceline.com made its debut in 1998, its name-your-own price system has turned fixed pricing on its head. Priceline matches sellers of perishable inventories such as airplane seats and hotel rooms with price-sensitive consumers. Bidders name their own prices, and sellers can decided whether to take it or leave it. But consumers aren't the only ones who benefit from this pricing model.

Name-your-own price is really about solving a vendor's problem—in the case of airlines, it's how to make money from the 500,000 airline seats that go unsold daily. Most businesses with excess merchandise cut prices over time, but airlines can't do this. They depend heavily on socking it to last-minute business travelers. Besides, many of those empty seats are on early or late flights, when not many people want to fly. Still, getting rid of excess product is just one benefit.

Looking deeper, this form of dynamic pricing lets vendors see, for the first time, the latent demand in the marketplace that exists beneath the estab- lished price of the product or service while protect- ing the brand's integrity and its published market- place prices. The seller never advertises that a lower price is being filled, and the buyer doesn't know which brand he or she is purchasing until the buyer's price is accepted. It provides an excellent opportu- nity for vendors to do some serious number crunch- ing to see where supply, demand, and price really do intersect. Moreover, it proves that for the right price people will buy something without knowing the brand, or in the case of airline tickets, without knowing when the flight takes off. And, it avoids the problem of free riders—people who buy at a pub- lished discounted price but would be willing to pay the full price anyway.

As name-your-own price and other dynamic strategies gain popularity, will the days of fixed prices disappear? Jay Walker, founder of Priceline, sure hopes they will. The idea of consumers naming their price is "absolutely revolutionary," notes Walker. While unlikely to become the standard any time soon, dynamic pricing will indeed touch many companies by its multifaceted potential. No wonder Star Trek's William Shatner keeps harping to audi- ences that Priceline is going to be big, *really* big.

QUESTIONS FOR CRITICAL THINKING

1. Why would a company agree to honor a cus- tomer's price even if that price is below the prod- uct's cost?

2. Why would a company not want to publish an agreed upon discounted price?

* *name-your-price,* where buyers specify how much they are willing to pay for a prod- uct and sellers can choose whether to sell at that price;
* *group buying,* where buyers obtain volume discount prices by joining buying groups.

All three are changing the way people buy airline tickets, hotels, mortgages, cars, elec- tronics, and much more. (Consult Part V of the E-business in Action online supplement at http://www.prenhall.com/ebusinessinaction for additional discussion of online pricing strategies.)

See It on the Web See It on the Web

UNCOVERING HIDDEN COSTS

When you buy something online, the selling price is usually only part of your *total* cost. Factor in hidden costs such as shipping and sales tax, and the total cost can vary dramatically from one Web site to another. Using comparison-shopping sites can help you ferret out hidden costs. Take a look at Best Book Buys, which compares the total cost of buying a book from a variety of Internet sources. Check out one of the best-selling books or search for your favorite book. Click to see a table comparing the item price, shipping cost, and total cost at different retail Web sites. What could be easier—then just click to buy.
http://www.bestbookbuys.com/

■ DEVELOPING PROMOTIONAL STRATEGIES

Although pricing is a critical ingredient in the marketing mix, promotion is perhaps the one element you associate most closely with the marketing function. **Promotion** is persuasive communication that motivates people to buy whatever an organization is selling—goods, services, or ideas. Promotion may take the form of direct, face-to-face communication or indirect communication through such media as television, radio, publications, direct mail, billboards, the Internet, and other channels. Your **promotional strategy** defines the direction and scope of the promotional activities you implement to meet your marketing objectives.

Promotional Goals

You can use promotion to achieve three basic goals: to inform, to persuade, and to remind. *Informing* is the first promotional priority, because people cannot buy a product until they are aware of it and know what it can do for them. Potential customers need to know where the item can be purchased, how much it costs, and how to use it. *Persuading* is also an important priority, because most people need to be encouraged to purchase something new or to switch brands. Advertising that meets this goal is classified as **persuasive advertising.** *Reminding* the customer of the product's availability and benefits is also important, because such reminders stimulate additional purchases. The term for such promotional efforts is **reminder advertising.**

Beyond these general objectives, your promotional strategy should accomplish specific objectives. These include attracting new customers, increasing usage among existing customers, aiding distributors, stabilizing sales, boosting brand-name recognition, creating sales leads, differentiating the product, and influencing decision makers.

Promotional Ethics and Regulations

Although promotion serves many useful functions, critics contend that sellers use promotional tools to persuade people to buy unnecessary or potentially harmful goods. Some people also argue that promotion encourages materialism at the expense of more worthwhile values, that it exploits stereotypes, and that it manipulates the consumer on a subconscious level. Another criticism is that the money spent on promotion could be put to better use inventing new products or improving the quality of existing items.

promotion
Wide variety of persuasive techniques used by companies to communicate with their target markets and the general public

promotional strategy
Statement or document that defines the direction and scope of the promotional activities that a company will use to meet its marketing objectives

persuasive advertising
Advertising designed to encourage product sampling and brand switching

reminder advertising
Advertising intended to remind existing customers of a product's availability and benefits

Although abuses do occur, some of those charges are not justified. Public concern about potential misuse of promotion has led to the passage of government regulations that limit promotional abuses. For example, the Federal Trade Commission (FTC) has developed strict rules for promotion. One rule is that *all statements of fact must be supported by evidence.* This rule prevents a company from using whipped cream in a shaving-cream commercial to create an impression of a firm, heavy lather. Another rule is that *sellers must not create an overall impression that is incorrect.* So they cannot claim that doctors recommend a product if doctors do not; nor can they dress an actor in a doctor's white jacket to deliver the message. Most states also regulate promotional practices by certain industries, such as liquor stores, stock brokerages, employment agencies, and loan companies.

Five Elements of the Promotional Mix

LEARNING OBJECTIVE 4
Identify the five basic categories of promotion

promotional mix
Particular blend of personal selling, advertising, direct marketing, sales promotion, and public relations that a company uses to reach potential customers

personal selling
In-person communication between a seller and one or more potential buyers

Within the framework of government regulations, marketers use a mix of five activities to achieve their promotional objectives: personal selling, advertising, direct marketing, sales promotion, and public relations. These elements can be combined in various ways to create a **promotional mix** for a particular product or idea (see Exhibit 12.6).

Personal Selling   **Personal selling** is direct, person-to-person selling, either face to face or by phone. Personal selling allows for immediate interaction between the buyer and the seller. It also enables the seller to adjust the message to the specific needs and interests of the individual customer. The chief disadvantage of personal selling is its relatively high cost.

By almost any measure, personal selling is the dominant form of promotional activity. Most companies spend twice as much on personal selling as on all other marketing activities combined, even as technology is drastically changing the entire selling process.[31] Computers, telecommunication, hardware, and software—such as online proposal-generation systems and order-management systems—are relieving salespeople from nonproductive tasks, freeing them to spend more time attending to customers' specific needs.

ACTIVITY	REACH	TIMING	COST FLEXIBILITY	EXPOSURE
Personal selling	Direct personal interaction with limited reach	Regular, recurrent contact	Message tailored to customer and adjusted to reflect feedback	Relatively high
Advertising	Indirect interaction with large reach	Regular, recurrent contact	Standard, unvarying message	Low to moderate
Direct marketing	Direct personal interaction with large reach	Intermittent, based on short-term sales objectives	Customized, varying message	Relatively high
Sales promotion	Indirect interaction with large reach	Intermittent, based on short-term sales objectives	Standard, unvarying message	Varies
Public relations	Indirect interaction with large reach	Intermittent, as newsworthy events occur	Standard, unvarying message	No direct cost

EXHIBIT 12•6

THE FIVE ELEMENTS OF PROMOTION

The promotional mix typically includes a blend of these five elements. The most effective mix depends on the nature of the product and the characteristics of the good or service being marketed. Over time, the mix for a particular product may change.

Advertising **Advertising** consists of messages paid for by an identified sponsor and transmitted through a mass-communication medium. The primary role of advertising is to create product awareness and stimulate demand by bringing a consistent message to a large audience economically. You have more control over advertising than over any other form of promotion. However, advertising is expensive: Together, the 100 largest U.S. advertisers spend well over $64 billion a year on this form of promotion.[32] Nevertheless, advertising isn't always as effective as personal selling in motivating customers to buy. For one thing, traditional forms of advertising are difficult to personalize and can't provide direct feedback, as personal selling can.

Keep in mind that advertising not only determines what people buy; it also shapes their view of the world. To be effective, your advertising messages must be persuasive and stand out from the competition's. Estimates suggest that the average person in the United States is exposed to hundreds or even thousands of ads every day.[33] Moreover, even if an ad is seen by 10 million people, only a small percentage will actually buy the product.[34] Still, many firms advertise year in and year out to create and maintain the image of their products.

Media Plans The key to effective advertising is to get your message to your target audience by choosing suitable **media,** or channels of communication. Your **media plan** is a document that shows your advertising budget, how you will divide your money among various media, and when your ads will appear. The goal of your media plan is to make the most effective use of your advertising dollars. In the course of developing a media plan, you will face the critical task of determining an appropriate **media mix**—the combination of print, broadcast, and other media for your advertising campaign. You can choose among several media categories: television, newspapers, direct mail, radio, Yellow Pages, magazines, business papers, outdoor, Internet, and others. Each medium has its own strengths and weaknesses for various advertising applications (see Exhibit 12.7).

advertising
Paid, nonpersonal communication to a target market from an identified sponsor using mass-communications channels

media
Communications channels, such as newspapers, radio, and television

media plan
Written plan that outlines how a company will spend its media budget, including how the money will be divided among the various media and when the advertisements will appear

media mix
Combination of various media options that a company uses in an advertising campaign

MEDIUM	ADVANTAGES	DISADVANTAGES
Newspapers	Extensive market coverage; low cost; short lead time for placing ads; good local market coverage; geographic selectivity	Poor graphic quality; short life span; cluttered pages; visual competition from other ads
Television	Great impact; broad reach; appealing to senses of sight, sound, and motion; creative opportunities for demonstration; high attention; entertainment carryover	High cost for production and air time; less audience selectivity; long preparation time; commercial clutter; short life for message; vulnerability to remote controls
Direct mail	Can deliver large amounts of information to narrowly selected audiences; excellent control over quality of message; personalization	High cost per contact; delivery delays; difficulty of obtaining desired mailing list; consumer resistance; generally poor image (junk mail)
Radio	Low cost; high frequency; immediacy; highly portable; high geographic and demographic selectivity	No visual possibilities; short life for message; commercial clutter; lower attention than television; easy to switch stations
Magazines	Good reproduction; long life; local and regional market selectivity; authority and credibility; multiple readers	Limited demonstration possibilities; long lead time between placing and publishing ads; high cost; less compelling than other major media
Internet	Fast-growing reach; low cost; ability to personalize; can appeal to senses of sight, sound, and motion	Difficulty in measuring audiences; consumer resistance; increasing clutter

EXHIBIT 12.7

ADVANTAGES AND DISADVANTAGES OF MAJOR ADVERTISING MEDIA

When selecting the media mix, companies attempt to match the characteristics of the media audiences with the characteristics of the customer segments being targeted. A typical advertising campaign involves the use of several media.

interactive advertising
Customer-seller communication in which the customer controls the amount and type of information received

Internet Advertising **Interactive advertising,** a two-way exchange between a company and a potential customer, has become a major focus as the Internet and other new media change the nature of advertising from a one-way announcement to a two-way dialogue. Spending for banners and other Internet-based ads now tops $2 billion yearly.[35] Of course, advertisers cannot control when Internet-delivered messages are received, since people can choose to click or not. Consequently, online ads must act as a "hook" to catch the audience's interest. On the other hand, people who choose to participate are often highly interested in the message and thus likely to buy—making the ad more effective (per viewer) than the same ad in other media.

On the Web, you can tailor your message to individuals and simultaneously gather data about each interaction. As the founder of Excite, notes, "The ultimate promise of the Internet is the ability to generate TV-sized audiences and to target a single individual."[36] Internet technology allows you to (1) track the exact information accessed by any particular visitor to your Web site, (2) profile each regular visitor, (3) present information of special interest to a particular visitor, and (4) alert customers to special savings or remind them of past purchases. Of course, before you can tailor a message, you need to gather and store personal data about your visitors. This ability concerns privacy experts, who worry about the type of information being collected and how it is being used. Ultimately, providing too much targeted content on your Web site could spark a backlash. "There's a fine line between adding value and the consumer feeling that you're being intrusive," notes one expert.[37]

direct marketing
Direct communication other than personal sales contacts designed to effect a measurable response

Direct Marketing **Direct marketing,** another element of the firm's promotional mix, is defined by the Direct Marketing Association as distributing one or more promotional materials directly to a consumer or business recipient for the purpose of generating (1) a response in the form of an order, (2) a request for further information, or (3) a visit to a store or other place of business for purchase of a specific product or service.[38] As this definition shows, direct marketing is both a distribution method and a form of promotion; this chapter covers the promotion side; Chapter 13 discusses the distribution side.

Direct marketing has become the promotion tool of choice for many companies because it enables them to more precisely target and personalize messages to specific consumer and business segments.[39] Overall revenues from direct-marketing activities are projected to reach $1.9 trillion by 2002.[40] In addition to the Internet, the main direct-marketing channels are direct mail, telemarketing, and infomercials.

direct mail
Advertising sent directly to potential customers, usually through the U.S. Postal Service

The principal vehicle for direct marketing is **direct mail,** which includes catalogs and other materials delivered through the U.S. Postal Service and private carriers. Mailing out

See It on the Web See It on the Web

MAKE IT A BANNER YEAR

Rev up traffic on your Web site by visiting the Website Promoters Resource Center (WPRC). Click on Banner Advertising, and then Useful Resources. Scroll down to the WPRC Library. Tour the Web site. See how to get started with banner advertising, and learn the dos and don'ts of online marketing. Find out how to optimize your Web site for search engine listings. Read the tip of the week and learn from the experience of others. Find out what's in a domain name. Get some free advice and make it a banner year.
http://www.wprc.com

letters, brochures, videotapes, disks, and other promotional items to customers and prospects can be an effective way to increase sales, although companies must take into account the cost of printing and postage.

Another popular form of direct marketing is **telemarketing,** or selling over the telephone, a low-cost way to efficiently reach many people. Time-pressed customers often appreciate the convenience of buying by phone.[41] With *outbound telemarketing,* companies place *cold calls* to potential customers who have not requested a sales call; *inbound telemarketing* establishes phone lines for customers to call in to place orders or request information. However, because outbound telemarketing has been criticized as being intrusive, some states are considering regulating or even banning this form of promotion.[42]

Television *infomercials* are long, informative commercials that have the appearance of regular programs. Although only one out of 40 infomercials turns a profit, some infomercials have been highly successful. For example, Ovation went from selling 2,000 Thigh Masters per week to selling 75,000 per week in a five-month period after using infomercials.[43]

Sales Promotion   **Sales promotion** includes a wide range of events and activities designed to stimulate immediate interest in your product. Over the past two decades, U.S. sales-promotion expenditures have grown so much they now exceed those for advertising.[44] Consumer sales promotion techniques, which include coupons, point-of-purchase displays, rebates, in-store demonstrations, samples, and premiums, are aimed directly at final users of the product and are used to stimulate repeat purchases and to entice new users. In contrast, trade sales promotion, which includes trade allowances and trade shows, is aimed at retailers and wholesalers.

Consumer Sales Promotions   The biggest category of consumer promotion—and the most popular with consumers—is **couponing,** used to spur sales by offering a discount through redeemable coupons.[45] Companies offer coupons on packages, in print ads, in direct mail, at the checkout, and on the Internet to encourage trial of new products, reach out to nonusers of mature products, encourage repeat buying, and temporarily lower a product's price.[46] Ford and General Motors, for example, have mailed coupons to owners of older-model vehicles to induce them to buy new cars.[47] Couponing is a fairly inefficient technique, however: A lot of money is wasted on advertising and delivering coupons that are never redeemed. Also, critics say couponing instills a bargain-hunting mentality, leading some people to avoid buying unless they have a coupon.[48]

Another widely used consumer promotion technique is the **point-of-purchase display,** a device for showing a product in a way that stimulates immediate sales. It may be simple, such as the end-of-aisle stacks of soda pop in a supermarket or the racks of gum and mints at checkout counters. Simple or elaborate, point-of-purchase displays really work: Studies show that in almost every instance, such displays significantly increase sales.[49]

Other consumer sales-promotion techniques include rebates, free samples, frequency programs such as frequent-flyer miles, and **premiums,** which are free or bargain-priced items offered to encourage the consumer to buy a product. Contests and sweepstakes are also quite

telemarketing
Selling or supporting the sales process over the telephone

sales promotion
Wide range of events and activities (including coupons, rebates, contests, in-store demonstrations, free samples, trade shows, and point-of-purchase displays) designed to stimulate interest in a product

couponing
Distribution of certificates that offer discounts on particular items

point-of-purchase display
Advertising or other display materials set up at retail locations to promote products to potential customers as they are making their purchase decisions

premiums
Free or bargain-priced items offered to encourage consumers to buy a product

Corporations promote their brands and products beyond the usual showrooms and supermarket shelves. Today, corporate logos are going on everything from T-shirts to shoes.

specialty advertising
Advertising that appears on various items such as coffee mugs, pens, and calendars, designed to help keep a company's name in front of customer

trade promotions
Sales-promotion efforts aimed at inducing distributors or retailers to push a producer's products

trade allowance
Discount offered by producers to wholesalers and retailers

trade shows
Gatherings where producers display their wares to potential buyers; nearly every industry has one or more trade shows each year focused on particular types of products

public relations
Nonsales communications that businesses have with their various audiences (included are both communication with the general public and relations with the press)

news release
Brief statement or video program released to the press announcing new products, management changes, sales performance, and other potential news items

news conference
Gathering of media representatives at which companies announce new information; also called a press briefing or press conference

popular in some industries. Particularly when valuable or unusual prizes are offered, contests and sweepstakes can generate a great deal of public attention. Special-event sponsorships are a fast-growing area of sales promotion: spending on festivals, fairs, and other events nearly doubled between 1995 and 1999, to $578 million.[50] **Specialty advertising** (on pens, calendars, T-shirts, and so on) helps keep a company's name in front of customers for a long period of time.

Trade Sales Promotions   **Trade promotions** are sales-promotion efforts aimed at inducing distributors or retailers to sell a company's products. Often, the lure is a discount on the product's price—a **trade allowance**—that enables the distributor or retailer to cut the price paid by ultimate consumers. Other techniques are used as well, including display premiums, dealer contests or sweepstakes, and travel bonus programs, all designed to motivate distributors or retailers to push particular merchandise.

Many companies targeting business buyers participate in **trade shows,** gatherings where producers display their wares to potential customers. According to one estimate, the average industrial exhibitor can reach 60 percent of all its prospects at a trade show, and some exhibitors do 25 percent or more of annual sales at one show. Apart from attracting likely buyers, trade shows have the advantages of enabling companies to demonstrate and explain their product and to talk to prospects about what they want and need.[51]

Public Relations   **Public relations,** which encompasses all the nonsales communications that businesses have with their various audiences, plays a vital role in the success of most companies. Smart businesspeople know that public relations can help them maintain positive relations with communities, investors, industry analysts, government agencies and officials, and the news media. This promotional tool is, in effect, the driving force behind an ongoing two-way conversation to make stakeholders "aware of the product, [to] listen to what [stakeholders] have to say, and [to] move . . . information back and forth," says one public relations expert.[52]

Two standard public relations tools are the news release and the press (or news) conference. A **news release** is a short memo sent to the media covering topics that are of potential news interest; a *video news release* is a brief video clip sent to television stations.[53] Companies use news releases to get favorable news coverage about themselves and their products. When a business has significant news to announce, it will often arrange a **news conference.** Both tools are used when the company's news is of widespread interest, when products need to be demonstrated, or when company officials want to be available to answer questions from the media.

Deciding on the Right Promotional Mix

With five major promotional methods available—personal selling, advertising, direct marketing, sales promotion, and public relations—how do you decide on the right mix for your product? There are no easy answers, because you must take many factors into account. In fact, when you consider all the ways that audiences can receive marketing messages today, the potential for confusion is not all that surprising. Besides the traditional media—television, radio, billboards, print ads, and direct-mail promotions—marketers are using Web sites, e-mail, faxes, kiosks, sponsorships, and many other channels to deliver messages to targeted audiences. Coordinating these diverse vehicles is vital if you are to send a consistent message and boost its effectiveness.

Integrated marketing communications (IMC) is a strategy of coordinating and integrating all your communications and promotion efforts to provide customers with clar-

integrated marketing communications (IMC)
Strategy of coordinating and integrating communications and promotions efforts with customers to ensure greater efficiency and effectiveness

ity, consistency, and maximum communications impact.[54] Properly implemented, IMC increases marketing and promotional effectiveness. The basics of IMC are quite simple: communicating with one voice and one message to the marketplace.

Southwest Airlines uses IMC to establish and maintain a consistent image of low-fare, no-frills, high-frequency service in new and existing markets. For example, when the Texas-based airline beefed up service on the East Coast, it used public relations, special events, and advertising to whip up excitement by promoting a special Thanksgiving Day cross-country flight from Baltimore, Maryland, to Oakland, California, at the bargain rate of $99. The resulting media coverage effectively communicated the airline's low-price, flyer-friendly position. "We always start out with the public relations side in announcing inaugural services. Then we integrate government relations, community affairs, service announcements, special events, advertising, and promotion," says the head of Southwest's ad agency. "We try to fire all guns at once so that by the time Southwest comes into the market, the airline is already part of the community."[55]

Besides integrating their marketing efforts, firms must consider other factors when deciding on the right promotional mix. For one thing, most companies have limited resources, so establishing a promotional budget is often the first step in developing a promotional strategy. Next, a firm should consider the nature and appeal of the product, its position in the life cycle, the size and interests of its targeted segments, its competitive situation, any country and cultural differences, and its desired market position.

In general, you can probably use advertising to explain simple consumer products such as laundry detergent, but you will likely need personal selling to communicate the features of business-oriented goods and services such as municipal waste-treatment facilities. Direct, personal contact is particularly important in promoting customized consumer or business services such as interior design, financial advice, or legal counsel.

Your product's price is also a factor in the selection of the promotional mix. Inexpensive items sold to a mass market are well suited to advertising and sales promotion, which have a relatively low per-unit cost. At the other extreme, you can justify the high cost of a personal sales call when marketing products with a high unit price to a well-defined customer segment.

To some extent, the right promotional mix depends on whether you plan to focus your marketing efforts on intermediaries or on final customers. If your focus is on intermediaries, you can use a **push strategy** to persuade wholesalers and retailers to carry your product. These outlets will then be responsible for selling the product to the end user. If your focus is on end users, you can use a **pull strategy** to appeal directly to the ultimate customer, using advertising, direct mail, contests, discount coupons, and so on. With this approach, consumers learn of your product through promotion and request it from retailers and other sources, who respond by buying it from wholesalers or directly from you.

Most companies use both push and pull tactics to increase the impact of their promotional efforts. For example, when Schering-Plough introduced Claritin antihistamine, it used push tactics to educate physicians about the prescription drug's use and efficacy while using pull tactics such as television and print advertising to increase market awareness and encourage consumers to ask for the new medication. This diverse, high-powered promotional mix helped Claritin capture a whopping 54 percent of the antihistamine drug market within a short time.[56] To properly execute this plan, Schering-Plough's marketers were careful to combine their promotional strategy with their distribution strategy, the final element of a firm's marketing mix, and the subject of Chapter 13.

LEARNING OBJECTIVE 5
Explain the use of integrated marketing communications

LEARNING OBJECTIVE 6
Distinguish between push and pull strategies of promotion

push strategy
Promotional approach designed to motivate wholesalers and retailers to push a producer's products to end users

pull strategy
Promotional strategy that stimulates consumer demand, which then exerts pressure on wholesalers and retailers to carry a product

Summary of Learning Objectives

1. **Describe the four stages in the life cycle of a product.**
   Products start in the introductory stage and progress through a growth stage and a maturity stage before eventually moving into a decline stage.

2. **Cite three levels of brand loyalty.**
   The first level of brand loyalty is brand awareness, in which the buyer is familiar with the product. The next level is brand preference, in which the buyer will select the product if it is available. The final level is brand insistence, in which the buyer will accept no substitute.

3. **List seven factors that influence pricing decisions.**
   Pricing decisions are influenced by marketing objectives, government regulations, consumer perceptions, manufacturing and selling costs, competition, consumer demand, and the needs of wholesalers and retailers who distribute the product to the final customer.

4. **Identify the five basic categories of promotion.**
   The five basic categories of promotion are personal selling, advertising, direct marketing, sales promotion, and public relations.

5. **Explain the use of integrated marketing communications.**
   Integrated marketing communications (IMC) is used to coordinate and integrate all of a company's communications and promotions efforts so they present only one voice and one message to the marketplace, increasing promotional and marketing effectiveness.

6. **Distinguish between push and pull strategies of promotion.**
   In the push strategy, the producer motivates distributors to carry a product, who in turn are responsible for "pushing," or selling, the item to end users. The pull approach, by contrast, stimulates consumer demand by using a variety of marketing tactics that appeal to consumers, who then "pull" the product through the distribution channel.

Key Terms

advertising (293)
brand (283)
brand awareness (284)
brand insistence (285)
brand loyalty (284)
brand mark (284)
brand names (283)
brand preference (284)
break-even analysis (288)
break-even point (288)
co-branding (286)
couponing (295)
direct mail (294)
direct marketing (294)
discount pricing (289)
family branding (285)
fixed costs (288)
generic products (284)

integrated marketing communications (IMC) (296)
interactive advertising (293)
media (293)
media mix (293)
media plan (293)
national brands (284)
news conference (296)
news release (296)
penetration pricing (289)
personal selling (292)
persuasive advertising (291)
point-of-purchase display (295)
premiums (295)
private brands (284)
product (278)
product life cycle (279)
product line (282)

product mix (281)
promotion (291)
promotional mix (292)
promotional strategy (291)
public relations (296)
pull strategy (297)
push strategy (297)
reminder advertising (291)
sales promotion (295)
skimming (289)
specialty advertising (296)
telemarketing (295)
trade allowance (296)
trade promotions (296)
trade shows (296)
trademark (284)
Universal Product Codes (UPCs) (286)
variable costs (288)

MEETING BUSINESS CHALLENGES AT LEVI STRAUSS

The once-proud Levi brand was humbled during the 1990s by a sharp decline in market share. Younger consumers were still buying jeans, but not Levi's. The company had refused to respond to the latest fashion trends, so consumers sought out more stylish versions made by competing manufacturers and jeans retailers. Once Levi's marketers recognized how out of touch they had become, they scrambled to revitalize the brand and its products.

The first step was to do a better job of researching two targeted consumer segments: youth (aged 13 to 25) and young adults (aged 25 to 35). The company assigned teams of marketers to learn more about these segments' perceptions and needs. They quickly learned that younger buyers were interested in unique, uncommon styles. This insight led to the development of the Limited Edition product line, a series of 12 tops, bottoms, and accessories inspired by the 1970s feel of the movie *Mod Squad*. The line, available for only 60 days, was promoted alongside the movie but was sold only through Levi's Web site and Original Levi stores. "We hear from kids that they want something different and exclusive, and this limited, short product offering is a new strategy for Levi," explained Levi's communications manager.

Next, the company moved away from its traditional "one brand fits all" strategy by creating a series of individual brands. Red Line jeans, for example, were positioned as fashionable and upscale, with distribution limited to 25 trendy stores. Other new brands included Dockers Equipment for Legs, casual pants sold only in Europe, and K-1 Khakis, a hipper version of the popular Dockers product line. These brands were designed specifically for the baby boomer segment.

Levi's Web site was an integral part of the company's marketing plan. Marketers got ideas and feedback from consumers who joined the online Be In Club. Going further, the company created Original Spin, a high-tech program that allowed con-sumers to order jeans customized to individual specifications. "Original Spin is all about providing choices to men and women that allow them to express their personal style," said one Levi spokesperson. "This consumer group has told us that individu-alized fashion is very important to them, because it tells people who they are." Accessing Original Spin on the Web or in com-puterized kiosks at selected stores, consumers were able to de-sign their own jeans by selecting among various fabrics, features, and fit choices.

Levi Strauss began to see some positive results soon after implementing these changes. However, given the rapid and un-predictable changes in consumer markets—especially in the fashion world—only time will tell whether the Levi brand has really regained its cool. [57]

Critical Thinking Questions

1. Why did Levi decide to use individual branding rather than family branding?
2. What does Levi's Limited Edition strategy mean for the product life cycle of such products?
3. In which stage of the product life cycle would you position bluejeans? How does this position influence Levi's strategic marketing planning?

■ LEARN MORE ONLINE

How is Levi Strauss using its Web site to position Original Spin in the minds of younger consumers? Visit the company's home-page at http://www.levi.com/ and follow the Original Spin link on the drop-down menu. How do the graphics and content re-flect the needs and interests of the targeted segment? What points of differentiation are being emphasized?

Test Your Knowledge

QUESTIONS FOR REVIEW

1. What are the four main subgroups of consumer products?
2. What are the functions of packaging?
3. How does cost-based pricing differ from price-based pricing?
4. What are the three basic goals of promotion?
5. What are some common types of consumer promotions?

QUESTIONS FOR ANALYSIS

6. Why do businesses continually introduce new products, given the high costs of the introduction stage of the product life cycle?
7. Why are brand names important?
8. How does electronic pricing benefit companies? How does it benefit customers?
9. What is the biggest advantage of personal selling over the other forms of promotion?
10. Why might an employee with high personal ethical standards act less ethically when developing packaging, labeling, pricing, or promotional strategies?

QUESTIONS FOR APPLICATION

11. In what ways might Mattel modify its pricing strategies during the life cycle of a toy product?
12. If you were the marketing manager for Ikea (a warehouse furniture store), how would you use persuasive advertising and reminder advertising to boost furniture sales?
13. After reviewing the theory of supply and demand in Chapter 1 (see pages 7–10), discuss how skimming and penetration pricing strategies would influence a product's supply and demand.
14. Review the discussion of cultural differences in international business in Chapter 3 (see pages 53–54). Which cultural differences did Disney have to consider when planning its product strategies for Disneyland Paris? Originally the company offered a standardized product but was later forced to customize many of the park's operations. What might have been some of the cultural challenges Disney experienced under a standardized product strategy?

Practice Your Knowledge

SHARPENING YOUR COMMUNICATION SKILLS

After scraping together enough money to purchase a new high-speed modem for your computer, you installed it, configured it, and were ready to cruise the Internet at high speed—or so you thought. But you've discovered that your apartment telephone line won't accommodate high-speed data transfer. Instead of 56 bps you're stuck at 28.8, and you're angry. For one thing, the store where you purchased the modem did not warn you that there might be a problem. For another, the only requirements listed on the product box or in the instructions were a computer and a phone line. Finally, the phone company has washed its hands of the problem altogether. Getting your money back is not a problem, of course, but you think company authorities should be advised of your dissatisfaction. Whom should you advise: the store? the manufacturer? the telephone company? Would it be most effective to communicate your dissatisfaction by phone, e-mail, or a letter? Explain your answers.

HANDLING DIFFICULT SITUATIONS ON THE JOB: WHO PAYS THE BILL FOR FREDDY PUMPKIN?

Allen White had a bit of a shock when he opened his March phone bill a while back—and April's bill was no better. The statements for both months listed $40 worth of phone calls that

White was sure he had not made. Finally, in May, when the mystery calls totaled $100, White figured out that his four-year-old son was placing calls to "Freddy Pumpkin"—a 900 telephone line advertised on children's television shows. The irate Mr. White paid the telephone bill but fired off a letter of protest to Robert H. Lorsch, president of Teleline, a company that operates children's phone-line services.

You are Mr. Lorsch's assistant, and you were in the office when White's letter arrived. Lorsch has asked you to draft a letter responding to this complaint. He believes that Teleline offers a legitimate service. Children who call the firm's 900 numbers hear a taped message featuring cartoon or fantasy characters. At $2.45 for the first minute and 45 cents for each additional minute, the calls aren't cheap; but they aren't a big problem unless a child develops a serious habit. Teleline receives fewer than 12 complaints a month. The company is careful to state its prices in its television ads for the phone lines, and it clearly warns children to ask their parents for permission before calling.[58]

1. Is pricing really the problem in this situation? What should you say about pricing in your letter to Mr. White?
2. What can you say in your letter about Teleline's promotional ethics?

3. What suggestions can you offer to Mr. Lorsch about changing Teleline's pricing or promotional strategies to minimize parents' complaints?

BUILDING YOUR TEAM SKILLS

When planning their pricing strategies, marketers need to understand their costs, both fixed and variable. Doing so is important not only for completing an accurate break-even analysis but also for setting prices that include sufficient profits. Consider pricing in the hotly competitive online brokerage industry, where Internet-based firms such as Ameritrade offer deeply discounted commissions on stock trades. At the higher end of the pricing spectrum are established brokerage firms such as Charles Schwab, which has moved into the booming online business with pricing well below the commissions it charges for trades that are not completed on the Internet. Schwab charges $29.95 per trade, whereas Ameritrade's pricing drops as low as $8 per buy or sell transaction.

Why are these companies' prices so different? Schwab has offices across the country and maintains a staff of registered brokers to work with customers who visit local branches or call to discuss trades. In contrast, Ameritrade operates only in cyberspace; its brokers are linked to customers by Internet or, when necessary, by phone. Both brokerage firms advertise heavily to attract and retain customers; both must factor taxes and stock exchange fees into their pricing. And thanks to its lower commission pricing, Ameritrade's profit margin is much thinner than Schwab's.[59]

With your team, brainstorm a listing of costs (such as paying brokers and buying computer equipment) that Ameritrade and Schwab must consider when pricing their trading services. Which of these costs are fixed, and which are variable? As the volume of online stock trading grows, which costs are likely to increase faster? Does Schwab have to bear certain costs that Ameritrade does not? What effect do you think these costs have on Schwab's pricing strategy?

Present your team's findings to your class. What additional costs did other teams identify? Did other teams categorize some costs as fixed that you thought were variable—or vice versa? Why did your categories differ? Why is it important to properly categorize costs when planning pricing?

Expand Your Knowledge

EXPLORING CAREER OPPORTUNITIES

Jobs in promotion—personal selling, advertising, direct marketing, sales promotion, and public relations—are among the most exciting and challenging in all of marketing. Choose a particular job in one of these five areas, such as public relations or media planning expert. Using personal contacts, local phone or Chamber of Commerce directories, or Internet resources such as Yahoo at http://www.yahoo.com, identify and arrange a brief phone or personal interview with a professional working in your chosen marketing field.

1. What are the daily activities of this professional? What tools and resources does this person use most often on the job? What does this professional like most and least about the job?

2. What talents and educational background does this professional bring to the job? How does the person apply his or her skills and knowledge to handle the job's daily activities?

3. What advice does the person you are interviewing have for newcomers entering this field? What can you do now to get yourself started on a career path toward this position?

DEVELOPING YOUR RESEARCH SKILLS

Developing a product strategy for international markets can be tricky, because of the diverse factors that affect a product's sales in different countries. Consider Unilever, the huge Anglo-Dutch consumer goods company that markets such well-known brands as Lipton tea and Ragu sauces. The company has successfully expanded throughout Europe, North America, Asia, and the Pacific by carefully studying local customers' tastes and preferences for various items before making product strategy decisions.[60]

1. Learn more about Unilever's international product strategies by checking several sources, such as *Hoover's Handbook of World Business,* Unilever's annual report, and Unilever's Web site at http://www.unilever.com. In which countries is the company marketing its food products? What new markets does it plan to enter soon?

2. On the basis of your research, do you think Unilever is standardizing, customizing, or using both approaches to market food products suited for different geographical areas?

3. Look at Unilever's recent acquisitions of food brands and companies. What effect are such acquisitions likely to have on the company's international product strategy?

SEE IT ON THE WEB EXERCISES
Protect Your Trademark, page 284

Visit the U.S. Patent and Trademark Office at http://www.uspto.gov/ to learn about trademarks.

1. Click on General Information and Trademark Information. Review the Basic Facts About Registering a Trademark. How do you establish trademark rights? Are you required to conduct a search for conflicting marks before applying with the Patent and Trademark Office (PTO)? Who is allowed to use the ® symbol?

2. Go to Frequently Asked Questions. How does a trademark differ from a service mark?

3. Go back Home and click on Databases, then Trademark Database with Images. What are the four ways you can search this database?

Uncovering Hidden Costs, page 291

Point your Web browser to Best Book Buys at http://www.bestbookbuys.com/ to compare prices of a best-selling book and uncover the hidden costs at various online bookstores.

1. Go to Bestsellers, select the top-selling book on the list, and hit *compare prices*. How do the item prices vary from store to store? How do the shipping cost, carrier, and delivery schedules vary?

2. In which states would a buyer pay sales tax from each store on the list? How does sales tax affect the total cost of the best-seller?

3. What is the lowest total cost for this book? What is the highest total cost? Why would a buyer choose to buy from an online store that does not have the lowest total cost?

Make It a Banner Year, page 294

Go to Website Promoters Resource Center at http://www.wprc.com and click on Banner Advertising to view two informative slide shows; click (1) Beginner's Guide to Banner Advertising and (2) Effective Banner Design. Now see how some of these principles are applied. View some effective banners at http://wprc.com.

1. What are some of the advantages of banner advertising? What is the most common method used for banner ad pricing?

2. What are some effective tools in designing banners?

3. Practice your skills. Visit a related site, The Banner Generator at http://www.coder.com/creations/banner. Scroll down and Make a Banner of your own.

13

DEVELOPING A DISTRIBUTION STRATEGY

LEARNING OBJECTIVES

After studying this chapter, you will be able to

1 Explain what a distribution channel is

2 Discuss how the Internet is influencing distribution channels

3 Differentiate between selective and exclusive distribution strategies

4 Explain how wholesalers and retailers function as intermediaries

5 Describe the growth in nonstore retailing and identify common types of nonstore retailers

6 List the five major modes of transportation used in physical distribution

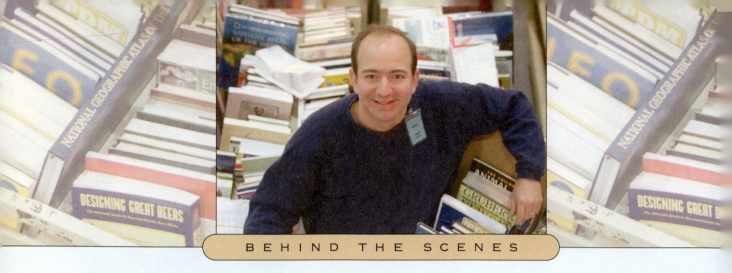

FACING BUSINESS CHALLENGES AT AMAZON.COM

Building the Earth's Biggest Online Department Store

The Internet was barely a blip on the world's business radar when Jeff Bezos read a report predicting that World Wide Web usage would grow 2,300 percent per year. That startling statistic was, he says, "a huge wake-up call." Sensing a major opportunity in the making, Bezos wasted no time. Within three months, he had quit his Wall Street job, packed up his belongings, and hopped into his car. As his wife drove them westward from New York, he drafted a business plan for a completely automated store on the Web.

First, Bezos had to decide what type of product to sell. He started with a list of 20 products and narrowed the list to five: books, CDs, videos, computers, and software. Examining market size, product choice, and pricing, the entrepreneur learned that book retailing was an $82 billion-a-year business with 3 million books selling in a wide price range. Books, he decided, would be his specialty, with a money-saving twist: He would minimize his on-hand inventory and buy most books from distributors after customers had placed their orders.

Working from a Seattle garage, Bezos, his wife, and three employees lined up investors, wholesalers, shippers, and software developers. Then in July 1995, Amazon.com (a name selected by Bezos to suggest enormous assortment) opened its electronic doors and ushered in a new era of low-price book retailing. Web surfers quickly found their way to the fledgling site, which offered personalized features made possible only by advanced computer technology.

Buoyed by growing customer acceptance of safe, convenient online channels, Amazon.com made the transition from newcomer to category killer in less than two years. But it wasn't long before Web sites established by Barnes and Noble, one of the country's largest chains, and Borders, another national chain, threatened to close in on Amazon's commanding lead as the premier online book retailer. With an eye toward the future, Bezos took the company public and raised millions of dollars through an initial public offering. He used the money to beef up advertising, upgrade systems, purchase warehouses, stock them with books, and diversify into other product lines—a costly endeavor, and a dramatic shift in strategy from Amazon's original "books only" and "no bricks and mortar" plan.

Had Bezos lost his mind? Even as annual sales topped $150 million, Amazon.com was unprofitable. But Bezos wasn't focusing on the bottom line. Instead he was obsessed with only one thing: staking out new Internet territory and generating sales before others did. What marketing changes would Bezos have to make to achieve his goal? How could he leverage the strength of the Amazon.com brand name to obtain a competitive advantage in the fast-paced world of e-commerce? Moreover, how could he convince investors to remain patient while Amazon.com racked up hefty losses?[1]

SELECTING THE MOST EFFECTIVE DISTRIBUTION ■ CHANNELS

Amazon.com's Jeff Bezos was a pioneer in recognizing the potential of the Internet as a method for making goods and services available to buyers. He reasoned that, given a choice, many people would prefer the ease and convenience of online shopping to visiting a store every time they wanted to buy a book. He also believed that publishers would welcome Amazon.com as yet another way to get their books into the hands of readers.

Getting products to consumers is the role of distribution, the fourth part of the marketing mix—also known as *place*. **Distribution channels,** or *marketing channels,* are an organized network of firms that work together to get goods and services from producer to consumer. Distribution channels come in all shapes and sizes. Some channels are short and simple; others are complex and involve many people and organizations. A company's decisions about which combination of channels to use—the **distribution mix**—and its overall plan for moving products to buyers—the **distribution strategy**—play major roles in the firm's success.

The Role of Marketing Intermediaries

Think of all the products you buy: food, toiletries, clothing, sports equipment, train tickets, haircuts, gasoline, stationery, appliances, CDs, videotapes, books, and all the rest. How many of these products do you buy directly from the producer? For most people, the answer is not many.

Most companies do not sell their goods directly to the final users, even though the Internet is making it easier to do so these days. Instead, producers in many industries work with **marketing intermediaries** (also called *middlemen*) to bring their products to market. In some cases, these "go-betweens" represent the producers but do not actually buy the products they sell; in others, the intermediaries buy and own what they sell.

Without marketing intermediaries, the buying and selling process would be expensive and time-consuming (see Exhibit 13.1). Intermediaries are instrumental in creating three of the four forms of utility mentioned in Chapter 11: place utility, time utility, and possession utility. By providing a way to transfer products from the producer to the customer, intermediaries ensure that goods and services are available at a convenient time and place. They also simplify the exchange process that drives commerce.

Overall, intermediaries such as stores perform a number of specific distribution functions that make life easier for both producers and customers. They

- *Provide a sales force.* Hiring, training, and paying salespeople to sell directly to customers can be expensive and inefficient, so many producers rely on intermediaries to sell their goods.
- *Provide market information.* Intermediaries such as Amazon.com collect valuable data about customer purchases: who buys, how often, and how much. Collecting these data allows them to spot buying patterns and to share marketplace information with producers.
- *Provide promotional support.* Many intermediaries create advertising, produce eye-catching displays, and use other promotional devices for some or all of the products they sell.
- *Gather an assortment of goods.* Amazon.com, Macy's, and other intermediaries receive bulk shipments from producers and break them into more convenient units by sorting, standardizing, and dividing bulk quantities into smaller packages.

LEARNING OBJECTIVE 1
Explain what a distribution channel is

distribution channels
Systems for moving goods and services from producers to customers; also known as marketing channels

distribution mix
Combination of intermediaries and channels a producer uses to get a product to end users

distribution strategy
Firm's overall plan for moving products to intermediaries and final customers

marketing intermediaries
Businesspeople and organizations that channel goods and services from producers to consumers

EXHIBIT 13·1

HOW INTERMEDIARIES SIMPLIFY COMMERCE

Intermediaries actually reduce the price customers pay for many goods and services, because they reduce the number of contacts between producers and consumers that would otherwise be necessary. They also create place, time, and possession utility.

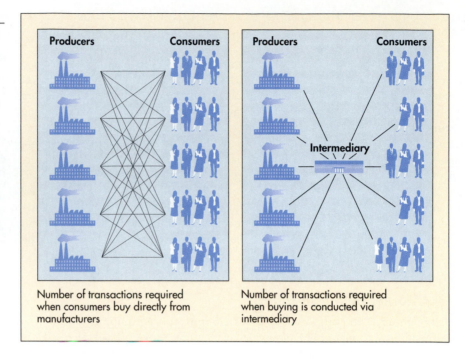

Number of transactions required when consumers buy directly from manufacturers

Number of transactions required when buying is conducted via intermediary

- *Stock and deliver the product.* Intermediaries such as retail stores maintain an inventory of merchandise that they acquire from manufacturers so they can quickly fill customers' orders. Some intermediaries, such as soda pop distributors, are responsible for delivering goods to retail buyers as well.
- *Assume risks.* When intermediaries accept goods from manufacturers, they take on the risks associated with damage, theft, product perishability, and obsolescence.
- *Provide financing.* Large intermediaries sometimes provide loans to smaller producers.
- *Match buyers and sellers.* By making sellers' products available to multiple buyers, intermediaries reduce the number of transactions between producers and customers.

Types of Distribution Channels

The number and type of intermediaries you select for your distribution mix depend on the kind of product you are selling and the marketing practices of your industry. An arrangement that works well for a power-tool and appliance manufacturer like Black & Decker or a book publisher like Prentice Hall would not necessarily work for an insurance company, a restaurant, a steel manufacturer, or a movie studio. In general, consumer goods and services tend to move through different channels than business goods and services do (see Exhibit 13.2).

Channel Levels   Most businesses purchase goods they use in their operations directly from producers, so the distribution channel is short. In contrast, the channels for consumer goods are usually longer and more complex than the channels for business goods. The four primary channels for consumer goods are:

- *Producer to consumer.* Producers who sell directly to consumers through catalogs, telemarketing, infomercials, and the Internet are using the shortest, simplest distribution channel. Dell Computer and other companies that deal directly with con-

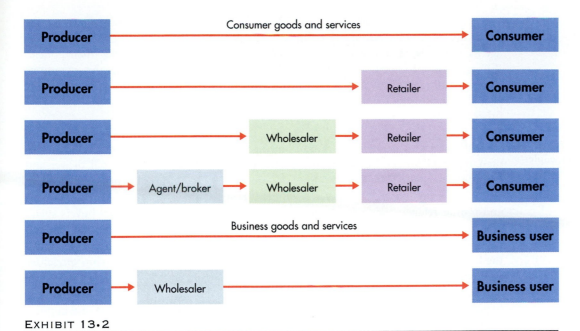

EXHIBIT 13·2

ALTERNATIVE CHANNELS OF DISTRIBUTION

Producers of consumer and business goods and services must analyze the alternative channels of distribution available for their products so they can select the channels that best meet their marketing objectives and their customers' needs.

sumers are seeking closer relationships with customers and more control over pricing, promotion, service, and delivery.[2] Although this approach eliminates payments to channel members, it also forces producers to handle distribution functions such as storing inventory and delivering products.

- *Producer to retailer to consumer.* Some producers create longer channels by selling their products to retailers, who then resell them to consumers. Ford vehicles, Benjamin Moore paint, and New Balance athletic shoes are typical of the many products distributed in this way.

- *Producer to wholesaler to retailer to consumer.* Most manufacturers of supermarket and drugstore items rely on even longer channels. They sell their products to wholesalers, who in turn sell to the retailers. This approach works particularly well for small producers who lack the resources to sell or deliver merchandise to individual retail sites.

- *Producer to agent/broker to wholesaler to retailer to consumer.* Additional channel levels are common in certain industries, such as agriculture, where specialists are required to negotiate transactions or to perform interim functions such as sorting, grading, or subdividing the goods.

Channels for Services   So far we have examined how producers of tangible goods use various channels to reach consumers and businesses, but how do producers of intangible services reach their customers? Because delivery of a service requires direct contact between providers and users, most service marketers use a direct channel to reach their customers. Hairstylists and lawyers, for example, deal directly with their clients, as do accounting firms such as H&R Block.

Some service businesses, however, do use other distribution channels. For example, Air France and other airlines typically sell tickets and vacation packages through travel agents. Similarly, State Farm and many other insurance companies market their policies through insurance agents and brokers. Technology is also increasing the number of options for distributing services. Banks, for instance, distribute financial services to customers all over the globe using automated teller machines in shopping centers, airports, and many other locations.

> The Internet doesn't replace salespeople. It makes them more efficient by enabling customers to do some things for themselves.[4]

LEARNING OBJECTIVE 2
Discuss how the Internet is influencing distribution channels

Internet Channels   The Internet is revolutionizing the way both goods and services are distributed. Using the Internet's efficient and effective global reach, companies can sell, deliver, and provide support for all kinds of products. Amazon.com, for example, sells products online to more than 12 million widely scattered customers.[3] Sears and a growing number of other brick-and-mortar retailers now sell a huge selection of goods online. In fact, tool buyers spend 27 percent more when they buy through the Sears Web site than when they buy at the store.[5] No product is too small or too large for Internet distribution: Stamps.com has partnered with the U.S. Postal Service to provide online delivery of postage, while Homebid.com specializes in auctioning homes on its Web site.[6]

Internet access is enabling more producers to streamline their channel arrangements, bypass some intermediaries, and pass the savings along to customers. A good case in point is Provident American Life & Health Insurance Company. After 110 years of offering medical insurance through 20,000 insurance agents, the company dropped its agent network, changed its name to HealthAxis.com, and launched a Web site to sell a full line of insurance products directly to consumers. CEO Michael Ashker says that eliminating "costly middlemen in an industry where distribution is inefficient" allowed the company to cut its prices by 15 percent.[7]

Although the rapid growth of the Internet is changing the entire distribution industry, traditional channels remain strong: 93 percent of all U.S. retail sales are still rung up in physical stores.[8] Besides, electronic commerce entails a variety of risks and costs that can complicate life for any company. As a result, the multifaceted role that intermediaries play in the distribution process is more important than ever. For one thing, consumers appreciate the convenience of buying from intermediaries who offer a variety of products from many different sources, rather than having to contact each individual

See It on the Web See It on the Web

CHANGE THE BLOOMIN' CHANNEL

New outlets for selling floral arrangements are blossoming all over the Internet, and competition is tough as florists try to distinguish themselves from the bloomin' lot. With Web sites such as iflowers (sponsored by Phillip's 1-800-Florals) springing up like weeds, FTD and 1-800-Flowers no longer have a competitive advantage. In fact, customers visiting iflowers can send digital postcards and personalized messages and then follow the site's links to many other Web sites offering free products, reference sources, live images, shareware, and multimedia tours. So what has all this got to do with romantic roses? Visit iflowers now, follow the links, and remember to think like a marketer.

http://www.iflowers.com

producer on the Internet. On the other side of the exchange, producers—especially new or small businesses—benefit from the assistance of experienced intermediaries who are knowledgeable about target markets and have long-term customer contacts.[9]

Factors to Consider When Selecting Channels

Should you sell directly to end users or rely on intermediaries? Which intermediaries should you choose? Should you try to sell your product in every available outlet or limit its distribution to a few exclusive shops? Should you use more than one channel? These are some of the critical decisions you face when designing and selecting marketing channels for any product.

Keep in mind that building an effective channel system takes years and, like all marketing relationships, requires commitment. Once you commit to your intermediaries, changing your distribution arrangements may prove difficult. As Chris DeNove, a channel expert puts it, "It's much more difficult to modify an existing system than [to start] with a clean slate." Citing the automobile industry, for example, DeNove points out that "if an auto maker could start over now, none of them would create a franchise distribution system that looks like the existing one."[10]

Effective channel selection depends on a number of factors; some are related to the type of product and the target market, and others are related to the company—its strengths, weaknesses, and objectives. In general, however, choosing one channel over another is a matter of making trade-offs among three factors: the number of outlets that sell your product, the cost of distribution, and the control of your product as it moves through the channel to the final customer.

Market Coverage The appropriate *market coverage*—the number of wholesalers or retailers that will carry your product—varies by type of product. Inexpensive convenience goods or organizational supplies such as Pilot pens sell best if they are available in as many outlets as possible. In contrast, shopping goods (goods that require some thought before being purchased) such as General Electric appliances require different market coverage, because customers shop for such products by comparing features and prices. For these items, the best strategy is usually **selective distribution,** selling through a limited number of outlets that can give the product adequate sales and service support.

If producers of expensive specialty or technical products do not sell directly to customers, they may choose **exclusive distribution,** offering products in only one outlet in each market area. Vehicle manufacturers have traditionally relied on exclusive distribution agreements to sell through one dealership in each local area. By contrast, other firms use multiple channels to increase their market coverage and reach several target markets. Apparel manufacturers such as Champion frequently sell through a combination of channels, including department stores, specialty stores, the Internet, and catalogs.

Cost Costs play a major role in determining a firm's channel selection. It takes money to perform all the functions that are handled by intermediaries. Small or new companies often cannot afford to hire a sales force large enough to sell directly to end users or to call on a host of retail outlets. Neither can they afford to build large warehouses and distribution centers or to buy trucks to ship their goods. These firms need the help of intermediaries who can spread the cost of such activities across a number of noncompeting products. With time and a larger sales base, a producer may build enough strength to take over some of these functions and reduce the length of the distribution channel.

Control A third issue to consider when selecting distribution channels is control of how, where, and when your product is sold. Remember, you can't force any intermediary to

LEARNING OBJECTIVE 3
Differentiate between selective and exclusive distribution strategies

selective distribution
Market coverage strategy that uses a limited number of outlets to distribute products

exclusive distribution
Market coverage strategy that gives intermediaries exclusive rights to sell a product in a specific geographical area

Exclusive distribution arrangements are being challenged by manufacturers in many industries as more and more consumers turn to kiosks, supercenters, and the Internet to purchase products. This automobile showroom offers the best of both worlds: A kiosk provides comprehensive product information and up-to-date ordering information while the showroom provides consumers with the chance to test drive their dream car.

properly promote, service, sell, or deliver your product. Longer distribution channels mean less control for producers, who become increasingly distant from sellers and buyers as the number of intermediaries multiplies.

On the other hand, companies may not want to concentrate too many distribution functions in the hands of too few intermediaries, as Ben & Jerry's Homemade once did. For years, Ben & Jerry's sold and distributed as much as 70 percent of its ice cream products through Dreyer's, a nationwide manufacturer and distributor. In 1998 Dreyer's offered to buy Ben & Jerry's, but the unsolicited bid was quickly rejected. Soon afterward, Ben & Jerry's drastically reduced Dreyer's distribution responsibilities, hired more employees to sell directly to retailers, and divided deliveries among a larger number of independent distributors. The reason? Control. "This distribution arrangement puts Ben & Jerry's in a better position to control our product sales and implement more efficient domestic distribution," said the CEO Perry Odak.[11]

Control also becomes critical when a firm's reputation is at stake. For instance, a designer of high-priced clothing might want to limit distribution to exclusive boutiques, because the brand could lose some of its appeal if the clothing were sold in discount stores. In addition, producers of complex technical products such as X-ray machines don't want their products handled by unqualified intermediaries who can't provide adequate customer service.

Other Factors   In addition to market coverage, cost, and control, you should consider several other factors when selecting distribution channels. These factors include the nature and price of your product, the market's growth rate, the geographical concentration of your customer base, your customers' need for service, the importance of rapid delivery, the strengths and weaknesses of the various types of intermediaries within the channel, and international laws and customs if you are selling your product in other countries.

Channel Conflict

No matter how well you design and manage your channels, conflict is bound to arise. What causes channel conflict? In many cases, conflict erupts when suppliers provide inadequate support, when markets are oversaturated with intermediaries, when one channel member places its own success above the success of the entire channel system, and when companies sell products in multiple channels and all the channels are competing for the same customers.

General Motors' recent decision to repurchase some independent dealerships, for instance, has met strong resistance from remaining dealers. These independents worry that company-owned stores will put them at a disadvantage in the marketplace even though GM has promised it will operate on a level playing field.[12] Similarly, Hallmark's decision to sell to mass-market outlets such as discount stores, supermarkets, and drugstores, has angered its 8,200 independent dealers. Hallmark responded by launching a $175 million ad campaign and creating new products exclusively for independents, but only time will tell whether these steps will be enough to save the card shops.[13]

Keep in mind that a limited amount of channel conflict can sometimes be productive, especially if it leads to a more dynamic, more efficient adaptation to changing environmental conditions. Therefore, the challenge is not to eliminate channel conflict but rather to effectively manage it so that the distribution system does not become dysfunctional. For instance, as new channels emerge, producers will want to modify their channel arrangements by adding the new channels while accommodating the needs of older, valued channel members.

DISTRIBUTING PRODUCTS THROUGH
■ INTERMEDIARIES

Depending on your customer base and the distribution patterns in your industry, you can distribute your products through two main types of intermediaries: wholesalers and retailers. **Wholesalers** sell primarily to retailers, to other wholesalers, and to organizational users such as government agencies, institutions, and commercial operations. In turn, the customers of wholesalers either resell the products or use them to make products of their own. Wholesalers that sell to organizational customers are often called **industrial distributors** to distinguish them from wholesalers that supply retail outlets.

Unlike wholesalers, **retailers** sell products to the final consumer for personal use. Retailers can operate out of a physical store (such as a supermarket or a gas station) or without a store (via telephones, catalogs, Web sites, vending machines, and other methods). These basic differences affect the way intermediaries work with producers and customers, as you will see in the following sections.

Selling Through Wholesalers

Because wholesalers seldom deal directly with consumers, you may not be familiar with this vital link in the distribution chain. Yet 453,000 U.S. wholesalers sell a whopping $4 trillion worth of goods every year.[14] Most U.S. wholesalers are independent, and they can be classified as *merchant wholesalers, agents,* or *brokers.*

The majority of wholesalers are **merchant wholesalers,** independently owned businesses that buy from producers, take legal title to the goods, then resell them to retailers or to organizational buyers. **Full-service merchant wholesalers** provide a wide variety of services, such as storage, selling, order processing, delivery, and promotional support. **Rack jobbers,** for example, are full-service merchant wholesalers that set up displays in retail outlets, stock inventory, and mark prices on merchandise displayed in a particular section of a store. **Limited-service merchant wholesalers,** on the other hand, provide fewer services. Natural resources such as lumber, grain, and coal are usually marketed through a class of limited-service wholesalers called **drop shippers,** which take ownership but not physical possession of the goods they handle.

In contrast to merchant wholesalers, **agents and brokers** never take title to the products they handle, and they perform fewer services. Their primary role is to bring buyers and sellers together; they are generally paid a commission (a percentage of the money received) for arranging sales. Real estate agents, insurance brokers, and securities brokers, for example, match up buyers and sellers for a fee or a commission, but they don't own what they sell. Producers of commercial parts often sell to business customers through brokers. Jerry Whitlock has built a $1 million business as a Georgia-based broker using the Internet to wholesale industrial seals made by nearly 100 producers to factories around the country.[15] Manufacturers' representatives, another type of agent, sell various noncompeting products to customers in a specific area and arrange for product delivery. By representing several manufacturers' products, these reps achieve enough volume to justify the high cost of a direct sales call.

Selling Through Store Retailers

In contrast to wholesalers, retailers are a highly visible element in the distribution chain. More than 1.1 million retail intermediaries ring up merchandise worth $2.5 trillion every year.[16] Store retailers include department stores, discount stores, off-price stores, warehouse clubs, factory outlets, specialty stores, category killers, supermarkets, hypermarkets,

LEARNING OBJECTIVE 4

Explain how wholesalers and retailers function as intermediaries

wholesalers
Firms that sell products to other firms for resale or for organizational use

industrial distributors
Wholesalers that sell to industrial customers rather than to retailers

retailers
Firms that sell goods and services to individuals for their own use rather than for resale

merchant wholesalers
Independent wholesalers that take legal title to goods they distribute

full-service merchant wholesalers
Merchant wholesalers that provide a wide variety of services to their customers, such as storage, delivery, and marketing support

rack jobbers
Merchant wholesalers that are responsible for setting up and maintaining displays in a particular section of a retail store

limited-service merchant wholesalers
Merchant wholesalers that offer fewer services than full-service merchant wholesalers; they often specialize in particular markets, such as agriculture

drop shippers
Limited-service merchant wholesalers that assume ownership of goods but don't take physical possession; commonly used to market agricultural and mineral products

agents and brokers
Independent wholesalers that do not take title to the goods they distribute but may or may not take possession of those goods

TYPE OF RETAILER	DESCRIPTION	EXAMPLES
Category killer	Type of specialty store focusing on specific products on giant scale and dominating retail sales in respective products categories	Office Depot Toys "R" Us
Convenience store	Offers staple convenience goods, long service hours, quick checkouts	7-Eleven
Department store	Offers a wide variety of merchandise under one roof in departmentalized sections and many customer services	Sears J. C. Penney Nordstrom
Discount store	Offers a wide variety of merchandise at low prices and few services	Kmart Wal-Mart
Factory/retail outlet	Large outlet store selling discontinued items, overruns, and factory seconds	Nordstrom Rack Nike outlet store
Hypermarket	Giant store offering food and general merchandise at discount prices	Super Kmart
Off-price store	Offers designer and brand-name merchandise at low prices and few services	T. J. Maxx Marshall's
Specialty store	Offers a complete selection in a narrow range of merchandise	Lucky
Supermarket	Large, self-service store offering a wide selection of food and nonfood merchandise	Kroger
Warehouse club	Large, warehouse style store that sells food and general merchandise at discount prices; some require club membership	Sam's Club

EXHIBIT 13·3

TYPES OF RETAIL STORES

The definition of retailer covers many types of outlets. This table shows some of the most common types.

convenience stores, and catalog stores (see Exhibit 13.3). They sell everything from rolling pins to Rolls-Royces, from hot dogs to haute cuisine.

Retail stores provide many benefits to consumers. Some, such as Sears and other department stores, save people time and money by providing an assortment of merchandise under one roof. Others, such as Pier One Imports, give shoppers access to goods and delicacies that they would have difficulty finding on their own. Still other retailers build traffic and add convenience by diversifying their product lines, a practice known as **scrambled merchandising.** For example, you can rent videos, eat pizza, and buy T-shirts at Grand Union supermarkets, and you can buy cosmetics, stationery, and toys at Walgreen's drugstores. Such mixed product assortments cut across retail classifications and blur store identities in the consumers' minds.

Many stores begin as discount operations and then upgrade their operations to become more like department stores in appearance, merchandise, and price. This process of store evolution, known as the **wheel of retailing,** follows a predictable pattern: An innovative retailer with low operating costs attracts a following by offering low prices and limited service. As this store adds more services over time to broaden its appeal, its prices creep upward, opening the door for lower-priced competitors. Eventually, these low-price competitors also upgrade their operations and are replaced by still other lower-priced stores that later follow the same upward pattern.

Specialty Stores, Category Killers, and Discount Stores   Although department stores account for about 10 percent of overall U.S. retail sales, a much higher percentage of store sales are racked up by other types of retailers.[17] When you shop in a pet store, a shoe store, or a stationery store, you are in a **specialty store**—a store that carries only particular types of goods. The basic merchandising strategy of a specialty shop is to offer a limited number of

scrambled merchandising
Policy of carrying merchandise that is ordinarily sold in a different type of outlet

wheel of retailing
Evolutionary process by which stores that feature low prices gradually upgrade until they no longer appeal to price-sensitive shoppers and are replaced by new low-price competitors

specialty store
Store that carries only a particular type of goods

product lines but an extensive selection of brands, styles, sizes, models, colors, materials, and prices within each line stocked. Specialty shops are particularly strong in certain product categories: books, children's clothing, or sporting goods, for example.

At the other end of the retail spectrum are the **category killers**—superstores that dominate a particular product category by stocking every conceivable variety of merchandise in that category. Toys "R" Us, Party City, Office Depot, and Barnes and Noble are category killers. And dominate they do: Category killers ring up as much as one-third of all U.S. retail sales.[18] Still, according to Arthur Martinez, CEO of Sears, "There's some evidence that category killers have gotten too big, too overwhelming, too frightening, and too confusing to shop."[19] Unfortunately, Tandy found this out too late. Its Incredible Universe chain was an incredible flop. After only months of operation, Tandy pulled the plug on its 26 superstores, including all 17 Incredible Universe stores with over 184,000 square feet of every electronic product imaginable.[20]

On the other hand, **discount stores** offer a wider variety of merchandise, lower prices, and fewer services than category killers. Discounters do especially well when the economy is struggling or when consumers are worried about the future.[21] Some discount stores, including Wal-Mart and Target, are stopping category killers like Toys "R" Us in their tracks. That's because a specific product category such as toys accounts for only a fraction of these general discounters' sales, so the discounters can afford to cut prices on that category as a way to lure shoppers. But toys are the only category at Toys "R" Us, so lowering prices has hurt this category killer far more than it has hurt the multiproduct discount store. In fact, Toys "R" Us has been losing market share in toy retailing, even as toy sales are going up.[22]

Another example is discount giant Wal-Mart's expansion into grocery retailing, which has the supermarket industry in an uproar. Since the early 1990s, Wal-Mart has opened nearly 500 U.S. supercenters with an average size of 182,000 square feet. The company continues to open 120 or more new supercenters each year, in addition to new supermarket-style Wal-Mart Neighborhood Markets. Counting all the food products sold throughout the chain, the company rings up an estimated $30 billion in grocery sales annually. Lower prices are a major advantage: Wal-Mart admits that it can sell groceries below cost because it compensates by selling other profitable merchandise. But the world's largest retailer is also counting on its high-efficiency distribution system to put fresher produce on the shelves and keep popular items in stock at all times.[23]

By leveraging its distribution and buying strengths, Wal-Mart is hoping that its new Neighborhood Markets, about the same size as traditional supermarkets, will be able to beat traditional grocery stores with lower everyday prices.

Retail Trends and Challenges   Today's fast-changing business environment is bringing changes and challenges to the retail industry. The average life cycle of a retail store today is considerably shorter than it used to be. It took 100 years for department stores to hit maturity, the period shortened to 10 years for warehouse stores, and now it takes just 5 to 6 years for a new concept to become tired. One reason for this compressed cycle is that retailers have opened too many stores. Today there is an estimated 20 square feet of retail space for every man, woman, and child in the United States, a one-third increase from the 14.7 square feet per person in 1986.[24]

Even though some of this retail space will get transformed by the next wave of ideas, the ongoing expansion has hurt the industry. For one thing, competition is more intense than ever, forcing continued mergers among store chains. In addition, shoppers are getting tired of tramping from one store to another; the average time that consumers spend shopping has dropped 25 percent since 1982, and the average number of stores visited during a mall trip has dropped by 32 percent.[25] Furthermore, many retail locations are looking their age: nearly half of the more than 2,800 enclosed malls in the United States have been around for 20 years or longer.[26]

To entice shoppers, some malls are getting new leases on life through extensive remodeling and the addition of newer stores, restaurants, and short-term shows and exhibits. New stores are also popping up everywhere—from airport terminals to tiny towns—offering any time, any place shopping convenience to draw consumers back again and again.[27] Some retailers are focusing on making their stores exciting, memorable, and fun. This trend toward "retail-tainment" is adding a touch of friendly theatrics to local outlets of giant chains. Customers who can attend a cooking class at Williams Sonoma or get tips from golf pros at the Sports Authority are likely to come back for the latest in-store event—and buy something when they do.[28]

Selling Through Nonstore Retailers

Nonstore retailing has its roots in the mail-order catalogs sent out by Sears and Montgomery Ward during the late 1800s, selling everything from household goods to ready-to-assemble housing materials. Today you can order clothing, electronics, flowers, and almost every other type of tangible and intangible product from anywhere in the world at any time of day without actually visiting a store. Nonstore retailing includes mail-order firms such as L.L. Bean, vending machines such as those selling candy bars and soft drinks, telemarketers such as those selling British Telecom services, door-to-door direct sellers such as Avon, and a variety of electronic venues such as the Internet, interactive kiosks, and television home shopping networks.

As you saw earlier, the overwhelming majority of goods and services are still sold through physical stores. Nonetheless, nonstore retailing is growing at a much faster rate than traditional store retailing, and an estimated one-third to one-half of all general merchandise could soon be sold through nonstore channels.[29] In many cases, producers are reaching shoppers through a carefully balanced blend of store and nonstore retail outlets. Nike, for example, has a button on its Web site to allow visitors to buy any product online at full price (plus shipping and handling charges). But, because most of the company's revenue

LEARNING OBJECTIVE 5
Describe the growth in nonstore retailing and identify common types of nonstore retailers

See It on the Web See It on the Web

EXPLORE THE WORLD OF RETAILING

Thinking about opening up a small store or building a career in retailing? Need some statistics? Find out what's hot in the retail industry by visiting the National Retail Federation Web site. Browse the FAQs and read the Washington Update. Learn which government proposals might affect your retail business and how to do something about them. Opening a retail store can be an exciting venture—especially if you're prepared.
http://www.nrf.com

comes from store intermediaries, it also lists retail locations on its Web site—and gives these retailers the extra advantage of being able to discount Nike products.[30] Despite the convenience of nonstore retailing, people will continue to shop in stores because they like to see, feel, smell, and try out goods before they buy.[31] This was the line of thinking behind Gateway's decision to open Gateway Country stores. The company hopes that giving customers the opportunity to test drive the computers and achieve a comfort level with the technology will eventually pay off.[33]

Mail-Order Firms Among the most popular types of nonstore retailers are **mail-order firms.** These firms provide customers and businesses with a wide variety of goods ordered from catalogs and shipped by mail or private carrier. Catalog shopping is big business, and it's growing at around 8 percent annually, faster than the 5 percent annual growth of all consumer shopping. In 1999, U.S. consumers spent over $265 billion on mail-order goods and services, and businesses ordered another $190 billion worth through catalogs.[34]

Many of the top mail-order firms, such as L.L. Bean, are set up like specialty stores, focusing on a narrow range of merchandise. Some companies, such as Nordstrom, use mail order to supplement and promote their base business, which is conducted primarily through retail stores. Others, such as Harry and David's Fruit-of-the-Month Club, rely almost entirely on mail-order sales. Still others, including Eddie Bauer, view retail stores as a logical expansion of their booming mail-order businesses.[35]

Direct Selling Variations on direct selling are also common forms of nonstore retailing. You have probably experienced telephone retailing, or *telemarketing*, in the form of calls from insurance agents, long-distance telephone companies, and assorted nonprofit organizations, all trying to interest you in their products and causes. Every year, U.S. consumers buy more than $186 billion worth of goods and services over the telephone, and business purchases by phone top $239 billion.[36]

Another form of direct selling is door-to-door sales, in which a large sales force calls directly on customers in their homes or offices to demonstrate merchandise, take orders, and make deliveries. Two famous names in door-to-door selling—and its variant, the party plan—are Avon and Tupperware. However, both companies are launching initiatives to sell directly to the customer over the Internet. Although Avon vows to keep most of its sales force and pay them a commission for sales booked via their individual homepages (which are linked to the company's Web site), the reps are concerned that eventually the company will bypass them and eliminate the commissions.[37]

Electronic Retailing Whether you call it electronic retailing, digital commerce, e-shopping, e-tailing, cybershopping, or virtual retail, the Internet provides a borderless shopping environment in which someone in London can browse through the newest offerings at a site in Los Angeles for products manufactured in Brazil. Many electronic retailers have no physical store outlets. Amazon.com, among the most successful of today's electronic retailers, offers an online-only assortment of CDs, videos, and scores of other products besides its extensive book listings. Other electronic retailers, such as Barnes and Noble, operate both physical stores and Web stores; this approach is becoming more and more common, as traditional store retailers open online outlets to remain competitive.[38] However, few store retailers have followed the lead of Egghead, a software retail chain that closed all its outlets and renamed itself Egghead.com to operate—at a much lower cost—only on the Internet. Recently merged with Onsale.com (an auction site specializing in computer equipment), Egghead.com expects to ring up more than $350 million in annual sales.[39]

Smart companies will combine Internet services and personal contact to give their customers the benefits of both kinds of interaction.[32]

mail-order firms
Companies that sell products through catalogs and ship them directly to customers

From the retailer's viewpoint, electronic retailing costs less (no expensive store rent and store payroll); from the customer's viewpoint, electronic retailing means being able to shop around the clock for products and information tailored to individual needs. These compelling benefits are encouraging companies that do not distribute through physical stores to make the Internet the cornerstone of their distribution strategies. Dell Computer, for example, sells computers through mail-order catalogs and telemarketing but wants to do even more business on the Internet, where it already generates an eye-popping $30 million in sales every day. "We're trying to transform the way Dell does business," explains the director of Dell Online. "We want the Net to become a core part of your experience with Dell."[40]

Selling Products Online

With electronic retailing still in its infancy, businesses selling everything from shoes to shoofly pie are rushing to sell online. But hanging out a shingle on the Internet does not guarantee visitors, let alone sales. Those products and selling approaches that best fit the Internet will succeed; less-appropriate products and selling approaches will fail.[41] Look at iPrint, an Internet-only printer of business cards, letterhead, and other stationery items. Although print-to-order products are commonly sold in person at Mail Boxes Etc. and many independent print shops, iPrint is thriving on a user-friendly, self-service approach. "The success of our Web site depends on the fact that it's as easy to use as a bank ATM," says Royal P. Farras, iPrint's founder.[42] Among the ways you can sell your products online are through electronic catalogs and via cybermalls with virtual storefronts. (Consult Part II of the E-Business in Action online supplement at http://www.prenhall.com/ebusinessinaction for additional discussion of how iPrint pursues outsourcing, co-branding, and partnering.)

Electronic Catalogs   Electronic catalogs (catalogs on computer disk or published over the Internet) allow you to reach an enormous number of potential customers at a relatively low cost. Consider AMP, an electronics manufacturer in Harrisburg, Pennsylvania. The company was spending about $8 million to $10 million a year on its paper-based catalog, and

Egghead.com takes full advantage of the Internet by offering customers such online programs as electronic auctions for about fifty different categories of hardware and software.

Focus on E-Business

E-TAILING: IT TAKES MORE THAN A WEB SITE

It seems like everyone is launching a Web site and taking orders these days. After all, the case for shopping online is compelling. Customers can save time and money by scouring for products and discounts with their keyboards. They can avoid crowded malls. And best of all they can shop day or night, in a tux or stark naked—not to mention that online stores offer many more items than their traditional counterparts, and the products are often easier to find.

In spite of these benefits, it doesn't take long for online retailers to discover that in many ways they aren't much different from brick-and-mortar stores. They run out of stock, sell damaged merchandise, and hire rude sales help. Above all, they can get overwhelmed at Christmas—a lesson many e-tailers have learned the hard way.

During their first major Internet Christmas in 1999, hordes of e-tailers flooded the market. Trouble is, many of them spent heavily to market and promote their brands but scrimped on the unglamorous side of business—the logistics or infrastructure—which focuses on servicing customers during and after the sale, and delivering their products efficiently. It's where people and imperfect technology collide. The results can be disastrous.

For example, no e-tailer did more to infuriate shoppers than toysrus.com. It kicked off the holiday season with a big ad campaign that lured thousands to its Web site. Traffic jumped more than 300 percent. Then, midway through the season the company announced it could not guarantee delivery by Christmas day. Countless shoppers were left empty-handed. Customers reported similar problems at Handspring.com. Launching its line of Visor hand-held computers in September 1999, Handspring was not prepared to handle the flood of orders that came pouring in. Overwhelmed by demand and plagued by glitches in its ordering software and shipping systems, the company lost shipments, delivered and billed customers for merchandise they never received, and kept scores of customers waiting months for products.

Batched logistics can indeed spell disaster as these companies and others have learned. If you can't provide the service, you're going to lose the customer. Seasoned e-tailers know that the hard part is after the customer hits the "buy" button. Order fulfillment and delivery is a critical part of e-tailing. That's why CDNow.com relies on tight relationships and electronic links with six music distributors in the United States and Europe to deliver music titles to more than two million customers. When a customer initiates an order, he or she triggers an automated process that sends the order information from the retailer's Web storefront to a distributor via an electronic data interchange network or over the Internet. Distributors send inventory and shipping information back to CDNow, which then updates the customer on the status of the order via e-mail.

Of course, everyone loves e-commerce when it works. Shopping online can be like having a personal assistant do your selecting, gift-wrapping, and mailing. But as these examples illustrate, many e-tailers are a long way from offering a shoppers' paradise.

QUESTIONS FOR CRITICAL THINKING

1. Why is the hard part of e-tailing after the customer hits the "buy" button?
2. How does the Internet raise consumer expectations for the shopping experience?

some of the information was already out of date by the time the catalog was mailed. So, like many companies, AMP switched to electronic catalogs. W. W. Grainger, a 71-year-old supplier of maintenance, repair, and operating supplies, is another company that has moved its catalog, with 80,000 items, to the Web; as a result, the company's Web sales have risen 60 to 100 percent per quarter. Electronic catalogs are an easy way to search for products as well as timely information about price and availability.[43]

Cybermalls and Virtual Storefronts   A *cybermall* is a Web-based retail complex that houses dozens of *virtual storefronts,* or Internet-based stores. Consumers can buy everything from computer software to gourmet chocolates in cybermalls maintained by Yahoo, America Online, and Microsoft. Like their physical counterparts, these Internet storefronts rely on a lot of "walk-in" traffic. For instance, cybermall shoppers looking to buy a CD might also click on the cyber shoe store. Besides exposure, another key advantage of a cybermall is that tenants do not have to create their own Web page or find a server to house it. Typically, the cybermall operator does all that for a sizable fee.[44]

Some cybermalls specialize. For example, MelaNet's African Marketplace specializes in goods and services provided by African Americans.[45] Other cybermalls feature a broader selection of retailers selling diverse goods and services. Yahoo's cybermall features well over 27,000 virtual storefronts, including big stores like J. C. Penney and smaller stores like the Amish Acres General Store. With cybermall sales increasing every day, Yahoo's chief operating officer predicts that online shopping will soon be bigger than catalog shopping.[46]

Reinventing the Roles of Producers and Intermediaries

A number of forces are changing the roles of producers and wholesale intermediaries today. Industry consolidation, intense competition, new technology, and the rush to the Web are just a few. As a result, the lines separating producers and their intermediaries are much fuzzier as some producers assume typical channel functions. Producer S.C. Johnson Wax, for example, warehouses goods, stocks store shelves with Johnson Wax products, and even handles some retail functions for rival products as part of its contractual arrangement with Wal-Mart.[47] Similarly, Northern Telecom doesn't just send one gigantic shipment of telephones to Wal-Mart and other large intermediaries. Instead, the company has to inventory shipments, label boxes so they look like they come directly from the intermediaries, and perform other functions that minimize the intermediaries' inventory and handling costs.[48]

As the Internet drives down the cost of transactions, the middleman will either add new value or disappear.[49]

Meanwhile, intermediaries are finding new value-added ways to solidify their role within the distribution system. Computer wholesaler Ingram Micro, for instance, has been taking on more tasks that were once the sole domain of manufacturers, such as assembling PCs and handling inquiries from customers. Among the big-name producers Ingram serves are Hewlett-Packard, Apple, and Compaq. Ingram also builds private-brand computers for dealers to resell to consumers. Ingram does not plan to sell directly to consumers, because its dealers and retailers are its sales force. "We have 120,000 resellers with more than one million feet on the street," says Ingram's CEO.[50]

One major trend that could potentially transform the role of intermediaries is the rapid growth of online auction sites such as eBay. Such sites directly connect buyers with sellers, facilitate auction pricing, and collect a commission from sellers after each auction. Consumers often pay bargain prices on auction sites, although they may actually overpay if they get caught up in the excitement of bidding. Some think the rise of eBay and other Internet sites that bring buyers and sellers together is the beginning of the end of middlemen; others see it as an opportunity for intermediaries to innovate and explore new functions that will benefit both consumers and other channel members.

SOMETHING OLD, SOMETHING NEW

Turbulent. That's the best way to describe the nature of distribution channels these days. Competition from Internet-based companies and rivals with Web sites, coupled with growing customer interest, is all but forcing firms into cyberspace. But here's the challenge: How can firms use the tremendous potential of the Internet as a distribution channel without disrupting their traditional channels?

Hewlett-Packard (HP) faced this dilemma in selling medical equipment such as ultrasound machines to hospitals around the world. Large hospitals were asking for one-click ordering on the Internet, but the company worried about the reaction of its 500 sales reps and its distributor network. With $1 billion in annual sales at stake, HP finally bowed to customer pressure and added a Web site for on-line ordering. Prices were in line with the prices offered through other channels. More important, sales reps still collected commissions when their accounts ordered over the Internet. "We have a big direct-sales force calling on hospitals," explained the head of HP's medical sales and marketing, "and it would be very demotivating for them if customers placed an order through this new e-channel and the sales force didn't get paid. At the same time, selling online could be more cost-effective. So maybe we will end up passing the savings on to the consumer."

Of course, companies such as HP know that ignoring the Internet could be a costly mistake. But before your company jumps on the Internet bandwagon, evaluate the Internet's potential by asking these questions:

- How will the Internet allow you to offer existing customers more information or services?
- How will the Internet help you meet the needs of new customer segments?
- How will the Internet help you generate additional revenues through the promotion of complementary products?
- How will your competitors use the Internet?

Finally, ask yourself: How will the Internet affect the company's current channel partners, and more important, how will you handle the conflict?

QUESTIONS FOR CRITICAL THINKING

1. Should Hewlett-Packard lower its prices on equipment sold over the Internet because the Internet is a more efficient distribution channel?
2. If your competitors are selling products over the Internet, must you follow suit?

MANAGING PHYSICAL DISTRIBUTION

Physical distribution encompasses all the activities required to move finished products from the producer to the consumer, including inventory control, order processing, warehousing, materials handling, and outbound transportation. This part of the distribution process may not appear very glamorous or exciting, but it is vital to a company's success.

To illustrate the importance of physical distribution, consider this: A typical box of breakfast cereal can spend as long as 104 days getting from factory to supermarket, moving haltingly through a series of wholesalers, distributors, brokers, diverters, and consolidators, each of which has a warehouse. In fact, so many physical distribution systems are burdened with duplication and inefficiency that in industry after industry, executives have been placing one item near the top of the corporate agenda: **logistics**—the planning and movement of goods and information throughout the supply chain.

Hard pressed to knock out competitors on quality or price, companies are trying to gain an edge through their ability to deliver the right stuff to the right place at the right time.

physical distribution
All the activities required to move finished products from the producer to the consumer

logistics
The planning, movement, and flow of goods and related information throughout the supply chain

For instance, PC Connection, a direct marketer selling computers and software, uses physical distribution to maintain an edge in customer service. Computer buyers who order as late as 2:45 A.M. can receive their purchases later that same day, nearly anywhere in the United States. PC Connection achieves this remarkable level of service by maintaining a warehouse at the Ohio airport used by its shipping partner, Airborne Express. When an order arrives by phone or fax, the merchandise can be loaded on the next Airborne flight. This dedication to customer service pays off for PC Connection in increased sales and a loyal customer base.[51] Plus, more skillful handling of logistics can put money back into a company's pocket by reducing inventory levels and holding time for finished goods.[52]

Keep in mind that streamlining processes that traverse companies and continents is not an easy task, but the payback can be enormous. Over a two-year period, National Semiconductor was able to cut its standard delivery time 47 percent, reduce distribution costs 2.5 percent, and increase sales 34 percent. How? By shutting down six warehouses around the globe and air-freighting its microchips to customers worldwide from a new distribution center in Singapore.[53]

Technology and Physical Distribution

Some of today's most advanced physical distribution systems employ satellite navigation and communication, voice-input computers, machine vision, robots, onboard computer logbooks, and planning software that relies on artificial intelligence. Kansas-based trucking firm OTR Express operates almost as if it were a giant computer system that just happens to use trucks to get the job done. By using custom software to track everything from the location of trucks to the best places in the country to buy tires, OTR racks up profits while keeping the firm's prices competitive.[54]

FedEx also fully exploits the benefits of technology to automate its services and provide superior customer service. The company's $180 million small-package sorting system processes over 400,000 packages an hour. Each parcel is scanned four times, weighed, and measured, and its digital image is recorded on computer. In addition, the company's world shipping software streamlines customer billing, reduces shipping paperwork, and allows customers to track their shipments over the Internet.[55]

Regardless of the technology you use, the key to success in managing physical distribution is to coordinate the activities of everyone involved, from the sales staff that is trying to satisfy demanding customers to the production staff that is trying to manage factory workloads. The overriding objective should be to achieve a competitive level of *customer-service standards* (the quality of service that a firm provides for its customers) at the lowest total cost. In general, as the level of service improves, the cost of distribution increases. A producer must analyze whether it is worthwhile to deliver the product in, say, three days as opposed to five, if doing so increases the price of the item.

This type of trade-off can be difficult because the steps in the distribution process are all interrelated. A change in one affects the others. For example, if you use slower forms of transportation, you reduce your shipping costs, but you probably increase your storage costs. Similarly, if you reduce the level of inventory to cut your storage costs, you run the risk of being unable to fill orders in a timely fashion. The trick is to optimize the *total* cost of achieving the desired level of service. This optimization requires a careful analysis of each step in the distribution process in relation to every other step.

Warehouse Operations

warehouse
Facility for storing inventory

Products held in inventory are physically stored in a **warehouse,** which may be owned by the manufacturer, by an intermediary, or by a private company that leases space to others. Some warehouses are almost purely holding facilities in which goods are stored for relatively long periods. Other warehouses, known as **distribution centers,** serve as command posts for moving products to customers. In a typical distribution center, goods produced at a company's various locations are collected, sorted, coded, and redistributed to fill customer orders.

An important part of warehousing activities is **materials handling,** the movement of goods within and between physical distribution facilities. One main area of concern is storage method—whether to keep supplies and finished goods in individual packages, in large boxes, or in sealed shipping containers. The choice of storage method depends on how the product is shipped, in what quantities, and to which locations. For example, a firm that typically sends small quantities of goods to widely scattered customers wouldn't want to use large containers. Materials handling also involves keeping track of inventory so that the company knows where in the distribution process its goods are located and when they need to be moved.

Here again, technology makes the difference. As orders come in at Amazon.com distribution centers, for example, workers known as pickers race around pulling the items off the shelves and loading them onto a giant conveyor belt that runs throughout the vast centers. The products move from belt to belt until they drop into one of the 2,000 long chute-like assembly bins assigned to customers when they click the "buy it now" button on the Web site. As the conveyer moves, other items for the same customer also fall into the bin. When the order is complete, a light flashes below the bin, and a worker puts all the binned items into a box, which then travels down another series of belts through machines that pack it, tape it, weigh it, affix a mailing label, and load it unto a truck at one of the loading docks.[56]

Transportation Operations

For any business, the cost of transportation is normally the largest single item in the overall cost of physical distribution. Firms that move freight are called *carriers*, and they fall into three basic categories. **Common carriers** offer their services to the general public; **contract carriers** haul freight for selected companies under written contract; and **private carriers** are company-owned systems that move their own company's products. Some firms use a combination, relying on common or contract carriers to help out when their own resources are stretched to the limit.

When choosing transportation, you must also consider other marketing concerns: storage, financing, sales, inventory size, and the like. The trick is to maximize the efficiency of your entire distribution process while minimizing the overall cost. Each of the five major

distribution centers
Warehouse facilities that specialize in collecting and shipping merchandise

materials handling
Movement of goods within a firm's warehouse terminal, factory, or store

Many Internet merchants are avoiding inventory and shipping snags by building their own giant distribution centers such as this Amazon.com distribution center in Seattle.

common carriers
Transportation companies that offer their services to the general public

contract carriers
Specialized freight haulers that serve selected companies under written contract

private carriers
Transportation operations owned by a company to move only its own products

See It on the Web See It on the Web

GET A MOVE ON

How much freight are companies moving around the United States? To find the answer, visit the Web site of the U.S. Department of Transportation's Commodity Flow Survey Program. Read the results of the latest survey to find out how many *billion* tons of raw materials and finished goods— worth *trillions* of dollars—are being shipped within the country. Surprisingly, more than half the shipments (as measured by tonnage) are headed to a destination less than 50 miles from their point of origin. So physical distribution is critical even when you are buying and selling locally.
http://www.bts.gov/ntda/cfs/

EXHIBIT 13·4

FREIGHT SHIPMENTS WITHIN THE UNITED STATES

Within the United States, most freight shipments move by railroad. In recent years, the amount of freight shipped by truck, air, and pipeline has increased, while the amount of freight shipped by water has decreased.

Freight (millions of ton-miles), 1996

Mode	Freight
Railroads	1,355,975
Trucks	986,000
Water	764,687
Pipeline (oil)	619,200
Air	12,861

LEARNING OBJECTIVE 6

List the five major modes of transportation used in physical distribution

modes of transportation described here has distinct advantages and disadvantages. Sometimes companies use intermodal transportation (a combination of multiple modes) to move a single shipment.

- *Rail.* Railroads can carry heavier and more diverse cargo and a larger volume of goods than any other mode of transportation (see Exhibit 13.4). However, trains are constrained to railroad tracks, so they rarely deliver goods directly to customers.

- *Truck.* Trucks are a favorite form of transportation for two reasons: (1) door-to-door delivery is convenient, and (2) operating on public highways does not require expensive terminals or right-of-way agreements (like air and rail transportation do). The main drawback of trucking is that trucks cannot carry all types of cargo cost effectively; for example, commodities such as steel and coal are too bulky.

- *Water.* The cheapest form of transportation, water is widely used for such low-cost bulk items as oil, coal, ore, cotton, and lumber. However, ships are slow, and service to any given location is infrequent. Furthermore, another form of transportation is usually needed to complete delivery to the final destination, like it is for rail.

- *Air.* Although airplanes offer the fastest form of transportation, they have numerous disadvantages. Many areas of the country are still not served by conveniently located airports. Also, airplanes can carry only certain types of cargo because of size, shape, and weight limitations. Furthermore, airplanes are the least dependable and most expensive form of transportation. Weather may cause flight cancellations, and even minor repairs may lead to serious delays. But when speed is a priority, air is usually the only way to go.

- *Pipeline.* For certain types of products, such as gasoline, natural gas, and coal chips or wood chips (suspended in liquid), pipelines are useful. Although they are expensive to build, they are extremely economical to operate and maintain. On the other hand, transportation via pipeline is slow (3 to 4 miles per hour), and routes are not flexible.

Summary of Learning Objectives

1. **Explain what a distribution channel is.**
   A distribution channel is an organized network of firms that work together to get a product from a producer to consumers.

2. **Discuss how the Internet is influencing distribution channels.**
   The Internet is allowing companies to sell, deliver, and provide support for goods and services all over the world. Producers can streamline their channel arrangements, shorten the channel in some cases, reduce costs, and, as a result, lower prices. The Internet is the driving force behind the increased use of electronic retailing, electronic catalogs, and virtual storefronts.

3. **Differentiate between selective and exclusive distribution strategies.**
   Companies that use a selective distribution strategy choose a limited number of retailers that can adequately support the product. Firms that use exclusive distribution grant a single wholesaler or retailer the exclusive right to sell the product within a given geographical area.

4. **Explain how wholesalers and retailers function as intermediaries.**
   Wholesalers buy from producers and sell to retailers, to other wholesalers, and to organizational customers such as businesses, government agencies, and institutions. Retailers buy from producers or wholesalers and sell the products to the final consumers.

5. **Describe the growth in nonstore retailing and identify common types of nonstore retailers.**
   Nonstore retailing is growing much faster than store retailing, although the vast majority of products are still bought in traditional stores. Common nonstore retailers are mail-order firms, vending machines, telemarketers, door-to-door direct sellers, and electronic approaches such as the Internet, interactive kiosks, and television home shopping.

6. **List the five major modes of transportation used in physical distribution.**
   The five most common methods of transporting goods are by truck, rail, ship, airplane, and pipeline.

Key Terms

agents and brokers (311)
category killers (313)
common carriers (321)
contract carriers (321)
discount stores (313)
distribution centers (321)
distribution channels (305)
distribution mix (305)
distribution strategy (305)
drop shippers (311)

exclusive distribution (309)
full-service merchant wholesalers (311)
industrial distributors (311)
limited-service merchant wholesalers (311)
logistics (319)
mail-order firms (315)
marketing intermediaries (305)
materials handling (321)
merchant wholesalers (311)

physical distribution (319)
private carriers (321)
rack jobbers (311)
retailers (311)
scrambled merchandising (312)
selective distribution (309)
specialty store (312)
warehouse (320)
wheel of retailing (312)
wholesalers (311)

Test Your Knowledge

QUESTIONS FOR REVIEW

1. What forms of utility do intermediaries create?
2. What are some of the main causes of channel conflict?
3. How does a specialty store differ from a category killer and a discount store?
4. What is the wheel of retailing?
5. Why is logistics becoming a corporate priority?

QUESTIONS FOR ANALYSIS

6. How does the presence of intermediaries in the distribution channel affect the price of products?
7. What are some of the challenges facing retailers today?
8. What are the benefits of electronic catalogs?
9. Why are customer-service standards so important in managing physical distribution?

BEHIND THE SCENES

MEETING BUSINESS CHALLENGES AT AMAZON.COM

The unprecedented success of Amazon.com is part of the legend of the early Internet years. Founder Jeff Bezos saw the immense business potential of the Internet when most people yawned or snickered. Amazon.com's sophisticated interface delivered a highly efficient, personalized shopping experience, allowing customers to register their preferences, find books, and make purchases with a click of the mouse. Discounting was also an integral part of Amazon.com's retail strategy, with books priced below what the largest chain stores charged. Of course, such discounting was financially possible because of Amazon's original streamlined channel of distribution: no physical retail outlets, no sales force, no expensive warehouses, and no complete product inventory. But that soon changed.

To make the most of his head start in online retailing and leverage the power of the Amazon.com brand name, Bezos decided that Amazon should be not just a bookstore but an everything store. So he spent $300 million to build five modern warehouses and developed automated systems to handle a wide range of merchandise. Then he expanded Amazon's product assortment to include videos, music, gifts, toys, consumer electronics, building supplies, and other merchandise. The entry into CD retailing was so successful that Amazon.com overtook the market-leading CDNow within three months. Next, eyeing the popularity of online auctions, Bezos opened an auction section on the Amazon.com site—auctioning everything from rare books to attic junk.

Meanwhile, Bezos also grew the business by purchasing big chunks of other online and mail-order retailers such as Drugstore.com (an Internet retailer targeting the $150 billion market for pharmaceutical products), Pets.com, HomeGrocer.com, Gear.com (featuring brand name sporting goods at closeout prices), and Tool Crib of the North, a closely held mail-order tool business. Then he topped it off by opening zShops, an online mall, where merchants of any size pay $9.99 a month plus a small percentage of their revenues for the privilege of gaining instant access to Amazon's 12-million-plus customers.

In its never-ending quest to be the world's biggest online department store, Amazon.com has picked up its share of challenges. For one thing, owning and operating its own warehouses means forfeiting the financial leverage enjoyed by others such as Yahoo and eBay, which run Web sites that serve millions of people without ever having to stock anything. For another, Amazon.com faces stiff competition from specialists in every product category that it sells: Barnesandnoble.com in books, Amazon's original product line; eToys, Toys "R" Us and KB Toys in toys; 800.com and circuitcity.com in electronics; eBay in auctions; Sears in tools; and Wal-Mart in everything else.

With Amazon's annual losses topping $600 million on sales of over $1.5 billion, even optimists agree that the company won't earn a penny for several years. But Bezos believes that concentrating on profitability would mean missing out on the big opportunities of the Internet, and that's something he's not willing to risk. As Bezos sees it, in ten years Amazon.com will become so huge, so omnipresent, that it will be hard to imagine that it started out as a tiny bookseller in 1995.[57]

Critical Thinking Questions

1. Jeff Bezos has said that the Internet "fundamentally shifts the balance of power from the merchant to the customer." What does he mean?

2. Why does Amazon.com pay as much attention to logistics as it does to the interface system that customers see when they log onto the Web site?

3. Although Bezos has expanded his offering beyond books, can you identify any products that would not fit well with Amazon.com's brand or style of retailing?

■ LEARN MORE ONLINE

Where is Amazon.com headed these days? Visit the Web site at http://www.amazon.com and count the product categories. Also notice the links to international Amazon.com sites, and read about the various shopping services. What other services might Amazon.com customers value? What else might Jeff Bezos do to attract new customers and reinforce the loyalty of current Amazon.com customers?

10. ▢ Direct-mail marketers often publish different prices in different catalogs targeted at different market segments. When you call to order, the sales representative asks for your customer number or catalog number first so that he or she knows what to charge you.[58] Is this practice ethical?

QUESTIONS FOR APPLICATION

11. Imagine that you own a small specialty store selling handcrafted clothing and jewelry. What are some of the nonstore retail options you might explore to increase sales? What are the advantages and disadvantages of each option?

12. Compare the prices of three products offered at a retail outlet with the prices charged if you purchase those products by mail order (catalog or phone) or over the Internet. Be sure to include hidden costs such as handling and delivery charges. Which purchasing format produced the lowest price for each of your products?

13. ▢ In Chapter 8 we discussed the fact that supply chain management integrates all the activities involved in the production of goods and services from suppliers to customers. How can companies involve distributors in the design, manufacturing, or sales of their products or services? What are the benefits of involving distributors in these activities?

14. ▢ Which of the four basic functions of management discussed in Chapter 6 would be involved in decisions that establish or change a company's channels of distribution? Explain your answer.

Practice Your Knowledge

SHARPENING YOUR COMMUNICATION SKILLS

Select a consumer product with which you are familiar, and trace its channel of distribution. The product might be fresh foods, cosmetics, clothing, or manufactured goods (ranging from something as simple as a fork to something as complex as a personal computer). For information you might contact a business involved in the manufacture or distribution of the product, either by letter or by telephone. Examine the various factors involved in the distribution of the product, and prepare a brief summary of your findings. Consider the following:

- The role of the intermediary in distribution
- The type of distribution: selective or exclusive
- The amount of control the manufacturer has over the distribution process
- The type of channel used in the distribution process and its influence on the cost of the product

HANDLING DIFFICULT SITUATIONS ON THE JOB: MERCEDES-BENZ STEERS INTO CATALOG SALES

Nearly every automobile company offers branded clothing and accessories for proud vehicle owners: ties, T-shirts, watches, shoes, hats, jackets, sweaters. Most are sold right in the showrooms, and they're extremely popular, whether they be Saturn sneakers or Land Rover tweeds. Some of the upscale auto manufacturers have been developing logo-bearing clothing and gadgets that meet their customers' higher-class budgets as well as their tastes. But pricing can be tricky because customers object to paying a lot more for an ordinary shirt dressed up with only a carmaker's trademark.

Steve Beaty, vice president of accessories marketing for Mercedes-Benz, is reaching out to car owners with a 55-page, glossy, full-color *Mercedes-Benz Personal & Automotive Accessories* catalog loaded with expensive logoed items. Mercedes-

Benz has recruited world-class, top-of-the-line manufacturers and designers to produce merchandise worthy of the company's highly refined clientele. The new catalog presents Wittnauer watches, Caran D'Ache ballpoints, Bally bomber jackets, and silk boxers designed by artist Nicole Miller—all emblazoned with the triangle logo or images of Mercedes-Benz models, past and present. The catalog even features a $3,300 collapsible aluminum mountain bike for slipping into the trunk of your 500SL.[59] As Beaty's assistant, you wonder whether mail-order retailing is the best—or the only—way to sell these items.

1. What are the advantages and disadvantages of using mail-order catalogs to sell Mercedes-Benz clothing and accessories?

2. Should Mercedes-Benz sell these accessories in its car showrooms? What challenges and opportunities do you see with this retail approach?

3. What nonstore retail options would you recommend for these logo products? What are the advantages and disadvantages of each?

BUILDING YOUR TEAM SKILLS

In managing the transportation side of physical distribution, companies have to look at more than cost. Paying less to ship products is certainly an important consideration, but dependability—knowing that carriers can be counted on to deliver products—is equally vital. Smaller businesses such as Noah's Ark Original Deli in Teaneck, New Jersey, can't afford to maintain their own fleet of delivery vans; they rely on FedEx and other common carriers to whisk their products to customers around the United States.

Noah's Ark is one of thousands of businesses that contract with FedEx to fulfill customer orders that come in via the Internet. But what can the deli do if FedEx employees go on strike?

David Sokolow, the deli's manager, is especially concerned about disrupting deliveries during the crucial year-end holiday gift-giving season, when orders for knishes and other specialty foods come from as far away as Puerto Rico and Hawaii.[60]

With your team, identify at least four transportation options that Noah's Ark might consider if FedEx is not able to make deliveries during the holidays. Next to each option, list both advantages and disadvantages. Then assess FedEx in the same way.

Now think about the way transportation will affect the deli's products during the delivery period. What product characteristics must Sokolow consider when he makes plans to deal with a possible FedEx strike? What additional information should he obtain about each transportation option before making a decision? What criteria should he use to choose among the many options? And what can he do in advance to be better prepared before any delivery disruptions occur?

Summarize and share your team's listing of options, advantages, and disadvantages with the class. Also share your team's thinking about additional information needed and criteria for deciding among the various options. Did other teams identify the same options and criteria as your team? Which option do most teams recommend for Noah's Ark? Why?

Expand Your Knowledge

EXPLORING CAREER OPPORTUNITIES

Retailing is a dynamic, fast-paced field with many career opportunities in both store and nonstore settings. In addition to hiring full-time employees when needed, retailers of all types often hire extra employees on a temporary basis for peak selling periods, such as the year-end holidays. You can find out about seasonal and year-round job openings by checking newspaper classified ads, looking for signs in store windows, and browsing the Web sites of online retailers.

1. Select a major retailer, such as a chain store in your area or a retailer on the Internet. Is this a specialty store, discount store, department store, or another type of retailer?
2. Contact the store manager or the human resources department of the retailer you have selected. What are this company's hiring procedures? What qualifications are needed for seasonal positions? For full-time positions? When is the best time to apply?
3. Research your chosen retailer using library sources, the company's annual report (if available), or online resources. Is this retailer expanding? Is it profitable? Has it recently acquired or been acquired by another firm? What are the implications of this acquisition for job opportunities?

DEVELOPING YOUR RESEARCH SKILLS

More and more producers are outsourcing their logistics activities, creating a $50 billion industry of companies specializing in warehouse operations, transportation, and related tasks.[61] Some major players in this third-party-logistics sector include Ryder Integrated Logistics, Emery Worldwide, and Penske Logistics. What exactly are these specialists providing, and who is buying their services? As you research third-party-logistics providers, list the resources you use and describe your search strategy, including sources and key words or phrases used.

1. Using printed sources such as *Industry Week* magazine, *Logistics Management and Distribution Report,* and company annual reports or online sources such as the LogLink Web site at http://www.loglink.net/3pl.htm, locate information about two logistics specialists. Where do these firms deliver?
2. Which physical distribution tasks (such as warehousing) does each firm handle for clients? What special functions (such as order fulfillment) are available?
3. Look for the names of clients that have used these firms' services. What kinds of companies are outsourcing to logistics specialists? What benefits do these clients gain by outsourcing logistics functions?

SEE IT ON THE WEB EXERCISES
Change the Bloomin' Channel, page (308)

Visit the iflowers Web site (sponsored by Phillip's 1-800-Florals) at http://www.iflowers.com. Tour the site. Be sure to check out the catalog by clicking on Order Flowers Online.

1. How can a small, local flower shop compete with Web sites like this? What type of distribution channel is Phillip's 1-800-Florals?
2. From iflowers' homepage, scroll down and click on Infospace.com. Why might an Internet flower shop feature a link like this?
3. From iflowers' homepage, scroll down and click on links to other interesting Free Sites. Explore some of the sites on this page. How does the Internet help companies give away products (or samples) for free? Why do companies do this?

Explore the World of Retailing, page (314)

Visit the National Retail Federation Web site at http://www.nrf.com to explore the world of retailing.

1. On the homepage, read About NRF. What does this organization do? Why should a retailer join this organization?
2. Click on FAQs and locate the question about finding information related to pursuing education and a career in retailing. Follow the link to read about retail careers. What

qualities should the ideal retail job seeker possess? What does a buyer do?

3. Click on Government Affairs, then click on Issues to read about some current retailing issues on the government agenda. Why must small retailers stay on top of these issues?

Get a Move On, page (321)

Point your Internet browser to the U.S. Department of Transportation's Commodity Flow Survey Program Web page at http://www.bts.gov/ntda/cfs/.

1. Click Detailed Description to read about this governmental survey of how commodity products are transported within the United States. What transportation modes are covered in this survey?

2. Return to the program homepage and click to read the summary of 1997 survey results. Did the movement of freight within the United States increase or decrease compared with the 1993 results? How much freight was transported in 1997?

3. From the program homepage, click Freight Planning and Policy to view a listing of other transportation reports. How would these reports be helpful to Wal-Mart and other major companies that move merchandise within the United States?

Developing Marketing Strategies to Satisfy Customers

Learning Objectives

1. Understand how effective relationship marketing can help a small business build customer loyalty and repeat business.
2. See how a small business prices products for various markets.
3. Learn how a company can use direct marketing to communicate with its customers.

Background Information

In developing a marketing strategy, a company divides its market into segments and niches, chooses its target markets and its position in those markets, and then creates a suitable marketing mix. Blausen Medical Communications (BMC), for example, subdivided the organizational market into specific segments. Regardless of whether they offer tangible or intangible products, all companies must adjust their marketing strategies as their products move through the life cycle from introduction and growth to maturity and eventual decline.

One of the most difficult marketing decisions is determining how to price a product, a decision that is affected by the firm's marketing objectives, government regulations, and customer perceptions. In setting promotional strategy, BMC and other companies first establish promotional goals and then decide on an appropriate mix of personal selling, advertising, direct marketing, sales promotion, and public relations. Although some firms, including BMC, prefer to sell through direct distribution channels, others get their products to customers through marketing intermediaries.

The Video

BMC serves customers in the industrial/commercial market, which is made up of companies that buy goods and services to produce their own goods and services. Although his firm is based in Houston, Blausen and his employees handle work for customers all over the world using the phone, overnight package delivery, and the Internet. BMC supports relationship marketing by maintaining a database of customer names, addresses, needs, and payment records. Every time BMC receives an inquiry through its Web site or from its advertising, Blausen enters the contact information in his database and follows up to determine that prospect's needs and budget. In addition, he so-

licits customer feedback during and after every project, checking that customers were well treated and satisfied with the accuracy of their animations or illustrations. This attention to detail and follow-through has helped Blausen establish a solid reputation in the niche of medical animation.

Discussion Questions

1. How is Blausen ensuring that his customers are satisfied? Why is this important for BMC?
2. What are the advantages and disadvantages of having BMC's vice president of sales handle sales transactions worth $250,000 or more?
3. What types of distribution channels does BMC use to reach its customers? What channels should BMC add, and for which products?

Next Steps

Select one of BMC's eight target segments (such as pharmaceuticals, museums, college publishing, or broadcast news). Which of the three basic promotional goals (to inform, to persuade, to remind) should BMC try to achieve in reaching out to this segment? Why? How can BMC use advertising to communicate with current and potential customers in this segment? What media might be most effective for advertising to this segment? How can BMC use sales promotion to stimulate response from this segment?

■ LEARN MORE ONLINE

How do BMC and two of its competitors use their Web sites for marketing? Go online and explore the following sites, looking for clues to each company's marketing strategy. What tangible and intangible products are offered on each site? What kinds of markets are being targeted by each firm? Which companies offer standardized products and which offer customized products? How do these Web sites handle the delicate question of pricing?

http://www.imagesofhealth.com/start.htm (BMC site)

http://www.GmedMedia.com (Gersony Medical Media)

http://www.alexanderandturner.com (Alexander & Turner)

Business Mystery

Natasha: Nick, didn't you visit the Saturn plant in Spring Hill, Tennessee, last year?
Nick: Yes, what an impressive operation. A sprawling complex where 7,200 workers produce the entire car—everything from engines to body panels to door modules to instrument panels.
Natasha: Well, according to this file, Saturn plans to turn over half of what it manufactures in Tennessee to outside suppliers and even share some key components with other GM divisions.
Nick: That's puzzling. I thought GM set up Saturn to be an entirely independent division. The dealerships were unique, too: no hard sales and very customer focused.
Natasha: Yes, I noticed the excellent service when I test drove a Saturn a few years ago. What a great car! But with two dogs, I needed something larger. Unfortunately, Saturn didn't have a model that met my needs.
Nick: You'd think that with so many new Buick, Chevy, and Oldsmobile models on the road, Saturn would have the same product line depth. After all it is a GM division. I wonder why GM limited Saturn to the same subcompact for nine years?
Natasha: Let's see if we can find the answers.

THE MYSTERY OF A START-UP CAUGHT IN THE CROSSFIRE OF SIBLING RIVALRY

In 1985 there was no Saturn, no plant to manufacture it in, no workers, and no dealers to sell it. Saturn, the newest member of GM's dysfunctional family, was built from scratch to become everything the other divisions weren't: self-sufficient, customer sensitive, labor friendly, service oriented, and very independent. In fact, from the outset, almost everything about Saturn was different: Cars were manufactured using a team-based process; dealers helped select car options; the union was a full partner in all decision making; and workers were paid under an innovative risk-and-reward compensation plan.

It didn't take long for GM's bright, young upstart to catch consumers' eyes—and win their hearts. By offering luxury-brand levels of quality and service, Saturn inspired cultlike customer devotion. Proud of its success, GM left Saturn alone and focused its resources on the weaker siblings, pumping billions into new models to revive Oldsmobile and Buick. In 18 months alone, these GM divisions introduced 15 new cars and minivans, while Saturn continued to produce a small sedan, a wagon, and a sports coupe—all built on the same platform. So when gas prices plunged and consumers began eyeing light trucks, vans, and sports utility vehicles, Saturn was stymied.

Customers loved their Saturns but its limited lineup forced many to defect. Nevertheless, GM refused to grant the stellar fledgling new products and instead continued to divert resources to its ailing siblings. Saturn's independence had backfired. Even if GM had a change of heart, lead time to market for new, larger models would take at least three years. Saturn knew that loyal customers wouldn't wait that long.

To get larger models on stream, Saturn agreed to share platforms with other GM brands, farm out production of key components, and move manufacturing to other GM locations. Union officials fumed and authorized a strike vote. Saturn had mortgaged its soul, clinging to its identity by a thread. No-haggle pricing, friendly sales and service, and some unique features would remain Saturn preserves; everything else would die.

In spite of a heavily promoted product launch, Saturn's new L-series midsize sedan and station wagon got off to a slow start. Lackluster sales of the new model forced Saturn to temporarily halt its production. Still, GM is confident that it can grow Saturn beyond its sma`ll-car niche and is now committing enormous resources to its prodigal child. But challenges exist. For one thing, the midsize-car segment is one of the most competitive in the U.S. market. For another, it may be too little, too late.[62]

SOLVING THE MYSTERY OF A START-UP CAUGHT IN THE CROSSFIRE OF SIBLING RIVALRY

1. Why didn't GM expand Saturn's product line sooner?
   CLUE: WHAT PRINCIPLE OF ECONOMICS PLAYED A KEY ROLE IN GM'S DECISION?
2. Look back at the margin clues in Parts I through V. What business principles did GM follow that contributed to Saturn's success?
3. Look back at the margin clues in Parts I through V. What business principles did GM overlook?

14

ANALYZING AND USING FINANCIAL INFORMATION

After studying this chapter, you will be able to

1 Discuss how managers and outsiders use financial information

2 Describe what accountants do

3 State the basic accounting equation and explain the purpose of double-entry bookkeeping

4 Cite the three major financial statements and discuss how companies and stakeholders use them

5 Explain the purpose of ratio analysis and list the four main categories of financial ratios

6 Cite four main activities performed during the financial planning process

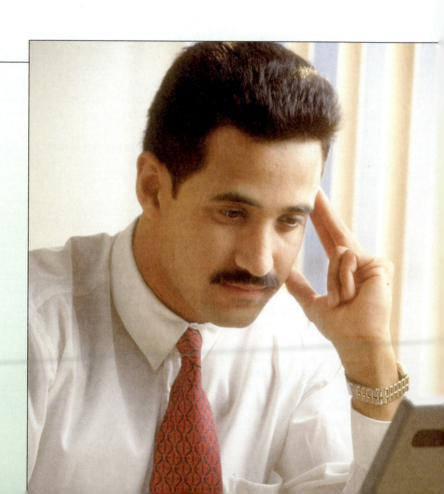

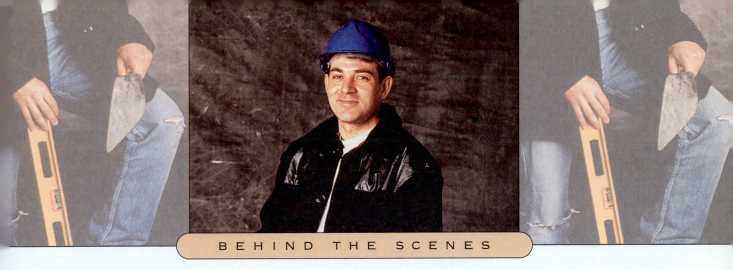

FACING BUSINESS CHALLENGES
AT THE CONCRETE DOCTOR

Making Cash Out of Concrete

Edward Weiner got the idea for his new business by looking down. As president of a waterproofing company in Milwaukee, Wisconsin, he noticed that the sidewalks and driveways at many customers' sites were several inches lower than the adjacent stoops or garage floors they abutted. This discrepancy was caused by poorly compacted soil, water infiltration, and voids below the concrete slabs. Weiner had heard about a process called slabjacking in which small holes were drilled into the concrete and a mudlike mortar was injected into the holes to stabilize the soil and lift the slab back to its original height. At one-third to one-half the cost of actual replacement, slabjacking was a cost-effective way of fixing the sinking mess. Only one company in the area was doing this type of work, but it concentrated on larger, commercial projects. Weiner sensed a concrete opportunity. He studied the market, found some investors, and before long he launched The Concrete Doctor, Inc. (TCDI).

As with most new businesses, things got off to a slow start. But one day the entrepreneur discovered an out-of-state company slabjacking a huge section of pavement on a major roadway. The company was using the same process TCDI used for residential driveways, but on a much larger scale. Weiner pulled off the road and talked to the site's construction engineer for several hours. Then he went home, called the state department of transportation, and began reading everything he could find on road repair. He learned how construction jobs were awarded by the state, how to bid on state transportation projects, how to meet the state's prequalification requirements, and more.

For instance, Weiner learned that state construction jobs were awarded to responsible companies that submitted bids with the lowest project costs. So he studied years of public bidding records for previously awarded slabjacking jobs. Then he added up the published bid prices, subtracted the estimated costs, and calculated the potential profit margin per job. It was a numbers game—and one that Weiner would have to master. He would have to develop accounting systems that would take the guesswork out of the bidding process by assigning costs to all the things that could go wrong—or perhaps right, if he got lucky.

If you were Edward Weiner, what types of accounting systems would you install to track, analyze, and predict the costs of repair jobs? How would you charge each construction job for the costs of expensive machinery and equipment used for multiple projects? How might you use a computerized accounting system and spreadsheet software to automate the bidding process?[1]

■ WHAT IS ACCOUNTING?

accounting
Measuring, interpreting, and communicating financial information to support internal and external decision making

Accounting is the system a business uses to identify, measure, and communicate financial information to others, inside and outside the organization. Financial information is important to businesses such as TCDI for two reasons: First, it helps managers plan and control a company's operation. Armed with such information, managers are better equipped to make informed business decisions. Second, it helps outsiders evaluate a business. Suppliers, banks, and other lenders want to know whether a business is creditworthy; investors and shareholders are concerned with a company's profit potential; government agencies are interested in a business's tax accounting.

LEARNING OBJECTIVE 1
Discuss how managers and outsiders use financial information

financial accounting
Area of accounting concerned with preparing financial information for users outside the organization

management accounting
Area of accounting concerned with preparing data for use by managers within the organization

Because outsiders and insiders use accounting information for different purposes, accounting has two distinct facets. **Financial accounting** is concerned with preparing financial statements and other information for outsiders such as stockholders and *creditors* (people or organizations that have lent a company money or have extended them credit); **management accounting** is concerned with preparing cost analyses, profitability reports, budgets, and other information for insiders such as management and other company decision makers. To be useful, all accounting information must be accurate, objective, consistent over time, and comparable to information supplied by other companies.

The Rules of Accounting

generally accepted accounting principles (GAAP)
Professionally approved U.S. standards and practices used by accountants in the preparation of financial statements

Much of accounting information is *proprietary*, which means it is not divulged to outsiders. Thus, managers and other internal users are free to organize and report a company's proprietary accounting information in a format that suits a company's needs. Published financial statements, on the other hand, must be prepared according to **generally accepted accounting principles (GAAP)**, basic accounting standards and procedures that have been agreed on by the accounting profession.

In the United States, the Financial Accounting Standards Board (FASB) is responsible for establishing GAAP, the accounting rules for U.S. public companies. Other countries have similar governing boards. Of course, this means that foreign companies such as Nissan or Mazda may report accounting data using rules that are different from those used by U.S. companies such as Ford or General Motors. As you can imagine, this difference makes it difficult to accurately compare the financial statements of Mazda (Japanese) with those of Ford (U.S.). Moreover, if a foreign company wishes to list its stock on a U.S. stock exchange, it must publish a set of financial statements that conform to GAAP. For example, when Toyota Motor Corporation listed its stock on the New York Stock Exchange, the company's earnings dropped 4 percent when it converted its financial results from Japanese accounting rules to U.S. rules.[2]

To eliminate the confusion that occurs from having multiple accounting rules in an economy where companies conduct business around the world, the London-based International Accounting Standards Committee (IASC) is mapping out new global rules for accounting. The committee hopes its proposed International Accounting Standards (IAS) will be adopted by all countries and accepted by stock exchanges anywhere on the planet. Not only would these international rules simplify bookkeeping for international companies, but they could pave the way for more and bigger international mergers. Nevertheless, such global rules are meeting strong resistance from the U.S. Securities and Exchange Commission (SEC) and FASB, which are concerned that many of the International Accounting Standards are inferior to GAAP.[3]

Keep in mind that accounting rules set forth the principles and guidelines that companies and accountants must follow when preparing financial reports or recording accounting transactions (which we will discuss later in this chapter). But, as with any rules, they can be interpreted aggressively or conservatively. Furthermore, management and accountants often make estimates and future projections in the course of their accounting work. Sometimes these estimates need to be adjusted because unexpected events happen or because the estimates were too optimistic or too pessimistic. In fact, pick up any newspaper business section and chances are you'll read about a company that is taking a "big charge against earnings" or is restating its financial reports because it is revising estimates. Interpreting accounting rules, establishing policy, and making and revising estimates are just some of the challenging work that accountants do.

What Accountants Do

Some people confuse the work accountants do with **bookkeeping,** which is the clerical function of recording the economic activities of a business. Although some accountants do perform some bookkeeping functions, their work generally goes well beyond the scope of this activity. Accountants design accounting systems, prepare financial statements, analyze and interpret financial information, prepare financial forecasts and budgets, prepare tax returns, interpret tax law, and do much more.

> **bookkeeping**
> Record keeping, clerical aspect of accounting

In fact, the entire accounting profession is undergoing sweeping changes. As Ronald Cohen, chairman of the American Institute of Certified Public Accounts (AICPA) puts it: "Users no longer want to look back—they want to look forward, and supplying forward-looking information is the kind of service businesses will be paying for in the future."[4] Of course, one of the forces driving this change is the availability of new technology (see Exhibit 14.1). Today, financial data are produced, collected, analyzed, and distributed faster and in greater detail than ever before. New software programs, more powerful computers, and the ability to store vast amounts of data now make it possible to automate many accounting tasks. Accountants now have time to redirect their efforts to more important business functions, such as helping clients improve business processes, plan for the future, evaluate product performance, analyze profitability by customer and product groups, and design and install new computer systems. Furthermore, many accountants are expanding their services to include *personal financial planning* (PFP). Personal financial planning is really an offshoot of income-tax planning, estate-tax planning, retirement planning, and profit sharing—services accountants have been providing for years.[5]

> **LEARNING OBJECTIVE 2**
> Describe what accountants do

Accountants perform a variety of services for their clients beyond tax preparation and auditing. Many serve on strategic planning teams and help companies plan for the future.

To prepare accountants for these additional responsibilities, most U.S. states have increased the educational eligibility requirement to sit for the *CPA examination* from 120 to 150 semester hours.[6] This exam is prepared by the AICPA and is a requirement for accountants to become **certified public accountants (CPAs).**

> **certified public accountants (CPAs)**
> Professionally licensed accountants who meet certain requirements for education and experience and who pass a comprehensive examination

Public Accountants   **Public accountants** are independent of the businesses, organizations, and individuals they serve. These accountants perform a variety of accounting functions for their clients. Perhaps the most widely recognized functions are compiling financial statements and preparing tax returns. Although all accountants can handle these tasks, only public accountants who have passed the CPA exam may ensure the integrity and reliability of a

> **public accountants**
> Professionals who provide accounting services to other businesses and individuals for a fee

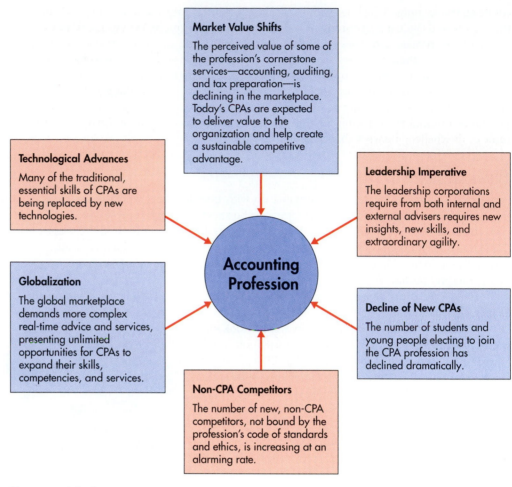

EXHIBIT 14·1

FORCES INFLUENCING THE ACCOUNTING PROFESSION

Today's accountants must expand their skills and services beyond traditional accounting and auditing as these forces pressure them to provide more value-added services.

audit
Formal evaluation of the fairness and reliability of a client's financial statements

internal auditors
Employees who analyze and evaluate a company's operations and data to determine their accuracy

company's financial statements. They do this by conducting an **audit**—a formal evaluation of the fairness and reliability of financial statements.

During an audit, independent CPAs review a client's financial records to determine whether the statements that summarize these records (1) have been prepared in accordance with GAAP and (2) fairly present the financial position and operating results of the firm. Once an auditor has completed an audit, he or she attaches a report summarizing the findings to the client's published financial statements. Sometimes these reports disclose information that might materially affect the client's financial position, such as the bankruptcy of a major supplier, a large obsolete inventory, costly environmental problems, or questionable accounting practices. For example, when auditors at Arthur Andersen discovered falsified shipping documents and purchase orders at Aviation Distributors, the auditors could no longer attest to the accuracy of the company's financial results.[7]

Keep in mind that many large companies also employ **internal auditors**—employees who investigate and evaluate a company's internal operations and data to determine whether they are accurate and whether they comply with GAAP, federal laws, and industry regulations. Although this self-checking process is vital to an organization's financial health, an internal audit is not a substitute for having an independent auditor look things over and render an unbiased opinion. Many people, such as creditors, shareholders, investors, and government agencies, rely on the integrity of a company's financial statements and place great trust and confidence in the independence of auditors whose detached position allows them to be objective and, when necessary, critical. Still, some regulators are concerned that the increasing amount of work performed by public accountants for their clients places this independent check and balance system at risk.[8]

Companies whose stock (ownership shares) is publicly traded in the United States are required to file audited financial statements with the SEC. Today, 90 percent of all publicly held U.S. corporations are audited by the world's five largest accounting firms: PricewaterhouseCoopers, KPMG Peat Marwick, Arthur Andersen, Ernst & Young, and Deloitte & Touche.[9] In addition to auditing services, these megafirms provide a variety of accounting and management consulting services for their clients all over the world. In fact, many accounting firms (big or small) earn only half of their revenues from performing auditing and accounting services. Most have become multiline service organizations in which accounting and auditing are rapidly becoming secondary activities.[10] Some have established

AUDITORS AND CLIENTS: TOO CLOSE FOR COMFORT?

Are today's auditors independent enough? Should the same accounting firm that tallies the books, installs complex computer software, and delivers managerial expertise to clients also provide the essential "second look" at numbers? These are some of the questions federal securities regulators are grappling with as more and more Big Five accounting firms become increasingly involved in the day-to-day operations of their audit clients.

Although no *major* problems have yet come to light in cases where the same firm provides both auditing and consulting functions, some experts say the double duties raise many uncertainties. For instance, will an accounting firm that is being paid $100 million to install complex software be willing to disagree with company executives on a controversial accounting issue and demand that financial statements be corrected if they fear they could anger management and lose the consulting job? Or, will an auditor who works for the same firm that installed a company's information system raise questions about flaws in that system when it was the accounting firm's consultants who installed it?

Accountants, of course, contend that by having a clearer understanding of a client's operations and systems they can perform a better audit. They also point out that many clients are demanding financial and consulting advice from their accountants, and accountants risk becoming irrelevant if they don't help their clients manage their money and enhance their operations.

Still, the SEC is concerned. It wants accountants to disclose in their audit reports the full range of consulting services their firm provides a client. But is this disclosure enough? After all, as one accounting professor puts it: "As auditors, they will have to express an opinion on something that they did. That is a conflict, and that is a problem."

QUESTIONS FOR CRITICAL THINKING

1. What are the main advantages and disadvantages of hiring an auditor who is familiar with a client's operation and industry?
2. Why are more and more accounting firms performing consulting services for their clients, even if it means losing them as audit clients?

See It on the Web See It on the Web

separate business consulting units—many of which now rank among the world's leading consulting firms.

Private Accountants   Of the 1.9 million accountants worldwide, only 35 percent are in public practice. The remaining 65 percent are, for the most part, **private accountants** (sometimes called corporate accountants) working for a business, a government agency (such as the Internal Revenue Service, a school, or a local police department), or a nonprofit corporation (such as a church, charity, or hospital).[11] Although many private accountants are CPAs, a growing number are **certified management accountants (CMAs),** who earn certification by passing a two-day exam (given by the Institute of Management Accountants) that is comparable in difficulty to the CPA exam.[12]

Some accountants specialize in certain areas of accounting, such as **cost accounting** (computing and analyzing production costs), **tax accounting** (preparing tax returns and tax planning), or **financial analysis** (evaluating a company's performance and the financial implications of strategic decisions such as product pricing, employee benefits, and business acquisitions). Most company accountants work together as a team under the supervision of the company **controller,** who reports to the vice president of finance. In smaller organizations like TCDI, the controller may be in charge of the company's entire finance operation and report directly to the president.

Of course, maintaining an accounting staff with the expertise businesses require to operate in today's competitive environment can be a costly proposition—even for large organizations. For this reason, more and more companies are assigning many of their accounting tasks and financial projects to outside accountants and consultants who specialize in an area of accounting or in an industry. Experts predict that outsourcing a company's accounting and finance functions will become even more widespread in the future.[13]

WHAT ARE THE FUNDAMENTAL ACCOUNTING CONCEPTS?

Regardless of who performs a company's accounting functions, all accountants must master the fundamental accounting concepts. Knowing the rules of accounting is critical to an organization's financial health. Without rules and standards, there would be no consistencies for comparisons. Moreover, assessing a company's performance or likelihood of continued success would be anyone's best guess.

---

private accountants
In-house accountants employed by organizations and businesses other than a public accounting firm; also called corporate accountants

certified management accountants (CMAs)
Accountants who have fulfilled the requirements for certification as specialists in management accounting

cost accounting
Area of accounting focusing on the calculation of manufacturing and storage costs of products for use or sale in a business

tax accounting
Area of accounting focusing on tax preparation and tax planning

financial analysis
Process of evaluating a company's performance and analyzing the costs and benefits of a strategic action

controller
Highest-ranking accountant in a company, responsible for overseeing all accounting functions

In their work with financial data, accountants are guided by three basis concepts: the *fundamental accounting equation, double-entry bookkeeping,* and *the matching principle.*

The Accounting Equation

For thousands of years, businesses and governments have kept records of their **assets**—valuable items they own or lease, such as equipment, cash, land, buildings, inventory, and investments. Claims against those assets are **liabilities,** or what the business owes to its creditors—such as banks and suppliers. For example, when a company borrows money to purchase a building, the lender or creditor has a claim against the company's assets. What remains after liabilities have been deducted from assets is **owners' equity:**

$$Assets - Liabilities = Owners' \ equity$$

Using the principles of algebra, this equation can be restated in a variety of formats. The most common is the simple **accounting equation,** which serves as the framework for the entire accounting process:

$$Assets = Liabilities + Owners' \ equity$$

This equation suggests that either creditors or owners provide all the assets in a corporation. Think of it this way: If you were starting a new business, you could contribute cash to the company to buy the assets you needed to run your business or you could borrow money from a bank (the creditor) or you could do both. The company's liabilities are placed before owners' equity in the accounting equation because creditors get paid first. After liabilities have been paid, anything left over belongs to the owners or, in the case of a corporation, to the shareholders. As a business engages in economic activity, the dollar amounts and composition of its assets, liabilities, and owners' equity change. However, the equation must always be in balance; in other words, one side of the equation must always equal the other side.

Double-Entry Bookkeeping

To keep the accounting equation in balance, companies use a **double-entry bookkeeping** system that records every transaction affecting assets, liabilities, or owners' equity. For example, if a company purchased a $4,000 computer on credit, assets would increase by $4,000 (the amount of the computer) and liabilities would also increase by $4,000 (the amount you owe the vendor), keeping the accounting equation in balance. But if the company paid cash outright for the computer (instead of arranging for credit), then the company's *total* assets would not change because the $4,000 increase in equipment would be offset by an equal $4,000 reduction in cash. In fact, the company would just be switching assets—cash for equipment.

Even though computers do much of the tedious recording of accounting transactions such as the one just discussed, accountants must program the computer software so that all transactions are recorded properly. Furthermore, once these individual transactions have been recorded and then summarized, accountants must review the resulting transaction summaries and adjust or correct all errors or discrepancies before they can **close the books,** or transfer net revenue and expense items to retained earnings.

The Matching Principle

The **matching principle** requires that expenses incurred in producing revenues be deducted from the revenue they generated during the same accounting period. This matching of expenses and revenue is necessary for the company's financial statements

---

assets
Any things of value owned or leased by a business

liabilities
Claims against a firm's assets by creditors

owners' equity
Portion of a company's assets that belongs to the owners after obligations to all creditors have been met

accounting equation
Basic accounting equation that assets equals liabilities plus owners' equity

LEARNING OBJECTIVE 3
State the basic accounting equation and explain the purpose of double-entry bookkeeping

double-entry bookkeeping
Way of recording financial transactions that requires two entries for every transaction so that the accounting equation is always kept in balance

close the books
The act of transferring net revenue and expense account balances to retained earnings for the period

matching principle
Fundamental principle requiring that expenses incurred in producing revenue be deducted from the revenues they generate during an accounting period

accrual basis
Accounting method in which revenue is recorded when a sale is made and expense is recorded when it is incurred

to present an accurate picture of the profitability of a business. Accountants match revenue to expenses by adopting the **accrual basis** of accounting, which states that revenue is recognized when you make a sale or provide a service, not when you get paid. Similarly, your expenses are recorded when you receive the benefit of a service or when you use an asset to produce revenue—not when you pay for it. Accrual accounting focuses on the economic substance of the event instead of on the movement of cash. It's a way of recognizing that revenue can be earned either before or after cash is received and that expenses can be incurred when you receive a benefit (such as a shipment of supplies) whether before or after you pay for it.

cash basis
Accounting method in which revenue is recorded when payment is received and expense is recorded when cash is paid

If a business runs on a **cash basis,** the company records revenue only when money from the sale is actually received. Your checkbook is an easy-to-understand cash-based accounting system: You record checks at the time of purchase and deposits at the time of receipt. Revenue thus equals cash received, and expenses equal cash paid. The trouble with cash-based accounting, however, is that it can be misleading. You can misrepresent expenses and income by the way you time payments. It's easy to inflate income, for example, by delaying the payment of bills. For that reason, few companies keep their books on a cash basis. In fact, manufacturers and retailers are required to use the accrual method.

depreciation
Accounting procedure for systematically spreading the cost of a tangible asset over its estimated useful life

Depreciation, or the allocation of the cost of a tangible long-term asset over a period of time, is another way that companies match expenses with revenue. During the normal course of business, a company enters into many transactions that benefit more than one accounting period—such as the purchase of buildings, inventory, and equipment. When you buy a piece of equipment or machinery, instead of deducting the entire cost of the item at the time of purchase, you depreciate it, or spread its cost over the asset's useful life (because the asset will likely generate income for years to come). If the company were to expense long-term assets at the time of purchase, the financial performance of the company would be distorted in the year of purchase as well as in all future years when these assets generate revenue.

■ HOW ARE FINANCIAL STATEMENTS USED?

An accounting system is made up of thousands of individual transactions—debits and credits to be exact. During the accounting process, sales, purchases, and other transactions are recorded and classified into individual accounts. Exhibit 14.2 presents the process for putting all of a company's financial data into standardized formats that can be used for decision making, analysis, and planning. To make sense of these individual transactions, accountants summarize them by preparing financial statements.

Understanding Financial Statements

LEARNING OBJECTIVE 4
Cite the three major financial statements and discuss how companies and stakeholders use them

Financial statements consist of three separate yet interrelated reports: the *balance sheet,* the *income statement,* and the *statement of cash flows.* Together these statements provide information about an organization's financial strength and ability to meet current obligations, the effectiveness of its sales and collection efforts, and how well the company manages its assets. Organizations and individuals use financial statements to spot opportunities and problems, to make business decisions, and to evaluate a company's past performance, present condition, and future prospects. In sum, they're indispensable.

In the following sections we will examine the financial statements of Computer Discount Warehouse (CDW), a Fortune 1000 company engaged in direct sales and distribution of brand name personal computers (such as Compaq, Toshiba, and Macintosh) and related computer products (such as software, printer cartridges, and scanners). The com-

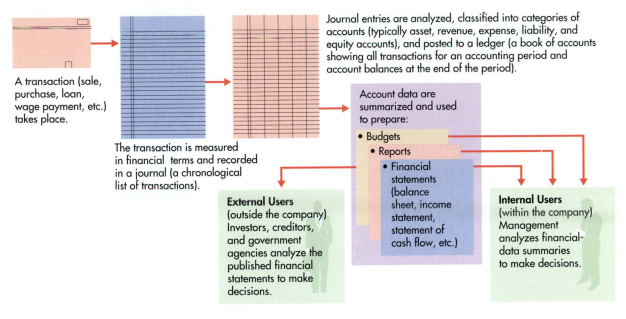

A transaction (sale, purchase, loan, wage payment, etc.) takes place.

The transaction is measured in financial terms and recorded in a journal (a chronological list of transactions).

Journal entries are analyzed, classified into categories of accounts (typically asset, revenue, expense, liability, and equity accounts), and posted to a ledger (a book of accounts showing all transactions for an accounting period and account balances at the end of the period).

Account data are summarized and used to prepare:
• Budgets
 • Reports
  • Financial statements (balance sheet, income statement, statement of cash flow, etc.)

External Users (outside the company) Investors, creditors, and government agencies analyze the published financial statements to make decisions.

Internal Users (within the company) Management analyzes financial-data summaries to make decisions.

Exhibit 14·2

THE ACCOUNTING PROCESS

The traditional printed accounting forms are shown here. Today, nearly all companies use the computer equivalents of these forms.

pany conducts its primary business from a combined telemarketing, corporate office, warehouse, and showroom facility located in Vernon Hills, Illinois. There, CDW's 600-plus account executives service over 634,000 customers annually. In 1998 the company shipped over 2.3 million orders, amounting to over $1.7 billion in sales—a 35 percent increase in sales from the prior year. CDW's daily sales volume has grown exponentially over the last decade—from $232,000 to $6.8 million. Because of this tremendous growth and the increasing demand for new computer products, the company recently built a new 218,000-square-foot facility. Keep these points in mind as we discuss CDW's financial statements in the next sections.[14]

Balance Sheet The **balance sheet,** also known as the statement of financial position, is a snapshot of a company's financial position on a particular date, such as December 31, 1999. In effect, it freezes all business actions and provides a baseline from which a company can measure change. This statement is called a balance sheet because it includes all elements in the accounting equation and shows the balance between assets on one side of the equation and liabilities and owners' equity on the other side. In other words, as in the accounting equation, a change on one side of the balance sheet means changes elsewhere. Exhibit 14.3 is the balance sheet for CDW as of December 31, 1998.

In reality, however, no business can stand still while its financial condition is being examined. A business may make hundreds of transactions of various kinds every working day. Even during a holiday, office fixtures grow older and decrease in value, and interest on savings accounts accumulates. Yet the accountant must set up a

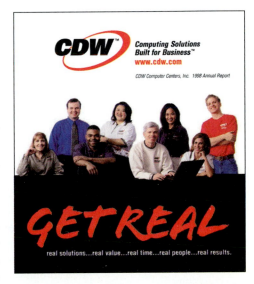

CDW continues to experience record growth and earnings despite facing such industry challenges as declining prices, product shortages, and an abundance of new entrants in the computer reselling arena.

balance sheet
Statement of a firm's financial position on a particular date; also known as a statement of financial position

EXHIBIT 14·3

BALANCE SHEET FOR COMPUTER DISCOUNT WAREHOUSE

The categories used on Computer Discount Warehouse's year-end balance sheet are typical.

Computer Discount Warehouse

Balance Sheet
As of December 31, 1998
(in thousands)

ASSETS

Current Assets

Cash	$ 4,230	
Marketable Securities	66,458	
Accounts Receivable	158,204	
Inventory	64,392	
Misc Prepaid and Deferred Items	6,504	
Total Current Assets		$299,788

Fixed Assets

Property and Equipment	$ 37,056	
Other Assets	4,977	
Total Fixed Assets		42,033
Total Assets		$341,821

LIABILITIES AND SHAREHOLDERS' EQUITY

Current Liabilities

Accounts Payable	$ 41,358	
Accrued Expenses	29,700	
Total Current Liabilities		$ 71,058

Long-Term Liabilities

		0
Total Liabilities		71,058

Shareholders' Equity

Common Stock		
(21,571 shares @ $.01 par value)	$ 216	
Less: Treasury Stock (50,000 shares)	(2,089)	
Paid-in Capital	81,352	
Retained Earnings	191,284	
Total Shareholders' Equity		270,763
Total Liabilities and Shareholders' Equity		$341,821

---

calendar year
Twelve-month accounting period that begins on January 1 and ends on December 31

fiscal year
Any 12 consecutive months used as an accounting period

balance sheet so that managers and other interested parties can evaluate the business's financial position as if it were static, rather than ever-changing.

Every company prepares a balance sheet at least once a year, most often at the end of the **calendar year,** covering from January 1 to December 31. However, many business and government bodies use a **fiscal year,** which may be any 12 consecutive months. For example, a company may use a fiscal year of June 1 to May 31 because its peak selling season ends in May. Its fiscal year would then correspond to its full annual cycle of manufacturing and selling. Some companies prepare a balance sheet more often than once a year, perhaps at the end of each month or quarter. Thus, every balance sheet is dated to show the exact date when the financial snapshot was taken.

By reading a company's balance sheet you should be able to determine the size of the company, the major assets owned, any asset changes that occurred in recent periods, how the company's assets are financed, and any major changes that have occurred in the company's debt and equity in recent periods. Most companies classify assets, liabilities, and owners' equity into categories like those shown in the CDW balance sheet.

Assets As discussed earlier in this chapter, an asset is something owned by a company that will be used to generate income. Assets can consist of cash, things that can be converted into cash (such as investments), and equipment needed to make products or to provide services. For example, CDW needs a warehouse and a sizable inventory in order to sell computer products to its customers. Most often, the asset section of the balance sheet is divided into *current assets* and *fixed assets*. **Current assets** include cash and other items that will or can become cash within the following year. **Fixed assets** (sometimes referred to as property, plant, and equipment) are long-term investments in buildings, equipment, furniture and fixtures, transportation equipment, land, and other tangible property used in running the business. Fixed assets have a useful life of more than one year. CDW's principal fixed asset is the company's warehouse facility.

Assets are listed in descending order by *liquidity*, or the ease with which they can be converted into cash. Thus, current assets are listed before fixed assets. The balance sheet gives a subtotal for each type of asset and then a grand total for all assets. CDW's current assets consist primarily of cash, investments in short-term marketable securities such as money-market funds, accounts receivable (or amounts due from customers), and inventory (such as computers, software, and other items the company sells to customers).

Liabilities Liabilities come after assets because they represent claims against the company's assets, as shown in the basic accounting equation: *Assets = Liabilities + Owners' equity*. Liabilities may be current or long-term, and they are listed in the order in which they will come due. The balance sheet gives subtotals for **current liabilities** (obligations that will have to be met within one year of the date of the balance sheet) and **long-term liabilities** (obligations that are due one year or more after the date of the balance sheet), and then it gives a grand total for all liabilities.

CDW's current liabilities consist of accounts payable and accrued expenses. Accounts payable includes the money CDW owes its suppliers (such as Compaq and Toshiba) as well as money it owes vendors for miscellaneous services (such as electricity and telephone charges). *Accrued expenses* are expenses that have been incurred but for which bills have not yet been received. According to the matching principle, CDW records its expenses when the company receives the benefit of the service, not when the company pays for it. For example, CDW's account executives earn commissions on computer sales to customers. The company has a liability to its account executives once the sale is made, regardless of when a check is issued to the employee. CDW must record this liability because it represents a claim against company assets. If such expenses and their associated liabilities were not recorded, CDW's financial statements would be misleading and would violate the matching principle (because the commission expenses that were earned at the time of sale would not be matched to the revenue generated from the sale).

Although its situation is highly unusual for a company this size, CDW has no long-term liabilities. Whereas most companies borrow sizable sums of money to finance the construction or acquisition of assets such as buildings and equipment, CDW paid for the costs of its new facility with money it had saved over many years. The company invests excess cash in short-term marketable securities so it can earn interest on these funds until they are needed for future projects.

Owners' Equity The owners' investment in a business is listed on the balance sheet under owners' equity (or shareholders' equity for a corporation such as CDW). Sole proprietorships list owner's equity under the owner's name with the amount (assets minus liabilities). Small partnerships list each partner's share of the business separately, and large partnerships list the total of all partners' shares. Shareholders' equity for a corporation is presented in

current assets
Cash and items that can be turned into cash within one year

fixed assets
Assets retained for long-term use, such as land, buildings, machinery, and equipment; also referred to as property, plant, and equipment

current liabilities
Obligations that must be met within a year

long-term liabilities
Obligations that fall due more than a year from the date of the balance sheet

terms of the amount of common stock that is outstanding, meaning the amount that is in the hands of the shareholders. The combined amount of the assigned or par value of the common stock plus the amount paid over the par value (paid-in capital) represents the shareholders' total investment. Roughly $81 million was paid into the corporation by CDW shareholders at the time the company's shares were issued. In 1998 CDW repurchased 50,000 shares of the company's own stock in the open market. CDW will use this *treasury stock* for its employee stock option plan and other general corporate purposes.

retained earnings
The portion of shareholders' equity earned by the company but not distributed to its owners in the form of dividends

Shareholders' equity also includes a corporation's **retained earnings**—the portion of shareholders' equity that is not distributed to its owners in the form of dividends. CDW's retained earnings amount to over $191 million. Most corporations like CDW keep or retain a portion of their earnings for future asset purchases and distribute the rest in the form of dividends.

income statement
Financial record of a company's revenues, expenses, and profits over a given period of time

Income Statement　If the balance sheet is a snapshot, the income statement is a movie. The **income statement** shows how profitable the organization has been over a specific period of time, typically one year. It summarizes all **revenues** (or sales), the amounts that have been or are to be received from customers for goods or services delivered to them, and all **expenses,** the costs that have arisen in generating revenues. Expenses and income taxes are then subtracted from revenues to show the actual profit or loss of a company, a figure known as **net income**—profit, or the *bottom line.* By briefly reviewing a company's income statements you should have a general sense of the company's size, its trend in sales, its major expenses, and the resulting net income or loss. Owners, creditors, and investors can evaluate the company's past performance and future prospects by comparing net income for one year with net income for previous years. Exhibit 14.4 is the 1998 income statement for CDW, showing net income of about $66 million. This is a 29 percent increase over the company's net income of $50 million for the previous year.

revenues
Amount earned from sales of goods or services and inflow from miscellaneous sources such as interest, rent, and royalties

expenses
Costs created in the process of generating revenues

net income
Profit earned or loss incurred by a firm, determined by subtracting expenses from revenues; also called the bottom line

Expenses, the costs of doing business, include both the direct costs associated with creating or purchasing products for sale and the indirect costs associated with operating the

EXHIBIT 14·4

INCOME STATEMENT FOR COMPUTER DISCOUNT WAREHOUSE

An income statement summarizes the company's financial operations over a particular accounting period, usually a year.

Computer Discount Warehouse

Income Statement
Year ended December 31, 1998
(in thousands)

Revenue		
Net Sales		$1,733,489
Costs of Goods Sold		
Beginning Inventory	$　61,941	
Add: Purchases During the Year	1,515,765	
Costs of Goods Available for Sale	1,577,706	
Less: Ending Inventory	64,392	
Costs of Goods Sold		(1,513,314)
Gross Profit		$　220,175
Operating Expenses		(115,537)
Net Operating Income		104,638
Other Income		4,373
Net Income Before Taxes		109,011
Income Taxes		(43,170)
Net Income		$　　65,841

business. Whether a company manufactures or purchases its inventory, the cost of storing the product for sale (such as heating the warehouse, paying the rent, and buying insurance on the storage facility) is added to the difference between the cost of the beginning inventory and the cost of the ending inventory in order to compute the actual cost of items that were sold during a period—or the **cost of goods sold.**

As shown in Exhibit 14.4, cost of goods sold is deducted from sales to obtain a company's **gross profit**—a key figure used in financial statement analysis. In addition to the costs directly associated with producing goods, companies deduct **operating expenses,** which include both *selling expenses* and *general expenses,* to compute a firm's *net operating income,* or the income that is generated from business operations. **Selling expenses** are operating expenses incurred through marketing and distributing the product (such as wages or salaries of salespeople, advertising, supplies, insurance for the sales operation, depreciation for the store and sales equipment, and other sales-department expenses such as telephone charges). **General expenses** are operating expenses incurred in the overall administration of a business. They include professional services (accounting and legal fees), office salaries, depreciation of office equipment, insurance for office operations, supplies, and so on.

A firm's net operating income is then adjusted by the amount of any nonoperating income or expense items such as the gain or loss on the sale of a building. The result is the firm's net income or loss before income taxes (losses are shown in parentheses), a key figure used in budgeting, cash flow analysis, and a variety of other financial computations. Finally, income taxes are deducted to compute the company's net income or loss for the period.

Statement of Cash Flows   In addition to preparing a balance sheet and an income statement, all public companies and many privately owned companies prepare a **statement of cash flows** to show how much cash the company generated over time and where it went (see Exhibit 14.5). The statement of cash flows reveals not only the increase or decrease in the company's cash for the period but also the accounts (by category) that caused that change. From

cost of goods sold
Cost of producing or acquiring a company's products for sale during a given period

gross profit
Amount remaining when the cost of goods sold is deducted from net sales; also known as gross margin

operating expenses
All costs of operation that are not included under cost of goods sold

selling expenses
All the operating expenses associated with marketing goods or services

general expenses
Operating expenses, such as office and administrative expenses, not directly associated with creating or marketing a good or a service

statement of cash flows
Statement of a firm's cash receipts and cash payments that presents information on its sources and uses of cash

EXHIBIT 14.5

STATEMENT OF CASH FLOWS FOR COMPUTER DISCOUNT WAREHOUSE

A statement of cash flows shows a firm's cash receipts and cash payments as a result of three main activities—operating, investing, and financing—for a period.

Computer Discount Warehouse Statement of Cash Flows Year ended December 31, 1998 (in thousands)		
Cash flows from operating activities:*		
Net Income	$ 65,841	
Adjustments to reconcile net income to net cash provided by operating activities	(61,317)	
Net cash provided by operations		$ 4,524
Cash flows from investing activities:		
Purchase of property and equipment	(15,110)	
Purchase of securities	(114,932)	
Redemptions of securities	112,463	
Net cash used in investment activities		(17,579)
Cash used in financing activities		(948)
Net (decrease) increase in cash		(14,003)
Cash and cash equivalents at beginning of year		$18,233
Cash and cash equivalents at end of year		$ 4,230

*Note: Numbers in parentheses indicate cash outflows.

a brief review of this statement you should have a general sense of the amount of cash created or consumed by daily operations, the amount of cash invested in fixed or other assets, the amount of debt borrowed or repaid, and the proceeds from the sale of stock or payments for dividends. In addition, an analysis of cash flows provides a good idea of a company's ability to pay its short-term obligations when they become due. CDW's statement of cash flow shows that the company used $15 million of its cash reserves in 1998 to pay for its new facility.

Analyzing Financial Statements

Once financial statements have been prepared, managers and outsiders use these statements to evaluate the financial health of the organization. They look at the company's performance in relation to its past performance, the economy as a whole, and the performance of its competitors. The process of comparing financial data from year to year in order to see how they have changed is known as **trend analysis.** You can use trend analysis to uncover shifts in the nature of the business over time. Most large companies provide data for trend analysis in their annual reports. Their balance sheets and income statements typically show three to five years or more of data (making comparative statement analysis possible). Changes in other key items—such as revenues, income, earnings per share, and dividends per share—are usually presented in tables and graphs.

trend analysis
Comparison of a firm's financial data from year to year to see how they have changed

Of course, when you are comparing one period with another, it's important to take into account the effects of extraordinary or unusual items such as the sale of major assets, the purchase of a new line of products from another company, weather, or economic conditions that may have affected the company in one period but not the next. These extraordinary items are usually disclosed in the text portion of a company's annual report or in the notes to the financial statements.

The Value of Ratio Analysis To facilitate the comparison of one company's financial results with those of competing firms and industry averages, managers compute financial ratios. **Ratio analysis** compares two elements from the same year's financial figures. They are called ratios because they are computed by dividing one element of a financial statement by another. The advantage of using ratios is that it puts companies on the same footing; that is, it makes it possible to compare different-sized companies and changing dollar amounts. For example, by using ratios, you can easily compare how well a large supermarket generates profit out of sales with a similar statistic for a small grocery store.

Bankers are particularly interested in the financial results of the companies that have borrowed money from them. They regularly meet with company owners and executives to assess the borrower's financial performance by reviewing key financial ratios.

ratio analysis
Use of quantitative measures to evaluate a firm's financial performance

The benefit of converting numbers into ratios can be explained by the following example: Suppose you wanted to know how well your favorite baseball player was performing this year. To find out, you would check his statistics—batting average, runs batted in (RBIs), hits, and home runs. In other words you would look at data that have been arranged into meaningful statistics that allow you to compare his present performance with his past performance and with the performance of other players in the league. Financial ratios do the same thing. They convert the raw numbers from the current and prior years' financial statements into ratios that highlight important relationships or measures of performance.[15]

See It on the Web See It on the Web

SHARPEN YOUR PENCIL

You never know what you'll find at a gallery these days. How about annual reports—lots of them! Sharpen your pencil and start thinking like an accountant. Take a virtual field trip to the Report Gallery, where you can click to view the annual reports of Allstate, Boeing, and many other U.S. and international firms. Be sure to bring along your calculator; this is a good site for locating solid corporate data for trend analysis.

http://www.reportgallery.com

Just as baseball statistics focus on various aspects of performance (such as hitting or pitching), financial ratios help companies understand their current operations and answer key questions: Is inventory too large? Are credit customers paying too slowly? Can the company pay its bills? Ratios also set standards and benchmarks for gauging future business by comparing a company's scores with industry averages that show the performance of competition. Every industry tends to have its own "normal" ratios, which act as yardsticks for individual companies. Dun and Bradstreet, a credit rating firm, and Robert Morris Associates publish both average financial figures and ratios for a variety of industries and company sizes.

Before reviewing specific ratios, consider two rules of thumb: First, avoid drawing too strong a conclusion from any one ratio. For instance, a baseball player's batting average may be low, but his RBIs may make him a valuable player in the lineup. Second, once ratios have presented a general indication, refer back to the specific data involved to see whether the numbers confirm what the ratios suggest. In other words do a little investigating, because statistics can be misleading. Remember, a baseball player who has been at bat only two times and has one hit has a batting average of .500.

Types of Financial Ratios   Financial ratios can be organized into the following groups, as Exhibit 14.6 shows: profitability, liquidity, activity, and leverage (or debt).

Profitability Ratios   You can analyze how well a company is conducting its ongoing operations by computing **profitability ratios,** which show the state of the company's financial performance or how well it's generating profits. Three of the most common profitability ratios are **return on sales,** or profit margin (the net income a business makes per unit of sales); **return on investment (ROI),** or return on equity (the income earned on the owner's investment); and **earnings per share** (the profit earned for each share of stock outstanding). Exhibit 14.6 shows how to compute these profitability ratios by using the financial information from CDW.

Liquidity Ratios   **Liquidity ratios** measure the ability of the firm to pay its short-term obligations. As you might expect, lenders and creditors are keenly interested in liquidity measures. Liquidity can be judged on the basis of *working capital*, the *current ratio*, and the *quick ratio*. A company's **working capital** (current assets minus current liabilities) is an indicator of liquidity because it represents current assets remaining after the payment of all current liabilities. The dollar amount of working capital can be misleading, however. For example, it may include the value of slow-moving inventory items that cannot be used to help pay a company's short-term debts.

LEARNING OBJECTIVE 5
Explain the purpose of ratio analysis and list the four main categories of financial ratios

profitability ratios
Ratios that measure the overall financial performance of a firm

return on sales
Ratio between net income after taxes and net sales; also known as profit margin

return on investment (ROI)
Ratio between net income after taxes and total owners' equity; also known as return on equity

earnings per share
Measure of a firm's profitability for each share of outstanding stock, calculated by dividing net income after taxes by the average number of shares of common stock outstanding

liquidity ratios
Ratios that measure a firm's ability to meet its short-term obligations when they are due

working capital
Current assets minus current liabilities

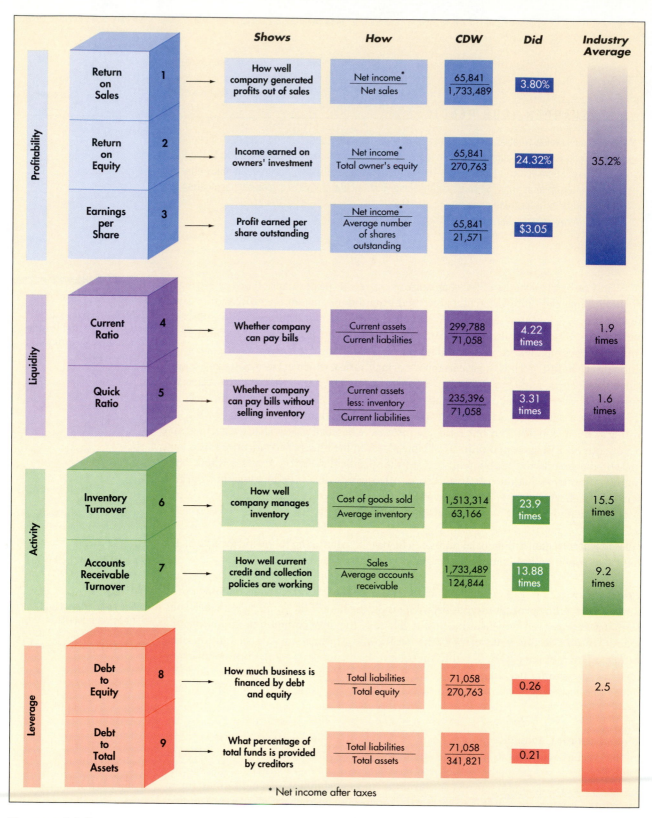

		Shows	How	CDW	Did	Industry Average
Profitability	1 Return on Sales	How well company generated profits out of sales	$\dfrac{\text{Net income}^*}{\text{Net sales}}$	$\dfrac{65,841}{1,733,489}$	3.80%	
	2 Return on Equity	Income earned on owners' investment	$\dfrac{\text{Net income}^*}{\text{Total owner's equity}}$	$\dfrac{65,841}{270,763}$	24.32%	35.2%
	3 Earnings per Share	Profit earned per share outstanding	$\dfrac{\text{Net income}^*}{\text{Average number of shares outstanding}}$	$\dfrac{65,841}{21,571}$	$3.05	
Liquidity	4 Current Ratio	Whether company can pay bills	$\dfrac{\text{Current assets}}{\text{Current liabilities}}$	$\dfrac{299,788}{71,058}$	4.22 times	1.9 times
	5 Quick Ratio	Whether company can pay bills without selling inventory	$\dfrac{\text{Current assets less: inventory}}{\text{Current liabilities}}$	$\dfrac{235,396}{71,058}$	3.31 times	1.6 times
Activity	6 Inventory Turnover	How well company manages inventory	$\dfrac{\text{Cost of goods sold}}{\text{Average inventory}}$	$\dfrac{1,513,314}{63,166}$	23.9 times	15.5 times
	7 Accounts Receivable Turnover	How well current credit and collection policies are working	$\dfrac{\text{Sales}}{\text{Average accounts receivable}}$	$\dfrac{1,733,489}{124,844}$	13.88 times	9.2 times
Leverage	8 Debt to Equity	How much business is financed by debt and equity	$\dfrac{\text{Total liabilities}}{\text{Total equity}}$	$\dfrac{71,058}{270,763}$	0.26	2.5
	9 Debt to Total Assets	What percentage of total funds is provided by creditors	$\dfrac{\text{Total liabilities}}{\text{Total assets}}$	$\dfrac{71,058}{341,821}$	0.21	

* Net income after taxes

EXHIBIT 14·6

HOW WELL DOES THIS COMPANY STACK UP?

Nearly all companies use ratios to evaluate how well the company is performing in relation to prior performance, the economy as a whole, and the company's competitors.

A different picture of the company's liquidity is provided by the **current ratio**—current assets divided by current liabilities. This figure compares the current debt owed with the current assets available to pay that debt. The **quick ratio,** also called the *acid-test ratio,* is computed by subtracting inventory from current assets and then dividing the result by current liabilities. This ratio is often a better indicator of a firm's ability to pay creditors than the current ratio because the quick ratio leaves out inventories—which at times can be difficult to sell. Analysts generally consider a quick ratio of 1.0 to be reasonable whereas a current ratio of 2.0 is considered a safe risk for short-term credit. Exhibit 14.6 shows that both the current and quick ratios of CDW are well above these benchmarks and industry averages.

current ratio
Measure of a firm's short-term liquidity, calculated by dividing current assets by current liabilities

quick ratio
Measure of a firm's short-term liquidity, calculated by adding cash, marketable securities, and receivables, then dividing that sum by current liabilities; also known as the acid-test ratio

Activity Ratios   A number of **activity ratios** may be used to analyze how well a company is managing its assets. The most common is the **inventory turnover ratio,** which measures how fast a company's inventory is turned into sales; in general, the quicker the better, because holding excess inventory can be expensive. When inventory sits on the shelf, money is tied up without earning interest; furthermore, the company incurs expenses for its storage, handling, insurance, and taxes. In addition, there is always a risk that the inventory will become obsolete before it can be converted into finished goods and sold. The firm's goal is to maintain enough inventory to fill orders in a timely fashion at the lowest cost.

activity ratios
Ratios that measure the effectiveness of the firm's use of its resources

inventory turnover ratio
Measure of the time a company takes to turn its inventory into sales, calculated by dividing cost of goods sold by the average value of inventory for a period

Keep in mind that it's difficult to judge a company by its inventory level. For example, lower inventories might mean one of many things: You're running an efficient operation; the right inventory is not being stocked; or sales are booming and you need to increase your orders. Likewise, higher inventories could signal a decline in sales, careless ordering, or stocking up because of favorable pricing. The "ideal" turnover ratio varies with the type of operation. In 1998 CDW turned its inventory 23.9 times (see Exhibit 14.6). This rate is unusually high when compared with industry averages, and it suggests that the company stocks only enough inventory to fill current orders and cover a product's reorder time, as discussed in Chapter 8.

Another popular activity ratio is the **accounts receivable turnover ratio,** which measures how well a company's credit and collection policies are working by indicating how frequently accounts receivable are converted to cash. The volume of receivables outstanding depends on the financial manager's decisions regarding several issues, such as who qualifies for credit and who does not, how long customers are given to pay their bills, and how aggressive the firm is in collecting its debts. Be careful here as well. If the ratio is going up, you need to determine whether the company is doing a better job of collecting or sales are rising. If the ratio is going down, it may be because sales are decreasing or because collection efforts are sagging. In 1998 CDW turned its accounts receivable 13.88 times—considerably higher than the industry average (see Exhibit 14.6).

accounts receivable turnover ratio
Measure of time a company takes to turn its accounts receivable into cash, calculated by dividing sales by the average value of accounts receivable for a period

Leverage, or Debt, Ratios   You can measure a company's ability to pay its long-term debts by calculating its **debt ratios,** or leverage ratios. Lenders look at these ratios to determine whether the potential borrower has put enough money into the business to serve as a protective cushion for the loan. The **debt-to-equity ratio** (total liabilities divided by total equity) indicates the extent to which a business is financed by debt, as opposed to invested capital (equity). From the lender's standpoint, the lower this ratio, the safer the company, because the company has less existing debt and may be able to repay additional money it wants to borrow. However, a company that is conservative in its long-term borrowing is not necessarily well managed; often a low level of debt is associated with a low growth rate. CDW's 1998 low debt-to-equity ratio of 26 percent (as shown in Exhibit 14.6) reflects the company's practice of financing its growth by using excess cash flow from operations and by selling shares of common stock to the public.

debt ratios
Ratios that measures a firm's reliance on debt financing of its operations (sometimes called leverage ratios)

debt-to-equity ratio
Measure of the extent to which a business is financed by debt as opposed to invested capital, calculated by dividing the company's total liabilities by owners' equity

debt-to-total-assets ratio
Measure of a firm's ability to carry long-term debt, calculated by dividing total liabilities by total assets

The **debt-to-total-assets ratio** (total liabilities divided by total assets) also serves as a simple measure of a company's ability to carry long-term debt. As a rule of thumb, the amount of debt should not exceed 50 percent of the value of total assets. For CDW, this ratio is a very low 21 percent and again reflects the company's policy not to finance its growth with long-term debt (see Exhibit 14.6). However, this ratio, too, is not a magic formula. Like

HOW TO READ AN ANNUAL REPORT

Whether you're thinking of investing in companies, becoming a supplier for them, or applying for a job with them, you'll need to know how to read annual reports in your career. Thus, it's worth your while to consider the advice of *Newsweek* columnist Jane Bryant Quinn, who provided these pointers:

READ THE LETTERS

First, turn to the report of the certified public accountant. This third-party auditor will tell you right off the bat if the report conforms with generally accepted accounting principles. Now turn to the letter from the chairman. This letter should tell you how the company fared this year, but more important, the letter should tell you why. Keep an eye out for sentences that start with "Except for . . ." and "Despite the . . ." They're clues to problems. The chairman's letter should also give you insights into the company's future. For example, look for what's new in each line of business. Is management getting the company in good shape to weather the tough and competitive years ahead?

DIG INTO THE NUMBERS

Check out the trend in the company's working capital (the difference between current assets and current liabilities). If working capital is shrinking, it could mean trouble. One possibility: The company may not be able to keep dividends growing rapidly.

Another important number to analyze is earnings per share. Management can boost earnings by selling off a plant or by cutting the budget for research and advertising. See the footnotes; they often tell the whole story. If earnings are down only be-cause of a change in accounting, maybe that's good! The company owes less tax and has more money in its pocket. If earnings are up, maybe that's bad. They may be up because of a special windfall that won't happen again next year. One good indicator is the trend in net sales. If sales increases are starting to slow, the company may be in trouble.

GET OUT YOUR CALCULATOR AND COMPARE

High and rising debt, relative to equity, may be no problem for a growing business. But it shows weakness in a company that's leveling out. So get out your calculator and divide long-term liabilities by shareholders' equity. That's the debt-to-equity ratio. A high ratio means the company borrows a lot of money to fund its growth. That's okay—if sales grow too, and if there's enough cash on hand to meet the payments. But if sales fall, watch out. The whole enterprise may slowly sink.

Remember, one ratio, one annual report, one chairman's letter, won't tell you much. You have to compare. Is the company's debt-to-equity ratio better or worse than it used to be? Better or worse than the industry norms? In company-watching, comparisons are all. They tell you if management is staying on top of things.

QUESTIONS FOR CRITICAL THINKING

1. Why might a job applicant want to read a company's annual report before applying for a job with that company?
2. What types of valuable nonfinancial information might an annual report disclose to a potential supplier?

grades on a report card, ratios are clues to performance. Managers, creditors, lenders, and investors can use them to get a fairly accurate idea of how a company is doing. But remember, one ratio by itself doesn't tell the whole story.

■ WHAT DOES FINANCIAL MANAGEMENT INVOLVE?

Every company, from the little corner store to General Motors, worries about money—how to get it and how to use it. This area of concern, known as **financial management,** or finance, involves making decisions about alternative sources and uses of funds with the goal of maximizing a company's value. To make these decisions, accountants and financial managers forecast and plan for the future, develop and implement a firm's financial plan, manage the company's cash flow, coordinate and control the efficiency of operations, decide on specific

financial management
Effective acquisition and use of money

investments and how to finance those investments, raise money needed to support growth, and interact with banks and capital markets. In smaller companies such as TCDI, the owner is responsible for the firm's financial decisions. In larger operations such as CDW, however, financial planning is the responsibility of the finance department, which reports to a vice president of finance or a chief financial officer (CFO). This department includes the accounting function. In fact, most financial managers are accountants.

Developing a Financial Plan

All companies need to pay their bills and still have some money left over to improve the business. Furthermore, a key goal of any business is to increase the value to its owners (and other stakeholders) by making it grow. Maximizing the owners' wealth sounds simple enough: Just sell a good product for more than it costs to make. Before you can earn any revenue, however, you need money to get started. Once the business is off the ground, your need for money continues—whether it's to buy new road repair equipment or to build a new warehouse.

When opportunities or problems crop up, financial managers will construct spreadsheets to analyze the financial impact of possible outcomes. Management will then use these analyses to identify the best course of action to take.

One way companies make sure they have enough money is by developing a **financial plan,** a document that shows the funds a firm will need for a period of time, as well as the sources and uses of those funds. When you prepare a financial plan for a company, you have two objectives: achieving a positive cash flow and investing any excess cash in **capital investments** such as major expenditures in buildings or equipment that will help your company grow. Most companies today use some type of computer software to assist them with the financial planning process, which includes (1) estimating the flow of money into and out of the business; (2) determining whether cash flow is negative or positive and how to use or create excess funds; (3) deciding whether to invest in major assets, which ones, and how to finance those undertaken—a process called **capital budgeting;** and (4) comparing actual results with projections to discover variances and take corrective action—a process known as **financial control.**

financial plan
A forecast of financial requirements and the financing sources to be used

capital investments
Money paid to acquire something of permanent value in a business

capital budgeting
Process for evaluating proposed investments in select projects that provide the best long-term financial return

financial control
Process of analyzing and adjusting the basic financial plan to correct for forecasted events that do not materialize

Monitoring Cash Flow   An underlying concept of financial management is that all money should be used productively. This concept is important because without cash a company cannot purchase the assets and supplies it needs to operate. Some companies use their

LEARNING OBJECTIVE 6
Cite four main activities performed during the financial planning process

The goal is not to save money but to make money.[16]

marketable securities
Stocks, bonds, and other investments that can be turned into cash quickly

budget
Planning and control tool that reflects expected revenues, operating expenses, and cash receipts and outlays

Every business has to manage its income and expenses. No company will prosper for long if products don't go out the door or if the bills and the employees don't get paid.[17]

excess cash to finance their growth just as CDW did. Using a company's own money instead of borrowing from an outside source such as a bank has one chief attraction: No interest payments are required. For this reason, many companies accumulate excess cash over a period of time instead of paying out dividends to shareholders.

One way financial managers improve a company's cash flow is by monitoring its *working capital accounts:* cash, inventory, accounts receivable, and accounts payable. They use commonsense procedures such as controlling the level of inventory, dispatching bills on a timely basis, shrinking accounts receivable collection periods, and paying bills no earlier than necessary.

Aggressive financial managers also earn as much interest as possible on their cash reserves. They use electronic cash management (the ability to access bank account information online) to move cash between accounts and pay bills on a daily basis; they also invest excess cash on hand in short-term investments called **marketable securities.** These interest-bearing or dividend-paying investments include money-market funds or publicly traded stocks such as IBM or Sears. They are said to be "marketable" because they can be easily converted back to cash. Because marketable securities are generally used as contingency funds, however, most financial managers invest these funds in securities of solid companies or the government—ones with the least amount of risk. (Risk management and debt versus equity financing are discussed in detail in Component Chapter B.)

Developing a Budget

Part of the financial planning process includes developing a **budget,** a financial blueprint for a given period (often one year). Budgets structure financial plans in a framework of estimated revenues, expenses, and cash flows. Companies prepare a master (or operating) budget—the overall estimate of revenues, costs, expenses, and cash flow—so that they can accomplish their objectives while controlling their costs. Accountants provide much of the data required for budgets and are important members of the budget development team because they have a complete understanding of the company's operating costs.

The master budget not only sets a standard for expenditures but also offers an integrated and detailed plan for the future. For example, by reviewing the budget of any airline you can determine whether the company plans on increasing its fleet of aircraft, adding more routes, hiring more employees, increasing employees' pay, or continuing or abandoning any discounts for travelers. No wonder companies like to keep their budgets confidential.

See It on the Web See It on the Web

LINK YOUR WAY TO THE WORLD OF ACCOUNTING

Looking for one supersite with links to resources for cash flow management, financial planning, internal audit issues, and many other financial matters? Check out the Accountant's Home Page, an online launching point for accountants. This is the place to find answers to all kinds of questions about accounting, financial management, and more. Scroll down to the miscellaneous resources to locate the Accounting Software Page, a comprehensive listing of accounting software for small and medium-sized businesses. Keep scrolling to find the link to Internal Control Resources for access to articles, books, and other information on internal auditing topics. Your instructor will even find a link to Great Ideas for Teaching Accounting on this site.
http://www.computercpa.com

Using Accounting Information to Make Financial Decisions

Suppose your company is considering changing the way it pays your sales force. Instead of paying them a fixed salary, the company would like to pay salespeople a base salary plus a commission, hoping that the commissions will motivate them to sell more product. How would you determine the best commission rate? Would this new pay structure cost the company more money? How could you guarantee that your sales force would benefit from this change? What if sales increased by 10 percent instead of the 20 percent you had projected? What if your commission structure was too high, and the company lost money? These are the types of questions accountants and financial managers deal with daily. Sometimes questions are even more complex because there are more variables. Asking "what-if" questions is certainly not new. What is new, however, is the application of computing technology to the process.

With electronic spreadsheet programs such as Microsoft Excel and Lotus 1-2-3, companies can plan for the future by analyzing the costs and benefits of just about any decision using the firm's financial data as a starting point. Data-rich financial reports allow users to drill down from summary report data to more detailed transaction data for further investigative analysis. Typically, the accountant will enter these data into an electronic spreadsheet and manipulate the numbers by converting total costs to unit costs such as cost per passenger-mile (for airlines) or cost per package delivered (for companies such as FedEx). Once the financial data have been entered into the spreadsheet, the accountant will compute a range of outcomes using expected, best-case, and worst-case scenarios—such as unit costs will increase by 5 percent, 2 percent, or 10 percent.

Using spreadsheet programs to build decision models is just one example of how companies analyze and use financial information to plan for the future. Component Chapter C discusses the role of information in business, how companies are processing and using information, and the challenges of managing increasing amounts of information in today's fast-paced, global economy.

Summary of Learning Objectives

1. **Discuss how managers and outsiders use financial information.**
Managers use financial information to control a company's operation and to make informed business decisions. Outsiders use financial information to evaluate whether a business is creditworthy or a good investment.

2. **Describe what accountants do.**
Accountants design accounting systems, prepare financial statements, analyze and interpret financial information, prepare financial forecasts and budgets, prepare tax returns, interpret tax law, provide business expertise and consulting services, and assist clients with personal financial planning.

3. **State the basic accounting equation and explain the purpose of double-entry bookkeeping.**
Assets = Liabilities + Owners' equity is the basic accounting equation. Double-entry bookkeeping is a system of recording financial transactions to keep the accounting equation in balance.

4. **Cite the three major financial statements and discuss how companies and stakeholders use them.**

Companies and stakeholders use the balance sheet, the income statement, and the statement of cash flows to evaluate an organization's financial strength, to make business decisions, to evaluate a company's past performance and present condition, and to spot opportunities and potential problems.

5. **Explain the purpose of ratio analysis and list the four main categories of financial ratios.**
Financial ratios provide information for analyzing the health and future prospects of a business while allowing for comparisons between different-sized companies. Most of the important ratios fall into one of four categories: profitability ratios, liquidity ratios, activity ratios, and debt ratios.

6. **Cite four main activities performed during the financial planning process.**
Financial planners estimate the flow of money into and out of the business, determine whether cash flow is negative or positive and how to use or create excess funds, decide whether to invest in major assets and how to finance such investments, and compare actual results with projections to discover variances and take corrective action.

BEHIND THE SCENES

MEETING BUSINESS CHALLENGES AT THE CONCRETE DOCTOR

Breaking into the lucrative market for slabjacking of sinking highways was harder than entrepreneur Edward Weiner had imagined. His company, TCDI, was unsuccessful on its first six bid attempts. Then the company struck pay dirt. Within five years, TCDI had boosted annual revenue to over $1 million. The data from each completed job were entered into the company's computerized accounting system, where they were later downloaded to financial spreadsheet models Weiner had built to take the guesswork out of the bidding process.

For instance, on one spreadsheet page he stored current payroll data: the hourly wage and benefit costs for workers in many states, plus other expenditures such as payroll taxes and workers' compensation insurance. On a second page he stored operational cost data such as travel costs, which he used for bidding on out-of-state projects. On a third page he stored equipment costs, either the daily cost of renting equipment or the daily depreciation and maintenance costs of company-owned equipment—most of which was quite expensive. Then on a fourth page he stored job experience data, such as that Project 70-99 took 37 days and 14 workers, drilling approximately 500 holes each day.

For each proposal, Weiner would use his spreadsheet software to run some 15 what-if scenarios, produce a range of outcomes, and factor these costs into his final bid price. To create these scenarios, he would ask a series of questions, such as: What if the workers could drill only 400 holes a day instead of 500? What if they had to put in overtime? Once the project began, TCDI's controller would prepare daily job cost-analysis reports. Weiner knew immediately whether he was on target or needed his job supervisor to smooth out some bumps here and there.

Looking ahead, Weiner knew he wanted to expand beyond slabjacking. "You can only fix a road so many times; eventually it has to be replaced," notes Weiner. But roads weren't the only thing sinking. Soil stabilization and foundation repair were becoming big industries. Using similar concepts, TCDI expanded its business into geotechnical contracting: hydraulically pushing steel piers into the earth to stabilize and lift settled buildings. Soon TCDI's sales exploded beyond $9 million a year.

One of TCDI's most challenging projects was its work on Chicago's Navy Pier, a major exposition center. Officials wanted to add six stories onto the parking garage, but construction could not proceed until the foundation support was strengthened. TCDI proposed to install 60 high-capacity steel micropiles drilled to bedrock 100 feet below grade. By using this innovative procedure, TCDI was able to shave a hundred thousand dollars off the project's total cost and capture this high-profile $650,000 contract.[18]

Critical Thinking Questions

1. Why did Weiner have to carefully track the depreciation of the equipment TCDI used for multiple projects?
2. If TCDI borrowed money to buy a new truck, under what heading on the balance sheet would this loan appear?
3. If Weiner wanted to check whether his customers were taking longer to pay the bills he submitted, which activity ratio would he use?

■ LEARN MORE ONLINE

Point your Internet browser to The Concrete Doctor's Web site at http://www.geomod.com and read about the kinds of construction projects the company is currently handling. Is TCDI expanding? Is it winning larger and more complex contracts? What are the implications for Edward Weiner's skill in preparing bids?

Key Terms

accounting (332)
accounting equation (337)
accounts receivable turnover ratio (347)
accrual basis (338)
activity ratios (347)
assets (337)
audit (334)
balance sheet (339)
bookkeeping (333)
budget (350)
calendar year (340)
capital budgeting (349)
capital investments (349)
cash basis (338)
certified management accountants (CMAs) (336)
certified public accountants (CPAs) (333)
close the books (337)
controller (336)
cost accounting (336)
cost of goods sold (343)
current assets (341)
current liabilities (341)

current ratio (347)
debt ratios (347)
debt-to-equity ratio (347)
debt-to-total-assets ratio (348)
depreciation (358)
double-entry bookkeeping (337)
earnings per share (345)
expenses (342)
financial accounting (332)
financial analysis (336)
financial control (349)
financial management (349)
financial plan (349)
fiscal year (340)
fixed assets (341)
general expenses (343)
generally accepted accounting principles (GAAP) (332)
gross profit (343)
income statement (342)
internal auditors (334)
inventory turnover ratio (347)
liabilities (337)

liquidity ratios (345)
long-term liabilities (341)
management accounting (332)
marketable securities (350)
matching principle (337)
net income (342)
operating expenses (343)
owners' equity (337)
private accountants (336)
profitability ratios (345)
public accountants (333)
quick ratio (347)
ratio analysis (344)
retained earnings (342)
return on investment (ROI) (345)
return on sales (345)
revenues (342)
selling expenses (343)
statement of cash flows (343)
tax accounting (336)
trend analysis (344)
working capital (345)

Test Your Knowledge

QUESTIONS FOR REVIEW

1. What is the primary difference between a public accountant and a private accountant?
2. What is the matching principle?
3. What is the purpose of an income statement, a balance sheet, and a statement of cash flows?
4. What are the three main profitability ratios, and how is each calculated?
5. Why do companies prepare budgets?

QUESTIONS FOR ANALYSIS

6. Why is accounting important to business?
7. How has technology changed the jobs of accountants?
8. Why have most states increased their requirement to sit for the CPA examination from 120 to 150 semester hours?
9. Why are the costs of fixed assets depreciated?

10. In the process of closing the company books, you encounter a problematic transaction. One of the company's customers was charged twice for the same project materials, resulting in a $1,000 overcharge. You immediately notify the controller of this billing error, and her response is, "Let it go, it happens often." What should you do?

QUESTIONS FOR APPLICATION

11. The senior partner of an accounting firm is looking for ways to increase the firm's business. What other services besides traditional accounting can the firm offer to its clients?
12. The financial manager for a small manufacturing firm wants to improve the company's cash flow position. What steps can he or she take?
13. Review the material in Chapter 5 discussing the advantages and disadvantages of going public. What

preliminary accounting steps might the controller of a company take to prepare the company for going public? Why?

14. ▪ Your appliance manufacturing company recently implemented a just-in-time inventory system for all parts used in the manufacturing process. How might you expect this move to affect the company's inventory turnover rate, current ratio, and quick ratio?

Practice Your Knowledge

SHARPENING YOUR COMMUNICATION SKILLS

Obtain a copy of the annual report of a business, and examine what the report shows about finances and current operations. In addition to other chapter material, use the information in "How to Read an Annual Report" on page 348 as a guideline for understanding the annual report's content.

- Consider the statements made by the CEO regarding the past year: Did the company do well, or are changes in operations necessary to its future well-being? What are the projections for future growth in sales and profits?
- Examine the financial summaries for information about the fiscal condition of the company: Did the company show a profit?
- If possible, obtain a copy of the company's annual report from the previous year, and compare it with the current report to determine whether past projections were accurate.
- Prepare a brief written summary of your conclusions.

HANDLING DIFFICULT SITUATIONS ON THE JOB: GIVING CREDIT WHERE CREDIT IS DUE

Selling music CDs, multimedia computers, stereo speakers, and other consumer electronics in a retail store on Saturday afternoons can create such loud and widely dispersed noise that no one can hear anything, including the sales pitch. Brown Innovations' virtual audio imager eliminates this problem by creating an "isolated" listening region directly beneath the speakers. This means that game arcade players can hear their own radical sound effects but no one else's. And consumer electronic stores can demo rap music on a boombox in one aisle while a salesperson explains the benefits of a laser printer in the next aisle—without shouting.

You work in the finance department of Brown Innovations, and you've been swamped with credit requests ever since a small item about the virtual audio imager appeared in *Newsweek*. Each day, Brown receives dozens of orders from music stores, arcades, and electronic equipment stores clamoring for your firm's noise-control equipment. Of course, none of these new customers expects to pay cash for the merchandise they are ordering; in this industry, it is common for commercial customers to obtain credit and pay 30 to 60 days after receiving the merchandise.

The head of finance at Brown has asked you to create a brief credit application and a process that will help the company screen out poor credit risks before the company sells them merchandise. This is your opportunity to save Brown Innovations a lot of money—and a lot of trouble.[19]

1. What basic information should you request on the credit application? Should you ask a new customer to provide the name and address of another vendor that has extended the business credit *or* the name of the company's public accountants so you can inquire about its creditworthiness?
2. Which financial statements should you ask each new customer to submit with the credit application? What do you expect to learn from these statements?
3. Of the various financial ratios, which ones do you think would be most helpful in gauging whether a music store will be able to pay in full and on time? Why?

BUILDING YOUR TEAM SKILLS

Owning a business is a dream for many people. In this exercise, you and two classmates are joining forces to launch a dry-cleaning business. Rather than start from scratch, however, you and your partners decide to look at two establishments that are for sale Ajax Services and Mallard Cleaners. The two are for sale at the same price, and they are located in equally attractive areas.

Your team manages to get enough financial data to compare the year-end condition of the two companies, as shown in Exhibit 14.7. Study the numbers carefully; the livelihood of you and your partners depends on choosing wisely between the two establishments.

Once you have examined all this financial information, decide on the specific factors your team will consider to help you select the best company to buy. Why is each factor important? Noting that net income is implied in the companies' data, what additional data might help you make your decision? Should you be concerned about the methods used to record revenues and expenses? Why?

On the basis of your team's analysis of the data, which company would you and your partners purchase? Prepare a brief presentation to the class about the decision your team has made and the process used to come to your decision. Compare your results with the decisions of other teams. How many decided to buy Ajax Services? How many decided to buy Mallard Cleaners? Hold a class discussion about these purchase decisions and the different rationales offered by the teams.

	AJAX SERVICES, INC.	MALLARD CLEANERS, INC.
ASSETS		
Cash	$10,000	$ 25,000
Accounts receivable	2,000	4,000
Cleaning equipment	50,000	80,000
Office equipment	11,000	18,000
Supplies	22,000	34,000
TOTAL ASSETS	$95,000	$161,000
LIABILITIES AND OWNERS' EQUITY		
Accounts payable	$21,000	$ 38,000
Bank loans payable	49,000	68,000
Owners' equity	25,000	55,000
TOTAL LIABILITIES AND OWNERS' EQUITY	$95,000	$161,000
OTHER DATA		
Personal withdrawals from cash during 2000	$40,000	$ 38,000
Owners' investments in business during 2000	$16,000	$ 32,000
Capital balances for each business on January 1, 2000	$30,000	$ 12,000

EXHIBIT 14·7

FINANCIAL DATA FOR TWO COMPANIES

December 31, 2000, year-end balance sheets.

Expand Your Knowledge

EXPLORING CAREER OPPORTUNITIES

People interested in entering the field of accounting can choose among a wide variety of careers with diverse responsibilities and challenges. Select one of the occupations mentioned in this chapter or in Appendix 2, under the section "Careers in Finance and Accounting." Using Appendix 2, library sources, or Internet Web sites from one of the major accounting firms or the AICPA, dig deeper to learn more about your chosen occupation.

1. What are the day-to-day duties of this occupation? How would these duties contribute to the financial success of a company?

2. What skills and educational qualifications would you need to enter this occupation? How do these qualifications fit with your current plans, skills, and interests?

3. What kinds of employers hire people for this position? According to your research, does the number of employers seem to be increasing or decreasing? How do you think this trend will affect your employment possibilities if you choose this career?

DEVELOPING YOUR RESEARCH SKILLS

From the Wall Street Journal, Business Week, or another business publication, select an article that discusses the quarterly or year-end performance of a company that industry analysts consider notable for either positive or negative reasons.

1. Did the company report a profit or a loss for this accounting period? What other performance indicators were reported? Did the company's performance improve or decline over previous accounting periods? What reasons were given for this change?

2. Did the company's performance match industry analysts' expectations, or was it a surprise? How did analysts or other experts respond to the firm's actual quarterly or year-end results?

3. Now research the industry. Was the company's performance outside the industry's norms, or did the entire industry experience similar performance?

SEE IT ON THE WEB EXERCISES
Size Them Up, page 336

Dealing with the most complex accounting and financial management issues is all in a day's work for the experts at Ernst & Young. Visit its Web site at http://www.ey.com/global/gcr.nsf/US/US_Home to find the answers to these questions:

1. Go to Services and scroll over to Assurance, and then Internal Audit. Why do you think a company would want to outsource its auditing function to an accounting firm?

2. Go to Services and scroll over to Corporate Finance, and then Cash Management. Read the main cash management page, then click on the link For Corporations at the right. What are some of the elements E&Y looks at when assessing a company's cash management system? How does a company benefit from better cash management?

3 Click on Career Center (on the left side of the screen) and scroll down. What does E&Y look for in recruits? What are the different career paths E & Y offers?

Sharpen Your Pencil, page 345

Learning about conditions and financial issues in various companies and industries is an important part of an accountant's job. Sharpen your pencil, go to the Report Gallery Web site at http://www.reportgallery.com, and click on Annual Reports to locate the latest annual report for a company of your choice. Now answer these questions:

1. Find the Chairman's Letter (also known as the *letter to shareholders*). Was it a good or a bad year for the company? Why?

2. Examine the company's Income Statement to find the company's annual revenues for the most recent year and the year before. By what percentage did revenues change from the prior year? (Hint: Use your calculator.) Does the chairman's letter explain this change?

3. Scan the financial section to find the Auditor's Report. Who are the company's auditors? Did the company get a clean audit report?

Link Your Way to the World of Accounting, page 350

The Accountant's Home Page is your launching pad for a wide variety of accounting-related Internet resources. Check out this Web site at http://www.computercpa.com so you can answer the questions below.

1. Which of the links listed might you, as a business student, find useful in your studies? How?

2. Under the heading of Accounting Profession, click on the link to AICPA. What is the full name and purpose of this association? What kind of information can accountants access at this site?

3. Under the heading of Government Resources, click on the FASB link and click through to read about the organization and about membership. What is the stated mission of FASB? What kinds of organizations become FASB members, and why?

UNDERSTANDING BANKING AND SECURITIES

LEARNING OBJECTIVES

After studying this chapter, you will be able to

1 Distinguish between deposit and nondeposit financial institutions

2 Discuss how customers and banks benefit from electronic and Internet banking

3 Identify the four ways the Federal Reserve System influences the U.S. money supply

4 Differentiate among a stock's par value, its market value, and its book value

5 Explain the advantages of investing in U.S. Treasury securities

6 Describe the two types of securities exchanges

FACING BUSINESS CHALLENGES AT E*TRADE

Pioneering Point-and-Click Securities Trading

In the early 1980s, Bill Porter was running a thriving business providing stock quotes and trading services electronically to Charles Schwab and other brokerage firms. A physicist and inventor, Porter began to wonder why he and other individual investors had to pay brokers hundreds of dollars each time they bought or sold stocks, bonds, and mutual funds. Although personal computing was still in its infancy, he envisioned a more efficient, more direct method of placing trades directly from his PC keyboard. By 1992, the doctor had translated this vision into E*Trade Securities, an all-electronic brokerage firm accessed through America Online and CompuServe. But E*Trade did not really take off until 1996, when the fledgling brokerage firm launched its multifaceted Web site, making online securities trading accessible and affordable for all Internet users.

E*Trade was at the forefront of a growing movement toward online investing, fueled in part by a healthy U.S. economy and investors eager to participate in U.S. securities markets that were trending upward and setting record highs. Some investors had long-term goals, such as saving for retirement or paying for their children's college education; others were seeking short-term profits; still others wanted a steady flow of returns to supplement their current income.

Unlike traditional full-service brokers, E*Trade did not offer extensive research reports written by experts who investigated specific stocks and bonds in detail. And it did not offer the constant hand-holding of a personal broker. What it did offer was a quick, easy, and inexpensive way to buy and sell securities over the Internet. Investors who knew exactly what they wanted could simply go to the E*Trade Web site, then point and click to make trades—paying a fraction of the commissions charged by full-service brokers.

To build E*Trade into a world-class brokerage firm, Porter brought in Christos Cotsakos, a former executive with Federal Express and A.C. Nielsen. Cotsakos took over just as E*Trade began selling its own shares through an initial public offering in 1996. He hired a management team of experts to enhance E*Trade's information systems and marketing programs. E*Trade soon kicked off an aggressive multimillion dollar ad campaign using the tagline "Someday we'll all invest this way" to increase brand awareness and to tout the benefits of online investing.

By early 1997, E*Trade had 145,000 brokerage customers, and Cotsakos was gearing up to handle many more as online investing mushroomed. But with competition heating up, how could E*Trade keep its lead? What pitfalls would Cotsakos have to watch for as E*Trade grew? How might competition affect E*Trade's pricing and services? How could the CEO reassure customers about the security of E*Trade's Web site?[1]

■ THE EVOLVING U.S. BANKING ENVIRONMENT

Just as E*Trade is using technology to let investors trade stocks and bonds over the Internet, U.S. banks are using technology to help individuals and businesses manage their money more efficiently than ever before. Banks of all sizes—from the largest multinational bank to the tiniest community bank—can now give customers access to their money and account information at any hour from almost anywhere, using some combination of automated teller machines, electronic funds transfer, telephone banking, and Internet banking. The human touch is still a big part of banking, but in today's time-pressured world, more people want to handle banking transactions from different locations and at different times, not during traditional bankers' hours.

Banking Services

A variety of financial institutions operate within the U.S. banking environment. *Deposit institutions* accept deposits from customers or members and offer checking and savings accounts, loans, and other banking services. Among the many deposit institutions are

LEARNING OBJECTIVE 1
Distinguish between deposit and nondeposit financial institutions

- Commercial banks, which operate under state or national charters.
- Thrifts, including savings and loan associations (which use most of their deposits to make home mortgage loans) and mutual savings banks (which are owned by their depositors).
- Credit unions, which take deposits only from members, such as one company's employees or one union's members or another designated group.

In addition, the banking environment includes *nondeposit institutions* that offer specific financial services. Insurance companies provide insurance coverage for life, property, and other potential losses; they invest the payments they receive in real estate, in construction projects, and in other ways. Pension funds are set up by companies to provide retirement benefits for employees; money contributed by the company and its employees is put into securities and other investments. Finance companies lend money to consumers and businesses for home improvements, expansion, purchases, and other purposes. Brokerage firms, as discussed later in this chapter, allow investors to buy and sell stocks, bonds, and other investments; many also offer checking accounts, high-paying savings accounts, and loans to buy securities.

Checking and Savings Accounts   Money you put into your checking account is a *demand deposit,* available immediately (on demand) through the use of **checks,** written orders that direct your bank to pay the stated amount of money to you or to someone else. Banks traditionally paid no interest on money in checking accounts. Since the laws changed in 1980, however, financial institutions have been allowed to offer interest-bearing NOW checking accounts. Most NOW accounts limit the number of checks customers can write and impose a fee if the account balance falls below a minimum level.

checks
Written orders that tell the user's bank to pay a specific amount to a particular individual or business

You earn interest on the money you put away in savings accounts; credit unions typically pay slightly higher savings rates than commercial banks. Originally, these accounts were known as *passbook savings accounts* because customers received a small passbook in which the bank recorded all deposits, withdrawals, and interest. Today, banks send out statements instead of passbooks, so these accounts have become known as *statement savings accounts.* In general, money in savings accounts can be withdrawn at any time. Money in a *money-market deposit account* earns more interest, but you are allowed only a limited number of monthly withdrawals. Money held in a *certificate of deposit (CD)* earns an even higher interest rate, but you cannot withdraw the funds for a stated period, such as six months or more. If you want to make an early withdrawal from a CD, you will lose some or all of the interest you've earned.

Loans   Banks are a major source of loans for customers who need money for a particular purpose. Individuals and businesses, for example, usually apply for mortgage loans when they want to buy a home or property. On such a loan, the buildings and land purchased serve as *collateral,* giving the bank the right to take over the property if the borrower does not repay the debt as promised. Consumers also look to banks and financial services firms for auto loans, home-improvement loans, student loans, and many other types of loans.

Businesses of all sizes gain access to short-term funds by applying for a *line of credit,* an arrangement in which the bank makes an approved amount of money available for the business to use as needed. Once a business draws on its line of credit, it begins to repay the loan through regular monthly payments to the bank. In addition, banks make long-term loans to businesses that want to expand by buying new equipment, building or renovating plants and facilities, or paying for other large-scale projects. Like consumers, businesses shop around to compare interest rates, fees, and repayment schedules before they take out a loan.

credit cards
Plastic cards that allow the user to buy now and repay the loaned amount at a future date

Credit, Debit, and Smart Cards   For everyday access to short-term credit, banks issue **credit cards,** plastic cards that entitle customers to make purchases now and repay the loaned amount later. Many banks charge an annual fee for Visa and MasterCard credit cards, and all charge interest on any unpaid credit-card balance. Nondeposit institutions such as American Express also issue credit cards.

Credit cards have become immensely popular with consumers because they are convenient and allow people to make purchases without cash. They also help people manage their finances by either choosing to repay the full amount when they are billed or making small payments month by month until the debt has been repaid. Credit-card companies make money by charging customers interest on their unpaid account balances and by charging businesses a processing fee, which can range from 2 to 5 percent of the value of each sales transaction paid by credit card. Nearly every store accepts credit cards, and mail-order merchants and Internet retailers are especially dependent on credit cards to facilitate purchases.

debit cards
Plastic cards that allow the bank to take money from the user's demand-deposit account and transfer it to a retailer's account

smart cards
Plastic cards with embedded computer chips that store money drawn from the user's demand-deposit account as well as information that can be used for purchases

In addition to credit cards, many banks offer **debit cards,** plastic cards that function like checks in that the amount of a purchase is electronically deducted from the user's checking account and is transferred to the retailer's account at the time of the sale. **Smart cards** are plastic cards with tiny computer chips that can store amounts of money (from the user's bank account) and selected data (such as frequent-flyer account numbers, health and insurance details, or other personal information). When a purchase is made, the store's equipment electronically deducts the amount from the value stored on the smart card. Users reload money from their bank accounts to their smart cards as needed. Although smart cards seem efficient in theory, many users have found them inconvenient for small purchases. This is one reason why recent smart-card tests in New York City and Guelph, Ontario, Canada, were not successful, even though smart cards for nonpayment purposes, such as holding the user's medical records, have caught on in Europe.[2]

automated teller machines (ATMs)
Electronic terminals that permit people to perform basic banking transactions 24 hours a day without a human teller

Electronic and Internet Banking   All over the world, customers rely on electronic banking to withdraw money from their demand-deposit accounts at any hour using **automated teller machines (ATMs).** In the United States, over 200,000 ATMs handle 11 billion electronic banking transactions every year. Look around: ATMs are everywhere, from banks, malls, and supermarkets to airports, resorts, and tourist attractions. By linking with regional, national, and international ATM networks, banks let customers withdraw cash far from home, make deposits, and handle other transactions. To compete, more banks are jazzing up their ATMs by allowing purchases of stamps, traveler's checks, movie tickets, ski lift tickets, and even foreign currency.[3]

Electronic funds transfer systems (EFTS) are another form of electronic banking. These computerized systems allow users to conduct financial transactions efficiently from remote locations. More than one-third of all U.S. workers take advantage of EFTS when their employers use *direct deposit* to transfer wages directly into employees' bank accounts. This procedure saves employers and employees the worry and headache of handling large amounts of cash.[4] Now the U.S. government is using EFTS for regular payments such as Social Security benefits.

In addition to electronic banking, most major banks and many thrifts and community banks now offer Internet banking to accommodate the growing number of individuals and businesses that want to transfer money between accounts, check account balances, pay bills, apply for loans, and handle other transactions at any hour. Online banking is not only fast and easy for customers; it's also extremely cost-efficient for banks (see Exhibit 15.1). As a result, Web-only banks such as Security First Network Bank and NetBank are setting up shop and attracting customers by passing the savings on in the form of higher interest rates on checking and savings deposits.[5]

On the Internet, Yahoo, America Online, eWallet, and several other firms are vying to create a widely accepted version of an *electronic wallet,* also known as *electronic cash.* After consumers register their credit-card numbers and shipping information at a secure electronic wallet Web site, they can make purchases at any participating Web site without having to repeatedly submit the same information. This type of electronic payment is expected to gain ground as Internet shopping grows even more.[6]

Automated teller machines (ATMs) allow customers to perform certain bank transactions 24 hours a day in places other than a branch. This ATM, installed in a food court of a shopping mall, offers customers the convenience of banking where they shop.

electronic funds transfer systems (EFTS)
Computerized systems for completing financial transactions

LEARNING OBJECTIVE 2
Discuss how customers and banks benefit from electronic and Internet banking

Deregulation and Competition

In the past, services such as checking, savings, and loans were not offered at all financial institutions; instead, each institution focused on offering a particular set of financial services for specific customer groups. However, the competitive situation changed dramatically after the passage of the Depository Institutions Deregulation and Monetary Control Act of

	Cost per transaction
Bank with live teller	$1.07
Bank through debit card	.29
Bank through ATM	.27
Bank on the Internet	.04

EXHIBIT 15·1

BANKING TRANSACTION COSTS

The average cost of having a teller handle a banking transaction is much higher than the cost for other ways of handling banking transactions. This is why banks want customers to bypass tellers whenever possible.

1980. This law deregulated banking and made it possible for all financial institutions to offer a wider range of services—blurring the line between banks and other financial institutions and encouraging more competition between different types of institutions.

Since 1980, the banking industry has changed radically in response to deregulation, competitive pressures, and financial problems. The most obvious evidence: a steep drop in the number of banks. In 1934, there were 14,146 main bank offices in the United States; by 1998, the number had plummeted to only 8,774.[7] Seeking strength, efficiency, and access to more customers and markets, U.S. banks underwent a series of mergers, acquisitions, and takeovers during the 1980s and 1990s. In many cases, failing institutions were taken over by stronger banks; in other cases, banks such as NationsBank and BankAmerica merged to cut costs and cover more territory with more services. Looking beyond U.S. borders, BankAmerica and other banks have gone global with branches in many countries—just as foreign banks such as Japan's Dai-Ichi Kangyo Bank have long done business in the United States and around the world.

Now the industry is being further transformed as institutions race to compete by becoming financial supermarkets. Merrill Lynch, a major brokerage firm, is offering checking accounts and credit services in addition to securities trading. Meanwhile, American Express has expanded beyond credit cards and now lends money to small businesses. Moreover, the merger of Travelers Group (insurance and investment services) with Citibank (to form Citigroup) paved the way for the repeal of Depression-era laws restricting banks, securities firms, and insurance companies from selling each other's products.[8]

The 1999 Financial Services Modernization Act The 1999 Financial Services Modernization Act repealed the Glass-Steagall Act (also known as the Banking Act of 1933) and portions of the 1956 Bank Holding Act, which for decades had kept banks out of the securities and insurance businesses. Originally enacted after the stock market crash of 1929 and the Great Depression, the Glass-Steagall Act restricted investment banks and commercial banks from crossing into each others' businesses. The law was designed to restore confidence in U.S. financial houses after investigations showed that large financial houses had abused their fiduciary duties at the expense of customers. Moreover, it insured that a catastrophic failure in one part of the finance industry did not invade every other part, as it did in 1929. The 1956 Bank Holding Company Act restricted what banks could do in the insurance business.[9]

Industry experts expect that the lifting of these restrictions will fuel a new raft of megamergers and create financial supermarkets that will offer customers a full range of services—from traditional loans to investment banking services to public stock offerings to insurance. Although consumers and financial institutions will both benefit from one-stop shopping and other provisions of the 1999 act, privacy advocates fear that the sharing of consumer data within a large corporate group could violate individual rights. For example, if a bank discovers that a customer has a deadly disease, it might use that information to keep the person from taking out a 30-year mortgage. The 1999 act does give consumers the right, by written request, to stop companies from sharing their data with firms outside the corporate group, but it does not restrict the sharing of personal data within affiliated financial companies.[10]

Community Banks and Interstate Banking

While large financial institutions offer consumers many benefits, *community banks*—smaller banks that concentrate on one particular market—are enjoying a resurgence by focusing on the needs of local consumers and businesses. Although the weakest will continue to be swallowed up through mergers, the strongest go out of their way to help their customers, thinking creatively to come up with special, customized services "that maybe a large

No Comfort for Borrowers in Tiers

How is it possible for banks to make so much money lending billions of dollars to people who may not be able to pay it back? The answer is easy: Charge a lot more to compensate for the extra risk. Tiered lending does just that. It adjusts loan rates on the basis of a customer's risk.

Banks say tiered lending is entirely ethical. Driven by intense competition for loan business and legislation that requires them to meet the credit needs of neighborhoods in which they do business, banks have been relaxing loan standards and charging tiered rates to compensate for lending to riskier borrowers. Banks know that the market for borrowers with spotty repayment records is large and lucrative. In fact, these customers will often pay between a third and a half more in interest than borrowers with good credit.

In the past, borrowers with poor credit records would go to finance companies such as the Money Store. These days, banks can use sophisticated computer models to identify borrowers who pose a greater risk of default and use this information to set loan fees and interest rates. Of course, lenders are not allowed to consider certain information, such as race, religion, or gender. But assessing risk can be subjective and at times discriminatory, because risk can be defined in many ways.

Minorities and women sometimes, for example, pay higher interest rates and fees for credit because loan officers may stereotype them as less astute and set charges as high as they think the borrower will accept. Critics of tiered lending say that these type of borrowers are therefore saddled with excessive interest rates. They want banks to provide loan counseling and to give borrowers an incentive to improve their credit records—something Chicago's Harris Trust and Savings Bank is already doing. For their part, banks claim they are being held to a higher standard than finance companies, which have been lending to less-than-perfect borrowers at higher rates for years. And so the controversy over tiered lending continues, with the people who can least afford it paying a higher price for access to credit.

QUESTIONS FOR CRITICAL THINKING

1. What steps can you, as a consumer, take to find the best loan rate possible?
2. Do you think the government should use one set of regulatory standards for the interest rates and fees charged by banks and by finance companies? Why or why not?

branching operation just simply does not have the flexibility to do," explains Robert J. Wingert of the Community Bankers Association of Illinois.[11]

As community banks continue to operate in smaller, well-defined areas, mid-sized and larger banks have been expanding into new markets by opening branch operations or merging with banks across state lines. Such interstate operations were made possible by the Riegle-Neal Interstate Banking and Branching Efficiency Act of 1994, a landmark law that reversed legislation dating back to 1927.[12] As a result, customers can now make deposits, cash checks, or handle any banking transaction in any branch of their bank, regardless of location.

Of course, technology plays a major role in interstate banking and mergers. Only with sophisticated computer systems can banks expand to offer more services to more customers in more locations at lower cost—and bigger institutions can afford bigger and better systems.[13] With interstate banking a reality, local branches are more than just a place to handle banking transactions. "We're transforming branches into financial service centers for advice and unique solutions," says Jeffrey Chisholm, a Bank of Montreal executive. "We're trying to move the routine to other channels."[14]

Bank Safety and Regulation

Regardless of where or how you conduct your financial transactions, everyone (including Congress, regulators, and the financial community) worries about bank failure. As many as 9,000 U.S. banks failed during the Depression years from 1929 to 1934. In response to concerns about bank safety during that period, the government established the Federal Deposit Insurance Corporation (FDIC) to protect money in customer accounts. Today, money on deposit in U.S. banks is insured by the FDIC up to a maximum of $100,000 through the Savings Association Insurance Fund (for thrifts) and the Bank Insurance Fund (for commercial banks). Similarly, the National Credit Union Association protects deposits in credit unions.

In addition, a number of government agencies supervise and regulate banks. State-chartered banks come under the watchful eyes of each state's banking commission; nationally chartered banks are under the federal Office of the Comptroller of the Currency; and thrifts are under the federal Office of Thrift Supervision. The overall health of the country's banking system is, ultimately, the responsibility of the Federal Reserve System.

■ THE FUNCTIONS OF THE FEDERAL RESERVE SYSTEM

The Federal Reserve System was created in 1913. Commonly known as the Fed, it is the most powerful financial institution in the United States, serving as the central bank. The Fed's primary role is to manage the money supply so that the country avoids both recession and inflation. It also supervises and regulates banks and serves as a clearinghouse for checks.

The Fed is a network of 12 district banks that controls the nation's banking system. The overall policy of the Fed is established by a seven-member board of governors who meet in Washington, D.C. To preserve the board's political independence, the members are appointed by the president to 14-year terms, staggered at two-year intervals. Although all national banks are required to be members of the Federal Reserve System, membership for state-chartered banks is optional. Still, the Fed exercises regulatory power over all deposit institutions, members and nonmembers alike. The Federal Reserve System has three major functions: influencing the U.S. money supply, supplying currency, and clearing checks.

Influencing the U.S. Money Supply

money
Anything generally accepted as a means of paying for goods and services

Money is anything generally accepted as a means of paying for goods and services. Before it was invented, people got what they needed by trading their services or possessions; in some societies, such as Russia, this system of trading, or bartering, still exists. However, barter is in-

See It on the Web See It on the Web

TAKE A FIELD TRIP TO THE FED

This is your chance to visit the Fed. Click on General Information to see who is serving on the Board of Governors and what the Federal Reserve System does. Check on monetary policy and follow the actions of the Federal Open Market Committee. Then browse the latest testimony and speeches to find out what Fed insiders are saying. Remember: When Fed members talk, the securities markets listen—and react.
http://www.bog.frb.fed.us/

Business PlanPro & Integrated Exercises

Business PlanPro is the top-rated, best-selling commercial software on the market for creating a business plan. This easy-to-use, Windows-based program is now available in an exclusive educational version that can be packaged with *Business in Action* at a substantially discounted price.

Business PlanPro is a superb tool for students:
- ✓ It's Easy. Wizards Walk students through the entire Business Plan process.
- ✓ It's Helpful. This CD-ROM contains 20 real sample plans to help students craft their own.
- ✓ It's attractive. The software automatically assemble text, tables, and charts into an easy-to-read report students will be proud to present.
- ✓ It's Internet-enhanced. Links to the Web allow students to seek assistance and additional resources from useful business planning Web sites.
- ✓ It's Complete. A complete user's manual is contained on the CD-ROM along with an online glossary. There's even audio help!

Appendix 3 contains exercises for each part that give students the opportunity to evaluate 20 sample plans from real start-up companies. They can then take what they have learned and apply it to developing their own personal business plan using our exclusive educational version of Business PlanPro Software. These intriguing exercises show students real companies in action and also allow the students to develop their own marketable skills. The software is totally interactive and provides students with a step-by-step approach to creating a comprehensive business plan. Business PlanPro can be shrinkwrapped with the text for $10.00. To order this special package, please use ISBN 0-13-055915-6.

PART 1: CONDUCTING BUSINESS IN THE GLOBAL ECONOMY

Think Like a Pro

Objective: By completing these exercises you will become acquainted with the sections of a business plan that address forms of competition, company and product/service descriptions, and the economic outlook for the related industry. You will use the sample business plan for Adventure Travel International (ATI) in this exercise.

Open the BPP software and explore the sample business plan Travel Agency.spd. Click on the "Plan Outline" icon to access the plan's Task Manager. Find the headings "What You're Selling" and "The Business You're In" and double click on each of the sections under these headings to read the text portion of the business plan that discusses these topics.

3. How has the Internet impacted this industry?

4. *Find the heading "What You're Selling." Double click on "Product and Service Description." The text view of BPP software provides helpful instructions for each section of a business plan. Click on the "Instructions" tab located at the top of your screen. What information should you include about a company's product and service in a business plan? Now return to the Task Manager and double click on "Competitive Comparison." Click on the "Instructions" tab. What are some of the things you should discuss about your competition in a business plan?*

convenient and impractical in a global economy, where many of the things we want are intangible, come from places all over the world, and require the combined work of many people.

To be an effective medium for exchange, money must have these important characteristics: It must be divisible, portable (easy to carry), durable, and difficult to counterfeit or secure; and it should have a stable value. In addition, money must perform three basic functions: First, it must serve as a medium of exchange—a tool for simplifying transactions between buyers and sellers. Second, it must serve as a measure of value so that you don't have to negotiate the relative worth of dissimilar items every time you buy something. Finally, money must serve as a temporary store of value—a way of accumulating your wealth until you need it.

The Fed's main job is to establish and implement *monetary policy,* guidelines for handling the nation's economy and the money supply. The U.S. money supply has three major components:

- **Currency:** Money in the form of coins, bills, traveler's checks, cashier's checks, and money orders
- **Demand deposits:** Money available immediately on demand, such as checking accounts
- **Time deposits:** Accounts that pay interest and restrict the owner's right to withdraw funds on short notice, such as savings accounts, certificates of deposit, and money-market deposit accounts

currency
Bills and coins that make up a country's cash money

demand deposits
Money that can be used by the customer at any time, such as checking accounts

time deposits
Bank accounts that pay interest and require advance notice before money can be withdrawn

The Fed influences the money supply to make certain that enough money and credit are available to fuel a healthy economy. However, it must act carefully, because altering the money supply affects interest rates, inflation, and the economy. When the money supply is increased, more money is available for loans, so banks can charge lower interest rates to borrowers. On the other hand, an increased money supply can lead to more consumer spending and can result in the demand for goods exceeding supply. When demand exceeds supply, sellers may raise their prices, leading to inflation. In turn, inflation can slow economic growth—a situation the Fed wants to avoid. And, because so many companies now buy and sell across national borders, Fed changes may affect the interlinked economies of many countries, not just the United States.[15] That's why the Fed moves cautiously and keeps a close eye on the size of the money supply.

How the Money Supply Is Measured   To get a rough idea of the size of the money supply, the Fed looks at various combinations of currency, demand deposits, and time deposits (see Exhibit 15.2). The narrowest measure, known as **M1,** consists of currency, demand deposits, and NOW accounts that are common forms of payment. **M2,** a broader measure of the money supply, includes M1 plus savings deposits, money-market funds, and time deposits under $100,000. **M3,** the broadest measure of the money supply, includes M2 plus time deposits of $100,000 and higher and other restricted deposits.

M1
The portion of the money supply consisting of currency, demand deposits, and NOW accounts

M2
A measure of the money supply consisting of M1 plus savings and small time deposits

M3
The broadest measure of the money supply, consisting of M1 and M2 plus large time deposits and other restricted deposits

Tools for Influencing the Money Supply   The Fed can use four basic tools to influence the money supply:

- *Changing the reserve requirement.* All financial institutions must set aside *reserves,* sums of money equal to a certain percentage of their deposits. The Fed can change the **reserve requirement,** the percentage of deposits that banks must set aside, to influence the money supply. However, the Fed rarely uses this technique because a small change can have a drastic effect. Increasing the reserve requirement slows down the economy: Banks have less money to lend, so businesses can't borrow to

LEARNING OBJECTIVE 3
Identify the four ways the Federal Reserve System influences the U.S. money supply

reserve requirement
Percentage of a bank's deposits that must be set aside

EXHIBIT 15•2

THE TOTAL MONEY SUPPLY

The U.S. money supply is measured at three levels: M1, M2, and M3. Here's a closer look at the size and composition of these three components.

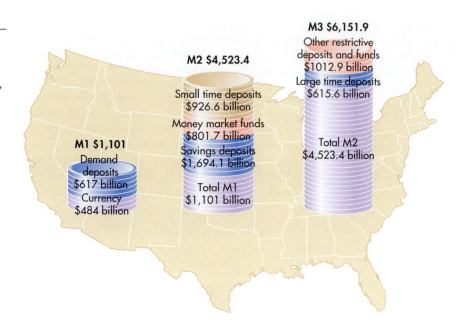

M3 $6,151.9
Other restrictive deposits and funds $1012.9 billion
Large time deposits $615.6 billion
Total M2 $4,523.4 billion

M2 $4,523.4
Small time deposits $926.6 billion
Money market funds $801.7 billion
Savings deposits $1,694.1 billion
Total M1 $1,101 billion

M1 $1,101
Demand deposits $617 billion
Currency $484 billion

discount rate
Interest rate the Federal Reserve charges on loans to commercial banks

prime interest rate (prime)
Lowest interest rate banks offer on short-term loans to preferred borrowers

open-market operations
Activity of the Federal Reserve in buying and selling government bonds on the open market

selective credit controls
Federal Reserve's power to set credit terms on various types of loans

expand and consumers can't borrow to buy goods and services. Conversely, reducing this requirement boosts the economy, because banks have more money to lend to businesses and consumers.

• *Changing the discount rate.* The Fed can also change the **discount rate,** the interest rate it charges on loans to commercial banks and other depository institutions. When the Fed raises the discount rate, member banks generally raise the **prime interest rate (prime),** the lowest interest rate offered on short-term bank loans to preferred borrowers. Raising the discount rate discourages loans, and in so doing tightens the money supply and slows down economic growth. Lowering the discount rate results in lower lending rates, thereby encouraging more borrowing and economic growth.

• *Conducting open-market operations.* The tool the Fed uses most often to influence the money supply is the power to buy and sell U.S. government bonds. Because anyone can buy these bonds on the open market, this tool is known as **open-market operations.** If the Fed is concerned about inflation, it can reduce the money supply by selling U.S. government bonds, which takes cash out of circulation. And when the Fed wants to boost the economy, it can buy back government bonds, putting cash into circulation and increasing the money supply.

• *Establishing selective credit controls.* The Fed can also use **selective credit controls** to set the terms of credit for various kinds of loans. This tool includes the power to set *margin requirements,* the percentage of the purchase price that an investor must pay in cash when purchasing a stock or a bond on credit. By altering the margin requirements, the Fed is able to influence how much cash is tied up in stock market transactions.

Exhibit 15.3 summarizes the effects of using these four tools.

Supplying Currency and Clearing Checks

The second function of the Fed is to supply currency to keep the U.S. financial system running smoothly. For example, regional Federal Reserve Banks are responsible for providing

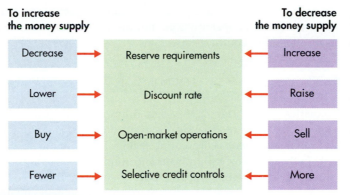

EXHIBIT 15·3

INFLUENCING THE MONEY SUPPLY

The Federal Reserve uses four tools to influence the money supply as it attempts to stimulate economic growth while keeping inflation and interest rates at acceptable levels.

member banks with adequate amounts of currency throughout the year. In preparation for potential disruptions due to year-2000 computer problems, the Fed was ready to provide U.S. banks with another $50 billion in cash.[16]

Another function of the Federal Reserve is to act as a clearinghouse for checks. Today, money on deposit in banks or other financial institutions is recorded in computerized ledger entries. When a customer deposits or cashes a check drawn on a bank in another city or town, the customer's bank uses the Fed's check-processing system to clear the check and receive payment. In clearing this check, the Fed's computer system charges and credits the appropriate accounts. Exhibit 15.4 shows the operation of this automated clearinghouse

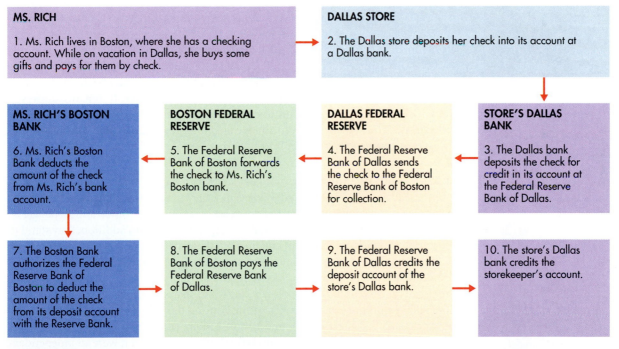

EXHIBIT 15·4

HOW THE FED CLEARS CHECKS

The Federal Reserve acts as a clearinghouse for checks in the United States. This example shows how the Fed clears a check that has been drawn on a bank in one city but deposited by a store in a bank in another city.

function, which is invisible yet indispensable to consumers and businesses. Similarly, the Fed's open-market operations are not directly visible but they do affect securities investments, the subject of the next section.

■ TYPES OF SECURITIES INVESTMENTS

securities
Investments such as stocks, bonds, options, futures, and commodities

Securities—stocks, bonds, options, futures, commodities, and other investments—are much in the news these days. Look at the business section of any newspaper or magazine, and you'll read about a corporation selling stocks or bonds to finance operations or expansion. In the same way, governments and municipalities issue bonds to raise money for building or public expenses—from national defense to road improvements. These securities are traded in organized markets where investors (individuals and institutions) can buy and sell them to meet their investment goals.

Stocks

stock certificate
Document showing ownership of a share of stock in a publicly held corporation

As you saw in Chapter 5, a share of stock represents ownership in a corporation; it is evidenced by a **stock certificate.** If you are a shareholder—someone who owns stock—you may vote on important issues but you have no say in day-to-day business activities. You and other shareholders have the advantage of limited liability if the corporation gets into trouble. At the same time, as part-owners, you share in the fortunes of the business and are eligible to receive dividends as long as you hold the stock.

LEARNING OBJECTIVE 4
Differentiate among a stock's par value, its market value, and its book value

Stock certificates issued to shareholders often include a **par value,** a dollar value assigned to the stock primarily for bookkeeping purposes and (for certain kinds of stock) for use in calculating dividends. Don't confuse par value with a stock's *market value*, the price at which a share currently sells, or its *book value*, the amount of net assets of a corporation represented by one share of common stock.

par value
As shown on the stock certificate, a value assigned to a stock for use in bookkeeping and in calculating dividends

The number of stock shares a company sells depends on the amount of equity capital the company will require and on the price of each share it sells. A corporation's board of directors sets a maximum number of shares into which the business can be divided. In theory, all these shares—called **authorized stock**—may be sold at once. In practice, however, the company sells only a part of its authorized stock. The part sold and held by shareholders is called **issued stock;** the unsold portion is called **unissued stock.** Common stock is one of two classes of stock an investor can buy; the other is preferred stock.

authorized stock
Maximum number of ownership shares into which a corporation's board of directors decides the business can be divided

issued stock
Portion of authorized stock sold to and held by shareholders

Common Stock Most investors buy common stock, which represents an ownership interest in a publicly traded corporation. As discussed in Chapter 5, shareholders of this class of stock vote to elect the company's board of directors, vote on other important corporate issues, and receive dividends, payments from the company's profits. In addition, they stand to make a profit if the stock price goes up and they sell their shares for more than the purchase price. The reverse is also true: shareholders of common stock can lose money if the market price drops and they sell the stock for less than they paid for it.

unissued stock
Portion of authorized stock not yet sold to shareholders

A special type of common stock is *tracking stock,* shares linked to the performance of a specific business unit of a public corporation. Among the corporations that have issued tracking stocks are AT&T, Ziff-Davis, and Perkin-Elmer. This type of stock allows a company to wring top market value from an attractive business unit as if it were an independent company. From the investor's perspective, tracking stock is a convenient way to own part of this business unit while taking advantage of the parent's financial stability. But tracking stocks are risky. The parent can do what it wishes with the unit's assets, and it does not always grant full voting rights to holders of such stock.[17] Conservative investors often prefer

Stock certificates represent a share of ownership of a company.

blue-chip stock, stock in a corporation such as General Electric that is well established and has a long record of solid earnings and dividends.

Dividends and voting rights are not the only benefits of common stock. From time to time a company may announce a **stock split,** in which it increases the number of shares that each stock certificate represents while proportionally lowering the value of each share. Companies generally use a stock split to make the share price more affordable. For instance, if a company with 1 million shares outstanding and a stock price of $50 per share announces a two-for-one split, it is doubling the number of shares. After the split, the company will have 2 million shares outstanding, and each original share will become two shares worth $25 a piece.

Preferred Stock Investors who own preferred stock, the second major class of stock, enjoy higher dividends and a better claim (after creditors) on assets if the corporation fails. The amount of the dividend on preferred stock is printed on the stock certificate and set when the stock is first issued. If interest rates fluctuate, the market price of preferred stock will go up or down to adjust for the difference between the market interest rate and the stock's dividend.

Preferred stock often comes with special privileges. *Convertible preferred stock* can be exchanged, if the shareholder chooses, for a certain number of shares of common stock issued by the company. *Cumulative preferred stock* has an additional advantage: If the issuing company stops paying dividends for any reason, the dividends on these shares will be held (accumulate) until preferred shareholders have been paid in full—before common stockholders are paid.

Corporate Bonds

Unlike stock, which gives the investor an ownership stake in the corporation, bonds are debt financing. (See Component Chapter B for a detailed discussion of debt versus equity financing.) A **bond** is a method of raising money in which the issuing organization borrows from an investor and issues a written pledge to make regular interest payments and then repay the borrowed amount later. When you invest in this type of security, you are lending money to the company, municipality, or government agency that issued the bond.

Corporate bonds—those issued by companies—are big business. The New York Stock Exchange lists more corporate bonds than stocks, and the market value of all outstanding corporate bonds exceeds $2 trillion.[18] Corporate bonds are usually issued in multiples of $1,000. Bond certificates show the issuer's name, the amount borrowed (the **principal**), the date this principal amount will be repaid, and the annual interest rate investors receive.

The certificate also indicates what type of corporate bond the investor has bought. **Secured bonds** are backed by company-owned property (such as airplanes or plant equipment) that will pass to the bondholders if the issuer does not repay the amount borrowed. *Mortgage bonds,* one type of secured bond, are backed by real property owned by the issuing corporation. **Debentures** are unsecured bonds, backed only by the corporation's promise to pay. Because debentures are riskier than other types of bonds, investors who buy these bonds receive higher interest rates. **Convertible bonds** can be exchanged at the investor's option, for a certain number of shares of the corporation's common stock. Because of this feature, convertible bonds generally pay lower interest rates.

Bonds are not guaranteed investments, so it is important to check the financial stability of the issuing companies before you buy. Bond-rating agencies such as Standard & Poor's (S&P) and Moody's rate bonds on the basis of the issuers' financial strength. Exhibit 15.5 shows that the safest corporate bonds are rated AAA (S&P) and Aaa (Moody's). Low-rated bonds, known as *junk bonds,* pay higher interest rates to compensate investors for the higher risk.

---

blue-chip stock
Stock in a well-established corporation with a long record of good earnings and dividends

stock split
Increase in the number of shares of ownership that each stock certificate represents, at a proportionate drop in each share's value

bond
Method of funding in which the issuer borrows from an investor and provides a written promise to make regular interest payments and repay the borrowed amount in the future

principal
Amount of money a corporation borrows from an investor through the sale of a bond

secured bonds
Bonds backed by specific assets that will be given to bondholders if the borrowed amount is not repaid

debentures
Corporate bonds backed only by the reputation of the issuer

convertible bonds
Corporate bonds that can be exchanged at the owner's discretion into common stock of the issuing company

BellSouth
Telecommunications
Bond Certificate
1. Name of corporation
   issuing the bond
2. Type of bond (debenture)
3. Face value of the bond
4. Annual interest rate
   (8.25%)
5. Maturity date (due 2032)

LEARNING OBJECTIVE 5

**Explain the advantages of
investing in U.S. Treasury
securities**

Treasury bills
Short-term debt securities issued
by the federal government; also
referred to as T-bills

Treasury notes
Debt securities issued by the
federal government that are
repaid within one to ten years
after issuance

Treasury bonds
Debt securities issued by the
federal government that are repaid
more than ten years after issuance

U.S. savings bonds
Debt instruments sold by the
federal government in a variety of
amounts

U.S. Government Securities and Municipal Bonds

Just as corporations raise money by issuing bonds, so too do federal, state, city, and local governments and agencies. As an investor, you can buy a variety of U.S. government securities, including three types of bonds issued by the U.S. Treasury, U.S. savings bonds, and bonds issued by various U.S. municipalities.

Treasury bills are short-term U.S. government bonds that are repaid in less than one year. **Treasury notes** are intermediate-term U.S. government bonds that are repaid from one to ten years after they were initially issued. **Treasury bonds** are long-term U.S. government bonds that are repaid more than ten years after they were initially issued. In total, investors worldwide hold about $3.5 trillion in these three types of securities. These U.S. government securities pay less interest than do corporate bonds because they are considered safer: There is very little risk that the government will fail to repay bondholders as promised. Another benefit is that investors pay no state or local income tax on interest earned on these bonds. Also, these bonds can easily be bought or sold through the Treasury or in organized securities markets.

A traditional choice for many individual investors, **U.S. savings bonds** are issued by the U.S. government in amounts ranging from $50 to $10,000. Investors who buy Series EE

See It on the Web See It on the Web

TRACK DOWN TREASURY SECURITIES

Want to do your share to finance the national debt (about $6 trillion)? Find out how to buy bills, bonds, and more at the U.S. Treasury's Bureau of the Public Debt Web site. Check the interest rate on Series EE savings bonds. See when T-bills, notes, and bonds are scheduled to be auctioned. Before you go, look at the exact amount of the national debt—to the penny—and click to meet the Savings Bond Wizard.

http://www.publicdebt.treas.gov

S&P	INTERPRETATION	MOODY'S	INTERPRETATION
AAA	Highest rating	Aaa	Prime quality
AA	Very strong capacity to pay	Aa	High grade
A	Strong capacity to pay; somewhat susceptible to changing business conditions	A	Upper-medium grade
BBB	More susceptible than A rated bonds	Baa	Medium grade
BB	Somewhat speculative	Ba	Somewhat speculative
B	Speculative	B	Speculative
CCC	Vulnerable to nonpayment	Caa	Poor standing; may be in default
CC	Highly vulnerable to nonpayment	Ca	Highly speculative; often in default
C	Bankruptcy petition filed or similar action taken	C	Lowest rated; extremely poor chance of ever attaining real investment standing
D	In default		

EXHIBIT 15·5

CORPORATE BOND RATINGS

Standard & Poor's (S&P) and Moody's Investors Service are two companies that rate the safety of corporate bonds. When its bonds receive a low rating, a company must pay a higher interest rate to compensate investors for the higher risk.

savings bonds pay just 50 percent of the stated value and receive the full amount in as little as 17 years, although they continue to earn interest until 30 years after the bonds were issued. Other savings bonds are Series HH, which can be bought only by exchanging Series EE bonds, and Series I, which pay interest indexed to the inflation rate.

Municipal bonds (often called *munis*) are issued by states, cities, and special government agencies to raise money for public services such as building schools, highways, and airports. Investors can buy two types of municipal bonds: general obligation bonds and revenue bonds. A **general obligation bond** is a municipal bond backed by the taxing power of the issuing government. When interest payments come due, the issuer makes payments out of its tax receipts. In contrast, a **revenue bond** is a municipal bond backed by the money to be generated by the project being financed. As an example, revenue bonds issued by a city airport are paid from revenues raised by the airport's operation. To encourage investment, the federal government doesn't tax the interest that investors receive from municipal bonds, and many municipal bonds are free from state and local taxes, as well. However, **capital gains**—the return investors get from selling a security for more than its purchase price—are taxed at both the federal and state levels.

Mutual Funds

Another way to invest in securities is to buy shares in a **mutual fund,** a financial organization that pools money from many investors to buy a diversified mix of stocks, bonds, or other securities. These funds are particularly well suited for investors who wish to spread a fixed amount of money over a variety of investments and do not have the time or experience to search out and manage investment opportunities. *No-load* funds charge no fee to buy or sell shares, whereas *load funds* charge investors a commission to buy or sell shares.

Various mutual funds have different investment priorities. Among the most popular mutual funds are **money-market funds,** which invest in short-term securities and other liquid investments. *Growth funds* invest in stocks of rapidly growing companies. *Income funds* invest in securities that pay high dividends and interest. *Balanced funds* invest in a carefully chosen mix of stocks and bonds. *Sector funds* (also known as specialty or industry funds) invest in

municipal bonds
Bonds issued by city, state, and government agencies to fund public services

general obligation bond
Municipal bond that is backed by the government's authority to collect taxes

revenue bond
Municipal bond backed by revenue generated from the project it is financing

capital gains
Return that investors receive when they sell a security for a higher price than the purchase price

mutual fund
Financial organization pooling money to invest in diversified blends of stocks, bonds, or other securities

money-market funds
Mutual funds that invest in short-term securities and other liquid investments

companies within a particular industry. *International funds* invest in foreign securities. And *index funds* buy stocks in companies included in specific market averages, such as the Standard & Poor's 500. You can buy shares in mutual funds through your broker or directly from the mutual fund company.

■ SECURITIES MARKETS

Where can you purchase bonds, stocks, and other securities? Stocks and bonds are bought and sold in two kinds of marketplaces: primary markets and secondary markets. As discussed in Chapter 5, corporations sell their stock to the public to generate funds for expansion or other purposes. Newly issued shares or initial public offerings (IPOs) are sold in the **primary market.** Once these shares have been issued, subsequent investors can buy and sell them in the organized **secondary market** known as **stock exchanges** (or securities exchanges). To have its stock traded on a securities exchange, a publicly held company must become a member of the exchange and meet certain listing requirements related to net income, the number of shares outstanding, and the total market value of all outstanding shares—its *market capitalization.* These listing requirements differ from exchange to exchange.

Auction and Dealer Exchanges

Investors can trade securities in two types of secondary marketplaces: *auction exchanges* (the traditional marketplace) and *dealer exchanges.* In an **auction exchange,** all buy and sell orders (and all information concerning companies traded on that exchange) are funneled onto an auction floor. There, buyers and sellers are matched by a *stock specialist,* a broker who occupies a post on the trading floor and conducts all the trades in a particular stock via a central clearinghouse. If buying or selling imbalances occur in that stock, the specialist can halt trading to prevent the price from plunging without adequate cause.[19] The NYSE (New York Stock Exchange), also known as the "Big Board," is the world's largest auction exchange. The stocks and bonds of nearly 3,100 companies, with a combined market value topping $9.4 trillion, are traded on the exchange's floor.[20]

The process for buying and selling securities is different in **dealer exchanges,** primarily because no central place exists for making transactions. Instead, all buy and sell orders are executed through computers by **market makers,** registered stock and bond representatives who sell securities out of their own inventories. The **over-the-counter (OTC) market** is a dealer exchange consisting of a network of registered stock and bond representatives who are spread out across the United States—in some cases, even around the world. Most use a nationwide computer network owned by the National Association of Securities Dealers (NASD). This network is called NASDAQ (National Association of Securities Dealers Automated Quotations).

The Changing Nature of Securities Exchanges

Despite its large size, the NYSE is feeling competitive pressure from regional and foreign exchanges. More than half of the NYSE-listed stocks can also be bought and sold at one or more of the regional exchanges, including the Pacific, Boston, and Chicago exchanges, and more than half of all the stocks around the world are traded outside the United States.[21] After the NYSE, some of the largest stock exchanges are located in Tokyo, London, Frankfurt, Paris, Toronto, and Montreal.

Over the years, NASDAQ has also developed into a formidable challenger to the NYSE. In part, this growth came about because NASDAQ's listing requirements were less stringent

---

primary market
Market where firms sell new securities issued publicly for the first time

secondary market
Market where subsequent owners trade previously issued shares of stocks and bonds

stock exchanges
Location where traders buy and sell stocks and bonds

LEARNING OBJECTIVE 6
Describe the two types of securities exchanges

auction exchange
Centralized marketplace where securities are traded by specialists on behalf of investors

dealer exchanges
Decentralized marketplaces where securities are bought and sold by dealers out of their own inventories

market makers
Registered representatives who trade securities from their own inventories on dealer exchanges, making a ready market for buyers and sellers

over-the-counter (OTC) market
Network of dealers who trade securities on computerized linkups rather than on a trading floor

than those of other exchanges, so younger companies with low market capitalizations could only be traded over the counter. Now that the NYSE has loosened its standards, however, fast-growth firms that once gravitated toward NASDAQ have more choice.[22] But NASDAQ has also expanded by acquiring the American Stock Exchange (the world's third largest exchange) and the Philadelphia Stock Exchange, putting more pressure on the NYSE.[23] In turn, NASDAQ is being challenged by new electronic broker systems that are working toward becoming exchanges where all kinds of stocks can trade at a lower cost.[24]

In addition to competitive pressures, securities exchanges are feeling the heat from consumers and large institutions who are pushing them to offer electronic trading options. For decades, the NYSE has resisted demands to automate the execution of stock orders, using specialists instead. But now the Big Board is exploring the possibility of permitting electronic trading for stock orders under 1,000 shares.[25]

At the same time, globalization is driving the move toward round-the-clock worldwide trading. Many securities exchanges are considering the possibilities of extending their traditional hours of 9:30 A.M. to 4 P.M. by adding early-morning and late-night trading sessions. The Chicago exchange has already extended its trading hours, and the Swedish exchange has moved to a 12-hour trading day. Furthermore, even when the traditional exchanges are closed, investors can buy and sell securities by using electronic systems such as Instinet, which offer after-hours trading. Extended trading hours are also on the horizon for stocks traded in the over-the-counter market.[26]

How to Buy and Sell Securities

For the present—even if you trade online—all trades must be executed by a securities broker. A **broker** is an expert who has passed a series of formal examinations and is legally registered to buy and sell securities on behalf of individual and institutional investors. As an investor, you pay *transaction costs* for every buy or sell order, to cover the broker's commission, which varies with the type of broker and the size of your trade: A *full-service broker* provides a full range of research and financial management services, such as investment counseling and planning; a *discount broker* provides fewer or limited services and generally charges lower commissions than a full-service broker. Remember, transaction costs can take a hefty bite out of your total return—especially if you trade frequently—so take these costs into consideration before you buy or sell securities.

broker
An expert who has passed specific tests and is registered to trade securities for investors

 Most of the data that brokerage firms provide to their customers are now available for free on the Internet.[27]

Trading Procedures Before you start to trade, take time to think about your objectives, both long term and short term. Next, look at how various securities match your objectives and your

 See It on the Web See It on the Web

STOCK UP AT THE NEW YORK STOCK EXCHANGE

Tour the New York Stock Exchange. Read about the NYSE and learn how the auction market works. Then visit the trading floor—online, not in person—and find out how stocks are actually traded. See how regulation protects investors and how you can become a better investor. Get the latest market information as well as a historical perspective of the NYSE. Don't leave without checking the price of your favorite stock. Is it time to buy or sell?
http://www.nyse.com

Once a buy or a sell order for stock listed on an auction exchange has been fulfilled, brokers must initial each other's order slips. Within minutes, the transaction is reported back to the brokerage houses and to the two customers.

attitude toward risk, since investing in stocks and bonds can involve potential losses. Finally, consider the many ways you can have your broker buy or sell securities: A *market order* tells the broker to buy or sell at the best price that can be negotiated at the moment. A *limit order* specifies the highest price you are willing to pay when buying or the lowest price at which you are willing to sell. A *stop order* tells the broker to sell if the price of your security drops to or below the price you set, protecting you from losing more money if prices are dropping. You can also place a time limit on your orders. An *open order* instructs the broker to leave the order open until you cancel it. A *day order* is valid only on the day you place it.

If you have special confidence in your broker's ability, you may place a *discretionary order,* which gives the broker the right to buy or sell your securities at his or her discretion. In some cases, discretionary orders can save you from taking a loss, because the broker may have a better sense of when to sell a stock. If the broker's judgment proves wrong, however, you cannot hold him or her legally responsible for the consequences; so investigate your broker's background and think carefully before you give anyone the right to trade your securities.

Investors sometimes borrow cash to buy stocks, a practice known as *margin trading.* Instead of paying for the stock in full, you borrow some of the money from your stockbroker, paying interest on the borrowed money and leaving the stock with the broker as collateral. As we mentioned earlier, the Federal Reserve Board establishes margin requirements. Be aware, however, that margin trading increases risk. If the price of a stock you bought on margin goes down, you will have to give your broker more money or the broker will sell your stock. Such forced sales can cause prices to fall even further, triggering a vicious cycle of sales and margin calls.[28]

short selling
Selling stock borrowed from a broker with the intention of buying it back later at a lower price, repaying the broker, and keeping the profit

If you believe that a stock's price is about to drop, you may choose a trading procedure known as **short selling.** With this procedure, you sell stock you borrow from a broker in the hope of buying it back later at a lower price. After you return the borrowed stock to the broker, you keep the price difference. For example, you might decide to borrow 25 shares that are selling for $30 per share and sell short because you think the share price is going to plummet. When the stock's price declines to $15, you buy 25 shares on the open market and make $15 profit on every share (minus transaction costs). Selling short is risky. If the stock had climbed to $32, you would have had to buy shares at that higher price, even though you would be losing money. (Consult part VI of the *E-Business in Action* online supplement at http://www.prenhall.com/ebusinessinaction for detailed discussion of buying shares in Internet IPOs.)

Trading Online   E*Trade is part of the online trading phenomenon that has revolutionized the way investors buy and sell securities. Already, online trading is responsible for an estimated one-third of all stock trades made by individual investors.[29] Convenience, control, and cost are the main advantages of trading online. Rather than talk with your broker each time you want to trade, you can now visit your brokerage firm's or mutual fund's Web site, enter your buy or sell instructions, and pay a much lower broker's commission. In fact, full-service brokerages initially resisted online trading because they were concerned about losing their lucrative percentage commissions. But now even traditional firms like Merrill Lynch have jumped on the cyber-bandwagon, offering online trading with lower, flat-fee commissions in line with transaction charges levied by Schwab and others for Internet trades.[31]

Only a few businesses will succeed by having the lowest price; most will need a strategy that includes customer service.[30]

PUT YOUR MONEY WHERE YOUR MOUSE IS!— INVESTMENT INFORMATION ON THE NET

Before you put a dollar (or a franc) into any investment, you need to learn as much as possible about the market, the security, its issuer, and its potential. This is where being wired really pays off, because the amount of investment information on the Internet is staggering.

For "how to" advice, try the Motley Fool (http://www.fool.com), Quicken's financial site (http://www.quicken.com/investments), or *Money's* Web site (http://www.money.com). Also look at the economic trend sites lined to Dr. Ed Yardeni's Economics Network (http://www.yardeni.com/). Then research individual securities using Yahoo! or another Internet search tool. Plug in the company name and click to see the latest news. Go to Hoover's Online (http://www.hoovers.com) to read a little about the company's history and recent results. Be sure to stop by the company's Web site to read its press releases and financial statements. You can burrow even further into potential investments using these Web sites:

- Corporate financial data filed with the SEC (http://www.freeedgar.com)
- Morningstar mutual fund reports (http://www.morningstar.net)
- Bond prices and market performance (http://www.investinginbonds.com)
- Investorama links to research and analysis sites (http://www.investorama.com)

Try your hand at trading stocks before you actually invest hard cash, using CNNfn's stock market simulation (http://www.sandbox.com/finalbell/pub-doc/home.html). Also, construct a hypothetical portfolio on Quicken, Yahoo!, or another financial Web site and watch how your investments fare. Track your favorite market index on S&P's Personal Wealth site (http://www.personalwealth.com) and compare it with the investments in your hypothetical portfolio. Are your proposed investments meeting, missing, or beating the market index?

Now you're in a better position to buy securities, but your research shouldn't end here. Even after you start trading, you need to stay on top of the latest news and industry developments that can affect the securities in which you have invested. And if a potential investment seems too good to be true, point your Web browser to the North American Securities Administrators Association primer on investment fraud (http://www.nasaa.org/investoredu/) to see if it's mentioned there. When it comes to investments, your Web surfing can really pay off.

QUESTIONS FOR CRITICAL THINKING

1. Why is it important to learn about a company's financial results and background before buying its stock or bonds?
2. What are the disadvantages of searching for investment information on the Internet?

Online trading is far from perfect. Some sites have had problems that prevented investors from placing online trades for minutes or even hours. And when you trade online, you trade alone, with no one to hold your hand, check for mistakes, or offer advice. Still, many online brokers such as Charles Schwab's Internet site, offer a range of services and resources, including free or low-cost research, customized tracking of securities, e-mails confirming trades, electronic newsletters packed with investment tips, and more.[32]

How to Analyze Financial News

Whether you trade online or off, you need to monitor financial news sources to see how your investments are doing. Start with daily newspaper reports on securities markets.

Other sources include newspapers aimed specifically at investors (such as *Investor's Daily* and *Barron's*) and general-interest business publications that follow the corporate world and give hints about investing (such as the *Wall Street Journal, Forbes, Fortune,* and *Business Week*). Standard & Poor's, Moody's Investor Service, and Value Line also publish newsletters and special reports on securities. Online sources include your brokerage firm's Web site plus Bloomberg (http://www.bloomberg.com/) and Smart Money (http://www.smartmoney.com/).

bull market
Rising stock market

bear market
Falling stock market

What types of financial information should you be looking for? First, you want to determine the general direction of stock prices. If stock prices have been rising over a long period, the industry and the media will often describe this situation as a **bull market.** The reverse is a **bear market,** one characterized by a long-term trend of falling prices. You can see these broad market movements in Exhibit 15.6. Once you have the general picture, look at the timing. Has a bull market lasted for too long, suggesting that stocks are overvalued and a *correction* (tumbling prices) might be imminent? Also watch the volume of shares traded each day. If the stock market is down on heavy volume (that is, if prices are moving downward and a lot of trading is going on), investors may be trying to sell before prices go down further—a bearish sign.

market indexes
Measures of market activity calculated from the prices of a selection of securities

One way to determine whether the market is bullish or bearish is to watch **market indexes** and averages, which use the performance of a representative sampling of stocks, bonds, or commodities as a gauge of broader market activity. The most famous U.S. stock average is the Dow Jones Industrial Average (DJIA), which tracks the prices of 30 blue-chip stocks, each representing a particular sector of the U.S. economy. Critics say the Dow is too narrow and too susceptible to short-term swings, lacks the right stocks, and gives too much weight to higher-priced shares. But advocates say the Dow's 30 stocks serve as a general barometer of market conditions. Regardless, a recent shuffling of the index by the *Wall Street Journal* editors (guardians of the Dow) should make it more representative of the "new economy"; in 1999 Microsoft, Intel, Home Depot, and SBC Communications replaced time-honored blue chips Chevron, Goodyear, Sears Roebuck, and Union Carbide.[33]

Another widely watched index is the Standard & Poor's 500 Stock Average (S&P 500), which tracks the performances of 500 corporate stocks, many more than the DJIA. This index is weighted by market value, not by stock price, so large companies carry far more weight than small companies.[34] The Wilshire 5000 Index, which actually covers some 7,000 stocks, is the broadest index measuring U.S. market performance. To get a sense of how technology stocks are doing, check the NASDAQ Composite Index, covering more than 3,000 over-the-counter stocks, including many high-tech firms. You can also look at indexes to learn about the performance of foreign markets, such as Japan's Nikkei 225 Index and the United Kingdom's FT-SE 100 Index.

In addition to watching market trends, you will want to follow the securities you own and others that look like promising investments. For stocks, you can turn to the stock exchange report in major daily newspapers. Exhibit 15.7 on page 378 shows how to read this report, which includes high and low prices for the past 52 weeks, the number of shares traded (volume), and the change from the previous day's closing price. U.S. securities markets began quoting security prices in decimals (dollars and cents) in 2000. Prior to that year, prices were quoted in fractions as small as 1/16.[35]

price-earnings ratio
Ratio calculated by dividing a stock's market price by its prior year's earnings per share

Included in the stock exchange report is the **price-earnings ratio,** or *p/e ratio* (also known as the price-earnings multiple), which is computed by dividing a stock's market price by its *prior* year's earnings per share. Some investors also calculate a forward p/e ratio using *expected* year earnings in the ratio's denominator. Bear in mind that if a stock's p/e ratio is well below the industry norm, either the company is in trouble or it's an undiscovered gem

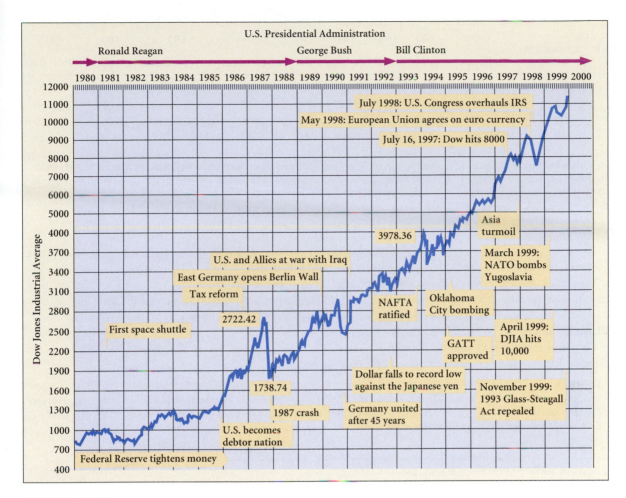

U.S. Presidential Administration

Ronald Reagan   George Bush   Bill Clinton

1980 1981 1982 1983 1984 1985 1986 1987 1988 1989 1990 1991 1992 1993 1994 1995 1996 1997 1998 1999 2000

July 1998: U.S. Congress overhauls IRS

May 1998: European Union agrees on euro currency

July 16, 1997: Dow hits 8000

3978.36

Asia turmoil

U.S. and Allies at war with Iraq

March 1999: NATO bombs Yugoslavia

East Germany opens Berlin Wall

Tax reform

2722.42

NAFTA ratified

Oklahoma City bombing

First space shuttle

GATT approved

April 1999: DJIA hits 10,000

Dollar falls to record low against the Japanese yen

1738.74

November 1999: 1993 Glass-Steagall Act repealed

1987 crash

Germany united after 45 years

U.S. becomes debtor nation

Federal Reserve tightens money

EXHIBIT 15·6

THE STOCK MARKET'S UPS AND DOWNS

The peaks and valleys on this chart represent swings in the Dow Jones Industrial Average, the most widely used indicator of U.S. stock prices.

with a relatively low stock price. For more detailed data on a stock, consult the company's annual reports or documents filed with the Securities and Exchange Commission (SEC).

To follow specific bonds, check the bond quotation tables in major newspapers (see Exhibit 15.8). When reading these tables, remember that the price is quoted as a percentage of the bond's value. For example, a $1,000 bond shown closing at 65 actually sold at $650. Newspapers and business publications also include tables of price quotations for investments such as mutual funds, commodities, options, and government securities. These same publications also carry news about securities frauds and investor protection.

Regulation of Securities Markets

Whenever you buy and sell securities, your trades are governed by a network of state and federal laws. Combined with industry self-regulation, these laws are designed to ensure that you and all investors receive accurate information and that no one artificially manipulates the market price of a given security. Trading in stocks and bonds is monitored by the Securities

(1) 52-WEEK HIGH	52-WEEK LOW	(2) STOCK	(3) SYM	(4) DIV	(5) YLD %	(6) PE	(7) VOL 100S	(8) HI	LOW	(9) CLOSE	(10) NET CHG
55.25	26.20	NtlDataCp	NDC	.30	.8	20	3580	40.75	38.20	39.95	−.70
56.25	17.00	Navistar	NAV		...	9	2570	45.95	44.40	45.75	+1.30
33.75	15.00	NeimanMarc	NMG		...	11	888	24.70	23.65	23.80	−.80
22.90	**10.75**	**NoblDrill**	**NE**		...	**26**	**15762**	**24.00**	**22.75**	**24.00**	**+1.25**

1. **52-week high/low:** Indicates the highest and lowest trading price of the stock in the past 52 weeks plus the most recent week but not the most recent trading day (adjusted for splits). Stocks are quoted in decimals. In most newspapers, boldfaced entries indicate stocks whose price changed by 5% or more if the previous closing price was $2 or higher.
2. **Stock:** The company's name abbreviated. A capital letter usually means a new word. In this example, NtlDataCp is National Data Corporation, NeimanMarc is Neiman-Marcus Group, and NoblDrill is Noble Drill.
3. **Symbol:** Symbol under which this stock is traded on stock exchanges.
4. **Dividend:** Dividends are usually annual payments based on the last quarterly or semiannual declaration, although not all stocks pay dividends. Special or extra dividends or payments are identified in footnotes.
5. **Yield:** The percentage yield shows dividends as a percentage of the share price.
6. **PE:** Price-to-earnings ratio, calculated by dividing the stock's closing price by the earnings per share for the latest four quarters.
7. **Volume:** Daily total of shares traded, in hundreds. A listing of 888 indicates 88,800 shares were traded during that day.
8. **High/Low:** The stock's highest and lowest price for that day.
9. **Close:** Closing price of the stock that day.
10. **Net change:** Change in share price from the close of the previous trading day.

Common Stock Footnotes: d—new 52 week low; n—new; pf—preferred; s—stock split or stock dividend of 25 percent or more in previous 52 weeks; u—new 52 week high; v—trading halted on primary market; vi—in bankruptcy; x—ex dividend (the buyer won't receive a recently declared dividend, but the seller will).

EXHIBIT 15·7

HOW TO READ A NEWSPAPER STOCK QUOTATION

Even before you invest, you will want to follow the latest quotations for your stock. This table shows you how to read the newspaper stock quotation tables.

EXHIBIT 15·8

HOW TO READ A NEWSPAPER BOND QUOTATION

When newspapers carry bond quotations, they show prices as a percentage of the bond's value, which is typically $1,000.

(1) COMPANY	(2) CUR YLD	(3) VOL	(4) CLOSE	(5) NET CHG
NYTel 6⅛ 10	6.6	11	93.40	−.25
PacBell 6¼ 05	6.4	10	98.40	+.25
Safwy 9⅞ 07	8.4	20	117.50	+3.60
StoneC 11½ 04	11.1	24	103.50	−1.10
TmeWar 9⅛ 13	8.3	30	109.75	−.50

1. **Company:** Name of company issuing the bond, such as New York Telephone, and bond description, such as 6⅛ percent bond maturing in 2010.
2. **Current yield:** Annual interest on $1,000 bond divided by the closing price shown. The yield for New York Telephone is $61.25 ÷ $933.75 = 0.06559, or approximately 6.6 percent.
3. **Volume:** Number of bonds traded that day.
4. **Close:** Price of the bond at the close of the last day's business.
5. **Net change:** Change in bond price from the close of the previous trading day.

and Exchange Commission. In addition, the SEC works closely with the stock exchanges and NASD to police securities transactions and maintain the system's integrity.

As mentioned earlier, companies must meet certain requirements (which include filing a blizzard of registration papers and reports) to be listed on any exchange. Similarly, brokers must operate according to the rules of the exchanges, rules that are largely designed to protect investors. (See Component Chapter A for a list of major federal legislation governing the securities industry.) Overseeing all these details keeps the SEC very busy indeed. Every year the SEC screens over 15,200 annual reports, 40,000 investor complaints, 14,000 prospectuses (a legal statement that describes the objectives of a specific investment), and 6,500 proxy statements (a shareholder's written authorization giving someone else the authority to cast his or her vote). The agency's Web site receives up to 300 complaints every day and contains a mountain of public documents that investors can browse, download, or print to learn more about publicly traded companies.[36]

One of the SEC's top priorities is to crack down on *insider trading,* in which a few people with access to secret information (say, a pending merger) profit by buying or selling a stock before the information becomes public and the price changes in reaction to the news. But monitoring insider information and securities fraud has become increasingly difficult now that stock promoters can quickly reach millions of investors through the Internet. As a result, the operators of some brokerage and financial Web sites voluntarily monitor chatroom and bulletin-board messages posted on their sites to avoid manipulation of smaller stocks in particular. Moreover, NASD has developed an Internet search engine to find phrases such as "too good to be true," and it monitors securities chat forums for fraudulent or misleading information.[37] As an investor, your best defense against fraud is to carefully research securities before you buy and to steer clear of any investment that seems too good to be true.

Summary of Learning Objectives

1. **Distinguish between deposit and nondeposit financial institutions.**
   Deposit institutions take deposits from customers and provide services such as checking accounts, savings accounts, and loans. Three types of deposit institutions are commercial banks, thrifts, and credit unions. Nondeposit institutions such as insurance companies and pension funds offer specific financial services.

2. **Discuss how customers and banks benefit from electronic and Internet banking.**
   Electronic and Internet banking offer customers the convenience of anywhere, anytime services. Moreover, customers get instant access to bank account information and benefit from expanded services offered via ATM machines and electronic wallets. Banks can draw from a potentially larger customer base, service their customers from anywhere in the world, and save significant dollars on lower processing and transaction costs.

3. **Identify the four ways the Federal Reserve System influences the U.S. money supply.**
   The Fed influences the U.S. money supply by changing reserve requirements, changing the discount rate, carrying out open-market operations, and setting selective credit controls.

4. **Differentiate among a stock's par value, its market value, and its book value.**
   Par value is the dollar value assigned to a stock for bookkeeping and for dividend calculations. Market value is the price at which a share of stock is currently selling. Book value is the portion of a corporation's net assets represented by a single share of common stock.

5. **Explain the advantages of investing in U.S. Treasury securities.**
   U.S. Treasury securities are considered safe investments because the government is highly unlikely to fail to make payments as promised. Interest from Treasury bills, notes, and bonds is exempt from state and local income taxes, and investors can easily buy and sell these securities through the Treasury or organized markets.

6. **Describe the two types of securities exchanges.**
   Auction exchanges such as the New York Stock Exchange funnel all buy and sell orders into one centralized location. Dealer exchanges such as NASDAQ are decentralized marketplaces in which dealers, known as market makers, are connected electronically to handle buy and sell orders without a single, centralized trading floor.

MEETING BUSINESS CHALLENGES AT E*TRADE

In early 1997, E*Trade was servicing 145,000 customers who traded securities on its Web site. Forecasts indicated that millions of investors would soon be trading online, and CEO Christos Cotsakos wanted E*Trade to capture a large share of this fast-growing market. Along the way, he and his management team had to juggle a variety of challenges.

One challenge was maintaining the company's broker registration in every state. By law, brokers are not allowed to buy and sell securities in a state if they do not complete the state's registration process. In early 1997, E*Trade personnel tracked state registrations by hand and inadvertently neglected to renew the Ohio registration. Although this problem was quickly corrected, regulators directed E*Trade to tell Ohio customers about the lapse—and to offer them the opportunity to reverse some trades made during that period. Unraveling these trades cost E*Trade $4.3 million. To avoid any repetition of this costly lapse, the company automated its registration process.

Another challenge was safeguarding the information in customers' accounts and maintaining the privacy of their trades. The company installed a super-secure server system using password authentication and data encryption to protect against unauthorized access. Every time customers accessed account information, they were prompted to enter both a user name and a password. Every time they placed a trade, they had to re-enter the password. In addition, E*Trade arranged for insurance to protect customers' assets against theft or misappropriation.

Meanwhile, Ameritrade and other brokers began offering Web-based trading with lower commissions, so E*Trade reduced its fees for some transactions. In addition, full-service and discount brokers were stepping up their Web services. But Cotsakos was committed to staying ahead of his competitors. He pushed E*Trade to continue adding services such as personalized screens, more securities research, and many other choices.

The company was growing rapidly and constantly upgrading its systems, which sometimes created glitches. On one occasion, E*Trade's system was down for three days. Then it malfunctioned again after new software was installed; customers could not trade online for nearly two hours (although they could trade by phone within an hour). E*Trade wasn't the only firm to suffer such problems, but it redoubled its efforts to ensure uninterrupted service.

By late 1999, E*Trade was the number three online brokerage firm. With over 1.5 million active customers, it was already handling more than 80,000 securities transactions each day. But Cotsakos continued expanding. He bought a stake in E-Offering, a new investment banking firm that handled initial public offerings, and he franchised the E*Trade business in 33 countries, pioneering more innovations in point-and-click trading for investors around the world.[38]

Critical Thinking Questions

1. Would you expect E*Trade to attract as many new customers in a bear market as in a bull market? Explain your answer.
2. Why would E*Trade invite noncustomers to check market indexes and averages on the company's Web site?
3. How would E*Trade's customers be likely to benefit from the company's stake in E-Offering?

■ LEARN MORE ONLINE

What has E*Trade done lately to enhance its site? Go to the company's homepage at http://www.etrade.com and browse the screens describing featured services such as the E*Trade Game and special sign-up deals. Also click on the link to the learning center. Why would E*Trade offer a free online trading game and a learning center? How are the new sign-up promotions helping the firm to compete more effectively?

Key Terms

auction exchange (372)

authorized stock (368)

automated teller machines (ATMs) (360)

bear market (376)

blue-chip stock (369)

bond (369)

broker (373)

bull market (376)

capital gains (371)

checks (359)

convertible bonds (369)

credit cards (360)

currency (365)

dealer exchanges (372)

debentures (369)

debit cards (360)

demand deposits (365)

discount rate (366)

electronic funds transfer systems (EFTS) (361)

general obligation bond (371)

issued stock (368)

M1 (365)

M2 (365)

M3 (365)

market indexes (376)

market makers (372)

money (364)

money-market funds (371)

municipal bonds (371)

mutual fund (371)

open-market operations (366)

over-the-counter (OTC) market (372)

par value (368)

price-earnings ratio (376)

primary market (372)

prime interest rate (prime) (366)

principal (369)

reserve requirement (365)

revenue bond (371)

secondary market (372)

secured bonds (369)

securities (368)

selective credit controls (366)

short selling (374)

smart cards (360)

stock certificate (368)

stock exchanges (372)

stock split (369)

time deposits (365)

Treasury bills (370)

Treasury bonds (370)

Treasury notes (370)

unissued stock (368)

U.S. savings bonds (370)

Test Your Knowledge

QUESTIONS FOR REVIEW

1. How do credit cards, debit cards, and smart cards work?
2. What is the main function of the Federal Reserve System?
3. What are the differences between a Treasury bill, a Treasury note, and a U.S. savings bond?
4. What happens during a 2-for-1 stock split?
5. What is the function of the Securities and Exchange Commission?

QUESTIONS FOR ANALYSIS

6. How has banking deregulation changed competition among financial institutions?
7. What are some of the advantages of mutual funds?
8. Why are debentures considered riskier than other types of bonds?
9. When might an investor sell a stock short? What risks are involved in selling short?

10. What issues regarding privacy of personal information must Citigroup and other financial supermarkets address to protect customers?

QUESTIONS FOR APPLICATION

11. What nontraditional locations might a growing community bank choose for its ATMs to better compete with larger banks that operate in the same city?
12. If you were thinking about buying shares of AT&T, under what circumstances would you place a market order, a limit order, an open order, and a discretionary order?
13. Which of the four forms of utility discussed in Chapter 11 do electronic banking and Internet stock trading create?
14. How does the money supply affect the economy and inflation? (Hint: Think about the theory of supply and demand discussed in Chapter 1.)

Practice Your Knowledge

SHARPENING YOUR COMMUNICATION SKILLS

One of the most important steps in preparing for an interview is developing a list of interview questions that are clear and concise. Practice your communication skills by developing two sets of questions:

1. Questions you might ask a stockbroker to help you decide whether you would use his or her services.
2. Questions you might pose to that broker to help you evaluate the merits of purchasing a specific security.

HANDLING DIFFICULT SITUATIONS ON THE JOB: BATTLING BESTBANK'S SCAMS

As a recent law-school graduate working for the Denver Free Legal Clinic, you help clients resolve all kinds of problems. Today, Angelina Bigelow's story about BestBank has you riled.

Neither BestBank's owner, Edward P. Mattar, nor his associates have been accused of any crimes. But their "virtual bank," which advertised on the Internet, was seized by state regulators after they discovered $134 million in soured loans and only $23 million in BestBank reserves to cover them. One of BestBank's scams was to offer credit cards to people with poor credit histories. Bigelow had signed up but hadn't read the fine print, which said she was also agreeing to join a travel club—with a fee of $498 charged to her new card. An additional $45 fee used up nearly all of the elderly woman's $600 credit limit and put her in serious debt for her modest income level. When she couldn't make her high monthly payments, the bank added interest charges and $20 late fees that put her over the credit limit. Then the bank started adding an additional $20 per month "overlimit fee."

The state's seizure stopped the card billings. However, you've made a few calls and learned that these debts have been bought and new bills might show up again any day.[39] Angelina Bigelow is distraught and doesn't know how to get out of this seemingly endless debt trap. You are determined to help.

1. How can you find out which federal regulators to contact to follow up on BestBank's treatment of its credit-card customers?
2. What specific actions will you ask regulators to take to solve Bigelow's problem?
3. What steps will you advise your clients to take to prevent similar credit-card problems in the future?

BUILDING YOUR TEAM SKILLS

You and your team are going to pool your money and invest $5,000. Before you plunge into any investments, how can you prepare yourselves to be good investors? First, consider your group's goals. What will you and your teammates do with any profits generated by your investments? Once you have agreed on a goal for your team's profits, think about how much money you will need to achieve this goal and how soon you want to achieve it.

Next, think about how much risk you personally are willing to take to achieve the goal. Bear in mind that safer investments generally offer lower returns than riskier investments—and certain investments, such as stocks, can lose money. Now hold a group discussion to find a level of risk that feels comfortable for everyone on your team.

Once your team has decided how much risk to take, consider which investments are best suited to your group's goals and chosen risk level. Will you choose stocks, bonds, a combination of both, or other securities? What are the advantages and disadvantages of each type of investment for your team's situation? Then come to a decision about specific investment opportunities—particular stocks, for example—that your group would like to investigate further.

Compare your group's goal, risk level, and investment possibilities with those of the other teams in your class and discuss the differences and similarities you see.

Expand Your Knowledge

EXPLORING CAREER OPPORTUNITIES

Is a career in branch banking for you? Bankers in local branch offices deal with a wide variety of customers, products, transactions, and inquiries every working day. To get a better idea of what branch bankers do, visit a local bank or a branch where you do business.

1. Talk with a customer service representative or an officer about the kinds of customers this branch serves. Does it handle a high volume of business banking transactions, or is it more geared to consumer banking needs? How does the mix of consumer and business customers affect the branch's staffing and working hours?
2. What banking services are offered by this branch? Does the branch have specialized experts on staff to service these customers? What kind of skills, experience, education, and licenses must these experts have?
3. What kinds of entry-level jobs in this branch are appropriate for your background? What are the advancement

opportunities within the branch and within the bank organization? Now that you have a better idea of what branch banking is, how does this career fit with your interests and goals?

DEVELOPING YOUR RESEARCH SKILLS

The Dow Jones Industrial Average (DJIA) is one of several indexes that reflect the performance of this country's securities markets. How do U.S. market trends compare with those in other countries? Choose one U.S. market index (such as the DJIA or the S&P 500) and one foreign market index to research, such as Japan's Nikkei 225, United Kingdom's FT-SE 100, or Germany's DAX. Using printed sources such as the *Wall Street Journal* and the *Financial Times* or online sources such as CNNfn (http://www.cnnfn.com), research the following questions, documenting your sources and your search methodology.

1. How many stocks are in the two indexes you selected? Does the foreign index cover more or fewer companies than the U.S. index?
2. Over the last year, how have the foreign index and the U.S. index performed? Which index showed the best performance?
3. How did the foreign index perform yesterday (or on the most recent business day), compared with the U.S. market index for that day?

SEE IT ON THE WEB EXERCISES
Take a Field Trip to the Fed, page 364

Visit the Fed at http://www.bog.frb.fed.us/ and explore the U.S. Federal Reserve System to answer the following questions.

1. Click to read General Information. Who is the current chairperson of the Federal Reserve System? How is he or she appointed, and for how long?

2. Where are the 12 Federal Reserve Banks located?
3. Click on Monetary Policy. Who serves on the Fed's Open Market Committee? What is the date of the next meeting? What happened at the most recent meeting?

Track Down Treasury Securities, page 370

Go to the U.S. Treasury's Bureau of the Public Debt Web site at http://www.publicdebt.treas.gov. Scan the homepage and follow the links to find the answers to these questions.

1. When is the next auction of U.S. securities scheduled? What type of security is being sold? How can investors use Treasury Direct to buy these securities?
2. What is the current interest rate paid on Series EE Savings Bonds?
3. What is the exact amount of the national debt right now?

Stock Up at the New York Stock Exchange, page 373

Tour the New York Stock Exchange at http://www.nyse.com and learn how the exchange operates.

1. Click on The NYSE at far left of the screen, then on the Historical Perspective link lower in that column, read the material under the Regulation/Structure heading at the far right. When were circuit breakers introduced, and what do they do?
2. Under the Auction Market link at far left of the screen, read about this type of exchange and then click on The Trading Floor. How many trading posts and trading booths are on the trading floor?
3. Click on Market Regulation at the far left and then on Surveillance. What is Stock Watch? List some of the steps involved.

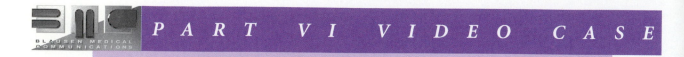

PART VI VIDEO CASE

Managing Financial Information and Resources

Learning Objectives

1. Understand why small business owners must pay close attention to financial statements and plans.
2. Learn how accountants can help small businesses prepare for future growth.
3. Become familiar with the various banking services needed by a growing business.

Background Information

Managers, as well as owners such as Bruce Blausen, need both financial accounting and management accounting information to effectively run their companies. Although they may have bookkeepers on staff to input invoices, record payments, and handle other day-to-day clerical functions, small and large businesses need professional accountants to prepare financial statements, analyze and interpret financial data, and offer advice on tax matters. Blausen Medical Communications (BMC), like other growing businesses, must find ways of managing cash flow to cover today's bills and payroll while planning to reinvest for tomorrow's expansion. Companies typically use a variety of banking services, including checking accounts, savings accounts, and loans.

The Video

When Blausen first started BMC, accounting was a minor concern because the company wasn't making much money. As the company began to grow, however, he realized that an accountant could take care of a variety of pressing tasks, such as tracking invoices, preparing tax documents, and developing profit and loss statements. In the early years, Blausen applied for—and promptly repaid—a series of small loans to buy more equipment and expand his business. With this solid repayment history, and Blausen's home as collateral for his personal guarantee, the company was able to qualify for a much larger loan to buy more expensive equipment. Because the company is still in an expansion drive, there is currently little surplus cash for investments, but this may change as BMC's sales continue to grow.

Discussion Questions

1. Why would a bank want to investigate BMC's liquidity ratios and debt ratios before approving the company's application for a loan?
2. How can Blausen use the information from BMC's financial management software package to make better decisions about the company's finances?
3. Why would Blausen prefer to invest his company's money in a money market deposit account rather than in a certificate of deposit?

Next Steps

In the future, Blausen may decide to take his company public by selling shares of stock in BMC. If he does this, why will it be important for his financial statements to be prepared according to generally accepted accounting principles (GAAP)? Once BMC is a public corporation, why would his certified public accountant (CPA) have to conduct periodic audits? What changes do you think BMC would have to make to its budgeting process if it goes public? Why?

■ LEARN MORE ONLINE

BMC and other small businesses can choose among a variety of software packages, including Intuit's QuickBooks programs and Peachtree Software's Accounting programs, to handle many routine accounting functions. Visit the Intuit and Peachtree sites to read about the QuickBooks and accounting packages for small businesses. What main features do these programs offer? How do these features help entrepreneurs and small business owners better manage their company's finances?

http:www.intuitmarket.com (Quicken site)
http://www.peachtree.com/html/product.htm (Peachtree site)

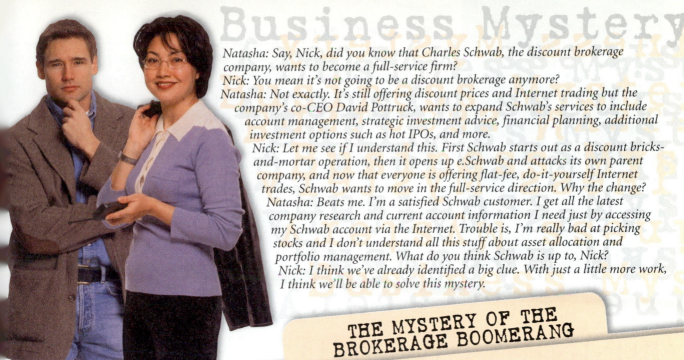

Business Mystery

Natasha: Say, Nick, did you know that Charles Schwab, the discount brokerage company, wants to become a full-service firm?

Nick: You mean it's not going to be a discount brokerage anymore?

Natasha: Not exactly. It's still offering discount prices and Internet trading but the company's co-CEO David Pottruck, wants to expand Schwab's services to include account management, strategic investment advice, financial planning, additional investment options such as hot IPOs, and more.

Nick: Let me see if I understand this. First Schwab starts out as a discount bricks-and-mortar operation, then it opens up e.Schwab and attacks its own parent company, and now that everyone is offering flat-fee, do-it-yourself Internet trades, Schwab wants to move in the full-service direction. Why the change?

Natasha: Beats me. I'm a satisfied Schwab customer. I get all the latest company research and current account information I need just by accessing my Schwab account via the Internet. Trouble is, I'm really bad at picking stocks and I don't understand all this stuff about asset allocation and portfolio management. What do you think Schwab is up to, Nick?

Nick: I think we've already identified a big clue. With just a little more work, I think we'll be able to solve this mystery.

THE MYSTERY OF THE BROKERAGE BOOMERANG

David Pottruck didn't seem like a cannibal, but in 1998 the co-CEO of Charles Schwab did the unthinkable: He let e.Schwab, the company's electronic brokerage unit, eat Schwab, turning Schwab's online business from a sideline to the very soul of the company.

In 1996 Pottruck set up a separate online unit called e.Schwab with its own building, employees, and freedom to make independent decisions. Customers at e.Schwab could trade over the Internet for a flat $29.95 fee. Regular Schwab customers still paid $65 for trades executed by phone. But having two companies confused Schwab customers. Some felt they had to choose between service and price. So to end the confusion, Pottruck dropped the two-tiered pricing structure and adopted the e.Schwab model of doing business for the entire company. All trades would be priced at $29.95, whether executed by phone or by Internet.

Schwab's directors had their doubts. So did industry analysts. After all, the move cut $150 million from expected revenue and sent Schwab's share price tumbling from $41 to $28. But eventually the short-term pain yielded long-term gain: Total customer accounts soon climbed from 3 million to over 6 million; $51 billion in new assets poured into the company within a six-month period; and the stock recovered and then soared. Not only did Schwab's huge $628 billion asset base dwarf the deep discount dot-com competitors, but Schwab's stock market value soon surpassed that of Merrill Lynch.

That jolted Merrill. Plunging into cyberinvesting at the turn of the century, Merrill matched Schwab's online trading fee, launched a Web site to rival Schwab's, and rolled out fee-based brokerage accounts to compete directly with Schwab's 5,400 independent financial advisors who used Schwab to process their trades and custody their customers' funds. After quietly grabbing assets from its bigger rivals for years, Schwab was now under attack. The predator had turned to prey. Schwab would have to decide the best direction for its future growth.

"Time for Schwab to become pioneers again," exclaimed Pottruck, who decided that Schwab was not going to just offer lower prices or online trading but set company sights higher up the food chain. Pottruck would turn Schwab into a different kind of full-service firm. "What we want is to be unlike anyone else," he announced in a Wall Street Journal press release. "We're changing because customers needs are changing."[40]

SOLVING THE MYSTERY OF THE BROKERAGE BOOMERANG

1. How were customers' needs changing at the turn of the century?

    CLUE: HOW DOES NATASHA EXEMPLIFY THE TYPICAL SCHWAB CUSTOMER?

2. Look back at the margin clues in Parts I through VI. Which business principles do you think Pottruck followed to help him navigate Schwab's future? Did Pottruck consider one principal to be more important than all others?

3. Look back at the margin clues in Parts I through VI. If you were Pottruck's assistant, to which business principles might you suggest Pottruck now pay close attention?

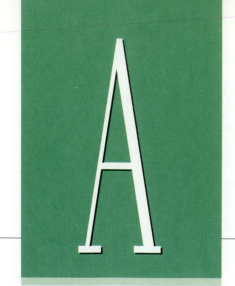

COMPONENT CHAPTER

BUSINESS LAW AND THE U.S. LEGAL SYSTEM

■ BUSINESS AND GOVERNMENT

Although the United States is philosophically committed to the free-market system, the government has often stepped in to enact laws and regulations that help resolve disputes between businesses, individuals, and communities. Two major areas in which the government regulates business activities are competition and stakeholder rights. Sometimes these areas overlap. For instance, laws designed to promote competition often have the ultimate goal of protecting consumers.

As you can imagine, keeping track of all these laws and regulations can be a costly and time-consuming undertaking. According to recent estimates, U.S. employers spend about $700 billion annually just to comply with federal laws and regulations.[1] Besides worrying about the federal government, businesses must also consider laws and regulations enacted by individual counties, states, and possibly foreign governments, many of which impose specific and sometimes conflicting restrictions. Of course, this plethora of laws makes it increasingly difficult to understand and stay current on what a business can or can't do. But it doesn't necessarily mean that businesses universally dislike regulation. Antitrust laws, for instance, make it possible for many small companies to compete with larger ones, while other laws encourage a safe, honest business environment. In addition, government regulation and deregulation of specific industries promote competition and protect consumers and other stakeholders.

Laws Promoting Competition

In most sectors of the economy, state and federal regulators work to ensure that all competitors have an equal chance of producing a product, reaching the market, and making a profit. By setting ground rules and establishing basic standards of proper business behavior, government helps prevent conflicts and facilitates the workings of the economic system. Laws concerning competition make up a huge and complex body of government regulation.

When regulators determine that the public can be best served by limiting competition in certain industries, they will consider restricting entry into those markets. However, in most industries, the government prefers to set ground rules that enable many companies to compete. Over the last century or so, a number of regulations have been established to help prevent individual companies or groups of companies from gaining control of markets in ways that restrain competition or harm consumers. Some of the earliest government moves in this arena produced such landmark pieces of legislation as the Sherman Antitrust Act, the Clayton Antitrust Act, and the Federal

Trade Commission Act, which generally sought to rein in the power of a few huge companies such as Standard Oil (see Exhibit A.1). These companies, usually referred to as *trusts* (hence the label *antitrust legislation,* discussed in Chapter 1), had financial and management control of a significant number of other companies in the same industry. The trusts thus controlled enough of the supply and distribution in their respective industries to muscle smaller competitors out of the way.

Whereas the Sherman Act got the regulatory ball rolling, the Clayton Act specifically prohibited **interlocking directorates,** or boards of directors made up of board members from competing firms; the practice of acquiring large blocks of competitors' stock; and discriminatory prices. The Clayton Act also restricted **tying contracts,** which attempt to force buyers to purchase unwanted goods along with goods actually desired. As Chapter 1 pointed out, the U.S. Justice Department found Microsoft guilty of bundling its Windows operating system with its Internet Explorer and with threatening to terminate contracts with computer manufacturers that did not install both software programs.[2] In his historic decision, Judge Jackson concluded that Microsoft was guilty of bundling and used such tactics to thwart the challenge posed by Internet software makers, especially Netscape Communications. The judge concluded that "Web browsers and operating systems are indeed separate products" and that tying them together actually harmed consumers by making the Windows operating system more likely to crash. Microsoft contended that integrating new functionality and features into products has been a longstanding company practice and that offering the two products together makes computers easier to use. The judge's decision is likely to lead to severe punishment for Microsoft, but remedies could be postponed while Microsoft appeals the case—a process that could take years.[3]

Besides monopolies and tying contracts, another key area of concern to regulators is mergers and acquisitions. The government won't grant approval of a merger or an acquisition if regulators think it will restrain competition, as Chapter 5 pointed out. Regulators also keep an eye on changes in technology that might give companies an unfair advantage and on the ability of large companies to control technological development, as evidenced by the U.S. Justice Department's case against Microsoft.

Laws Protecting Stakeholders

As Chapter 2 discussed, businesses have many stakeholders, including employees, consumers, investors, and society as a whole. In the course of serving one or more of these stakeholders, the enterprise may sometimes neglect

REGULATION	YEAR	EFFECT
Interstate Commerce Act	1887	Regulates business practices, specifically railroad operations and shipping rates
Sherman Antitrust Act	1890	Fosters competition by preventing monopolies and noncompetitive mergers; establishes competitive market environment as national policy
Pure Food and Drug Act	1906	Prohibits misbranding and adulteration of food and drugs, specifically those transported across state lines
Meat Inspection Act	1906	Encourages purity of meat and meat products, specifically those transported across state lines
Federal Trade Commission Act	1914	Creates the Federal Trade Commission (FTC) to monitor activities that might be unfair and to control illegal trade practices (The FTC's authority was later expanded to cover practices that harmed the public, such as marketing unsafe products.)
Clayton Antitrust Act	1914	Restricts practices such as price discrimination, tying contracts, exclusive dealing, and interlocking boards of directors that give large businesses an advantage over smaller firms
Robinson Patman Act	1936	Prohibits price differentials that substantially weaken competition unless they can be justified by actual lower production and selling costs

EXHIBIT A·1

EARLY GOVERNMENT REGULATIONS PERTAINING TO BUSINESS

In response to public outcry against a few large and powerful companies, in the late 1800s and early 1900s Congress passed a number of laws to prevent monopolies and to encourage competition.

the interests of other stakeholders in the process. For example, managers who are too narrowly focused on generating wealth for shareholders might not spend the funds necessary to create a safe work environment for employees or to reduce waste. On the other hand, by withholding information about the company's financial performance, managers may hamper the ability of investors to make solid decisions, thereby possibly limiting investors' returns. As a result, government has passed many laws and has established several regulatory agencies that protect consumers, employees, shareholders, and the environment from the potentially harmful actions of business (see Exhibits A.2 and A.3). The Occupational Safety and Health Administration (OSHA), the Equal Employment Opportunity Commission (EEOC), the Securities and Exchange Commission (SEC), and the Environmental Pro-

LEGISLATION	YEAR	EFFECT
Food, Drug, and Cosmetic Act	1938	Puts cosmetics, foods, drugs, and therapeutic products under Food and Drug Administration (FDA) jurisdiction; outlaws false and misleading labeling
Wool Products Labeling Act	1939	Requires manufacturers to identify the type and percentage of wool content in products
Flammable Fabrics Act	1953, 1967	Prohibits interstate shipment of apparel or fabric made of flammable materials; sets stronger standards for clothing flammability
Automobile Information Disclosure Act	1958	Requires automobile manufacturers to put suggested retail prices on all new passenger vehicles
Textile Fiber Products Identification Act	1958	Requires labeling of fiber content on textile products
National Traffic Safety Act	1958	Establishes safety standards for cars and tires
Federal Hazardous Substances Act	1960	Requires warning labels on items with dangerous chemicals
Cigarette Labeling Act	1965	Mandates warnings on cigarette packages and in ads
Child Protection Act	1966	Prohibits the sale of hazardous toys; amended in 1969 to include products that pose electrical, mechanical, or thermal hazards
Fair Packaging and Labeling Act	1966, 1972	Requires honest, informative package labeling; labels must show origin of product, quantity of contents, and uses or applications
Truth-in-Lending Act (Consumer Protection Credit Act)	1968	Requires creditors to disclose finance charge and annual percentage rate; limits cardholder liability for unauthorized use
Land Sales Disclosure Act	1968	Protects consumers from unfair practices in sales of land conducted across state lines
Fair Credit Reporting Act	1970	Requires credit-reporting agencies to set process for ensuring accuracy; requires creditors who deny credit to tell consumers the source of information
Consumer Product Safety Act	1972	Creates Consumer Product Safety Commission
Magnuson-Moss Warranty Act	1975	Requires complete written warranties in ordinary language; requires warranties to be available before purchase
Alcohol Labeling Legislation	1988	Requires warning labels on alcohol products saying that alcohol impairs abilities and that women shouldn't drink when pregnant
Nutrition Education and Labeling Act	1990	Requires specific, uniform product labels detailing nutritional information on every food regulated by the FDA
American Automobile Labeling Act	1992	Requires car makers to identify where cars are assembled and where their individual components are manufactured

EXHIBIT A·2

MAJOR FEDERAL CONSUMER LEGISLATION

Major federal legislation aimed at consumer protection has focused on food and drugs, false advertising, product safety, and credit protection.

tection Agency (EPA) are just a few of the federal regulatory agencies that most companies must deal with. In addition, the Nutrition Education and Labeling Act of 1990, the Fair Credit Reporting Act, the Americans with Disabilities Act, and the Clean Air Act represent only a fraction of the laws that most businesses must adhere to.

Industry Regulation and Deregulation

In addition to these agencies and laws, the government imposes another layer of regulations on specific industries. From mining to banking to advertising, government officials keep tabs on companies to ensure fair competition, safe working conditions, and generally ethical business practices. For instance, the Federal Aviation Administration (FAA) sets rules for the commercial airline industry; the Federal Reserve Board and the Treasury Department look after the banking industry; and the Federal Commu-

nications Commission (FCC) oversees telephone services and radio and television broadcasts.[4] Some lawmakers and citizens have recently called upon the FCC to also regulate Internet development and content more closely. However, top FCC officials have emphatically stated their belief that passing laws to regulate the Internet would be a mistake. Opponents of Internet regulation scored a huge victory in 1997 when the U.S. Supreme Court struck down the Communications Decency Act—a law signed in 1996 that prohibited the transmission of "indecent" material on the Internet—on the grounds that the act restricted the constitutional right to freedom of speech.[5]

In past years, some industries were under strict government control. In the most extreme cases, regulators decided who could enter an industry, what customers they had to serve, and how much they could charge. Consequently, companies that operated in heavily regulated industries had

LEGISLATION	YEAR	EFFECT
Securities Act	1933	Known as the Truth in Securities Act; requires full disclosure of relevant financial information from companies that want to sell new stock or bond issues to the general public
Securities Exchange Act	1934	Creates the Securities and Exchange Commission (SEC) to regulate the national stock exchanges and to establish trading rules
Maloney Act	1938	Creates the National Association of Securities Dealers to regulate over-the-counter securities trading
Investment Company Act	1940	Extends the SEC's authority to cover the regulation of mutual funds
Amendment to the Securities Exchange Act	1964	Extends the SEC's authority to cover the over-the-counter market
Securities Investor Protection Act	1970	Creates the Securities Investor Protection Corporation (SIPC) to insure individual investors against losses in the event of dealer fraud or insolvency
Commodity Futures Trading Commission Act	1974	Creates the Commodity Futures Trading Commission (CFTC) to establish and enforce regulations governing futures trading
Insider Trading and Securities Fraud Act	1988	Toughens penalties, authorized bounties for information, requires brokerages to establish written policies to prevent employee violations, and makes it easier for investors to bring legal action against violators
Securities Market Reform Act	1990	Increases SEC market control by granting additional authority to suspend trading in any security for ten days, to restore order in the event of a major disturbance, to establish a national system for settlement and clearance of securities transactions, to adapt rules for actions affecting market volatility, and to require more detailed record keeping and reporting of brokers and dealers
Private Securities Litigation Reform Act	1995	Protects companies from frivolous lawsuits by investors: limits how many class-action suits can be filed by the same person in a three-year period, and encourages judges to penalize plaintiffs that bring meritless cases

EXHIBIT A·3

MAJOR FEDERAL LEGISLATION GOVERNING THE SECURITIES INDUSTRY

Although you have no guarantee that you'll make money on your investments, you are protected by laws against unfair securities trading practices.

In response to EPA pressure for a cleaner environment, automobile manufacturers are experimenting with several gas alternatives referred to as zero-emission vehicles. DaimlerChrysler recently unveiled one such prototype called NECAR 4. Powered by a liquid hydrogen fuel cell, this four-passenger Mercedes A-Class can go 280 miles before refueling and can attain a speed of 90 miles per hour. Future revisions of this prototype will use methane for fuel.

little or no competition. The telecommunications, airline, and banking industries fell under such control until the last few decades, when several waves of *deregulation,* the abandonment or relaxation of existing regulations, opened up competition.

When new competitors enter the market, they often drive down prices and create more choices for consumers. Consider the telecommunications industry, for example. In 1982 the federal government broke AT&T up into seven local telephone companies and one long-distance provider to allow smaller carriers such as MCI (now MCI Worldcom-Sprint) to compete for long-distance telephone business. Some observers cite the AT&T breakup as the event that triggered the development of new technologies such as cellular networks and that facilitated the mainstreaming of the Internet.[6] The telecommunications industry was further deregulated with the passage of the Telecommunications Reform Act of 1996, which opened up opportunities for smaller businesses to compete in areas once dominated by large conglomerates. This act allowed long-distance carriers to enter local telephone markets and ended the seven local telephone companies' monopolies (although some claim that recent mergers among these seven companies have in effect reassembled the original AT&T monopoly). The 1996 act also deregulated the cable

television industry, enabling telephone companies and others to compete for cable television viewers.[7]

Recent state initiatives to allow consumers to buy gas and electricity from several sources are spearheading the introduction of federal government bills in Congress to deregulate the last of the major U.S. monopolies: the electric-power industry. Although many states have moved ahead with local power deregulation, some industry analysts cite public nervousness over too many unknowns as the reason that competition is getting off to a slow start.[8] Others are more optimistic, pointing out that overall deregulation is good for consumers. For instance, after adjustment for inflation, air fares have decreased by almost one-third since 1978 when Congress deregulated the airlines, and long-distance telephone rates have been cut by about 50 percent since the breakup of AT&T.[9]

■ THE U.S. LEGAL SYSTEM

In addition to government agencies and regulations, one of the most pervasive ways that government affects business is through the U.S. legal system. The law protects both businesses and individuals against those who threaten society. It also spells out accepted ways of performing many essential business functions—along with the penalties for failing to comply. In other words, like the average person, companies must obey the law or face the consequences. Although this situation limits a company's freedom, it also provides protection from wrongdoers.

Types of Law

The U.S. Constitution, including the Bill of Rights, is the foundation for our laws. Because the Constitution is a general document, laws offering specific answers to specific problems are constantly embellishing its basic principles. However, law is not static; it develops in response to changing conditions and social standards. Individual laws originate in various ways: through legislative action (*statutory law*), through administrative rulings (*administrative law*), and through customs and judicial precedents (*common law*). To one degree or another, all three forms of law affect businesses. In addition, companies that conduct business overseas must be familiar with **international law,** the principles, customs, and rules that govern the relationships between sovereign states and international organizations and persons.[10] Successful global business requires an understanding of the domestic laws of trading partners as well as of established international trading standards and legal guidelines.

Statutory Law   **Statutory law** is law written by the U.S. Congress, state legislatures, and local governments. One very important part of statutory law affecting businesses is the **Uniform Commercial Code (UCC).** Designed to mitigate differences between state statutory laws and to simplify interstate commerce, this code is a comprehensive, systematic collection of statutes in a particular legal area.[11] For example, the UCC provides a nationwide standard in many issues of commercial law, such as sales contracts, bank deposits, and warranties. The UCC has been adopted in its entirety in 49 states and the District of Columbia, and about half of it has been adopted in Louisiana.

Administrative Law   Once laws have been passed by a state legislature or Congress, an administrative agency or commission typically takes responsibility for enforcing them. That agency may be called on to clarify a regulation's intent, often by consulting representatives of the affected industry. The administrative agency may then write more specific regulations, which are considered **administrative law.**

Government agencies cannot, however, create regulations out of thin air; the agency's regulations must be linked to specific statutes to be legal. For example, the FTC (Federal Trade Commission) issues regulations and enforces statutory laws concerning such deceptive trade practices as unfair debt collection and false advertising. Recently the FTC cracked down on germ-fighting claims being made by Unilever, producer of Vaseline Intensive Care products. The FTC said that Unilever's claims that the lotion "stops germs for hours" lacked scientific proof and deceived consumers into thinking they would be shielded from disease-causing germs if they used the lotion. Unilever agreed to stop making such claims.[12]

Administrative agencies also have the power to investigate corporations suspected of breaking administrative laws. A corporation found to be misbehaving may agree to a **consent order,** which allows the company to promise to stop doing something without actually admitting to any illegal behavior. For example, Stone Container signed a 1998 consent order with the FTC settling the alleged charges that the company attempted to orchestrate an industrywide price increase in violation of federal antitrust laws. Admitting no guilt, Stone Container entered into the consent order to avoid costly and time-consuming litigation.[13]

As an alternative to entering into a consent order, the administrative agency may start legal proceedings against the company in a hearing presided over by an administrative law judge. For instance, the Securities and Exchange Commission required KPMG Peat Marwick to go before an administrative law judge to answer charges that the company violated the SEC's auditor independence rules when it audited the client of a former KPMG-affiliated company.[14] During such a hearing, witnesses are called and evidence is presented to determine the facts of the situation. The judge then issues a decision, which may impose corrective actions on the company. If either party objects to the decision, the party may file an appeal to the appropriate federal court.[15]

Common Law   **Common law,** the type of law that comes out of courtrooms and judges' decisions, began in England many centuries ago and was transported to the United States by the colonists. It is applied in all states except Louisiana (which follows a French model). Common law is sometimes called the "unwritten law" to distinguish it from legislative acts and administrative-agency regulations, which are written documents. Instead, common law is established through custom and the precedents set in courtroom proceedings.

Despite its unwritten nature, common law has great continuity, which derives from the doctrine of *stare decisis* (Latin for "to stand by decisions"). What the *stare decisis* doctrine means is that judges' decisions establish a precedent for deciding future cases of a similar nature. Because common law is based on what has gone before, the legal framework develops gradually.

In the United States, common law is applied and interpreted in the system of courts (see Exhibit A.4). Common law thus develops through the decisions in trial courts, special courts, and appellate courts. The U.S. Supreme Court (or the highest court of a state when state laws are involved) sets precedents for entire legal systems. Lower courts must then abide by those precedents as they pertain to similar cases.

In all but six states, business cases are heard in standard trial courts. However, many corporations are pushing for the establishment of a network of special business courts. Advocates say that the special nature of business legal disputes requires experienced judges who understand business issues. They also feel that a system of business courts would go a long way toward reducing the expense and unpredictability of business litigation. However, opponents say that business courts are likely to favor local companies in disputes involving out-of-state litigants. Moreover, they say that the courts are likely to come under the influence of powerful business special-interest groups. It remains to be seen whether more states establish special business courts, but at least nine are currently considering it.[16]

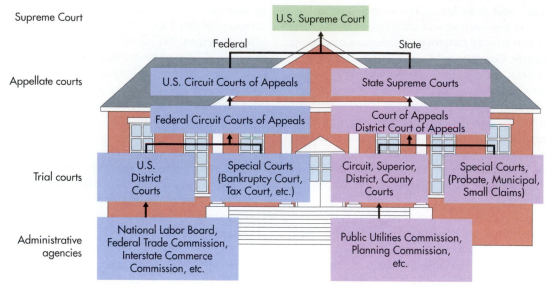

EXHIBIT A·4

THE U.S. COURT SYSTEM

A legal proceeding may begin in a trial court or an administrative agency (examples of each are given here). An unfavorable decision may be appealed to a higher court at the federal or state level. (The court of appeals is the highest court in most states that have no state supreme court; some other states have no intermediate appellate court.) The U.S. Supreme Court, the country's highest court, is the court of final appeal.

In legal proceedings, common law, administrative law, and statutory law may all be applicable. If they conflict, statutory law generally prevails. However, the three forms of law overlap to such an extent that the differences between them are often indistinguishable. For instance, if you bought what you thought was a goose-down coat and then found out that the coat was actually filled with reprocessed polyester, you could sue the coat manufacturer for misrepresentation. Although the basis for this suit is an old concept in common law, it has also been incorporated in state and federal legislation against fraudulent and misleading advertising, which is further interpreted and enforced by the Federal Trade Commission.

Business Law

Although businesses must comply with the full body of laws that apply to individuals, a subset of laws can be defined more precisely as **business law.** This includes those elements of law that directly affect business activities. For example, laws pertaining to business licensing, employee safety, and corporate income taxes can all be considered business law. For the remainder of this chapter, we will examine some of the specific categories of laws affecting business, including torts; contracts; agency; property

transactions; patents, trademarks, and copyrights; negotiable instruments; and bankruptcy.

Torts   A **tort** is a noncriminal act (other than breach of contract) that results in injury to a person or to property.[17] A tort can be either intentional or the result of negligence. The victim of a tort is legally entitled to some form of financial compensation, or **damages,** for his or her loss and suffering. This compensation is also known as a *compensatory damage award.* In some cases, the victim may also receive a *punitive damage award* to punish the wrongdoer if the misdeed was glaringly bad. You may have heard about cases of excessively high punitive damage awards, such as the $4 million punitive judgment against BMW for retouching a car that had paint damage and selling it as new or the $1.2 million awarded a former Home Depot worker after a jury found that she had been sexually harassed and unfairly terminated. However, a recent Cornell University study found that punitive damages are awarded in only about 6 percent of cases nationwide and that the majority of damages are commensurate with compensatory damage awards.[18]

Intentional Torts   An **intentional tort** is a willful act that results in injury. For example, accidentally hitting a softball through someone's window is a tort, but purposely cutting down someone's tree because it obscures your view is an intentional tort. Note that *intent* in this case does not mean the intent to cause harm; it is the intent to commit a specific physical act. Some intentional torts involve communication of false statements that harm another's reputation. If the communication is in writing or on television, it is called *libel*; if it is spoken, it is *slander*.[19] For example, a group of Texas cattlemen sued television talk show host Oprah Winfrey for more than $12 million in damages because they said her disparaging remarks about beef in a 1996 television program caused beef prices to plummet. The jury found Winfrey not guilty of food-libel laws designed to protect perishable food products from disparagement or misinformation that could diminish their market value.[20]

Negligence and Product Liability   In contrast to intentional torts, torts of **negligence** involve a failure to use a reasonable amount of care necessary to protect others from unreasonable risk of injury.[21] Cases of alleged negligence often involve **product liability,** which is a product's capacity to cause damages or injury for which the producer or seller is held responsible. Product-liability lawsuits cost business owners as much as $150 billion every year.[22]

Consider American Home Products, for instance. The company recently agreed to pay about $4 billion to thousands of individuals who contended they were injured by taking the company's popular diet pill combination fen-phen. The product, which had been hailed as a miracle weight-loss pill for the obese, was removed from the market at the request of the FDA after studies linked the drugs to heart valve damage. Over six million people took fen-phen, but only those who developed problems are eligible to collect an injury award; others will be reimbursed for out-of-pocket costs.[23]

A company may also be held liable for injury caused by a defective product even if the company used all reasonable care in the manufacture, distribution, or sale of its product. Such **strict product liability** makes it possible to assign liability without assigning fault. It must only be established that (1) the company is in the business of selling the product; (2) the product reached the customer or user without substantial change in its condition; (3) the product was defective; (4) the defective condition rendered the product unreasonably dangerous; and (5) the defective product caused the injury.[24]

Although few people would argue that individual victims of harmful products shouldn't be entitled to some sort of compensation, many people question whether such strict interpretation of product-liability laws is good for

society. Many individuals try to take advantage of the system by filing "frivolous" lawsuits. The large compensatory, and sometimes punitive, damages that plaintiffs are awarded make it difficult for many companies to obtain product-liability insurance at a reasonable price. As a result, manufacturers have withheld products from the market that might otherwise benefit society. Although Congress passed a bill in 1996 that restricted the amounts of compensatory and punitive damages awarded in product-liability suits, the bill was vetoed by President Clinton, who felt that it was too restrictive and would have a negative impact on consumers. Nonetheless, the issue continues to be a priority with lawmakers.[25]

Contracts   Broadly defined, a **contract** is an exchange of promises between two or more parties that is enforceable by law. Many business transactions—including buying and selling products, hiring employees, purchasing group insurance, and licensing technology—involve contracts. Contracts may be either express or implied. An **express contract** is derived from the words (either oral or written) of the parties; an **implied contract** stems from the actions or conduct of the parties.[26] Iris Kapustein learned the hard way how important written contracts can be in the business world. When she first started her trade show management and consulting firm, she operated on the principle of "my word is my bond." But after losing $15,000 to clients who didn't pay, she adopted a new principle: All clients must sign contracts, and all contracts supplied by clients must be reviewed by her attorney.[27]

Elements of a Contract   The law of contracts deals largely with identifying the exchanges that can be classified as contracts. The following factors must usually be present for a contract to be valid and enforceable:

- *An offer must be made.* One party must propose that an agreement be entered into. The offer may be oral or written, but it must be firm, definite, and specific enough to make it clear that someone intends to be legally bound by the offer. Finally, the offer must be communicated to the intended party or parties.

- *An offer must be accepted.* For an offer to be accepted, there must be clear intent (spoken, written, or by action) to enter into the contract. An implied contract arises when a person requests or accepts something and the other party has indicated that payment is expected. If, for example, your car breaks down on the road and you call a mobile mechanic and ask him or her to repair it, you are obligated to pay the reasonable value for the services, even if you didn't agree to specific charges beforehand. However, when a specific offer is made, the acceptance must satisfy the terms of the offer. For example, if someone offers you a car for $18,000, and you say you would take it for $15,000, you have not accepted the offer. Your response is a *counteroffer*, which may or may not be accepted by the salesperson.

- *Both parties must give consideration.* A contract is legally binding only when the parties have bargained with each other and have exchanged something of value, which is called the **consideration.** The relative value of each party's consideration does not generally matter to the courts. In other words, if you make a deal with someone and later decide you didn't get enough in the deal, that result is not the court's concern. You entered into the deal with the original consideration in mind, and that fact is legally sufficient.[28]

- *Both parties must give genuine assent.* To have a legally enforceable contract, both parties must agree to it voluntarily. The contract must be free of fraud, duress, undue influence, and mutual mistake.[29] If only one party makes a mistake, it ordinarily does not affect the contract. On the other hand, if both parties made a mistake, the agreement would be void. For example, if both the buyer and the seller of a business believed the business was profitable, when in reality it was operating at a loss, their agreement would be void.

- *Both parties must be competent.* The law gives certain classes of people only a limited capacity to enter into contracts. Minors, people who are senile or insane, and in some cases those who are intoxicated cannot usually be bound by a contract for anything but the bare necessities: food, clothing, shelter, and medical care.

- *The contract must not involve an illegal act.* Courts will not enforce a promise that involves an illegal act. For example, a drug dealer cannot get help from the courts to enforce a contract to deliver illegal drugs at a prearranged price.

- *The contract must be in proper form.* Most contracts can be made orally, by an act, or by a casually written document; however, certain contracts are required by law to be in writing. For example, the transfer of goods worth $500 or more must be accompanied by a written document. The written form is also required for all real estate contracts.

A contract need not be long; all these elements of a contract may be contained in a simple document (see Exhibit A.5). In fact, a personal check is one type of simple contract.

Contract Performance   Contracts normally expire when the agreed-to conditions have been met, called *performance* in legal terms. However, not all contracts run their expected course. Both parties involved can agree to back out of the contract, for instance. In other cases, one party fails to live up to the terms of the contract, a situation called **breach of contract.** The other party has several options at that point:

- *Discharge.* When one party violates the terms of the agreement, generally the other party is under no obligation to continue with his or her end of the contract. In other words, the second party is discharged from the contract.

- *Damages.* A party has the right to sue in court for damages that were foreseeable at the time the contract was entered into and that result from the other party's failure to fulfill the contract. The amount of damages awarded usually reflects the amount of profit lost and often includes court costs as well.

> The band entitled XYZ agrees to provide entertainment at the Club de Hohenzollern on April 30, 2000 between 8:30 P.M. and midnight.
>
> The band will be paid $500.00 for its performance.
>
> Signed on the date of
> *February 19, 2000*
>
> *Violetta Harvey*
>
> Violetta Harvey,
> Manager,
> Club de Hohenzollern
> and
>
> *Ralph Perkins*
>
> Ralph Perkins,
> Manager, XYZ

EXHIBIT A·5

ELEMENTS OF A CONTRACT
This simple document contains all the essential elements of a valid contract.

- *Specific performance.* A party can be compelled to live up to the terms of the contract if money damages would not be adequate.

Jeffrey Katzenberg, former Walt Disney studio chief, recently settled a bitter breach-of-contract lawsuit after contending that he was owed as much as $581 million stemming from a unique contractual bonus arrangement with the Walt Disney Company. Katzenberg, who left the company upon learning he would not be promoted to president, argued that he was due a lump sum equal to 2 percent of the projected future profits of films and television shows created during the ten years he oversaw Disney's movie and television operations. The settlement figure is private, but analysts speculate that Katzenberg received about $250 million.[30]

To control the increasing costs of litigation, more and more companies are now experimenting with alternatives to the courtroom. These include independent mediators, who sit down with the two parties and try to hammer out a satisfactory solution to contract problems, and mandatory arbitration, in which an impartial arbitrator or arbitration panel hears evidence from both sides and makes a legally binding decision. However, mandatory arbitration has come under fire by consumer groups because it can wipe out a customer's right to sue. For example, Gateway includes a clause in the purchase agreement documents it ships with every computer stating that any dispute or controversy arising from an agreement to purchase a Gateway product "shall be settled exclusively and finally by arbitration." Moreover, the courts have ruled that failure to read such documents constitutes acceptance of Gateway's terms. Although some consumers prefer to use alternative dispute resolution, those who do not wish to waive their right to sue are advised to read the fine print of all contracts and purchase agreements. The same advice applies to employment and service contracts. [31]

Warranties   The Uniform Commercial Code specifies that everyday sales transactions are a special kind of contract (although this provision applies only to tangible goods, not to services), even though they may not meet all the exact requirements of regular contracts. Related to the sales contract is the notion of a **warranty,** which is a statement specifying what the producer of a product will do to compensate the buyer if the product is defective or if it malfunctions. Warranties come in several flavors. One important distinction is between *express warranties,* which are specific, written statements, and *implied warranties,* which are unwritten but in-

volve certain protections under the law. Also, warranties are either *full* or *limited.* The former obligates the seller to repair or replace the product, without charge, in the event of any defect or malfunction, whereas the latter imposes restrictions on the defects or malfunctions that will be covered. Warranty laws also address a number of other details, including giving consumers instructions on how to exercise their rights under the warranty. [32]

Agency   These days it seems that nearly every celebrity has an agent. Basketball players hire agents to get them athletic shoe commercials and handle their contract negotiations; authors' agents sell manuscripts to the publishers that offer the largest advances; actors' agents try to find choice movie and television roles for their clients. These relationships illustrate a common legal association known as **agency,** which exists when one party, known as the *principal,* authorizes another party, known as the *agent,* to act on his or her behalf in contractual matters.[33]

All contractual obligations come into play in agency relationships. The principal usually creates this relationship by explicit authorization. In some cases—when a transfer of property is involved, for example—the authorization must be written in the form of a document called **power of attorney,** which states that one person may legally act for another (to the extent authorized).

Usually, an agency relationship is terminated when the objective of the relationship has been met or at the end of a period specified in the contract between agent and principal. It may also be ended by a change of circumstances, by the agent's breach of duty or loyalty, or by the death of either party.

Property Transactions   Anyone interested in business must know the basics of property law. Most people think of property as some object they own (a book, a car, a house). However, **property** is actually the relationship between the person having the rights to any tangible or intangible object and all other persons. The law recognizes two primary types of property: real and personal. **Real property** is land and everything permanently attached to it, such as trees, fences, or mineral deposits. **Personal property** is all property that is not real property; it may be tangible (cars, jewelry, or anything having a physical existence) or intangible (bank accounts, stocks, insurance policies, customer lists). A piece of marble in the earth is real property until it is cut and sold as a block, when it becomes personal property. Property rights are subject to various limitations and restrictions. For example, the government monitors the use of real property for the welfare of the public, to the point of explicitly prohibiting some property uses and abuses.[34]

Two types of documents are important in obtaining real property for factory, office, or store space: a deed and a lease. A **deed** is a legal document by which an owner transfers the *title,* or right of ownership, to real property to a new owner. A lease is used for a temporary transfer of interest in real property. The party that owns the property is commonly called the landlord; the party that occupies or gains the right to occupy the property is the tenant. The tenant pays the landlord, usually in periodic installments, for the use of the property. Generally, a lease may be granted for any length of time that the two parties agree on.

Patents, Trademarks, and Copyrights If you invent a product, write a book, develop some new software, or simply come up with a unique name for your business, you probably want to prevent other people from using or prospering from your **intellectual property** without fairly compensating you. Several forms of legal protection are available for your creations. They include patents, trademarks, and copyrights. Which one you should use depends on what you have created. Having a patent, copyright, or trademark still doesn't guarantee that your idea or product will not be copied. However, they do provide you with legal recourse if your creations are infringed upon.

Patents A patent protects the invention or discovery of a new and useful process, an article of manufacture, a machine, a chemical substance, or an improvement on any of these. Issued by the U.S. Patent Office, a patent grants the owner the right to exclude others from making, using, or selling the invention for 17 years. After that time, the patented item becomes available for common use. On the one hand, patent law guarantees the originator the right to use the discovery exclusively for a relatively long period of time, thus encouraging people to devise new machines, gadgets, and processes. On the other hand, it also ensures that rights to the new item will be released eventually, allowing other enterprises to discover even more innovative ways to use it.

Trademarks A trademark is any word, name, symbol, or device used to distinguish the product of one manufacturer from those made by others. A service mark is the same thing for services. McDonald's golden arches are one of the most visible of modern trademarks. Brand names can also be registered as trademarks. Examples are Exxon, Polaroid, and Chevrolet.

If properly registered and renewed every 20 years, a trademark generally belongs to its owner forever. Among the exceptions are popular brand names that have become generic terms, meaning that they describe a whole class of products. A brand-name trademark can become a generic term if the trademark has been allowed to expire, if it has been incorrectly used by its owner (as in the case of Borden's ReaLemon lemon juice, which the Federal Trade Commission ruled was being used by Borden to maintain a monopoly in bottled lemon juice), or if the public comes to equate the name with the class of products, as was the case with zipper, linoleum, aspirin, Xerox, and many other brand names.

Trade dress, defined as the general appearance or image of a product, has been easier to legally protect since 1992 when the U.S. Supreme Court extended trademark protection to products with "inherently distinctive" appearances. For instance, Apple Computer recently filed suit against Future Power for allegedly infringing on the iMac trade dress with its lookalike E-Power PC and asked

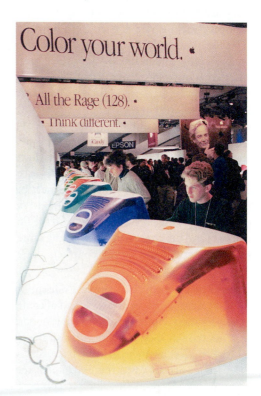

"We've invested a lot of money and effort to create and market our award-winning designs, and we intend to protect them under law," says Apple's CEO Steve Jobs in reference to the company's suit against Future Power for allegedly copying the popular design of the iMac.

the court to prohibit the sale of E-Power in addition to an award of actual and punitive damages. Although a U.S. District Court granted a preliminary injunction against Future Power from making, distributing, and selling their personal computers, the court will not rule on the case until both parties have had a chance to present their arguments in court.[35]

Copyrights   Copyrights protect the creators of literary, dramatic, musical, artistic, scientific, and other intellectual works. Any printed, filmed, or recorded material can be copyrighted. The copyright gives its owner the exclusive right to reproduce (copy), sell, or adapt the work he or she has created. Copyright law covers reproduction by photocopying, videotape, and magnetic storage.

The Library of Congress Copyright Office will issue a copyright to the creator or to whomever the creator has granted the right to reproduce the work. (A book, for example, may be copyrighted by the author or the publisher.) Copyrights issued through 1977 are good for 75 years. Copyrights issued after 1977 are valid for the lifetime of the creator plus 50 years.

Copyright protection on the Internet has become an especially important topic as more businesses and individuals publish Web sites. Technically, copyright protection exists from the moment material is created. Therefore, anything you post on a Web site is protected by copyright law. However, loose Internet standards and a history of sharing information via the 'Net has made it difficult for some users to accept this situation. But the No Electronic Theft Act (enacted in 1998) makes it clear that the sanctity of the copyright extends into the area of cyberspace. This law makes it a crime to possess or distribute multiple copies of online copyrighted material for profit or not. Specifically, it closes the loophole that had allowed the distribution of copyrighted material as long as the offender didn't seek profit. Penalties include fines up to $250,000 and five years in prison.[36] To avoid potential copyright infringements, experts suggest that authors include copyright and trademark notices on Web pages that contain protected material, include a link on each page to a detailed copyright notice that explains what users can and cannot do, and place disclaimers on all pages that contain links to other sites. (Consult Part VII of the *E-Business in Action* online supplement at http://www.prenhall.com/ebusinessinaction for additional discussion of intellectual property issues in e-business).[37]

Negotiable Instruments   Whenever you write a personal check, you are creating a **negotiable instrument,** a trans-

ferable document that represents a promise to pay a specified amount. (*Negotiable* in this sense means that it can be sold or used as payment of a debt; an *instrument* is simply a written document that expresses a legal agreement.) In addition to checks, negotiable instruments include certificates of deposit, promissory notes, and commercial paper. To be negotiable, an instrument must meet several criteria:[38]

- It must be in writing and signed by the person who created it.
- It must have an unconditional promise to pay a specified sum of money.
- It must be payable either on demand or at a specified date in the future.
- It must be payable either to some specified person or organization or to the person holding it (the bearer).

You can see how a personal check meets those criteria; when you write one, you are agreeing to pay the amount of the check to the person or organization to whom you're writing it.

Bankruptcy   Even though the U.S. legal system establishes the rules of fair play and offers protection from the unscrupulous, it can't prevent most businesses from taking

Planet Hollywood, the movie-themed restaurant chain that has been financially bleeding despite backing from a star-studded roster of investors, recently filed for Chapter 11 bankruptcy reorganization to protect the company from creditors, bond owners, and especially leaseholders as it attempts to financially restructure. The restructuring is expected to end with most of the company's restaurants shattered.

Step 1: All current legal proceedings against the firm are halted. A decision is made to either liquidate or reorganize the firm, based on the value of the firm's assets. If liquidation is chosen, the firm's assets are transferred to a trustee, who sells them to pay the firm's debts. If reorganization is chosen, go to step 2.

Step 2: The courts may appoint a trustee to operate the firm, or current management may continue to operate it. A reorganization plan is developed either by current management, by the trustee, or by a committee of creditors. When plan is developed, go to step 3.

Step 3: Creditors and shareholders vote on the reorganization plan. Plan is ratified if (1) at least one-half of creditors vote in favor and if their claims against the company represent at least two-thirds of total claims; (2) at least two-thirds of shareholders approve the plan; and (3) the plan is confirmed by the court. When plan is ratified, go to step 4.

Step 4: The plan guarantees creditors new securities, and sometimes cash, in exchange for dismissal of their claims. With the firm discharged from its debts, it is free to start anew without the weight of past failures.

EXHIBIT A·6

STEPS IN CHAPTER 11 BANKRUPTCY PROCEEDINGS

Chapter 11 bankruptcy may buy a debtor time to reorganize finances and continue operating. However, using this device to evade financial obligations is extremely risky from a legal standpoint, and declaring bankruptcy may severely damage the reputation and credit rating of a firm or an individual.

on too much debt. The legal system does, however, provide help for businesses that find themselves in deep financial trouble. **Bankruptcy** is the legal means of relief for debtors (either individuals or businesses) who are unable to meet their financial obligations.[39]

Voluntary bankruptcy is initiated by the debtor; *involuntary bankruptcy* is initiated by creditors. The law provides for several types of bankruptcy, which are commonly referred to by chapter number of the Bankruptcy Reform Act. In a Chapter 7 bankruptcy, the debtor's assets will be sold and the proceeds divided equitably among the creditors. Under Chapter 11 (which is usually aimed at businesses but does not exclude individuals other than stockbrokers), a business is allowed to get back on its feet and continue functioning while it arranges to pay its debts.[40] For the steps involved in a Chapter 11 bankruptcy, see Exhibit A.6.

By entering Chapter 11, a company gains time to cut costs and streamline operations. Many companies emerge from Chapter 11 as leaner, healthier organizations. Creditors often benefit too. If the company can get back on its financial feet, creditors may be able to retrieve more of the money they are owed. Consider Carson Pirie Scott & Co. The Milwaukee-based department store chain entered Chapter 11 in 1991 with an $800 million mountain of debt. Today the company is out of bankruptcy, is virtually debt-free, and brings in $1 billion a year in revenue.[41] However, filing for bankruptcy is an extremely risky venture and should not be pursued lightly. Bankruptcy can damage a company's or an individual's credit rating and reputation for a long time to come. It should never be used as a tactic to avoid paying creditors.

Test Your Knowledge

QUESTIONS FOR REVIEW

1. What are the major areas in which governments regulate business?

2. How did the deregulation of the telecommunications industry benefit consumers?

3. What are the three types of U.S. laws, and how do they differ? What additional laws must global companies consider?

4. What is the difference between negligence and intentional torts?

5. What are the seven elements of a valid contract?

QUESTIONS FOR ANALYSIS

6. What is precedent, and how does it affect common law?

7. What does the concept of strict product liability mean to businesses?

8. Why is agency important to business?

9. What is the advantage of declaring Chapter 11 bankruptcy? What is the disadvantage?

10. For a small investment, anyone can purchase a CD copier, called a CD burner, and record a free CD by downloading music off the Internet. If the 1998 Electronic Theft Act makes it a crime to possess or distribute multiple copies of online copyrighted material, for profit or not, why doesn't the government simply ban such copying devices?

QUESTIONS FOR APPLICATION

11. If you wrote a poem or a short story and published it on your own Web site, would your work be protected under copyright law? What steps should you take to make sure your work is not stolen or misused?

12. As the owner of a small manufacturing firm, why might you be in favor of a law limiting the amount of compensatory and punitive damages awarded in product-liability lawsuits? Why might you be against such a law?

13. When Jefferson County school district in Colorado needed a new football stadium, it signed an exclusive contract with PepsiCo to eliminate the competition's products from school vending machines and concession stands in exchange for a $630,000 "sponsorship fee" and an eventual payment of $1.5 million toward a new stadium. The contract states that "Pepsi products shall be the exclusive carbonated soft drinks, juice and juice-based products, isotonics, ready-to-drink tea, ready-to drink coffee, bottled water, and other nonalcoholic beverage products that may be sold, dispensed or otherwise made available by the district at any of the district's schools and athletic facilities or at district-sponsored events."[42] Using the knowledge you gained in Part 5, "Developing Marketing Strategies to Satisfy Customers," explain how such a contract benefits PepsiCo.

14. When you consider all the departments that are directly and indirectly responsible for a product's safety—research, design, manufacturing, marketing, and finance—it's no surprise that more and more companies are winding up in court these days. How can companies redesign their organizational structures (as discussed in Chapter 7) to open up the lines of communication between departments? How might cross-departmental communication help lessen the potential for product-liability lawsuits?

Chapter Glossary

administrative law   Rules, regulations, and interpretations of statutory law set forth by administrative agencies and commissions

agency   Business relationship that exists when one party (the principal) authorizes another party (the agent) to enter into contracts on the principal's behalf

bankruptcy   Legal procedure by which a person or a business that is unable to meet financial obligations is relieved of debt

breach of contract   Failure to live up to the terms of a contract, with no legal excuse

business law   Those elements of law that directly influence or control business activities

common law   Law based on the precedents established by judges' decisions

consent order   Settlement in which an individual or organization promises to discontinue some illegal activity without admitting guilt

consideration   Negotiated exchange necessary to make a contract legally binding

contract   Legally enforceable exchange of promises between two or more parties

damages   Financial compensation to an injured party for loss and suffering

deed   Legal document by which an owner transfers the title, or ownership rights, to real property to a new owner

express contract   Contract derived from words, either oral or written

implied contract   Contract derived from actions or conduct

intellectual property   Intangible personal property, such as ideas, songs, trade secrets, and computer programs, that are protected by patents, trademarks, and copyrights

intentional tort   Willful act that results in injury

interlocking directorate   Situation in which members of the board of one firm sit on the board of a competing firm

international law   Principles, customs, and rules that govern the international relationships between states, organizations, and persons

negligence   Tort in which a reasonable amount of care to protect others from risk of injury is not used

negotiable instrument   Transferable document that represents a promise to pay a specified amount

personal property   All property that is not real property

power of attorney   Written authorization for one party to legally act for another

product liability   The capacity of a product to cause harm or damage for which the producer or seller is held accountable

property   Rights held regarding any tangible or intangible object

real property   Land and everything permanently attached to it

stare decisis   Concept of using previous judicial decisions as the basis for deciding similar court cases

statutory law   Statute, or law, created by a legislature

strict product liability   Liability for injury caused by a defective product when all reasonable care is used in its manufacture, distribution, or sale; no fault is assigned

tort   Noncriminal act (other than breach of contract) that results in injury to a person or to property

tying contracts   Contracts forcing buyers to purchase unwanted goods along with goods actually desired

Uniform Commercial Code (UCC)   Set of standardized laws, adopted by most states, that govern business transactions

warranty   Statement specifying what the producer of a product will do to compensate the buyer if the product is defective or if it malfunctions

FINANCIAL AND RISK MANAGEMENT

■ FINANCING THE ENTERPRISE

Most companies can't operate and grow without a periodic infusion of money. Firms need money to cover the day-to-day expenses of running a business, such as paying employees and purchasing inventory. They also need money to acquire new assets such as land, production facilities, and equipment. Furthermore, as Chapter 4 pointed out, start-up companies need money to fund the costs involved in launching a new business.

Where can existing firms obtain the money they need to operate and grow? The most obvious source would be revenues: cash received from sales, rentals of property, interest on short-term investments, and so on. Another likely source would be suppliers who may be willing to do business on credit, thus enabling the company to postpone payment. Most firms also obtain money in the form of loans from banks, finance companies, or other commercial lenders. In addition, public companies can raise funds by selling shares of stock, and large corporations can sell bonds.

As you can imagine, financing an enterprise is a complex undertaking. The process begins by assessing the firm's financing needs and determining whether funds are needed for the short or the long term. Next, the firm must assess the cost of obtaining those funds. Finally, it must weigh the advantages and disadvantages of financing through debt or equity, taking into consideration the firm's special needs and circumstances. The financing process is further complicated by the fact that many sources of long-term and short-term funding exist—each with their own special attributes, risks, and costs.

Cost of Capital

In general, a company wants to obtain money at the lowest cost and least amount of risk. However, lenders and investors want to receive the highest possible return on their investment, also at the lowest risk. A company's cost of capital, the average rate of interest it must pay on its debt and equity financing, depends on three main factors: the risk associated with the company, the prevailing level of interest rates, and management's selection of funding vehicles. Obviously, the more financially solid a company is, the less risk investors face. However, time also plays a vital role. Because a dollar will be worth less tomorrow than it is today, lenders need to be compensated for waiting to be repaid. As a result, long-term financing generally costs a company more than short-term financing.

Interest Regardless of how financially solid a company is, the cost of money will vary over time because interest

Financial managers help their companies determine how much money they need for operations and for expansion. They're also responsible for identifying the right combination of funding sources at the lowest cost.

rates fluctuate. Companies must take such interest rate fluctuations into account when making financing decisions. For instance, a company planning to finance a short-term project when the prime rate is 8.5 percent would want to reevaluate the project if the prime rose to 10 percent a few months later. Even though companies try to time their borrowing to take advantage of drops in interest rates, this option is not always possible. A firm's need for money doesn't always coincide with a period of favorable rates. At times, a company may be forced to borrow when rates are high and then renegotiate the loan when rates drop. Sometimes projects must be put on hold until interest rates become more affordable.

Opportunity Cost   Using a company's own cash to finance its growth has one chief attraction: No interest payments are required. Nevertheless, such internal financing is not free; this money has an *opportunity cost.* That is, a company might be better off investing its excess cash in external opportunities, such as another company's projects or stocks of growing companies, and borrowing money to finance its own growth. Doing so makes sense as long as the company can earn a greater *rate of return,* the percentage increase in the value of an investment, on external investments than the rate of interest paid on borrowed money. Still, most companies require some degree of external financing from time to time. Thus, the issue is not so much

whether to use outside money; rather, it's a question of how much should be raised, by what means, and when. The answers to such questions determine the firm's **capital structure,** the mix of debt and equity.

Debt Versus Equity Financing

Debt financing refers to what we normally think of as a loan. A creditor agrees to lend money to a debtor in exchange for repayment, with accumulated interest, at some future date. *Equity financing* is achieved by selling shares of a company's stock. (The advantages and disadvantages of selling stock to the public are discussed in Chapter 5.) When choosing between debt and equity financing, companies consider a variety of issues, including whether the financing is for the short or the long term; the cost of the financing, including interest, fees, and other charges; and the desire for ownership control (see Exhibit B.1):

- *Length of term.* Financing can be either short-term or long-term. **Short-term debt** is any debt that will be repaid within one year, whereas **long-term debt** is any debt that will be repaid in a period longer than one year. The primary purpose of short-term debt financing is to ensure that a company maintains its liquidity, or its ability to meet financial obligations (such as inventory payments) as they become due. By contrast, long-term financing is used to acquire long-term assets such as buildings and equipment or to fund expansion via any number of growth options.

- *Fees and charges.* Small privately held companies seeking from $1 million to $5 million would probably not issue and sell securities to the public because of the high costs involved in issuing stock and the cumbersome and costly federal registrations and filing requirements with the SEC. Nevertheless, these costs must be weighed against the costs of financing with debt—especially when interest rates are high and the amount required is large. For example, a company can sell stock and survive rough times by omitting dividend payments, but if it can't meet its loan and bond commitments, it could be forced into bankruptcy.

- *Ownership control.* Two of the biggest benefits of debt financing are (1) the lender does not gain an ownership interest in the business, and (2) a firm's obligations are limited to repaying the loan. By contrast, equity financing involves an exchange of money for a share of business ownership: It allows firms to obtain funds without

CHARACTERISTIC	DEBT	EQUITY
Maturity	**Specific:** Specifies a date by which it must be repaid.	**Nonspecific:** Specifies no maturity date.
Claim on income	**Fixed cost:** Company must pay interest on debt held by bondholders and lenders before paying any dividends to shareholders. Interest payments must be met regardless of operating results.	**Discretionary cost:** Shareholders may receive dividends after creditors have received interest payments; however, company is not required to pay dividends.
Claim on assets	**Priority:** Lenders have prior claims on assets.	**Residual:** Shareholders have claims only after the firm satisfies claims of lenders.
Influence over management	**Little:** Lenders are creditors, not owners. They can impose limits on management only if interest payments are not received.	**Varies:** As owners of the company, shareholders can vote on some aspects of corporate operations. Shareholder influence varies, depending on whether stock is widely distributed or closely held.

EXHIBIT B·1

DEBT VERSUS EQUITY

When choosing between debt and equity financing, companies evaluate the characteristics of both types of funding.

pledging to repay a specific amount of money at a particular time, but in exchange for this benefit the firm must give up some ownership control. (The advantages and disadvantages of equity financing are discussed in Chapter 5.)

Common Types of Debt Financing

Aside from internal financing, the three most common types of short-term financing are (1) **trade credit** (or open-account purchases) from suppliers, allowing purchasers to obtain products before paying for them, (2) short-term commercial loans, and (3) **commercial paper**—short-term promissory notes of major corporations sold in minimum investments of $25,000 with a maturity or due date of 30 to 90 days. By contrast, when companies need money for the long term they typically finance with bank loans, leases, or the sale of company bonds.

Loans can be secured or unsecured. **Secured loans** are those backed by something of value, known as **collateral,** which may be seized by the lender in the event that the borrower fails to repay the loan. The most common types of collateral are accounts receivable, inventories, and property such as marketable securities, buildings, and other assets. **Unsecured loans** are ones that require no collateral. Instead, the lender relies on the general credit record and the earning power of the borrower. To increase the returns

on such loans and to obtain some protection in case of default, most lenders insist that the borrower maintain some minimum amount of money on deposit at the bank—a **compensating balance**—while the loan is outstanding. Exhibit B.2 shows some of the key factors lenders look for when analyzing the merits of a loan request.

One example of an unsecured loan is a working capital **line of credit,** which is an agreed-on maximum amount of money a bank is willing to lend a business during a specific period of time, usually one year. Once a line of credit has been established, the business may obtain unsecured loans for any amount up to that limit, provided the bank has funds. The line of credit can be canceled at any time, so companies that want to be sure of obtaining credit when needed should arrange a revolving line of credit, which guarantees that the bank will honor the line of credit up to the stated amount.

Rather than borrowing from a commercial lender to buy a piece of property or equipment, a firm may enter into a **lease,** under which the owner of an item allows another party to use it in exchange for regular payments. Leasing may be a good alternative for a company that has difficulty obtaining loans because of a poor credit rating. Creditors are more willing to provide a lease than a loan because, should the company fail, the lessor need not worry about a default on loan payments; it can simply repossess equipment it legally owns. Some firms use leases

EXHIBIT B·2

THE FIVE Cs OF BASIC LENDING

Lenders look at these five factors when analyzing the merits of a loan request.

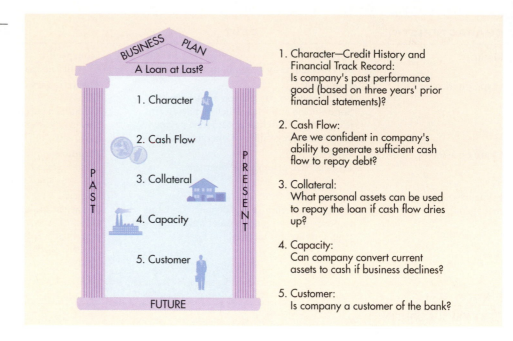

BUSINESS PLAN

A Loan at Last?

1. Character

2. Cash Flow

3. Collateral

4. Capacity

5. Customer

PAST   PRESENT

FUTURE

1. Character—Credit History and Financial Track Record: Is company's past performance good (based on three years' prior financial statements)?

2. Cash Flow: Are we confident in company's ability to generate sufficient cash flow to repay debt?

3. Collateral: What personal assets can be used to repay the loan if cash flow dries up?

4. Capacity: Can company convert current assets to cash if business declines?

5. Customer: Is company a customer of the bank?

to finance up to 35 percent of their total assets, particularly in industries such as airlines, where assets are mostly large, expensive pieces of equipment.

When a company needs to borrow a large sum of money, it may not be able to get the entire amount from a single source. Under such circumstances, it may borrow from many individual investors by issuing bonds—certificates that obligate the company to repay a certain sum, plus interest, to the bondholder on a specific date. (Both bonds and stocks are traded on organized securities exchanges and are discussed in detail in Chapter 15.)

PROTECTING THE ENTERPRISE AGAINST RISK

In addition to providing for and protecting a firm's financial well-being, managers must also protect companies from a number of business risks. For instance, all businesses face the risk of loss. Fire, lawsuits, accidents, natural disasters, theft, illness, disability, and death are common occurrences that can devastate any business—large or small—if they are not prepared for. Of course, managers cannot guard against every conceivable threat of loss. Still, they know that in any given situation, the greater the number of outcomes that may occur, the greater their company is at *risk*.

Risk is a daily fact of life for both businesses and individuals. Most businesses accept the possibility of losing

money in order to make money. In fact, risk prompts people to go into business in the first place. Although the formal definition of **risk** is the variation, based on chance, in possible outcomes of an event, it's not unusual to sometimes hear the term used to mean exposure to loss. This second definition is helpful, because it explains why people purchase **insurance,** a contractual arrangement whereby one party agrees to compensate another party for losses.

Speculative risk refers to those exposures that offer the prospect of making a profit or loss—such as investments in stock. Because in most cases speculative risks are not insurable, the idea is to identify the risks, take steps to minimize them, and provide for the funding of potential losses. **Pure risk,** on the other hand, is the threat of loss without the possibility of gain. Disasters such as an earthquake or a fire at a manufacturing plant are examples of pure risk. Nothing good can come from an exposure to pure risk.

An **insurable risk** is one that meets certain requirements in order for the insurer to provide protection, whereas an **uninsurable risk** is one that an insurance company will not cover (see Exhibit B.3). For example, most insurance companies are unwilling to cover potential losses that can occur from general economic conditions such as a recession. Such uncertainties are beyond the realm of insurance. In general, a risk is insurable if it meets these requirements:

INSURABLE	UNINSURABLE
Property risks: Uncertainty surrounding the occurrence of loss from perils that cause 1. Direct loss of property 2. Indirect loss of property	Market risks: Factors that may result in loss of property or income, such as 1. Price changes, seasonal or cyclical 2. Consumer indifference 3. Style changes 4. Competition offered by a better product
Personal risks: Uncertainty surrounding the occurrence of loss due to 1. Premature death 2. Physical disability 3. Old age	Political risks: Uncertainty surrounding the occurrence of 1. Overthrow of the government 2. Restrictions imposed on free trade 3. Unreasonable or punitive taxation 4. Restrictions on free exchange of currencies
Legal liability risks: Uncertainty surrounding the occurrence of loss arising out of 1. Use of automobiles 2. Occupancy of buildings 3. Employment 4. Manufacture of products 5. Professional misconduct	Production risks: Uncertainties surrounding the occurrence of 1. Failure of machinery to function economically 2. Failure to solve technical problems 3. Exhaustion of raw-material resources 4. Strikes, absenteeism, labor unrest
	Personal risks: Uncertainty surrounding the occurrence of 1. Unemployment 2. Poverty from factors such as divorce, lack of education or opportunity, loss of health from military service

EXHIBIT B•3

INSURABLE AND UNINSURABLE RISKS

Insurance companies consider some pure risks insurable. They usually view speculative risks as uninsurable. (Some pure risks, such as flood and strike, are considered uninsurable.)

- *The loss must be accidental and beyond the insured's control.* For example, a fire insurance policy excludes losses caused by the insured's own arson, but losses caused by an employee's arson would be covered.
- *The loss must be financially measurable.* Although the loss of an apartment building is financially measurable, the loss suffered by having an undesirable tenant is not.
- *A large number of similar cases must be subject to the same peril.* In order for the likelihood of a loss to be predictable, insurance companies must have data on the frequency and severity of losses caused by a given peril. If this information covers a long period of time and is based on a large number of cases or observations, the **law of large numbers** will usually allow insurance companies to predict accurately how many losses will occur in the future. For example, insurers keep track of the number of automobile accidents by age group in the United States so they can estimate the likelihood of a customer's becoming involved in a collision.

- *The risk should be spread over a wide geographical area.* Unless an insurance company spreads its coverage over a large geographical area or a broad population base, a single disaster might force it to pay out on all its policies at once. Consider Hurricane Andrew. This catastrophe caused over $16.3 billion in insured losses, the largest dollar amount of damage claims ever made on the insurance system from a single natural event. Even though all insured claims for the damage caused by Hurricane Andrew were honored, many insurers now restrict the amount of insurance they provide in Florida.[1]
- *The possible loss must be financially serious to the insured.* An insurance company could not afford the paperwork involved in handling numerous small **claims** (demands by the insured that the insurance company pay for a loss) of a few dollars each; nor would a business be likely to insure such a small loss. For this reason, many policies have a clause specifying that the insurance company will pay only that part of a loss greater than an amount stated in the policy. This amount, the

deductible, represents small losses (such as the first $250 of covered repairs) that the insured has agreed to absorb.

Managing risk is indeed an important part of running a business. The process of reducing the threat of loss from uncontrollable events and funding potential losses is called **risk management,** which includes assessing risk, controlling risk, and financing risk by shifting it to an insurance company or by self-insuring to cover possible losses.

Assessing Risk

One of the first steps in managing risk is to identify where it exists. Those areas of risk in which a potential for loss exists, called **loss exposures,** fall under four headings: (1) loss of property (due to destruction or theft of tangible or intangible assets), (2) loss of income (either through decreased revenues or through increased expenses resulting from an accidental event), (3) legal liability to others, including employees, and (4) loss of the services of key personnel (through accidental injury or death).

Consider just one of the many loss exposures that a manufacturer of stuffed toys must face: First, the manufacturer must identify the ways a consumer (most likely a child) can be injured by a stuffed toy. The child might choke on button eyes, get sick from eating the stuffing, or have an allergic reaction to any material in the toy. Second, the company must identify any possible flaws in the production or marketing of the toy that might lead to one of these injuries. For example, a child may have an allergic

reaction to the toy if its materials are not carefully tested for allergenic substances, if impurities enter the toy during manufacture, or if the toy is not properly packaged (allowing foreign substances to reach it). Third, the manufacturer must analyze these possibilities in order to predict product-liability losses accurately.

Controlling Risk

Once you've assessed your potential risk, the next step is to try to control it. Here are some of the *risk-control techniques* managers use to minimize an organization's losses:

- *Risk avoidance.* A risk manager might try to eliminate the chance of a particular type of loss. With rare exceptions, such risk avoidance is not practical. The stuffed-toy manufacturer could avoid being sued for a child's allergic reaction by not making stuffed toys, but, of course, the company would also be out of business.

- *Loss prevention.* A risk manager may try to reduce (but not totally eliminate) the *chance* of a given loss by removing hazards or taking preventive measures. Security guards at banks, warnings on medicines and dangerous chemicals, and safety locks are examples of loss prevention measures.

- *Loss reduction.* A risk manager may try to reduce the *severity* of the losses that do occur. Examples include installing overhead sprinklers to reduce damage during a fire and paying the medical expenses of an injured consumer to reduce the likelihood of litigation and punitive damages.

- *Risk-control transfer.* A risk manager may try to eliminate risk by transferring to some other person or group either (1) the actual property or activity responsible for the risk or (2) the responsibility for the risk. For example, a firm can sell a building to eliminate the risks of ownership.

Of course, not all risk is controllable. Whereas some companies choose to fully accept the financial consequences of a loss themselves—especially when the potential loss costs are small or can be financed by the company itself—others choose to shift risk to an outside insurance company or to self-insure against risk.

Shifting Risk to an Insurance Company

Insurance is an intangible good—a contingent promise to be delivered in the future. When companies purchase insurance, they transfer a group's (but not an individual's)

Theft and destruction of company information are two loss exposures that more and more companies are taking seriously. "High-tech crime is the wave of the future," says Lewis Schiliro, head of the FBI's computer crime department. According to a recent FBI survey of 563 corporations, 49 percent acknowledged unauthorized use of their computer systems.

predicted losses to an insurance pool. The pool combines the cost of the potential losses to be financed and then redistributes them back to the individuals exposed (in advance) by charging them a fee known as a **premium.**

Actuaries determine how much income insurance companies need to generate from premiums by compiling statistics of losses, predicting the amount needed to pay claims over a given period, and calculating the amount needed to cover these expenses plus any anticipated operating costs. Keep in mind that insurance companies don't count on making a profit on any particular policy, nor do they count on paying for a single policyholder's losses out of the premium paid by that particular policyholder. Rather, the insurance company pays for a loss by drawing the money out of the pool of funds it has received from all its policyholders in the form of premiums (see Exhibit B.4). In this way, the insurance company redistributes the cost of predicted losses from a single individual or company to a large number of policies.

If you were starting a business, what types of insurance would you need? To some extent, the answer to that question would depend on the nature of your business and your potential for loss. In general, however, you would probably want to protect yourself against the loss of property, loss of income, liability, and loss of services of key personnel.

Property Insurance   Property loss can have a variety of causes, including accidental damage, natural disaster, and theft. Property can also be lost through employee dishonesty and nonperformance. When a cannery in California ships jars of pizza sauce by a truck to New York, for example, the goods face unavoidable risks in transit. One wrong turn could cover a whole hillside with broken glass and gallons of sauce, which would represent a sizable loss to the manufacturer. The factory itself is vulnerable to fire, flood, and (especially in California) earthquake. **Property insurance** covers the insured for physical damage to or destruction of property and also for its loss by theft.

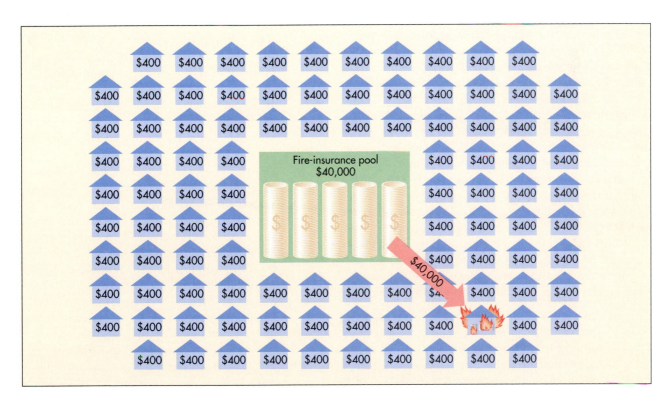

EXHIBIT B•4

HOW INSURANCE WORKS

An insurance company covers the cost of a policyholder's loss out of the premiums paid by a large pool of policyholders. Thus, if 100 policyholders pay $400 each to insure against fire damage, the insurance company can afford to compensate one policyholder who actually suffers fire damage with $40,000.

Consequential Loss Insurance When a disaster strikes, such as a fire or a flood, property loss is only one part of the story. Disasters not only disrupt the business operation; they often result in temporary shutdown, costing the company far more than the equipment repairs or replacement of damaged stock. That's because expenses continue—salaries, interest payments, rent—even though the company is not earning revenues. Disruption also results in extra expenses: leasing of temporary space, paying overtime to meet work schedules with a reduced capacity, buying additional advertising to assure the public that the business is still a going concern. In fact, a prolonged interruption of business could even cause bankruptcy.

For this reason, many companies carry *consequential loss insurance.* Available coverage includes **business-interruption insurance,** which protects the insured against lost profits and pays continuing expenses when a fire or other disaster causes a company to shut down temporarily; **extra-expense insurance,** which pays the additional costs of maintaining the operation in temporary quarters; and **contingent business-interruption insurance,** which protects against a company's loss of profit due to the misfortune of another business, such as a fire or other disaster that interrupts the operation of an important supplier or the closing of an anchor store in the mall where the business is located.

Liability Insurance Liability insurance provides protection against a number of perils. **Liability losses** are financial losses suffered by firms or individuals held responsible for property damage or for injuries suffered by others. In general, liability losses arise from three sources: (1) A company must pay legal damages awarded by a court to the injured party if it is found negligent; (2) the costs of a legal defense can be quite expensive; and (3) the costs of loss prevention or identifying potential liability problems so they may be handled in an appropriate way can also add up. To accommodate theses sources of liability, the insurance industry has created these types of liability policies:

- *Commercial general liability.* This basic coverage automatically provides protection against all forms of liability not specifically excluded under the terms of the policy. Examples would be liability for operations on business premises, product liability, completed operations, and operations of independent contractors.
- *Product liability.* Manufacturers of a product have a legal duty to design and produce a product that will not injure people in normal use. In addition,

products must be packaged carefully and accompanied by adequate instructions and warnings so consumers may use them properly and avoid injury. If these duties are not fulfilled and result in an injured user, a potential for a product-liability lawsuit exists. **Product-liability coverage** protects insured companies from being threatened financially when someone claims that one of their products caused damage, injury, or death.

- *Automobile liability.* Many companies also carry insurance that specifically covers liability connected with any vehicles owned or operated by the company. Some states have **no-fault insurance laws,** which means that all parties involved in an automobile accident receive compensation for their injuries from their own insurer, regardless of who causes the accident. According to current no-fault plans, after some threshold of damage has been reached, the injured party may revert to the liability system to seek compensation for loss. In some cases this threshold is so low that the term *no-fault* hardly seems descriptive.[2]
- *Professional liability.* Also known as *malpractice insurance* or *errors and omissions insurance,* **professional liability insurance** covers people who are found liable for professional negligence. Because this type of coverage protects professionals from financial ruin if sued by dissatisfied clients, it is very expensive.
- *Employment practices liability.* Recent increases in employee lawsuits and hefty judgments against employers have generated increased interest in employment practices liability insurance. Such insurance reimburses employers for defense costs, settlements, and judgments arising from employment claims related to discrimination, sexual harassment, wrongful termination, breach of employment contract, negligent evaluation, failure to employ or promote, wrongful discipline, deprivation of career opportunity, wrongful infliction of emotional stress, and mismanagement of employee benefits.[3]
- *Umbrella liability.* Because many liability policies have limits, or maximum amounts that may be paid out, businesses sometimes purchase **umbrella policies** to provide coverage after underlying liability policies have been exhausted. Some-

times an umbrella policy is called *excess liability insurance.*

Key-Person Insurance Sometimes one executive or employee has expertise or experience that is crucial to the company's operation. If a business loses this key person by illness, disability, death, or unplanned retirement, the effect may be felt in lost income. **Key-person insurance** can be purchased to protect a company against the financial impact of losing such a key employee under the circumstances described. Part of identifying the key-employee exposure is developing an estimate of where, at what cost, and how quickly a replacement may be hired and trained. For example, when fashion designer Gianni Versace was murdered, his key-man policy paid $21 million to his company.[4]

Self-Insuring Against Risk

Self-insurance is becoming an increasingly popular method of insuring against risk. Because self-insurance plans are not subject to state regulation, mandates, and premium taxes (typically 2 percent), companies that use **self-insurance** often save quite a bit of money. Deciding to self-insure with a liability reserve fund means putting aside a certain sum each year to cover predicted liability losses. Unless payments to the self-insurance fund are calculated scientifically and paid regularly, a true self-insurance system does not exist.

Keep in mind that self-insurance differs greatly from "going bare," or having no reserve funds. Self-insurance implies an attempt by business to combine a sufficient number of its own similar exposures to predict the losses accurately. It also implies that adequate financial arrangements have been made in advance to provide funds to pay for losses should they occur. For instance, companies that self-insure often set aside a revenue or self-insurance contingency fund to cover any unexpected or large losses. That way, if disaster strikes, companies won't have to borrow funds to cover their losses, or be forced out of business. In addition, they generally protect themselves from unexpected losses or disasters by purchasing excess insurance from commercial insurers, called *stop-loss insurance.* This additional insurance is designed to cover losses that would exceed a company's own financial capabilities.

Experts advise companies to consider self-insurance plans only if they are prepared to handle the worst-case scenario (usually the point at which stop-loss insurance kicks in) and to use self-insurance only as a long-term strategy. That's because in some years the cost to self-insure

Most self-insurers protect themselves from disasters by purchasing stop-loss insurance.

will be lower than the cost of commercial insurance, whereas in other years it will be higher. In the long run, however, statistics show that the good and bad years should average out in the company's favor.[5]

Monitoring the Risk-Management Program

Risk management is an ongoing activity. Managers must periodically reevaluate the company's loss exposures by asking these questions: What does the company have? What can go wrong? What's the minimum we need to stay in business? What's the best way to protect the company's assets?[6] By answering these questions, managers can then revise a company's risk-management program to address changing needs and circumstances. Of course, smart managers recognize that risk management is really everybody's job. Practically every employee can take steps to reduce his or her company's exposure to risk by preventing it or controlling it.

■ INSURING EMPLOYEES

Besides protecting company property and assets, most businesses look out for the well-being of employees by providing them with health, disability, workers' compensation, and life insurance coverage. Disease and disability may cost employees huge sums of money unless they are insured. In addition, death carries the threat of financial hardship for an employee's family.

Health Insurance

Approximately 90 percent of the people who have private health insurance acquire their benefits as part of a company employee benefit program. Employers providing group health insurance typically cover the employee and eligible dependents. Traditionally, group insurance includes health expense coverage as well as a coverage guaranteeing income in the event of a disabling illness or injury. Most group policies place limits on the amount they will pay for mental health and substance abuse claims. Exhibit B.5 lists the most common types of health expense coverage offered by employers.[7]

Employers typically pay a large portion of the premium costs of health insurance for their employees; however, as costs rise, many employers are shifting more of the cost burden to employees by requiring them to pay a larger portion of their own premiums and larger deductibles through a payroll deduction plan. Small companies often get hit the hardest. Because their insurance groups are smaller, premiums tend to be more costly, forcing some small companies to drop health insurance altogether.

Some companies choose to contain their health insurance costs by joining **health maintenance organizations (HMOs),** which are comprehensive, prepaid, group-practice medical plans in which consumers pay a set fee (called a capitation payment) and in return receive most of their health care at little or no additional costs. Because the capitation payment does not change with usage, HMOs shift the risk from the employer to the health-care provider. Unlike hospitals and doctors in private practice, which charge on a fee-for-service basis, HMOs charge a fixed fee with which they must cover all their expenses.

As an alternative to HMOs, some employers opt for **preferred-provider organizations (PPOs),** health-care providers that contract with employers, insurance companies, or other third-party payers to deliver health-care services to an employee group at a reduced fee. In most companies, employees are not required to use preferred providers, but they are offered incentives to do so—such as reduced deductibles, lower co-payments, and wellcare. Preferred-provider organizations not only save employers money but also allow them to control the quality and appropriateness of services provided. However, employees are restricted in their choice of hospitals and doctors, and preventive services are generally not covered.

Disability Income Insurance

Disability income insurance, which replaces income not earned because of illness or accident, is often included as part of the health insurance package provided by employers. Such policies are designated as either short-term

Cutting health-care costs by improving employees' health is the goal of the Xerox Corporate Fitness Center.

Basic medical	Designed to pay for most inpatient and some outpatient hospital costs
Major medical	Protects the insured against catastrophic financial losses by covering medical expenses that exceed the coverage limits of the basic policies
Disability income	Designed to protect against the loss of short-term or long-term income while the insured is disabled as a result of an illness or accident
Medicare supplemental	Designed specifically to supplement benefits provided under the Medicare program
Long-term care	Designed to cover stays in long-term care facilities

EXHIBIT B·5

COMMON TYPES OF HEALTH INSURANCE

Here are five of the most common types of health insurance policies sold by insurers.

or long-term, depending on the period for which coverage is provided. Short-term policies are more common and provide a specific number of weeks of coverage (often 30), after a brief waiting or elimination period—a period that must elapse before an employee is eligible to receive insurance payments. The purpose of the elimination period is to exclude payments for minor illness. Long-term disability income, on the other hand, provides a number of years of protection after a substantial elimination period has elapsed (generally six months of continuous disability).

The amount of disability payment depends on whether the disability is partial or total, temporary or permanent, short-term or long-term. In general, the amount received is decreased by the amount of disability payments received from Social Security. To encourage employees to return to work as soon as possible, some policies will continue partial payments if an employee is able to perform some type of work, even if he or she is unable to maintain the same pace of career advancement or hours of labor per week as before the disability.

Workers' Compensation Insurance

Each year, thousands of workers die or are injured permanently because of job-related injuries. **Workers' compensation insurance** pays the medical bills of employees who are hurt or become ill as a result of their work. It covers loss of income by occupationally injured or diseased workers, full payment of medical expenses, and rehabilitation expenses for these workers. Plus, it provides death benefits to the survivors of any employee killed on the job. In most cases, it covers both full- and part-time employees.

Workers' compensation insurance is required by U.S. law, and the benefits are enumerated in the workers' compensation statute. Premiums for workers' compensation insurance are based on the employer's payroll and past experience. Thus, employers with relatively good safety results will pay lower workers' compensation insurance rates than employers with poor safety records. This approach rewards loss prevention and loss reduction efforts. Insurers also classify employers by industry, giving recognition to the fact that some industries involve more danger to workers than others. For instance, an employer in a mining industry would pay higher rates than an employer in the food services industry.

Life Insurance

One of the most unfortunate circumstances that could strike a family would be the loss of its main source of income. Life insurance policies provide some protection against the financial problems associated with premature death by paying predetermined amounts to **beneficiaries** when the covered individual dies. Life insurance is the closest thing to a universal employee benefit: It is offered to roughly 90 percent of the employees in the United States.[8]

There are many types of life insurance, and each is used for a variety of purposes. For example, *credit life insurance* is required by many lending institutions to guarantee that a mortgage or other large loan will be paid off in the case of the borrower's death.[9] Some life insurance policies provide a type of savings fund for retirement or other purposes by building a *cash value* from excess premiums. In some policies, owners can borrow against the cash value by paying interest to the insurer (sometimes at a lower rate than banks charge), and they can withdraw the accumulated cash value in one lump sum or in annual payments if they want to end the policy.

Term insurance, as the name implies, covers a person for a specific period of time—the term of the policy. If the insured outlives the period, no payment is made by the insurer, and the policy has no cash value. Group life insurance is term insurance that is commonly purchased by employers for their employees. It may generally be renewed without the proof of insurability (also known as guaranteed renewable), but not past the age of 65. **Whole life insurance** provides a combination of insurance and savings. The policy stays in force until the insured dies, provided that the premiums are paid. In addition to paying death benefits, whole life insurance accumulates cash value. Because this type of insurance tends to be more expensive than term insurance, it is not typically provided by employers.

Test Your Knowledge

QUESTIONS FOR REVIEW

1. What are three major types of short-term financing and three major types of long-term financing?
2. What is the difference between a secured and an unsecured loan?
3. What is the difference between pure risk and speculative risk?
4. What are the five characteristics of insurable risks?
5. What are the four types of loss exposure?

QUESTIONS FOR ANALYSIS

6. What are some of the things a company should consider before selecting an appropriate type of financing?
7. Why would a company lease a piece of property or equipment instead of purchasing it?
8. How can you control risk?
9. How do insurance companies calculate their premiums?
10. As the new company finance manager, you would like to revise some of the overly aggressive interest rate estimates that were made by your predecessor. The problem is, these revisions will negatively affect (one time only) the company's financial statements and will likely upset your shareholders. What should you do? Should you leave things as they are—after all, they are not your estimates—or should you make the accounting changes and handle the consequences?

QUESTIONS FOR APPLICATION

11. If you were starting a new accounting practice with 15 employees, what types of insurance might you need?

12. One of your smaller clients is seeking your advice on ways he might lower or control his rising health insurance premium costs. Currently he offers his 25 employees a group health policy with few restrictions. What advice might you offer him?

13. The president of your vending machine company wants to expand your $20 million local operation nationwide. To start things rolling, your company will initially require about $50 million. But first management has to decide whether to finance this growth with debt or with equity. Review the material in Chapter 4 on "Financing a New Business," the material in Chapter 5 on "Advantages and Disadvantages of Going Public," and the financing material in this chapter. Then write a brief memo to the company president discussing the many options the company has for financing its growth. Be sure to highlight the advantages and disadvantages of each option.

14. To keep pace with the changing work force, your company recently adopted several alternative work arrangements (as discussed in Chapter 9). These include flextime, telecommuting, and job sharing. In the past, your company has always provided full-time employees with group health insurance, disability income insurance, and term life insurance. Now that many employees will be switching to part-time, flexible arrangements, the company may change its employee insurance benefits. What are some of the arguments employees might make for keeping insurance benefits as they are? What are some of the arguments management might make for changing these benefits to reflect the new flexible working arrangements?

Chapter Glossary

actuaries People employed by an insurance company to compute expected losses and to calculate the cost of premiums

beneficiaries People named in a life insurance policy who receive the proceeds of an insurance contract when the insured dies

business-interruption insurance Insurance that covers losses resulting from temporary business closings

capital structure The financing mix of a firm

claims Demands for payments from an insurance company because of some loss by the insured

collateral Tangible asset a lender can claim if a borrower defaults on a secured loan

commercial paper An IOU, backed by the corporation's reputation, issued to raise short-term capital

compensating balance Portion of an unsecured loan that is kept on deposit at the lending institution to protect the lender and increase the lender's return

contingent business-interruption insurance Insurance that protects a business from losses due to losses sustained by other businesses such as suppliers or transportation companies

deductible Amount of loss that must be paid by the insured before the insurer will pay for the rest

disability income insurance Short-term or long-term insurance that protects an individual against loss of income while that individual is disabled as the result of an illness or accident

extra-expense insurance Insurance that covers the added expense of operating the business in temporary facilities after an event such as a fire or a flood

health maintenance organizations (HMOs) Prepaid medical plans in which consumers pay a set fee in order to receive a full range of medical care from a group of medical practitioners

insurable risk Risk for which an acceptable probability of loss may be calculated and that an insurance company might, therefore, be willing to cover

insurance Written contract that transfers to an insurer the financial responsibility for losses up to specified limits

key-person insurance Insurance that provides a business with funds to compensate for the loss of a key employee by unplanned retirement, resignation, death, or disability

law of large numbers Principle that the larger the group on which probabilities are calculated, the more accurate the predictive value

lease Legal agreement that obligates the user of an asset to make payments to the owner of the asset in exchange for using it

liability losses Financial losses suffered by a business firm or individual held responsible for property damage or injuries suffered by others

line of credit Arrangement in which the financial institution makes money available for use at any time after the loan has been approved

long-term debt Borrowed funds used to cover long-term expenses (generally repaid over a period of more than one year)

loss exposures Areas of risk in which a potential for loss exists

no-fault insurance laws Laws limiting lawsuits connected with auto accidents

preferred-provider organizations (PPOs) Health-care providers offering reduced-rate contracts to groups that agree to obtain medical care through the providers' organization

premium Fee that the insured pays the insurer for coverage against loss

product-liability coverage Insurance that protects companies from claims for injuries or damages that result from use of a product the company manufactures or distributes

professional liability insurance Insurance that covers losses arising from damages or injuries caused by the insured in the course of performing professional services for clients

property insurance Insurance that provides coverage for physical damage to or destruction of property and for its loss by theft

pure risk Risk that involves the chance of loss only

risk Uncertainty of an event or exposure to loss

risk management Process used by business firms and individuals to deal with their exposures to loss

secured loans Loans backed up with something of value that the lender can claim in case of default, such as a piece of property

self-insurance Accumulating funds each year to pay for predicted liability losses, rather than buying insurance from another company

short-term debt Borrowed funds used to cover current expenses (generally repaid within a year)

speculative risk Risk that involves the chance of both loss and profits

term insurance Life insurance that provides death benefits for a specified period

trade credit Credit obtained by the purchaser directly from the supplier

umbrella policies Insurance that provides businesses with coverage beyond what is provided by a basic liability policy

uninsurable risk Risk that few, if any, insurance companies will assume because of the difficulty of calculating the probability of loss

unsecured loans Loans requiring no collateral but a good credit rating

whole life insurance Insurance that provides both death benefits and savings for the insured's lifetime, provided premiums are paid

workers' compensation insurance Insurance that partially replaces lost income and that pays for employees' medical costs and rehabilitation expenses for work-related injuries

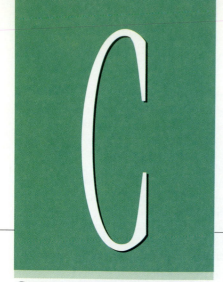

COMPONENT CHAPTER

INFORMATION MANAGEMENT, THE INTERNET, AND E-BUSINESS

WHAT IS EFFECTIVE INFORMATION MANAGEMENT?

We live in the Information Age. Today's workers have instant access to all the data they could ever want. But this ease of information exchange also has its drawbacks. E-mail, fax machines, voice mail, Web sites, snail mail, pagers, cell phones, and overnight express couriers are pelting employees with a surplus of data like a relentless Seattle rain (see Exhibit C.1). As a result, employees are finding it difficult to discriminate between useful and useless information and between what is truly important and what is routine. Moreover, experts worry about the human capacity to absorb this ever-increasing amount of information, especially when the channels are already full and flowing at top speed—and they predict that information overload is only going to get worse.[1]

Businesspeople use information to increase organizational efficiencies, stay ahead of competitors, find new customers, keep current customers loyal, and achieve a competitive advantage. As a businessperson, you will be expected to know how to use technology to manage information effectively in the workplace. But what exactly does effective information management mean? For one thing, information is most useful to those people who can act on it. A salesperson, for example, doesn't need to know

the salaries of other employees, and an administrative assistant in human resources typically doesn't benefit from seeing inventory control data. Therefore, a key element of an effective information management system is the ability to *filter* information: making sure that the *right information* reaches the *right people* at the *right time* in the *right form*.[2] Moreover, for information to be useful, it must be accurate, timely, complete, relevant, and concise.[3] Of

This Planet Advertising employee finds it difficult to cope with the daily glut of faxes, memos, reports, e-mail, and other messages he receives.

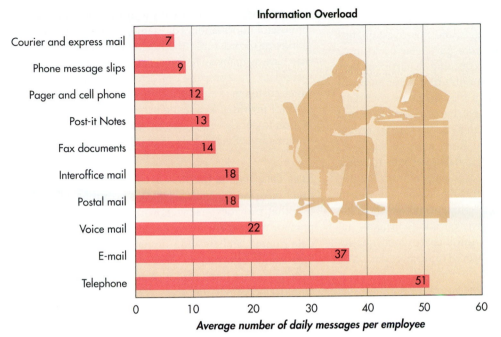

Information Overload

Courier and express mail — 7
Phone message slips — 9
Pager and cell phone — 12
Post-it Notes — 13
Fax documents — 14
Interoffice mail — 18
Postal mail — 18
Voice mail — 22
E-mail — 37
Telephone — 51

0   10   20   30   40   50   60
Average number of daily messages per employee

EXHIBIT C·1

MESSAGE MANIA

The average U.S. office worker sends or receives 201 messages of all kinds each day.

course, information in the real world is rarely perfect, and managers must often make do with whatever information they can get. However, the closer information comes to meeting these five criteria, the more it will facilitate the company's decision-making process.

Effective information management is of such strategic importance in business today that many companies hire a top-level manager, called a **chief information officer (CIO),** to design and develop the company's information management systems. The CIO is responsible for finding out who in the organization needs what types of information, how these individuals will use this information, how often they will need it, and how they will share it with others. The CIO oversees the purchase and installation of computer equipment and assists in designing systems to collect, track, store, process, and retrieve **data** (recorded facts and statistics that flow through the organization) so the data can be converted into useful information and reports.

Processing Data with Computer Application Software

Computer applications in today's business world are almost limitless. Companies use them to set goals, hire employees, order supplies, manage inventory, sell products, communicate with employees, store data, and perform countless other tasks. **Hardware** represents the tangible equipment used in a computer system, such as disk drives, keyboards, modems,

and integrated circuits (small pieces of silicon containing thousands of transistors and electronic circuits). By contrast, **software** encompasses the computer's operating systems and **application software**—programs that perform specific user functions such as word processing, spreadsheets, desktop publishing, database management, and business graphics. These programs automate and facilitate clerical, numerical, graphical, and analytical tasks.

A **spreadsheet** program, for example, lets users organize and manipulate data in a row-column matrix. Among the spreadsheet's biggest strengths is the ability to quickly update masses of calculations when conditions change. Businesspeople use spreadsheets to solve a variety of problems and to facilitate managerial decision making. **Desktop publishing** (DTP) software goes a step beyond typical word processors by allowing users to lay out pages that incorporate artwork, photos, and a large variety of typographic elements. Flyers, brochures, user manuals, annual reports, and newsletters are just a few of the documents that can be produced in camera-ready formats that can go directly to the print shop or to digital printers. **Database management** is an application that uses software to create, store, maintain, rearrange, and retrieve the contents of **databases,** collections of data that are usually stored in a computerized format. Such programs convert data into useful information by allowing users to look at the data from various perspectives.

Turning Data into Information

Every company collects, generates, and stores vast quantities of data that are relevant to a particular decision or problem. For example, the accounting department may have price and sales data for hundreds of different products, the marketing department may have customer data, the purchasing department may have inventory data, and so on (see Exhibit C.2). Through a process known as **data warehousing,** data are moved from separate databases into a well-organized central database where they are sorted, summarized, and stored. Managers from the different functional areas can then make complex *queries,* or ask questions of the central database to review the data, analyze it, solve problems, answer questions, or make decisions (see Exhibit C.3). Such multidepartmental queries are not possible when data are stored in separate databases throughout the organization.[4]

When a query is made, the computer software sifts through huge amounts of data, identifying what is valuable to the specific query and what is not. This process, known as **data mining,** allows managers to turn mountains of data into useful information. For example, MCI WorldCom has marketing records on 140 million households, each of which may have as many as 10,000 separate attributes. By mining these data, the company can detect patterns that indicate which customers are most likely to switch to a different long-distance provider. Marketing personnel can use this information to decide which customers to target for special promotions and which incentives to offer current customers.[5]

Using Computers to Facilitate Decision Making   A **management information system (MIS)** is a computer-based system that provides managers with information and support for making effective routine decisions. An MIS takes data from a database and summarizes or restates the data into useful information such as monthly sales figures, daily inventory levels, product manufacturing schedules, employee earnings, and so on. This information is generally organized in a report or graphical format, making it easier for managers to read and interpret.

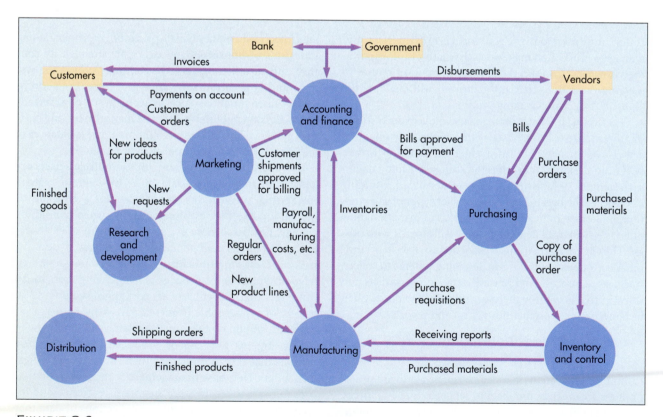

EXHIBIT C.2

INFORMATION FLOW IN A TYPICAL MANUFACTURING COMPANY

Many kinds of manipulations and transfers of information support daily operations and decision making in a manufacturing company.

Whereas a management information system provides structured, routine information for managerial decision making, a **decision support system (DSS)** assists managers in solving highly unstructured and nonroutine problems with the use of decision models and specialized databases. Compared with an MIS, a DSS is more interactive (allowing the user to interact with the system instead of simply receiving information), and it usually relies on both internal and external information.[6] Similar in concept to a DSS is an **executive information system (EIS),** which helps executives make the necessary decisions to keep the organization moving forward. An EIS usually has a more strategic focus than a DSS, and it is used by higher management to plan for the future.

Perhaps the greatest potential for computers to aid decision making and problem solving lies in the development of **artificial intelligence**—the ability of computers to solve problems through reasoning and learning and to simulate human sensory perceptions.[7] One type of computer system that can simulate human reasoning by responding to questions, asking for more information, and making recommendations is the **expert system.**[8] As its name implies, an expert system essentially takes the place of a human expert by helping less knowledgeable individuals make critical decisions.

Using Computers to Share Information To facilitate the sharing of data among employees and departments, most companies today maintain computer network systems. A **network** is a collection of hardware, software, and communications media that enables computers to communicate and share information. Networks differ by the size of their geographic area. A **wide area network (WAN)** links together computers at different geographic locations, whereas a **local area network (LAN)** links computers within a small area, such as a single office building. Any computer can be part of a network, provided it has the

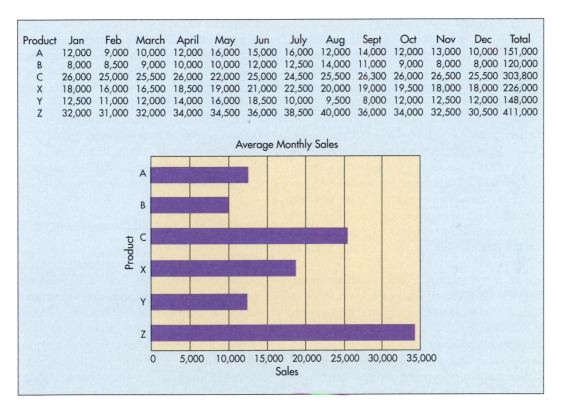

Product	Jan	Feb	March	April	May	Jun	July	Aug	Sept	Oct	Nov	Dec	Total
A	12,000	9,000	10,000	12,000	16,000	15,000	16,000	12,000	14,000	12,000	13,000	10,000	151,000
B	8,000	8,500	9,000	10,000	10,000	12,000	12,500	14,000	11,000	9,000	8,000	8,000	120,000
C	26,000	25,000	25,500	26,000	22,000	25,000	24,500	25,500	26,300	26,000	26,500	25,500	303,800
X	18,000	16,000	16,500	18,500	19,000	21,000	22,500	20,000	19,000	19,500	18,000	18,000	226,000
Y	12,500	11,000	12,000	14,000	16,000	18,500	10,000	9,500	8,000	12,000	12,500	12,000	148,000
Z	32,000	31,000	32,000	34,000	34,500	36,000	38,500	40,000	36,000	34,000	32,500	30,500	411,000

Exhibit C·3

DATA VERSUS INFORMATION

The table at the top represents sales data for a small company's six products. In this form, the data are just statistics that answer no particular question and solve no particular problem. Therefore, they are not considered information. When a manager queries the database to identify the average monthly sales for each product, he or she is asking for specific information. The sales data are used to generate the graph that illustrates the requested information.

right hardware, software, and transmission media. For instance, to communicate over standard telephone lines, a computer must be equipped with a **modem** (modulator-demodulator). This device converts digital information into analog signals (such as sound waves) and then reverses this process so that information can be passed back and forth between computers over telephone lines. Some Internet-ready digital phones, pagers, computers, and other wireless communication devices transmit digital information over networks through antennas, satellites, cables, and special phone lines.[9]

■ WHAT IS THE INTERNET?

The **Internet** is the world's largest computer network. Started in 1969 by the U.S. Department of Defense, the Internet is a voluntary, cooperative undertaking; no one individual, organization, or government owns it. The Internet is accessible to individuals, companies, colleges, government agencies, and other institutions in countries all over the world. It links thousands of smaller computer networks and millions of individual computer users in homes, businesses, government offices, and schools worldwide. You can learn more about the Internet by taking an Internet tour at http://www.whatis.com/tour.htm or http://www.provide.net/~bfield/polaris/tour0000.htm.

To connect to the Internet, all you need is a computer with a modem, a standard telephone line, and an **Internet service provider** (**ISP**)—a company that provides access to the Internet. For a flat monthly fee or a per-use fee, you can dial into one of the ISP's host computers, which will link you to any number of the computers that make up the Internet network. Organizations can also lease their own direct Internet access lines, which provide Internet access to every user wired to the organization's LAN.

The most widely used part of the Internet is the **World Wide Web** (**WWW** or **Web**). Developed in 1990, the Web uses a **graphical user interface (GUI)** system rather than text commands, enabling users to search for, display, and save **multimedia** resources such as graphics, text, audio, and video files. This information is typically stored in a **Web site,** which consists of one or more Web pages located on one of the Internet's many networked computers. To read Web pages, you need a Web **browser**—software such as Netscape Navigator or Microsoft's Internet Explorer.

The **homepage** of a Web site is the primary screen that users first access when visiting a site. Furthermore, each page in a Web site is identified by a unique address known as a **uniform resource locator** (**URL**). Take http://www.amazon.com, for example. The address begins with *http*, which is the abbreviation for **hypertext transfer protocol** (**HTTP**), the communications protocol that allows you to navigate the Web. The address continues with *www*, indicating that the site is located on the World Wide Web. The next part of the address is the site's registered **domain name** (in this case *amazon.com*). No other Web site may use this name. The abbreviation following the *period* indicates whether the site is hosted by a business (com), an educational institution (edu), a government (gov), an international source (int), the military (mil), network resources (net), or a nonprofit organization (org).

Fortunately, you don't have to remember URLs because just about every bit of information on the Web has a **hyperlink** or *hot link*, which means you can click on words in **hypertext markup language** (**HTML**)—colored, underlined, or highlighted words—with your mouse and automatically jump to another Web page or a different Internet site. Once you get to your new destination, you can **bookmark** the site by using a browser feature that places the site's URL in a file on your computer for future use. Then, whenever you click on a bookmark while online, you automatically go to that site's address. Another handy browser feature is the ability to navigate your trail backward or forward at any time by using the *back* and *forward* buttons on your browser software.

Of course, you can't really get a picture of what the Internet is until you have a better idea of how to use it and how it is changing the way companies do business.

How Do You Find Information on the Internet?

The Internet is rich in business information, ranging from current news, issues, and industry trends to company-related data such as financial performance, products, goals, and employment. In fact, the Web is so vast and changes so constantly that it's easy to get sidetracked. If you've ever been lost in cyberspace, take heart—it happens to everybody. Chances are good that you'll find information on the Internet about almost any research topic. However, finding that information can be frustrating if you don't know how to conduct an effective database search.

One important thing to keep in mind when looking for business information on the Internet is that anyone (including you) can post anything on a Web site. No one filters it. No one checks it for accuracy. And no one can be sure of who is producing the information or why it is being placed on the Internet. For that reason, it's best to refrain from seriously surfing the Web for business information until you've had a chance to learn a bit about your topic from journals, books, and commercial databases. That way you'll be able to detect skewed or erroneous information, and you can be more selective about the Web sites and documents you choose to use as a resource.

If you are looking for specific company information, your best source may be the company's own Web site (assuming it maintains one). Web sites generally include detailed information about the company's products, services, history, mission, strategy, financial performance, and employment needs. Furthermore, many sites provide links to related company information, such as SEC filings, press releases, and more.

You can obtain press releases and general company news from news release sites such as PR Newswire at http://www.prnewswire.com and Business Wire at http://www.businesswire.com. These sites offer free databases of news releases from companies subscribing to their services. News release sites are also good places to look for announcements of new products, management changes, earnings, dividends, mergers, acquisitions, and other company information. If you subscribe to a commercial online database system, you can also use the Internet to access company and business information from the provider's database.

Keep in mind that a lot of the information that you may want simply isn't on the Web. If you're researching small organizations, for instance, you may find nothing or just an address and phone number. Furthermore, even if the information you're seeking does exist on the Web, you may not be able to locate it. The Internet holds more than 800 million Web pages, with hundreds of pages being added every day. But even the best **search engines**—Internet tools for finding Web sites—manage to index only about a third of the pages on the Web.[10] When a search engine does turn up what you're looking for, it will probably also turn up a mountain of stuff you won't need. Suppose you're looking for information about available jobs for writers. The search engine may turn up information on being an accountant at an insurance company. Why? Because the insurance company described itself on the Web as one of the largest *writers* of insurance policies. You can produce more targeted search results by learning how to conduct an effective database search.

Conducting an Effective Database Search Whether you are using a library database or an Internet search engine such as the ones listed in Exhibit C.4, use the following search strategies and tips to conduct an effective database search:[11]

- *Select an appropriate database or databases.* In most cases you'll want a good business database. However, it could be that the journals covering your topic are located in the database that includes journals on psychology, computers, or medicine.

- *Use multiple search engines.* Not all search engines are the same. Don't limit yourself to a single search engine—especially if you are looking for less popular topics. To improve your results, read the help file and learn how the search engine works.

- *Choose search terms by translating concepts into key words and phrases.* For instance, if you want to determine the "effect of TQM on company profits," select the key words *TQM, total quality management, profits, sales, companies,* and *corporations.* Remember, use synonyms or word equivalents whenever possible, and use quotes around phrases to look for the entire phrase instead of separate words.

- *Do not use a long phrase when a short phrase or single term will do.* The computer searches for the words exactly as you have keyed them in. If the words occur, but not in the same order, you may miss relevant hits.

- *Do not use stopwords.* Consult the database documentation for any stopwords in addition to the common ones: *a, an, the, of, by, with, for,* and *to.* The computer disregards such words and will not search for them.

- *Do not use words contained in the name of the database.* Words such as *business* or *finance* in the ABI Inform database will work, but they will slow down the processing time and yield no better results.

- *Do enter variations of your terms.* Use acronyms (*CEO, CPA*), synonyms (*man, male*), related terms (*child, adolescent, youth*), different spellings (*dialog, dialogue*), singular and plural forms (*man, men*), nouns and adjectives (*manager, management, managerial*), and simple and compound forms (*online, on line, on-line*).

- *Specify a logical relationship between the key words.* Does the document need to have both *companies* and *corporations,* or is either word fine? Do you need to have both *profits* and *companies* in the same document, or is it more important to have *TQM* or *total quality management* and *profits* or *sales*?

MAJOR SEARCH ENGINES

Alta Vista	http://altavista.digital.com
	Indexes data from millions of Web pages and articles from thousands of Usenet newsgroups.
Ask Jeeves	http://www.ask.com
	Finds answers to natural-language questions such as "Who won Super Bowl XXV?"
Excite	http://www.excite.com
	All-purpose site loaded with options.
Fedstats	http://www.fedstats.gov/search.html
	Simultaneously queries 14 federal agencies for specified statistics and numerical data.
Google	http://www.google.com
	A simple directory that is especially useful for finding home pages of companies and organizations.
GoTo	http://www.goto.com
	Companies can pay to be placed higher in this engine's search results.
HotBot	http://www.hotbot.com
	Wired magazine packs all kinds of searching possibilities into this site.
Infoseek	http://www.infoseek.com
	Sites with red check marks are recommended by Infoseek.
LookSmart	http://www.looksmart.com
	Closest rival to Yahoo! In terms of being a human-compiled directory. Choose the "Your Town" for local directories.
Lycos	http://www.lycos.com
	One of the oldest of the major search engines, provides short abstracts for each match.
Northern Light	http://www.northernlight.com
	Categorizes returns by subject. Has "special collection" of over 2 million documents not readily accessible to search engine spiders.
Snap	http://www.snap.com
	CNET's Snap does a great job of sifting through and organizing some of the best material on the Web and presenting it in a logical fashion.
WebCrawler	http://www.webcrawler.com
	Allows you to either search the entire site or browse any of the preselected categories.
Yahoo!	http://www.yahoo.com
	The oldest major Web site directory, listing over 500,000 sites.

MULTIPLE SEARCH ENGINE SITES—METACRAWLERS

Cyber411	http://www.cyber411.com
	Search up to 16 popular search engines at the same time. The query is reformulated to fit the syntax of each search engine.
Dogpile	http://www.dogpile.com
	Despite the silly name, just enter one query and this hound sniffs through dozens of FTP, Usenet, and Web sites.
IXQuick	http://www.ixquick.com
	Search up to 14 search engines at the same time. Results are ranked by relevancy.
Mamma	http://www.mamma.com
	Claiming to be the "Mother of All Search Engines," this multilegged spider queries the major search engines for fast results.
ProFusion	http://www.profusion.com
	The University of Kansas spider retrieves only the "best" results from selected search engines.
Zworks	http://www.zworks.com
	Results are ranked based on the cumulative score of all the engines used in the search. Duplicate results are eliminated.

EXHIBIT C·4

BEST OF INTERNET SEARCHING

Searchers can get the most dependable results from well-known, commercially backed search engines. These major search engines (and directories) are likely to be well maintained and upgraded when necessary to keep pace with the growing Web. Most have simple or advanced search features, plus extras such as interactive maps and weather, travel information, phone and e-mail directories, and company profiles.

- *Evaluate the precision and quality of your search results, and refine or redo your search if necessary.* Generally, if you end up with more than 60 to 100 references to sort through, you probably need to refine your search strategy. Experts recommend that if your first page of results doesn't have something of interest, you've probably entered the wrong words or too few words. In addition, pay attention to whether you are searching in the title, subject, or document fields of the database. Each will return different results.

Of course, having too much information can be just as bad as having no information. To enhance your search results, use Boolean operators, proximity operators, and wildcards.

Enhancing Your Search Results **Boolean operators** include the words AND, OR, and NOT. As Exhibit C.5 shows, the AND operator narrows a search because it indicates that all the key words (joined by the word AND) must be found in the same document or Web page. By contrast, the OR operator broadens the search because it indicates that either key word must be present. Finally, the NOT operator (sometimes expressed as AND NOT) narrows a search because it indicates that a certain key word must not appear in the document or Web page. For example, say that you are trying to search for the *gross national product of Jordan,* and you keep getting sports sites about Michael Jordan. By using the operator NOT to exclude the word *Michael,* you'll trim a few hundred thousand irrelevant results right away.

Boolean operators can help you create complex, precise search strategies. For example, you could create a search strategy such as "(marketing OR advertising) AND (organizations OR associations) AND NOT consultants." In plain English this means that qualifying documents or Web sites must have either the word *marketing* or *advertising* and must have either the word *organizations* or *associations,* but they can't have the word *consultants.*

SEARCH OPERATOR	EFFECT	STRATEGY	RESULTS
AND	Narrows the results. Searches for records containing both of the words it separates. Words separated by AND may be anywhere in the document—and far away from each other.	Rock AND roll	Music
OR	Broadens the results. This is a scattergun search that will turn up lots of matches and is not particularly precise. Searches for records containing either of the words it separates.	Rock OR roll	Igneous rocks; gemstones; crescent rolls; music
NOT AND NOT	Limits the results. Searches for records containing the first word(s) but not the second one. Depending on the database, AND is not always included in combination with NOT.	Snow skiing NOT water skiing; Snow skiing AND NOT water skiing.	snow skiing; cross-country skiing
NEAR	Proximity operator. Searches for words that all appear in a specified word range.	Snow NEAR/2 skiing	Terms in which *skiing* is withing 2 words of *snow*
ADJ	Adjacency operator. Searches for records in which second word immediately follows first word (two words are next to each other).	Ski ADJ patrol	Ski patrol
?	Wildcard operator for single character; matches any one character.	Ski?	Skit; skid; skin; skip
*	Wildcard operator for string of characters.	Ski*	Ski; skiing; skies; skill; skirt; skit; skinny, skimpy
""	Exact match. Searches for string of words placed within quotation marks.	"1999 budget deficit"	1999 budget deficit

EXHIBIT C·5

IMPROVING YOUR SEARCH RESULTS

Using these Boolean operators, proximity operators, and wildcards will vastly improve the effectiveness of your electronic searches.

Many search engines automatically include Boolean operators in their search strategies even though you can't see them on the screen. For instance, some search engines insert the OR operator between key words. Others may insert the word AND. For this reason, either insert these operators yourself (in most cases they will override the automatic operators inserted by the engine) or review the instructions to learn the inner workings of the specific search engine you are using.

Proximity operators let you specify how close one of your key words should be to another. The most common proximity operator is NEAR, which tells the database engine to find documents in which one key word is a certain number of words away from another. For example, the search phrase "marketing NEAR2 organizations" means *marketing* must be within two words of *organizations*.

Wildcard characters help you find plurals and alternate spellings of your key words. For example, by using a question mark in the word *organi?ations,* you'll find documents with both *organisations* (British spelling) and *organizations*. Similarly, by using an asterisk at the end of the stem *chair*,* you'll find *chairman, chairperson, chairs,* and *chairlift*.

How Does the Internet Facilitate Communication?

Businesses are using the Internet to communicate with employees, customers, suppliers, shareholders, and other stakeholders anywhere in the world. Because the Internet is platform independent, all computers can link to it and communicate with each other even if they have different internal operating systems. The Internet makes these types of communications possible:

- *E-mail.* Electronic mail, generally called **e-mail,** enables users to create, transmit, and read written messages entirely on computer. An e-mail document may be a simple text message, or it might include long and complex files or programs. In addition to facilitating communication, e-mail also offers speed, low cost, portability, convenience, and ease of record keeping.
- *Telnet.* **Telnet** is a class of Internet application programs that allows you to connect with a remote host computer even though your computer is not a permanent part of the network that the host supports. This enables you to run a normal interactive session with other computers on the network as if you were sitting at an on-site terminal. For instance, you would use Telnet to access

Where are you? Your employees? Your clients? Doesn't matter. Thanks to the latest virtual-office technology, staying connected has never been easier.

your county library's electronic card catalog from your home computer.

- *Internet telephony.* It is now possible for Internet users to converse vocally over the Internet. Although the telephone has handled this job for decades, converting traditional voice calls to digital signals and sending them over the Internet is much less expensive than calling over standard analog phone lines. It can also be more efficient, allowing an organization to accommodate more users on a single line at once. Developers of this technology are still working out the bugs, but experts say that Internet telephony could capture 4 percent of U.S. telephone company revenues by 2004.[12]
- *File transfers.* **File transfer protocol (FTP)** is an Internet service that enables you to **download** files or transfer data from a server to your computer, and **upload** files, or transfer data from your computer to a server or host system.[13] Millions of useful files, including art, music, educational materials, games, maps, photos, software, and books, are available on the Internet. FTP also allows you to attach formatted documents to your e-mail messages. When you download a file, the FTP software breaks it down and reassembles it on your computer in a usable form.[14] Sometimes users compress or *zip* large files into smaller packets to make them easier and faster to transfer. If you receive a zipped file, you must use special software (usually provided with your Web browser) to unzip it before you can read it.

- *Discussion mailing lists.* **Discussion mailing lists,** also known as a *listservs,* are discussion groups to which you subscribe by sending a message to the list's e-mail address. From then on, copies of all messages posted by any other subscriber are sent to you via e-mail. It's like subscribing to an electronic newsletter to which everyone can contribute.
- *Newsgroups.* **Usenet newsgroups** consist of posted messages on a particular subject and responses to them. They differ from discussion mailing lists in two key ways. First, messages are posted at the newsgroup site, which you must access by using a news reader program. Second, messages posted to a newsgroup can be viewed by anyone. In other words, think of a newsgroup as a *place* you visit to read posted messages, whereas a discussion mailing list *delivers* posted messages to you.
- *Chat.* **Chat** is an online conversation in which any number of computer users can type in messages to each other and receive responses in real time.

An intranet set up by his law firm enables attorney David Beckman to view documents and other legal resources whether he's in his office or in the courtroom.

Intranets   Not all Web sites are available to anyone cruising the Net. Some are reserved for the private use of a single company's employees and stakeholders. An **intranet** is a private corporate network that connects company computers in various locations. Intranets use the same technologies as the Internet and the World Wide Web, but the information provided and the access allowed are restricted to the boundaries of a companywide computer network. Sensitive corporate data that reside on intranets are protected from unauthorized access via the Internet by security software called a **firewall,** a special type of gateway that controls access to the company's local network. When anyone tries to get into the internal web, the firewall requests a password and other forms of identification. Whereas people on an intranet can get out to the Internet, unauthorized people on the Internet can't get in.

More than half of companies with 500 employees or more have corporate intranets. One of the biggest advantages of an intranet is that it enables employees to communicate and collaborate. At Arthur Andersen, for instance, employees use the company's intranet, *AA Online,* to access the company's wealth of expert knowledge and to search the company's on-line databases. Ford Motor Company uses its intranet to enable engineers and designers worldwide to collaborate in real time on the design of new car models. Every car and truck model has its own internal Web site to track design, production, quality control, and delivery processes.[15]

Besides sharing information, other uses for these networks include sending e-mail, filing electronic forms and reports, gaining access to the company database from remote locations, and publishing electronic phone directories, company newsletters, and other company material.[16]

- *Policy manuals.* The most current version is always available to all employees without having to reprint hundreds of copies when policies change.
- *Employee benefits information.* Employees can find out what their benefits are, reallocate the funds in their employee benefit plans, fill out electronic W-4 forms, view an electronic pay stub, and sign up for employee training programs.
- *Job openings.* New positions are posted, and current employees can submit job applications over the intranet.
- *Presentation materials used by marketing and sales departments.* Sales representatives can download sales and marketing materials at customer sites all over the world. In addition, changes made by marketing representatives at company headquarters are immediately available to field salespeople.
- *Company records and information.* Company directories, customer information, employee skills inventories, project status reports, company calendars and events, and many other records are stored on an intranet and are accessible from anywhere in the world; all you need is an Internet connection and the right password.

Putting this material on an intranet allows employees to find information quickly and easily. Companies are finding that performing an electronic search on a well-designed intranet is far more efficient than digging through multiple filing cabinets stuffed with papers.

Extranets Once a company has an intranet in place, the cost of adding *extranet* capabilities is minimal, but the benefits can be substantial. An **extranet** is simply an organized network that allows people to communicate and exchange data within a secured network.[17] Unlike intranets, which limit network access to a single organization, extranets allow prequalified people from the outside—such as suppliers and customers—to use the network.

Take Arthur Andersen's KnowledgeSpace. This extranet is rich in the latest business practices and business news. Company clients can access this information by entering their proper security codes.[18] Similarly, some executive search firms and employment agencies are allowing clients to tap into their private Web sites to search for job prospects. Doctors and hospitals are also using extranets to share best practices among their individual organizations. In the past they faxed this information to each other, but there was no guarantee that the right person would see a fax or even know it existed before the information became obsolete.

In addition to increasing communication with clients, suppliers, and colleagues, extranets can save companies time and money. Consider this: One management consultant has seen an organization save as much as $70,000 simply by offering online information to its health-care providers and eliminating the need to print special booklets.[19]

How Is the Internet Changing the Way Companies Do Business?

The Internet is revolutionizing all facets of business life. Large and small companies are using the Internet to find and share information; find new business partners; sell and deliver products and services 24 hours a day; attract new customers; market their products and themselves; deliver news; order supplies; maintain investor relations; shorten the time for product design; communicate with their manufacturers, suppliers, customers, employees, and stakeholders; determine customer preferences; invest funds; recruit employees; and much, much more. In fact, most companies are just beginning to realize the Net's potential (see "Here Comes the Electronic Economy" on page 20).[20]

In spite of the many things the Internet allows businesses to do, it is the selling of goods and services over the Internet, or electronic commerce (e-commerce), that's in the spotlight today.

■ WHAT IS ELECTRONIC COMMERCE?

In Chapter 1 we defined electronic commerce (e-commerce) as the buying and selling of goods and services over an electronic network. Specifically, e-commerce is classified into two broad categories. **Business-to-consumer e-commerce** involves interactions and transactions between a company and its consumers, with a strong focus on selling goods and services and marketing to the consumer. Typical business-to-consumer transactions take place via electronic storefronts, auctions, and e-mail. As Exhibit C.6 shows, these transactions include sales, marketing (promotions, advertising, coupons, catalogs), order processing and tracking, credit authorization, customer service, and electronic payments.

By contrast, **business-to-business e-commerce** implies the selling of products and services between companies. This category of e-commerce typically involves a company and its suppliers, distributors, manufacturers, and retailers, but not consumers. Generally, the types of goods sold in business-to-business transactions include office materials, manufacturing supplies, equipment, and other goods

Each Procter & Gamble product has its own Web site. The Crisco site offers consumers product information, tips, recipes, and a newsletter, in addition to reinforcing the product's quality and versatility.

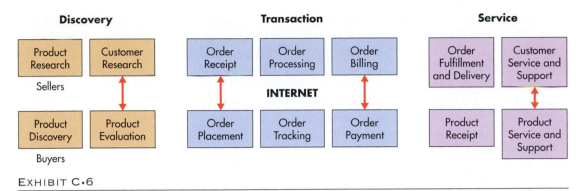

Discovery   **Transaction**   **Service**

EXHIBIT C·6

WHAT IS E-COMMERCE?

In general, e-commerce enables both the buying and selling of goods and services over the Internet.

the company needs to operate. Companies from Honeywell to Chevron, W.W. Grainger, Sears, and the big three automakers (Ford, GM, and DaimlerChrysler) have all started electronic marketplaces to purchase supplies and transact business.[21] (See "This Cyberbazaar Is Strictly Business-to-Business" on page 190.) Industry experts predict that the business-to-business segment of e-commerce will grow five times faster than transactions between businesses and consumers. By 2006, it could represent over 9 percent of all business conducted in the United States.[22]

Even though business-to-consumer electronic commerce currently represents only a fraction of today's sales, it's a fraction that didn't exist a few years ago. Because selling online is so new, companies are just beginning to figure out the best ways to do it and how to make money at it (see Exhibit C.7). In addition to selling products directly to customers, companies are making money from referral fees, service and pay-per use charges, advertising, online subscriptions, and license fees. For example, www.1-800-Flowers.com adds a service charge to a customer's bill that varies according to the price of the order. Others such as insurance carriers charge companies a license fee to become a member of their referral network.[23]

COMPANY	ADDRESS	INDUSTRY
DoubleClick	www.doubleclick.com	Advertising
eBay	www.ebay.com	Auctions
AutoByTel	www.autobytel.com	Auto retailing
Amazon	www.amazon.com	Books
Monster	www.monster.com	Employment
1-800-Flowers	www.1800flowers.com	Flowers
Webvan	www.webvan.com	Groceries
Yahoo!	www.yahoo.com	Information
CDNow	www.cdnow.com	Music
CNBC	www.cnbc.com	News
iPrint	www.iprint.com	Printing
E*Trade	www.etrade.com	Stock brokerage
eToys	www.etoys.com	Toys
Travelocity	www.travelocity.com	Travel reservations

EXHIBIT C·7

E-COMMERCE SUCCESSES

Without the Internet, these companies would not exist.

What Is the Difference Between E-Commerce and E-Business?

As discussed earlier, e-commerce is the buying and selling of goods and services over electronic networks. An **electronic business (e-business)** uses Internet technology to do much more than set up a Web site to sell or deliver goods. An e-business takes full advantage of Internet technology to transform its key business processes in order to maximize customer value. E-commerce is indeed an important part of becoming an e-business, but it is only one step of the evolutionary process.

How a Typical E-Business Evolves   Typically, a company moves through three distinct stages to become an e-business:[24]

• *Stage 1: The e-aware company.* The company feels a sense of urgency about the Internet. It launches a Web site, provides information to prospective customers and other interested parties, and then wonders what to do next. It has not yet developed specific e-commerce strategies; nor has it addressed the internal structural or cultural changes that must be made to transact e-commerce successfully (see "Living with the E-Cultures of Hype and Craft" on page 210).

- *Stage 2: The e-launch company.* The company begins to sell goods over the Internet and begins making some noticeable changes: It shifts to a paperless order-to-delivery process; it rapidly acknowledges the profound opportunity e-commerce offers; and it develops some new strategies and makes operational changes to take advantage of these opportunities.

- *Stage 3: The e-organization.* The company's e-commerce vision is now apparent to all employees and business partners. An entrepreneurial culture takes root and knowledge is shared freely throughout the organization and at all levels, facilitated by intranets and extranets. Business units seamlessly access needed resources from both inside and outside the organization. The company adopts a flexible and efficient organizational structure and begins to integrate technology into every part of the company's operation. It reorganizes the company's operation, creating a fundamentally new enterprise and making "e" such a core part of its business operation that the difference between "e" and everything else is nonexistent (see "Seven Habits of Highly Effective E-Managers" on page 136).

In short, visionary companies understand that they must radically change their current systems and operations to meet the challenges of doing business in the e-commerce era. To become an e-business, they must develop systems and structures that facilitate the company's ability to innovate constantly, react rapidly, and handle dynamic change. The company begins the transformation process by asking some difficult questions. Then it uses the answers to those questions to reinvent the enterprise one piece at a time, as Exhibit C.8 suggests.[25]

The Role of Technology in the Evolution Process   In an e-business, technology is no longer an afterthought in the strategic process but the actual driver. A company evolves into an e-business by integrating technology and the Internet into every phase of the business process—production, marketing, sales, customer support, advertising, public relations, and more—with one goal in mind: to meet customers' changing needs and priorities.[26]

Earlier in this chapter we discussed the importance of data mining and effective information management. In Chapter 8 we discussed how companies are using technology to streamline the production process and improve operating deficiencies. And in Chapter 13 we discussed the importance of technology in physical distribution. Running a successful e-business means seamlessly coordinating all of these processes so that they are transparent to the customer.

Studies show that companies that have woven technology and the Internet into every part of their operations are more successful in transacting e-commerce.[27] Look at Amazon, for example. The company started with two employees in a rundown Seattle warehouse, grew revenues in just three short years to more than $600 million, and outmaneuvered the two industry gorillas, Barnes & Noble and Borders Books & Music.[28] Here's how they did it.

To create a satisfying shopping experience, Amazon created an e-retail infrastructure to meets its customers' needs. Amazon's Web site includes author interviews, sales information, customized book recommendations, instant order confirmation, editorial analysis, sample chapters, and more. If a customer inquires about an out-of-print book, the special orders department contacts suppliers to check availability and, if a copy is located, notifies the customer by e-mail for price approval. As Chapter 13 discussed, Amazon's order fulfillment process is built around state-of-the art, high-tech distribution centers that operate seamlessly with the company's Web site. As a result, Amazon can provide a level of customer service that is unprecedented in the book retailing industry.[29]

Still, providing end-to-end process integration is a huge undertaking. *Fortune* magazine reports that fewer than 10 percent of e-business strategies are effectively executed. Moreover, for a business to become a successful e-business it must not only meet the needs and priorities of its customers, but it must anticipate and prepare for the unexpected.[30] Consider the debacle online auctioneer eBay faced in June 1999 when its computers went down for 22 hours. Such outage was the cyber equivalent of hanging a huge "closed" sign on eBay's front door. Ebay was unprepared for such a major technological failure, even though its entire business operation depends on functioning computer systems. The event cost eBay an estimated $3 million to $5 million in potential revenue, drove down its stock price by 9 percent, and created a round of unimaginable headaches—not to mention a huge public embarrassment.[31]

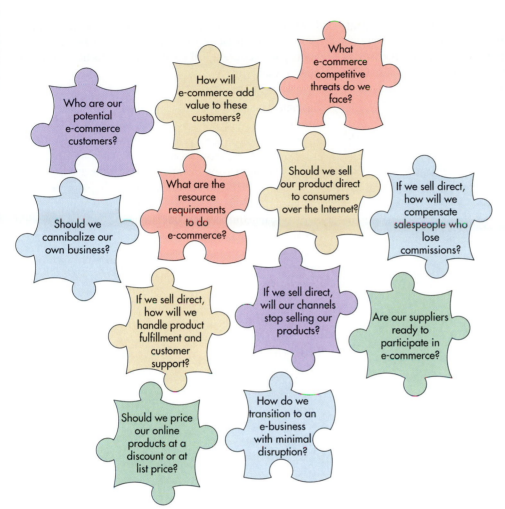

EXHIBIT C·8

BECOMING AN E-BUSINESS

Puzzled by what it takes to become an e-business? So are many of today's leading companies. Experts advise companies to start the transformation process by asking the right questions and by making sure they have all the right pieces. Then it's a matter of trial and error until everything fits in the right place.

What Is Driving the Growth of E-Commerce?

The Internet (the backbone of electronic commerce), faster computers, and faster connections via high-speed modems and cable lines are binding consumers and companies in a low-cost way just as the inventions of the steam engine, electricity, and the telephone did. Affordable technology facilitates the growth of electronic commerce by making it accessible to more and more people. Additionally, the costs to build a Web site and transact business electronically can be relatively small when compared to setting up a physical site and stocking it with inventory. As a result, just about any company can enter the electronic marketplace.

As more and more businesses set up shop on the Web, competition increases. In some cases, it even forces reluctant traditional businesses to migrate their business to the Web. Barnesandnoble.com is a perfect example of a traditional chain that was forced to sell books online because of the rapid consumer acceptance and enthusiasm for online book retailer Amazon. Nevertheless, most companies today aren't being forced into electronic commerce. Instead, they're marching into cyberspace willingly and at unprecedented speeds because e-commerce offers substantial benefits to both companies and consumers (see "Is the End of the Beginning Near?" on page 112).

Company Benefits   Two of the biggest benefits driving companies into the e-commerce arena are cost savings and new growth opportunities.

Cost Savings   As more and more manufacturers watch their profit margins get squeezed, they are seeking ways to cut their distribution, operating, and inventory costs.

Electronic commerce can reduce publishing, printing, marketing, selling, and customer support costs. Although designing and creating online catalogs can be as costly as creating a print catalog, the variable costs to distribute electronic catalogs are negligible. This is true whether the online catalog is viewed by one potential customer or millions. Similarly, although the electronic processing of customer orders is not free, it too can be done at a fraction of the cost of doing business with traditional paper-based and labor-intensive processes. Dell Computer reports that prior to its Web site launch, customers called an average of once or twice per purchase to check on the status of their orders. Now with online order tracing, customers check their order status electronically instead of calling a customer service rep. This reduces Dell's costs significantly.[32]

New Growth Opportunities   CEOs everywhere are facing shareholder demands for double-digit revenue growth, no matter what business they're in. Many companies have already reengineered, downsized, and cut costs. Now they are focusing on generating additional revenue. But it is becoming increasingly difficult for retailers in particular to expand their market share in the crowded physical marketplace. Shifting attention to the new Internet markets gives retailers a chance to redefine their market shares. This new opportunity comes from (1) creating new online markets for existing products, (2) creating new products specifically designed for online markets, and (3) expanding existing or new products into international markets.[33]

CDW, a leading seller of computer equipment and computer supplies, launched its e-commerce Web site in 1998. Today the Web site gets over 400,000 hits daily and generates well over $20 million annually in e-commerce sales.

If you are a small company, electronic commerce makes it economically feasible to expand your market reach beyond your geographical location and into new locations and new customer segments.

Customer Benefits   While companies are flocking to the Internet to expand their sales and cut costs, at the same time they are recognizing that e-commerce is a valuable tool for servicing customers, building customer relationships, and increasing customer loyalty. As a result, customers stand to gain as much, and perhaps more, from e-commerce than companies do. Because informed consumers can compare products and prices from a wide range of suppliers, faster and more easily than ever before, the producer-consumer relationship has turned upside down, putting today's consumers in an unprecedented position of control.[34]

Power Shift to Customers   The Internet is an empowerment tool, providing customers with options they never had before—countless brands from which to choose, searchable databases, personalized attention, shipping options, built-to-order merchandise, instant access to information, auction items, and more. With a click of the mouse, American Airlines' customers can plan and price trips, purchase tickets, receive travel confirmations, review current reservations, and review the status of their AAdvantage mileage rewards accounts.

Similarly, Auto-By-Tel has revolutionized the way cars are bought and sold. Prior to the Internet, consumers had no way of knowing actual dealer invoice price, dealer rebates, and other purchasing incentives. Many car dealers liked it that way. After all, ill-informed prospects are easily manipulated whereas educated buyers are not. Today prospective car buyers walk into car dealerships with printouts of dealer invoice prices. They know what dealers pay for cars and they don't let dealers make big profits.[35] What does this new process mean for traditional car companies? As Robert Eaton, past co-chairman of Daimler-Chrysler put it, "The customer is going to grab control of the process, and we are all going to salute smartly and do exactly what the customer tells us if we want to stay in business."[36]

So what exactly do e-commerce customers want besides affordable prices? Here's just a few of their demands:[37]

- *Give me what I want when I need it and don't waste my time.* Most of today's online shoppers are time deprived and usually come to a Web site with a specific purpose in mind. This is true of both

iPrint, the leading online print shop, makes it easy for Internet users of any level to design and order personalized print products via the Internet 24 hours a day, 365 days a year. The site features a full collection of design templates, type styles, features, and colors.

businesses and individual consumers. To them, visiting Web sites is about getting a job done—not cruising. Customers want companies to anticipate and offer what they need in one cohesive experience. They want one-stop shopping and better integration among order entry, fulfillment, and delivery.

- *Give me meaningful content.* Customers want engaging content—not propaganda. Productive Web sites offer practical information such as pricing, product specifications, quick and easy access to technical support, and comparative information. Users will "click away" if the content does not hold their attention and empower them with useful information.

- *Don't exploit me.* Many people resent having to register at Web sites and give companies personal information—such as income, age, education, and address—especially if this information is irrelevant to the task at hand. Customers become angry when companies misuse this personal information to send them unsolicited junk e-mail, know as **spam,** or sell that information to third parties.

- *Let me take care of myself.* E-commerce is a big enabler of self-service. Today's market leaders are giving customers the means to serve themselves whenever possible. At Gateway's Web site, for example, customers can assess their computer needs, configure and price an order, pay for new systems, and get limited technical support—without even talking to a person. Online stock trading is another example of self-service. Companies such as E*Trade and eSchwab make it easy for customers to buy and sell stock without the help of a broker.[38]

- *Make the experience entertaining.* In addition to information, customers want entertainment. Marriott is introducing sophisticated multimedia capabilities into its Web site to give potential guests and travel planners a visual experience of a property including views of the lobby and other facilities. Marriott has found that the more interactive a site is, the more business activity it gets from its visitors. A dynamic Web site creates more bookings and more business. In addition to multimedia, companies such as Marriott are offering customers an opportunity to share their product or service experiences or common interests with others via chat rooms and discussion groups. "We've gone from monologue to dialogue in our Web site. Now we need to move from dialogue to forum," says Mike Pusateri, Marriott's head of interactive sales and marketing.[39]

- *Answer my questions.* Consumers want companies to answer their questions in real time. By some estimates, two-thirds of shoppers abandon their electronic "shopping cart" in the middle of a transaction. Studies show that shoppers often terminate the transaction because they are unable to ask a question that arises at the moment of a sale. For example, they may have questions about return policies, using their credit cards, or complimentary products and services. They become frustrated when there is no one to answer their questions when they need help.

Lands' End clearly understands that making customer service easy, friendly, and convenient is one of the most important trends in business today. Recently, the company introduced Lands' End Live, a feature which allows customers to immediately engage a customer service representative in an electronic or phone conversation. The service reps, known as personal shoppers, can answer customer questions, solve problems, and even make suggestions about appropriate merchandise—all in real time. Customers who click the Lands' End Live button are immediately trading e-mail messages (chatting) with a personal shopper. If they prefer to talk on the phone, they simply tell the rep and he or she will call them back.

At the Lands' End Web site, customers can get more than answers to their questions. Personal shoppers also recommend additional products that match customers' preferences. They can even split the computer screen and display apparel combinations (such as a shirt and tie) to help the customer make a decision.

Personalized Treatment   Where companies used to rely on differentiating their products and services to gain a competitive edge, now more and more companies are competing by differentiating the customer experience, making it more personal and compelling. By using the Internet to gather customer data, smart companies are learning how to anticipate what individual customers are likely to purchase next, and then deliver exactly what the customer wants.[40]

Powerful, new technologies give companies the ability to interact with customers, remember customer preferences and priorities, capture insights about customers in great detail, and calculate customers' profitability and future potential. Using customer relationship management software, companies build sophisticated but easily accessible customer profiles and share these data throughout the organization. Now salespeople, marketers, and service representatives all have access to a single, unified view of the customer.[41]

Over time, these customer profiles allow a Web site to greet each user by name, serve up personalized marketing messages, create Web pages that display products and services that suit the customer's specific requirements, and even present specific segments of a company's catalog instead of requiring the customer to sift through thousands of pages. Customers benefit from such personalized

treatment by saving time and finding solutions that better meet their needs.[42]

Hot Topics and Issues in E-Commerce and E-Business

Electronic commerce may be a merchant's and consumer's dream, but once the Web site is up and running, companies must confront a variety of hot topics and issues as they begin to do business in the e-world. These hot topics and issues include channel management, security, privacy, pricing strategies, and legal issues—to name a few.

Channel Management   The Internet presents an opportunity for the producer to sell directly to the consumer. But the decision to modify the traditional channel structure is a critical one, and it has consequences unique to each situation. Many dealers and distributors are up in arms about the possibility of being cut out of the picture and are seeking ways to protect themselves. Automobile dealers have threatened manufacturers with boycotts as a result of direct car sales by some dealers over the Internet.[43]

As discussed in Chapter 13, some producers are using the Internet to eliminate the middleman; others are using it to restructure their distribution structures to make them more cost-effective; still others are using the Internet to expand their reach. Herman Miller, an office furniture manufacturer, uses the Internet to target the home-office market, a segment that its dealer network wasn't servicing. The company sees this as a terrific opportunity for both the supplier and the distributor. It hopes that home-office customers will eventually grow into corporate accounts (typically serviced by dealers).[44] Funjet, a vacation vendor, also creates a compelling online presence without undermining the role of its travel agents. Funjet uses its Web site to advertise its charter vacations and provide potential customers with enough information so they can plan and price their trips. To book the trip, however, customers must still use an authorized travel agent.[45]

Security   Before computers, a typical company conducted the vast majority of its business on paper. Important files and documents were kept under lock and key, and when something was sent to someone across the office or in another part of the country, security precautions were almost always used. Furthermore, only a limited number of people had access to vital company data. But today's move from paper-based systems to electronic data management poses a real threat to corporate security.[46]

Global networks increase the possibility that crucial information sent over the Internet can fall into the wrong hands. Recently, a group of scientists claimed to have broken an international security code used to protect millions of daily e-mail messages and credit card transactions transmitted over the Internet.[47] Although *cyberterrorism*—orchestrated attacks on a company's information systems for political or economic purposes—is indeed a very real threat, an even greater security threat is a company network without proper safeguards. Vulnerable networks can become a high-tech sieve that lets crooks steal or destroy sensitive data. That's because digital data are far easier to duplicate and disseminate. Furthermore, a PC without the proper password protections can easily become a fountain of insider information.

Consider this: According to one recent study, 75 percent of companies have suffered financial losses from fraud, theft of proprietary information, and sabotage as a result of breaches in computer security. The study also found that the biggest threat typically comes from inside the organization. Violators include laid-off workers, contractors, consultants, and even good employees who inadvertently destroy, alter, or expose critical data.[48]

Computer viruses, hidden programs that can work their way into computer systems and erase or corrupt data and programs, also pose a major security threat in the workplace. Computer viruses behave much like human viruses by invisibly attaching themselves to any computer data or programs that come into contact with them. Viruses can be spread by diskettes, electronic bulletin boards, or computer networks, including the Internet. There is no way to entirely stop the spread of computer viruses because new ones are created all the time. However, a number of excellent "vaccine" programs exist that

search for and destroy viruses and prevent new ones from infecting your computer system.

To reduce the chances of sabotage, companies today are taking these steps: screening all programs and files before they are loaded onto computers; scanning existing hardware and software for new computer viruses; providing employees with ongoing data security education; conducting background checks on all new employees; and establishing security policies that at a minimum encourage employees to use passwords, turn computer systems off when not in use, and rely on encryption when sending sensitive e-mail.

Privacy Invasions of privacy can take various forms on the Internet: Unwanted e-mail fills electronic mailboxes to the brim; Web sites place electronic bits of data on a visitor's computer called a **cookie** to obtain a visitor's e-mail address and monitor which parts of a Web site he or she looks at, and more; employers legally monitor the Web sites employees access from a company computer and the content of their company e-mail or voice-mail messages.

In addition to these privacy issues, many companies are learning the hard way that e-mail and voice mail can be used as evidence in court cases. Moreover, deleting e-mail from a company computer does not erase the record. Electronic postings and other archived matter from the Internet and company network are preserved on network backup storage devices long after they've been deleted from an employee's computer. Thus, companies are advising employees not to say anything in e-mail or voice mail that they would not want to see published in the *New York Times.*[49]

For a closer look at Internet privacy and security, and other e-commerce hot topics such as online pricing strategies and emerging legal issues, consult this text's online supplement *E-Business in Action* at http://www.prenhall.com/ebusinessinaction.

Test Your Knowledge

QUESTIONS FOR REVIEW

1. Would employee records be considered data or information? Explain your answer.
2. Besides the World Wide Web, what else resides on the Internet?
3. What are some of the key benefits of company intranets?
4. What are some of the information challenges companies are facing in the Information Age?
5. What are the demands of today's e-commerce customers?

QUESTIONS FOR ANALYSIS

6. What are some of the ways to improve database searching?
7. What is the difference between e-commerce and e-business?
8. What is driving the growth of e-commerce?
9. Why do today's customers have more power in the relationship between buyers and sellers?
10. When constructing a Web site, is it ethical to use the same design features and functions you find on another company's Web site?

QUESTIONS FOR APPLICATION

11. Your instructor has given you the assignment to write a research paper on the topic "advantages and disadvantages of franchising." Using the Internet as a resource:

    a. What are some key words and phrases you might use in your search strategy?

    b. Using Boolean operators, how might you narrow your search?

    c. Which wildcards might you use and how?

12. Select a well-known e-commerce Web site and using Exhibit C.6 as a guide, answer these questions:

    a. What kinds of product and company information does the Web site provide customers?

    b. What information does the Web site ask customers to provide about themselves?

    c. Describe some of the features the site includes to facilitate the product ordering process. (Example: Can you check the status of your order? Does the site advise you if the product is out of stock?)

    d. How does the Web site provide customers with assistance if they have a question or concern?

13. Using some of the examples cited throughout this text, explain how the Internet is transforming the way companies communicate and do business.

14. How can companies use databases and the Internet to learn more about their customers and build stronger relationships with them?

Chapter Glossary

application software Programs that perform specific functions for users, such as word processing or spreadsheet analysis

artificial intelligence Ability of computers to reason, to learn, and to simulate human sensory perceptions

bookmark A browser feature that places selected URLs in a file for quick access, allowing you to automatically return to the Web site by clicking on the site's name

Boolean operators From a system of logical thought developed by the English mathematician George Boole, it uses the operators AND, OR, and NOT in Internet searches

browser Software, such as Netscape Navigator or Microsoft's Internet Explorer, that enables a computer to search for, display, and download the multimedia information that appears on the World Wide Web

business-to-business e-commerce Electronic commerce that involves transactions between companies and their suppliers, manufacturers, or other companies

business-to-consumer e-commerce Electronic commerce that involves transactions between businesses and the end user or consumer

chat A form of interactive communication that enables computer users in separate locations to have real-time conversations; usually takes place at Web sites called chat rooms

chief information officer (CIO) Top corporate executive with responsibility for managing information and information systems

computer viruses Computer programs that can work their way into a computer system and erase or corrupt data or programs

cookie A text file that is stored on a visitor's computer to identify each time the user visits the Web site; the cookie can contain data about subscriptions and memberships to online services and other information

data Recorded facts and statistics; data need to be converted to information before they can help people solve business problems

database management Creating, storing, maintaining, rearranging, and retrieving the contents of databases

databases Collection of related data that can be cross-referenced in order to extract information

data mining Sifting through huge amounts of data to identify what is valuable to a specific question or problem

data warehousing Building an organized central database out of files and databases gathered from various functional areas, such as marketing, operations, and accounting

decision support system (DSS) Information system that uses decision models, specialized databases, and artificial intelligence to assist managers in solving highly unstructured and nonroutine problems

desktop publishing (DTP) Ability to prepare documents using computerized typesetting and graphics-processing capabilities

discussion mailing lists E-mail lists that allow people to discuss a common interest by posting messages, which are received by everyone in the group

domain name The portion of an Internet address that identifies the host and indicates the type of organization it is

download Transmitting a file from one computer system to another; on the Internet, bringing data from the Internet into your computer

electronic business (e-business) A company that has transformed its key business processes to incorporate Internet technology into every phase of the operation

e-mail Communication system that enables computers to transmit and receive written messages over electronic networks

executive information system (EIS) Similar to decision support system but customized to strategic needs of executives

expert system Computer system that simulates the thought processes of a human expert who is adept at solving particular problems

extranet   Similar to an intranet but extending the network to select people outside the organization

file transfer protocol (FTP)   A software protocol that lets you copy or move files from a remote computer—called an FTP site—to your computer over the Internet; it is the Internet facility for downloading and uploading files

firewall   Computer hardware and software that protect part or all of a private computer network attached to the Internet by preventing public Internet users from accessing it

graphical user interface (GUI)   A user-friendly program that enables computer operators to enter commands by clicking on icons and menus with a mouse

hardware   Physical components of a computer system, including integrated circuits, keyboards, and disk drives

homepage   The primary Web site for an organization or individual; the first hypertext document displayed on a Web site

hyperlink   A highlighted word or image on a Web page or document that automatically allows people to move to another Web page or document when clicked on with a mouse

hypertext markup language (HTML)   The software language used to create, present, and link pages on the World Wide Web

hypertext transfer protocol (HTTP)   A communications protocol that allows people to navigate among documents or pages linked by hypertext and to download pages from the World Wide Web

Internet   A worldwide collection of interconnected networks that enables users to share information electronically and provides digital access to a wide variety of services

Internet service provider (ISP)   A company that provides access to the Internet, usually for a monthly fee, via telephone lines or cable; ISPs can be local companies or specialists such as America Online

intranet   A private network, set up within a corporation or organization, that operates over the Internet and may be used to link geographically remote sites

local area network (LAN)   Computer network that encompasses a small area, such as an office or a university campus

management information system (MIS)   Computer system that supplies information to assist in managerial decision making

modem   Hardware device that allows a computer to communicate over a regular telephone line

multimedia   Typically used to mean the combination of more than one presentation medium—such as text, sound, graphics, and video

network   Collection of computers, communications software, and transmission media (such as telephone lines) that allows computers to communicate

search engines   Internet tools for finding Web sites on the topics of your choice

software   Programmed instructions that drive the activity of computer hardware

spam   Unsolicited e-mail; from the sender's point of view, it's a form of bulk mail, to the receiver it seems like junk e-mail

spreadsheet   Program that organizes and manipulates data in a row-column matrix

Telnet   A way to access someone else's computer (the host computer), and to use it as if it were right on your desk

uniform resource locator (URL)   Web address that gives the exact location of an Internet resource

upload   To send a file from your computer to a server or host system

Usenet newsgroups   One or more discussion groups on the Internet in which people with similar interests can post articles and reply to messages

Web site   A related collection of files on the World Wide Web

wide area network (WAN)   Computer network that encompasses a large geographic area

World Wide Web (WWW)   A hypertext-based system for finding and accessing Internet resources such as text, graphics, sound, and other multimedia resources

PART VII VIDEO CASE

Focusing on Special Topics in Business

Learning Objectives

1. Become familiar with some of the legal issues affecting small businesses.
2. See how insurance can help a company manage various risks.
3. Understand the role of computers and the Internet in the operation of a small business.

Background Information

Companies such as Blausen Medical Communications (BMC), which sell to customers in other countries, must be familiar with a variety of domestic and international laws and regulations. In turn, they are protected by statutory law governing commerce, administrative law regulating business practices, common law covering litigation, and business law affecting business activities. BMC and many other firms are also concerned about protecting intellectual property such as illustrations. In addition, owners and managers seek to protect company assets through appropriate financial and risk management strategies. And every business, regardless of size, is looking at ways to harness technology and the Internet to manage information more effectively.

The Video

Bruce Blausen, BMC's founder, uses contracts to protect his company's intellectual property by licensing, not selling, his copyrighted medical images. This allows Blausen to maintain complete control over where and when BMC's images are used. He shifts his risk of loss by carrying four types of insurance: key-person insurance on Blausen; property insurance on the BMC building and contents, health insurance for employees, and equipment insurance on expensive equipment. Technology plays a major role in BMC's daily operations. Not only are images and animations produced and stored electronically, but the company depends heavily on the Internet and e-mail for contact with out-of-town customers. Blausen has several techniques for securing his company's data, including regular use of virus detection software and separate passwords for individual computer systems and files.

Discussion Questions

1. In a typical BMC contract, what consideration would be offered by the company? What consideration would be offered by the customer?
2. Why is it important for BMC to buy key-person insurance for founder Bruce Blausen?
3. Why is Blausen so concerned about data security? In addition to running virus protection programs and using passwords for confidential files, what other measures might he take to safeguard BMC data files?

Next Steps

As BMC expands, Bruce Blausen may want to change his risk management strategies. One possibility is self-insurance. What advantages and disadvantages should Blausen consider before self-insuring against risk? Another approach is minimizing the chance of a particular loss. What loss prevention measures might Blausen take to guard against loss of property (tangible and intangible) and loss of income?

■ LEARN MORE ONLINE

BMC is concerned about unauthorized use of its animations and other proprietary images. One way BMC prevents potential problems is by clearly marking its work as copyrighted. Look at the copyright notices on BMC's homepage and on the Products page. What, exactly, is BMC protecting? What is it prohibiting by posting these notices? Now go to the copyright page at Yahoo! and read how that site guards the intellectual property rights of others. Under what circumstances might BMC have to follow these steps to contact Yahoo! officials?

http://www.imagesofhealth.com/start.html (BMC site)
http://docs.yahoo.com/info/copyright/copyright.html (Yahoo! copyright page)

THE EMPLOYMENT SEARCH

■ THINKING ABOUT YOUR CAREER

Getting the job that's right for you takes more than sending out a few letters and signing up with the college placement office. Planning and research are important if you want to find a company and a position that suit you. Before you limit your job search to a particular industry or functional specialty, analyze what you have to offer and what you hope to get from your work. Then you can identify employers who are likely to want you and vice versa.

What Do You Have to Offer?

What are your marketable skills? You can analyze them in three steps.

First, jot down ten achievements you're proud of, such as learning to ski, taking a prizewinning photo, tutoring a child, or editing the school paper. Look carefully at each of these achievements. What specific skills did they demand? For example, leadership skills, speaking ability, and artistic talent may have helped you coordinate a winning presentation to the college administration. As you analyze your achievements, you'll begin to recognize a pattern of skills. Which of them might be valuable to potential employers?

Second, look at your educational preparation, work experience, and extracurricular activities. What kinds of jobs are you qualified to do on the basis of your knowledge and experience? What have you learned from volunteer work or class projects that could benefit you on the job? Have you held any offices, won any awards or scholarships, or mastered a second language?

Third, take stock of your personal characteristics so that you can determine the type of job you'll do best. Are you aggressive, a born leader, or would you rather follow? Are you outgoing, articulate, great with people, or do you prefer working alone? Make a list of what you believe are your four or five most important qualities.

For help with figuring out your interests and capabilities, consult your college placement office or career guidance center. Many schools administer tests designed to help you identify your interests, aptitudes, and personality traits. Although these tests won't reveal the "perfect" job for you, they'll help you focus on the types of work that best suit your personality. (Consult Part VIII of the *E-Business in Action* online supplement at http://www.prenhall.com/ebusinessinaction for links to a number of online job-hunting resources and self-assessment tests.)

What Do You Want to Do?

Knowing what you *can* do is one thing. Knowing what you *want* to do is another. Don't lose sight of your own values. Discover the things that will bring you satisfaction and happiness on the job.

- *Decide what you'd like to do every day.* Talk to people in various occupations. You might consult relatives, local businesses, or former graduates (through your school's alumni relations office). Read about various occupations. Start with your college library or placement office. One of the liveliest books aimed at college students is Lisa Birnbach's *Going to Work.* Another useful source is the 13-volume *Career Information Center* encyclopedia of jobs and careers. Also consider how much independence you want on the job, how much variety you like, and whether you prefer to work with products, machines, people, ideas, figures, or some combination. Do you like physical work, mental work, or a mix? Constant change or predictable routine?

- *Establish some specific compensation targets.* What do you hope to earn in your first year on the job?

What kind of pay increase do you expect each year? What's your ultimate earnings goal? Would you be comfortable with a job that pays on commission, or would you prefer a steady paycheck? What occupations offer the kind of money you're looking for? Are these occupations realistic for someone with your qualifications? Are you willing to settle for less money in order to do something you really love? Consider where you'd like to start, where you'd like to go, and the ultimate position you'd like to attain. How soon after joining the company would you like to receive your first promotion? Your next one? What additional training or preparation will you need to achieve them?

• *Consider the type of work environment you'd prefer.* Think in broad terms about the size and type of operation you find appealing, the location you prefer, the facilities you envision, and especially the corporate culture you're most comfortable with. Do you like the idea of working for a small, entrepreneurial operation or a large company? A profit-making company or a nonprofit organization? A service business or a manufacturing operation? Do you want a predictable work schedule or flexible, varied hours? Would you enjoy a seasonally varied job such as education (which may give you summers off) or retailing (with its selling cycles)? Would you like to work in a city, a suburb, a small town, or an industrial area? Do you favor a particular part of the country or a country abroad? Do you like working indoors or outdoors? Is it important to you to work in an attractive place, or will simple, functional quarters suffice? Do you need a quiet office to work effectively, or can you concentrate in a noisy, open setting? Is access to public transportation or freeways important? Would you be happy in a well-defined hierarchy, where roles and reporting relationships are clear, or would you prefer a less structured situation? What qualities do you want in a boss? Are you looking for a paternalistic organization or one that fosters individualism? Do you like a competitive environment or one that rewards teamwork?

SEEKING EMPLOYMENT OPPORTUNITIES AND INFORMATION

Whether your major is business, biology, or political science, once you know what you have to offer and what you want, you can start finding an employer to match. If you haven't already committed yourself to any particular career field, review Appendix 2, "Careers in Business," and other sources of employment information to find out where the job opportunities are. Which industries are strong? Which parts of the country are booming, and which specific job categories offer the best prospects for the future?

Sources of Employment Information

Begin your job search by reviewing professional and trade journals in the career fields that interest you. Talk to people in these fields. You may be able to network with executives in your field by joining or participating in student business organizations, especially those with ties to real-world organizations such as the American Marketing Association or the American Management Association.

Keep abreast of business and financial news by subscribing to a major newspaper and scanning the business pages every day. Watch television programs that focus on business, such as *Wall Street Week*. You can find information about the future for specific jobs in *The Dictionary of Occupational Titles* (U.S. Employment Service), *Occupational Outlook Handbook* (U.S. Bureau of Labor Statistics), and the employment publications of Science Research Associates.

Once you've identified a promising career field, compile a list of specific organizations that appeal to you. Consult directories of employers such as *The College Placement Annual* and *Career: The Annual Guide to Business Opportunities*. Write to selected companies and ask for an annual report and any descriptive brochures or newsletters. Check to see if the organization you're interested in maintains a Web site. Such Web sites generally include a company profile, press releases, financial information, and employment opportunities. If possible, visit some of the organizations on your list, contact their human resources departments, or talk with key employees.

You can find ads for specific job openings by looking in local and major newspapers and by visiting your college placement office. Of course, a source of growing importance to your job search is the World Wide Web. An increasing number of large and small companies are posting job openings on the Internet.

Employment Information on the Web

The World Wide Web offers an amazing amount of employment information.[1] Is the Web the answer to all your employment dreams? Perhaps . . . or perhaps not. But as the Web grows, the employment information it provides is constantly expanding. For helpful hints and useful Web addresses, you can consult innumerable books such as *What Color Is Your Parachute?* by Richard Nelson Bolles.

When you're dealing with the Internet, the one thing you can count on is rapid change. Using the Web effectively in your job search will depend on how well you prepare your job-search strategy, how many employers (especially in your field) accept the Web as a source of potential employees, and how quickly current resources expand and adapt to the ever-changing Web environment. The Web offers information not only from employers seeking applicants but also from people seeking work. You can use the World Wide Web for a variety of job-seeking tasks:

- *Finding career counseling.* Use the Web to analyze your skills and work expectations. For example, begin your self-assessment with the *Keirsey Temperament Sorter II,* an online personality test at http://keirsey.com/. The Web offers job-seeking pointers and counseling from online career centers, many of which are run by colleges and universities. Make sure the advice you get is useful and sensible, since some career centers are commercial sites. One good commercial site is Monster.com: The Job-smart Coach at http://campus.monster.com/experts/bradley.

- *Making contacts.* Use the Web to locate and communicate with potential employers. One way to locate people is through Usenet newsgroups dedicated to your field of interest. Newsgroup members can leave and send messages on an electronic bulletin board. You might also try listservs (or Internet mailing lists). These discussion groups mail each message to every member's e-mail address. Commercial systems such as Prodigy, America Online, and CompuServe have their own special interest discussion groups (called Special Interest Groups, RoundTables, Clubs, Forums, or Bulletin Boards). E-mail allows you to communicate quickly and nonintrusively for requesting information or contacting a potential employer.

- *Researching companies.* By visiting a company's Web site, you can find out its mission, products, annual reports, employee benefits, and job openings. You can locate company Web sites through URLs (Web addresses), links from other sites, or search engines such as Alta Vista, Lycos, Yahoo!, or Excite.

- *Searching for job vacancies.* Many Web sites list job openings from multiple companies. Popular online indexes include Job Trak (which partners with 750 college campuses nationwide and specializes in entry-level jobs), Online Career Center (which specializes in engineering, health care, and business resources), Career Mosaic, America's Job Bank, CareerPath, and The Monster Board. Some allow you to search by region, industry, job title, company, skills, or requirements.

- *Posting your résumé online.* You can post your résumé online either through an index service or on your own homepage. To post your résumé on an index service, you'll need to adapt it to an electronic format and transmit it by mail, fax, modem, or e-mail (see "Adapting Your Résumé to an Electronic Format" later in this chapter). Once your information is input into the service's database, your résumé will be sent to any employers whose requests match key words in your information. Posting your résumé on your own homepage allows you to retain a nicer-looking format. You can even include sound or video clips and links to papers you've written or recommendations you've received.

Using the World Wide Web to find employment allows you to respond directly to job postings (without going through recruiters), post résumés (tailored to match the skills and qualifications necessary to fill a particular position), send résumés through e-mail (which is faster and less expensive than printing and mailing them), send focused cover letters directly to the executives doing the hiring, and quickly gain detailed information about prospective employers. Moreover, most campus placement offices are retooling to help you take advantage of Web opportunities. Still, experts claim that at least 10 million U.S. employers don't think of the Internet when it's time to hire. In short, the Web cannot replace other techniques for finding employment; it's just one more tool in your overall strategy.

For any job, your ultimate goal is an interview with potential employers. The fastest way to obtain an interview is to get a referral from someone you know. In fact, many companies pay their employees handsome referral bonuses if they recommend a candidate who subsequently is hired and stays for a designated period of time.[2] Some organizations recruit students for job openings by sending representatives to college campuses for interviews, usually coordinated by the campus placement office. Employers also recruit candidates through campus publications and the employment bureaus operated by some trade associations. Unsolicited résumés can also be vital for obtaining interviews. Most companies will keep unsolicited résumés on file or scan them into a database.[3]

■ PREPARING YOUR RÉSUMÉ

A **résumé** is a structured, written summary of a person's education, employment background, and job qualifications. It's a form of advertising, designed to stimulate an employer's interest in meeting you and learning more about you. A good résumé inspires the prospective employer to pick up the phone and ask you to come in for an interview. Your objective in writing your résumé is to create interest rather than tell everything about yourself. If hints leave the reader wanting more, a potential employer will have more reasons to reach for the phone.

Build the reader's interest by calling attention to your best features and downplaying your weaknesses, without distorting or misrepresenting the facts.[4] A good résumé conveys seven specific qualities that employers seek. It shows that a candidate (1) thinks in terms of results, (2) knows how to get things done, (3) is well-rounded, (4) shows signs of progress, (5) has personal standards of excellence, (6) is flexible and willing to try new things, and (7) possesses strong communication skills. As you put your résumé together, think about how the format, style, and content convey these seven qualities.

Controlling the Format and Style

A typical recruiter devotes less than 45 seconds to each résumé before tossing it into either the "maybe" or the "reject" pile. In fact, most recruiters scan rather than read a résumé from top to bottom. If your résumé doesn't *look* sharp, and if you don't grab the reader's interest in the first few lines, chances are nobody will read it carefully enough to judge your qualifications.

To give your résumé a sharp look, use a clean typeface on high-grade, letter-size bond paper (in white or some light earth tone). Make sure that your stationery and envelope match. Leave ample margins all around, and be certain any corrections are unnoticeable. Avoid italic typefaces, which can be difficult to read, and use a quality laser printer.

In general, try to write a one-page résumé. If you have a great deal of experience and are applying for a higher-level position, you may prepare a somewhat longer résumé. Give yourself enough space to present a persuasive, accurate portrait of your skills and accomplishments.

Lay out your résumé so that the information is easy to grasp.[5] Break up the text with headings that call attention to various aspects of your background, such as work experience and education. Underline or capitalize key points, or set them off in the left margin. Use indented lists to itemize your most important qualifications. Leave plenty of white space, even if you're forced to use two pages. Pay attention to mechanics and details. Make sure that headings and itemized lists are grammatically parallel and that grammar, spelling, and punctuation are correct.

Write in a simple and direct style to save your reader time. Use short, crisp phrases instead of whole sentences, and focus on what your reader needs to know. Absolutely avoid using the word *I*. You might say, "Coached a Little League team to the regional playoffs" or "Managed a fast-food restaurant and four employees."

Think about your résumé from the employer's perspective. Ask yourself: What key qualifications will an employer be looking for? Which of these are my greatest strengths? What will set me apart from other candidates in their eyes? What are my greatest accomplishments, and what was produced as a result? Then tailor your résumé to appeal to the employer's needs.

Tailoring the Contents

Most potential employers expect to see certain items in any résumé. The bare essentials are name and address, academic credentials, and employment history. Otherwise, it's up to you to emphasize your strongest, most impressive qualifications and combine your experiences into a straightforward message that communicates what you can do for your potential employer.[6] Don't exaggerate, don't alter the past or claim skills you don't have, and don't dwell on negatives. By focusing on your strengths, you can convey the desired impression without distorting the facts.

Choosing the Best Organizational Plan

Your résumé should emphasize information that has a bearing on your career objective and should minimize or exclude any that is irrelevant or counterproductive. Adopt an organizational plan—chronological, functional, or combination—that focuses on your strongest points. The "right" choice depends on your background and goals.

- *Chronological résumés.* The most common and most traditional type of résumé is the **chronological résumé.** The "Work Experience" section dominates the chronological résumé in the most prominent slot, immediately after the name and address and the career objective. Develop this section by listing your jobs sequentially in reverse order, beginning with the most recent position. Under each listing, describe your responsibilities and accomplishments, giving the most space to the most recent positions. If you're a recent college grad, focus attention on your academic credentials by putting your educational qualifications before your experience. The key advantages of the chronological pattern are (1) employers are familiar with it and can easily find things; (2) it highlights growth and career progression; and (3) it highlights employment continuity and stability.[7] The chronological approach is especially appropriate if you have a strong employment history and are aiming for a job that builds on your current career path (see Exhibit A1.1).

EXHIBIT A1·1

CHRONOLOGICAL RÉSUMÉ

Roberto Cortez calls attention to his most recent achievements by setting them off in list form with bullets. The section titled "Intercultural and Technical Skills" emphasizes his international background, fluency in Spanish, and extensive computer skills—all of which are important qualifications for his target position.

ROBERTO CORTEZ
5687 Crosswoods Drive
Falls Church, Virginia 22046
Home: (703) 987-0086   Office: (703) 549-6624

OBJECTIVE

Accounting management position requiring a knowledge of international finance

EXPERIENCE

March 1995 to present   Staff Accountant/Financial Analyst, Inter-American Imports (Alexandria, VA)
- Prepare accounting reports for wholesale giftware importer ($15 million annual sales)
- Audit financial transactions with suppliers in 12 Latin American countries
- Create computerized models to adjust accounts for fluctuations in currency exchange rates
- Negotiate joint-venture agreements with major suppliers in Mexico and Colombia

October 1991 to March 1995   Staff Accountant, Monsanto Agricultural Chemicals (Mexico City, Mexico)
- Handled budgeting, billing, and credit-processing functions for the Mexico City branch
- Audited travel/entertainment expenses for Monsanto's 30-member Latin American sales force
- Assisted in launching an online computer system to automate all accounting functions

EDUCATION

1989 to 1991   MBA with emphasis in international business
George Mason University (Fairfax, Virginia)

1985 to 1989   BBA, Accounting
University of Texas (Austin, Texas)

INTERCULTURAL AND TECHNICAL SKILLS

- Fluent in Spanish and German
- Traveled extensively in Latin America
- Excel
- Access
- HTML
- Visual Basic

- *Functional résumés.* In a **functional résumé,** you organize your résumé around a list of skills and accomplishments and then identify your employers and academic experience in subordinate sections. This pattern stresses individual areas of competence, and it's useful for people who are just entering the job market, people who want to redirect their careers, and people who have little continuous career-related experience. The key advantages of this organizational pattern are (1) it helps readers clearly see what you can do for them, rather than having to read through job descriptions to find out; (2) it allows job seekers to emphasize an earlier job experience; and (3) it deemphasizes lack of career progress or lengthy unemployment. Bear in mind that many seasoned employment professionals are suspect of this résumé style; they assume candidates who use it are trying to hide something.

- *Combination résumés.* A **combination résumé** includes the best features of the chronological and functional formats. This format emphasizes a candidate's skills and accomplishments while including a complete job history. Nevertheless, it is not commonly used and has two major disadvantages: (1) It tends to be longer, and (2) it can be repetitive because you may have to list your accomplishments and skills in both the functional section and the chronological job descriptions.

Adapting Your Résumé to an Electronic Format

Along with a traditional, paper résumé, you'll need an electronic version to submit to potential employers by e-mail or via the Internet. You may also need an HTML-coded document to post as a Web page should you choose to go that route.

Most Fortune 1000 companies today encourage applicants to submit electronic or scannable résumés. By scanning these résumés into their electronic database, companies can narrow down the pile of applicants quickly.

Electronic or scannable résumés should convey the same information as a traditional résumé, but the format and style must be computer-friendly. This means you must eliminate any graphics, boldface print, underlines, italics, small print, and formatting codes such as tab settings.[8] To change your traditional paper résumé into a scannable one, you convert it into plain text (ASCII) for-

mat, provide a list of key words, and balance common language with jargon (see Exhibit A1.2):

- *Convert your résumé to ASCII format.* ASCII is a common plain-text language that allows your résumé to be read by any scanner and accessed by any computer regardless of the word-processing software you used to prepare the document. All word-processing programs allow you to save files as plain text. To convert your résumé to an ASCII plain-text file, remove all formatting such as bolding, centering, bullets, and graphic lines, and use a popular typeface such as Times, Helvetica, or Courier with a 10- to 14-point font size. To indicate a bullet, use an asterisk or a lowercase letter *o*. Add some blank spaces (rather than tabs) to align text and a few blank lines to create headings and separate paragraphs, as white space allows scanners and computers to recognize when one topic ends and another begins.

- *Provide a list of key words.* Emphasize certain key words to help potential employers select your résumé from the thousands they scan. When employers scan résumés, they generally search for nouns because verbs tend to be generic rather than specific to a particular position or skill. To maximize the number of matches, or "hits," include a key word summary of 20 to 30 words and phrases that define your skills, experience, education, and professional affiliations. Place this list right after your name and address. A key word summary for an accountant, for example, might include these terms: Accountant, Corporate Controller, Fortune 1000, Receivables, Payables, Inventory, Cash Flow, Financial Analysis, Payroll Experience, Corporate Taxes, Activity Based Accounting, Problem Solving, Computer Skills, Excel, Access, Networks, HTML, Peachtree, Quick Books, BA Indiana University–Accounting, CPA, Dean's List, Articulate, Team Player, Flexible, Willing to Travel, Fluent Spanish.

- *Balance common language with current jargon.* To maximize hits between your résumé and an employer's search, use words that potential employers will understand. For example, don't call a keyboard an input device. Also, use only common abbreviations such as BA or MBA. Include the important buzz words in your field. You can find appropriate buzz words in the classified ads of

EXHIBIT A1.2

ELECTRONIC RÉSUMÉ

Because some of his target employers will be scanning his résumé into a database, and because he wants to submit his résumé via e-mail or post it on the Internet, Roberto Cortez created an electronic résumé by changing his formatting and adding a list of key words. However, the information remains essentially the same and appears in the same order.

Roberto Cortez
5687 Crosswoods Drive
Falls Church, Virginia 22046
Home: (703) 987-0086   Office: (703) 549-6624
RCortez@silvernet.com

KEY WORDS

Financial executive, accounting management, international finance, financial analyst, accounting reports, financial audit, computerized accounting model, exchange rates, joint-venture agreements, budgets, billing, credit processing, online systems, MBA, fluent Spanish, fluent German, Excel, Access, Visual Basic, team player, willing to travel

OBJECTIVE

Accounting management position requiring a knowledge of international finance

EXPERIENCE

Staff Accountant/Financial Analyst, Inter-American Imports (Alexandria, Virginia)
March 1995 to present
o Prepare accounting reports for wholesale giftware importer, annual sales of $15 million
o Audit financial transactions with suppliers in 12 Latin American countries
o Create computerized models to adjust for fluctuations in currency exchange rates
o Negotiated joint-venture agreements with suppliers in Mexico and Colombia
o Implemented electronic funds transfer for vendor disbursements, improving cash flow and eliminating payables clerk position

Staff Accountant, Monsanto Agricultural Chemicals (Mexico City, Mexico)
October 1991 to March 1995
o Handled budgeting, billing and credit-processing functions for the Mexico City branch
o Audited travel/entertainment expenses for Monsanto's 30-member Latin American sales force
o Assisted in launching an online computer system to automate all accounting functions

EDUCATION

MBA with emphasis in international business, George Mason University (Fairfax, Virginia), 1989 to 1991

BBA, Accounting, University of Texas (Austin, Texas), 1985 to 1989

INTERCULTURAL AND TECHNICAL SKILLS

Fluent in Spanish and German
Traveled extensively in Latin America
Excel, Access, HTML, Visual Basic

An attractive and fully formatted hard copy of this document is available upon request.

major newspapers such as the *Wall Street Journal* and in résumés that are posted online. Be careful to check and recheck the spelling, capitalization, and punctuation of any jargon you include, and use only those words you see most often.

If an employer gives you an option of submitting a scannable résumé by mail, by fax, or by e-mail, choose e-mail. Sending your résumé by e-mail in a plain-text format puts your résumé directly into the employer's database, bypassing the scanning process. If you send your résumé in a paper format by regular mail or by fax, you still run the risk that a scanning program will create an error when reading your résumé.

If you submit your résumé by e-mail, don't attach it as a separate document. Most human resources departments won't accept attached files because of concern about computer viruses. Instead, paste your résumé into the body of your e-mail message, using the "insert text file" command to bring the ASCII-formatted résumé into the file. Always include reference numbers or job ad numbers in the subject line of your e-mail if they are available.

If you're posting your electronic résumé to an employer's online résumé builder, copy and paste the appropriate sections from your electronic file directly into the employer's form. Doing so will avoid rekeying and will eliminate errors.

If you fax your electronic résumé, set your machine to "fine" mode to result in a higher-quality printout on the receiving end. If you're mailing your résumé, you may want to send both a well-designed traditional résumé and a scannable one. Attach Post-it Notes, labeling one copy "visual résumé," and the other "scannable résumé."

Preparing Your Application Letter

The purpose of your cover letter is to get the reader interested enough to read your résumé. Always send the two together because each has a unique job to perform.

Before you write your application letter, learn something about the organization you're applying to. When composing the letter, show that you've done your homework. Imagine yourself in the recruiter's situation and show how your background and talents will solve a particular company problem or fill a need. The more you can learn about the organization, the better you'll be able to capture the reader's attention and convey your desire to join the company.[9] The letter in Exhibit A1.3 makes an impression by focusing on the employer's needs.

During your research, find out the name, title, and department of the person you're writing to. Reaching and addressing the right person is the most effective way to gain attention. Always avoid phrases such as "To Whom It May Concern" and "Dear Sir."

Following Up on Your Application

If your application letter and résumé fail to bring a response within a month or so, follow up with a second letter to keep your file active. This follow-up letter also gives you a chance to update your original application. Even if you receive a letter acknowledging that your application will be kept on file, don't hesitate to send a follow-up letter after three months. Such a letter demonstrates that you are sincerely interested in working for the organization and that you are persistent in pursuing your goals and upgrading your skills to make yourself a better employee—and it might just get you an interview.

INTERVIEWING WITH POTENTIAL EMPLOYERS

Approach job interviews with a sound appreciation of their dual purpose: The organization's main objective is to find the best person available for the job; the applicant's main objective is to find the job best suited to his or her goals and capabilities.

In general, the easiest way to connect with a big company is through your campus placement office; the most efficient way to approach a smaller business is by contacting the company directly. In either case, you move to the next stage and prepare to meet with a recruiter during an **employment interview,** a formal meeting during which an employer and an applicant ask questions and exchange information to see whether the applicant and the organization are a good match.

Most employers conduct two or three interviews before deciding whether to offer a person a job. The first interview, generally held on campus, is the **preliminary screening interview,** which helps employers eliminate unqualified applicants from the hiring process. Those candidates who best meet the organization's requirements are invited to visit company offices for further evaluation. Some organizations make a decision at that point, but many schedule a third interview to complete the evaluation process before extending a job offer.

Because the interview takes time, start seeking interviews well in advance of the date you want to start work. It takes an average of ten interviews to get one job offer. If you hope to have several offers to choose from, you can expect to go through 20 or 30 interviews during your job search.[10] Some students start their job search as early as nine months before graduation. Early planning is even more crucial during downturns in the economy because many employers become more selective when times are tough.

What Employers Look For

In general, employers are looking for two things: proof that a candidate can handle a specific job and evidence that the person will fit in with the organization. Employers are usually most concerned with the candidate's experience, intelligence, communication skills, enthusiasm, creativity, and motivation.

- *Qualifications for the job.* The interviewer may already have some idea of whether you have the right qualifications, based on a review of your résumé. During the interview, you'll be asked to describe your education and previous jobs in

Glenda S. Johns

Home: 457 Mountain View Road, Clear Lake, IA 50428 (515) 633-5971
College: 1254 Main Street, Council Bluffs, IA 51505 (712) 438-5254

June 16, 2000

Ms. Patricia Downings, Store Manager
Wal-Mart
840 South Oak
Iowa Falls, Iowa 50126

Dear Ms. Downings:

You want retail clerks and managers who are accurate, enthusiastic, and experienced. You want someone who cares about customer service, who understands merchandising, and who can work with others to get the job done. When you're ready to hire a manager trainee or a clerk who is willing to work toward promotion, please consider me for the job.

Working as a clerk and then as an assistant department manager in a large department store has taught me how challenging a career in retailing can be. Moreover, my AA degree in retailing (including work in such courses as retailing, marketing, and business information systems) will provide your store with a well-rounded associate. Most important, I can offer Wal-Mart's Iowa Falls store more than my two years' of study and field experience. You'll find that I'm interested in every facet of retailing, eager to take on responsibility, and willing to continue learning throughout my career. Please look over my résumé to see how my skills can benefit your store.

I understand that Wal-Mart prefers to promote its managers from within the company, and I would be pleased to start out with an entry-level position until I gain the necessary experience. Do you have any associate positions opening up soon? Could we discuss my qualifications? I will phone you early next Wednesday to arrange a meeting at your convenience.

Sincerely,

Glenda Johns

Glenda Johns

Enclosure

EXHIBIT A1·3

APPLICATION LETTER

In her unsolicited application letter, Glenda Johns manages to give a snapshot of her qualifications and skills without repeating what is said in her résumé.

---

more depth so that the interviewer can determine how well your skills match the requirements. In many cases, the interviewer will be seeking someone with the flexibility to apply diverse skills in several areas.[11]

- *Personality traits.* A résumé can't show whether a person is lively and outgoing, subdued and low-key, able to take direction, or able to take charge. Each job requires a different mix of personality traits, so the task of the interviewer is to find out whether a candidate will be effective in a particular job.

- *Physical appearance.* Clothing and grooming reveal something about a candidate's personality and professionalism. Even in companies where interviewers may dress casually, show good judgment by dressing (and acting) in a professional manner. Interviewers also consider such physical factors as posture, eye contact, handshake, facial expression, and tone of voice.

- *Age.* Job discrimination against middle-aged people is prohibited by law, but if you feel your youth could count against you, counteract its influence by emphasizing your experience, dependability, and mature attitudes.

- *Personal background.* You might be asked about your interests, hobbies, awareness of world events, and so forth. You can expand your potential along these lines by reading widely, meeting new people, and participating in discussion groups, seminars, and workshops.

- *Attitudes and personal style.* Openness, enthusiasm, and interest are likely to impress an interviewer. So are courtesy, sincerity, willingness to learn, and a positive, self-confident style—all of which help a new employee adapt to a new workplace and new responsibilities.

What Applicants Need to Find Out

What things should you find out about the prospective job and employer? By doing a little advance research and asking the right questions during the interview, you can probably find answers to these questions and more:

- Are these my kind of people?
- Can I do this work?
- Will I enjoy the work?
- Is this job what I want?
- Does the job pay what I'm worth?
- What kind of person would I be working for?
- What sort of future can I look forward to with this organization?

How to Prepare for a Job Interview

It's perfectly normal to feel a little anxious before an interview. Don't worry too much, however; preparation will help you perform well. Here are some pointers to guide that preparation:

- *Do some basic research.* Learning about the organization and the job is important because it enables you to review your résumé from the employer's point of view.

- *Think ahead about questions.* Most job interviews are essentially question-and-answer sessions: You answer the interviewer's questions about your background, and you ask questions of your own to determine whether the job and the organization are right for you. By planning for your interviews, you can handle these exchanges intelligently (see Exhibits A1.4 and A1.5). Of course, you don't want to memorize responses or sound overrehearsed.

- *Bolster your confidence.* By overcoming your tendencies to feel self-conscious or nervous during an interview, you can build your confidence and make a better impression. If some aspect of your background or appearance makes you uneasy, correct it or exercise positive traits to offset it, such as warmth, wit, intelligence, or charm. Instead of dwelling on your weaknesses, focus on your strengths so that you can emphasize them to an interviewer.

- *Polish your interview style.* Confidence helps you walk into an interview and give the interviewer an impression of poise, good manners, and good judgment. In the United States, you're more likely to be invited back for a second interview or offered a job if you maintain eye contact, smile frequently, sit in an attentive position, and use frequent hand gestures. These nonverbal signals convince the interviewer that you're alert, assertive, dependable, confident, responsible, and energetic.[12] Work on eliminating speech mannerisms such as "you know," "like," and "um." Speak in your natural tone, and try to vary the pitch, rate, and volume of your voice to express enthusiasm and energy.

- *Plan to look good.* The best policy is to dress conservatively. Wear the best-quality businesslike clothing you can, preferably in a dark, solid color. Avoid flamboyant styles, colors, and prints. Clean, unwrinkled clothes, well-shined shoes, neatly styled and combed hair, clean fingernails, and fresh breath help make a good first impression. Don't spoil the effect by smoking cigarettes before or during the interview. Finally, remember that one of the best ways to look good is to smile at appropriate moments.

- *Be ready when you arrive.* Be sure you know when and where the interview will be held. Take a small notebook, a pen, a list of your questions, a folder with two copies of your résumé, an outline of your research findings about the organization, and any correspondence about the position. You may also want to take a small calendar, a transcript of your college grades, a list of references,

COLLEGE

- What courses in college did you like most? Least? Why?
- Do you think your extracurricular activities in college were worth the time you devoted to them? Why?
- When did you choose your college major? Did you ever change your major? If so, why?
- Do you feel you did the best scholastic work you are capable of?
- Which of your college years was the toughest? Why?

EMPLOYMENT HISTORY

- What jobs have you held? Why did you leave?
- What percentage of your college expenses did you earn? How?
- Why did you choose your particular field of work?
- What are the disadvantages of your chosen field?
- Have you served in the military? What rank did you achieve? What jobs did you perform?
- What do you think about how this industry operates today?
- Why do you wish to change employment?
- What do you like the least about your current position?
- What goals do you expect to achieve in your current job that you have not already accomplished?

THE NEW POSITION

- Why do you think you would like this particular type of job?
- What are your expectations of this position?
- What do you anticipate will be the most challenging aspects of this job?
- What can you contribute to this position?
- What would be your first goal in this position?
- How would you handle a 10 percent budget cut in your area of responsibility?

PERSONAL ATTITUDES AND PREFERENCES

- Do you prefer to work in any specific geographical location? If so, why?
- How much money do you hope to be earning in five years? In ten years?
- What do you think determines a person's progress in a good organization?
- What personal characteristics do you feel are necessary for success in your chosen field?
- Tell me a story.
- Do you like to travel?
- Do you think grades should be considered by employers? Why or why not?

WORK HABITS AND COMPANY "FIT"

- Are you a team player, or are you more satisfied working alone?
- What type of boss do you prefer?
- Have you ever had any difficulty getting along with colleagues or supervisors? With other students? With instructors?
- Would you prefer to work in a large or a small organization? Why?
- How do you feel about overtime work?
- What have you done that shows initiative and willingness to work?
- Do you praise the contributions of others?
- What characteristics do you believe an outstanding employee should possess? A peer? A supervisor?
- How would you handle a "problem" employee?
- How would you deal with a colleague who has competed with you for a position, feels better qualified than you, and now works for you?

CAREER GOALS

- What are your long-term goals?
- How have you moved from each stage in your career to the next?
- What factors are most important to you in terms of job satisfaction?
- When do you anticipate a promotion?

EXHIBIT A1·4

COMMON INTERVIEW QUESTIONS

- What are this job's major responsibilities?
- What qualities do you want in the person who fills this position?
- Do you want to know more about my related training?
- What is the first problem that needs the attention of the person you hire?
- What are the organization's major strengths? Weaknesses?
- Who are your organization's major competitors, and what are their strengths and weaknesses?
- What makes your organization different from others in the industry?
- What are your organization's major markets?
- Does the organization have any plans for new products? Acquisitions?
- What can you tell me about the person I would report to?
- How would you define your organization's managerial philosophy?
- What additional training does your organization provide?
- Do employees have an opportunity to continue their education with help from the organization?
- Would relocation be required, now or in the future?
- Why is this job now vacant?

EXHIBIT A1•5

APPLICANT QUESTIONS FOR INTERVIEWERS

and, if appropriate, samples of your work. After you arrive, relax. You may have to wait, so bring something to read or to occupy your time (the less frivolous or controversial, the better).

How to Follow Up After the Interview

Touching base with the prospective employer after the interview, either by phone or in writing, shows that you really want the job and are determined to get it. It also brings your name to the interviewer's attention again and reminds him or her that you're waiting to know the decision.

The two most common forms of follow-up, the thank-you message and the inquiry, are generally handled by letter. But a phone call can be just as effective, particularly if the employer favors a casual, personal style. Express your thanks within two days after the interview, even if you feel you have little chance for the job. In a brief message, acknowledge the interviewer's time and courtesy, convey your continued interest, and ask politely for a decision. If you're not advised of the interviewer's decision by the promised date or within two weeks, you might make an inquiry, particularly if you don't want to accept a

job offer from a second firm before you have an answer from the first. Assume that a simple oversight is the reason for the delay, not outright rejection.

■ BUILDING YOUR CAREER

Having the right skills is one way to build toward a career. Employers seek people who are able and willing to adapt to diverse situations, who thrive in an ever-changing workplace, and who continue to learn throughout their careers. In addition, companies want team players with strong work records and leaders who are versatile. Many companies encourage managers to get varied job experience.[13] In some cases, your chances of being hired are better if you've studied abroad or learned another language. Many employers expect college graduates to have a sound understanding of international affairs, and they're looking for employees with intercultural sensitivity and an ability to adapt in other cultures.[14]

Compile an employment portfolio. Get a three-ring notebook and a package of plastic sleeves that open at the top. Collect anything that shows your ability to perform, such as classroom or work evaluations, certificates, awards, and papers you've written. An employment portfolio serves as an excellent resource when writing your résumé and provides employers with tangible evidence of your professionalism.

As you search for a permanent job that fulfills your career goals, take interim job assignments, participate in an internship program, and consider temporary work or freelance jobs. Not only will these temporary assignments help you gain valuable experience and relevant contacts, but they will also provide you with important references and with items for your portfolio.[15] Employers will be more willing to find (or even to create) a position for someone they've learned to respect, and your temporary or freelance work gives them a chance to see what you can do.

If you're unable to find actual job experience, work on polishing and updating your skills. Network with professional colleagues and friends who can help you stay abreast of your occupation and industry. While you're waiting for responses to your résumé or your last interview, take a computer course or gain some other educational or life experience that would be difficult while working full time. Become familiar with the services offered by your campus career center (or placement office). These centers offer individual placement counseling, credential services, job fairs, on-campus interviews, job listings, advice on computerized résumé-writing software, workshops in job-search techniques, résumé preparation, interview techniques, and more.[16]

Once an employer hires you and you're on the job, don't think you've reached the end of the process. The best thing you can do for your long-term career is to continue learning. Listen to and learn from those around you who have experience. Be ready and willing to take on new responsibilities, and actively pursue new or better skills. Employers appreciate applicants and employees with willingness and enthusiasm to learn, to listen, and to gain experience.

Chapter Glossary

chronological résumé   Most traditional type of résumé, listing employment history sequentially in reverse order so that the most recent experience is listed first

combination résumé   Résumé that combines the best features of the chronological and functional formats by including a candidate's skills, accomplishments, and complete job history

employment interview   Formal meeting during which an employer and an applicant ask questions and exchange information to see whether the applicant and the organization are a good match

functional résumé   Résumé organized around a list of skills and accomplishments, subordinating employers and academic experience in order to stress individual areas of competence

preliminary screening interview   Meeting between an employer's representative and a candidate for the purpose of eliminating unqualified applicants from the hiring process

résumé   Form of advertising that lists a person's education, employment background, and job qualifications in order to obtain an interview

CAREERS IN BUSINESS

STARTING YOUR CAREER IN BUSINESS

As you look ahead to starting your business career, you should consider employment trends and job possibilities for the occupations that interest you. Your opportunities for finding the perfect job will be affected by the demands of the marketplace. Are jobs plentiful or scarce in your chosen field of work? Is the number of jobs in your field of interest projected to grow or decline?

Career charts on the following pages indicate the duties, qualifications, salary levels, and career outlook through 2006 for selected jobs in management, human resources, computers and information systems, sales and marketing, finance and accounting, communications, and other business careers.[1] Although entry, median, and average salary levels will vary by employer and geographical location, salaries normally correspond to educational requirements for a position. Statistics show that both earnings and unemployment rates are directly related to levels of educational attainment (see Exhibit A2.1).

Job growth varies widely by education and training requirements. Jobs that require college degrees, for example, are expected to grow substantially in the near future. Categories that do not require a college degree are projected to grow slower than those that require college degrees, through 2006 (see Exhibit A2.2).

The hottest jobs in today's business world demand technological and computer skills. Even if you're interested in finance, human resources, or marketing positions, you'll need basic computer skills to snare the best jobs in your desired field of work. As business becomes increasingly dependent on technology, computer-related careers have become the fastest-growing occupations among all jobs in the work force (see Exhibit A2.3 on page 450).

CAREERS IN MANAGEMENT

Today's business environment requires the skills of effective managers to reduce costs, streamline operations, develop marketing strategies, and supervise workers (see

EXHIBIT A2·1

UNEMPLOYMENT AND EARNINGS FOR YEAR-ROUND, FULL-TIME WORKERS AGE 25 AND OVER, BY EDUCATIONAL ATTAINMENT

EDUCATION ATTAINED	UNEMPLOYMENT RATE IN 1998 (PERCENT)	MEDIAN EARNINGS IN 1997
Professional degree	1.4	$72,700
Doctorate	1.3	62,400
Master's degree	1.6	50,000
Bachelor's degree	1.9	40,100
Associate degree	2.5	31,700
Some college, no degree	3.2	30,400
High school graduate	4.1	26,000
Less than a high school diploma	7.1	19,700

Exhibit A2.4 on page 451). Facing increased competition, many businesses are becoming more dependent on the expertise of outside management consultants—one of the fastest-growing occupations of all jobs through the year 2006.

CAREERS IN HUMAN RESOURCES

Large numbers of job openings are expected in the human resources field through 2006 (see Exhibit A2.5 on page 452). Efforts to recruit quality employees and to provide more employee training programs should create new human resources positions. With a vast supply of qualified workers and new college graduates, however, the job market for human resources is likely to remain competitive.

CAREERS IN COMPUTERS AND INFORMATION SYSTEMS

Job opportunities abound for trained information technology workers. As competition and advanced technologies force companies to upgrade and improve their computer systems, the number of computer-related positions continues to escalate. Computer jobs hold the top spots in the fastest-growing occupations and rank among the top 20 in the number of newly created jobs projected through 2006 (see Exhibit A2.6 on page 453).

Within the computer field, only two categories of jobs are expected to decrease: computer operators and data entry clerks. More user-friendly computer software has greatly reduced the need for operators and data entry processors, but displaced workers who keep up with changing technology should have few problems moving into other areas of computer support.

CAREERS IN SALES AND MARKETING

Increasing competition in products and services should create greater needs for effective sales and marketing personnel in the future. The number of securities and financial services sales representatives is projected to increase much faster than average to meet the needs of the growing numbers of investors putting their money into stocks, bonds, and other securities. Employment for insurance and real estate agents, however, is expected to grow more slowly than average (see Exhibit A2.7 on page 454). Computer technology will allow established agents to increase their sales volume and will eliminate the need for additional marketing personnel in these fields.

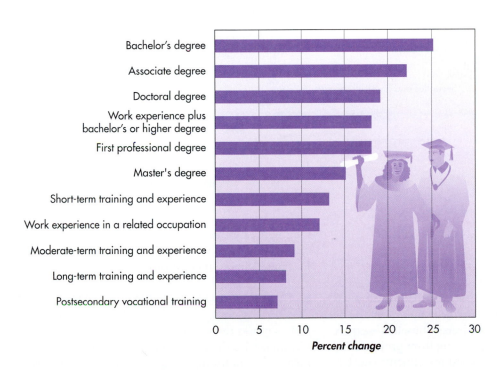

EXHIBIT A2.2

JOB GROWTH BY EDUCATION AND TRAINING, PROJECTED 1996–2006

Research by the Bureau of Labor Statistics shows that earning a bachelor's degree pays off.

EXHIBIT A2·3

THE 25 FASTEST-GROWING OCCUPATIONS, 1996–2006

The 25 occupations with the largest and fastest employment growth, higher-than-average pay, and lower-than-average unemployment will account for 5 million new jobs, or 27 percent of all job growth, between 1996 and 2006. Of the 25 occupations, 18 require at least a bachelor's degree.

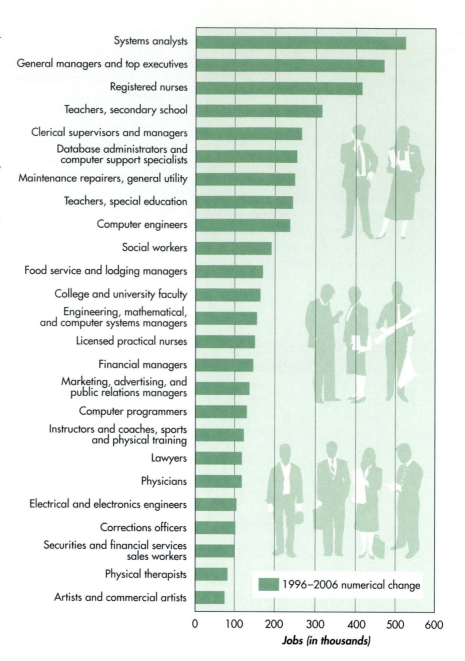

1996–2006 numerical change

Jobs (in thousands)

CAREERS IN FINANCE AND ACCOUNTING

Most positions in finance and accounting are expected to grow as fast as the average for all occupations through 2006. Three exceptions—bill and account collectors, financial planners, and loan officers/counselors—expect faster than average growth, stemming from projected increases in the number of loans and investments (see Exhibit A2.8 on page 455). Continued growth in the economy and population is expected to create more demand for trained financial personnel.

CAREERS IN COMMUNICATIONS

As businesses recognize the need for effective communications with their customers and the public, employment of communications personnel is expected to

JOB TITLE	DUTIES	QUALIFICATIONS	SALARY	OUTLOOK THROUGH 2006
Building services/ facilities manager	Oversees physical aspects of facilities	Bachelor's degree; background in management, architecture, or real estate	Average: $53,800	Average growth
Chief executive officer, public company	Formulates policies; directs operations	Bachelor's degree or higher	Median: $714,000	Average growth
Chief executive officer, nonprofit organization	Sets strategies to meet objectives; directs operations	Bachelor's degree or higher	Average: less than $135,000	Average growth
Clerical supervisor	Supervises duties of clerical and administrative staff	Office and supervisory skills	Median: $28,900	Average growth
Food and beverage director	Directs food service operations	College degree or training in hotel/restaurant management	Average: $43,000	Average growth
Hotel manager	Responsible for overall operations of hotel	College degree or postsecondary training in hotel/restaurant management	Average: $54,000+ bonuses	Average growth
Industrial production manager	Oversees production staff and equipment	Varies; most manufacturers prefer college degree in business or engineering	Average: $60,000	Slight decline
Management analyst/consultant	Collects and analyzes data; recommends and implements ideas	Master's degree in business plus 5 years of experience	Entry: $35,200; median: $39,500	Faster than average
Merchandise buyer/manager	Obtains highest-quality items at lowest possible cost	Bachelor's degree in business	Average: $33,200 for buyers (higher for managers)	Slower than average
Office/administrative services manager	Coordinates and directs office support services	Associate or bachelor's degree in business or management	Average: $41,400	Average growth
Property manager	Organizes, staffs, and manages real estate operations	College degree in real estate, finance, or business	Median: $28,500	Average growth

EXHIBIT A2·4

CAREERS IN MANAGEMENT

grow as fast or faster than the average for almost all communications occupations through 2006 (see Exhibit A2.9 on page 456). Recent college graduates may face keen competition for entry positions in communications as the number of applicants is expected to exceed the number of job openings. Newly created jobs in the ever-expanding computer world—such as graphic designers for Web sites or technical writers for instruction manuals—are expected to improve the career outlook for new communications graduates through 2006.

■ OTHER BUSINESS CAREERS

Many career opportunities exist outside the realm of traditional business career paths. Federal government positions, for example, offer opportunities in a variety of fields, ranging from environmental health to occupational safety. Other careers, such as industrial designer or insurance adjuster, provide chances to utilize a variety or combination of skills on the job (see Exhibit A2.10 on page 457).

JOB TITLE	DUTIES	QUALIFICATIONS	SALARY	OUTLOOK THROUGH 2006
Affirmative action/ EEO specialist	Investigates and resolves EEO grievances; files EEO reports	College degree preferred; familiarity with laws and regulations necessary	Median: $38,200	Likely to remain competitive
Compensation and benefits director	Oversees pay and evaluation systems; develops and coordinates employee benefits program	Master's degree in human resources, labor relations, or business recommended	Median: $90,500	Likely to remain competitive
Employee assistance specialist	Assists with employee programs ranging from safety to child care	College graduate preferred	Median: $39,000	Likely to remain competitive
Employee benefits specialist	Handles employee benefit programs; assists employees with filing claims	College degree preferred; certification in employee benefits desirable	Median: $38,300	Likely to remain competitive
Employment interviewer	Searches for promising job applicants; screens, interviews, and tests applicants	High school diploma sufficient	Entry: $25,300; commissions possible	Average growth
Human resources information systems specialist	Develops and applies computer programs to process personnel information	Bachelor's degree in computer science, math, or information systems	Median: $38,800	Faster than average growth
Human resources manager	Oversees all personnel activities: employment, compensation, benefits, training, and employee relations	College degree preferred; master's degree in human resources desirable	Median: $64,400	Likely to remain competitive
Industrial/labor relations director	Forms labor policy; oversees labor relations; negotiates bargaining agreements	College degree preferred; graduate study in labor relations may be necessary	Median: $106,100	Likely to remain competitive
Interviewing clerk	Assists with forms, applications, and questionnaires	High-school diploma	Median: $18,512	Faster than average growth
Job analyst	Collects and examines detailed data about job duties to prepare job descriptions	College degree in business or human resources	Median: $39,600	Likely to remain competitive
Occupational health and safety manager	Detects and corrects unsafe machinery or working conditions	Training in applicable laws or safety procedures; college degree may be required	Median: $36,140	Slower than average growth
Payroll and timekeeping clerk	Computes wages for payroll records, usually by computer	High school diploma necessary; higher degree favored	Median: $23,100	Little or no change
Personnel clerk	Maintains employee records	High school diploma necessary; higher degree favored	Median: $23,100	Little or no change
Recruiting manager	Recruits and interviews employees; advises on hiring decisions	College degree preferred	Median: $63,800	Likely to remain competitive
Training specialist	Plans, organizes, and directs training activities; evaluates training effectiveness	College degree in business, human resources, or personnel administration	Median: $37,200	Likely to remain competitive

EXHIBIT A2.5

CAREERS IN HUMAN RESOURCES

JOB TITLE	DUTIES	QUALIFICATIONS	SALARY	OUTLOOK THROUGH 2006
Computer-aided design (CAD) specialist	Develops and designs products with computer-aided design (CAD) software	Portfolio with formal CAD training or certification; associate or bachelor's degree in specialty field	Median: $30,680	Faster than average growth
Computer engineer	Designs hardware, software, networks, and processes; develops and tests systems	Bachelor's degree in computer science, computer engineering, or electrical engineering	Entry: $39,722	Much faster than average growth
Computer operator	Oversees the operation of computer hardware systems	Minimum of high school diploma; some postsecondary education or training may be required	Median: $22,400	Sharp decline expected
Computer programmer	Writes, tests, and maintains software programs; updates and expands existing programs	Bachelor's or two-year degree in computer-related field	Median: $40,100	Faster than average growth
Computer support specialist	Provides assistance and advice to computer users; interprets problems and provides technical support	Bachelor's degree in computer-related field	Entry: $25,000–$36,500 for help-desk support technicians	Much faster than average growth
Computer systems analyst	Designs computer solutions to meet needs; plans and develops new systems or revises existing resources to new operations	Bachelor's degree in computer-related field	Entry: $36,261; median: $46,300	Fastest-growing occupation of all jobs
Computer systems manager	Plans, coordinates, and directs computer programming, hardware, systems design, and software	Bachelor's degree in computer-related field; master's degree often preferred	Median entry: $60,900; average range: $33,000–$100,000+	Much faster than average growth
Data entry clerk/ word processor	Enters information into computers or word processors	High school graduate with skills in keyboarding and/or computer software packages	Entry: $18,100	Decline expected
Database administrator	Implements computer databases; coordinates changes and tests; plans and coordinates security	Bachelor's degree in computer-related field	Entry: $54,000–$67,500	Much faster than average growth
Information systems manager	Installs, configures, and supports systems or portions of systems	Bachelor's degree in computer-related field	Entry: $36,261	Much faster than average growth
Software developer	Designs and develops software; creates custom software applications	Bachelor's degree in computer-related field	Range: $49,000–$67,500	Much faster than average growth
Webmaster	Responsible for all aspects of maintaining Web site	Knowledge of HTML, Java, and/or specific databases; experience desirable	Range: $40,000–$90,000	Much faster than average growth

EXHIBIT A2·6

CAREERS IN COMPUTERS AND INFORMATION SYSTEMS

JOB TITLE	DUTIES	QUALIFICATIONS	SALARY	OUTLOOK THROUGH 2006
Account executive	Maintains and services accounts	Bachelor's degree in business with marketing emphasis	Entry for marketing majors: $29,000	Faster than average growth
Advertising sales representative	Markets advertising services	College degree in business, advertising, or marketing	Median: $26,000	Much faster than average growth
Insurance agent/ broker	Sells and services insurance policies; helps policyowners settle claims	College graduate with proven sales ability	Median commissions: $31,500	Slower than average growth
Manufacturers' and wholesale sales representative	Markets products or services to manufacturers or to wholesale and retail establishments	High school diploma with desire to sell	Median: $36,100; commissions possible	Average growth
Marketing manager	Develops detailed marketing strategies; directs the sale of products and services	College degree in almost any major; certification desirable	Median: $46,000; bonuses possible	Faster than average growth
Marketing research analyst	Researches and analyzes data of past sales to predict future sales	Graduate degree in business, economics, marketing, or statistics	Median entry: $35,000 with master's degree	Average growth
Real estate agent/ broker	Solicits property listings; sells properties; negotiates and conducts real estate transactions	License required; most states require 30–90 classroom hours; continuing education needed for license renewal	Median commissions: $31,500	Slower than average growth
Retail sales manager	Serves customers, supervises workers, and coordinates retail operations	Associate or bachelor's degree preferred	Median: $24,400	Slower than average growth
Sales representative, business services	Sells business products and services	High school diploma with proven sales record	Median: $30,264; commissions possible	Much faster than average growth
Stockbroker/ securities sales representative	Advises investors on stocks, bonds, and market conditions; conducts buy/sell orders	College degree and sales ability; state license	Median: $38,800 (commissions after licensure)	Much faster than average growth
Travel agent	Organizes and schedules travel activities	Minimum of high school diploma; formal or specialized training desirable	Entry: $16,400; commissions possible	Faster than average growth

EXHIBIT A2•7

CAREERS IN SALES AND MARKETING

JOB TITLE	DUTIES	QUALIFICATIONS	SALARY	OUTLOOK THROUGH 2006
Accountant/ auditor	Prepares, analyzes, and verifies financial reports and taxes	Bachelor's degree in accounting or related field	Entry: $29,400	Average growth
Actuary	Determines probabilities of income or loss based on various risk factors	Bachelor's degree in math, actuarial science, business, accounting, or statistics	Entry: $37,600	Slower than average growth
Bank examiner	Investigates financial institutions to enforce laws and regulations; approves mergers and acquisitions	Bachelor's degree	Median: $36,140	Slower than average growth
Bank teller	Services banking customers by processing money, checks, and other financial items	High school diploma	Median: $16,300	Little or no change
Bill and account collector	Ensures that customers pay overdue accounts; locates and notifies customers of delinquent accounts	High school diploma	Median: $21,320	Much faster than average growth
Bookkeeper/ accounting clerk	Maintains financial data in computer and paper files	High school diploma	Median: $20,700	Little or no change
Budget analyst	Reviews, analyzes, and interprets financial data; makes recommendations for future	Bachelor's degree in accounting, finance, business, public administration, or economics	Entry: $24,000–$38,700	Average growth
Controller	Directs preparation of all financial reports; oversees accounting, audit, or budget departments	Bachelor's degree in accounting, finance, business, public administration, or economics	Range: $47,000–$138,000	Average growth
Cost estimator	Compiles and analyzes data on factors that influence costs	Bachelor's degree in construction management, engineering, math, accounting, or related field	Entry: $20,000–$31,949	Average growth
Credit analyst	Establishes credit rating criteria; determines credit ceilings and monitors credit extensions	Bachelor's degree in finance, accounting, economics, or business	Average: $40,500	Average growth
Financial manager	Oversees cash flow; monitors credit extensions; assesses risk of transactions; and analyzes investments	Minimum of bachelor's degree in finance or related field; master's degree preferred	Median: $40,700	Average growth
Financial planner	Determines financial objectives and analyzes data; develops and implements financial plans	College graduate with sales experience	Median: $38,800	Much faster than average growth
Insurance underwriter	Identifies and analyzes risk of loss; establishes premium rates and writes policies	College degree in business administration, finance, or accounting	Median: $31,400	Slower than average growth
Loan officer/ counselor	Prepares, analyzes, and verifies loan applications; extends credit; helps borrowers with loan transactions	Bachelor's degree in finance, economics, or related field	Mortgage loan: $30,600–$73,000; consumer loan: $28,900–$48,000	Faster than average growth
Loan and credit authorizer	Reviews credit histories and obtains data to determine creditworthiness of loan applicants	No specific training needed; on-the-job training usually provided	Average: $24,000–$24,700	Slight decline
Operations research analyst	Applies mathematical principles to organizational problems; evaluates options and chooses best alternative	Master's degree in operations research or management science and bachelor's in computer science or math	Median: $42,400	Slower than average growth
Treasurer	Prepares financial reports and ensures compliance with tax and regulatory requirements	Bachelor's degree in accounting, finance, business, public administration, or economics	Total compensation with bonuses: $122,500	Average growth

EXHIBIT A2·8

CAREERS IN FINANCE AND ACCOUNTING

JOB TITLE	DUTIES	QUALIFICATIONS	SALARY	OUTLOOK THROUGH 2006
Advertising/public relations manager	Directs advertising activities and communication of information	Bachelor's degree in advertising, journalism, or public relations	Entry for advertising majors: $27,000; median for managers: $46,000	Faster than average growth
Graphic designer	Creates artistic works to communicate ideas; designs images with computer software	Portfolio with training through bachelor's or master's degree in fine arts or graphic design	Median: $27,100	Faster than average growth
Public relations specialist	Creates favorable attitudes through effective communications	College degree in journalism, public relations, advertising, or communications	Median: $34,000	Faster than average growth
Radio news announcer	Researches, prepares, and presents news; interviews news guests; reports on community activities	Successful audition and broadcast journalism training from college or technical school	Average: $31,251	Slight decline; keen competition
Reporter/ correspondent	Gathers and reports information; investigates issues and composes reports	Bachelor's degree in journalism	Median entry: $23,296	Decline expected; keen competition
Technical writer	Prepares understandable scientific and technical information for nontechnical audiences	College degree in communications, English, journalism, or specialized field	Median: $44,000	Faster than average growth
Television news anchor	Presents news stories; introduces videotaped news or live transmissions from reporters	Successful audition and broadcast journalism training from college or technical school	Average: $65,520	Keen competition
Writer/editor	Communicates ideas and information; develops material for publication or broadcasts	College degree in communications, English, or journalism	Average entry: $21,000	Faster than average growth

EXHIBIT A2·9

CAREERS IN COMMUNICATIONS

JOB TITLE	DUTIES	QUALIFICATIONS	SALARY	OUTLOOK THROUGH 2006
Environmental protection specialist	Conducts investigations to ensure that food, water, and air comply with government standards	Bachelor's degree in environmental health or physical or biological sciences; some states require license	Average: $52,940 (federal government employee)	Slower than average growth
Industrial designer	Develops and designs manufactured products using computer-aided industrial design (CAID) software	Bachelor's degree in related field	Average entry: $27,000	Faster than average growth
Insurance adjuster	Investigates claims; inspects damage; negotiates and settles claims	College degree preferred with major in any field; many states require license	Median: $22,880	Faster than average growth
Quality assurance inspector/manager	Examines and inspects products or services to ensure high standards of quality	Varies by employer and specific job function; usually a combination of experience and education	Average: $47,020 (federal government employee)	Slower than average growth
Record clerk	Maintains and updates records; enters data into computer and performs basic data analysis	High school diploma	Median: $17,100–$23,700	Little or no change

EXHIBIT A2·10

OTHER BUSINESS CAREERS

YOUR BUSINESS PLAN

GETTING STARTED WITH BUSINESS PLANPRO SOFTWARE

Business PlanPro (BPP) software is a template for crafting a winning business plan. The software is designed to stimulate your thinking about the many tasks and decisions that go into planning and running a business. The software does not do your thinking for you; instead it leads you through a thought process by asking you to respond to questions about your business and provide data for the pre-formatted tables and charts. Accompanying instructions, examples, and sample business plans provide you with a full range of assistance you can use to draft your own comprehensive business plan. By working through these exercises, you will gain a practical skill for your business career.

When installing the software disk, be sure to install the *Getting Started* manual. This electronic guide is in a PDF format and can be read by using Adobe Acrobat Reader software. You can download the software for free by visiting the Adobe Acrobat Web site at http://www. adobe.com/products/acrobat/readstep.html. To read the online *Getting Started* manual, open the Adobe Acrobat Reader software, and then the Getting Started file. This file is located in the Bus PlanPro files which are stored in the Pas file folder in your Program files.

NAVIGATING THE SOFTWARE

One of the best ways to become familiar with the BPP software is by navigating one of the BPP sample business plans. The BPP start-up screen offers you four choices. Click on "Open a Sample Plan" and select any sample plan. Read the *Getting Started* manual to learn about the different screen modes available in BPP. Navigate the sample plan as you read about the features available in each

mode. As with most software, you have multiple options for accessing the same information. Once you navigate a few sample business plans, you'll see how easy it is to get around. You will use the same navigational process to enter information for your own business plan.

To access the text mode option, select the "Your Text" icon from the Plan Manager Screen. Use the "Previous" and "Next" buttons at the bottom of the text screen to move backward and forward through the sample plan. To view related tables and charts, click on the Text Manager tab. Then click on the "Go To Table" or "Go To Chart" buttons.

If you prefer to view topics in your own sequence, access the plan outline by clicking on the "Plan Outline" icon at the bottom of your screen. To read a specific section of a sample plan, simply double click on its topic heading. You can return to the plan outline at any time by clicking on that icon.

The Task Manager (also accessed from the Plan Outline screen) is another way to navigate a business plan. The Task Manager uses descriptive headings to direct you to sections in the business plan that address related topics. For example, access the Task Manager in the sample plan and select "Competitive Edge" in the Your Marketing Plan section to read about how the company will gain a competitive edge in the marketplace. Click on the "Plan Outline" icon at the bottom of the screen, then click on the "Plan Outline" tab to find the related section in the plan outline.

You may find it helpful to print out a full copy of the sample plan you have selected and review it as you navigate its contents on your screen. This way you can see how the software uses the information to construct a formal business plan. To print out the sample plan, click on the "Printer" icon on the Plan Manager screen. Make sure both the "Print Tables" and "Print Chart" boxes are checked. You can view the plan on your screen by selecting the "Preview" option, or you can print it on paper.

CREATING A WINNING BUSINESS PLAN

The exercises included in this appendix allow you to use the knowledge you've gained from reading a specific part in this textbook. Each exercise has two tasks: Think Like a Pro tasks require you to navigate the software, find and review information in the sample business plans, and evaluate and critique some of the thinking that went behind these plans. By reviewing these sample plans with a critical eye you will begin to sharpen your own business planning skills. Create Your Own Business Plan tasks provide you with an opportunity to apply your business planning skills to create your own winning business plan. So, begin thinking now about the type of business you'd like to own or manage someday. Then, develop and refine your business strategies as you work through the exercises on the pages that follow.

Business PlanPro

PART 1: CONDUCTING BUSINESS IN THE GLOBAL ECONOMY

Think Like a Pro

OBJECTIVE: By completing these exercises you will become acquainted with the sections of a business plan that address forms of competition, company and product/service descriptions, and the economic outlook for the related industry. You will use the sample business plan for Adventure Travel International (ATI) in this exercise.

Open the BPP software and explore the sample business plan Travel Agency.spd. Click on the "Plan Outline" icon to access the plan's Task Manager. Find the headings "What You're Selling" and "The Business You're In" and double click on each of the sections under these headings to read the text portion of the business plan that discusses these topics.

1. What products and services does ATI provide? Will ATI compete on price, speed, quality, service, or innovation to gain a competitive advantage?

2. What is the economic outlook for the travel industry? What are the principal categories of this industry? What percentage of the industry involves international travel?

3. How has the Internet affected this industry?

4. *Find the heading "What You're Selling." Double click on "Product and Service Description." The text view of BPP software provides helpful instructions for each section of a business plan. Click on the "Instructions" tab located at the top of your screen.* What information should you include about a company's product and service in a business plan? *Now return to the Task Manager and double click on "Competitive Comparison." Click on the "Instructions" tab.* What are some of the things you should discuss about your competition in a business plan?

Create Your Own Business Plan

Think about your own business. Describe in detail the product or service your company will provide. Indicate whether you will compete on price, speed, quality, service, or innovation. In what industry will you compete? What is the economic outlook for that industry? What kinds of competition do you expect to face?

PART 2: STARTING A SMALL BUSINESS

Think Like a Pro

OBJECTIVE: By completing these exercises you will become acquainted with the sections of a business plan that address forms of ownership, financing the enterprise, and the franchising alternative. You will use the sample business plan for Golf Masters Pro Shops in this exercise.

Open the BPP software and explore the sample business plan Golf Pro Shop.spd. Click on the "Plan Outline" icon to access the plan's Task Manager.

1. *Find the heading "What You're Selling." Double click on the sections "Product and Service Description" and "Competitive Comparison" and read*

Superb Supplements

An unparalleled supplements package rounds out our teaching and learning materials.

Instructor's Manual

The complete instructors manual focuses on *Business In Action* with "how to handle a situation" in mind. All answers and guidelines parallel the features in the book, including: "Behind the Scenes," "Handling Difficult Situations on the Job," "Business Mysteries," "See It on the Web" exercises, "Video Cases," among others. Complete lecture notes are also provided.

Study Guide

The study guide gives complete support for students. It reflects and balances what is emphasized in the Instructor's Manual for optimum usefulness to students.

Test Item File

The Test Item File includes multiple-choice, true/false and essay questions. The questions are broken down into easy, moderate, and difficult types. A computerized Test Item File is also available.

Web Site

The myPHLIP Companion Web site is the most advanced, text-specific site available on the Web! Students can log on and have a dialogue with their peers, talk to a tutor, take a quiz and get immediate feedback, read articles about current events—all with the click of a mouse.

Unique E-Business In Action Online supplement

These additional online chapters cover the latest trends in e-commerce, include learning objectives, discussions of e-commerce issues and specific real-world examples, discussion questions, group exercises, Internet exercises, and business mystery exercises picking up on the "Business Mystery" feature in the book. A grid is also included showing how to integrate each online chapter within a specific chapter or part in the book. Lastly, a special career feature with hotlinks to career-oriented sites and tips for building e-commerce careers are features as well!

PowerPoints

Comprehensive PowerPoints that support the lecture notes in the Instructor's Manual are animated, interesting, and useful. These are also available in hard copy form.

Beginning Your Career Search Guide

This supplement offers straightforward, practical advice on how to write a résumé, where and how to find company information, how to conduct yourself during an interview, and tips on the interviewing process. Also included are sample introductory, cover, follow-up, and thank-you letters. This supplement can be shrink-wrapped with the text at no additional cost. Contact your local sales representative for more information.

more ⟶

Video Cases

Closely integrated with the content of the text are brand new and professionally produced video cases. Each video case includes questions and exercises that help students understand how business principles and chapter concepts apply to the workplace. The cases and related videos feature BMC, a business animation company.

E-BIZ: PRENTICE HALL GUIDE TO E-BUSINESS AND E-COMMERCE (FREE VALUE-PACK ITEM UPDATED ANNUALLY)

Take your students behind the scenes to explore the dynamic world of e-business with this new multidisciplinary supplement. The supplement's printed component offers ten modules that examine the challenges and opportunities e-businesses face in such disciplines as strategy, marketing, management, finance, and more.

those sections of the business plan. Using the Task Manager, find the heading "The Business You're In" and read the section titled "Industry Participants." What products and services does Golf Master Pro Shops provide? How will it differentiate its products and services from those of its competitors?

2. *Find the heading "Your Company" and read the section titled "Company Ownership."* What form of ownership will Golf Master Pro Shops use? What are the advantages of selecting that form of ownership? *Read the company's financial plan summary under the Task Manager heading "Financial Plan."* How will Golf Master Pro Shops finance its start-up expenses and its growth?

3. *Find the heading "Finish and Polish" and read the "Strategy Pyramid" section. Now read about the company's pricing strategy under the heading "Your Sales Forecast."* Explain the company's master franchise strategy. How will Golf Master Pro Shops use franchising to expand their business? What fees will master franchises pay? What commissions and royalties will master franchises earn? What fees will store franchises pay? As a potential franchise owner, what might you want to know about the required advertising contribution?

4. *Access the "Company Ownership" section of the business plan and, in text view, click on the "Instructions" tab located at the top of your screen.* What information should you include about company ownership in a business plan? Which outside resources might you use to help you select the best form of ownership?

Create Your Own Business Plan

Think about your own business. What form of ownership will you choose? Why? How much start-up money will you need? How will you finance your start-up costs? Where will you obtain the money that you will need to expand your business?

PART 3: MANAGING A BUSINESS

Think Like a Pro

OBJECTIVE: By completing these exercises you will become acquainted with the sections of a business plan that address a company's mission, goals and objectives, and management team. You will use the sample business plan for Salvador's in this exercise.

Open the BPP software and explore the sample business plan Salvador's Sauces Food Dis.spd. Click on the "Plan Outline" icon to access the plan's Task Manager and use it to navigate the company's business plan. Find the sections titled "Your Company" and "What You're Selling" to acquaint yourself with Salvador's product and goals.

1. What products does Salvador's sell? How does the company compete? What is the outlook for the Hispanic food industry?

2. *Find the section titled "Initial Assessment" and read the company's mission statement.* Evaluate Salvador's mission statement. Does it summarize why the organization exists, what it seeks to accomplish, and the principles that the company will adhere to as it tries to reach its' goals? How might you improve Salvador's mission statement?

3. *Find the section titled "Initial Assessment" and review and evaluate the company's objectives.* Are they clearly stated? Are they measurable? Do they seem realistic? Which objectives might need some refining?

4. *Locate the section titled "Your Management Team" and review each of the sections under that heading.* Evaluate the strengths and weaknesses of the company's management team. What important management skills is the team lacking? How will the company address these gaps? *Now click on the "Instructions" tab (in text view).* What information should you include about your management team in a business plan? Should you mention the team's weaknesses in addition to its strengths? Why?

Create Your Own Business Plan

Make a list of your company's goals and objectives. Be sure they are clearly stated and measurable. What accomplishments do they assume? How will you reach these goals and objectives? What might prevent you from doing so?

PART 4: MANAGING HUMAN RESOURCES AND LABOR RELATIONS

Think Like a Pro

OBJECTIVE: By completing these exercises you will become acquainted with the sections of a business plan that address staffing the enterprise and managing employees. You will use the sample business plan for Puddle Jumpers Airlines in this exercise.

Open the BPP software and explore the sample business plan Puddle Jumpers Airline.spd. Click on the "Plan Outline" icon to access the plan's Task Manager and use it to navigate the company's business plan. Familiarize yourself with this firm's service and operation by reading the "Executive Summary" (see "Finish and Polish") and by reading the "Competitive Comparison" (see "What You're Selling").

1. According to the Competitive Comparison, Puddle Jumper's will achieve its low cost operation by using fewer crew members and utilizing its flight crews 85 hours a month vs. an industry average of 50–60 hours. How might this affect employee motivation and job stress? What programs might management implement to help pilots and flight crews achieve a work/life balance?

2. *Find the heading "What You're Selling" and read the business plan section titled "Fulfillment."* What service does Puddle Jumpers intend to outsource? Why does it make good sense to outsource these services?

3. *Find the heading "Your Company" and read about the section titled "Company's Ownership."* What form of compensation will the company use to motivate and reward managers? *Read the section titled "Management Team." Consider the team's qualifications and experience.* What specific traits should you look for to evaluate whether the management team is capable of understanding and satisfying employees' needs?

4. *Review the company's personnel plan by double clicking on the "Personnel" table under the "Your Management Team" heading.* Write a brief job description and job specification for three positions listed in the table. *With the table displayed on your computer screen, click on the "Instructions" tab and then on "Table Help". Play the Audio instructions.* How does BPP software use the information in this table in other segments of the business plan?

Create Your Own Business Plan

The success of your business depends on hiring, training, and motivating the right employees. How many employees will your business require? Of these, how many will be managers? How will you motivate your staff? Will you pay them a salary or a commission? Will you offer them alternative work arrangements? If so, which ones? Will you use part–time and temporary em-

PART 5: DEVELOPING MARKETING STRATEGIES TO SATISFY CUSTOMERS

Think Like a Pro

OBJECTIVE: By completing these exercises you will become acquainted with the sections of a business plan that address a firm's target market and pricing, promotion, sales, and distribution strategies. You will use the sample business plan for Boulder Stop Gear in this exercise.

Open the BPP software and explore the sample business plan Boulder Stop Gear.spd. Click on the "Plan Outline" icon to access the plan's Task Manager and use it to navigate the company's business plan. Familiarize yourself with this firm's service and operation by reading the "Executive Summary" (see "Fin-

ish and Polish") and by reading the sections listed under "Your Company," "What You're Selling," and "Your Sales Forecast."

1. Define the target market for Boulder Stop Gear. How will Boulder Stop Gear differentiate its products and services from its competitors?

2. Describe the company's pricing, promotion, sales, and distribution strategies. Which distribution channels will the company use to deliver its products?

3. *Find "Your Market" and read the plan sections listed under this heading. View the market analy-*

sis graphic by double clicking on the "Market Analysis Summary" and then clicking on the "Chart" icon at the top of the screen. Click on the "Text" icon to return to the summary. Rank the company's three market segmentation categories according to their importance.

4. *Find the heading "Initial Assessment" and read the "Keys to Success" section.* What must Boulder Stop Gear do to be successful? *Use the BPP instructions to learn about this section of a business plan.* How do you benefit by preparing this section of a business plan?

Create Your Own Business Plan

Consider your own target market and customers. How will you segment your target market? Which customers are likely to buy your product or service? Describe your pricing, promotion, sales, and distribution strategies. Now make some preliminary sales forecasts. Review the BPP *Task Manager.* Under which section headings will you present this information?

PART 6: MANAGING FINANCIAL INFORMATION AND RESOURCES

Think Like a Pro

OBJECTIVE: By completing these exercises you will become acquainted with the sections of a business plan that address a company's financial and operational projections. You will use the sample business plan for Fantastic Florals in this exercise.

Open the BPP software and explore the sample business plan Flower Importer.spd. Click on the "Plan Outline" icon to access the plan's Task Manager and use it to navigate the company's business plan. Familiarize yourself with this firm's products by reading the "Executive Summary" section (see "Finish and Polish") and by reading the sections listed under "Your Company," "What You're Selling," and "Your Sales Forecast."

1. *Review the "Start-up Summary" and "Start-up Table" under the "Your Company" heading, and the "Start-up Chart" under the "Financial Plan" heading.* Identify the two sources Fantastic Florals will use to fund its start-up costs. Why is it important to indicate how much start-up money will be used to fund assets versus expenses?

2. *Review the tables and graphs included in the Fantastic Florals business plan by double clicking on the table and graph icons in the Task Manager. (Note: When viewing financial statements in BPP software use the toolbar—accessible from the table view—to adjust your screen view. For example, to view detail by years only, select "Years Only" from the "View" menu. To view a larger portion of the table on your screen, select "Hide Table Instructions" from the "Table" menu.)* Assuming the financial projections included in the business plan are on target, would an investment of $75,000 for a 20 percent ownership stake in the company be prudent? Explain your answer. Which financial statement(s) did you use to make your decision?

3. Use the latest yearly financial figures from the company's projected profit and loss statement to determine the company's most profitable product. (Hint: Which of the seven product types listed produces the most gross profit?) How did you arrive at your answer?

4. Graphs and tables are important features of a well-written business plan. They give the reader necessary detail and present data visually so they are easy to interpret and analyze. Why is it a good idea to use only summary tables in the plan's body and place the detail in the plan's appendix?

Create Your Own Business Plan

Think about your own business. How will you categorize your revenue and expense items? Will you break down your sales by product type? By service? By location? What general operating and product-related expenses will you incur? Now take out a sheet of paper and list your revenue and expense categories and build the framework for your profit and loss statement without entering amounts. How do your categories compare to those used by Fantastic Florals?

REFERENCES

■ Notes

CHAPTER 1

1. KARA SWISHER, "How Steve Case Morphed Into a Media Mogul," *Wall Street Journal,* 11 January 2000, B1, B12; MARTIN PEERS, NICK WINGFIELD, AND LAURA LANDRO, "AOL, Time Warner Set Plan to Link in Mammoth Merger," *Wall Street Journal,* 11 January 2000, A1, A6; THOMAS E. WEBER, MARTIN PEERS, AND NICK WINGFIELD, "Two Titans in a Strategic Bind Bet on a Futuristic Megadeal," *Wall Street Journal,* 11 January 2000, B1, B12; "AOL and Time Warner Will Merge to Create World's First Internet-Age Media and Communications Company," America Online Web site, http://media.web.aol.com/media/press.cfm, [accessed 11 January 2000]; "AOL Profits Set Another Record," *Wired,* 27 April 1999 [accessed 30 April 1999], http://www.wired.com/news/news/business/story/19369.html; "Making AOL A-OK," *Business Week,* 11 January 1999, 65; KATE GERWIG, "AOL's Challenge—Taking Care of Business," *Internetweek,* 30 November 1998, PG1; HEATHER GREEN AND CATHERINE YANG, "Not So Odd a Couple After All," *Business Week,* 21 December 1998, 77–78; IRA SAGER AND CATHERINE WANG, "A New Cyber Order," *Business Week,* 7 December 1998, 27–31; CATHERINE YANG, "America Online: Often Down, Never Out," *Business Week,* 20 July 1998, 16; JOSHUA COOPER RAMO, "How AOL Lost the Battles But Won the War," *Time,* 22 September 1997, 46.
2. "IBM Managed Messaging Offerings Expanded," *Corporate IT Update,* 1 July 1997, *Electric Library,* Online [accessed 14 August 1997]; CHERYL GERBER, "IBM Sports a New Attitude," *Computerworld,* 28 July 1997, S5; "IBM Introduces Broad Array of Mobile and Wireless Services," *M2 PressWIRE,* 30 July 1997, *Electric Library* [accessed 14 August 1997]; Gary Hoover, ALTA CAMPBELL, AND PATRICK J. SPAIN, eds., *Hoover's Handbook of American Business* (Austin, Tx.: Reference Press, 1994), 640–641.
3. GARY HAMEL AND C. K. PRAHALAD, *Competing for the Future* (Boston: Harvard Business School Press, 1994), 159–161.

4. THOMAS STEWART, "Brain Power," *Fortune,* 17 March 1997, 105–110; "Post-Capitalist Society," *Soundview Executive Book Summaries* 17, no. 3 (March 1995).
5. PETER F. DRUCKER, *Management Challenges for the 21st Century* (New York: HarperBusiness, 1999), 135.
6. JAMES WILFONG AND TONI SEGER, *Taking Your Business Global* (Franklin Lakes, N.J.: Career Press, 1997).
7. ROBERT L. HEILBRONER AND LESTER C. THUROW, *Economics Explained* (New York: Simon & Schuster, 1994), 29–30.
8. HEILBRONER AND THUROW, *Economics Explained,* 250.
9. HEILBRONER AND THUROW, *Economics Explained,* 250.
10. COLLIN MCMAHON, "Russians at a Critical Crossroad," *Chicago Tribune,* 29 August 1998, 1; PATRICIA KRANZ, "Russia; Is There a Solution?" *Business Week,* 7 September 1998, 27–29; ROBERT J. SAMUELSON, "Global Capitalism, R.I.P.?" *Newsweek,* 14 September 1998, 40–42; EMILY THORTON, "Russia—What Happens When Markets Fail," *Business Week,* 26 April 1999, 50–52; BRUCE NUSSBAUM, "Time to Act," *Business Week,* 14 September 1998, 34–37.
11. LARRY DERFNER, "The Fight over Privatization: Netanyahu Has Pledged to End Israel's," *The Jewish Week,* 9 August 1996, 14; "Israel to Privatize 49% of El Al Airlines," *New York Times,* 2 June 1998, C5; PIERRE TRAN, "Air France Head Hopes for Privatization," *Reuters Business Report,* 8 June 1997, 6; NATHAN GARDELS, "Socialism Fate Awaits the Welfare State," *New Perspectives Quarterly,* 22 March 1996, 2; "Air France Shares Jump on First Day of Trading," *New York Times,* 23 February 1999, C3; GREG STEINMETZ, "Her Majesty May Sell Part of London's Tube, Angering Some in U.K.," *Wall Street Journal,* 14 October 1999, A1, A12.
12. ERIK ECKHOLM, "Chinese Restate Goals to Reorganize State Companies," *New York Times,* 23 September 1999, A10; MARK L. CLIFFORD, DEXTER ROBERTS, JOYCE BARNATHAN, AND PETE ENGARDIO, "Can China Reform Its Economy?" *Business Week,*

29 September 1997, 116–123; NICHOLAS D. KRISTOF AND SHERYL WUDUNN, "The World's Ills May Be Obvious, But Their Cure Is Not," *New York Times,* 15 February 1999 [accessed 16 February 1999], http://www.nytimes.com/library/world/global/021699global-econ.html.
13. GARY HAMEL AND JEFF SAMPLER, "The E-Corporation," *Fortune,* 7 December 1998, 81–92.
14. BRIAN O'REILLY, "The Rent-a-Car Jocks Who Made Enterprise #1," *Fortune,* 28 October 1996, 125–128.
15. JEFF WISE, "How Skiboarding Became the New Snowboarding," *New York Times Magazine,* 21 March 1999, 58–61.
16. ROBERT PEAR, "In Bush Presidency, the Regulators Ride Again," *New York Times,* 28 April 1991, sec. 4, 5.
17. JOHN R. WILKE AND DON CLARK, "Federal Judge Orders Microsoft Not to Bundle Windows Browser," *Wall Street Journal Interactive Edition,* 12 December 1997 [accessed 12 December 1997], http://www.wsj.com; MARTIN WOLK, "FOCUS—As Microsoft Power Grows, So Do Legal Battles," *Reuters Business Report,* 7 October 1997; JOEL BRINKLEY, "As Microsoft Trial Gets Started, Gates's Credibility Is Questioned," *New York Times,* 20 October 1998, A1, C4; SUSAN B. GARLAND AND STEVE HAMM, "The Cops Converge on Microsoft," *Business Week,* 18 May 1998, 34–36; JOSEPH NOCERA, "Microsoft Goes to Court," *Fortune,* 26 October 1998, 35–36.
18. PATRICK M. REILLY, "Barnes & Noble Closes Book on Attempt to Buy Ingram Amid FTC Objections," *Wall Street Journal,* 3 June 1999, B16.
19. JAMES F. PELTZ AND ROBERT A. ROSENBLATT, "FTC Opposes Staples–Office Depot Merger," *Los Angeles Times,* 11 March 1997, D1; DAVID LAWSKY, "Government Wins Major Court Victory Against Staples," *Reuters Business Report,* 30 June 1997.
20. MARTIN KASINDORF AND KEN FIREMAN, "The Clinton Budget/2002 Solution," *Newsday,* 7 February 1997, A4; GILBERT C. ALSTON, "Balancing the Federal Budget," *Los Angeles*

Times, 14 February 1997, B8; JENNIFER OLDHAM, "The Budget Battle; Deficit and Debt: A Primer," *Los Angeles Times,* 6 January 1996, D1; BRIAN NAYLOR, JACKI LYNDEN, AND ROBERT SIEGEL, "House Budget Debate," *1997 National Public Radio,* 30 July 1997; U.S. Department of Treasury [accessed 19 April 1999], http://www.treas.gov.

21. ELIA KACAPYR, "The Well-Being Index," *American Demographics,* February 1996, 32–35; BETH BELTON, "U.S. Brings Economy into Information Age," *USA Today,* 17 March 1999, B1.

22. MICHAEL MOYNIHAN, *The Coming American Renaissance* (New York: Simon & Schuster, 1987), 25.

23. CLAYTON M. CHRISTENSEN, *The Innovator's Dilemma* (Boston: Harvard Business School Press, 1997), 136.

24. MICHAEL VAN BIEMA AND BRUCE GREENWALD, "Managing Our Way to Higher Service-Sector Productivity," *Harvard Business Review,* July/August 1997, 87–95.

25. MOYNIHAN, *The Coming American Renaissance,* 42–43; "Through Seven Decades, Tracking Business and the World," *Business Week,* 4 October 1999, 118A–118P.

26. EVERETTE JAMES, "Services—U.S. Firms Are Leaders in the Global Economy," *Business America,* April 1998, 5–7.

27. U.S. Department of Commerce, Bureau of Economic Analysis [accessed 24 September 1999], http://beadata.bea.doc.gov/bea/dn2/gpoc.htm; "Fortune 1000 Ranked Within Industry," *Fortune,* 26 April 1999, F51–F73.

28. *Survey of Current Business* (Washington, D.C.: GPO, November 1997), Table B8, 132; Infoplease Almanac, Infoplease.com [accessed 22 September 1999], http://www.infoplease.com/ipa/A0302210.html.

29. *Statistical Abstract of the United States, 1996* (Washington, D.C.: GPO, 1996), 56–59, 394, 396.

30. COURTLAND L. BOVÉE, MICHAEL J. HOUSTON, AND JOHN V. THILL, *Marketing,* 2d ed. (New York: McGraw-Hill, 1995), 301.

31. MICHAEL J. MANDEL, "The Internet Economy: The World's Next Growth Engine," *Business Week,* 4 October 1999, 72–77.

32. NANETTE BYRNES AND PAUL C. JUDGE, "Internet Anxiety," *Business Week,* 28 June 1999, 79–88.

33. BYRNES AND JUDGE, "Internet Anxiety."

34. ROBERT D. HOF, "THE NET IS OPEN FOR BUSINESS—BIG TIME," *BUSINESS WEEK,* 31 August 1998, 108–109.

35. GARY L. NEILSON, BRUCE A. PASTERNACK, AND ALBERT J. VISCIO, "UP THE E ORGANIZATION," *STRATEGY & BUSINESS,* First Quarter 2000, 52–61; Craig Fellenstein and Ron Wood, *Exploring E-Commerce, Global E-Business, and E-Societies* (Upper Saddle River, New Jersey: Prentice Hall, 1999), 54–55.

36. CHRISTENSEN, *The Innovator's Dilemma,* xi, 48.

37. "AOL Profits Set Another Record"; "Making AOL A-OK"; Gerwig, "AOL's Challenge"; GREEN AND YANG, "Not So Odd a Couple After All"; SAGER AND WANG, "A New Cyber Order"; Yang, "America Online"; RAMO, "How AOL Lost the Battles But Won the War."

38. ANDREW GOLDSMITH, "Beanie Babies Just Will Not Go Away," *Fortune,* 12 October 1998, 58.

39. Adapted from KENDALL HAMILTON, "Getting Up, Getting Air," *Newsweek,* 13 May 1996, 68.

CHAPTER 2

1. MICHAEL LEAR-OLIMPI, "Management Mountaineer," *Warehousing Management,* January–February 1999, 23–30; LARRY ARMSTRONG, "Patagonia Sticks to Its Knitting," *Business Week,* 7 December 1998, 68; NANCY RIVERA BROOKS, "Companies Give Green Power the Green Light," *Los Angeles Times,* 27 September 1998, D8; CHARLENE MARMER SOLOMON, "A Day in the Life of Terri Wolfe: Maintaining Corporate Culture," *Workforce,* June 1998, 94–95; JACQUELINE OTTMAN, "Proven Environmental Commitment Helps Create Committed Customers," *Marketing News,* 2 February 1998, 5–6; DAWN HOBBS, "Patagonia Ranked 24th by Magazine," *Los Angeles Times,* 23 December 1997, B1; JIM COLLINS, "The Foundation for Doing Good," *Inc.,* December 1997, 41–42; "It's Not Easy Being Green," *Business Week,* 24 November 1997, 180; PAUL C. JUDGE AND MELISSA DOWNING, "A Lean, Green Fulfillment Machine," *Catalog Age,* June 1997, 63; "Patagonia, A Green Endeavor," *Apparel Industry Magazine,* February 1997, 46–48; POLLY LABARRE, "Patagonia Comes of Age," *Industry Week,* 3 April 1995, 42; JOHN STEINBREDER, "Yvon Chouinard, Founder and Owner of the Patagonia Outdoor," *Sports Illustrated,* 2 November 1991, 200.

2. THOMAS EASTON AND STEPHAN HERRERA, "J&J's Dirty Little Secret," *Forbes,* 12 January 1998, 42–44.

3. EASTON AND HERRERA, "J&J's Dirty Little Secret."

4. "For Heavy Drinkers, a Written Warning," *New York Times Abstracts,* 27 October 1998, sec. F, 8 [accessed 24 May 1999], http://nrstg2s.djnr.com/cgi-binDJ.

5. MILTON BORDWIN, "The Three R's of Ethics," *Management Review,* June 1998, 59–61.

6. BORDWIN, "The Three R's of Ethics."

7. TINA KELLEY, "Ethics Officers Guide Workers to Right Choices," *San Diego Union-Tribune,* 2 March 1998, C2, C3.

8. KELLEY, "Ethics Officers Guide Workers to Right Choices"; SUSAN GAINES, "Handing Out Halos," *Business Ethics,* March–April 1994, 20–24.

9. MARK SEIVAR, personal communication, 2 April 1998; "1-800-Jus-tice or 1-800-Rat-fink," *Reputation Management,* March–April 1995, 31–34; MARGARET KAETER, "The 5th Annual Business Ethics Awards for Excellence in Ethics," *Business Ethics,* December 1993, 26–29.

10. KURT EICHENWALD, "Blowing the Whistle, and Now Facing the Music," *New York Times,* 16 March 1997, sec. 3, 1; LAURA MANSNERUS, "Sounding the Trumpets for Whistle-Blowers," *New York Times,* 15 December 1996, sec. Earning It, 14; SUSAN ANTILLA, "Of Whistle-Blowers and Layoffs," *New York Times,* 9 October 1994, sec. Money, 11; JOHN R. BOATRIGHT, *Ethics and the Conduct of Business,* 2d ed. (Upper Saddle River, N.J.: Prentice Hall, 1997), 114.

11. DOUGLAS S. BARASCH, "God and Toothpaste," *New York Times Magazine,* 22 December 1996, 28.

12. See letters in *New York Times,* 25 August 1918, and *New York Herald,* 1 October 1918.

13. "Does It Pay to Be Ethical?" *Business Ethics,* March–April 1997, 14–16; DON L. BOROUGHS, "The Bottom Line on Ethics," *U.S. News & World Report,* 20 March 1995, 61–66.

14. EDWARD O. WELLES, "Ben's Big Flop," *Inc.,* September 1998, 40; CONSTANCE L. HAYS, "Getting Serious at Ben & Jerry's," *New York Times,* 22 May 1998, C1, C3.

15. THOMAS A. FOGARTY, "Corporations Use Causes for Effect," *USA Today,* 10 November 1997, 7B; Peaceworks Web site [accessed 22 June 1999], http://www.peaceworks.net; FLORENCE FABRICANT, "A Young Entrepreneur Makes Food, Not War," *New York Times,* 30 November 1996, sec. International Business, 21.

16. Wal-Mart Web site [accessed 22 June 1999], http://www.walmartfoundation.org/cmn.html; Microsoft Web site [accessed 22 June 1999], http://www.microsoft.com/giving/pages//Ogivann.htm; American Express Web site [accessed 22 June 1999], http://www6.americanexpress.com/corp/philanthropy/community.asp.

17. CARRIE SHOOK, "Dave's Way," *Forbes,* 9 March 1998, 126–127.

18. ANNA MUOIO, ed., "Ways to Give Back," *Fast Company,* December–January 1998, 113.

19. WILLIAM H. MILLER, "Cracks in the Green Wall," *Industry Week,* 19 January 1998, 58–65.

20. GIL ADAMS, "Cleaning Up," *International Business,* February 1996, 32; Susan Moffat, "Asia Stinks," *Fortune,* 9 December 1996, 120–132; PETE ENGARDIO, JONATHAN MOORE, AND CHRISTINE HILL, "Time for a Reality Check in Asia," *Business Week,* 2 December 1996, 58–66.

21. CHRIS BURY AND TED KOPPEL, "The Ad Campaign and the Kyoto Summit," *ABC Nightline,* 9 December 1997; PETER PASSELL, "Trading on the Pollution Exchange,"

New York Times, 24 October 1997, C1, C4;
JULIA FLYNN, HEIDI DAWLEY, AND NAOMI
FREUNDLICH, "Green Warrior in Gray
Flannel," *Business Week,* 6 May 1996, 96.
22. MICHAEL CASTLEMAN, "Tiny Particles, Big
Problems: Our Air Is Cleaner, Yet the Body
Count Climbs," *Sierra,* 21 November 1995, 26.
23. KIRK SPITZER, "Companies Divert
Enough Waste to Fill Five Astrodomes,"
Gannett News Service, 2 November 1995;
MICHAEL SATCHELL, BETSY CARPENTER,
AND KENAN POLLACK, "A New Day for Earth
Lovers," *U.S. News & World Report,* 24 April
1994, 58–62.
24. BRUCE B. AUSTER, "Enviro-intelligence:
The CIA Goes Green," *U.S.News & World
Report,* 16 March 1998, 34.
25. DAVID BRINKERHOFF, "Honda Unveils
Electric Car to Rival GM Version," *Reuters
Business Report,* 3 January 1997; "Manhattan
Beach Offers Free Charging for Electric Cars,"
Los Angeles Times, 27 March 1997, B5;
HOWARD ROTHMAN, "Interview: Amory
Lovins," *Business Ethics,* March–April, 1996,
34–36.
26. GREGG EASTERBROOK, "Cleaning Up,"
Newsweek, 24 July 1989, 27–42; SATCHELL,
CARPENTER, AND POLLACK, "A New Day for
Earth Lovers."
27. DAN CHARLES, "Industrial Symbiosis,"
Morning Edition (NPR), 31 July 1997.
28. "Money to Burn?" *The Economist* 345, 6
December 1997; DONNA BECKLEY,
"Industrial Pollution Still Haunts Hudson,
Group Says," *Gannett News Service,* 24
September 1996, S12; Jim Bradley, "Buying
High, Selling Low," *E Magazine,* 17 July 1996,
14–15; BRIAN DOHERTY, "Selling Air
Pollution," *Reason,* 1 May 1996, 32–37; BILL
NICHOLS, "Four Years of Work, Debate
Produce First Phase of EPA's Cluster Rules,"
Pulp & Paper, 1998, 71.
29. SATCHELL, CARPENTER, AND POLLACK,
"A New Day for Earth Lovers."
30. SPITZER, "Companies Divert Enough
Waste to Fill Five Astrodomes."
31. "The IW Survey: Encouraging Findings,"
Industry Week, 19 January 1998, 62.
32. CONSTANCE L. HAYS, "Since 70's the
World Has Become Safer for Consumerism,"
New York Times, 5 January 1998, C6.
33. CHRIS BURRITT, "Fallout from the
Tobacco Settlement," *Atlanta Journal and
Constitution,* 22 June 1997, A14; JOLIE
SOLOMON, "Smoke Signals," *Newsweek,* 28
April 1997, 50–51; MARILYN ELIAS,
"Mortality Rate Rose Through '80s," *USA
Today,* 17 April 1997, B3; MIKE FRANCE,
MONICA LARNER, AND DAVE LINDORFF,
"The World War on Tobacco," *Business Week,*
11 November 1996, 99; RICHARD LACAYO,
"Put Out the Butt, Junior," *Time,* 2 September
1996, 51; ELIZABETH GLEICK, "Smoking
Guns," *Time,* 1 April 1996, 50.
34. LAURA SHAPIRO, "The War of the
Labels," *Newsweek,* 5 October 1992, 63, 66.

35. KAREN FRIEFELD, "As Subtle As a Slap in
the Face: New Ad Campaign Makes Certain
Its Messages Are Absolutely Clear," *Newsday,*
21 May 1995, A56.
36. ROGER FILLION, "Law Could Curb
Phone Company Use of Customer Data,"
Reuters Business Report, 23 October 1996;
BRUCE KNIGHT, "A New Casualty in Legal
Battles: Your Privacy," *Wall Street Journal,* 11
April 1995, B1; THOMAS B. ROSENSTIEL,
"Someone May Be Watching," *Los Angeles
Times,* 18 May 1994, A1.
37. LESLIE MILLER, "AOL Won't Sell Phone
Numbers," *USA Today,* 25 July 1997, A1;
"Telemarket Deal Irks AOL Members,"
Atlanta Journal and Constitution, 24 July
1997, A1; FILLION, "Law Could Curb Phone
Company Use of Customer Data"; KNIGHT,
"A New Casualty in Legal Battles";
ROSENSTIEL, "Someone May Be Watching."
38. ANNE FAIRCLOTH, "Denny's Changes Its
Spots," *Fortune,* 13 May 1996, 133–142;
NICOLE HARRIS, "A New Denny's—Diner by
Diner," *Business Week,* 25 March 1996,
166–168; ERIC SMITH, "Not Paid in Full,"
Black Enterprise, April 1996, 16; MARK
LOWERY, "Denny's New Deal Ends Blackout,"
Black Enterprise, 20 February 1995, 43;
"Denny's Does Some of the Right Things,"
Business Week, 6 June 1994, 42; "Making
Amends at Denny's," *Business Week,* 21
November 1994, 47.
39. SUZANNE WOOLEY, "The Hustlers Queue
Up on the Net," *Business Week,* 20 November
1995, 146–148.
40. ARTHUR LEVITT, JR. Chairman, SEC, as
reported in Nanette Byrnes, "Needed:
Accounting the World Can Trust," *Business
Week,* 12 October 1998, 46.
41. "Does It Pay to Be Ethical?" 15.
42. JOHN A. BYRNE, LESLIE BROWN, AND
JOYCE BARNATHAN, "Directors in the Hot
Seat," *Business Week,* 8 December 1997, 100,
102, 104.
43. ROBERT PEAR, "U.S. Proposes Rules to
Bar Obstacles to the Disabled," *New York
Times,* 22 January 1991, A1, 12.
44. "Vital Facts 1999," OSHA Web site
[accessed 29 September 1999], http://www.
oshaslc.gov/OSHAFacts/OSHAFacts.html.
45. WENDY BOUNDS AND HILARY STOUT,
"Sweatshop Pact: Good Fit or Threadbare?"
Wall Street Journal, 10 April 1997, A2; ELLEN
NEUBORNE, "Nike to Take a Hit in Labor
Report," *USA Today,* 27 March 1997, B1;
WILLIAM J. HOLSTEIN, "Santa's Sweatshop,"
U.S. News & World Report, 16 December
1996, 50–60; STEPHANIE STROM, "From
Sweetheart to Scapegoat," *New York Times,*
27 June 1996, C1, 16; NANCY GIBBS, "Cause
Celeb: Two High-Profile Endorsers Are
Props in a Worldwide Debate over
Sweatshops and the Use of Child Labor,"
Time, 17 June 1996; ELLEN NEUBORNE,
"Labor's Shopping List: No Sweatshops,"
USA Today, 5 December 1995, B1; BOB

HERBERT, "A Sweatshop Victory," *New York
Times,* 22 December 1995, A15.
46. SKIP KALTENHEUSER, "Bribery Is Being
Outlawed Virtually Worldwide," *Business
Ethics,* May–June 1998, 11; THOMAS
OMESTAD, "Bye-bye to Bribes," *U.S.News &
World Report,* 22 December 1997, 39, 42–44.
47. KATE MURPHY, "Fighting Pollution—
and Cleaning Up, Too," *Business Week,*
January 19, 1998, 90.
48. MARTIN WALKER, "How Green Is
Europe?" *Europe,* February 1998, 26, 28–29.
49. EDWARD A. ROBINSON, "China's Spies
Target Corporate America," *Fortune,* 30
March 1998, 118–122.
50. ANDREW TANZER, "Tech-Savvy Pirates,"
Forbes, 7 September 1998 [accessed 28 June
1999], http://www.forbes.com/forbes/
98/0907/6205162a.htm; RICHARD RAPAPORT,
"Singapore Sting," *Forbes,* 7 April 1997
[accessed 28 June 1999], http://www.forbes.
com/asap/97/0407/084.htm.
51. LEAR-OLIMPI, "Management
Mountainer"; ARMSTRONG, "Patagonia Sticks
to Its Knitting"; BROOKS, "Companies Give
Green Power the Green Light"; SOLOMON, "A
Day in the Life of Terri Wolfe"; OTTMAN,
"Proven Environmental Commitment Helps
Create Committed Customers"; HOBBS,
"Patagonia Ranked 24th by Magazine";
COLLINS, "The Foundation for Doing Good";
"It's Not Easy Being Green"; JUDGE AND
DOWNING, "A Lean, Green Fulfillment
Machine"; "Patagonia, A Green Endeavor";
LaBarre, "Patagonia Comes of Age";
STEINBREDER, "Yvon Chouinard, Founder
and Owner of the Patagonia Outdoor."
52. MATT MURRAY, "Hey Kids! Marketers
Want Your Help!" *Wall Street Journal,* 6 May
1997, B1, B8.

CHAPTER 3

1. Adapted from REGINA FAZIO MARUCA,
"The Right Way to Go Global," *Harvard
Business Review,* March–April 1994, 135–145;
DEBORAH DUARTE AND NANCY SNYDER,
"From Experience: Facilitating Global
Organizational Learning in Product
Development at Whirlpool Corporation,"
Journal of Product Innovation Management 14,
no. 1 (January 1997): 48–55; JOE JANCSURAK,
"Whirlpool: U.S. Leader Pursues Global
Blueprint," *Appliance Manufacturer* 45, no. 2
(February 1997): G21; CARL QUINTANILLA,
"Despite Setbacks, Whirlpool Pursues
Overseas Markets," *Wall Street Journal,* 9
December 1997, B4; Ian Katz, "Whirlpool: In
the Wringer," *Business Week,* 14 December
1998, 831; GALE CUTLER, "Asia Challenges
Whirlpool Technology," *Research Technology
Management,* September–October 1998, 4–6;
"Whirlpool Europe and Tupperware Europe
Announce Strategic Alliance," Whirlpool
Investor Relations, 28 April 1999, Whirlpool
Web site, [accessed 5 May 1999],
http://www.whirlpoolcorp.com.

2. JOHN ALDEN, "What in the World Drives UPS?" *International Business,* March/April 1998, 6–7.

3. THOMAS L. FRIEDMAN, *The Lexus and the Olive Tree* (New York: Farrar, Straus, & Giroux, 1999), 10.

4. JAMES WILFONG AND TONI SEGER, *Taking Your Business Global* (Franklin Lakes, N.J.: Career Press, 1997), 216–219.

5. "Getting It Right in Japan," *International Business,* May–June 1997, 19.

6. GARY M. WEDERSPAHN, "Exporting Corporate Ethics," *Global Workforce,* January 1997, 29–30; DANA MILBANK AND MARCUS W. BRAUCHLI, "Greasing Wheels," *Wall Street Journal,* 29 September 1995, A1, A7.

7. U.S. Census Bureau Web site [accessed 7 May 1999], http://www.census.gov/statab/freq/98s1323.txt.

8. President, Proclamation, "World Trade Week, 1997," M2 PressWIRE, 22 May 1997, *Electric Library,* Online, 17 July 1997; JAMES TOEDTMAN, "Battle over U.S. Trade Fought across 1,000 Fronts," *Newsday,* 23 April 1997, *Electric Library* [accessed 17 July 1997].

9. WILFORN AND SEGER, *Taking Your Business Global,* 289.

10. "Padgett Surveys Franchise/Small Business Sectors," *Franchising World,* March–April 1995, 46; JOHN STANSWORTH, "Penetrating the Myths Surrounding Franchise Failure Rates—Some Old Lessons for New Business," *International Small Business Journal,* January–March 1995, 59–63; LAURA KOSS-FEDER, "Building Better Franchise Relations," *Hotel & Motel Management,* 6 March 1995, 18; CAROL STEINBERG, "Franchise Fever," *World Trade,* July 1992, 86, 88, 90–91; JOHN O'DELL, "Franchising America," *Los Angeles Times,* 25 June 1989, sec. IV, 1.

11. SCOTT MCCARTNEY, SUSAN CAREY, AND MARTHA BRANNIGAN, "Delta Blues," *Wall Street Journal,* 27 January 1998, A1, A10; STACY PERMAN, "Allied Air Force," *Time,* 9 February 1998, 76, 79.

12. LEWIS M. SIMONS, "High-Tech Jobs for Sale," *Time,* 22 July 1996, 59.

13. ALDEN, "What in the World Drives UPS?" 6–7.

14. ERNEST BECK AND EMILY NELSON, "As Wal-Mart Invades Europe, Rivals Rush to Match Its Formula," *Wall Street Journal,* 6 October 1999, A1, A6.

15. "Foreign Investment in U.S. Reaches 54.4 Billion Dollars in 1995," *Xinhua News Agency,* 1996.

16. THOMAS G. CONDON AND KURT BADENHAUSEN, "Spending Spree," *Forbes,* 26 July 1999, 208–218.

17. *Big Emerging Markets: 1996 Outlook* (Washington D.C.: GPO, 1996); NICHOLAS D. KRISTOF AND SHERYL WUDUNN, "The World's Ills May Be Obvious, But Their Cure Is Not," *New York Times,* 18 February 1999 [accessed 19 February 1999], http://www.nytimes.com/library/world/global/021699global-econ.html.

18. PATRICK LANE, "World Trade Survey: Why Trade Is Good for You," *The Economist,* 3 October 1998, S4–S6.

19. HOLLEY H. ULBRICH AND MELLIE L. WARNER, *Managerial Economics* (New York: Barron's Educational Series, 1990), 190.

20. "U.S. International Trade in Goods & Services September 21, 1999 News Release," Bureau of Economic Analysis Web site [accessed 3 October 1999], http://www.bea.doc.gov/ bea/di/tradgs-d.htm.

21. MARIA MALLORY, "Wheels of Fortune," *U.S. News & World Report,* 4 March 1996, 49–50.

22. Table 1—U.S. International Transactions, Bureau of Economic Analysis Web site [accessed 27 October 1999], http://www.bea.doc.gov/bea/di/bopq/bop1./htm.

23. PETER F. DRUCKER, "Change Leaders," *Inc.,* June 1999, 65–72.

24. ROBERT J. SAMUELSON, "Trading with the Enemy," *Newsweek,* 1 April 1996, 41; AMY BORRUS, PETE ENGARDIO, AND DEXTER ROBERTS, "The New Trade Superpower," *Business Week,* 16 October 1995, 56–57; DAVID A. ANDELMAN, "Marco Polo Revisited," *American Management Association,* August 1995, 10–12; JOHN GREENWALD, "Get Asia Now, Pay Later," *Time,* 10 October 1994, 61; SIMONS, "High-Tech Jobs for Sale," 59.

25. ERIC SCHMITT, "U.S. Backs off Sanctions, Seeing Poor Effect Abroad," *New York Times,* 31 July 1998, A1, A6; ROBERT T. GRAY, "Book Review," *Nation's Business,* January 1999, 47.

26. "Saudi Arabia Hopes to Join WTO by 2002," *Reuters Business Report,* 3 August 1997.

27. "Airbus to Resume Talks on Status," *New York Times,* 5 May 1999, C4.

28. ELLYN FERGUSON, "Here Are Details of New Farm Law," *Gannett News Service,* 4 April 1996, S12.

29. STEVE HOLLAND, "China Decries Anti-Dumping Actions by U.S., E.U.," *Reuters,* 23 January 1996.

30. SEELEY LODWICK, "Reviewing the World Trade Organization," *Choices: The Magazine of Food, Farm, & Resources Issues,* 1 January 1996, 29; BRUCE BARNARD, "WTO," *Europe,* November 1994, 22–23; ELIZABETH OLSON, "Many Steps to Go Before China Can Become a Full Member," *New York Times,* 16 November 1999, [accessed online 16 November 1999], http://www.nytimes.com/library/world/asia/111699china-us-moore.html.

31. "APEC Ministers Commit to Sustainable Development," *Xinhau News Agency,* 11 June 1997; FRED C. BERGSTEN, "An Asian Push for World-Wide Free Trade: The Case For APEC," *The Economist,* 6 January 1996, 62; "U.S. Must Press to Reduce Trade Barriers in Asia, Pacific, Congress Told," *Gannett News Service,* 1995.

32. MICHAEL M. PHILLIPS, "One by One," *Wall Street Journal,* 26 April 1999, R4, R7.

33. CHRISTOPHER KOCH. "It's a Wired, Wired World," *Webmaster,* March 1997, 50–55.

34. MASAAKI KOTABE AND MARIA CECILIA COUTINHO DE ARRUDA, "South America's Free Trade Gambit," *Marketing Management,* Spring 1998, 39–46.

35. "Grand Illusions," *The Economist,* 4 March 1995, 87; Bob Davis, "Global Paradox: Growth of Trade Binds Nations, But It Also Can Spur Separatism," *Wall Street Journal,* 20 June 1994, A1, A6; BARBARA RUDOLPH, "Megamarket," *Time,* 10 August 1992, 43–44; PETER TRUELL, "Free Trade May Suffer from Regional Blocs," *Wall Street Journal,* 1 July 1991, A1.

36. EMERIC LEPOURTE, "Europe's Challenge to the U.S. in South America's Biggest Market," *Christian Science Monitor,* 8 April 1997, 19; MARIO OSAVA, "Mercosur: Free Trade with Europe More Advantageous Than FTAA," *Inter Press English News Wire,* 6 May 1997; ROBERT MAYNARD, "At a Crossroads in Latin America," *Nation's Business,* April 1996, 38–39; GREGORY L. MILES AND LOUBNA FREIH, "Join the Caribbean Revolution," *International Business,* September 1994, 42–54; MATT MOFFETT, "Spreading the Gospel," *Wall Street Journal,* 28 October 1994, R12.

37. JOEL RUSSELL, "NAFTA in the Real World," *Hispanic Business,* June 1996, 22–28; SCOT J. PALTROW, "NAFTA's Job Impact Slight, Study Says," *Los Angeles Times,* 19 December 1996, D3.

38. "Sweden Says EU Enlargement Outweighs NATO Expansion," *Xinhua News Agency,* 16 July 1996; HELENE COOPER, "The Euro: What You Need to Know," *Wall Street Journal,* 4 January 1999, A5, A6.

39. THOMAS KAMM, "EU Certifies Participants for Euro," *Wall Street Journal,* 26 March 1998, A14.

40. THANE PETERSON, "The Euro," *Business Week,* 27 April 1998, 90–94; JOAN WARNER, "The Great Money Bazaar," *Business Week,* 27 April 1998, 96–98; GAIL EDMONDSON, "Industrial Evolution," *Business Week,* 27 April 1998, 100–101.

41. MICHAEL R. SESIT, "Currency Contenders," *Wall Street Journal,* 28 September 1998, R18; LOUIS UCHITELLE, "Euro Has Plenty of Time to Challenge the Dollar," *New York Times,* 25 April 1999, BU4; MICHAEL R. SESIT, "It's Much Too Early for Angst over Euro," *Wall Street Journal,* 7 June 1999, A1.

42. TOM PETRUNO AND ART PINE, "Indonesian Currency Fall Deepens Asia Crisis," *Los Angeles Times,* 9 January 1998, A1.

43. PETE ENGARDIO, CHRISTINA HOAG, AND PETER COY, "Déjà Vu?" *Business Week,* 21 December 1998, 34–35.

44. MARK WHITEHOUSE, "Capital Flight Remains Draining Problem for Russia," *Wall Street Journal,* 19 April 1999, A19.

45. JEFFREY D. SACHS, "Rule of the Ruble"; *New York Times,* 4 June 1998, A27; RICHARD

LACAYO, "IMF to the Rescue," *Time,* 8 December 1997, 37–39; PAUL KRUGMAN, "Saving Asia: It's Time to Get Radical," *Fortune,* 7 September 1998, 75–80.

46. SACHS, "Rule of the Ruble," LACAYO, "IMF to the Rescue."

47. SACHS, "Rule of the Ruble"; LACAYO, "IMF to the Rescue."

48. NICHOLAS D. KRISTOF AND DAVID E. SANGER, "How U.S. Wooed Asia to Let Cash Flow In," *New York Times* Web site, 15 February 1999 [accessed 15 February 1999], http://www. nytimes.com/library/world/global/021699global-econ.html; KRUGMAN, "Saving Asia"; PHILLIPS, "One by One."

49. KRISTOF AND SANGER, "How U.S. Wooed Asia to Let Cash Flow In."

50. KRISTOF AND WUDUNN, "The World's Ills May Be Obvious, But Their Cure Is Not."

51. JEAN-MICHAEL PAUL, "Asian Economies May Suffer a Relapse," *Wall Street Journal,* 5 May 1999, A22; MICHAEL SCHUMAN, "Korea's Fast Recovery Suggests That Reform Isn't the Only Answer," *Wall Street Journal,* 14 May 1999, A1, A6.

52. LAURENCE ZUCKERMAN, "Boeing's Leaders Losing Altitude," *New York Times,* 13 December 1998, BU1, 11.

53. JUSTIN FOX, "Forecast for the U.S. Economy: Still Mostly Sunny," *Fortune,* 15 February 1999, 92–98; DAVID E. SANGER, "U.S. Trade Deficit Soared in '98, Reaching Record $168.8 Billion," *New York Times,* 20 February 1999, A1, B2; MICHAEL M. PHILLIPS, "How Long Can the U.S. Stay Immune to What Ails the Economy?" *Wall Street Journal,* 5 February 1999, A1, A10.

54. PHILLIPS, "How Long Can the U.S. Stay Immune to What Ails the Economy?"

55. GEORGE MELLOAN, "Best Laid Plans Go Awry When Currencies Fail," *Wall Street Journal,* 29 September 1998, A23; MARK L. CLIFFORD AND PETE ENGARDIO, "There's No Wishing This Crisis Away," *Business Week,* 31 August 1998, 28–29.

56. Adapted from MARUCA, "The Right Way to Go Global"; DUARTE AND SNYDER, "From Experience"; JANCSURAK, "Whirlpool"; QUINTANILLA, "Despite Setbacks, Whirlpool Pursues Overseas Markets"; KATZ, "Whirlpool"; Cutler, "Asia Challenges Whirlpool Technology"; "Whirlpool Europe and Tupperware Europe Announce Strategic Alliance."

57. Associated Press, "Flood of Imports into Argentina Delights Shoppers, Riles Local Industry," *Los Angeles Times,* 6 January 1992, D4.

58. ADAM ZAGORIN, "The Great Banana War," *Time,* 8 February 1999 [accessed 11 May 1999], http://www.pathfinder.com.

59. "USAJobs: International Trade Specialist," USA Jobs Web site [accessed 17 June 1999], http://www.usajobs.opm.gov/wfjic/jobs/BL2896.htm.

60. Adapted from DAVID KIRKPATRICK, "Intel's Amazing Profit Machine," *Fortune,* 17

February 1997, 60–72; ANDY REINHARDT, IRA SAGER, AND PETER BURROWS, "Intel," *Business Week,* 22 December 1997, 70–77; JOHN H. SHERIDAN, "Andy Grove: Building an Information Age," *IW,* 15 December 1997, 65–77; DAVID KIRPATRICK, "Intel's Got a Bigger Problem Than the FTC," *Fortune,* 6 July 1998, 30–32; ANDY REINHARDT AND PETER BURROWS, "It's Not Easy Being Cheap," *Business Week,* 17 August 1998, 62–63; ANDY REINHARDT, "Who Says Intel's Chips Are Down," *Business Week,* 7 December 1998, 103–104; ANDY REINHARDT, "Intel Is Taking No Prisoners," *Business Week,* 12 July 1999, 38; ELIZABETH CORCORAN, "Reinventing Intel," *Forbes,* 3 May 1999, 154–159; DEAN TAKAHASHI, "AMD Reports Record Loss for 2nd Period," *Wall Street Journal,* 15 July 1999, A3, A6; DEAN TAKAHASHI, "Intel Posts Earning Below Expectations," *Wall Street Journal,* 14 July 1999, A3, A10.

CHAPTER 4

1. TOM DUFFY, "Baking Up Millions," *Self Employed Professional,* May–June 1997, 22–27; CAROLE MATTHEWS, "Grassroots Marketing," *Self-Employed Professional,* May–June 1997, 22; "Gordon: The 6-Foot 9-Inch Pieguy . . ." *Top of the Tree Baking Company* [accessed 24 March 1999], http://www.gordonpies.com/gordons3.htm.

2. DAVID BIRCH, "Thinking About Tomorrow," *Wall Street Journal,* 24 May 1999, R30–R31.

3. CLAUDIA H. DEUTSCH, "When a Big Company Hatches a Lot of Little Ideas," *New York Times,* 23 September 1998, D4.

4. "Matters of Fact," *Inc.,* April 1985, 32.

5. ELIZABETH MACDONALD, "Slim Pickings," *Wall Street Journal,* 22 May 1997, R6; STEPHANIE N. MEHTA, "Small Talk," *Wall Street Journal,* 23 May 1996, R28–R30; *Small Business Association* Web site [accessed 16 May 1999], http://smallbusinesssuccess.sba. gov/stats.html.

6. JANICE CASTRO, "Big vs. Small," *Time,* 5 September 1988, 49; STEVE SOLOMON, *Small Business USA* (New York: Crown, 1986), 124.

7. LLOYD GITE AND DAWN M. BASKERVILLE, "Black Women Entrepreneurs on the Rise," *Black Enterprise,* August 1996, 73–74.

8. RACHEL BECK, *Wall Street Journal Interactive Edition—Small Business Suite,* 28 March 1998 [accessed 21 April 1998], http://interactive.wsj.com/public/currentarticles/SB891025783545694000.htm.

9. MEHTA, "Small Talk."

10. PETER F. DRUCKER, *Management Challenges for the 21st Century* (New York: HarperBusiness, 1999), 37; MICHAEL MOELLER, STEVE HAMM, AND TIMOTHY J. MULLANEY, "Remaking Microsoft," *Business Week,* 17 May 1999, 106–116.

11. MICHAEL MOELLER, STEVE HAMM, AND TIMOTHY J. MULLANEY, "Remaking Microsoft," *Business Week,* 17 May 1999, 106–116.

12. TIMOTHY D. SCHELHARDT, "David in Goliath," *Wall Street Journal,* 23 May 1996, R14; DEUTSCH, "When a Big Company Hatches a Lot of Little Ideas."

13. *Inc. Special Edition—The State of Small Business 1997,* 20 May 1997, 121.

14. JAMES WILFONG AND TONI SEGER, *Taking Your Business Global* (Franklin Lakes, NJ: Career Press, 1997), 301.

15. JOSHUA MACHT, "The Two Hundred Million Dash," *Inc. Technology 1997,* 16 September 1997, 48–55.

16. TIM McCOLLUM, "A High-Tech Edge for Home Offices," *Nation's Business,* December 1998, 52–54.

17. *Inc. Special Edition—The State of Small Business 1997,* 112; JAMES WILFONG AND TONI SEGER, *Taking Your Business Global* (Franklin Lakes, N.J.: Career Press, 1997), 84.

18. JANE FRITSCH, "Big in Small Business, Straining to Grow," *New York Times,* 23 September 1998, D2.

19. STEPHANIE ARMOUR, "Many Turn to Start-Ups for Freedom," *USA Today,* 8 June 1998, 1B, 2B; "The Top 500 Women-Owned Businesses," *Working Woman,* May 1998, 50.

20. GORDON FAIRCLOUGH, "P&G to Slash 13,000 Jobs, Shut 10 Plants," *Wall Street Journal,* 10 June 1999, A3, A10.

21. CAROLYN BROWN, "How to Make Your Ex-Boss Your Client," *Black Enterprise,* 30 April 1994, 95.

22. TOM RICHMAN, "Creators of the New Economy," *Inc.—Special Edition: The State of Small Business 1997,* 20 May 1997, 44–48.

23. BRIAN O'REILLY, "The New Face of Small Business," *Fortune,* 2 May 1994, 82–88.

24. DONNA FENN, "The Buyers," *Inc.,* June 1996, 46–52.

25. MARK ROBICHAUX, "Business First, Family Second," *Wall Street Journal,* 12 May 1989, B1.

26. RICK MENDOSA, "A Side Order of Success," *Hispanic Business,* August 1995, 48–50.

27. JANE APPLEGATE, *Succeeding in Small Business* (New York: Plume/Penguin, 1992), 1.

28. WILFONG AND SEGER, *Taking Your Business Global,* 78–80; KELLY J. ANDREWS, "Born or Bred?" *Entrepreneurial Edge* 3 (1998): 24–28.

29. LISA J. MOORE AND SHARON F. GOLDEN, "You Can Plan to Expand or Just Let It Happen," *U.S. News & World Report,* 23 October 1989, 78; JOHN CASE, "The Origins of Entrepreneurship," *Inc.,* June 1989, 56.

30. WARREN BENNIS, "Becoming a Leader of Leaders," *Rethinking the Future* (London: Nicholas Brealey Publishing, 1997), 159.

31. J. TOL BROOME JR., "How to Write a Business Plan," *Nation's Business,* February 1993, 29–30; ALBERT RICHARDS, "The Ernst & Young Business Plan Guide," *R & D Management,* April 1995, 253; DAVID LANCHNER, "How Chitchat Became a Valuable Business Plan," *Global Finance,* February 1995, 54–56; MARGUERITA

ASHBY-BERGER, "My Business Plan—and What Really Happened," *Small Business Forum,* Winter 1994–1995, 24–35; STANLEY R. RICH AND DAVID E. GUMPERT, *Business Plans That Win $$$* (New York: Harper Row, 1985).

32. RICH AND GUMPERT, *Business Plans That Win $$$.*

33. JOSEPH W. DUNCAN, "The True Failure Rate of Start-Ups," *D&B Reports,* January–February 1994; MAGGIE JONES, "Smart Cookies," *Working Woman,* April 1995, 50–52; JANICE MALONEY, "Failure May Not Be So Bad After All," *New York Times,* 23 September 1998, 12.

34. JERRY USEEM "Failure," *Inc.,* May 1998, 67–80.

35. JAMES A. BELASCO AND RALPH C. STAYER, *Flight of the Buffalo* (New York, Warner Books, 1993), 317–321.

36. MALONEY, "Failure May Not Be So Bad After All."

37. GERDA D. GALLOP AND ROZ AYRES-WILLIAMS, "Five Things You Should Know Before Starting a Business," *Black Enterprise,* September 1998, 66–72.

38. *SCORE* Web site [accessed September 18, 1997], http://www.score.org; J. TOL BROOME JR., "SCORE's Impact on Small Firms"; *Nation's Business,* January 1999, 41–43.

39. BROOME, "SCORE's Impact on Small Firms,"; ROBERT MCGARVEY, "Peak Performance," *American Way,* July 1996, 56–60.

40. DALE BUSS, "Bringing New Firms out of Their Shell," *Nation's Business,* March 1997, 48–50.

41. BUSS, "Bringing New Firms out of Their Shell."

42. Data provided by the National Business Incubation Association, 153 South Hanover Street, Carlisle, Penn. 17013; DAVID RIGGLE, "Great Places to Grow a Business," *In Business,* September–October 1990, 20–22.

43. MCGARVEY, "Peak Performance."

44. NORM BRODSKY, "Caveat Emptor," *Inc.,* August 1998, 31–32; "Why Buy a Business?" *CCH Toolkit Web site* [accessed 20 May 1999], http://aol.toolkit.cch.com/text/PO1_0820.asp.

45. DALE BUSS, "New Dynamics for a New Era," *Nation's Business,* January 1999, 45–48.

46. CAROLYN M. BROWN, "All Talk, No Action," *Black Enterprise,* September 1995, 60–64; "Franchising Fellowship," *Marketing Management* 4, no. 2 (Fall 1995): 4–6; ROBERTA MAYNARD, "The Changing Landscape," *Nation's Business,* January 1997, 54–55.

47. NICOLE HARRIS AND MIKE FRANCE, "Franchisees Get Feisty," *Business Week,* 24 February 1997, 65–66; ROBERTA MAYNARD, "Prospecting for Gold," *Nation's Business,* June 1996, 69–74.

48. ROGER RICKLEFS, "Road to Success Becomes Less Littered with Failures," *Wall Street Journal,* 10 November 1989, B2.

49. CONSTANCE MITCHELL, "Franchising Fever Spreads," *USA Today,* 13 September 1985, 4B.

50. MAYNARD, "The Changing Landscape."

51. ROBERTA MAYNARD, "Choosing a Franchise," *Nation's Business,* October 1996, 56–63.

52. LATONYA WEST, "Success Is Convenient," *Minorities in Business* [undated], 22–26.

53. JEFFREY A. TANNENBAUM, "Taking a Bath," *Wall Street Journal,* 22 June 1998, 27.

54. BOB ZIDER, "How Venture Capital Works," *Harvard Business Review,* November/December 1998, 131–139.

55. CARYN BROWN, "The Best Ways to Finance Your Business," *Black Enterprise,* June 1993, 270–278.

56. JANE EASTER BAHLS, "Cyber Cash," *Entrepreneur,* March 1999, 109–113; "Startup Financing: Finding an Angel to Get Going," *CCH Business Owners Toolkit Web site* [accessed 20 May 1999], http://aol.toolkit.cch.com/columns/Starting/225-99AngelR.asp.

57. PAUL CARROLL, "More High-Tech Entrepreneurs Turn to Angels," *Wall Street Journal,* 20 May 1996, B1; "Who's Funding Today's Emerging Businesses?" *Inc.—Special Edition: State of Small Business 1997,* 20 May 1997, 118.

58. RODNEY HO, "Banking on Plastic," *Wall Street Journal,* 9 March 1998, A1, A8.

59. JOEL RUSSELL, "Credit Card Capitalism," *Hispanic Business,* March 1998, 40.

60. WILFONG AND SEGER, *Taking Your Business Global,* 20.

61. RONALEEN R. ROHA, "Big Loans for Small Businesses," *Changing Times,* April 1989, 105–109; "Small Loans, Big Problems," *Economist,* 28 January 1995, 73; ELIZABETH KADETSKY, "Small Loans, Big Dreams," *Working Woman,* February 1995, 46–49; REID RUTHERFORD, "Securitizing Small Business Loans: A Banker's Action Plan," *Commercial Lending Review,* Winter 1994–1995, 62–74.

62. ROHA, "Big Loans for Small Businesses," 105.

63. SUSAN HODGES, "Microloans Fuel Big Ideas," *Nation's Business,* February 1997, 34–35.

64. KAREN GUTLOFF, "Five Alternative Ways to Finance Your Business," *Black Enterprise,* March 1998, 81–85.

65. SHARON NELTON, "Coming to Grips with Growth," *Nation's Business,* February 1998, 26–32.

66. NELTON, "Coming to Grips with Growth."

67. NELTON, "Coming to Grips with Growth."

68. NELTON, "Coming to Grips with Growth."

69. MICHAEL SELZ, "Here's the Problem," *Wall Street Journal—Breakaway Special Report Winter 1999,* 22 February 1999, 12.

70. LOUISE LEE, "A Company Failing from Too Much Success," *Wall Street Journal,* 17 March 1995, B1.

71. DUFFY, "Baking Up Millions"; Matthews, "Grassroots Marketing"; "Gordon: The

6-Foot 9-Inch Pieguy . . ." *Top of the Tree Baking Company* [accessed 24 March 1999], http://www.gordonpies.com/gordons3.htm.

72. PATTI BOND, "Hispanics Display Growing Muscle in Entrepreneurship," *Atlanta Journal-Constitution,* 11 July 1996, B1.

CHAPTER 5

1. Adapted from *Kinko's* Web site http://www.kinkos.com/info [accessed 13 December 1998]; SHAWN TULLY, "A Better Taskmaster Than the Market," *Fortune,* 26 October 1998, 277–286; LAURIE J. FLYNN, "For the Officeless, A Place to Call Home," *New York Times,* 6 July 1998, 1, 4; MICHELE MARCHETTI, "Getting the Kinks Out," *Sales and Marketing Management,* March 1997, 56–64; "Man of Few Words," *Sales and Marketing Management,* March 1997, 63; "Kinko's Improves Image of Businesses with Top-Notch Proposals and Presentations Capabilities; Presentations a Growing Percentage of Customer Work at Kinko's," *Business Wire,* 28 September 1997; "Kinko's Strengthens Office Product Assortment," *Discount Store News,* 17 November 1997, 6, 70; ANN MARSH, "Kinko's Grows Up—Almost," *Forbes,* 1 December 1997, 270–272; "Kinko's Strikes Deal for Mideast Growth," *Graphic Arts Monthly,* January 1998, 22; LORI IOANNOU AND PAUL ORFALEA, "Interview: The Brains Behind Kinko's," *Your Company,* 1 May 1999, 62.

2. DAVID WHITFORD, "Arthur, Arthur," *Fortune,* 10 November 1997, 169.

3. JAMES W. CORTADA, "Do You Take This Partner," *Total Quality Review,* November–December 1995, 11.

4. MARCIA VICKERS, "How Tight Is the Knot in Partnership Pacts?" *New York Times,* 8 June 1997, F9.

5. LAURENCE ZUCKERMAN, "UPS Hears Market's Song, And Plans to Sell Some Stock," *New York Times,* 22 July 1999, A1, C23.

6. ROBERTA MAYNARD, "Are You Ready to Go Public," *Nation's Business,* January 1995, 30–32.

7. ROBERT A. MAMIS, "Face to Face—Andy Klein," *Inc.,* July 1996, 39–40; SHARON NELTON, "Using the Internet to Find Funds," *Nation's Business,* August 1998, 35–36.

8. NELTON, "Using the Internet to Find Funds."

9. STEPHANIE GRUNER, "When Mom & Pop Go Public," *Inc.,* December 1996, 66–73.

10. ROBERT G. GOLDSTEIN, RUSSELL SHAPIRO, AND EDWARD A. HAUDER, "So Many Choices of Business Entities—Which One Is Best for Your Needs?" *Insight (CPA Society),* February/March 1999, 10–16.

11. RANA DOGAR, "Crony Baloney," *Working Woman,* January 1997; RICHARD H. KOPPES, "Institutional Investors, Now in Control of More Than Half the Shares of U.S. Corporations, Demand More Accountability," *National Law Journal,* 14

April 1997, B5; JOHN A. BYRNE, "The Best & Worst Boards," *Business Week,* 25 November 1996, 82–84; ANTHONY BIANCO, JOHN BYRNE, RICHARD MELCHER, AND MARK MAREMONT, "The Rush to Quality on Corporate Boards," *Business Week,* 3 March 1997, 34–35.

12. CLIFF EDWARDS, "President of United Airlines Reigns Under Union Pressure—Edwardson Steps Down to Sidestep Turmoil," *Denver Rocky Mountain News,* 19 September 1998, 2B.

13. BARBARA ETTORRE, "Changing the Rules of the Board Game," *Management Review,* April 1996, 13–15; JOHN A. BYRNE, "Listen Up: The National Association of Corporate Directors' New Guidelines Won't Tolerate Inattentive, Passive, Uninformed Board Members," *Business Week,* 25 November 1996, 100; DOGAR, "Crony Baloney," 34–35; BYRNE, "The Best & Worst Boards" Bianco et al., "The Rush to Quality on Corporate Boards."

14. MARTHA T. MOORE, "Firms Look Globally to Diversify Boards," *USA Today,* 4 December 1995, B7.

15. VIVIEN KELLERMAN, "A Growing Business Takes the Corporate Plunge," *New York Times,* 23 July 1994, sec. Your Money, 31.

16. NELSON D. SCHWARTZ, "A Tale of Two Economies," *Fortune,* 26 April 1999, 198–204; "Fortune 500—Ranked within States," *Fortune,* 26 April 1999, F33–F50.

17. "WorldCom and MCI Announce $37 Billion Merger," *Cambridge Telecom Report,* 17 November 1997, *Electric Library,* Online [accessed 21 January 1998]; LAURA M. HOLSON AND SETH SCHIESEL, "MCI to Buy Sprint in Swap of Stock for $108 Billion," *New York Times,* 5 October 1999, A1, C13; Matt Hamblen, "MCI WorldCom Responds to Sprint Merger Concerns," *Computerworld,* 18 October 1999, 66.

18. SAUL HANSELL, "Pitfalls Loom in Possible Merger of Two Exchanges," *New York Times,* 16 March 1998, C5; SUZANNE MCGEE, "Nasdaq Opts for Options After All," *Wall Street Journal,* 13 March 1998, C1, C13.

19. DAVID A. NADLER, "10 Steps to a Happy Merger," *New York Times,* 15 March 1998, BU14.

20. PETER PASSELL, "Do Mergers Really Yield Big Benefits?" *New York Times,* 14 May 1998, C1, C2.

21. "Merger Mania, Sobering Statistics," *The Economist,* 20 June 1998, 89.

22. ALEX TAYLOR III, "More Mergers. Dumb Idea," *Fortune,* 15 February 1999, 26–27.

23. TOM PETERS, *Thriving on Chaos* (New York: HarperPerennial, 1988), 9.

24. NADLER, "10 Steps to a Happy Merger"; GLENN RIFKIN, "How IBM and Lotus Work Together," *Strategy and Business,* Third Quarter 1998, 42–61.

25. J. ROBERT CARLETON, "Cultural Due Diligence," *Training,* November 1997, 67–75; "How to Merge," *The Economist.*

26. ALMAR LATOUR, "Detroit Meets a Worker Paradise," *Wall Street Journal,* 3 March 1999, B1, B4.

27. "How to Merge," *The Economist,* 9 January 1999, 21–23.

28. DAVID LIEBERMAN, "Experts Doubt Co-CEO's Can Share Power," *USA Today,* 7 April 1998, 1B.

29. RAM CHARAN, "Two on Top," *Fortune,* 25 May 1998, 193–194.

30. TOM PETERS, *Thriving on Chaos* (New York: HarperPerennial, 1988), 333.

31. SUSAN CHANDLER, "Tracing Trouble at Wards," *Chicago Tribune,* 13 July 1997, sec. 5, 1.

32. MICHAEL ONEAL, BRIAN BREMNER, JONATHAN B. LEVINE, TODD VOGEL, ZACHARY SCHILLER, AND DAVID WOODRUFF, "The Best and Worst Deals of the '80s," *Business Week,* 15 January 1990, 52.

33. IRVING W. BAILEY II AND ALVIN H. SCHECHTER, "The Corporation As Brand: An Identity Dilemma," *Chief Executive,* October 1994, 42.

34. "1999 Mergers and Acquisitions Stack Up to a Remarkable Year," *Weekly Corporate Growth Report,* 15 February 1999, 10025–10030.

35. WILLIAM GLASSALL, JOHN ROSSANT, AND THANE PETERSON, "The Citicorp-Travelers Deal May Point the Way to the Future of Financial Services," *Business Week,* 20 April 1998, 35–37.

36. MARTIN PEERS, NICK WINGFIELD AND LAURA LANDRO, "AOL, Time Warner Set Plan to Link in Mammoth Merger," *The Wall Street Journal,* 11 January 2000, A1, A6; THOMAS E. WEBER, MARTIN PEERS, AND NICK WINGFIELD, "Two Titans in a Strategic Bind Bet on a Futuristic Megadeal," *Wall Street Journal,* 11 January 2000, B1, B12; "AOL and Time Warner Will Merge to Create World's First Internet-Age Media and Communications Company," America Online Web site, http://media.web.aol.com/media/press.cfm, [accessed 11 January 2000].

37. TIM JONES, "FCC Questions Phone Deal," *Chicago Tribune,* 6 October 1999, sec. 1, 1.

38. JEFFREY TAYLOR, "Alarm Bells," *Wall Street Journal,* 12 May 1998, A1, A8; TIM JONES AND FRANK JAMES, "FCC Head: No Ring of Certainty for Deal," *Chicago Tribune,* 13 May 1998, sec. 1, 1, 22; JEFFREY A. TANNENBAUM, "The Consolidators: Acquisitive Companies Set Out to 'Roll Up' Fragmented Industries," *Wall Street Journal,* 3 March 1997, A1; JON VAN, "Ameritech Deal Targets Stocks over Consumers," *Chicago Tribune,* 12 May 1998, sec. 1, 1, 10.

39. MICHAEL ARNDT, "A Baby Bell, No More, Ameritech Has New Parent," *Chicago Tribune,* 10 October 1999, sec. 5, 2.

40. ELEENA DE LISSER, "Banking on Mergers," *Wall Street Journal,* 24 May 1999, R25.

41. STEPHEN LABATON, "U.S. Set to Clear a Merger between Exxon and Mobil," *New York Times,* 27 November 1999, A1, B2.

42. MERRILL GOOZNER AND JOHN SCHMELTZER, "Mass Exodus Hits Corporate Names," *Chicago Tribune,* 12 May 1998, sec. 3, 1, 3; Bill Vlasic, "The First Global Car Colossus," *Business Week,* 18 May 1998, 40–43; ABID ASLAM, "Exxon-Mobil Merger Could Poison the Well," *Inter Press Service English News Wire,* 2 December 1998, *Electric Library* [accessed 2 June 1999]; AGIS SALPUKAS, "Do Oil and Bigger Oil Mix?" *New York Times,* 2 December 1998, C1, C4.

43. STEVE LIPEN, "Concentration: Corporations' Dreams Converge in One Idea: It's Time to Do a Deal," *Wall Street Journal,* 26 February 1997, A1, A8.

44. JOANN S. LUBLIN, " 'Poison Pills' Are Giving Shareholders a Big Headache, Union Proposals Assert," *Wall Street Journal,* 23 May 1997, C1.

45. THOMAS MULLIGAN, "ITT Takes Starwood Offer," *Los Angeles Times,* 13 November 1997, D2; KATHLEEN MORRIS, "Behind the New Deal Mania," *Business Week,* 3 November 1997, 36.

46. MARTHA GROVES AND STUART SILVERSTEIN, "Levi Strauss Offers Year's Pay As Incentive Bonus," *Los Angeles Times,* 13 June 1996, A1.

47. Adapted from *Kinko's* Web site http://www.kinkos.com/info [accessed 13 December 1998]; TULLY, "A Better Taskmaster Than the Market"; FLYNN, "For the Officeless, A Place to Call Home"; Marchetti, "Getting the Kinks Out"; "Man of Few Words"; "Kinko's Improves Image of Businesses with Top-Notch Proposals and Presentations Capabilities"; "Kinko's Strengthens Office Product Assortment"; Marsh, "Kinko's Grows Up"; "Kinko's Strikes Deal for Mideast Growth"; IOANNOU AND ORFALEA, "Interview".

48. "Entrepreneurs across America," *Entrepreneur Magazine Online* [accessed 12 June 1997], http://www.entrepreneurmag.com/entmag/50states5.hts.

49. JEFFREY BALL AND SCOTT MILLER, "Full Speed Ahead: Stuttgart's Control Grows With Shakeup at DaimlerChrysler," *Wall Street Journal,* 24 September 1999, A1, A8; ROBERT L. SIMISON AND SCOTT MILLER, "Making Digital Decision," *Wall Street Journal,* 24 September 1999, B1, B4; KEITH BRADSHER, "A Struggle Over Culture and Turf at Auto Giant," *New York Times,* 25 September 1999, B1, B14; "Message from DaimlerChrysler Chairmen to Company Employees," *Wall Street Journal,* 24 September 1999, A15; JOANN MULLER, KATHLEEN KERWIN, AND JACK EWING, "Man With a Plan," *Business Week,* 4 October 1999, 34–35; FRANK GIBNEY JR., "Worldwide Fender Bender," *Time,* 24 May 1999, 58–62; DANIEL MCGINN AND STEFAN THEIL, "Hands on the Wheel," *Newsweek,* 12 April 1999, 49–52; ALEX TAYLOR III, "The Germans Take Charge," *Fortune,* 11 January 1999, 92–96; BARRETT SEAMAN

AND RON STODGHILL II, "The Daimler-Chrysler Deal; Here Comes the Road Test," *Time,* 18 May 1999, 66–69; BILL VLASIC, KATHLEEN KERWIN, DAVID WOODRUFF, THANE PETERSON, AND LEAH NATHANS SPIRO, "The First Global Car Colossus," *Business Week,* 18 May 1998, 40–43; JOANN MULLER, "Lessons From a Casualty of the Culture Wars," *Business Week,* 29 November 1999, 198.

CHAPTER 6

1. CHRIS BLACKHURST, "At the Court of King Richard," *Management Today,* April 1998, 38–44; "Business: Behind Branson," *The Economist,* 21 February 1998, 63–66; JULIA FLYNN, "Then Came Branson," *Business Week,* 26 October 1998, 116, 118, 120; MANFRED F. R. KETS DE VRIES, "Charisma in Action: The Transformational Abilities of Virgin's Richard Branson and ABB's Percy Barnevik," *Organizational Dynamics,* Winter 1998, 6–21; GLENN RIFKIN, "How Richard Branson Works Magic," *Strategy and Business,* Fourth Quarter 1998, 44–52.
2. RICHARD L. DAFT, *Management,* 4th ed. (Fort Worth: Dryden Press, 1997), 8.
3. STEPHEN P. ROBBINS, *Managing Today* (Upper Saddle River, N.J.: Prentice Hall, 1997), 452.
4. DAVID BANK AND DON CLARK, "Microsoft Broadens Vision Statement Beyond PCs," *Wall Street Journal,* 23 July 1999, A3, A4.
5. JERRY USEEM, "Internet Defense Strategy: Cannibalize Yourself," *Fortune,* 6 September 1999, 121–134.
6. LEONARD GOODSTEIN, TIMOTHY NOLAN, AND J. WILLIAM PFEIFFER, *Applied Strategic Planning* (New York: McGraw-Hill, 1993), 169–192.
7. AIMEE L. STERN, "Management: You Can Keep Your Staff on the Competitive Track If You . . . Inspire Your Team with a Mission Statement," *Your Company,* 1 August 1997, 36, *Electric Library,* Online [accessed 2 September 1997].
8. STEPHANIE ARMOUR, "Once Plagued by Pink Slips, Now They're in Driver's Seat," *USA Today,* 14 May 1998, 1B–2B.
9. DAFT, *Management,* 219–221.
10. COURTLAND L. BOVÉE, JOHN V. THILL, MARIAN BURK WOOD, AND GEORGE P. DOVEL, *Management* (New York: McGraw-Hill, 1993), 220; DAVID H. HOLT, *Management: Principles and Practices,* 2d ed. (Upper Saddle River, N.J.: Prentice Hall, 1990), 10–12; JAMES A. F. STONER, *Management,* 4th ed. (Upper Saddle River, N.J.: Prentice Hall, 1989), 15–18.
11. ROBERT L. KATZ, "Skills of an Effective Administrator," *Harvard Business Review,* September–October 1974. Reprinted in *Paths Toward Personal Progress: Leaders Are Made, Not Born* (Boston: Harvard Business Review, 1983), 23–35; MIKE DAWSON, "Leaders Versus Managers," *Systems Management,*

March 1995, 32; R. S. DREYER, "Do Good Bosses Make Lousy Leaders?" *Supervision,* March 1995, 19–20; MICHAEL MACCOBY, "Teams Need Open Leaders," *Research-Technology Management,* January–February 1995, 57–59.
12. RIFKIN, "How Richard Branson Works Magic."
13. COURTLAND L. BOVÉE AND JOHN V. THILL, *Business Communication Today,* 6th ed. (Upper Saddle River, N.J.: Prentice Hall, 2000), 4.
14. DAFT, *Management,* 128; KATHRYN M. BARTOL AND DAVID C. MARTIN, *Management* (New York: McGraw-Hill, 1991), 268–272.
15. BARTOL AND MARTIN, *Management,* 268–272; RICKY W. GRIFFIN, *Management,* 3d ed. (Boston: Houghton Mifflin, 1990), 131–137.
16. ROBBINS, *Managing Today,* 72.
17. BARTOL AND MARTIN, *Management,* 268–272.
18. DAFT, *Management,* 132–136; Bartol and Martin, *Management,* 172–173.
19. PAUL N. ROMANI, "MBO by Any Other Name Is Still MBO," *Supervision,* December 1997, 6–8.
20. BOVÉE et al., *Management,* 218–220.
21. WILLIAM B. WERTHER JR. AND KEITH DAVIS, *Human Resources and Personnel Management,* 4th ed. (New York: McGraw-Hill, 1993), 359–360; Daft, *Management,* 225–227.
22. GARY HAMEL AND C. K. PRAHALAD, *Competing for the Future* (Boston, MA: Harvard Business School Press, 1994), 73.
23. EDWARD A. ROBINSON, "America's Most Admired Companies," *Fortune,* 3 March 1997, 68, *Electric Library,* Online [accessed 2 September 1997]; SUSAN CHANDLER, "Crisis Management: How TWA Faced the Nightmare," *Business Week,* 5 August 1996, 30; KERRI SELLAND, "Experts Say Corporations Ill-Prepared for Crises," *Reuters,* 23 July 1996, *Electric Library,* Online [accessed 2 September 1997]; THOMAS S. MULLIGAN, "TWA Garners Weak Marks for Crisis Management," *Los Angeles Times,* 20 July 1996, D1; TOM INCANTALUPO, "TWA's Image Polishing," *Newsday,* 23 July 1996, A49.
24. BRIAN RUBERRY, "Danger Zone," *Entrepreneur,* November 1998, 153–157.
25. WILLIAM ECHIKSON, STEPHEN BAKER, AND DEAN FROST, "Things Aren't Going Better with Coke," *Business Week,* 28 June 1999, 49.
26. MICHAEL MOELLER, STEVE HAMM, AND TIMOTHY J. MULLANEY, "Remaking Microsoft," *Business Week,* 17 May 1999, 106–116.
27. GARY A. YUKL, *Leadership in Organizations,* 2d ed. (Upper Saddle River, N.J.: Prentice Hall, 1989), 9, 175–176.
28. DANIEL GOLEMAN, "What Makes a Leader?" *Harvard Business Review,* November–December 1998, 92–102.

29. DAFT, *Management,* 498–499.
30. RAM CHARAN AND GEOFFREY COLVIN, "Why CEOs Fail," *Fortune,* 21 June 1999, 69–78.
31. MICHAEL A. VERESPEJ, "Lead, Don't Manage," *Industry Week,* 4 March 1996, 58.
32. STRATFORD SHERMAN, "Secrets of HP's 'Muddled' Team," *Fortune,* 18 March 1996, 116–120.
33. CHARLES M. FARKAS AND SUZY WETLAUFER, "The Ways Chief Executive Officers Lead," *Harvard Business Review,* May–June 1996, 114.
34. STEPHEN P. ROBBINS AND DAVID A. DE CENZO, *Fundamentals of Management,* 2d ed. (Upper Saddle River, N.J.: Prentice Hall, 1998), 55–56; James Waldroop and Timothy Butler, "The Executive As Coach," *Harvard Business Review,* November–December 1996, 113.
35. "The Advantage of Female Mentoring," *Working Woman,* October 1991, 104.
36. PETER F. DRUCKER, *Management Challenges for the 21st Century* (New York: HarperBusiness, 1999), 74.
37. JAMES A. BELASCO AND RALPH C. STAYER, *Flight of the Buffalo* (New York: Warner Books, 1993), 138.
38. MICHAEL BARRIER, "Managing Workers in Times of Change," *Nation's Business,* May 1998, 31–32.
39. J. ROBERT CARLETON, "Cultural Due Diligence," *Training,* November 1997, 67–75.
40. JOANNE COLE, "Flying High at Southwest," *HR Focus,* May 1998, 8.
41. KOSTAS N. DERVITSIOTIS, "The Challenge of Managing Organizational Change," *Total Quality Management,* February 1998, 109–122.
42. BOVÉE et al., *Management,* 680.
43. JAMES R. LACKRITZ, "TQM Within Fortune 500 Corporations," *Quality Progress,* February 1997, 69–72.
44. DAVID SIROTA, BRIAN USILANER, AND MICHELLE S. WEBER, "Sustaining Quality Improvement," *Total Quality Review,* March–April 1994, 23; JOE BATTEN, "A Total Quality Culture," *Management Review,* May 1994, 61; RAHUL JACON, "More Than a Dying Fad?" *Fortune,* 18 October 1993, 66–72.
45. LACKRITZ, "TQM Within Fortune 500 Corporations," 69–72.
46. BLACKHURST, "At the Court of King Richard," "Business: Behind Branson"; FLYNN, "Then Came Branson"; DE VRIES, "Charisma in Action"; RIFKIN, "How Richard Branson Works Magic".
47. "Starters: Spearing the Best," *Bon Appétit,* March 1997, 20; MARY ALICE KELLOGG, "The Reel Dish," *Bon Appétit,* March 1997, 38.

CHAPTER 7

1. MICHAEL BARRIER, "Creating a Violence-Free Company Culture," *Nation's Business,* February 1, 1995, 22; MICHAEL A. VERESPEJ, "Wainwright Industries," *Industry Week,* 21 October 1996, 72; "CEO of Baldrige-Winner

Wainwright Industries Shares Learnings on Leadership and Change," Center for Quality of Management (n.d.) [accessed 6 March 1999] http://www.cqm. org/whats_new/wainright.htm; ARTHUR D. WAINWRIGHT, "People-First Strategies Get Implemented," *Strategy and Leadership,* January–February 1997, 12–17.

2. RICHARD L. DAFT, *Management,* 4th ed. (Fort Worth: Dryden Press, 1997), 358.

3. ROB GOFFEE AND GARETH JONES, "What Holds the Modern Company Together?" *Harvard Business Review,* November–December 1996, 134–145.

4. PETER F. DRUCKER, "Management's New Paradigms," *Forbes,* 5 October 1998, 152–176.

5. PETER F. DRUCKER, *Management Challenges for the 21st Century* (New York: HarperBusiness, 1999), 13.

6. STEPHEN P. ROBBINS, *Managing Today!* (Upper Saddle River, N.J.: Prentice Hall, 1997), 193; Daft, *Management,* 320.

7. STEPHEN P. ROBBINS AND DAVID A. DE CENZO, *Fundamentals of Management,* 2d ed. (Upper Saddle River, N.J.: Prentice Hall, 1998), 201; Daft, *Management,* 321.

8. ALAN WEBBER, "The Best Organization Is No Organization," *USA Today,* 13A, *Electric Library,* Online [accessed 25 September 1997]; EVE TAHMINCIOGLU, "How GM's Team Approach Works," *Gannett News Service,* 24 April 1996, S11, *Electric Library,* Online [accessed 25 September 1997].

9. FRED R. DAVID, *Strategic Management,* 6th ed. (Upper Saddle River, N.J.: Prentice Hall, 1997), 225; KATHRYN M. BARTOL AND DAVID C. MARTIN, *Management* (New York: McGraw-Hill, 1991), 352.

10. JEANNE DUGAN, ALISON REA, AND JOSEPH WEBER, "The BW 50: Business Week's Performance Rankings of the S&P 500 Best Performers," *Business Week,* 24 March 1997, 80, *Electric Library,* Online [accessed 25 September 1997].

11. DAFT, *Management,* 325.

12. BARTOL AND MARTIN, *Management,* 345.

13. COURTLAND L. BOVÉE, JOHN V. THILL, MARIAN WOOD, GEORGE DOVEL, *Management* (New York: McGraw-Hill, 1993), 285.

14. BARTOL AND MARTIN, *Management,* 370–371.

15. GARY IZUMO, "Teamwork Holds Key to Organization Success," *Los Angeles Times,* 20 August 1996, D9, *Electric Library,* Online [accessed 18 September 1997]; DAFT, *Management,* 328–329; DAVID, *Strategic Management,* 223.

16. DAFT, *Management,* 329–333; David, *Strategic Management,* 223–225; ANN MAJCHRZAK AND QIANWEI WANG, "Breaking the Functional Mind-Set in Process Organizations," *Harvard Business Review,* September–October 1996, 95–96.

17. JOHN A. BYRNE, "The Horizontal Corporation," *Business Week,* 20 December 1993, 76–81; "Is a Horizontal Organization

for You?" *Fortune,* 3 April 1995, 96; RAHUL JACOB, "The Struggle to Create an Organization for the 21st Century," *Fortune,* 3 April 1995, 90–96.

18. DAFT, *Management,* 332, 328–329; David, *Strategic Management,* 223; Bartol and Martin, *Management,* 376.

19. DAN DIMANCESCU AND KEMP DWENGER, "Smoothing the Product Development Path," *Management Review,* 1 January 1996, 36(6), *Electric Library,* Online [accessed 18 September 1997].

20. DIMANCESCU AND DWENGER, "Smoothing the Product Development Path."

21. ROBBINS, *Managing Today!,* 209; DAFT, *Management,* 333–336.

22. DAFT, *Management,* 340–343; ROBBINS, *Managing Today!,* 213–214.

23. DONNA FENN, "Managing Virtual Employees," *Inc.,* July 1996, 91.

24. DAFT, *Management,* 340–343; ROBBINS, *Managing Today!,* 213–214.

25. "The Horizontal Organization," *Soundview Executive Book Summaries* 21, no. 3, (March 1999): 1–8.

26. "Sharing Knowledge Through BP's Virtual Team Network," *Harvard Business Review,* September–October 1997, 152–153.

27. "The Horizontal Organization."

28. "The Horizontal Organization."

29. DAFT, *Management,* 352–353; RICHARDS, *Strategic Management,* 217; BARTOL AND MARTIN, *Management,* 357–358.

30. ROSS SHERWOOD, "The Boss's Open Door Means More Time for Employees," *Reuters Business Report,* 30 September 1996, *Electric Library,* Online [accessed 18 September 1997].

31. DAFT, *Management,* 591; ROBBINS, *Managing Today!,* 295.

32. TOM PETERS, *Thriving on Chaos* (New York: HarperPerennial, 1988), 638.

33. "Microsoft Teamwork," *Executive Excellence,* 6 July 1996, 6–7.

34. JEFFREY PFEFFER, "When It Comes to 'Best Practices'—Why Do Smart Organizations Occasionally Do Dumb Things?" *Organizational Dynamics,* 1 June 1996, 33(12), *Electric Library,* Online [accessed 18 September 1997]; LAMAR A. TREGO, "Reengineering Starts with a 'Clean Sheet of Paper,' " *Manage,* 1 July 1996, 17(4), *Electric Library,* Online [accessed 18 September 1997].

35. SCOTT KIRSNER, "Every Day, It's a New Place," *Fast Company,* April–May 1998, 132–134.

36. DAFT, *Management,* 338.

37. WAINWRIGHT, "People-First Strategies Get Implemented."

38. DAFT, *Management,* 612–615.

39. ELLEN NEUBORNE, "Companies Save, But Workers Pay," *USA Today,* 25 February 1997, B2; CHARLES L. PARNELL, "Teamwork: Not a New Idea, But It's Transforming the Workplace," *Vital Speeches of the Day,* 1 November 1996, 46.

40. ROBBINS AND DE CENZO, *Fundamentals of Management,* 151.

41. MIKE VERESPEJ, "Drucker Sours on Teams," *Industry Week,* 6 April 1998, 16.

42. DAFT, *Management,* 594–595; Robbins and De Cenzo, *Fundamentals of Management,* 336; ROBBINS, *Managing Today!,* 309.

43. PFEFFER, "When It Comes to 'Best Practices.' "

44. DAFT, *Management,* 594; Robbins and De Cenzo, *Fundamentals of Management,* 336.

45. SETH LUBOVE, "Destroying the Old Hierarchies," *Forbes,* 3 June 1996, 62–64.

46. W. V. BUSSMANN, "Making a Difference at Chrysler," *Business Economics,* July 1998, 10–12.

47. DAFT, *Management,* 594; Robbins and De Cenzo, *Fundamentals of Management,* 338; Robbins, *Managing Today!,* 310–311.

48. JENNY C. MCCUNE, "On the Train Gang: In the New Flat Organizations, Employees Who Want to Be Competitive Must Be Versatile Enough to Perform a Variety of Tasks," *Management Review,* 1 October 1994, 57(4), *Electric Library,* Online [accessed 18 September 1997].

49. NEUBORNE, "Companies Save, But Workers Pay," B1; DAFT, *Management,* 594; Robbins and De Cenzo, *Fundamentals of Management,* 338; Robbins, *Managing Today!,* 310.

50. RICHARD MODEROW, "Teamwork Is the Key to Cutting Costs," *Modern Healthcare,* 29 April 1996, 138.

51. DAFT, *Management,* 594.

52. "Sharing Knowledge Through BP's Virtual Team Network," *Harvard Business Review,* September–October 1997, 152–153.

53. ROBBINS AND DE CENZO, *Fundamentals of Management,* 334–335; Daft, *Management,* 602–603.

54. ROBBINS, *Managing Today!,* 297–298; Daft, *Management,* 604–607.

55. DAFT, *Management,* 609–612.

56. STEVEN CROM AND HERBERT FRANCE, "Teamwork Brings Breakthrough Improvements in Quality and Climate," *Quality Progress,* March 1996, 39–41.

57. DAVID, *Strategic Management,* 221.

58. PHYLLIS GAIL DOLOFF, "Beyond the Org Chart," *Across the Board,* February 1999, 43–47.

59. STEPHANIE ARMOUR, "Failure to Communicate Costly for Companies," *USA Today,* 30 September 1998, 1A.

60. BARRIER, "Creating a Violence-Free Company Culture" VERESPEJ, "Wainwright Industries"; "CEO of Baldrige-Winner Wainwright Industries Shares Learnings on Leadership and Change," Center for Quality of Management (n.d.) [accessed 6 March 1999] http://www.cqm.org/whats_new/ wainright.htm; WAINWRIGHT, "People-First Strategies Get Implemented."

61. DONNA FENN, "Teams: Formula for Success," *Inc.,* May 1996, 111.

CHAPTER 8

1. Adapted from VINCENT J. ORANGE AND DAVID E. ROBINSON, "The Role of Certification in the Buyer/Planner Position: A Case Study at Harley-Davidson Motor Company," *Hospital/Materiel Management Quarterly,* February 1999, 28–36; LESLIE P. NORTON, "Potholes Ahead?" *Barron's,* 1 (February 1999), 16–17; Bruce Caldwell, "Harley-Davidson Revs Up IT Horsepower," *Internetweek,* 7 December 1998, PG63; PETER BRADLEY, "Harley-Davidson Keeps Its Eyes on the Road," *Logistics Management and Distribution Report,* August 1998, 68–73; "Harley-Davidson History" [accessed 23 April 1999], http://www.harley-davidson.com/company/history/history.asp; Harley-Davidson 1998 Annual Report [accessed 23 April 1999] http://www.harley-davidson.com/company/investor/ar/1998/growing/supply.asp.

2. ROBERTA S. RUSSELL AND BERNARD W. TAYLOR III, *Operations Management: Focusing on Quality and Competitiveness,* 2d ed. (Upper Saddle River, N.J.: Prentice Hall, 1998), 21.

3. JUSTIN MARTIN, "Are You As Good As You Think You Are?" *Fortune,* 30 September 1996, 143–144.

4. JOHN GREENWALD, "Cruise Lines Go Overboard," *Time,* 11 May 1998, 42–45.

5. RUSSELL AND TAYLOR, *Operations Management,* 501; Courtland L. Bovée, JOHN V. THILL, MARIAN WOOD, AND GEORGE DOVEL, *Management* (New York: McGraw-Hill, 1993), 644.

6. JOSEPH G. MONKS, *Operations Management, Theory and Problems* (New York: McGraw-Hill, 1987), 77–78.

7. MARK M. DAVIS, NICHOLAS J. AQUILANO, AND RICHARD B. CHASE, *Fundamentals of Operations Management* (Boston: Irwin McGraw-Hill, 1999), 241–242.

8. JAE K. SHIM AND JOEL G. SIEGEL, *Operations Management* (Hauppauge, N.Y.: Barron's Educational Series, 1999), 206.

9. MONKS, *Operations Management, Theory and Problems,* 2–3.

10. SHIM AND SIEGEL, *Operations Management,* 206.

11. MONKS, *Operations Management, Theory and Problems,* 125.

12. RUSSELL AND TAYLOR, *Operations Management,* 291–292; DAVIS, AQUILANO, AND CHASE, *Fundamentals of Operations Management,* 254; Richard L. Daft, *Management,* 4th ed. (Fort Worth: Dryden Press, 1997), 718.

13. KATHRYN M. BARTOL AND DAVID C. MARTIN, *Management* (New York: McGraw-Hill, 1991), 307–308.

14. LARRY E. LONG AND NANCY LONG, *Introduction to Computers and Information Systems,* 5th ed. (Upper Saddle River, N.J.: Prentice Hall, 1997), 1997, AT 84.

15. STUART F. BROWN, "Giving More Jobs to Electronic Eyes," *Fortune,* 16 February 1998, 104B–104D.

16. "IBM and Dassault Awarded Boeing CATIA Contract," *CAD/CAM Update,* 1 January 1997, 1–8.

17. RUSSELL AND TAYLOR, *Operations Management,* 211.

18. "CAD/CAM Industry Embracing Intranet-Based Technologies," *Computer Dealer News* 12 (28 November 1996), 21.

19. DREW WINTER, "C3P: New Acronym Signals Big Change at Ford," *Ward's Auto World* 32 (1 August 1996): 34; THOMAS HOFFMAN, "Ford to Cut Its Prototype Costs," *Computerworld,* 30 September 1996, 65; DREW WINTER, "Massive Changes Coming in Computer Engineering," *Ward's Auto World* 32 (1 April 1996): 34.

20. DAVIS, AQUILANO, AND CHASE, *Fundamentals of Operations Management,* 64; RUSSELL AND TAYLOR, *Operations Management,* 257–258.

21. BRIAN S. MOSKAL, "Born to Be Real," *Industry Week,* 2 August 1993, 14–18.

22. RUSSELL AND TAYLOR, *Operations Management,* 255–256.

23. JOHN H. SHERIDAN, "Agile Manufacturing: Stepping Beyond Lean Production," *Industry Week,* 19 April 1993, 30–33, 36–38, 40–41, 44, 46.

24. BRIAN McWILLIAMS, "Re-engineering the Small Factory," *Inc. Technology,* 1 (1996): 44–45.

25. JOHN H. SHERIDAN, "Lessons from the Best," *Industry Week,* 19 February 1996, 16.

26. NEAL M. GOLDSMITH AND ED ROSENFELD, "Shooting the Rapids—Business Process Reengineering Can Be a Wild Ride, But There Are a Number of Tools and Services Available to Help Companies Manage Change and Maximize Growth," *Information Week,* 25 November 1996, 65; SHERIDAN, "Lessons from the Best," 16–17; BARTOL AND MARTIN, *Management,* 688.

27. RONALD HENKOFF, "Boeing's Big Problem," *Fortune,* 12 January 1998, 96–103; JAMES WALLACE, "How Boeing Blew It," *Sales and Marketing Management,* February 1998, 52–57; JOHN GREENWALD, "Is Boeing out of Its Spin?" *Time,* 13 July 1998, 67–69; JOHN T. LANDRY, "Supply Chain Management: The Case for Alliances," *Harvard Business Review,* November–December 1998, 24–25.

28. JOHN T. LANDRY, "Supply Chain Management: The Case for Alliances," *Harvard Business Review,* November–December 1998, 24–25.

29. DAVIS, AQUILANO, AND CHASE, *Fundamentals of Operations Management,* 382.

30. RUSSELL AND TAYLOR, *Operations Management,* 440.

31. LANDRY, "Supply Chain Management."

32. TIMOTHY M. LASETER, "Balanced Sourcing the Honda Way," *Strategy and Business,* Fourth Quarter 1998, 24–31.

33. DAVID WOODRUFF, IAN KATZ, AND KEITH NAUGHTON, "VW's Factory of the Future," *Business Week,* 7 October 1996, 52, 56.

34. J. TOL BROOME JR., "The Benefits of Smart Inventory Management," *Nation's Business,* June 1999, 18–19.

35. RUSSELL AND TAYLOR, *Operations Management,* 652–653.

36. LAWRENCE A. BERARDINIS, ed., "Factory Monitoring Via the Internet," *Machine Design,* 20 March 1997.

37. SHIM AND SIEGEL, *Operations Management,* 326.

38. RUSSELL AND TAYLOR, *Operations Management,* 712–733.

39. PATRICIA W. HAMILTON, "Getting a Grip on Inventory," *D&B Reports,* March–April 1994, 32.

40. ROBERT O. KNORR AND JOHN L. NEUMAN, "Quick Response Technology: The Key to Outstanding Growth," *Journal of Business Strategy,* September–October 1992, 63.

41. TOM PETERS, *Thriving on Chaos* (New York: HarperPerennial, 1988), 90.

42. KARL RITZLER, "A Mercedes Made from Scratch," *Atlanta Journal and Constitution,* 30 May 1997, S1.

43. DEL JONES, "Training and Service at Top of Winners' List," *USA Today,* 17 October 1996, 5B.

44. JOHN A. BYRNE, "Never Mind the Buzzwords. Roll up Your Sleeves," *Business Week,* 22 January 1996, 84.

45. DAVIS, AQUILANO, AND CHASE, *Fundamentals of Operations Management,* 177–179; RUSSELL AND TAYLOR, *Operations Management,* 131.

46. WILLIAM M. CARLEY, "Charging Ahead: To Keep GE's Profits Rising, Welch Pushes Quality-Control Plan," *Wall Street Journal,* 13 January 1997, A1, A6.

47. RUSSELL AND TAYLOR, *Operations Management,* 131.

48. HUGH D. MENZIES, "Global Guide: Quality Counts When Wooing Overseas Clients," *Your Company,* 1 June 1997, 64; MICHAEL E. RAYNOR, "Worldwide Winners," *Total Quality Management,* July–August 1993, 43–48; GREG BOUNDS, LYLE YORKS, MEL ADAMS, AND GIPSIE RANNEY, *Beyond Total Quality Management: Toward the Emerging Paradigm* (New York: McGraw-Hill, 1994), 212; RUSSELL AND TAYLOR, *Operations Management,* 115–116.

49. SAUL HANSELL, "Is This the Factory of the Future?" *New York Times,* 26 July 1998, sec. 3, 1, 12–13; PETE ENGARDIO, "Souping Up the Supply Chain," *Business Week,* 31 August 1998, 110–112.

50. HANSELL, "Is This the Factory of the Future?" sec. 3, p. 1, 12–13; ENGARDIO, "Souping Up the Supply Chain," 110–112.

51. HANSELL, "Is This the Factory of the Future?"; ENGARDIO, "Souping Up the Supply Chain," 110–112.

52. LAURENCE ZUCKERMAN, "The Jet Wars of the Future," *New York Times,* 9 July 1999, C1, C5.

53. Adapted from ORANGE AND ROBINSON, "The Role of Certification in the

Buyer/Planner Position"; Norton, "Potholes Ahead?"; CALDWELL, "Harley-Davidson Revs Up IT Horsepower"; BRADLEY, "Harley-Davidson Keeps Its Eyes on the Road"; "Harley-Davidson History," http://www.harley-davidson.com/company/history/history.asp; Harley-Davidson 1998 Annual Report, http://www.harley-davidson.com/company/investor/ar/1998/growing/supply.asp.

54. "How Microsoft Reviews Suppliers," *Fast Company, 17* [accessed 3 September 1998], http://fastcompany.com/online/17/msoftreviews.html.

55. Adapted from RONALD HENKOFF, "Boeing's Big Problem," *Fortune,* 12 January 1998, 96–103; DAVID FIELD, "Mistake No. 1: Disregarding Competition," *USA Today,* 6 May 1998, B1; JOHN GREENWALD, "Is Boeing Out of Its Spin?" *Time,* 13 July 1998, 67–69; JAMES WALLACE, "How Boeing Blew It," *Sales and Marketing Management,* February 1998, 52–57; "Business: Boeing Woeing," *The Economist,* 8 August 1998, 55; ANDY REINHARDT AND SEANNA BROWDER, "Can a New Crew Buoy Boeing?" *Business Week,* 14 September 1998, 53; ANDY REINHARDT AND SEANNA BROWDER, "Fly, Damn It, Fly," *Business Week,* 9 November 1998, 150–156; SEANNA BROWDER, "Boeing's Revised Flight Plan," *Business Week,* 21 December 1998, 39; LAURENCE ZUCKERMAN, "Boeing Sees Big Job Cuts Over 2 Years," *New York Times,* 2 December 1998, C1, C8; LAURENCE ZUCKERMAN, "Boeing's Leasers Losing Altitude," *New York Times,* 13 December 1998, BU1, 11; HOLMAN W. JENKINS, JR., "Boeing's Trouble: Not Enough Monopolistic Arrogance," *Wall Street Journal,* 16 December 1998, A23; FREDERIC M. BIDDLE AND ANDY PASZTOR, "Boeing May Be Hurt Up to 5 Years by Asia," *Wall Street Journal,* 3 December 1998, A3, A6; DAVID FIELD, "Airbus Plans Humongous, 2-Decker Jet," *USA Today,* 28 April 1999, 1A; LAURENCE ZUCKERMAN, "The Jet Wars of the Future," *New York Times,* 9 July 1999, C1, C5; GEORGE TIBBITS, "New Boeing Jet Comes Together for Debut," *Chicago Tribune,* 11 July 1999, sec. 5, 7.

CHAPTER 9

1. Adapted from LINDA GRANT, "How UPS Blew It," *Fortune,* 29 September 1997, 29–30; SHARI CAUDRON, "Part-Timers Make Headline News—Here's the Real HR Story," *Workforce,* November 1997, 40–50; "UPS, Pilots Quickly Reach Agreement," *Logistics Management and Distribution Report,* February 1998, 26–27; JOHN SCHMELTZER, "A Year After UPS Strike, Its Rivals Are Real Victors," *Chicago Tribune,* August 2, 1998, sec. 5, 1, 2; ROBERT J. GROSSMAN, "Trying to Heal the Wounds," *HR Magazine,* September 1998, 85–92; "UPS's 4th Quarter Results Cap Year of Leadership in Key Growth Areas," UPS news release, 18 February 1999 [accessed 6 April 1999], http://www.ups.com/bin/

shownews.cgi?19990218earnings; David Rocks, "UPS: Will This IPO Deliver?" *Business Week,* 15 November 1999, 41.

2. ROBERT B. REICH, "The Company of the Future," *Fast Company,* November 1998, 124–150.

3. DONALD J. McNERNEY, "Employee Motivation: Creating a Motivated Workforce," *HR Focus* 73, 1 August 1996, *Electric Library* [accessed 14 October 1997].

4. TERESA M. AMABILE, "How to Kill Creativity," *Harvard Business Review,* September–October 1998, 77–87.

5. DENNIS C. KINLAW, "What Employees See Is What Organizations Get," *Management Solutions,* March 1988, 38–41.

6. FREDERICK HERZBERG, *Work and the Nature of Man* (New York: World, 1971).

7. DOUGLAS McGREGOR, *The Human Side of Enterprise* (New York: McGraw-Hill, 1960).

8. JENNIFER LAABS, "Has Downsizing Missed Its Mark?" *Workforce,* April 1999, 31–38.

9. AARON BERNSTEIN, "We Want You to Stay. Really," *Business Week,* 22 June 1998, 67–72.

10. REICH, "The Company of the Future."

11. KELLY BARRON AND ANN MARSCH, "The Skills Gap," *Forbes,* 23 February 1998, 44–45; "Nine HR Challenges for 1999," *HR Focus,* December 1998, 1, 14–16.

12. U.S. Bureau of Labor Statistics, *Employment Statistics* [accessed 23 August 1999], www.bls.gov.

13. SAMUEL GREENGARD, "Economic Forces Are Squeezing Growth Potential," *Workforce,* March 1998, 44–54.

14. GREG JAFFE AND DOUGLAS A. BLACKMON, "Just in Time. When UPS Demanded Workers, Louisville Did the Delivering," *Wall Street Journal,* 24 April 1998, A1, A10.

15. BARRON AND MARSCH, "The Skills Gap."

16. PETER F. DRUCKER, *Management Challenges for the 21st Century* (New York: HarperBusiness, 1999), 90.

17. BERNSTEIN, "We Want You to Stay. Really"; CAROL KLEIMAN, "The New Loyalty: A Work in Progress," *Chicago Tribune,* 15 August 1999, sec. 6, 1.

18. JENNIFER LAABS, "The New Loyalty: Grasp It. Earn It. Keep It." *Workforce,* November 1998, 35–39.

19. EMILY THORNTON, "No Room at the Top," *Business Week,* 9 August 1999, 50; Michael A. Lev, "Lifetime Jobs May Be at Death's Door As Japan Tradition," *Chicago Tribune,* 11 October 1998, sec. 5, 1, 18.

20. JULIA LAWLOR, "Busters Have Work Ethic All Their Own," *USA Today,* 20 July 1993, 1B–2B.

21. JOHN GREENWALD, "Spinning Away," *Time,* 26 August 1996, 30–31.

22. STEPHANIE ARMOUR, "Blame It on Downsizing, E-Mail, Laptops, and Dual-Career Families," *USA Today,* 13 March 1998, B1; JENNIFER LAABS, "Workforce Overload," *Workforce,* January 1999, 30–37.

23. SUE SHELLENBARGER, "More Executives Cite Need for Family Time As Reason for Quitting," *Wall Street Journal,* 11 March 1998, B1.

24. RICHARD L. DAFT, *Management,* 4th ed. (Fort Worth: Dryden Press, 1997), 771.

25. STEPHANIE ARMOUR, "Workplace Demands Taking Up More Weekends," *USA Today,* 24 April 1998, B1; Laabs, "Workforce Overload."

26. ARMOUR, "Workplace Demands Taking Up More Weekends."

27. LAABS, "Workforce Overload."

28. STEPHANIE ARMOUR, "Workplace Hazard Gets Attention," *USA Today,* 5 May 1998, B1.

29. JOHN W. NEWSTROM AND KEITH DAVIS, *Organizational Behavior: Human Behavior at Work,* 9th ed. (New York: McGraw-Hill, 1993), 345.

30. JENNIFER BRESNEHAN, "The Elusive Muse," *CIO Enterprise,* 15 October 1997, 52; KERRY A. DOLAN, "When Money Isn't Enough," *Forbes,* 18 November 1996, 164–170.

31. JOAN CROCKETT, "Winning Competitive Advantage Through a Diverse Workforce," *HRFocus,* May 1999, 9–10.

32. DAVID A. THOMAS AND ROBIN J. ELY, "Making Differences Matter: A New Paradigm for Managing Diversity," *Harvard Business Review,* September–October 1996, 85.

33. NINA MUNK, "Finished at Forty," *Fortune,* 1 February 1999, 50–66.

34. MUNK, "Finished at Forty."

35. MUNK, "Finished at Forty."

36. LINDA HIMELSTEIN AND STEPHANIE FOREST, "Breaking Through," *Business Week,* 17 February 1997, 64; "Study Says U.S. Women Make Workplace Gains," *Reuters Business Report,* 2 January 1997, *Electric Library* [accessed 28 July 1997]; MARTHA GROVES, "Women Still Bumping Up Against Glass Ceiling," *Los Angeles Times,* 26 May 1996, D1; CHRISTOPHER FARRELL, "Women in the Workplace: Is Parity Finally in Sight?" *Business Week,* 9 August 1999, 35.

37. DAFT, *Management,* 462–463.

38. JOSEPH WHITE AND CAROL HYMOWITZ, "Broken Glass: Watershed Generation of Women Executives Is Rising to the Top," *Wall Street Journal,* 10 February 1997, A1, 6; ANDREA ADELSON, "Casual, Worker-Friendly, and a Moneymaker, Too: At Patagonia, Glass Ceiling Is Sky-High," *New York Times,* 30 June 1996, sec. Earning It, 8; JOAN S. LUBLIN, "Women at Top Still Are Distant from CEO Jobs," *Wall Street Journal,* 28 February 1996, B1, 12; "Firm's Diversity Efforts Even the Playing Field," *Personnel Journal,* January 1996, 56; HIMELSTEIN AND FOREST, "Breaking Through," 64–70; GROVES, "Women Still Bumping Up Against Glass Ceiling," D1, 5; FARRELL, "Women in the Workplace"; REED ABELSON, "A Push from the Top Shatters a Glass Ceiling," *New York Times,* 22 August 1999, Y21, Y23.

39. SUSAN CRAWFORD, "A Wink Here, a Leer There: It's Costly," *New York Times,* 28 March 1993, C17; ELIZABETH KOLBERT, "Sexual Harassment at Work Is Pervasive, Survey Suggests," *New York Times,* 11 October 1991, A1, 11.

40. MICHAEL BARRIER, "Sexual Harassment," *Nation's Business,* December 1998, 15–19.

41. MARIANNE LAVELLE, "The New Rules of Sexual Harassment," *U.S. News & World Report,* 6 July 1998, 30–31.

42. MAHLON APGAR IV, "The Alternative Workplace: Changing Where and How People Work," *Harvard Business Review,* May–June 1998, 121–136.

43. GENEVIEVE CAPOWSKI, "The Joy of Flex," *Management Review,* March 1996, 13.

44. CHARLENE MARMER SOLOMON, "Flexibility Comes out of Flux," *Personnel Journal,* June 1996, 38–40.

45. SOLOMON, "Flexibility Comes Out of Flux."

46. SHARI CAUDRON, "Workers' Ideas for Improving Alternative Work Situations," *Workforce,* December 1998, 42–46; CAROL LEONETTI DANNHAUSER, "Who's in the Home Office?," *American Demographics,* June 1999, 50–56.

47. DANNHAUSER, "Who's in the Home Office?"

48. APGAR, "The Alternative Workplace."

49. APGAR, "The Alternative Workplace."

50. MELANIE WARNER, "Working at Home—The Right Way to Be a Star in Your Bunny Slippers," *Fortune,* 3 March 1997, 166; LIN GRENSING-POPHAL, "Employing the Best People—From Afar," *Workforce,* March 1997, 30–32.

51. LISA CHADDERDON, "Merrill Lynch Works—At Home," *Fast Company,* April–May 1998, 70–72.

52. CAUDRON, "Workers' Ideas for Improving Alternative Work Situations."

53. CAUDRON, "Workers' Ideas for Improving Alternative Work Situations."

54. THOMAS A. KOCHAN AND HARRY C. KATZ, *Collective Bargaining and Industrial Relations* (Homewood, Ill.: Irwin, 1988), 165.

55. MARTHA IRVINE, "Organizing Twentysomethings," *Los Angeles Times,* 7 September 1997, D5, *Electric Library* [accessed 13 November 1997].

56. U.S. Bureau of Labor Statistics, "Union Members Summary," *Developments in Labor-Management Relations* [accessed 1 November 1997], http://www.bls.gov:80/newsrels.htm; International Labour Organization, "ILO Highlights Global Challenge to Trade Unions," *International Labour Organization 1997 Press Releases,* 4 November 1997 [accessed 7 November 1997], http://www.ilo.org; International Labour Organization, *World Labour Report,* 4 November 1997 [accessed 7 November 1997], http://www.ilo.org.

57. International Labour Organization, *World Labour Report,* 4 November 1997 [accessed 7 November 1997], http://www.ilo.org.

58. LLOYD G. REYNOLDS, STANLEY H. MASTERS, AND COLLETTA H. MOSER, *Labor Economics and Labor Relations,* 11th ed. (Upper Saddle River, N.J.: Prentice Hall, 1998), 497; Indiana University News Bureau, "Trends in U.S. Labor Movement," *Futurist,* January–February 1996, 44; BARBARA PRESLEY NOBLE, "Reinventing Labor: An Interview with Union President Lynn Williams," *Harvard Business Review,* July–August 1993, 115–125.

59. AARON BERNSTEIN, "Sweeney's Blitz," *Business Week,* 17 February 1997, 56–62; MARC LEVINSON, "It's Hip to Be Union," *Newsweek,* 8 July 1996, 44–45; JAMES WORSHAM, "Labor Comes Alive," *Nation's Business,* February 1996, 16–24; E. EDWARD HERMAN, *Collective Bargaining and Labor Relations,* 4th ed. (Upper Saddle River, N.J.: Prentice Hall, 1998); MICHAEL HICKINS, "Unions: New Activism or Old Adversarial Approach?" *HR Focus,* May 1999, 7–8.

60. MICHAEL A. VERESPEJ, "What's Behind the Strife?" *Industry Week,* 1 February 1999, 58–62; KEITH BRADSHER, "General Motors and the U.A.W. Agree on End to Strike," *New York Times,* 29 July 1998, A1, C6.

61. *World Almanac and Book of Facts* (New York: Scripps Howard, 1989), 161.

62. STEPHANIE OVERMAN, "Unions: New Activism or Old Adversarial Approach?" *HRFocus,* May 1999, 7–8; LAURENCE ZUCKERMAN, "Pilots Lose a Battle, Not the War," *New York Times,* 17 April 1999, B1, B14.

63. EUGENE H. METHVIN, "The Union Label: With the Level of Union Violence on the Rise, Congress Must, Again, Deal with the Courts," *National Review,* 29 September 1997, 47, *Electric Library* [accessed 11 November 1997]; ANYA SACHAROW, "Walking the Line in Detroit," *Newspapers,* 22 July 1996, 8–13; Worsham, "Labor Comes Alive," 17.

64. HERMAN, *Collective Bargaining and Labor Relations,* 61; "NLRB Permits Replacements During Legal Lockout," *Personnel Journal,* January 1987, 14–15.

65. DAVID FIELD, "Airline Chief Has Become Key Figure in Labor Dispute," *USA Today,* 6 March 1997, B1, B2; DONNA ROSATO, "American Airlines Pilots Ask to Extend Deadline for Talks," *USA Today,* 18 March 1997, 2B, *Electric Library,* Online [accessed 11 November 1997]; DAVID FIELD, "Clinton Unlikely to Act Unless Both Sides Ask," *USA Today,* 10 February 1997, 2A, *Electric Library,* Online [accessed 11 November 1997].

66. Adapted from GRANT, "How UPS Blew It"; CAUDRON, "Part-Timers Make Headline News"; "UPS, Pilots Quickly Reach Agreement"; Schmeltzer, "A Year After UPS Strike, Its Rivals Are Real Victors"; GROSSMAN, "Trying to Heal the Wounds";

"UPS's 4th Quarter Results Cap Year of Leadership in Key Growth Areas," UPS news release, 18 February 1999 [accessed 6 April 1999], http://www.ups.com/bin/shownews.cgi?19990218earnings; Rocks, "UPS: Will This IPO Deliver?"

67. ED EMDE, "Employee Values Are Changing Course," *Workforce,* March 1998, 83–84.

68. "US West Labor Strike Ends," *CNNfn,* *CNN Interactive* [accessed 31 August 1998], http://cnnfn.com:80/hotstories/companies/9808/31/uswest.

CHAPTER 10

1. Adapted from Howard Schultz, "Starbucks' Secret Weapon," *Fortune,* 29 September 1997, 268; SCOTT S. SMITH, "Grounds for Success," *Entrepreneur,* May 1998, 120–126; NAOMI WEISS, "How Starbucks Impassions Workers to Drive Growth," *Workforce,* August 1998, 60–64; JOANNE LEE-YOUNG, "Starbucks' Expansion in China Is Slated," *Wall Street Journal,* 5 October 1998, B13E; KELLY BARRON, "The Cappuccino Conundrum," *Forbes,* 22 February 1999, 54–55.

2. TIMOTHY EGAN, "A Temporary Force to Be Reckoned With," *New York Times,* 20 May 1996, C1, C10; JAN LARSEN, "Temps Are Here to Stay," *American Demographics,* February 1996, 26–31; BRENDA PAIK SUNOO, "From Santa to CEO—Temps Play All Roles," *Personnel Journal,* April 1996, 34–44; MAX MESSMER, "Strategic Staffing for the 90s," *Personnel Journal,* October 1990, 94.

3. STEVEN GREENHOUSE, "Equal Work, Less-Equal Perks," *New York Times,* 30 March 1998, C1, C6; AARON BERNSTEIN, "When Is a Temp Not a Temp?" *Business Week,* 7 December 1998, 90–92.

4. JOHN A. BYRNE, "Has Outsourcing Gone Too Far?" *Business Week,* 1 April 1996, 26–28; SANA SIWOLOP, "Outsourcing: Savings Are Just the Start," *Business Week/Enterprise,* 13 May 1996, ENT 24–ENT 25; DALE D. BUSS, "Growing More by Doing Less," *Nation's Business,* December 1995, 18.

5. SHEILA M. POOLE, "Hoping to Net That Ideal Job," *Atlanta Journal and Constitution,* 13 April 1997, H1, *Electric Library,* Online [accessed 29 October 1997]; "Oracle Leverages IntelliMatch and the Power of Its Own Web Technology to Fill Key Job Openings," M2 PressWIRE, 4 March 1997, *Electric Library,* Online [accessed 29 October 1997]; JULIA KING, "Point-and-Click Recruiting Falls Short," *Computerworld,* 10 February 1997, 1, Electric Library, Online [accessed 29 October 1997]; ALICE M. STARCKE, "Internet Recruiting Shows Rapid Growth," HR Magazine 41, 1 August 1996, 61, *Electric Library,* Online [accessed 29 October 1997].

6. AUDREY ARTHUR, "How Much Should Employees Know?" *Black Enterprise,* October 1997, 56; Anthony Ramirez, "Name, Résumé,

References. And How's Your Credit? *New York Times,* 31 August 1997, F8.

7. DOROTHY LEONARD AND SUSAN STRAUS, "Putting Your Company's Whole Brain to Work," *Harvard Business Review,* July–August 1997, 111–121.

8. JONATHAN SEGAL, "When Norman Bates and Baby Jane Act Out at Work," *HR Magazine* 41 (1 February 1996), 31, *Electric Library,* Online [accessed 30 October 1997]; JENNY C. MCCUNE, "Companies Grapple with Workplace Violence," *Management Review,* March 1994, 52–57.

9. ELLIS HENICAN, "Nightmare at Saks Fifth Ave.," *Newsday,* 5 June 1996, A2, *Electric Library,* Online [accessed 3 November 1997].

10. "Substance Abuse in the Workplace," *HR Focus,* February 1997, 1, 41; TYLER D. HARTWELL, PAUL D. STEELE, AND NATHANIEL F. RODMAN, "Workplace Alcohol-Testing Programs: Prevalence and Trends," *Monthly Labor Review,* June 1998, 27–34.

11. RANDALL S. SCHULER, *Managing Human Resources* (Cincinnati: South-Western College Publishing, 1998), 386.

12. KATHARINE MIESZKOWSKI, "Report from the Future," *Fast Company,* February–March 1998, 28–30.

13. TONIA L. SHAKESPEARE, "High-Tech Training, Wal-Mart Style," *Black Enterprise,* July 1996, 54.

14. MICHAEL BARRIER, "Develop Workers— and Your Business," *Nation's Business,* December 1998, 25–27.

15. STEPHEN BAKER AND LARRY ARMSTRONG, "The New Factory Worker," *Business Week,* 30 September 1996, 59–60.

16. SHAKESPEARE, "High-Tech Training, Wal-Mart Style"; Charles Bermant, "For the Latest in Corporate Training, Try a CD-ROM," *New York Times,* 16 October 1995, C5.

17. LARRY STEVENS, "The Intranet: Your Newest Training Tool?" *Personnel Journal,* July 1996, 27.

18. ADOLPH HAASEN AND GORDON F. SHEA, *A Better Place to Work* (New York: American Management Association, 1997), 19–20.

19. GINA IMPERATO, "How to Give Good Feedback," *Fast Company,* September 1998, 144–156.

20. IMPERATO, "How to Give Good Feedback."

21. BRADELY R. SCHILLER, *State Minimum Wage Laws: Youth Coverage and Impact* (Washington, D.C.: George Mason University, 1994), *Electric Library,* Online [accessed 18 February 1998].

22. TERESA M. AMABILE, "How to Kill Creativity," *Harvard Business Review,* September–October 1998, 77–87.

23. JACK STACK, "The Problem with Profit Sharing," *Inc.,* November 1996, 67–69; ELLEN NEUBORNE, "Meeting Goals Just Got More Rewarding," *USA Today,* 15 October 1996, B1–B2.

24. NEUBORNE, "Meeting Goals Just Got More Rewarding."

25. PETER V. LEBLANC, "Pay for Work: Reviving an Old Idea for the New Customer Focus," *Compensation & Benefits Review* 26, 1 July 1994, *Electric Library,* Online [accessed 30 October 1997]; KEVIN J. PARENT AND CAROLINE L. WEBER, "Case Study: Does Knowledge Pay Off?" *Compensation & Benefits Review* 26, 1 September 1994, *Electric Library,* Online [accessed 30 October 1997]; EARL INGRAM, "Compensation: The Advantages of Knowledge-Based Pay," *Personnel Journal,* April 1990, 138–140.

26. KEITH H. HAMMONDS, WENDY ZELLNER, AND RICHARD MELCHER, "Writing a New Social Contract," *Business Week,* 11 March 1996, 60; DON L. BOROUGHS, "The Bottom Line on Ethics," *U.S. News & World Report,* 20 March 1995, 63–65; DAWN GUNSCH, "Benefits Leverage Hiring and Retention Efforts," *Personnel Journal,* November 1992, 91–92, 94–97.

27. ALAN R. EARLS, "True Friends of the Family," *Computerworld,* 17 February 1997, 83, *Electric Library,* Online [accessed 30 October 1997]; ROBERT BRYCE, "Need an Extra Week Off? Visit the Company Store," *New York Times,* 16 July 1995, 10F.

28. PAT WECHSLER, "Firms Brace for Rising Health Costs," *USA Today,* 9 October 1997, 3B, *Electric Library,* Online [accessed 30 October 1997]; U.S. Census Bureau, "Health Insurance Coverage: 1997," [accessed 27 August 1999], http: www.census.gov.

29. BOROUGHS, "The Bottom Line on Ethics," 64.

30. Bureau of Labor Statistics, "Employee Benefits Survey: Incidence of Defined Benefit Pension," http://www.bls.gov/cgi-bin/surveymost, Online [accessed 30 October 1997]; ROGER THOMPSON, "The Threat to Pension Plans," *Nation's Business,* March 1991, 18–24.

31. JAMES LARDINER, "OK, Here Are Your Options," *U.S. News & World Report,* 1 March 1999, 44.

32. DEL JONES, "More Workers Get Options, Too," *USA Today,* 7 April 1999, 3B.

33. *Workforce,* January 1997 (Supplement), 5; BARBARA PRESLEY NOBLE, "At Work: We're Doing Just Fine, Thank You," *New York Times,* 20 March 1994, 25.

34. "Workplace Briefs," Gannett News Service, 24 April 1997, *Electric Library,* Online [accessed 30 October 1997]; JULIA LAWLOR, "The Bottom Line," *Working Woman,* July/August 1996, 54–58, 74–76.

35. SUE SHELLENBARGER, "Employees Who Value Time As Much As Money Now Get Their Reward," *Wall Street Journal,* 22 September 1999, B1.

36. DEL JONES, "Firms Take New Look at Sick Days," *USA Today,* 8 October 1996, 8B.

37. VALERIE L. WILLIAMS AND JENNIFER E. SUNDERLAND, "New Pay Programs Boost Retention," *Workforce,* May 1999, 36–40.

38. GILLIAN FLYNN, "Heck No—We Won't Go!" *Personnel Journal,* March 1996, 37–43.

39. RODNEY HO, "AT&T's Offer of $10,000 May Test Entrepreneurship of Laid-Off Workers," *Wall Street Journal,* 12 March 1997; DAVID FISCHER AND KEVIN WHITELAW, "A New Way to Shine Up Corporate Profits," *U.S. News and World Report,* 15 April 1996, 55.

40. GILLIAN FLYNN, "Why Rhino Won't Wait 'til Tomorrow," *Personnel Journal,* July 1996, 36–39.

41. Adapted from SCHULTZ, "Starbucks' Secret Weapon"; SMITH, "Grounds for Success"; WEISS, "How Starbucks Impassions Workers to Drive Growth"; LEE-YOUNG, "Starbucks' Expansion in China Is Slated"; BARRON, "The Cappuccino Conundrum."

42. SAL D. RINALLA AND ROBERT J. KOPECKY, "Recruitment: Burger King Hooks Employees with Educational Incentives," *Personnel Journal,* October 1989, 90–99.

43. Adapted from: QUENTIN HARDY, "Strained Relations: A Software Star Sees Its Family Culture Turn Dysfunctional," *Wall Street Journal,* 15 May 1999, A1, A12; RICHARD BRANDT, "Cha-Cha-Changes," *Upside,* June 1999, 40; CRAIG STEDMAN, "Change in the Wind at Slumping ERP Vendors," *Computerworld,* 15 March 1999, 27; STEPHAN HERRERA, "Bad Karma," *Forbes,* 8 March 1999, 134; WILLIAM SCHAFF, "New Math for PeopleSoft," *Informationweek,* 18 October 1999, 194; CRAIG STEDMAN, "PeopleSoft Plans Changes," *Computerworld,* 30 August 1999, 6; Tom Stein, "PeopleSoft's Brain Drain," *Informationweek,* 22 March 1999, 26; "PeopleSoft's Duffield Passes CEO Position to New President," *Wall Street Journal,* 22 September 1999, B6.

CHAPTER 11

1. "BusinessFirst," *Continental Airlines* [accessed 27 April 1999], http://www.continental.com/products/bfirst; "Continental Airlines Moves Up to No. 2 in National Airline Quality Rating Study," *Continental Airlines,* 19 April 1999 [accessed 27 April 1999], http://www.continental.com; "Continental Reports Record March Load," *Houston Business Journal,* 5 April 1999 [accessed 27 April 1999], http://www.amcity.com/houston/stories/1999/04/05/daily1.html?h=Continentall/Airlines; "Continental to Pay Profit Sharing to Employees," *Houston Business Journal,* 11 February 1999 [accessed 27 April 1999], http://www.amcity.com/ houston/stories/1999/02/08/daily11.html?h=Continentall/Airlines; GORDON BETHUNE, "From Worst to First," *Fortune,* 25 May 1, 1998, 185–190; STACY PERMAN, "Allied Air Force," *Time,* 9 February 1998, 76, 79; "Continental Airlines: A Turnaround Case Study," *Aviation Week and Space Technology,* 16 December 1996, S3–S30; SHELIA M. PUFFER, "Continental Airlines CEO Gordon Bethune on Teams

and New Product Development," *Academy of Management Executive,* August 1999, 28–35.

2. "AMA Board Approves New Marketing Definition," *Marketing News,* 1 March 1985, 1.

3. PHILIP KOTLER, *Marketing Management* (Upper Saddle River, N.J.: Prentice Hall, 1997), 24.

4. AL RIES AND JACK TROUT, *The 22 Immutable Laws of Marketing* (New York: HarperCollins, 1994), 19–25.

5. FRANKLIN S. HOUSTON, "The Marketing Concept: What It Is and What It Is Not," *Journal of Marketing,* April 1986, 81–87.

6. WILLIAM C. TAYLOR, "Permission Marketing," *Fast Company,* April–May 1998, 198–212.

7. ROBERTA MAYNARD, "New Directions in Marketing," *Nation's Business,* July 1995, 25–26.

8. KEVIN MANEY, "Consumers Latch onto Speedy Way to Get Gas," *USA Today,* 26 February 1998, 8B.

9. B. JOSEPH PINE II, DON PEPPERS, AND MARTHA ROGERS, "Do You Want to Keep Your Customers Forever?" *Harvard Business Review,* March–April 1995, 103–114; ERICK SCHONFELD, "The Customized, Digitized, Have-It-Your-Way Economy," *Fortune,* 28 September 1998, 115–124.

10. GARY MCWILLIAMS, "Small Fry Go Online," *Business Week,* 20 November 1995, 158–164.

11. TERRY G. VAVRA, "The Database Marketing Imperative," *Marketing Management,* 2, no. 1 (1993): 47–57.

12. THOMAS L. FRIEDMAN, *The Lexus and the Olive Tree,* (New York: Ferrar Straus Giroux, 1999), 69.

13. SUZANNE OLIVER, "Spoiled Rotten," *Forbes,* 15 July 1996, 70–73; "Skymall's Web Sales Take Flight As Shares Soar Nearly Threefold," *Wall Street Journal,* 29 December 1998, B9.

14. RON ZEMKE AND DICK SCHAAF, *The Service Edge: 101 Companies That Profit from Customer Care* (New York: New American Library, 1989), 50.

15. MANFRED F. R. KETS DE VRIES, "Charisma in Action: The Transformational Abilities of Virgin's Richard Branson and ABB's Percy Barnevik," *Organizational Dynamics,* Winter 1998, 6–21.

16. WILLIAM H. DAVIDOW AND BRO UTTAL, *Total Customer Service: The Ultimate Weapon* (New York: Harper & Row, 1989), 8; VALARIE A. ZEITHAML, A. PARASURAMAN, AND LEONARD L. BERRY, *Delivering Quality Service* (New York: Free Press, 1990), 9; GEORGE J. CASTELLESE, "Customer Service . . . Building a Winning Team," *Supervision,* January 1995, 9–13; ERICA G. SOROHAN AND CATHERINE M. PETRINI, "Dumpsters, Ducks, and Customer Service," *Training and Development,* January 1995, 9.

17. BILL SAPORITO, "What's for Dinner?" *Fortune,* 15 May 1995, 50–64; ROBERT F. LUSCH, DEBORAH ZIZZO, AND JAMES M.

KENDERDINE, "Strategic Renewal in Distribution," *Marketing Management* 2, no. 2, 27; JODI S. COHEN, "On-Line Grocers Make Fans, But Not Profits," *Chicago Tribune,* 27 July 1998, 4.

18. THOMAS A. STEWART, "A Satisfied Customer Isn't Enough," *Fortune,* 21 July 1997, 112–113.

19. FREDERICK F. REICHHELD, "Learning from Customer Defections," *Harvard Business Review,* March–April 1996, 56–69; FREDERICK F. REICHHELD, "Loyalty and the Renaissance of Marketing," *Marketing Management* 2, no. 4 (1994): 10–21; MICHAEL MUELLER, "FedEx Adds Shipping to Web," *PC Week,* July 1996, 100; WILLIAM H. DAVIDOW AND BRO UTTAL, *Total Customer Service: The Ultimate Weapon* (New York: Harper & Row, 1989), 34–35.

20. RONALD B. LIEBER, "Storytelling: A New Way to Get Close to Your Customer," *Fortune,* 3 February 1997, 102–110.

21. STEVE SCHRIVER, "Customer Loyalty: Going Going . . ." *American Demographics,* September 1997, 20–23.

22. JANET WILLEN, "The Customer Is Wrong," *Business97,* October–November 1997, 40–42.

23. PETER BURROWS, "HP: No Longer Lost in Cyberspace?" *Business Week,* 31 May 1999, 124, 126.

24. AVERY COMAROW, "Broken? No Problem," *U.S. News & World Report,* 11 January 199, 68–69.

25. SCOTT WOOLLEY, "Get Lost, Buster," *Forbes,* 23 February 1998, 90; JON VAN, "$5 Question: When Does Not Calling Not Add Up?" *Chicago Tribune,* 8 April 1999, sec. 1, 1, 14.

26. HAL LANCASTER, "Managing Your Career: Giving Good Service, Never an Easy Task, Is Getting a Lot Harder," *Wall Street Journal,* 9 June 1998, B1.

27. MARY J. CRONIN, *Doing More Business on the Internet* (New York: Van Nostrand Reinhold, 1995), 13.

28. LIEBER, "Storytelling."

29. HARRY S. DENT JR., "Individualized Marketing," *Small Business Reports,* April 1991, 36–45.

30. DAVID SHANI AND SUJANA CHALASANI, "Exploring Niches Using Relationship Marketing," *Journal of Business and Industrial Marketing* 8, no. 4 (1993): 58–66; JANET NOVACK, "The Data Miners," *Forbes,* 12 February 1996, 96–97; DON PEPPERS AND MARTHA ROGERS, *Enterprise One to One* (New York: Doubleday, 1997), 120–121.

31. WILLIAM J. HOLSTEIN, "Data-Crunching Santa," *U.S. News & World Report,* 21 December 1998, 45–46, 48.

32. JOSHUA MACHT, "The New Market Research," *Inc.,* July 1998, 87–94.

33. BRUCE HOROVITZ, "Malls Are Like, Totally Uncool, Say Hip Teens," *USA Today,* 1 May 1996, 1.

34. COURTLAND L. BOVÉE, MICHAEL J. HOUSTON, AND JOHN V. THILL, *Marketing,* 2d ed. (New York: McGraw-Hill, 1996), 188.

35. MALCOLM H. B. MCDONALD, "Ten Barriers to Marketing Planning," *Journal of Product and Brand Management,* Fall 1992, 51–64.

36. AL RIES AND JACK TROUT, The 22 *Immutable Laws of Marketing* (New York: HarperBusiness, 1993), 99.

37. VANESSA O'CONNELL, "Changing Tastes Dent Campbell's Canned-Soup Sales," *Wall Street Journal,* 28 April 1998, B1, B25.

38. NORIHIKO SHIROUZU, "Japan's High-School Girls Excel in Art of Setting Trends," *Wall Street Journal,* 24 April 1998, B1, B7.

39. LESLIE KAUFMAN, "Playing Catch-Up at the On-Line Mall," *New York Times,* 21 February 1999, sec. 3, 1, 6.

40. PHILIP KOTLER, *Marketing Management,* 9th ed. (Upper Saddle River, New Jersey: Prentice Hall, 1997), 147.

41. STAN DAVIS, "Business Wins, Organization Kills," *Forbes ASAP,* 7 April 1997, 49–50.

42. MALCOLM MCDONALD AND JOHN W. LEPPARD, *Marketing by Matrix* (Lincolnwood, Ill.: NTC, 1993), 10; H. IGOR ANSOFF, "Strategies for Diversification," *Harvard Business Review,* November–December 1957, 113–124; H. IGOR ANSOFF, *Corporate Strategy* (New York: McGraw-Hill, 1965).

43. ALEX TAYLOR III, "How to Murder the Competition," *Fortune,* 22 February 1993, 87, 90.

44. SCOTT HAYS, "Exceptional Customer Service Takes the 'Ritz' Touch," *Workforce,* January 1999, 99–102.

45. ANN OLDENBURG, "Market Responds Slowly to a Growing Population," *USA Today,* 18 March 1998, 9D.

46. SHANI AND CHALASANI, "Exploring Niches Using Relationship Marketing."

47. LARRY CARPENTER, "How to Market to Regions," *American Demographics,* November 1987, 45.

48. MICHAEL J. WEISS, *The Clustering of America* (New York: Harper & Row, 1988), 41.

49. DON PEPPERS AND MARTHA ROGERS, "One-to-One Business Travel," *Inside 1to1,* 17 September 1998 [via e-mail 16 September 1998].

50. SHANI AND CHALASANI, "Exploring Niches Using Relationship Marketing."

51. "Logitech Posts Fourth-Quarter and Year-End Results," *Logitech,* 29 April 1999 [accessed 7 May 1999], http://www.logitech.com/us/about/al_006_34.html.

52. PEPPERS AND ROGERS, *Enterprise One to One,* 145–146.

53. JUSTIN MARTIN, "Give 'Em Exactly What They Want," *Fortune,* 10 November 1997, 283–285.

54. MARC BALLON, "Sale of Modern Music Keyed to Customization," *Inc.,* May 1998, 23–25.

55. Bovée, Houston, and Thill, *Marketing,* 224.

56. Daniel Roth, "First: From Poster Boy to Whipping Boy," *Fortune,* 6 July 1998, 28–29.

57. Faye Brookman, "Brushing Up," *Supermarket Business,* February 1998, 57–62; Laurie Freeman, "Maintaining the Momentum," *Supermarket Business,* February 1999, 57–58.

58. Kotler, *Marketing Management,* 294–297.

59. "BusinessFirst," *Continental Airlines* [accessed 27 April 1999], http://www. continental.com/products/bfirst; "Continental Airlines Moves Up to No. 2 in National Airline Quality Rating Study," *Continental Airlines,* 19 April 1999 [accessed 27 April 1999], http://www.continental.com; "Continental Reports Record March Load," *Houston Business Journal,* 5 April 1999 [accessed 27 April 1999], http://www.amcity. com/houston/stories/1999/04/05/daily1.html ?h=Continental/Airlines/; "Continental to Pay Profit Sharing to Employees," *Houston Business Journal,* 11 February 1999 [accessed 27 April 1999], http://www.amcity.com/ houston/stories/1999/02/08/daily11.html? h=Continental/Airlines; Bethune, "From Worst to First"; Perman, "Allied Air Force"; "Continental Airlines"; Puffer, "Continental Airlines CEO Gordon Bethune on Teams and New Product Development."

60. Adapted from John Case and Jerry Useem, "Six Characters in Search of a Strategy," *Inc.,* March 1996, 46–49.

61. Fred Vogelstein, "Corporate America Loves the Weather," *U.S. News & World Report,* 13 May 1998, 48.

CHAPTER 12

1. Suzette Hill, "Levi Strauss Puts a New Spin on Brand Management," *Apparel Industry Magazine,* November 1998, 46–47; Suzette Hill, "Levi Strauss & Co.: Icon in Revolution," *Apparel Industry Magazine,* January 1999, 66–69; Wayne D'Orio, "Clothes Make the Teen," *American Demographics,* March 1999, 34–37; Nina Munk, "How Levi's Trashed a Great American Brand," *Fortune,* 12 April 1999, 83–86, 88, 90.

2. Philip Kotler, *Marketing Management* (Upper Saddle River, N.J.: Prentice Hall, 1997), 434.

3. Bill Gates, *Business @ the Speed of Thought* (New York: Warner Books, 1999), 155.

4. Gary Hamel, *Lessons in Leadership Lecture,* Northern Illinois University, 23 October 1997.

5. "Preparing for a Point to Point World," *Marketing Management* 3, no. 4 (Spring 1995): 30–40.

6. Mark Maremont, "How Gillette Brought Its Mach3 to Market," *Wall Street Journal,* 15 April 1998, B1, B4; Jeremy Kahn, "Gillette Loses Face," *Fortune,* 8 November 1999, 147–148.

7. Michele Rosen, "Apple Escapes PC Market Crunch," *Forbes Digital Tool,* 15 April 1999 [accessed 16 June 1999], http://www. forbes.com/tool/html/99/apr/0415/mu2.htm.

8. Bill Saporito, "Can Nike Get Unstuck?" *Time,* 30 March 1998, 48–53.

9. Peter F. Drucker, *Management Challenges for the 21st Century,* (New York: HarperBusiness, 1999), 75.

10. John C. Dvorak, "Razors with No Blades," *Forbes,* 18 October 1999, 168.

11. Marcia Mogelonsky, "Product Overload?" *American Demographics,* August 1998, 65–69.

12. Lisa Bannon, "Goodbye, Dolly: Mattel Tries to Adjust as 'Holiday Barbie' Leaves Under a Cloud," *Wall Street Journal,* 7 June 1999, A1, A8; Dana Canedy, "Beyond Barbie's Midlife Crisis," *New York Times,* 6 April 1999, C1, C8.

13. Al Ries and Jack Trout, "Focused in a Fuzzy World," *Rethinking the Future,* (London: Nicholas Brealey Publishing, 1997), 183.

14. Zachary Schiller, "Make It Simple," *Business Week,* 9 September 1996, 96–104; Katrina Brooker, "Can Procter & Gamble Change Its Culture, Protect Its Market Share, and Find the Next Tide?" *Fortune,* 26 April 1999, 146–152.

15. Tara Parket-Pope, "Custom-Made," *Wall Street Journal,* 26 September 1996, R22–R23.

16. Ernest Beck and Rekha Balu, "Europe Is Deaf to Snap! Crackle! Pop!" *Wall Street Journal,* 2 June 1998, B1, B12.

17. David Leonhardt, "It Was a Hit in Buenos Aires—So Why Not in Boise?" *Business Week,* 7 September 1998, 56, 58.

18. Constance L. Hays, "No More Brand X," *New York Times,* 12 June 1998, C1, C4.

18. Kelly Barron, "The Cappuccino Conundrum," *Forbes,* 22 February 1999, 54–55.

19. Nina Munk, "Gap Gets It," *Fortune,* 3 August 1998, 68–82.

20. Scott Davis, "When Brand Extension Becomes Brand Abuse," *Brandweek,* 26 October 1998, 20–22.

21. Steven Flax, "The Big Brand Stretch," *The Marketer,* September 1990, 32–35; Michael McDermott, "Too Much of a Good Thing?" *Adweek's Marketing Week,* 4 December 1989, 20–25; Tom Bunday, "Capitalizing on Brand Extensions," *Journal of Consumer Marketing,* Fall 1989, 27–30; Joshua Levine, "But in the Office, No," *Forbes,* 16 October 1989, 272–273.

22. Jagdish N. Sheth and Rajendra S. Sisodia, "Feeling the Heat," *Marketing Management* 4, no. 2 (Fall 1995): 9–23.

23. David Leonhardt, "Cereal-Box Killers Are on the Loose," *Business Week,* 12 October 1998, 72.

24. Dean Takahashi, "Intel Steps Up Use of Price Cuts to Protect Its Turf and to Expand," *Wall Street Journal,* 9 June 1998, B6.

25. Terril Yue Jones, "Fearing the Old Shoddy Image," *Forbes,* 12 January 1998 [accessed 16 June 1999], http://www.forbes. com/forbes/98/0112/6101064a.htm.

26. Thomas T. Nagle, "Managing Price Competition," *Marketing Management* 2, no. 1 (1993): 38–45; Sheth and Sisodia, "Feeling the Heat," 21.

27. Gurumurthy Kalyanaram and Ragu Gurumurthy, "Market Entry Strategies: Pioneers Versus Late Arrivals," *Strategy & Business,* Third quarter 1998 [accessed 16 June 1999], http://www.strategy- business.com.

28. Tim Klass, "Web Bookstores Discount Bestsellers," *Associated Press Online,* 17 May 1999 [accessed 21 May 1999], http://www.cbsmarketwatch.com.

29. Edwin McDowell, "Winging It, with Internet Fares," *New York Times,* 7 March 1999, sec. 3, 1, 10.

30. "Sales Costs Higher for Small Firms," *Small Business Reports,* November 1990, 18.

31. Craig Endicott, "Ad Volume Soars 6.9% to $64.6 Billion for Top Marketers," *Advertising Age,* 27 September 1999, S1–S6.

32. Kenneth R. Sheets, "3-D or Not 3-D? That's the Question for Advertisers," *U.S. News & World Report,* 25 January 1988, 59; authors' estimates.

33. Frank Koelsch, *The Infomedia Revolution* (Whitby, Ontario, Canada: McGraw-Hill Ryerson, 1995), 235.

34. "Web Ad Revenue Keeps Growing," *CyberAtlas,* 3 May 1999 [accessed 21 May 1999], http://www.cyberatlast.com/ segments/advertising/rev.html.

35. Marc Gunther, "The Trouble with Web Advertising," *Fortune,* 12 April 1999, 147–148.

36. Amy Cortese, "A Way Out of the Web Maze," *Business Week,* 24 February 1997, 95–108.

37. *Direct Marketing Association* [accessed 23 November 1997], http://www.the-dma.org/ services1/libres-home1b.shtml.

38. "Direct Hit," *The Economist,* 9 January 1999, 55–57.

39. *Direct Marketing Association* [accessed 23 November 1997], http://www.the-dma.org/ services1/libres-home1b.shtml.

40. Roger Reece, "The New Generation of Integrated Inbound/Outbound Telemarketing Systems," *Telemarketing,* March 1995, 58–65; Malynda H. Madzel, "Outsourcing Telemarketing: Why It May Work for You," *Telemarketing,* March 1995, 48–49; "Despite Hangups, Telemarketing a Success," *Marketing News,* 27 March 1995, 19.

41. Courtland L. Bovée, Michael J. Houston, and John V. Thill, *Marketing,* 2d ed. (New York: McGraw-Hill, 1994), 475.

42. Steve Dworman, "Trends That Hurt Infomercials," *Target Marketing,* February 1997, 46; Peter Bieler, "The ThighMaster

Exerciser Bonanza," *Success,* July/August 1996, 59.

43. "Promotional Trends Survey Caps Two Decades," *Cox Direct,* 14 September 1998 [accessed 24 May 1999], http://www. justdelivered.com/itm/pressreleases/ pr-091498.htm.

44. "Coupons, Samples Drive Consumer Shopping Decisions," *Cox Direct,* 8 September 1998 [accessed 24 May 1999], http://www.justdelivered.com/itm/ pressreleases/pr-090898-2.htm.

45. PAULETTE THOMAS, " 'Clicking' Coupons On-Line Has a Cost: Privacy," *Wall Street Journal,* 18 June 1998, B1, B8.

46. MICHELINE MAYNARD, "Ford Follows GM's Lead into Coupon Competition," *USA Today,* 24 April 1998, B1.

47. JOHN PHILIP JONES, "The Double Jeopardy of Sales Promotions," *Harvard Business Review,* September–October 1990, 145–152; LAURIE PETERSEN, "The Pavlovian Syndrome," *Adweek's Marketing Week,* 9 April 1990, P6–P7; "Coupons—Still the Shopper's Best Friend," *Progressive Grocer,* February 1995, SS11.

48. LISA Z. ECCLES, "Point of Purchase Advertising," *Advertising Age Supplement,* 26 September 1994, 1–6.

49. JAMES HECKMAN, "Local Festivals Attracting More Sponsorship Dollars," *Marketing News,* 24 May 1999, 3.

50. "Trade Shows: An Alternative Method of Selling," *Small Business Reports,* January 1985, 67; KATE BERTRAND, "Trade Shows Can Be Global Gateways," *Advertising Age's Business Marketing,* March 1995, 19–20.

51. KATHARINE MIESZKOWSKI, "The Power of Public Relations," *Fast Company,* April–May 1998, 182–196.

52. CYNDEE MILLER, "VNRs Are Still Hot, But They're Drawing Fire," *Marketing News,* 12 November 1990, 6.

53. COURTLAND L. BOVÉE, JOHN V. THILL, GEORGE P. DOVEL, AND MARIAN BURK WOOD, *Advertising Excellence* (New York: McGraw-Hill, 1994), 16.

54. WENDY ZELLNER, "Southwest's New Direction," *Business Week,* 8 February 1999, 58–59; JENNIFER LAWRENCE, "Integrated Mix Makes Expansion Fly," *Advertising Age— Special Integrated Marketing Report,* 4 November 1993, S10–S12.

55. DAVID J. MORROW, "From Lab to Patient, by Way of Your Den," *New York Times,* 7 June 1998, sec. 3, 1, 10.

56. HILL, "Levi Strauss Puts a New Spin on Brand Management"; HILL, "Levi Strauss & Co."; D'ORIO, "Clothes Make the Teen"; MUNK, "How Levi's Trashed a Great American Brand."

57. JOANNE LIPMAN, "Do Toll Phone Services Play Fair by Advertising Directly to Kids?" *Wall Street Journal,* 7 July 1989, B1.

58. AMY OLMSTEAD, "Economics of On-Line Trading: Clicking for Dollars," *New York Times Magazine,* 11 April 1999, 30; SEAN T. KELLY, "The Top Ten Discount Brokers," *Time Digital,* 17 May 1999, 38–39.

59. "Unilever's Foods Business," *Unilever* [accessed 26 May 1999], http://www.unilever. com/public/brands/foods/food0001.htm.

CHAPTER 13

1. DOREEN CARVAJAL, "Trying to Read a Hazy Future," *New York Times,* 18 April 1999, sec. 3, 1, 6; PETER DE JONGE, "Riding the Wild, Perilous Waters of Amazon.com," *New York Times Magazine,* 14 March 1999, 36–41, 54, 68, 79, 81; ROBERT D. HOF, "Amazon.com: The Wild World of E-Commerce," *Business Week,* 14 December 1998, 106–108, 110, 112, 114, 119; JODI MARDESICH AND MARC GUNTHER, "Is Competition Closing In on Amazon.com?" *Fortune,* 9 November 1998, 229–230, 234; Bernhard Warner, "Jeff Bezos: Volume Discounter," *Brandweek,* 12 October 1998, S18–S22; LESLEY HAZLETON, "Jeff Bezos," *Success,* July 1998, 58, 60; SAUL HANSELL, "Amazon.com Gets into Two New Businesses," *New York Times,* 13 July 1999, C1, C7; GEORGE ANDERS, "The View from the Top," *Wall Street Journal,* 12 July 1999, R52; KATRINA BROOKER, "Amazon vs. Everybody," *Fortune,* 8 November 1999, 120–128; GEORGE ANDERS AND NICK WINGFIELD, "Amazon.com, in Yet Another Expansion, Will Launch Credit Card with NextCard," *Wall Street Journal,* 10 November 1999, A3, A14; ROBERT D. HOF AND STEVE HAMM, "Amazon.com Throws Open the Doors," *Business Week,* 11 October 1999, 44; LESLIE KAUFMAN, "Amazon.com Plans to Reposition Itself As Internet Bazaar," *New York Times,* 30 September 1999, A1, C25; GEORGE ANDERS, "Different Strokes," *Wall Street Journal,* 2 November 1999, A1, A10.

2. LISA CHADDERDON, "How Dell Sells on the Web," *Fast Company,* September 1998, 58, 60.

3. BROOKER, "Amazon vs. Everybody."

4. BILL GATES, *Business @ the Speed of Thought* (New York: Warner Books, 1999), 95.

5. MARCIA STEPANEK, "Closed, Gone to the Net," *Business Week,* 7 June 1999, 113–114, 116.

6. ANDREA ADELSON, "Getting in on the Ground Floor in the Cyberpostage Market," *New York Times,* 18 February 1999, D8; STEPANEK, "Closed, Gone to the Net."

7. STEPANEK, "Closed, Gone to the Net."

8. JULIA KING, "Retailers, Manufacturers Find Ways to Co-exist on Electronic Frontier," *Computerworld,* 17 May 1999 [accessed 21 May 1999], http://www. computerworld.com/home/print.nsf/all/ 990517a69e.

9. WARREN COHEN, "Same Price.com," *U.S. News & World Report,* 25 May 1998, 59; JOSEPH CONLIN, "The Art of the Dealer Meeting," *Sales and Marketing Management,* February 1997, 76.

10. GREGORY L. WHITE, "GM Is Forming Unit to Buy Dealerships," *Wall Street Journal,* 24 September 1999, A3; JOANN MULLER, "Meet Your Local GM Dealer: GM," *Business Week,* 11 October 1999, 48.

11. LAURA JOHANNES, "Ben & Jerry's Plans to End Ties with Dreyer's," *Wall Street Journal,* 1 September 1998, A4; "Dreyer's Grand Ice Cream and Ben & Jerry's Complete Ongoing Distribution Agreement," Dreyer's Grand Ice Cream, 25 January 1999 [accessed 3 June 1999], http://www.dreyers.com/ thecompany/press/main_press_benjerry.html; Ben & Jerry's Announced Distribution Redesign," Ben & Jerry's Homemade, 31 August 1998 [accessed 3 June 1999], http://lib. benjerry.com/press-rel/dist-redesign98.htm

12. WHITE, "GM Is Forming Unit to Buy Dealerships."

13. "Hallmark, a New Name in Mass Retailing," *Supermarket Business,* March 1997, 84; DANIEL ROTH, "Card Sharks," *Forbes,* 7 October 1996, 14; JULIE RYGH, "Hallmark Cards Find Success with New Expressions Brand," *Knight-Ridder/Tribune Business News,* 31 August 1997, 831B0958.

14. "1997 Economic Census: Advance Summary Statistics for the United States 1997 NAICS Basis," U.S. Census Bureau, 16 March 1999 [accessed 7 June 1999], http://www. census.gov/epcd/wwww/ advanc1ahtm.

15. MARCIA STEPANEK, "Middlemen: Rebirth of the Salesman," *Business Week,* 22 June 1998, 146–147.

16. "1997 Economic Census," U.S. Census Bureau.

17. LINNEA ANDERSON, "Industry Zone: Industry Snapshot: Retail & Wholesale," Hoover's Online [accessed 7 June 1999], http://www.hoovers.com/features/industry/ retail.html.

18. ANDERSON, "Industry Zone: Industry Snapshot: Retail & Wholesale," Hoover's Online [accessed 7 June 1999], http://www. hoovers.com/features/industry/retail.html.

19. PATRICIA SELLERS, "Giants of the Fortune Five Hundred: Sears: The Turnaround Is Ending; The Revolution Has Begun," *Fortune,* 28 April 1997, 106.

20. JULIE SCHMIT, "Tandy Pulls Plug on 35 Superstores," *USA Today,* 31 December 1996, B1.

21. "Economic Trends: Third Quarter 1998," International Mass Retailers Association, 3 December 1998 [accessed 7 June 1999], http://www.imra. org/economic_trends.html.

22. PAUL KLEBNIKOV, "Trouble in Toyland," *Forbes,* 1 June 1998, 56, 58, 60; I. JEANNE DUGAN, "The Corporation: Strategies: Can Toys "R" Us Get on Top of Its Game?" *Business Week,* 7 April 1997, 124.

23. WENDY ZELLNER, "Look Out, Supermarkets—Wal-Mart Is Hungry," *Business Week,* 14 September 1998, 98, 100; ZINA MOUKHEIBER, "The Great Wal-Mart Massacre, Part II," *Forbes,* 22 January 1996, 44–45.

24. WILLIAM J. HOLSTEIN AND KERRY HANNON, "They Drop Till You Shop," *U.S. News & World Report,* 21 July 1997, 51–52.

25. HOLSTEIN AND HANNON, "They Drop Till You Shop."

26. MICHELLE PACELLE, "The Aging Shopping Mall Must Either Adapt or Die," *Wall Street Journal,* 16 April 1996, B1, B14.

27. JENNIFER STEINHAUER, "It's a Mall . . . It's an Airport," *New York Times,* 10 June 1998, B1, B4; CHRIS WOODYARD, "Hamlets Feature Fewer Rivals, Higher Profits," *USA Today,* 3 February 1998, B1, B2.

28. GINIA BELLAFANTE, "That's Retailtainment!" *Time,* 7 December 1998, 64–65.

29. PHILIP KOTLER, *Marketing Management,* 9th ed. (Upper Saddle River, N.J.: Prentice Hall, 1997), 567.

30. JULIA KING, "Retailers, Manufacturers Find Ways to Co-exist on Electronic Frontier," Computerworld, 17 May 1999 [accessed 21 May 1999], http://www.computerworld.com/home/print.nsf/all/990517a69e.

31. RICHARD A. FEINBERG, "Sobering Thoughts on Cybermalls," *Computerworld,* 14 April 1997, 35.

32. BILL GATES, *Business @ the Speed of Thought* (New York: Warner Books, 1999), 109.

33. SUSAN CHANDLER, "Opening the Retail Gates for PCs," *Chicago Tribune,* 27 October 1999, B1, B2.

34. "Value of U.S. DM Driven Sales Compared to Total U.S. Sales," Direct Marketing Association [accessed 8 June 1999], http://www.thedma.org/services1/charts/dmsales_ussales.html.

35. HOWARD RUDNITSKY, "Growing Pains," *Forbes,* 27 February 1995, 32; SIGMUND KIENER, "The Future of Mail Order," *Direct Marketing,* 15 February 1995, 17.

36. CATHERINE ROMANO, "Telemarketing Grows Up," *Management Review,* June 1998, 31–34.

37. "Is the Bell Tolling for Door-to-Door Selling?" *Business Week E.Biz,* 1 November 1999 EB58–EB60.

38. CHRIS WOODYARD AND LORRIE GRANT, "E-tailers Dash to Wild, Wild Web," *USA Today,* 13 January 1999, B1, B2.

39. TIMOTHY HANRAHAN, "Lessons Learned," *Wall Street Journal Reports: The Internet, Selling Points,* 7 December 1998, R16; ROBERT SCALLY, "Egghead Merger Expected Soon," *Discount Store News,* 22 November 1999, 6; "Onsale and Egghead Merger Creates a Leader in Online Retailing of Technology Products," *Business Wire,* 22 November 1999 [accessed online at Electric Library Web site, 5 December 1999].

40. PHIL WAGA, "Dell's Prowess on the Net," *Gannett News Service,* 23 November 1999, 1; LISA CHADDERDON, "How Dell Sells on the Web," *Fast Company,* September 1998, 58, 60; WILLIAM J. HOLSTEIN, SUSAN GREGORY THOMAS, AND FRED VOGELSTEIN, "Click 'Til

You Drop," *U.S. News & World Report,* 7 December 1998, 42–45.

41. HEATHER PAGE, "Open for Business," *Entrepreneur,* December 1997, 51–53.

42. KELLY J. ANDREWS, "Value-Added E-Commerce," *Entrepreneurial Edge,* 3 (1998), 62–64.

43. ROBERT D. HOF, "Electronic Commerce: The Net Is Open for Business—Big Time," *Business Week,* 31 August 1998, 108–109; MARY BRANDEL, "On-line Catalogs Are Booting Up." *Computerworld Electronic Commerce-Journal,* 29 April 1996, 5.

44. DANIEL S. JANAL, "Net Profit Now", *Success,* July/August 1997, 57–63.

45. TARIQ K. MUHAMMAD, "Marketing Online," *Black Enterprise,* September 1996, 85–88.

46. HOLSTEIN, THOMAS, AND VOGELSTEIN, "Click 'Til You Drop."

47. NEIL GROSS, "The Supply Chain: Leapfrogging a Few Links," *Business Week,* 22 June 1998, 140–142.

48. LISA H. HARRINGTON, "The New Warehousing," *Industry Week,* 20 July 1998, 52, 54, 57–58.

49. BILL GATES, *Business @ the Speed of Thought* (New York: Warner Books, 1999), 90.

50. SAUL HENSELL, "Is This the Factory of the Future?" *New York Times,* 26 July 1998, sec. 3, 1, 12.

51. "You, Me, and All Those Others Just Like Us," *Inc.,* 19 May 1998, 51–52; PC Connection Catalog, vol. 4, no. 6B, 1994, 2–3.

52. LISA H. HARRINGTON, "Coping with Adolescence," *Industry Week,* 19 October 1998, 110, 112, 114, 117; "Neiman Marcus Selects Circle As Global Logistics Supplier," Circle International, 21 April 1999 [accessed 8 June 1999], http://www.circleintl.com/news/releases/Neiman.html.

53. RONALD HENKOFF, "Delivering the Goods," *Fortune,* 28 November 1994, 64–78.

54. EDWARD O. WELLES, "Riding the High-Tech Highway," *Inc.,* March 1993, 72–85.

55. COLLEEN GOURLEY, "Retail Logistics in Cyberspace," *Distribution,* December 1996, 29; DAVE HIRSCHMAN, "FedEx Starts Up Package Sorting System at Memphis Tenn. Airport," *Knight-Ridder/Tribune Business News,* 28 September 1997, 928B0953; "FedEx and Technology—Maintaining a Competitive Edge," *PresWIRE,* 2 December 1996.

56. SAUL HANSELL, "For Amazon, a Holiday Risk: Can It Sell Acres of Everything?" *New York Times,* 28 November 1999, sec. 3, 1, 15; BROOKER, "Amazon vs. Everybody."

57. CARVAJAL, "Trying to Read a Hazy Future"; DE JONGE, "Riding the Wild, Perilous Waters of Amazon.com"; Hof, "Amazon.com"; MARDESICH AND GUNTHER, "Is Competition Closing In on Amazon.com?"; WARNER, "Jeff Bezos"; HAZLETON, "Jeff Bezos"; HANSELL, "Amazon.com Gets into Two New Businesses"; ANDERS, "The View from the Top"; BROOKER, "Amazon vs. Everybody";

ANDERS AND WINGFIELD, "Amazon.com, in Yet Another Expansion, Will Launch Credit Card with NextCard"; HOF AND HAMM, "Amazon.com Throws Open the Doors"; KAUFMAN, "Amazon.com Plans to Reposition Itself as Internet Bazaar"; ANDERS, "Different Strokes."

58. BILL GATES, *Business @ the Speed of Thought* (New York: Warner Books, 1999), 76; ELIZABETH WEISE, "Sizing Up Web Shoppers for the Perfect Fit," USA Today, 21 April 1999, 4D.

59. PAUL DEAN, "Auto Makers Shift into New Gear," *Los Angeles Times,* 15 January 1997, E1, E6.

60. BILL DEDMAN, "Holiday Vigil for FedEx Customers," *New York Times,* 8 November 1998, sec. 3, 4.

61. HARRINGTON, "Coping with Adolescence."

62. GREGORY L. WHITE, "GM's Saturn Unit Temporarily Closes Plants on Slow Sales, Launch Problems," *Wall Street Journal,* 7 January 2000, A4; KATHLEEN KERWIN AND KEITH NAUGHTON, "A Different Kind of Saturn," *Business Week,* 5 July 1999, 28–29; MIKE ARNHOLT, "Saturn Grows Up," *Ward's Auto World,* July 1999, 43–45; Jeff Green, "Saturn's 'L' Pitch: Next Big Thing," *Brandweek,* 14 June 1999, 8; Greg Gardner, "Is This the End of Saturn?" *Ward's Auto World,* September 1998, 41; JENNIFER LAABS, "Saturn Workers Vote to Retain Innovative Risk-and-Reward Pay Package," *Workforce,* May 1998, 14; KATHLEEN KERWIN, "Why Didn't GM Do More for Saturn?" *Business Week,* 16 March 1998, 62; DON L. BOHL, "Case Study: Saturn Corp—A Different Kind of Pay," *Compensation and Benefits Review,* November/December 1997, 51–56; SARAH LORGE, "Saturn," *Sales and Marketing Management,* October 1997, 63.

CHAPTER 14

1. Adapted from "Highway Retrofit Project Showcases New Capabilities," TCDI Web site [accessed 27 April 1999], http://www.geomod.com/tcdinews4.html; "Exciting Projects Mark Another Year of Growth for TCDI," TCDI Web site [accessed 27 April 1999], http://www.geomod.com/tcdinews3.html; EDWARD WEINER, chief operating officer, TCDI, personal communication, March 1998.

2. Elizabeth MacDONALD, "U.S. Accounting Board Faults Global Rules," *Wall Street Journal,* 18 October 1999, A1.

3. JEFFREY E. GARTEN, "Global Accounting Rules? Not So Fast," *Business Week,* 5 April 1999, 26; MacDonald, "U.S. Accounting Board Faults Global Rules."

4. JOHN VON BRACHEL, "AICPA Chairman Lays the Foundation for the Future," *Journal of Accountancy,* November 1995, 64–67.

5. TOM KENNEDY SMITH, "The Changing Face of Accounting Services," *Corporate Report—Minnesota,* 1 August 1996, 61.

6. MELODY PETERSEN, "Shortage of Accounting Students Raises Concern on Audit Quality," *New York Times,* 19 February 1999, C1, C3.

7. RICHARD MELCHER, "Where Are the Accountants?" *Business Week,* 5 October 1998, 144–146.

8. DANIEL MCGINN, "Sherlocks of Finance," *Newsweek,* 24 August 1998, 38–39.

9. JENNIFER REINGOLD AND RICHARD A. MELCHER, "Then There Were Four," *Business Week,* 3 November 1997, 37; SALLIE L. GAINES, "KPMG and Ernst Call Off Merger," *Chicago Tribune,* 14 February 1998, B1,B3.

10. RALPH SAUL, "Keeping the Watchdog Healthy," *Financial Executive,* November–December 1995, 10–13; Melcher, "Where are the Accountants?"

11. ROBERT STUART, "Accountants in Management—A Globally Changing Role," *CMA Magazine,* 1 February 1997, 5.

12. JACK L. SMITH, ROBERT M. KEITH, AND WILLIAM L. STEPHENS, *Accounting Principles,* 4th ed. (New York: McGraw-Hill, 1993), 16–17.

13. STANLEY ZAROWIN, "The Future of Finance," *Journal of Accountancy,* August 1995, 47–49.

14. 1998 Annual Report of Computer Discount Warehouse.

15. FRANK EVANS, "A Road Map to Your Financial Report," *Management Review,* October 1993, 39–47.

16. ELI GOLDRATT, "Focusing On Constraints, Not Costs." *Rethinking the Future* (London: Nicholas Brealey Publishing. 1997, 106.

17. BILL GATES, *Business @ the Speed of Thought,* (New York: Warner Books, 1999), 23.

18. Adapted from "Highway Retrofit Project Showcases New Capabilities," TCDI Web site [accessed 27 April 1999], http://www.geomod.com/tcdinews4.html; "Exciting Projects Mark Another Year of Growth for TCDI," TCDI Web site [accessed 27 April 1999], http://www.geomod.com/tcdinews3.html; EDWARD WEINER, chief operating officer, TCDI, personal communication, March 1998.

19. Adapted from "Technology: Sound Chamber," *Newsweek,* 13 May 1996, 10.

CHAPTER 15

1. "E*Trade Records 1 Million Active Customer Accounts," E*Trade, 26 April 1999 [accessed 28 April 1999], http://www.etrade.com; "The Story of E*Trade," E*Trade (n.d.) [accessed 28 April 1999], http://www.etrade.com; "More Secure Securities," E*Trade (n.d.) [accessed 28 April 1999], http://www.etrade.com; KATHLEEN OHLSON, "E*Trade Revenue Soars, Losses Continue," Computerworld, 20 April 1999 [accessed 28 April 1999], http://www.computerworld.com/home/news.nsf/all/9904202etrade; SAUL HANSELL, "Trading on E*Trade's Success," *New York Times,* 16 March 1999, C1, C11; LEAH NATHANS SPIRO,

"Will E*Trade Move Beyond E*Tragedy?" *Business Week,* 22 February 1999, 118; SHARON MACHLIS, "Glitch Snuffs Out Online Broker for Hours," Computerworld, 4 February 1999 [accessed 28 April 1999], http://www.computerworld.com/home/news.nsf/all/9902044etrade; KIMBERLY WEISUL, "E*Trade Snafu Results in $4 Million Earnings Hit," *Investment Dealer's Digest,* 14 July 1997, 6–7; "E*Trade Solidifies Industry Leadership by Adding over 1,000,000 Net New Active Accounts in 12 months," E*Trade, 13 October 1999 [accessed 10 December 1999], http://www.etrade.com.

2. PAUL BECKET, "Smart Card Still Needs More Answers, Sponsors Concede, As Big Test Nears End," *Wall Street Journal,* 4 November 1998, A8; INKA RESCH, "Medical Care on a Card," *Business Week,* 14 September 1998, 94.

3. BETH KWON, "Need Stamps, Stocks, Plane Tickets? Step Up to an ATM," *Newsweek,* 25 January 1999, 15; KARA K. CHOQUETTE, "Super ATMs Sell Lift Tickets, Exchange Currencies," *USA Today,* 19 January 1998, B1; CONNIE GUGLIELMO, "Here Come the Super-ATMs," *Fortune,* 14 October 1996, 232–234.

4. THOMAS MCCARROLL, "No Checks. No Cash. No Fuss?" *Time,* 9 May 1994, 60–61.

5. SCOTT WOOLLEY, "Virtual Banker," *Forbes,* 15 June 1998 [accessed 28 July 1999], http://www.forbes.com/forbes/98/0615/6112127a.htm; DEAN FOUST, "Will Online Banking Replace the ATM?" *Yahoo! Internet Life,* November 1998, 114–118.

6. THOMAS E. WEBER, "On the Web, the Race for a Better Wallet," *New York Times,* 16 December 1998, B1, B4.

7. "FDIC Statistics on Banking: Number of FDIC-Insured Commercial Banks, 1934 Through 1998," FDIC Databank [accessed 28 July 1999], http://www.fdic.gov/databank/sob/9812/nmbank.gif.

8. LEAH NATHANS SPIRO, "The 'Coca-Cola of Personal Finance,'" *Business Week,* 20 April 1998, 37–38; JOSEPH NOCERA, "'Banking Is Necessary—Banks Are Not,'" *Fortune,* 11 May 1998, 84–85.

9. STEPHAN LABATON, "Accord Reached on Lifting Depression-Era Barriers Among Financial Industries," *New York Times,* 23 October 1999, A1, B4.

10. LABATON, "Accord Reached on Lifting Depression-Era Barriers Among Financial Industries" JOSEPH KAHN, "Financial Services Industry Faces a New World," *New York Times,* 23 October 1999, B1, B5; MICHAEL SCHROEDER, "Glass-Steagall Compromise Is Reached," *Wall Street Journal,* 25 October 1999, A2, A20; MARCY GORDON, "Clinton Signs Historic Bank Overhaul Bill," *Desert Sun,* 31 November 1999, A1, A9.

11. SHARON NELTON, "You Can Bank on the Personal Touch," *Nation's Business,* June 1999, 49–51.

12. "Important Banking Legislation," FDIC [accessed 28 July 1999], http://www.fdic.gov/publish/banklaws.html; "Interstate Branching," The Federal Reserve Board [accessed 23 July 1999], http://www.bog.frb.fed.us/generalinfo/isb.

13. MATT MURRAY AND RAJU NARISETTI, "Bank Mergers' Hidden Engine: Technology," *Wall Street Journal,* 23 April 1998, B1, B9; DAVID GREISING, "$1,000,000,000,000 Banks," *Business Week,* 27 April 1998, 32–39.

14. MELISSA WAHL, "Banking Branches Out on the Internet," *Chicago Tribune,* 8 July 1998, sec. 3, 1, 3.

15. JEFFREY E. GARTEN, "The Fed Should Look Farther Than Its Own Backyard," *Business Week,* 31 August 1998, 18.

16. LAURA COHN, "Are T-Bills Y2K Insurance?" *Business Week,* 26 July 1999, 34.

17. PETER COY, "Tracking Stocks Are Accidents Waiting to Happen," *Business Week,* 2 August 1999, 33; MARCIA VICKERS, "Are Two Stocks Better Than One?" *Business Week,* 28 June 1999, 98–99.

18. "An Investor's Guide to Corporate Bonds: How Big Is the Market and Who Buys?" Bond Market Association [accessed 27 July 1999], http://www.investinginbonds.com/info/igcorp/big.htm.

19. JULIE BORT, "Trading Places," *Computerworld,* 27 May 1996, 105.

20. DAVID BARBOZA, "An Expert at Trades," *New York Times,* 24 June 1998, C1, C17.

21. CATHERINE FRIEND WHITE, "At Home in the Global Marketplace," *Business Ethics,* September–October, 1993, 39–40.

22. GREG IP, "Big Board Overhauls Its Standards," *Wall Street Journal,* 5 June 1998, C1, C16.

23. GREG BURNS, "Amex Members Say Yes to Merger," *Chicago Tribune,* 26 June 1998, sec. 3, 1, 4.

24. MIKE MCNAMEE, "Faster, Cheaper Trading—Can the Regulators Keep Up?" *Business Week,* 9 August 1999, 84–85.

25. GREG IP, "NYSE Studying Electronic System to Fill Small Trades Automatically," *Wall Street Journal,* 5 November 1999, C1.

26. MIKE MCNAMEE, "A Revolt at NASD?" *Business Week,* 2 August 1999, 70–71; DEAN FOUST, "Open All Night," *Business Week,* 14 June 1999, 42–44; TERRI CULLEN, "Making the Trade: After Hours," *Wall Street Journal Online Investing,* 14 June 1999, R12; "Today, Late Access Begins for NYSE-Listed Stocks," *Wall Street Journal,* 29 October 1999, C2.

27. BILL GATES, *Business @ the Speed of Thought,* (New York: Warner Books, 1999), 80.

28. JOHN R. DORFMAN, "Crash Courses," *Wall Street Journal,* 28 May 1996, R12–R13.

29. REBECCA BUCKMAN, "Making the Trade: What Now?" *Wall Street Journal Online Investing,* 14 June 1999, R6.

30. BILL GATES, *Business @ the Speed of Thought,* (New York: Warner Books, 1999), 90.

31. LEAH NATHANS SPIRO, "Bullish on the Internet," *Business Week,* 14 June 1999, 45–46.

32. NANETTE BYRNES, "How Schwab Grabbed the Lion's Share," *Business Week,* 28 June 1998, 88.

33. KATRINA BROOKER, "Could the Dow Become Extinct?" *Fortune,* 15 February 1999, 194–195; ANITA RAGHAVAN AND NANCY ANN JEFFREY, "What, How, Why—So What Is the Dow Jones Industrial Average, Anyway?" *Wall Street Journal,* 28 May 1996, R30; E. S. BROWNING, "New Economy Stocks Join Industrials," *Wall Street Journal,* 27 October 1999, C1, C15.

34. JEFFREY M. LADERMAN, "Why It's So Tough to Beat the S&P," *Business Week,* 24 March 1997, 82–38.

35. "SEC Orders Decimal Stock Prices," *Chicago Tribune,* 29 January 2000, sec 2, 2; "SEC Orders Securities Markets to Begin Trading in Decimals on July 3, 2000," SEC Web site, [accessed 20 January 2000], http://www.sec.gov/news/decimals.htm.

36. DAVID DIAMOND, "The Web's Most Wanted," *Business 2.0,* August 1999, 120–128.

37. AARON LUCCHETTI, "Some Web Sites Getting Tough on Stock Chat," *Wall Street Journal,* 28 May 1999, C1, C20; REBECCA BUCKMAN, "NASD Maps War on Claims on Internet," *Wall Street Journal,* 24 March 1997, B98W.

38. "E*Trade Records 1 Million Active Customer Accounts," E*Trade, 26 April 1999 [accessed 28 April 1999], http://www.etrade. com; "The Story of E*Trade," E*Trade (n.d.) [accessed 28 April 1999], http://www.etrade. com; "More Secure Securities," E*Trade (n.d.) [accessed 28 April 1999], http://www.etrade. com; KATHLEEN OHLSON, "E*Trade Revenue Soars, Losses Continue," *Computerworld,* 20 April 1999 [accessed 28 April 1999], http:// www.computerworld.com/home/news.nsf/ all/9904202etrade; SAUL HANSELL, "Trading on E*Trade's Success," *New York Times,* 16 March 1999, C1, C11; LEAH NATHANS SPIRO, "Will E*Trade Move Beyond E*Tragedy?" *Business Week,* 22 February 1999, 118; SHARON MACHLIS, "Glitch Snuffs Out Online Broker for Hours," *Computerworld,* 4 February 1999 [accessed 28 April 1999], http://www.computerworld.com/home/ news.nsf/all/9902044etrade; KIMBERLY WEISUL, "E*Trade Snafu Results in $4 Million Earnings Hit," *Investment Dealer's Digest,* 14 July 1997, 6–7; "E*Trade Solidifies Industry Leadership by Adding over 1,000,000 Net New Active Accounts in 12 months," E*Trade, 13 October 1999 [accessed 10 December 1999], http://www.etrade.com.

39. JOSEPH B. CAHILL, "Regulators Discover There Is No There at a 'Virtual' Bank," *Wall Street Journal,* 1 September 1998, A1, A6.

40. Adapted from NANETTE BYRNES, "How Schwab Grabbed the Lion's Share," *Business Week,* 28 June 1999, 88; ANDREW SERWER, "Online and Off, Schwab's the One," *Fortune,* 10 May 1999, 181–182; ERICK SCHONFELD,

"Schwab Puts It All Online," *Fortune,* 7 December 1998, 94–100; REBECCA BUCKMAN, "Schwab, Once a Predator, Is Now Prey," *Wall Street Journal,* 8 December 1999, C1; JERRY USEEM, "Internet Defense Strategy: Cannibalize Yourself," *Fortune,* 6 September 1999, 121–134; PATRICK MCGEEHAN, "Competitors Don't Seem to Hurt Schwab," *New York Times Online,* 30 December 1999, http://www.nytimes.com/library/financial/ colums/123099broker-place.html; Schwab press release, *Wall Street Journal,* 28 December 1999, B10; PUI-WING TAM AND RANDALL SMITH, "Schwab to Acquire U.S. Trust, Bring in High-End Clients," *Wall Street Journal,* 14 January 2000, C1.

COMPONENT CHAPTER A

1. WILLIAM H. MILLER, "Growth of Government," *Industry Week,* 21 September 1998, 83–94.

2. STEVE HAMM, SUSAN B. GARLAND, AND OWEN ULLMANN, "Going After Gates," *Business Week,* 3 November 1997, 34.

3. STEVE LOHR, "Judge Wakes Up Investors Who Shrugged Off the Antitrust Case," *New York Times* on the Web, 6 November 1999, http://www.nytimes.com/library/tech/99/11/ biztech/articles/07assess.html; JOEL BRINKLEY, "U.S. Judge Declares Microsoft a Monopoly That Stifles Industry," *New York Times* on the Web, 6 November 1999, http://www.nytimes. com/library/tech/99/11/biztech/articles/06soft. html; STEVE LOHR, "A Clear-Cut Finding in Blunt Language," *New York Times* on the Web, 6 November 1999, http://www.nytimes.com/ library/tech/99/11/biztech/articles/06assess. html; SAM HOWE VERHOVEK, "Gates Takes a Long View and Promises to Fight On," *New York Times* on the Web, 6 November 1999, http://www.nytimes.com/library/tech/99/11/ biztech/articles/06react.html.

4. WILLIAM C. FREDERICK, KEITH DAVIS, AND JAMES E. POST, *Business and Society,* 6th ed. (New York: McGraw-Hill, 1990), 158.

5. "Hundt Calls Internet Key to Competition," *Newsbytes News Network,* 28 August 1997, *Electric Library,* Online [accessed 11 December 1997]; SUSAN BENKELMAN, "Free Cyberspeech Ruling Strikes Indecency Law," *Newsday,* 26 June 1997, A5, *Electric Library* [accessed 12 December 1997]; "FCC Paper Seeks to Limit Internet Regulation," *Newsbytes News Network,* 31 March 1997, *Electric Library,* Online [accessed 11 December 1997].

6. "The United States: The Electric Acid Test," *The Economist,* 25 September 1999, 29–30.

7. WENDY M. BEECH, "Deregulation: Bonanza or Bust?" *Black Enterprise,* May 1998, 93–99.

8. AGIS SALPUKAS, "California's Effort to Promote Plan for Electricity Is Off to a Slow Start," *New York Times,* 26 February 1998, C1, C6; JAMES WORSHAM, "States Plug In to Deregulation," *Nation's Business,* April 1998, 66.

9. ROBERT J. SAMUELSON, "The Joy of Deregulation," *Newsweek,* 3 February 1997, 39.

10. BILL SHAW AND ART WOLFE, *The Structure of the Legal Environment: Law, Ethics, and Business,* 2d ed. (Boston: PWS-Kent, 1991), 635.

11. SHAW AND WOLFE, *The Structure of the Legal Environment;* 146.

12. CAROLINE E. MAYER, "FTC Challenges Anitbacterial Claims," *Washington Post,* 17 September 1999, A9.

13. "Stone Settles FTC Price Fix Charger," *Pulp & Paper,* April 1998, 19.

14. ELIZABETH MACDONALD, "SEC Alleges KPMG Violated Rules by Auditing Client of Former Affiliate," Wall Street Journal Interactive Edition [accessed 5 December 1997], http://www.wsj.com.

15. GEORGE A. STEINER AND JOHN F. STEINER, *Business, Government, and Society* (New York: McGraw-Hill, 1991), 149.

16. MIKE FRANCE, "Order in the Business Court," *Business Week,* 9 December 1996, 138–140.

17. THOMAS W. DUNFEE, FRANK F. GIBSON, JOHN D. BLACKBURN, DOUGLAS WHITMAN, F. WILLIAM MCCARTY, AND BARTLEY A. BRENNAN, *Modern Business Law* (New York: Random House, 1989), 164.

18. JACQUELINE BUENO, "Home Depot to Fight Sex-Bias Charges," *Wall Street Journal,* 19 September 1997, B5; EDWARD FELSENTHAL, "Punitive Awards Are Called Modest, Rare," *Wall Street Journal,* 17 June 1996, B2.

19. BARTLEY A. BRENNAN AND NANCY K. KUBASEK, *The Legal Environment of Business* (New York: McGraw-Hill, 1990), 183.

20. "For the Record, What's the Beef, Oprah," *London Free Press,* 14 February 1998, F5; DEBORAH FRAZIER, "Cattlemen Have Beef with Oprah—Stock Raisers Angry That TV Host Maligned Food They're Proud Of," *Denver Rocky Mountain News,* 21 January 1998, 30A; "United States: No Beef with Oprah," *The Economist,* 7 March 1998, 29; SCOTT BALDAUF, "In Oprah Trial, Food Libel Charges Prove Hard to Swallow," *Christian Science Monitor,* 27 February 1998, 3.

21. BRENNAN AND KUBASEK, *The Legal Environment of Business,* 184.

22. "Reasonable Product-Liability Reform," *Nation's Business,* 1 September 1997, 88.

23. DAVID J. MORROW, "Maker of Diet Pill Agrees to Pay $3.75 Billion to Settle Liability Case," *New York Times* Web site, [accessed 8 October 1999], http://www.nytimes.com.

24. DUNFEE et al., *Modern Business Law,* 569.

25. "Reasonable Product-Liability Reform"; STEPHEN BLAKELY, "Getting a Handle on Liability Coverage," *Nation's Business,* 1 September 1997, 87; JOHN M. BRODER, "Clinton Vetoes Bill to Limit Product-Liability Lawsuits," *Los Angeles Times,* 3 May 1996, A1.

26. DUNFEE et al., *Modern Business Law,* 236.

27. ETHAN A. BLUMEN, "Legal Land Mines," *Business 96,* June/July 1996, 53.

28. DUNFEE et al., *Modern Business Law,* 284–297; Brennan and Kubasek, *The Legal Environment of Business,* 125–127; DOUGLAS WHITMAN AND JOHN WILLIAM GERGACZ,

The Legal Environment of Business, 2d ed. (New York: Random House, 1988), 196–197; *The Lawyer's Almanac* (Englewood Cliffs, N.J.: Prentice Hall Law & Business, 1991), 888.

29. BRENNAN AND KUBASEK, *The Legal Environment of Business,* 128.

30. JAMES BATES, "Disney Settles Up with Its Former Studio Boss," *Los Angeles Times,* 8 July 1999, 1; BRUCE ORWALL, "Katzenberg Wins Round in Lawsuit with Walt Disney," *Wall Street Journal,* 20 May 1999, B16.

31. ROY FURCHGOTT, "Opposition Builds to Mandatory Arbitration at Work," *New York Times,* 20 July 1997, F11; BARRY MEIER, "In Fine Print, Customers Lose Ability to Sue," *New York Times,* 10 March 1997, A1, C7.

32. RICHARD M. STEUER, *A Guide to Marketing Law: What Every Seller Should Know* (New York: Harcourt Brace Jovanovich, 1986), 151–152.

33. DUNFEE et al., *Modern Business Law,* 745, 749.

34. BRENNAN AND KUBASEK, *The Legal Environment of Business,* 160; Whitman and Gergacz, *The Legal Environment of Business,* 260.

35. DAVID P. HAMILTON, "Apple Sues Future Power and Daewood, Alleging They Copied Design of iMac," *Wall Street Journal,* 2 July 1999, B4; "Injunction Is Issued Against Makers of iMac Look Alikes," *Wall Street Journal,* 9 November 1999, B25.

36. MIKE SNIDER, "Law Targets Copyright Theft Online," *USA Today,* 18 December 1998, A1.

37. TARIQ K. MUHAMMAD, "Real Law in a Virtual World," *Black Enterprise,* December 1996, 44.

38. JERRY M. ROSENBERG, *Dictionary of Business and Management* (New York: Wiley, 1983), 340.

39. RONALD A. ANDERSON, IVAN FOX, AND DAVID P. TWOMEY, *Business Law* (Cincinnati: South-Western Publishing, 1987), 635.

40. BRENNAN AND KUBASEK, *The Legal Environment of Business,* 516–517.

41. DALE KASLER, "Carson's Department Store Chain Manager Stronger After Bankruptcy," *Gannett News Service,* 21 November 1994.

42. CONSTANCE L. HAYS, "Be True to Your Cola, Rah! Rah!" *New York Times,* 10 March 1998, C1, C4.

COMPONENT CHAPTER B

1. "Hurricanes and the Insurance Crisis," *American Business Review,* 21 September 1997, 2; Matt Walsh, "Deeper Pockets," *Forbes,* 26 September 1994, 42–44.

2. MARK S. DORFMAN, *Introduction to Risk Management and Insurance,* 6th ed. (Upper Saddle River, N.J.: Prentice Hall, 1999), 322–323.

3. BRANDA PAIK SUNNO, "After Everything Else—Buy Insurance," *Workforce,* October 1998, 45–50.

4. JUDY FELDMAN, "What Daredevil CEO's Can Cost," *Money,* April 1999, 32.

5. LAURA M. LITVAN, "Switching to Self-Insurance," *Nation's Business,* March 1996, 16–21; JOSEPH B. TREASTER, "Protecting Against the Little Risks," *New York Times,* 31 December 1996, C1, C15.

6. JOHN S. DEMOTT, "Think Like a Risk Manager," *Nation's Business,* June 1995, 30–32.

7. DORFMAN, *Introduction to Risk Management and Insurance,* 505.

8. *Employee Benefits* (Washington, D.C.: U.S. Chamber of Commerce, 1991), 28.

9. *1991 Life Insurance Fact Book, Update* (Washington, D.C.: American Council of Life Insurance, 1991), 4.

COMPONENT CHAPTER C

1. JAY STULLER, "Overload," *Across the Board,* April 1996, 16–22.

2. LARRY LONG AND NANCY LONG, *Computers,* 5th ed. (Upper Saddle River, NJ: Prentice Hall, 1998), MIS 5.

3. KATHRYN M. BARTOL AND DAVID C. MARTIN, *Management* (New York: McGraw-Hill, 1991), 703–705.

4. RICHARD L. DAFT, *Management,* 4th ed. (Fort Worth, TX: Dryden, 1997), 688.

5. JOHN W. VERITY, "Coaxing Meaning out of Raw Data," *Business Week,* 3 February 1997, 134.

6. BARTOL AND MARTIN, *Management,* 709–710.

7. DAVID MORSE, ed., *CyberDictionary* (Santa Monica, CA: Knowledge Exchange, 1996), 19; Long and Long, *Computers,* G1.

8. LONG AND LONG, *Computers,* 21–22.

9. G. CHRISTIAN HILL, "First Voice, Now Data," *Wall Street Journal,* 20 September 1999, R4; NICOLE HARRIS, "All Together Now," *Wall Street Journal,* 20 September 1999, R10; G. CHRISTIAN HILL, "Siber-Talk," *Wall Street Journal,* 20 September 1999, R27.

10. JASON ZIEN, "Measuring the Internet," *About.com,* 13 July 1999 [accessed 17 July 1999]., http://internet.about.com/library/weekly/1999/aa071399a.htm; "FAST Aims for Largest Index," *Search Engine Watch,* 4 May 1999 [accessed 17 July 1999], http://searchenginewatch.internet.com/sereport/99/05-fast.htm.

11. ERNEST L. MAIER, ANTHONY J. FARIA, PETER KAATRUDE, AND ELIZABETH WOOD, *The Business Library and How to Use It* (Detroit, MI: Omnigraphics, 1996), 84–97; MATT LAKE, "Desperately Seeking Susan OR Suzie NOT Sushi," *New York Times,* 3 September 1998, D1, D7.

12. ANNE ZIEGER, "Enterprise Computing: IP Telephony Gets Real," *InfoWorld,* 5 January 1998, 20; LAURA KUJUBU, "Telcos Answer Wake-Up Call from Internet," *InfoWorld,* 15 December 1997, 19.

13. DAVID MORSE, ed., *CyberDictionary: Your Guide to the Wired World* (Santa Monica, CA: Knowledge Exchange, 1996), 113.

14. MORSE, *CyberDictionary,* 233.

15. CHARLENE MARMER SOLOMON, "Sharing Information Across Borders and Time Zones," *Global Workforce,* March 1998, 13–18; ERYN BROWN, "9 Ways to Win on the Web," *Fortune,* 24 May 1999, 112.

16. Material for this section was taken from COURTLAND L. BOVEÉ AND JOHN V. THILL, *Business Communication Today,* 6th ed. (Upper Saddle River, NJ: Prentice Hall, 1999), 348–352.

17. SAMUEL GREENGARD, "Extranets Linking Employees with Your Vendors," *Workforce,* November 1997, 28–34.

18. "The Extranet Habit: The Web Becomes the New Business Platform," *Fortune-Technology Buyer's Guide,* Summer 1998, 243.

19. SAMUEL GREENGARD, "Extranets Linking Employees with Your Vendors," 28–34.

20. ROBERT D. HOF, GARY MCWILLIAMS, AND GABRIELLE SAVERI, "The Click Here Economy," *Business Week,* 22 June 1998, 122–128.

21. ROBERT D. HOF, DAVID WELCH, MICHAEL ARNDT, AMY BARRETT, AND STEPHEN BAKER, "E-Mail for Business," *Business Week,* 13 March 2000, 32–34.

22. STEFFANO KORPER AND JUANITA ELLIS, *The E-Commerce Book: Building the E-Empire* (San Diego, CA: Academic Press, 2000), 80; RODES FISHBURNE, ALEX FRANKEL, MICHELLE JEFFERS, SCOTT LAJOIE, AND LEE PATTERSON, "Voices of the Revolution," *Forbes ASAP,* 21 February 2000, 80–86.

23. LAURIE WINDHAM, *Dead Ahead* (New York: Allworth Press, 1999), 80–85.

24. GARY L. NEILSON, BRUCE A. PASTERNACK, AND ALBERT J. VISCIO, "Up the E Organization," *Strategy & Business,* First Quarter 2000, 52–61; PETER FINGAR, HARSHA KUMAR, AND TARUN SHARMA, *Enterprise E-Commerce* (Tampa, FL: Meghan-Kiffer Press, 2000), 48–53; RAVI KALAKOTA AND MARCIA ROBINSON, *e-Business Roadmap for Success* (Reading, MA: Addison-Wesley: 1999), 2–3; STEWART ALSOP, "E or Be Eaten," *Fortune,* 8 November 1999, 87.

25. KALAKOTA AND ROBINSON, *e-Business Roadmap for Success,* 1–7; IBM e-Business Web site [accessed 10 March 2000], http://www.ibm.com/e-business/info; KORPER AND ELLIS, *The E-Commerce Book: Building the E-Empire,* 4–5; CHRISTINA FORD HAYLOCK AND LEN MUSCARELLA, *Net Success* (Holbrook, MA: Adams Media Corporation, 1999), 10–11.

26. KORPER AND ELLIS, *The E-Commerce Book: Building the E-Empire,* 4.

27. KORPER AND ELLIS, *The E-Commerce Book: Building the E-Empire,* 232.

28. KALAKOTA AND ROBINSON, *e-Business Roadmap for Success,* 2.

29. KALAKOTA AND ROBINSON, *e-Business Roadmap for Success,* 15.

30. KALAKOTA AND ROBINSON, *e-Business Roadmap for Success,* 22–23.

31. BILL LABERIS, "Jumping the e-gun," *Ent,* 8 September 1999, 46; JIM THOMPSON, "EBay Outage Could Strike You," *Boardwatch,* August 1999, 68.

32. WINDHAM, *Dead Ahead,* 31–32.

33. WALID MOUGAYAR, *Opening Digital Markets* (New York: McGraw Hill, 1998), 29–35.
34. FINGAR, KUMAR, AND SHARMA, *Enterprise E-Commerce,* 24, 109.
35. WINDHAM, *Dead Ahead,* 29; Hof, McWilliams, and Saveri, "The Click Here Economy," 122–128.
36. KALAKOTA AND ROBINSON, *e-BUSINESS ROADMAP FOR SUCCESS,* 19.
37. WINDHAM, *Dead Ahead,* 22–23.
38. KALAKOTA AND ROBINSON, *e-Business Roadmap for Success,* 33.
39. BILL GATES, *Business @ The Speed of Thought* (New York: Warner Books, 1999), 101–105.
40. WILLIAM S. HOPKINS AND BRITTON MANASCO, "The Coming Customer Free-For-All," *New York Times Supplement—Customer Relationships in a Wired World,* 14 February 2000, CU1–CU2.
41. WILLIAM S. HOPKINS AND BRITTON MANASCO, "The Coming Customer Free-For-All," CU6.
42. FINGAR, KUMAR, AND SHARMA, *Enterprise E-Commerce,* 30; Windham, *Dead Ahead,* 35; DANIEL AMOR, *The E-Business (R)evolution* (Upper Saddle River, NJ: Prentice Hall RTR, 2000), 13.
43. IBM e-Business Web site [accessed 10 March 2000], http://www.ibm.com/e-business/info.
44. IBM e-Business Web site [accessed 10 March 2000], http://www.ibm.com/e-business/info.
45. KORPER AND ELLIS, *"The E-Commerce Book: Building the E-Empire,"* 71–72.
46. SAMUEL GREENGARD, "How Secure Is Your Data?" *Workforce,* 52–60; NIKHIL HUTHEESING AND PHILIP E. ROSS, "Hackerphobia," *Forbes,* 23 March 1998, 150–154.
47. "Researchers Say They Cracked Internet's Global Security System," *Chicago Tribune,* 28 August 1999, Sec. 1, 9.
48. GREENGARD, "How Secure Is Your Data?" 52–60.
49. JULIE DEARDORFF, "With Voice Mail, You Never Know Who's Listening," *Chicago Tribune,* 6 July 1998, Sec. 1.

APPENDIX 1

1. RICHARD NELSON BOLLES, *The 1997 What Color Is Your Parachute?* (Berkeley, Calif.: Ten Speed Press, 1996), 129–166; Karen W. Arenson, "Placement Offices Leave Old Niches to Become Computerized Job Bazaars," *New York Times,* 17 July 1996, B12; LAWRENCE J. MAGID, "Job Hunters Cast Wide Net Online," *Los Angeles Times,* 26 February 1996, 20; RICHARD VAN DOREN, "On-Line Career Advice Speeds Search for Jobs," *Network World,* 4 March 1996, 54; ALEX MARKELS, "Job Hunting Takes Off in Cyberspace," *Wall Street Journal,* 20 September 1996, B1, B2; MICHAEL CHOROST, "Jobs on the Web," *Hispanic,* October 1995, 50–53; ZANE K. QUIBLE, "Electronic Résumés: Their Time Is Coming," *Business Communication Quarterly* 58, no. 3 (1995): 5–9; MARGARET MANNIX, "The Home-Page Help Wanteds," *U.S. News & World Report,* 30 October 1995, 88, 90; PAM DIXON AND SILVIA TIERSTEN, *Be Your Own Headhunter Online* (New York: Random House, 1995), 53–69; MICHELE HIMMELBERG, "Internet an Important Tool in Employment Search," *San Diego Union-Tribune,* 7 September 1998, D2; RICHARD N. BOLLES, "Career Strategizing, or What Color Is Your Web Parachute?" *Yahoo! Internet Life,* May 1998, 116–122; VALERIE FRAZEE, "Online Job Services Explode," *Personnel Journal,* August 1996, 21.
2. CHRISTOPER CAGGIANO, "Recruiting Secrets," *Inc.,* October 1998, 29–42; DONNA FENN, "The Right Fit," *Inc. 500,* 1997, 104.
3. CAGGIANO, "Recruiting Secrets."
4. PAM STANLEY-WEIGAND, "Organizing the Writing of Your Résumé," *Bulletin of the Association for Business Communication* 54, no. 3 (September 1991): 11–12.
5. JANICE TOVEY, "Using Visual Theory in the Creation of Résumés: A Bibliography," *The Bulletin of the Association for Business Communication* 54, no. 3 (September 1991): 97–99.
6. SAL DIVITA, "If You're Thinking Résumé, Think Creatively," *Marketing News,* 14 September 1992, 29.

7. RICHARD H. BEATTY AND NICHOLAS C. BURKHOLDER, *The Executive Career Guide for MBAs* (New York: Wiley, 1996), 133.
8. WILLIAM H. BAKER, KRISTEN DETIENNE, AND KARL L. SMART, "How Fortune 500 Companies Are Using Electronic Résumé Management Systems," *Business Communication Quarterly,* 61, no. 3 (September 1998): 8–19.
9. WILLIAM J. BANIS, "The Art of Writing Job-Search Letters," *CPC Annual, 36th Edition* 2 (1992): 42–50.
10. SYLVIA PORTER, "Your Money: How to Prepare for Job Interviews," *San Francisco Chronicle,* 3 November 1981, 54.
11. JOEL RUSSELL, "Finding Solid Ground," *Hispanic Business,* February 1992, 42–44, 46.
12. ROBERT GIFFORD, CHEUK FAN NG, AND MARGARET WILKINSON, "Nonverbal Cues in the Employment Interview: Links Between Applicant Qualities and Interviewer Judgments," *Journal of Applied Psychology* 70, no. 4 (1985): 729.
13. AMANDA BENNETT, "GE Redesigns Rungs of Career Ladder," *Wall Street Journal,* 15 March 1993, B1, B3.
14. ROBIN WHITE GOODE, "International and Foreign Language Skills Have an Edge," *Black Enterprise,* May 1995, 53.
15. NANCY M. SOMERICK, "Managing a Communication Internship Program," *Bulletin of the Association for Business Communication* 56, no. 3 (1993): 10–20.
16. CHERYL L. NOLL, "Collaborating with the Career Planning and Placement Center in the Job-Search Project," *Business Communication Quarterly* 58, no. 3 (1995): 53–55.

APPENDIX 2

1. Source for career information in charts: Bureau of Labor Statistics, *1998–99 Occupational Outlook Handbook* [accessed 10 August 1999], http://www.bls.gov/ocohome.htm; Webmaster career information from Excite Careers, Internet Industry Focus [accessed 10 August 1999], http://careers.excite.com/cgi-cls/display.exe?xcxca+Career+WetFeet+Industry+HiTech_InternetWebmaster.

■ Illustration and Text Credits

CHAPTER 1

5 Exhibit 1.1, Christopher Caggiano, "Will the Real Bootstrappers Please Stand Up?" *Inc.,* August 1995, 34; Mike Hofman, "Capitalism—A Bootstrappers' Hall of Fame," *Inc.,* August 1997, 54–57.
8 Exhibit 1.2, Adapted from Chris Woodyard, "Firms Stretch Travel Dollars," *USA Today,* 16 March 1999, Sec. B, 1–2.
11 (Enterprise Rent-A-Car Tries Harder, and It Pays Off): Adapted from Brian O'Reilly, "The Rent-a-Car Jocks Who Made

Enterprise #1," *Fortune,* 28 October 1996, 125–128; Del Jones, "Enterprise Rides on 'Spare Car' Niche," *USA Today,* 24 November 1997, 13B; Fred Faust, "Enterprise Is Independent at the Top," *St. Louis Post-Dispatch,* 25 January 1998 [accessed 19 April, 1999], http://www.pickenterprise.com; Enterprise press release [accessed 19 April 1999], http://www.pickenterprise.com.
15 Exhibit 1.5, Roger LeRoy Miller, Reprinted by permission of Glencoe/McGraw-Hill. *Economics Today and Tomorrow,* 1999.

18 Exhibit 1.6, U.S. Department of Commerce, Bureau of Economic Analysis, [accessed 24 September 1999], http://beadata.bea.doc.gov/bea/dn2/gpoc.htm.
20 (Here Comes the Electronic Economy): Adapted from Tim McCollum, "End Your Internet Anxieties Now," *Nation's Business,* April 1999, 19–26; Robert D. Hof, Gary McWilliams, and Gabrielle Saveri, "The Click Here Economy," *Business Week,* 22 June 1998, 122–128; Robert D. Hof, "The Net is Open For Business—Big Time," *Business Week,* 31 August 1998, 108–109; Stewart Alsop, "E or

Be Eaten," *Fortune,* 8 November 1999, 87; Charles V. Callahan and Bruce A. Pasternack, "Corporate Strategy in the Digital Age," *Strategy & Business,* Second Quarter 1999, http://www.strategy-business.com/research/99202/page1.html, [accessed online 9 February 2000].

CHAPTER 2

29 Exhibit 2.1, Manuel G. Velasquez, *Business Ethics: Concepts and Cases* (Upper Saddle River, N.J.: Prentice Hall, 1998), 87; Joseph L. Badaracco Jr. "Business Ethics: Four Spheres of Executive Responsibility," *California Management Review,* Spring 1992, 64–79; Kenneth Blanchard and Norman Vincent Peale, *The Power of Ethical Management* (Reprint, 1989; New York: Fawcett Crest, 1991), 7–17; John R. Boatright, *Ethics and the Conduct of Business* (Upper Saddle River, N.J.: Prentice Hall, 1996), 35–39, 59–64, 79–86.
30 Exhibit 2.2, © 1999 IEEE. Reprinted, with permission.
31 (Actions Speak Louder Than Codes): Adapted from Dr. Craig Dreilinger, "Get Real (and Ethics Will Follow)," *Workforce,* August 1998, 101–102; Louisa Wah, "Workplace Conscience Needs a Boost," *American Management Association International,* July–August 1998, 6; "Ethics Are Questionable in the Workplace," *HRFocus,* June 1998, 7.
36 (Eco-invasion: A Global Threat to the Environment): Adapted from Ellen Licking, "They're Here, and They're Taking Over," *Business Week,* 24 May 1999, 69–70; Lee Dye, "Beetlemania Attacks Trees," ABCNEWS, 1999 [accessed 15 July 1999] http://abcnews.go.com/sections/science/DyeHard/dye990519.html; David Phinney, "The Global Species Invasion," ABCNEWS, 1998 [accessed 15 July 1999] http://abcnews.go.com/sections/science/DailyNews/bioinvaders100998.html; Laura Gatland, "Polka-Dot Pest Hits Chicago," *Christian Science Monitor,* 28 August 1998 [accessed 15 July 1999], http://abcnews.go.com/sections/science/DailyNews/asianbeetle980828.html.
44 Exhibit 2.3, Adapted from "Workplace Injuries and Illnesses in 1997," *Bureau of Labor Statistics,* Table 7 [accessed 30 September 1999], http://www.osha.gov/oshstats/bls/osnr0007.txt.

CHAPTER 3

57 Exhibit 3.1, Brian Zajac, "Spanning the World," Forbes, 26 July 1999, 202–206.
59 Exhibit 3.2, Adapted from Fedstats, Exhibit 6: Exports and Imports of Goods by Principal End-Use Category, January–December 1997 [accessed 8 May 1999], http://beadata.bea.doc.gov/bea/newsrel/trad0998.htm; "U.S. International Trade in Goods and Services—Table 1: Private Services Transactions by Type, 1986–96," Bureau of Economic Analysis [accessed 3 October 1999], http://www.bea.dog.gov/bea/ai/1097/srv/table1.htm.

61 Exhibit 3.3, Adapted in part from Clemens P. Work and Robert F. Black, "Uncle Sam As Unfair Trader," *U.S. News & World Report,* 12 June 1989, 42–44; Todd G. Buchholz, "Free Trade Keeps Prices Down," *Consumers' Research Magazine,* 1995, excerpted from Todd G. Buchholz, *From Here to Economy: A Shortcut to Economic Literacy* (New York: Dutton Signet, 1995).
66 (Focus on E-Business: Roadblocks on the European Superhighway) Martin Vander Weyer, "Globalism vs. Nationalism vs. E-Business, the World Debates," *Strategy & Business,* First Quarter 2000, 63–72; Charles Thurston, "E-Commerce Waves Wash Onto All Shores," *Global Finance,* January 2000, 121–123; Peter McGrath, "You are a Data Subject," *Newsweek Supplement,* December 1999–February 2000, 80; Matthew Friedman, "E-Commerce Players Agree to Disagree," *Computing Canada,* 13 August 1999, 1, 6.
70 (The Rise and Fall of a Mighty Empore—GUM Department Store) Adapted from Nicholas D. Kristof and Sheryl WuDunn, "Of World Markets, None an Island," New York Times, 17 February 1998, A1, A8; Marcus Warren, "International: A Leap in the Price of Luxury," Daily Telegraph, 19 August 1998; Greg Myre, "Yeltsin Touts Russian Products—Kremlin Has to Admit That Many Foreign Goods Are Better, More Reliable," Denver Rocky Mountain News, 20 April 1997, 56A.

CHAPTER 4

83 (Focus on E-Business: Create a Winning Web Site): Adapted from Brian Hurley and Peter Birkwood, *A Small Business Guide to Doing Big Business on the Internet* (Bellingham, Wash.: International Self-Counsel Press),1996, 124–134; "Design a Better Web Site," *Journal of Accountancy,* August 1998, 18; Anita Dennis, "A Home on the Web," *Journal of Accountancy,* August 1998, 29–31.
84 Exhibit 4.2, Republished with permission of Dow Jones and Company, Inc., adapted from Carrie Dolan, "Entperneurs Often Fail as Managers," *Wall Street Journal,* 15 May 1989, B1.; permission conveyed through Copyright Clearance Center, Inc.
86 Exhibit 4, Adapted from Carol Lawson, "Life's Miraculous Transmissions," *New York Times,* 6 June 1996, B3; Nancy Rotenier, "La Tempesta," *Forbes,* 18 December 1995, 134–135; Anne Murphy, "Entrepreneur of the Year," *Inc.,* December 1995, 38–51; Christina F. Watts and Loyde Gite, "Emerging Entrepreneurs," *Black Enterprise,* November 1995, 100–110; Marc Ballon, "Pretzel Queen," *Forbes,* 13 March 1995, 112–113; Robert La Franco, "Beach Bum Makes Good," *Forbes,* 19 June 1995, 80–82.
89 (Are You Crazy?): Adapted from "Secrets of a Start-Up," *Success,* September 1998, 61; Martha Vissner, "Phenomenon," *Success,* September 1998, 62; Marc Ballon, "Concierge Makes Hay in Corporate Fields," *Inc.,*

September 1998, 23–25; Michelle Conlin, "It's in the Bag," *Forbes,* 28 December 1998, 86, 90.
92 Exhibit 4.3, *Business Know How* [accessed 19 September 1997], http://www.businessknowhow.com.
95 Exhibit 4.4, Adapted from Alfred Edmond Jr., "The B.E. Franchise Start-Up Guide," *Black Enterprise,* September 1990, 75. Reprinted by permission of Earl G. Graves Publishing Co.

CHAPTER 5

107 Exhibit 5.1, Adapted with the permission of Simon & Schuster, Inc. from the Macmillian College text, *The Legal Environment of Business,* 2d ed., by Charles R. McGuire. Copyright © 1986, 1989 by Merrill Publishing, an imprint of Macmillan College Publishing Company, Inc., 216.
112 (Focus on E-Business: Is the End of the Beginning Near?): Adapted from Kathleen Melymuka, "Internet Intuition," *Computerworld,* 10 January 2000, 48–50; John Steele Gordon, "The Golden Spike," *Forbes ASAP,* 21 February 2000, 118–122; Eric W. Pfeiffer, "Where Are We in the Revolution?" *Forbes ASAP,* 21 February 2000, 68–70; Christopher Byron, "Balance Due," *Forbes ASAP,* 21 February 2000, 102–108; Stewart Alsop, "E or Be Eaten," *Fortune,* 8 November 1999, 87.
116 (How Cisco Bought Its Way to the Top): Adapted from Henry Goldblatt, "Cisco's Secrets," *Fortune,* 8 November 1999, 177–181; Kimberly Caisse, "Cisco's Buying Binge Goes On," *Computer Reseller News,* 4 January 1999, 123, 128; Stacy Collett, "A Guide to Cisco's Acquisition and Investment Strategy," *Computerworld,* 4 October 1999, 20; Glenn Drexhage, "How Cisco Bought Its Way to the Top," *Corporate Finance,* May 1999, 26–30; Scott Thurm, "Under Cisco's System, Mergers Usually Work; That Defies the Odds," *Wall Street Journal,* 1 March 2000, A1, A12.

CHAPTER 6

132 Exhibit 6.1, Adapted from Dell Computer home page, (accesssed 15 June 1999), http://www.dell.com/corporate/vision/mission.htm. Reprinted by permission.
135 Exhibit 6.3, Stuart Crainer, "The 75 Greatest Management Decisions Ever Made," *Management Review,* November 1998, 17–23.
136 (Focus on E-Business: Seven Habits of Highly Effective E-Managers): Adapted from George Anders, "The Auctioneer," *Wall Street Journal,* 22 November 1999, R68–R70; George Anders, "The View From the Top," *Wall Street Journal,* 12 July 1999, R52; James M. Citrin and Thomas J. Neff, "Digital Leadership," *Strategy & Business,* First Quarter 2000, 42–50; Gary L. Neilson, Bruce A. Pasternack, and Albert J. Viscio, "Up the E-Organization," *Strategy and Business,* First Quarter 2000, 52–61; Beverly Goldberg and John G. Sifonis, "Focusing Your E-Commerce Vision," *American Management Association International,* September 1998, 48–51;

Christian Ford Haylock and Len Muscarella, *Net Success,* (Holbrook, Massachusetts: Adams Media Corporation, 1999), 12; Meryl Davids, "The IPO CEO's Reality," *Chief Executive,* January 2000, 22–26.

142 Exhibit 6.5, Reprinted by permission of *Harvard Business Review.* Exhibit from "How to Choose a Leadership Pattern" by Robert Tannenbaum and Warren H. Schmidt in Harvard Business Review, May-June 1973, 164. © 1973 by the President and Fellows of Harvard College; all rights reserved.

144 (How Michael Dell Works his Magic): Adapted from Michael V. Verespej, "Michael Dell's Magic," *Industry Week,* 16 November 1998, 57–64; Richard Murphy, "Michael Dell," *Success,* January 1999, 50–53.

145 Exhibit 6.6, Adapted with permission of *Harvard Business Review,* an exhibit from "How to Choose a Leadership Pattern" by Robert Tannenbaum and Warren H. Schmidt, May–June 1973. Copyright © 1973 by the President and Fellows of Harvard College. All Rights Reserved.

CHAPTER 7

164 (Office Ethics: Teams Make It Hard to Tattle): Adapted from Stephanie Armour, "Office Ethics: Teams Make It Hard to Tattle," *USA Today,* 17 February 1998.

168 (Mervyn's Calls SWAT Team to the Rescue): Adapted from Peter Carvonara, "Mervyn's Calls in the SWAT Team," *Fast Company,* April–May 1998, 54–56; Richard Halverson, "Ulrich Delivers Ultimatum to Mervyn's: Improve Sales Performance, or Else," *Discount Store News,* 26 October 1998, 3, 126.

167 Exhibit 7.6, Exhibit from *Management, Fourth Edition,* by Richard L. Daft copyright © 1977 by Harcourt Inc., reproduced by permission of the publisher.

CHAPTER 8

180 Exhibit 8.1, From Mark M. Davis, Nicholas J. Aquilano, and Richard B. Chase, *Fundamentals of Operations Management, 2e,* 1995. Reprinted by permission of The McGraw-Hill Companies.

185 Exhibit 8.2, Adapted from Courtland L. Bovée, et al., *Management* (New York; McGraw-Hill, 1993), 648: Roberta S. Russell and Bernard W. Taylor III, *Operations Management: Focusing on Quality and Competitiveness,* 2d ed. (Upper Saddle River, N.J.: Prentice Hall, 1998), 294.

186 Exhibit 8.4, Adapted from Gerald H. Graham, *The World of Business* (Reading, Mass.: Addison-Wesley, 1985), 1999.

190 (Focus on E-Business: This Cyberbazaar is Strictly Business-to-Business) Adapted from Robert L. Simison, Fara Warner, and Gregory L. White, "GM, Ford, DaimlerChrysler to Create a Single Firm to Supply Auto Parts," *Wall Street Journal Interactive,* 28 February 2000, http://interactive.wsj.com/articles/ SB951493383958527087.htm; Keith Bradsher, "3 Automakers Plan Private Online Purchasing System," *New York Times,* 26 February 2000, B1, B4: Kathleen Kerwin, Marcia Stepanek, and David Welch, "At Ford, E-Commerce is Job 1," *Business Week,* 28 February 2000, 74–78; "3 Automakers to Create Cheaper Supply Network," *Washington Times,* 26 February 2000, C9.

195 (Chek Lap Kok's Turbulent Takeoff): Adapted from Bruce Dorminey, "Overconfidence, Poor Planning Led to Hong Kong Airport Woes," *Aviation Week and Space Technology,* 15 February 1999, 53; Sherrie E. Zhan, "No Kudos for Chek Lap Kok Airport," *World Trade,* October 1998, 32; Martyn Warwick, "Not Tried, Not Tested," *Communications International,* August 1998, 24; "Hong Kong Opens New Airport," *Material Handling Engineering,* August 1998, 12; "Trouble-Shooting at Chek Lap Kok," *Transportation and Distribution,* August 1998, 12; Bruce Dorminey and Carole A. Shifrin, "Hong Kong Investigates What Went Wrong," *Aviation Week and Space Technology,* 20 July 1998, 45; Megan Scott, "Vendors Take Blame for System Woes," *Computerworld,* 20 July 1998, 29–32; Kristin S. Krause, "Order out of Chaos," *Traffic World,* 20 July 1998, 23–24; Murray Hiebert, "Opening-Day Blues," *Far-Eastern Economic Review,* 16 July 1998, 62–63; Mark Landler, "Problems Continue to Mount at New Hong Kong Airport," *New York Times,* 9 July 1998, C6.

CHAPTER 9

208 Exhibit 9.2, From *Management, Fourth Edition,* by Richard L. Daft copyright © 1997 by Harcourt Inc., reproduced by permission of the publisher.

208 Exhibit 9.3, Douglas McGregor, *The Human Side of Enterprise* (New York: McGraw-Hill, 1960).

210 (Focus on E-Business: Living with the E-Cultures of Hype and Craft): Adapted from Art Kleiner, "Corporate Culture in Internet Time," *Strategy & Business,* First Quarter 2000, 18–24; Peter Buxbaum, "The Talent War—Where's Dilbert?" *Chief Executive,* January 2000, 28–29; Robert J. Spitzer, "The Spirit of Teams," *Executive Excellence,* May 1999, 13; Bob Nelson, "Top 10 Ironies of Employee Motivation Programs," *Potentials,* May 1999, 901.

211 Exhibit 9.4, Jennifer Laabs, "The New Loyalty: Grasp It. Earn It. Keep It." *Workforce,* November 1998, 35–39.

216 Exhibit 9.5, Exhibit from "Dual-Career Couples Speak Out," *HR Focus,* August 1998. Reprinted by permission of IOMA.

218 (Is Telecommuting Right for You?): Adapted from Bronwyn Fryer, "WorkShop," *Working Woman,* April 1997, 59–60; Lisa Chadderdon, "Merrill Lynch Works—At Home," *Fast Company,* April–May 1998, 70–72; Peg Verone, "House Rules," *Success,* July 1998, 22–23.

CHAPTER 10

232 (Are Temp Workers Becoming a Full-Time Headache?): Adapted from Aaron Bernstein, "When Is a Temp, Not a Temp?" *Business Week,* 7 December, 1998, 90–92; Daniel Eisenberg, "Rise of the Permatemp," *Time,* 12 July 1999, 48; Aaron Bernstein, "Now, Temp Workers Are a Full-Time Headache," *Business Week,* 31 May 1999, 46; Barb Cole-Gomolski, "Reliance on Temps Creates New Problems," *Computerworld,* 31 August 1998, 1, 85; "Temp Work Force Rising Up for Benefits," *Salt Lake Tribune,* 30 June 1999, B5; John Cook, "Temp Ruling Far Reaching," *Seattle Post,* 14 May 1999, B1; Dan Richman, "Despite Changes, Microsoft's Temp Force Precariously Discontent," *Seattle Post,* 12 June 1999, A1; Jennifer Laabs, "Microsoft Battles Permatemp Issue," *Workforce,* March 1999, 16; Aaron Bernstein, "TempWars: Why Microsoft May Cry Uncle," *Business Week,* 15 November 1999, 48.

242 (It's Okay to Fall Asleep on the Job): Adapted from Anna Mulrine, "Take a Nap; It's on the House," *U.S.News & World Report,* 20 July 1998, 61; Janet Gemignani, "The Latest Productivity Booster," *Business and Health,* September 1997, 12; "Take an Afternoon Nap on Your Way to the Top," *Management Today,* March 1998, 12–13; Shane McLaughlin, "A Real Dream Job," *Inc.,* January 1999, 80; Mark Sabourin, "Sleeping on the Job," *OH & S Canada,* June/July 1998, 32–37.

CHAPTER 11

259 Exhibit 11.2, Joan O. Fredericks and James M. Salter, "Beyond Customer Satisfaction," *Management Review,* May 1995, 29.

260 Exhibit 11.3, Courtland L. Bovée, Michael J. Houston, and John V. Thill, *Marketing,* 2d ed. (New York: McGraw-Hill, 1994), 109.

261 (Your Right to Privacy Versus the Marketing Databases): Adapted from Amy Harmon, "F.T.C. to Propose Laws to Protect Children on Line," *New York Times,* 4 June 1998, C1, C6; Andrew L. Shapiro, "Privacy for Sale," *The Nation,* 23 June 1997, 11–16; Bruce Horovitz, "Marketers Tap Data We Once Called Our Own," *USA Today,* 19 December 1995, 1A–2A; Stephen Baker, "Europe's Privacy Cops," *Business Week,* 2 November 1998, 49, 51.

264 Exhibit 11.5, Adapted from Courtland L. Bovée, Michael J. Houston, and John V. Thill, *Marketing,* 2d ed. (New York: McGraw-Hill, 1994), 30.

268 (Move Over, Boomers and Gen Xers: Here Comes Generation Y): Adapted from Ellen Neuborne, "Generation Y," *Business Week,* 15 February 1999, 80–88; Mary Purpura and Paolo Pontoniere, "A Look at the New N-Gen of the Economy," *Los Angeles Times,* 20 April 1988, D4; Molly O'Neill,

"Feeding the Next Generation," *New York Times,* 14 March 1998, B1, B14.

259 (Exhibit 11.2, From "Beyond Customer Satisfaction" by Joan O. Fredericks and James M. Salter, *Management Review,* May 1995, p. 29. Reprinted by permission of Eliot Bergman.

260 Exhibit 11.3, From Courtland Bovee, Michael Houston, and John V. Thill, *Marketing, 2nd ed.* (New York: McGraw-Hill, 1994), p. 109. Reprinted by permission.

264 Exhibit 11.5, From Courtland Bovee, Michael Houston, and John V. Thill, *Marketing, 2nd ed.* (New York: McGraw-Hill, 1994), p. 30. Reprinted by permission.

CHAPTER 12

278 Exhibit 12.1, Courtland Bovee, Michael Houston, and John V. Thill, *Marketing, 2nd ed.* (New York: McGraw-Hill, 1994), p. 240. Reprinted by permission.

280 Exhibit 12.2, Adapted from Charles D. Schewe, *Marketing Principles and Strategies* (New York: McGraw-Hill, 1987). Reprinted by permission of the author.

282 Exhibit 12.3, Adapted from Charles D. Schewe, *Marketing Principles and Strategies* (New York: McGraw-Hill, 1987), 294. Reprinted by permission of the publisher.

285 (It's the Brand, Stupid): Adapted from "The *Business Week* Best-Sellers of 1998," *Business Week,* 8 February 1999, 18; Silvia Sansoni, "It's the Stupid *Name,* Stupid!" *Forbes,* 10 August 1998, 60–61.

290 (Focus on E-Business: The Electronic Price Isn't Always Right): Adapted from Peter Elkind, "The Hype is Big, Really Big, at Priceline," *Fortune,* 6 September 1999, 193–202; Regina Fazio Maruca, "Redesigning Business," *Harvard Business Review,* November–December 1999, 19–21; "Finance and Economics: The Heyday of the Auction," *Economist,* 24 July 1999, 67–68; Adam Cohen, "The Attic of E," *Time,* 27 December 1999, 74–80; Michael Schrage, "To Hal Varian the Price is Always Right," *Strategy & Business,* First Quarter 2000, 82–93.

CHAPTER 13

306 Exhibit 13.1, Adapted from Philip Kotler, *Marketing Management,* 10th ed. (Upper Saddle River, N.J.: Prentice Hall, 2000), 491.

317 (Focus on E-Business: E-Tailing: It Takes More Than a Web Site): Adapted from Katrina Brooker, "First: The Nightmare Before Christmas," *Fortune,* 24 January 2000, 24–25; Alorie Gilbert, "Rule No. 1: Don't Annoy Your Customers," *InformationWeek,* "13 December 1999, 134–136; Jodi Mardesich, "The Web is No Shopper's Paradise," *Fortune,* 8 November 1999, 188–198.

319 (Something Old, Something New): Adapted from Mary Beth Grover, "Lost in Cyberspace," *Forbes,* 8 March 1999, 124–128; George Anders, "Discomfort Zone: Some Big Companies Long to Embrace Web But Settle for Flirtation," *Wall Street Journal,* 4

November 1998, A1, A13; Shikhar Ghosh, "Making Business Sense of the Internet," *Harvard Business Review,* March–April 1998, 126–135.

322 Exhibit 13.4, Adapted from Charles D. Schewe, *Marketing Principles and Strategies* (New York: McGraw-Hill, 1987). Reprinted by permission of the author.

CHAPTER 14

335 (Auditors and Clients: Too Close for Comfort?): Adapted from Melody Petersen, "Consulting by Auditors Stirs Concern," *New York Times,* 13 July 1998, B1, B4; Nanette Byrnes, "Auditors and Clients: Too Close for Comfort," *Business Week,* 22 February 1999, 92; Reed Abelson, "As Accounting Changes, Conflicts Are First Items to Audit," *New York Times,* 25 November 1997, C1, C10; Elizabeth MacDonald, "SEC Steps Up Scrutiny of Accountants," *Wall Street Journal,* 8 January 1999, A3; Elizabeth MacDonald, "Small Accounting Firms Losing Independence," *Wall Street Journal,* 10 September 1998, B8; Richard Melcher, "Where Are the Accountants?" *Business Week,* 5 October 1998, 144–146.

340 Exhibit 14.3, 1998 Annual Report for CDW Computer Centers, Inc. Reprinted by permission of CDW Computer Centers, Inc.

342 Exhibit 14.4, 1998 Annual Report for CDW Computer Centers, Inc. Reprinted by permission of CDW Computer Centers, Inc.

343 Exhibit 14.5, 1998 Annual Report for CDW Computer Centers, Inc. Reprinted by permission of CDW Computer Centers, Inc.

346 Exhibit 14.6, 1998 Annual Report for CDW Computer Centers, Inc. Reprinted by permission of CDW Computer Centers, Inc.

348 (How to Read an Annual Report): Adapted from Manual Schiffres, "All the Good News That Fits," *U.S. News and World Report,* 14 April 1998, 50–51.

CHAPTER 15

361 (No Comfort for Borrowers in Tiers): Adapted from Christine Dugas, "Tiered Lending Adjusts Rates to Each Customer," *USA Today,* 16 November 1995, 1A; Andrew Brimmer, "The Cost of Bank Bias," *Black Enterprise,* July 1992, 43; Adam Zagorin, "Sub-Prime Time," *Time,* 4 November 1996, 67–68; Ilyce Glink, "Where to Look for Money Now," *Working Woman,* October 1994, 56–60.

366 Exhibit 15.2, "Money Stock and Debt Measures," Federal Reserve Release, 29 July 1999 [accessed 3 August 1999], http://www.bog.frb.fed.us/releases/H6/.

375 (Put Your Money Where the Mouse Is!—Investment Information on the Net): Adapted from Jim Frederick, "Internet Tools: The Web Workshop," *Money,* April 1999, 84; Gretchen Morgenson, "Don't Be a Victim," *Forbes,* 2 June 1997, 42–43; Randy Myers, "The Wired World of Investment Information," *Nation's Business,* March 1997,

58–60; Joseph Garber, "Click Before You Leap," *Forbes,* 24 February 1997, 108–100.

377 Exhibit 15.6, "A Big Test for Dow Jones Industrial's Long Bull Run," *Wall Street Journal,* 28 October 1997, C17; Standard & Poor's, Telescan, Inc. 1995; "A Centennial View: Dow Jones Industrial Average," *Wall Street Journal,* centennial edition, B15, and reprinted by permission of *The Wall Street Journal,* © 1991 Dow Jones & Company, Inc. All rights reserved worldwide.

COMPONENT CHAPTER A

398 Exhibit A.5, Adapted from Richard A. Brealely and Stewart C. Myers, *Principles of Corporate Finance,* 4th ed. (New York: McGraw-Hill, 1991), 761–765.

COMPONENT CHAPTER B

410 Exhibit B.5, Adapted from *Introduction to Risk Management and Insurance, 6th Ed.,* by Mark S. Dorfman, © 1996. Adapted by permission of Prentice-Hall, Inc., Upper Saddle River, NJ.

COMPONENT CHAPTER C

415 Exhibit C.1 Source: Don Clark, "Managing the Mountain," *Wall Street Journal,* 21 June 1999, R4.

420 Exhibit C.4 Source: Adapted from *Search Engines Fact and Fun* [accessed 11 March 1998], http://searchenginewatch.internet.com/facts/major.html; "Getting Started—What You Need to Know to Begin Using the Internet," *Fortune Technology Buyer's Guide,* Winter 1998, 232–240; Matt Lake, "Desperately Seeking Susan OR Suzie NOT Sushi," *New York Times,* 3 September 1998, D1, D7; "Notable Websites," *Fortune Technology Buyer's Guide,* Winter 1999; Stephen H. Wildstrom, "Search Engines with Smarts," *Business Week,* 8 February 1999, 22.

425 Exhibit C.6 Source: Adapted from Craig Fellenstein and Ron Wood, *Exploring E-Commerce, Global E-Business, and E-Societies* (Upper Saddle River, NJ: Prentice Hall, 1999), 28.

427 Exhibit C.8 Source: Adapted from Peter Fingar, Harsha Kumar, and Tarun Sharma, *Enterprise E-Commerce* (Tampa, FL: Meghan-Kiffer Press, 2000), 228–229; Laurie Windham, *Dead Ahead* (New York: Allworth Press, 1999), 57; Craig Fellenstein and Ron Wood, *Exploring E-Commerce, Global E-Business,* and *E-Societies* (Upper Saddle River, NJ: Prentice Hall, 1999), 34.

APPENDIX 2

449 Exhibit A2.1, Adapted from Bureau of Labor Statistics, unpublished data from the Current Population Survey; Bureau of the Census, Current Population Survey, *PPL-99, Educational Attainment in the United States: March 1998,* Table 9 (unpublished data), and *Current Population Reports,* P20-513, October 1998, "Educational Attainment in the United States: March 1998 (Update)" (earnings).

■ Photo Credits

CHAPTER 1
1 Super Stock, Inc.
2 (Waiting for credit)
4 Dakota Studios/Liaison Agency
6 Joe Traver/Liaison Agency
10 Davis Barber/Photo Edit

CHAPTER 2
26 FPG International LLC
27 Jean-Marc Giboux/Liaison Agency, Inc.
33 Jason Funari/Corbis Sygma Photo News
34 Marilynn K. Yee/New York Times Pictures
39 Reuters/Ira Schwartz/Archive Photos
40 Liaison Agency, Inc.

CHAPTER 3
50 Stewart Cohen/Tony Stone Images
51 Kraipit Phahvut/SIPA Press
55 Greg Girard/Contact Press Images
57 Greg Girard/Contact Press Images
68 Archive Photos
71 Ted Soqui/New York Times Pictures

CHAPTER 4
78 Norman Lono/New York Times Pictures
79 Larry Dunn/Larry Dunn Photography
85 Philip Saltonstall Photographer
90 T. Michael Keza Photography
95 Matrix International, Inc.
97 Richard Howard Photography

CHAPTER 5
104 The Stock Market
105 Dan Lamont Photography
108 Frank Siteman/Monkmeyer aPress
110 Giboux/Liaison Agency, Inc.
117 Frances Roberts/Richard B. Levine/
Frances M. Roberts
120 Richard Drew/AP/Wide World Photos

CHAPTER 6
129 Lonny Kalfus/Tony Stone Images
130 Photo 20-20, Inc.
140 Thierry Charlier/AP/Wide World Photos
141 John Abbott Photography
147 L.L. Bean

CHAPTER 7
152 Sharpshooters
153 Wainwright Indusriers, Inc.

161 Rob Crandall/Stock Boston
162 Jay Daniel/Photo 20-20, Inc.
169 Stephen Simpson/FPG International LLC
171 Charles Gupton/Tony Stone Images

CHAPTER 8
177 SuperStock, Inc.
178 Ron Kimball Photography
181 Jonathan Atkin
187 AP/Wide World Photos
196 Reuters/Larry Chain/Archive Photos
197 Mark Richards

CHAPTER 9
204 FPG International LLC
205 The Terry Wild Studio
209 Pacific Crest Outward Bound School
214 Brian Coats Photography
222 Santa Fabio Photography

CHAPTER 10
228 SuperStock, Inc.
229 PhotoEdit
234 Bob Daemmrich/The Image Works
236 Grant/Monkmeyer Press
241 C.J. Gunther, Photographer
245 Bill Sikes/AP/Wide World Photos

CHAPTER 11
252 PhotoEdit
253 Photo 20-20, Inc.
258 SABA Press Photos, Inc.
260
262 Rhoda Sidney/PhotoEdit

CHAPTER 12
276 Andy Sacks/Tony Stone Images
277 Jim Whitmer Photography
280 Dick Blume/The Image Works
282 Ted Rice
283 Peter Blakely/SABA Press Photos, Inc.
295 Marilyn Yee/The New York Times

CHAPTER 13
303 John Zoiner/Photo Network
304 Jeff Reinking Photography
310 Dick Blume/The Image Works
313 Jim Argo
316 (Waiting for Egghead credit)
321 Dan Lamont Photography

339 1998 Annual Report for CDW Computer
Centers, Inc. Reprinted by permission of
CDW Computer Centers, Inc

CHAPTER 14
330 The Stock Market
331 Picture Perfect USA, Inc.
333 SuperStock, Inc.
344 Terry Vine/Tony Stone Images
349 Gabe Palmer/The Stock Market

CHAPTER 15
357 Jake Evans/Tony Stone Images
358 Copyright ©1999 E*TRADE Securities,
Inc. All rights reserved. E*TRADE® is a
registered trademark of E*TRADE Securities,
Inc. Other marks of E*TRADE that appear on
its website are owned worldwide exclusively by
E*TRADE Group, Inc., or its subsidiaries.
361 Cathlyn Melloan/Tony Stone Images
368 Ron Sherman/Ron Sherman,
Photographer
370 Bellsouth Corporation
374 C.J. Pickerell/The Image Works

CHAPTER A
390 Liaison Agency, Inc.
397 Ben Margot/AP/Wide World Photos
398 Peter Cosgrove/AP/Wide World Photos

CHAPTER B
402 Uniphoto Stock Agency New York
406 Stan Godlweski
409 Susan Holtz
410 Ken Kerbs/Twin Vision Productions, Inc.

CHAPTER C
415 Collins/Monkmeyer Press
422 Ariel Skelley/The Stock Market
424 (Left) Chris Stewart/Black Star
424 (Right) Crisco Web Page. Copyright ©
Procter & Gamble Company. Used by
Permission.
428 1998 Annual Report for CDW Computer
Centers, Inc. Reprinted by permission of
CDW Computer Centers, Inc.
429 Courtesy of iPrint.com.
430 Courtesy of Lands' End, Inc.

GLOSSARY

absolute advantage A nation's ability to produce a particular product with fewer resources per unit of output than any other nation

accountability Obligation to report results to supervisors or team members and to justify outcomes that fall below expectations

accounting Measuring, interpreting, and communicating financial information to support internal and external decision making

accounting equation Basic accounting equation that assets equals liabilities plus owners' equity

accounts receivable turnover ratio Measure of time a company takes to turn its accounts receivable into cash, calculated by dividing sales by the average value of accounts receivable for a period

accrual basis Accounting method in which revenue is recorded when a sale is made and expense is recorded when it is incurred

acquisition Form of business combination in which one company buys another company's voting stock

activity ratios Ratios that measure the effectiveness of the firm's use of its resources

actuaries People employed by an insurance company to compute expected losses and to calculate the cost of premiums

administrative law Rules, regulations, and interpretations of statutory law set forth by administrative agencies and commissions

administrative skills Technical skills in information gathering, data analysis, planning, organizing, and other aspects of managerial work

advertising Paid, nonpersonal communication to a target market from an identified sponsor using mass-communications channels

affirmative action Activities undertaken by businesses to recruit and promote women and minorities, based on an analysis of the work force and the available labor pool

agency Business relationship that exists when one party (the principal) authorizes another party (the agent) to enter into contracts on the principal's behalf

agents and brokers Independent wholesalers that do not take title to the goods they distribute but may or may not take possession of those goods

application software Programs that perform specific functions for users, such as word processing or spreadsheet analysis

arbitration Process for resolving a labor-contract dispute in which an impartial third party studies the issues and makes a binding decision

artificial intelligence Ability of computers to reason, to learn, and to simulate human sensory perceptions

assets Any things of value owned or leased by a business

auction exchange Centralized marketplace where securities are traded by specialists on behalf of investors

audit Formal evaluation of the fairness and reliability of a client's financial statements

authority Power granted by the organization to make decisions, take actions, and allocate resources to accomplish goals

authorized stock Maximum number of ownership shares into which a corporation's board of directors decides the business can be divided

autocratic leaders Leaders who do not involve others in decision making

automated teller machines (ATMs) Electronic terminals that permit people to perform basic banking transactions 24 hours a day without a human teller

balance of payments Sum of all payments one nation receives from other nations minus the sum of all payments it makes to other nations, over some specified period of time

balance of trade Total value of the products a nation exports minus the total value of the products it imports, over some period of time

balance sheet Statement of a firm's financial position on a particular date; also known as a statement of financial position

bankruptcy Legal procedure by which a person or a business that is unable to meet financial obligations is relieved of debt

barriers to entry Factors that make it difficult to launch a business in a particular industry

bear market Falling stock market

behavior modification Systematic use of rewards and punishments to change human behavior

behavioral segmentation Categorization of customers according to their relationship with products or response to product characteristics

beneficiaries People named in a life insurance policy who receive the proceeds of an insurance contract when the insured dies

blue-chip stock Stock in a well-established corporation with a long record of good earnings and dividends

board of directors Group of people, elected by the shareholders, who have the ultimate authority in guiding the affairs of a corporation

bond Method of funding in which the issuer borrows from an investor and provides a written promise to make regular interest payments and repay the borrowed amount in the future

bonus Cash payment, in addition to the regular wage or salary, that serves as a reward for achievement

bookkeeping Record-keeping, clerical aspect of accounting

bookmark A browser feature that places selected URLs in a file for quick access, allowing you to automatically return to the Web site by clicking on the site's name

Boolean operators From a system of logical thought developed by the English mathematician George Boole, it uses the operators AND, OR, and NOT in Internet searches

boycott Union activity in which members and sympathizers refuse to buy or handle the product of a target company

brand A name, term, sign, symbol, design, or combination of those used to identify the products of a firm and to differentiate them from competing products

brand awareness Level of brand loyalty at which people are familiar with a product; they recognize it

brand insistence Level of brand loyalty at which people will accept no substitute for a particular product

brand loyalty Commitment to a particular brand

brand mark Portion of a brand that cannot be expressed verbally

brand name Portion of a brand that can be expressed orally, including letters, words, or numbers

brand preference Level of brand loyalty at which people habitually buy a product if it is available

breach of contract Failure to live up to the terms of a contract, with no legal excuse

break-even analysis Method of calculating the minimum volume of sales needed at a given price to cover all costs

break-even point Sales volume at a given price that will cover all of a company's costs

broadbanding Payment system that uses wide pay grades, enabling the company to give pay raises without promotions

broker An expert who has passed specific tests and is registered to trade securities for investors

browser Software, such as Netscape Navigator or Microsoft's Internet Explorer, that enables a computer to search for, display, and download the multimedia information that appears on the World Wide Web

budget Planning and control tool that reflects expected revenues, operating expenses, and cash receipts and outlays

bull market Rising stock market

business Activity and enterprise that provides goods and services that a society needs

business cycle Fluctuations in the rate of growth that an economy experiences over a period of several years

business-interruption insurance Insurance that covers losses resulting from temporary business closings

business law Those elements of law that directly influence or control business activities

business plan A written document that provides an orderly statement of a company's goals and how it intends to achieve those goals

business-to-business e-commerce Electronic commerce that involves transactions between companies and their suppliers, manufacturers, or other companies.

business-to-consumer e-commerce Electronic commerce that involves transactions between businesses and the end user or consumer

buyers' market Marketplace characterized by an abundance of products

calendar year Twelve-month accounting period that begins on January 1 and ends on December 31

capacity planning A long-term strategic decision that determines the level of resources available to an organization to meet customer demand

capital The physical, human-made elements used to produce goods and services, such as factories and computers; can also refer to the funds that finance the operations of a business

capital budgeting Process for evaluating proposed investments in select projects that provide the best long-term financial return

capital gains Return that investors receive when they sell a security for a higher price than the purchase price

capital-intensive business Businesses that require large investments in capital assets

capital investments Money paid to acquire something of permanent value in a business

capital structure The financing mix of a firm

capitalism Economic system based on economic freedom and competition

cash basis Accounting method in which revenue is recorded when payment is received and expense is recorded when cash is paid

category killer A discount chain that sells only one category of products

cause-related marketing Identification and marketing of a social issue, cause, or idea to selected target markets

cellular layout Method of arranging a facility so that parts with similar shapes or processing requirements are processed together in work centers

centralization Concentration of decision-making authority at the top of the organization

certified management accountants (CMAs) Accountants who have fulfilled the requirements for certification as specialists in management accounting

certified public accountants (CPAs) Professionally licensed accountants who meet certain requirements for education and experience and who pass a comprehensive examination

chain of command Pathway for the flow of authority from one management level to the next

chat A form of interactive communication that enables computer users in separate locations to have real-time conversations; usually takes place at Web sites called chat rooms

checks Written orders that tell the user's bank to pay a specific amount to a particular individual or business

chief executive officer (CEO) Person appointed by a corporation's board of directors to carry out the board's policies and supervise the activities of the corporation

chief information officer (CIO) Top corporate executive with responsibility for managing information and information systems

chronological résumé Most traditional type of résumé, listing employment history sequentially in reverse order so that the most recent experience is listed first

claims Demands for payments from an insurance company because of some loss by the insured

close the books The act of transferring net revenue and expense account balances to retained earnings for the period

coaching Helping employees reach their highest potential by meeting with them, discussing problems that hinder their ability to work effectively, and offering suggestions and encouragement to overcome these problems

co-branding Partnership between two or more companies to closely link their brand names together for a single product

code of ethics Written statement setting forth the principles that guide an organization's decisions

cognitive dissonance Anxiety following a purchase that prompts buyers to seek reassurance about the purchase; commonly known as *buyer's remorse*

cohesiveness A measure of how committed the team members are to their team's goals

collateral Tangible asset a lender can claim if a borrower defaults on a secured loan

collective bargaining Process used by unions and management to negotiate work contracts

combination résumé Résumé that combines the best features of the chronological and functional formats by including a candidate's skills, accomplishments, and complete job history

commercial paper An IOU, backed by the corporation's reputation, issued to raise short-term capital

commissions Payments to employees equal to a certain percentage of sales made

committee Team that may become a permanent part of the organization and is designed to deal with regularly recurring tasks

common carriers Transportation companies that offer their services to the general public

common law Law based on the precedents established by judges' decisions

common stock Shares whose owners have voting rights and have the last claim on distributed profits and assets

communism Economic system in which all productive resources are owned and operated by the government, to the elimination of private property

comparative advantage theory Theory which states that a country should produce and sell to other countries those items it produces most efficiently

compensating balance Portion of an unsecured loan that is kept on deposit at the lending institution to protect the lender and increase the lender's return

compensation Money, benefits, and services paid to employees for their work

competition Rivalry among businesses for the same customer

competitive advantage Ability to perform in one or more ways that competitors cannot match

computer-aided design (CAD) Use of computer graphics and mathematical modeling in the development of products

computer-aided engineering (CAE) Use of computers to test products without building an actual model

computer-aided manufacturing (CAM) Use of computers to control production equipment

computer-integrated manufacturing (CIM) Computer-based systems, including CAD and CAM, that coordinate and control all the elements of design and production

computer viruses Computer programs that can work their way into a computer system and erase or corrupt data or programs

conceptual skills Ability to understand the relationship of parts to the whole

conglomerate mergers Combinations of companies that are in unrelated businesses, designed to augment a company's growth and to diversify risk

consent order Settlement in which an individual or organization promises to discontinue some illegal activity without admitting guilt

consideration Negotiated exchange necessary to make a contract legally binding

consolidation Combination of two or more companies in which the old companies cease to exist and a new enterprise is created

consumer buying behavior Behavior exhibited by consumers as they consider and purchase various products

consumer market Individuals or households that buy goods or services for personal use

consumer price index (CPI) Monthly statistic that measures changes in the prices of about 400 goods and services that consumers buy

consumerism Movement that pressures businesses to consider consumer needs and interests

contingency leadership Adapting the leadership style to what is most appropriate, given current business conditions

contingent business-interruption insurance Insurance that protects a business from losses due to losses sustained by other businesses such as suppliers or transportation companies

contract Legally enforceable exchange of promises between two or more parties

contract carriers Specialized freight haulers that serve selected companies under written contract

controller Highest-ranking accountant in a company, responsible for overseeing all accounting functions

controlling Process of measuring progress against goals and objectives and correcting deviations if results are not as expected

convertible bonds Corporate bonds that can be exchanged at the owner's discretion into common stock of the issuing company

cookie A text file that is stored on a visitor's computer to identify each time the user visits the Web site; the cookie can contain data about subscriptions and memberships to online services and other information

corporation Legally chartered enterprise having most of the legal rights of a person, in-

cluding the right to conduct business, to own and sell property, to borrow money, and to sue or be sued; owners of the corporation enjoy limited liability

cost accounting Area of accounting focusing on the calculation of manufacturing and storage costs of products for use or sale in a business

cost of goods sold Cost of producing or acquiring a company's products for sale during a given period

couponing Distribution of certificates that offer discounts on particular items

credit cards Plastic cards that allow the user to buy now and repay the loaned amount at a future date

crisis management System for minimizing the harm that might result from some unusually threatening situations

critical path In a PERT network diagram, the sequence of operations that requires the longest time to complete

cross-functional teams Teams that draw together employees from different functional areas

currency Bills and coins that make up a country's cash money

current assets Cash and items that can be turned into cash within one year

current liabilities Obligations that must be met within a year

current ratio Measure of a firm's short-term liquidity, calculated by dividing current assets by current liabilities

customer divisions Divisional structure that focuses on customers or clients

damages Financial compensation to an injured party for loss and suffering

data Recorded facts and statistics; data need to be converted to information before they can help people solve business problems

data mining Sifting through huge amounts of data to identify what is valuable to a specific question or problem

data warehousing Building an organized central database out of files and databases gathered from various functional areas, such as marketing, operations, and accounting

database management Creating, storing, maintaining, rearranging, and retrieving the contents of databases

database marketing Process of building, maintaining, and using customer databases for the purpose of contacting customers and transacting business

databases Collection of related data that can be cross-referenced in order to extract information

dealer exchanges Decentralized marketplaces where securities are bought and sold by dealers out of their own inventories

debentures Corporate bonds backed only by the reputation of the issuer

debit cards Plastic cards that allow the bank to take money from the user's demand-deposit account and transfer it to a retailer's account

debt ratios Ratios that measures a firm's reliance on debt financing of its operations (sometimes called coverage ratios)

debt-to-equity ratio Measure of the extent to which a business is financed by debt as opposed to invested capital, calculated by dividing the company's total liabilities by owners' equity

debt-to-total-assets ratio Measure of a firm's ability to carry long-term debt, calculated by dividing total liabilities by total assets

decentralization Delegation of decision-making authority to employees in lower-level positions

decision making Process of identifying a decision situation, analyzing the problem, weighing the alternatives, choosing an alternative and implementing it, and evaluating the results

decision support system (DSS) Information system that uses decision models, specialized databases, and artificial intelligence to assist managers in solving highly unstructured and nonroutine problems

deductible Amount of loss that must be paid by the insured before the insurer will pay for the rest

deed Legal document by which an owner transfers the title, or ownership rights, to real property to a new owner

deflation Economic condition in which prices fall steadily throughout the economy

delegation Assignment of work and the authority and responsibility required to complete it

demand Buyers' willingness and ability to purchase products

demand curve Graph of relationship between various prices and the quantity demanded at each price

demand deposits Money that can be used by the customer at any time, such as checking accounts

democratic leaders Leaders who delegate authority and involve employees in decision making

demographics Study of statistical characteristics of a population

departmentalization Grouping people within an organization according to function, division, matrix, or network

departmentalization by division Grouping departments according to similarities in product, process, customer, or geography

departmentalization by function Grouping workers according to their similar skills, resource use, and expertise

departmentalization by matrix Assigning employees to both a functional group and a project team (thus using functional and divisional patterns simultaneously)

departmentalization by network Electronically connecting separate companies that perform selected tasks for a small headquarters organization

depreciation Accounting procedure for systematically spreading the cost of a tangible asset over its estimated useful life

deregulation Removal or relaxation of rules and restrictions affecting businesses

desktop publishing (DTP) Ability to prepare documents using computerized typesetting and graphics-processing capabilities

direct mail Advertising sent directly to potential customers, usually through the U.S. Postal Service

direct marketing Direct communication other than personal sales contacts designed to effect a measurable response

disability income insurance Short-term or long-term insurance that protects an individual against loss of income while that individual is disabled as the result of an illness or accident

discount pricing Offering a reduction in price

discount rate Interest rate the Federal Reserve charges on loans to commercial banks

discount stores Retailers that sell a variety of goods below the market price by keeping their overhead low

discrimination In a social and economic sense, denial of opportunities to individuals on the basis of some characteristic that has no bearing on their ability to perform in a job

discussion mailing lists E-mail lists that allow people to discuss a common interest by posting messages, which are received by everyone in the group

dispatching Issuing work orders and schedules to department heads and supervisors

distortion Misunderstanding that results when a message passes through too many links in the organization

distribution centers Warehouse facilities that specialize in collecting and shipping merchandise

distribution channels Systems for moving goods and services from producers to customers; also known as marketing channels

distribution mix Combination of intermediaries and channels a producer uses to get a product to end users

distribution strategy Firm's overall plan for moving products to intermediaries and final customers

diversity initiatives Company policies designed to enhance opportunities for minorities and to promote understanding of diverse cultures, customs, and talents

dividends Distributions of corporate assets to shareholders in the form of cash or other assets

domain name The portion of an Internet address that identifies the host and indicates the type of organization it is

double-entry bookkeeping Way of recording financial transactions that requires two entries for every transaction so that the accounting equation is always kept in balance

download Transmitting a file from one computer system to another; on the Internet, bringing data from the Internet into your computer

drop shippers Limited-service merchant wholesalers that assume ownership of goods but don't take physical possession; commonly used to market agricultural and mineral products

dumping Charging less than the actual cost or less than the home-country price for goods sold in other countries

e-mail Communication system that enables computers to transmit and receive written messages over electronic networks

earnings per share Measure of a firm's profitability for each share of outstanding stock, calculated by dividing net income after taxes by the average number of shares of common stock outstanding

ecology Study of the relationships between living things in the water, air, and soil, their environments, and the nutrients that support them

economic indicators Statistics that measure variables in the economy

economic system Means by which a society distributes its resources to satisfy its people's needs

economies of scale Savings from manufacturing, marketing, or buying in large quantities

electronic business (e-business) A business that transforms its processes to take full advantage of Internet technology, generates a large share of its revenue from Internet sales, focuses on earning a profit, and is always open for business

electronic business (e-business) A company that has transformed its key business processes to incorporate Internet technology into every phase of the operation

electronic commerce (e-commerce) The general term for buying and selling of goods and services on the Internet

electronic data interchange (EDI) Information systems that transmit documents such as invoices and purchase orders between computers, thereby lowering ordering costs and paperwork

electronic funds transfer systems (EFTS) Computerized systems for completing financial transactions

embargo Total ban on trade with a particular nation (a sanction) or of a particular product

employee benefits Compensation other than wages, salaries, and incentive programs

employee stock-ownership plan (ESOP) Program enabling employees to become partial owners of a company

employment at will Employer's right to keep or terminate employees as it wishes

employment interview Formal meeting during which an employer and an applicant ask questions and exchange information to see whether the applicant and the organization are a good match

entrepreneurs People who accept the risk of failure in the private enterprise system

equilibrium price Point at which quantity supplied equals quantity demanded

ethical dilemma Situation in which both sides of an issue can be supported with valid arguments

ethical lapse Situation in which an individual makes a decision that is morally wrong, illegal, or unethical

ethics The rules or standards governing the conduct of a person or group

euro A planned unified currency used by European nations that meet certain strict requirements

exchange process Act of obtaining a desired object from another party by offering something of value in return

exchange rate Rate at which the money of one country is traded for the money of another

exclusive distribution Market coverage strategy that gives intermediaries exclusive rights to sell a product in a specific geographical area

executive information system (EIS) Similar to decision support system but customized to strategic needs of executives

expenses Costs created in the process of generating revenues

expert system Computer system that simulates the thought processes of a human expert who is adept at solving particular problems

exporting Selling and shipping goods or services to another country

express contract Contract derived from words, either oral or written

extra-expense insurance Insurance that covers the added expense of operating the business in temporary facilities after an event such as a fire or a flood

extranet Similar to an intranet but extending the network to select people outside the organization

factors of production Basic inputs that a society uses to produce goods and services, including natural resources, labor, capital, and entrepreneurship

family branding Using a brand name on a variety of related products

file transfer protocol (FTP) A software protocol that lets you copy or move files from a remote computer—called an FTP site—to your computer over the Internet; it is the Internet facility for downloading and uploading files

financial accounting Area of accounting concerned with preparing financial information for users outside the organization

financial analysis Process of evaluating a company's performance and analyzing the costs and benefits of a strategic action

financial control Process of analyzing and adjusting the basic financial plan to correct for forecasted events that do not materialize

financial management Effective acquisition and use of money

financial plan A forecast of financial requirements and the financing sources to be used

firewall Computer hardware and software that protect part or all of a private computer network attached to the Internet by preventing public Internet users from accessing it

first-line managers Those at the lowest level of the management hierarchy; they supervise the operating employees and implement the plans set at the higher management levels; also called supervisory managers

fiscal policy Use of government revenue collection and spending to influence the business cycle

fiscal year Any 12 consecutive months used as an accounting period

fixed assets Assets retained for long-term use, such as land, buildings, machinery, and equipment; also referred to as property, plant, and equipment

fixed costs Business costs that remain constant regardless of the number of units produced

fixed-position layout Method of arranging a facility so that the product is stationary and equipment and personnel come to it

flat organizations Organizations with a wide span of management and few hierarchical levels

flexible manufacturing system (FMS) Production system using computer-controlled machines that can adapt to various versions of the same operation

flextime Scheduling system in which employees are allowed certain options regarding time of arrival and departure

floating exchange rate system World economic system in which the values of all currencies are determined by supply and demand

forecasting Making educated assumptions about future trends and events that will have an impact on the organization

foreign direct investment (FDI) Investment of money by foreign companies in domestic business enterprises

foreign exchange Trading one currency for the equivalent value of another currency

form utility Consumer value created by converting raw materials and other inputs into finished goods and services

formal communication network Communication network that follows the official structure of the organization

franchise Business arrangement in which a small business obtains rights to sell the goods or services of the supplier (franchisor)

franchisee Small-business owner who contracts for the right to sell goods or services of the supplier (franchisor) in exchange for some payment

franchisor Supplier that grants a franchise to an individual or group (franchisee) in exchange for payments

free riders Team members who do not contribute sufficiently to the group's activities because members are not being held individually accountable for their work

free trade International trade unencumbered by restrictive measures

free-market system Economic system in which decisions about what to produce and in what quantities are decided by the market's buyers and sellers

full-service merchant wholesalers Merchant wholesalers that provide a wide variety of services to their customers, such as storage, delivery, and marketing support

functional résumé Résumé organized around a list of skills and accomplishments, subordinating employers and academic experience in order to stress individual areas of competence

functional teams Teams whose members come from a single functional department and that are based on the organization's vertical structure

gain sharing Plan for rewarding employees not on the basis of overall profits but in relation to achievement of goals such as cost savings from higher productivity

Gantt chart Bar chart used to control schedules by showing how long each part of a production process should take and when it should take place

general expenses Operating expenses, such as office and administrative expenses, not directly associated with creating or marketing a good or a service

general obligation bond Municipal bond that is backed by the government's authority to collect taxes

general partnership Partnership in which all partners have the right to participate as co-owners and are individually liable for the business's debts

generally accepted accounting principles (GAAP) Professionally approved U.S. standards and practices used by accountants in the preparation of financial statements

generic products Products characterized by a plain label, with no advertising and no brand name

geodemographics Method of combining geographical data with demographic data to develop profiles of neighborhood segments

geographic divisions Divisional structure based on location of operations

geographic segmentation Categorization of customers according to their geographical location

glass ceiling Invisible barrier attributable to subtle discrimination that keeps women out of the top positions in business

globalization Tendency of the world's economies to act as a single interdependent system

goal Broad, long-range target or aim

goods-producing businesses Businesses that produce tangible products

graphical user interface (GUI) A user-friendly program that enables computer operators to enter commands by clicking on icons and menus with a mouse

gross domestic product (GDP) Dollar value of all the final goods and services produced by businesses located within a nation's borders; excludes receipts from overseas operations of domestic companies

gross national product (GNP) Dollar value of all the final goods and services produced by domestic businesses, including receipts from overseas operations; excludes receipts from foreign-owned businesses within a nation's borders

gross profit Amount remaining when the cost of goods sold is deducted from net sales; also known as gross margin

hardware Physical components of a computer system, including integrated circuits, keyboards, and disk drives

health maintenance organizations (HMOs) Prepaid medical plans in which consumers pay a set fee in order to receive a full range of medical care from a group of medical practitioners

high-growth ventures Small businesses intended to achieve rapid growth and high profits on investment

holding company Company that owns most, or all, of another company's stock but that does not actively participate in the management of that other company

homepage The primary Web site for an organization or individual; the first hypertext document displayed on a Web site

horizontal coordination Coordinating communication and activities across departments

horizontal mergers Combinations of companies that are direct competitors in the same industry

hostile takeover Situation in which an outside party buys enough stock in a corporation to take control against the wishes of the board of directors and corporate officers

human resources All the people who work for an organization

human resources management (HRM) Specialized function of planning how to obtain employees, oversee their training, evaluate them, and compensate them

hygiene factors Aspects of the work environment that are associated with dissatisfaction

hyperlink A highlighted word or image on a Web page or document that automatically allows people to move to another Web page or document when clicked on with a mouse

hypertext markup language (HTML) The software language used to create, present, and link pages on the World Wide Web

hypertext transfer protocol (HTTP) A communications protocol that allows people to navigate among documents or pages linked by hypertext and to download pages from the World Wide Web

implied contract Contract derived from actions or conduct

importing Purchasing goods or services from another country and bringing them into one's own country

incentives Cash payments to employees who produce at a desired level or whose unit (often the company as a whole) produces at a desired level

income statement Financial record of a company's revenues, expenses, and profits over a given period of time

incubators Facilities that house small businesses during their early growth phase

industrial distributors Wholesalers that sell to industrial customers rather than to retailers

inflation Economic condition in which prices rise steadily throughout the economy

informal communication network Communication network that follows the organization's unofficial lines of activity and power

informal organization Network of informal employee interactions that are not defined by the formal structure

injunction Court order prohibiting certain actions by striking workers

inside trading The use of unpublicized information that an individual gains from the course of his or her job to benefit from fluctuations in the stock market

insurable risk Risk for which an acceptable probability of loss may be calculated and that an insurance company might, therefore, be willing to cover

insurance Written contract that transfers to an insurer the financial responsibility for losses up to specified limits

integrated marketing communications (IMC) Strategy of coordinating and integrating communications and promotions efforts with customers to ensure greater efficiency and effectiveness

intellectual property Intangible personal property, such as ideas, songs, trade secrets, and computer programs, that are protected by patents, trademarks, and copyrights

intentional tort Willful act that results in injury

interactive advertising Customer-seller communication in which the customer controls the amount and type of information received

interlocking directorate Situation in which members of the board of one firm sit on the board of a competing firm

internal auditors Employees who analyze and evaluate a company's operations and data to determine their accuracy

international law Principles, customs, and rules that govern the international relationships between states, organizations, and persons

Internet A worldwide collection of interconnected networks that enables users to share information electronically and provides digital access to a wide variety of services

Internet service provider (ISP) A company that provides access to the Internet, usually for a monthly fee, via telephone lines or cable; ISPs can be local companies or specialists such as America Online

interpersonal skills Skills required to understand other people and to interact effectively with them

intrafirm trade Trade between global units of a multinational corporation

intranet A private network, set up within a corporation or organization, that operates over the Internet and may be used to link geographically remote sites

inventory Goods kept in stock for the production process or for sales to final customers

inventory control System for determining the right quantity of various items to have on hand and keeping track of their location, use, and condition

inventory turnover ratio Measure of the time a company takes to turn its inventory into sales, calculated by dividing cost of goods sold by the average value of inventory for a period

ISO 9000 Global standards set by the International Organization for Standardization establishing a minimum level of acceptable quality

issued stock Portion of authorized stock sold to and held by shareholders

job analysis Process by which jobs are studied to determine the tasks and dynamics involved in performing them

job description Statement of the tasks involved in a given job and the conditions under which the holder of the job will work

job enrichment Reducing work specialization and making work more meaningful by adding to the responsibilities of each job

job redesign Designing a better fit between employees' skills and their work to increase job satisfaction

job sharing Splitting a single full-time job between two employees for their convenience

job specification Statement describing the kind of person who would be best for a given job—including the skills, education, and previous experience that the job requires

joint venture Cooperative partnership in which organizations share investment costs, risks, management, and profits in the development, production, or selling of products

just-in-time (JIT) system Continuous system that pulls materials through the production process, making sure that all materials arrive just when they are needed with minimal inventory and waste

key-person insurance Insurance that provides a business with funds to compensate for the loss of a key employee by unplanned retirement, resignation, death, or disability

knowledge Expertise gained through experience or association

knowledge-based pay Pay tied to an employee's acquisition of skills; also called skill-based pay

labor unions Organizations of employees formed to protect and advance their members' interests

labor-intensive business Businesses in which labor costs are more significant than capital costs

laissez-faire leaders Leaders who leave the actual decision making up to employees

law of large numbers Principle that the larger the group on which probabilities are calculated, the more accurate the predictive value

layoffs Termination of employees for economic or business reasons

lead time Period that elapses between the ordering of materials and their arrival from the supplier

leading Process of guiding and motivating people to work toward organizational goals

lease Legal agreement that obligates the user of an asset to make payments to the owner of the asset in exchange for using it

leveraged buyout (LBO) Situation in which individuals or a group of investors purchase a company primarily with debt secured by the company's assets

liabilities Claims against a firm's assets by creditors

liability losses Financial losses suffered by a business firm or individual held responsible for property damage or injuries suffered by others

licensing Agreement to produce and market another company's product in exchange for a royalty or fee

lifestyle businesses Small businesses intended to provide the owners with a comfortable livelihood

limited liability companies (LLCs) Organizations that combine the benefits of S corporations and limited partnerships without the drawbacks of either

limited partnership Partnership composed of one or more general partners and one or more partners whose liability is usually limited to the amount of their capital investment

limited-service merchant wholesalers Merchant wholesalers that offer fewer services than full-service merchant wholesalers; they often specialize in particular markets, such as agriculture

line-and-staff organization Organization system that has a clear chain of command but that also includes functional groups of people who provide advice and specialized services

line of credit Arrangement in which the financial institution makes money available for use at any time after the loan has been approved

line organization Chain-of-command system that establishes a clear line of authority flowing from the top down

liquidity The level of ease with which an asset can be converted to cash

liquidity ratios Ratios that measure a firm's ability to meet its short-term obligations when they are due

local area network (LAN) Computer network that encompasses a small area, such as an office or a university campus

lockout Management tactic in which union members are prevented from entering a business during a strike in order to force union acceptance of management's last contract proposal

logistics The planning, movement, and flow of goods and related information throughout the supply chain

long-term debt Borrowed funds used to cover long-term expenses (generally repaid over a period of more than one year)

long-term liabilities Obligations that fall due more than a year from the date of the balance sheet

loss exposures Areas of risk in which a potential for loss exists

M1 The portion of the money supply consisting of currency, demand deposits, and NOW accounts

M2 A measure of the money supply consisting of M1 plus savings and small time deposits

M3 The broadest measure of the money supply, consisting of M1 and M2 plus large time deposits and other restricted deposits

mail-order firms Companies that sell products through catalogs and ship them directly to customers

management Process of coordinating resources to meet organizational goals

management accounting Area of accounting concerned with preparing data for use by managers within the organization

management by objectives (MBO) A motivational tool whereby managers and employees work together to structure goals and objectives for every individual, department, and project to mesh with the organization's goals

management information system (MIS) Computer system that supplies information to assist in managerial decision making

management pyramid Organizational structure comprising top, middle, and lower management

mandatory retirement Required dismissal of an employee who reaches a certain age

manufacturing resource planning (MRP II) Computer-based system that integrates data from all departments to manage inventory and production planning and control

market People or businesses who need or want a product and have the money to buy it

market indexes Measures of market activity calculated from the prices of a selection of securities

market makers Registered representatives who trade securities from their own inventories on dealer exchanges, making a ready market for buyers and sellers

market segmentation Division of total market into smaller, relatively homogeneous groups

market share A firm's portion of the total sales in a market

marketable securities Stocks, bonds, and other investments that can be turned into cash quickly

marketing Process of planning and executing the conception, pricing, promotion, and distribution of ideas, goods, and services to create and maintain relationships that satisfy individual and organizational objectives

marketing concept Approach to business management that stresses customer needs and wants, seeks long-term profitability, and integrates marketing with other functional units within the organization

marketing intermediaries Businesspeople and organizations that channel goods and services from producers to consumers

marketing mix The four key elements of marketing strategy: product, price, distribution (place), and promotion

marketing research The collection and analysis of information for making marketing decisions

marketing strategy Overall plan for marketing a product

mass customization Producing customized goods and services through mass production techniques

mass production Manufacture of uniform products in great quantities

matching principle Fundamental principle requiring that expenses incurred in producing revenue be deducted from the revenues they generate during an accounting period

material requirements planning (MRP) Method of getting the correct materials where they are needed, on time, and without carrying unnecessary inventory

materials handling Movement of goods within a firm's warehouse terminal, factory, or store

media Communications channels, such as newspapers, radio, and television

media mix Combination of various media options that a company uses in an advertising campaign

media plan Written plan that outlines how a company will spend its media budget, including how the money will be divided among the various media and when the advertisements will appear

mediation Process for resolving a labor-contract dispute in which a neutral third party meets with both sides and attempts to steer them toward a solution

mentor Experienced manager or employee with a wide network of industry colleagues who can explain office politics, serve as a role model for appropriate business behavior, and help other employees negotiate the corporate structure

merchant wholesalers Independent wholesalers that take legal title to goods they distribute

merger Combination of two companies in which one company purchases the other and assumes control of its property and liabilities

middle managers Those in the middle of the management hierarchy; they develop plans to implement the goals of top managers and coordinate the work of first-line managers

mission statement A statement of the organization's purpose, basic goals, and philosophies

modem Hardware device that allows a computer to communicate over a regular telephone line

monetary policy Government policy and actions taken by the Federal Reserve Board to regulate the nation's money supply

money Anything generally accepted as a means of paying for goods and services

money-market funds Mutual funds that invest in short-term securities and other liquid investments

monopolistic competition Situation in which many sellers differentiate their products from those of competitors in at least some small way

monopoly Market in which there are no direct competitors so that one company dominates

morale Attitude an individual has toward his or her job and employer

motivation Force that moves someone to take action

motivators Factors of human relations in business that may increase motivation

multimedia Typically used to mean the combination of more than one presentation medium—such as text, sound, graphics, and video

multinational corporations (MNCs) Companies with operations in more than one country

municipal bonds Bonds issued by city, state, and government agencies to fund public services

mutual fund Financial organization pooling money to invest in diversified blends of stocks, bonds, or other securities

national brands Brands owned by the manufacturers and distributed nationally

natural resources Land, forests, minerals, water, and other tangible assets usable in their natural state

need Difference between a person's actual state and his or her ideal state; provides the basic motivation to make a purchase

negligence Tort in which a reasonable amount of care to protect others from risk of injury is not used

negotiable instrument Transferable document that represents a promise to pay a specified amount

net income Profit earned or loss incurred by a firm, determined by subtracting expenses from revenues; also called the bottom line

network Collection of computers, communications software, and transmission media (such as telephone lines) that allows computers to communicate

news conference Gathering of media representatives at which companies announce new information; also called a press briefing or press conference

news release Brief statement or video program released to the press announcing new products, management changes, sales performance, and other potential news items

no-fault insurance laws Laws limiting lawsuits connected with auto accidents

norms Informal standards of conduct that guide team behavior

not-for-profit organizations Firms whose primary objective is something other than returning a profit to their owners

objective Specific, short-range target or aim

oligopoly Market dominated by a few producers

open-market operations Activity of the Federal Reserve in buying and selling government bonds on the open market

operating expenses All costs of operation that are not included under cost of goods sold

operational objectives Objectives that focus on short-term issues and describe the results needed to achieve tactical objectives and strategic goals

operational plans Plans that lay out the actions and the resource allocation needed to achieve operational objectives and to support tactical plans; usually defined for less than one year and developed by first-line managers

operations management Management of the conversion process that transforms inputs into outputs in the form of finished goods and services

organization chart Diagram showing how employees and tasks are grouped and where the lines of communication and authority flow

organization structure Framework enabling managers to divide responsibilities, ensure employee accountability, and distribute decision-making authority

organizational culture A set of shared values and norms that support the management system and that guide management and employee behavior

organizational market Customers who buy goods or services for resale or for use in conducting their own operations

organizing Process of arranging resources to carry out the organization's plans

orientation Session or procedure for acclimating a new employee to the organization

outsourcing Subcontracting work to outside companies

over-the-counter (OTC) market Network of dealers who trade securities on computerized linkups rather than on a trading floor

owners' equity Portion of a company's assets that belongs to the owners after obligations to all creditors have been met

par value As shown on the stock certificate, a value assigned to a stock for use in bookkeeping and in calculating dividends

parent company Company that owns most, or all, of another company's stock and that takes an active part in managing that other company

participative management Sharing information with employees and involving them in decision making

partnership Unincorporated business owned and operated by two or more persons under a voluntary legal association

pay for performance Accepting a lower base pay in exchange for bonuses based on meeting production or other goals

penetration pricing Introducing a new product at a low price in hopes of building sales volume quickly

pension plans Company-sponsored programs for providing retirees with income

performance appraisal Evaluation of an employee's work according to specific criteria

perpetual inventory System that uses computers to monitor inventory levels and automatically generate purchase orders when supplies are needed

personal property All property that is not real property

personal selling In-person communication between a seller and one or more potential buyers

persuasive advertising Advertising designed to encourage product sampling and brand switching

philanthropic Descriptive term for altruistic actions such as donating money, time, goods, or services to charitable, humanitarian, or educational institutions

physical distribution All the activities required to move finished products from the producer to the consumer

picketing Strike activity in which union members march before company entrances to persuade nonstriking employees to walk off the job and to persuade customers and others to cease doing business with the company

place marketing Marketing efforts to attract people and organizations to a particular geographical area

place utility Consumer value added by making a product available in a convenient location

planned economy Economic system in which the government controls most of the factors of production and regulates their allocation

planning Establishing objectives and goals for an organization and determining the best ways to accomplish them

point-of-purchase display Advertising or other display materials set up at retail locations to promote products to potential customers as they are making their purchase decisions

pollution Damage to or destruction of the natural environment caused by the discharge of harmful substances

positioning Using promotion, product, distribution, and price to differentiate a good or service from those of competitors in the mind of the prospective buyer

possession utility Consumer value created when someone takes ownership of a product

power of attorney Written authorization for one party to legally act for another

preferred stock Shares that give their owners first claim on a company's dividends and assets after all debts have been paid and whose owners do not have voting rights

preferred-provider organizations (PPOs) Health-care providers offering reduced-rate contracts to groups that agree to obtain medical care through the providers' organization

preliminary screening interview Meeting between an employer's representative and a candidate for the purpose of eliminating unqualified applicants from the hiring process

premium Fee that the insured pays the insurer for coverage against loss

premiums Free or bargain-priced items offered to encourage consumers to buy a product

price-earnings ratio Ratio calculated by dividing a stock's market price by its prior year's earnings per share

primary market Market where firms sell new securities issued publicly for the first time

prime interest rate (prime) Lowest interest rate banks offer on short-term loans to preferred borrowers

principal Amount of money a corporation borrows from an investor through the sale of a bond

private accountants In-house accountants employed by organizations and businesses other than a public accounting firm; also called corporate accountants

private brands Brands that carry the label of a retailer or a wholesaler rather than a manufacturer

private carriers Transportation operations owned by a company to move only its own products

private corporation Company owned by private individuals or companies

privatizing The conversion of public ownership to private ownership

problem-solving team Informal team of 5 to 12 employees from the same department who meet voluntarily to find ways of improving quality, efficiency, and the work environment

process divisions Divisional structure based on the major steps of a production process

process layout Method of arranging a facility so that production tasks are carried out in separate departments containing specialized equipment and personnel

product Good or service used as the basis of commerce

product divisions Divisional structure based on products

product layout Method of arranging a facility so that production proceeds along a line of workstations

product liability The capacity of a product to cause harm or damage for which the producer or seller is held accountable.

product-liability coverage Insurance that protects companies from claims for injuries or damages that result from use of a product the company manufactures or distributes

product life cycle Four basic stages through which a product progresses: introduction, growth, maturity, and decline

product line A series of related products offered by a firm

product mix Complete list of all products that a company offers for sale

production Transformation of resources into goods or services that people need or want

production efficiency Minimizing cost by maximizing the level of output from each resource

production forecasts Estimates of how much of a company's goods and services must be produced in order to meet future demand

professional liability insurance Insurance that covers losses arising from damages or injuries caused by the insured in the course of performing professional services for clients

profit Money left over after expenses and taxes have been deducted from revenue generated by selling goods and services

profit sharing System for distributing a portion of the company's profits to employees

profitability ratios Ratios that measure the overall financial performance of a firm

program evaluation and review technique (PERT) A planning tool that managers of complex projects use to determine the optimal order of activities, the expected time for project completion, and the best use of resources

promotion Wide variety of persuasive techniques used by companies to communicate with their target markets and the general public

promotional mix Particular blend of personal selling, advertising, direct marketing, sales promotion, and public relations that a company uses to reach potential customers

promotional strategy Statement or document that defines the direction and scope of the promotional activities that a company will use to meet its marketing objectives

property Rights held regarding any tangible or intangible object

property insurance Insurance that provides coverage for physical damage to or destruction of property and for its loss by theft

protectionism Government policies aimed at shielding a country's industries from foreign competition

proxy Document authorizing another person to vote on behalf of a shareholder in a corporation

proxy fight Attempt to gain control of a takeover target by urging shareholders to vote for directors favored by the acquiring party

psychographics Classification of customers on the basis of their psychological makeup

public accountants Professionals who provide accounting services to other businesses and individuals for a fee

public corporation Corporation that actively sells stock on the open market

public relations Nonsales communications that businesses have with their various audiences (included are both communication

with the general public and relations with the press)

pull strategy Promotional strategy that stimulates consumer demand, which then exerts pressure on wholesalers and retailers to carry a product

purchasing Acquiring the raw materials, parts, components, supplies, and finished products needed to produce goods and services

pure competition Situation in which so many buyers and sellers exist that no single buyer or seller can individually influence market prices

pure risk Risk that involves the chance of loss only

push strategy Promotional approach designed to motivate wholesalers and retailers to push a producer's products to end users

quality A measure of how closely a product conforms to predetermined standards and customer expectations

quality assurance System of policies, practices, and procedures implemented throughout the company to create and produce quality goods and services

quality control Routine checking and testing of a finished product for quality against an established standard

quality of work life (QWL) Overall environment that results from job and work conditions

quick ratio Measure of a firm's short-term liquidity, calculated by adding cash, marketable securities, and receivables, then dividing that sum by current liabilities; also known as the acid-test ratio

quotas Fixed limits on the quantity of imports a nation will allow for a specific product

rack jobbers Merchant wholesalers that are responsible for setting up and maintaining displays in a particular section of a retail store

ratio analysis Use of quantitative measures to evaluate a firm's financial performance

real property Land and everything permanently attached to it

recession Period during which national income, employment, and production all fall

recruiting Process of attracting appropriate applicants for an organization's jobs

relationship marketing A focus on developing and maintaining long-term relationships with customers, suppliers, and distributors for mutual benefit

reminder advertising Advertising intended to remind existing customers of a product's availability and benefits

reserve requirement Percentage of a bank's deposits that must be set aside

responsibility Obligation to perform the duties and achieve the goals and objectives associated with a particular position

résumé Form of advertising that lists a person's education, employment background, and job qualifications in order to obtain an interview

retailers Firms that sell goods and services to individuals for their own use rather than for resale

retained earnings The portion of shareholders' equity earned by the company but not distributed to its owners in the form of dividends

return on investment (ROI) Ratio between net income after taxes and total owners' equity; also known as return on equity

return on sales Ratio between net income after taxes and net sales; also known as profit margin

revenue bond Municipal bond backed by revenue generated from the project it is financing

revenues Amount earned from sales of goods or services and inflow from miscellaneous sources such as interest, rent, and royalties

risk Uncertainty of an event or exposure to loss

risk management Process used by business firms and individuals to deal with their exposures to loss

robots Programmable machines that can complete a variety of tasks by working with tools and materials

roles Behavioral patterns associated with or expected of certain positions

routing Specifying the sequence of operations and the path the work will take through the production facility

S corporation Corporations with no more than 75 shareholders that may be taxed as a partnership; also known as a subchapter S corporation

salaries Fixed weekly, monthly, or yearly cash compensation for work

sales promotion Wide range of events and activities (including coupons, rebates, contests, in-store demonstrations, free samples, trade shows, and point-of-purchase displays) designed to stimulate interest in a product

scheduling Process of determining how long each production operation takes and then setting a starting and ending time for each

scientific management Management approach designed to improve employees' efficiency by scientifically studying their work

scrambled merchandising Policy of carrying merchandise that is ordinarily sold in a different type of outlet

search engines Internet tools for finding Web sites on the topics of your choice

secondary market Market where subsequent owners trade previously issued shares of stocks and bonds

secured bonds Bonds backed by specific assets that will be given to bondholders if the borrowed amount is not repaid

secured loans Loans backed up with something of value that the lender can claim in case of default, such as a piece of property

securities Investments such as stocks, bonds, options, futures, and commodities

selective credit controls Federal Reserve's power to set credit terms on various types of loans

selective distribution Market coverage strategy that uses a limited number of outlets to distribute products

self-directed team Teams in which members are responsible for an entire process or operation

self-insurance Accumulating funds each year to pay for predicted liability losses, rather than buying insurance from another company

sellers' market Marketplace characterized by a shortage of products

selling expenses All the operating expenses associated with marketing goods or services

service businesses Businesses that provide intangible products or perform useful labor on behalf of another

setup costs Expenses incurred each time a producer organizes resources to begin producing goods or services

sexism Discrimination on the basis of gender

sexual harassment Unwelcome sexual advance, request for sexual favors, or other verbal or physical conduct of a sexual nature within the workplace

shareholders Owners of a corporation

short selling Selling stock borrowed from a broker with the intention of buying it back later at a lower price, repaying the broker, and keeping the profit

short-term debt Borrowed funds used to cover current expenses (generally repaid within a year)

skimming Charging a high price for a new product during the introductory stage and lowering the price later

small business Company that is independently owned and operated, is not dominant in its field, and meets certain criteria for the number of employees and annual sales revenue

smart cards Plastic cards with embedded computer chips that store money drawn from the user's demand-deposit account as well as information that can be used for purchases

software Programmed instructions that drive the activity of computer hardware

social audit Assessment of a company's performance in the area of social responsibility

social responsibility The idea that business has certain obligations to society beyond the pursuit of profits

socialism Economic system characterized by public ownership and operation of key industries combined with private ownership and operation of less-vital industries

sole proprietorship Business owned by a single individual

spam Unsolicited e-mail; from the sender's point of view, it's a form of bulk mail, to the receiver it seems like junk e-mail

span of management Number of people under one manager's control; also known as span of control

special-purpose teams Temporary teams that exist outside the formal organization hierarchy and are created to achieve a specific goal

specialty advertising Advertising that appears on various items such as coffee mugs, pens, and calendars, designed to help keep a company's name in front of customer

specialty store Store that carries only a particular type of goods

speculative risk Risk that involves the chance of both loss and profits

spreadsheet Program that organizes and manipulates data in a row-column matrix

stakeholders Individuals or groups to whom business has a responsibility

standards Criteria against which performance is measured

stare decisis Concept of using previous judicial decisions as the basis for deciding similar court cases

start-up companies New ventures

statement of cash flows Statement of a firm's cash receipts and cash payments that presents information on its sources and uses of cash

statistical process control (SPC) Use of random sampling and control charts to monitor the production process

statistical quality control (SQC) Monitoring all aspects of the production process to see whether the process is operating as it should

statutory law Statute, or law, created by a legislature

stock Shares of ownership in a corporation

stock certificate Document showing ownership of a share of stock in a publicly held corporation

stock exchanges Location where traders buy and sell stocks and bonds

stock option plan Program enabling employees to purchase a certain amount of stock at a discount after they have worked for the company a specified length of time or after the company's stock reaches a specific market price

stock split Increase in the number of shares of ownership that each stock certificate represents, at a proportionate drop in each share's value

strategic alliance Long-term relationship in which two or more companies share ideas, resources, and technologies in order to establish competitive advantages

strategic goals Goals that focus on broad organizational issues and aim to improve performance

strategic plans Plans that establish the actions and the resource allocation required to accomplish strategic goals; usually defined for periods of two to five years and developed by top managers

strict product liability Liability for injury caused by a defective product when all reasonable care is used in its manufacture, distribution, or sale; no fault is assigned

strike Temporary work stoppage by employees who want management to accept their union's demands

strikebreakers Nonunion workers hired to replace striking workers

subsidiary corporations Corporations whose stock is owned entirely or almost entirely by another corporation

supply Specific quantity of a product that the seller is able and willing to provide

supply-chain management Integrating all of the facilities, functions, and processes associated with the production of goods and services, from suppliers to customers

supply curve Graph of relationship between various prices and the quantity supplied at each price

tactical objectives Objectives that focus on departmental issues and describe the results necessary to achieve the organization's strategic goals

tactical plans Plans that define the actions and the resource allocation necessary to achieve tactical objectives and to support strategic plans; usually defined for a period of one to three years and developed by middle managers

tall organizations Organizations with a narrow span of management and many hierarchical levels

target markets Specific customer groups or segments to whom a company wants to sell a particular product

tariffs Taxes levied on imports

task force Team of people from several departments who are temporarily brought together to address a specific issue

tax accounting Area of accounting focusing on tax preparation and tax planning

team A unit of two or more people who share a mission and collective responsibility as they work together to achieve a goal

technical skills Ability and knowledge to perform the mechanics of a particular job

technology Knowledge, tools, techniques, and activities used in the production of goods and services

telecommuting Working from home and communicating with the company's main office via computer and communication devices

telemarketing Selling or supporting the sales process over the telephone

Telnet A way to access someone else's computer (the host computer), and to use it as if it were right on your desk

tender offer Invitation made directly to shareholders by an outside party who wishes to buy a company's stock at a price above the current market price

term insurance Life insurance that provides death benefits for a specified period

termination Act of getting rid of an employee through layoffs or firing

Theory X Managerial assumption that employees are irresponsible, unambitious, and distasteful of work and that managers must use force, control, or threats to motivate them

Theory Y Managerial assumption that employees like work, are naturally committed to certain goals, are capable of creativity, and seek out responsibility under the right conditions

time deposits Bank accounts that pay interest and require advance notice before money can be withdrawn

time utility Consumer value added by making a product available at a convenient time

top managers Those at the highest level of the organization's management hierarchy; they are responsible for setting strategic goals, and they have the most power and responsibility in the organization

tort Noncriminal act (other than breach of contract) that results in injury to a person or to property

total quality management (TQM) Comprehensive, strategic management approach that builds quality into every organizational process as a way of improving customer satisfaction

trade allowance Discount offered by producers to wholesalers and retailers

trade credit Credit obtained by the purchaser directly from the supplier

trade deficit Unfavorable trade balance created when a country imports more than it exports

trade promotions Sales-promotion efforts aimed at inducing distributors or retailers to push a producer's products

trade shows Gatherings where producers display their wares to potential buyers; nearly every industry has one or more trade shows each year focused on particular types of products

trade surplus Favorable trade balance created when a country exports more than it imports

trademark Brand that has been given legal protection so that its owner has exclusive rights to its use

trading blocs Organizations of nations that remove barriers to trade among their members and that establish uniform barriers to trade with nonmember nations

transaction Exchange between parties

Treasury bills Short-term debt securities issued by the federal government; also referred to as T-bills

Treasury bonds Debt securities issued by the federal government that are repaid more than ten years after issuance

Treasury notes Debt securities issued by the federal government that are repaid within one to ten years after issuance

trend analysis Comparison of a firm's financial data from year to year to see how they have changed

trusts Monopolistic arrangements established when one company buys a controlling share of the stock of competing companies in the same industry

tying contracts Contracts forcing buyers to purchase unwanted goods along with goods actually desired

umbrella policies Insurance that provides businesses with coverage beyond what is provided by a basic liability policy

Uniform Commercial Code (UCC) Set of standardized laws, adopted by most states, that govern business transactions

uniform resource locator (URL) Web address that gives the exact location of an Internet resource

uninsurable risk Risk that few, if any, insurance companies will assume because of the difficulty of calculating the probability of loss

unissued stock Portion of authorized stock not yet sold to shareholders

Universal Product Codes (UPCs) A bar code on a product's package that provides information read by optical scanners

unlimited liability Legal condition under which any damages or debts attributable to the business can also be attached to the owner because the two have no separate legal existence

unsecured loans Loans requiring no collateral but a good credit rating

upload To send a file from your computer to a server or host system

U.S. savings bonds Debt instruments sold by the federal government in a variety of amounts

Usenet newsgroups One or more discussion groups on the Internet in which people with similar interests can post articles and reply to messages

utility Power of a good or service to satisfy a human need

variable costs Business costs that increase with the number of units produced

venture capitalists Investment specialists who provide money to finance new businesses or turnarounds in exchange for a portion of the ownership, with the objective of making a considerable profit on the investment; also called VCs

vertical mergers Combinations of companies that participate in different phases of the same industry (e.g., materials, production, distribution)

vertical organization Structure linking activities at the top of the organization with those at the middle and lower levels

virtual team Team that uses communication technology to bring geographically distant employees together to achieve goals

vision A viable view of the future that is rooted in but improves on the present

wages Cash payment based on the number of hours the employee has worked or the number of units the employee has produced

wants Things that are desirable in light of a person's experiences, culture, and personality

warehouse Facility for storing inventory

warranty Statement specifying what the producer of a product will do to compensate the buyer if the product is defective or if it malfunctions

Web site A related collection of files on the World Wide Web

wheel of retailing Evolutionary process by which stores that feature low prices gradually upgrade until they no longer appeal to price-sensitive shoppers and are replaced by new low-price competitors

whole life insurance Insurance that provides both death benefits and savings for the insured's lifetime, provided premiums are paid

wholesalers Firms that sell products to other firms for resale or for organizational use

wide area network (WAN) Computer network that encompasses a large geographic area

work specialization Specialization in or responsibility for some portion of an organization's overall work tasks; also called division of labor

worker buyout Distribution of financial incentives to employees who voluntarily depart, usually undertaken in order to reduce the payroll

workers' compensation insurance Insurance that partially replaces lost income and that pays for employees' medical costs and rehabilitation expenses for work-related injuries

working capital Current assets minus current liabilities

World Wide Web (WWW) A hypertext-based system for finding and accessing Internet resources such as text, graphics, sound, and other multimedia resources

wrongful discharge Firing an employee with inadequate advance notice or explanation

NAME/ORGANIZATION/BRAND/ COMPANY INDEX

SUBJECT INDEX